Student Solutions Manual

John Garlow
Tarrant County Community College

Introductory Algebra

Second Edition

K. Elayn Martin-Gay

Prentice Hall

D1418229

Upper Saddle River, NJ 07458

Editor in Chief: Chris Hoag
Executive Editor: Karin E. Wagner
Editorial Assistant: Kanarian Kindred
Assistant Managing Editor: John Matthews
Production Editor: Donna Crilly
Supplement Cover Manager: Paul Gourhan
Supplement Cover Designer: Joanne Alexandris
Manufacturing Buyer: Ilene Kahn

Prentice Hall

© 2003 by Pearson Education, Inc.
Pearson Education, Inc.
Upper Saddle River, NJ 07458

Printed in the United States of America

10 9 8 7 6 5 4 3

ISBN 0-13-035068-0

Pearson Education Ltd., *London*
Pearson Education Australia Pty. Ltd., *Sydney*
Pearson Education Singapore, Pte. Ltd.
Pearson Education North Asia Ltd., *Hong Kong*
Pearson Education Canada, Inc., *Toronto*
Pearson Educacíon de Mexico, S.A. de C.V.
Pearson Education—Japan, *Tokyo*
Pearson Education Malaysia, Pte. Ltd.
Pearson Education, *Upper Saddle River, New Jersey*

Table of Contents

Chapter R

Chapter R Pretest

1. $12 = 1 \cdot 12, \ 12 = 2 \cdot 6, \ 12 = 3 \cdot 4$
   Factors: $1, 2, 3, 4, 6, 12$

2. $150 = 2 \cdot 3 \cdot 5 \cdot 5$

3. $8 = 2 \cdot 2 \cdot 2$
   $14 = 2 \cdot 7$
   $20 = 2 \cdot 2 \cdot 5$
   $\text{LCM} = 2 \cdot 2 \cdot 2 \cdot 5 \cdot 7 = 280$

4. $\dfrac{7}{8} = \dfrac{7 \cdot 5}{8 \cdot 5} = \dfrac{35}{40}$

5. $\dfrac{24}{40} = \dfrac{2 \cdot 2 \cdot 2 \cdot 3}{2 \cdot 2 \cdot 2 \cdot 5} = \dfrac{3}{5}$

6. $\dfrac{120}{250} = \dfrac{2 \cdot 2 \cdot 2 \cdot 3 \cdot 5}{2 \cdot 5 \cdot 5 \cdot 5} = \dfrac{2 \cdot 2 \cdot 3}{5 \cdot 5} = \dfrac{12}{25}$

7. $\dfrac{2}{9} \cdot \dfrac{3}{8} = \dfrac{2 \cdot 3}{3 \cdot 3 \cdot 2 \cdot 2 \cdot 2} = \dfrac{1}{3 \cdot 2 \cdot 2} = \dfrac{1}{12}$

8. $\dfrac{1}{4} + \dfrac{5}{6} = \dfrac{1 \cdot 3}{4 \cdot 3} + \dfrac{5 \cdot 2}{6 \cdot 2} = \dfrac{3}{12} + \dfrac{10}{12} = \dfrac{3+10}{12} = \dfrac{13}{12}$

9. $\dfrac{3}{7} \div \dfrac{7}{10} = \dfrac{3}{7} \cdot \dfrac{10}{7} = \dfrac{3 \cdot 10}{7 \cdot 7} = \dfrac{30}{49}$

10. $\dfrac{2}{3} - \dfrac{5}{9} = \dfrac{2 \cdot 3}{3 \cdot 3} - \dfrac{5}{9} = \dfrac{6}{9} - \dfrac{5}{9} = \dfrac{6-5}{9} = \dfrac{1}{9}$

11. $\begin{array}{r} 76 \\ 0.5 \\ +2.03 \\ \hline 78.53 \end{array}$

12. $\begin{array}{r} 18. \\ -12.76 \\ \hline 5.33 \end{array}$

13. $\begin{array}{r} 12.8 \\ \times\ 0.19 \\ \hline 1152 \\ 128 \\ \hline 2.432 \end{array}$

14. $\begin{array}{r} 34.9 \\ 75\overline{)\ 2617.5} \\ -225 \\ \hline 367 \\ -300 \\ \hline 675 \\ -675 \\ \hline 0 \end{array}$

15. $7.16 = \dfrac{716}{100}$

16. $\dfrac{3}{16} = 16\overline{)\ 3.0000} = 0.1875$
$$\begin{array}{r} 0.1875 \\ 16\overline{)\ 3.0000} \\ -16 \\ \hline 140 \\ -128 \\ \hline 120 \\ -112 \\ \hline 80 \\ -80 \\ \hline 0 \end{array}$$

1

17. $\dfrac{5}{6} = 6\overline{)\,5.0000}^{0.8333} = 0.8\overline{3}$

$$\underline{-48}$$
$$20$$
$$\underline{-18}$$
$$20$$
$$\underline{-18}$$
$$20$$
$$\underline{-18}$$
$$2$$

18. $78.6159 \Rightarrow 78.6$

19. $78.6159 \Rightarrow 78.62$

20. $80.6\% = 0.806$

21. $0.3 = 0.3 \cdot 100\% = 30\%$

Practice Problems R.1

1. $4 = 1 \cdot 4, \ 4 = 2 \cdot 2$
Factors: $1, 2, 4$

2. $18 = 1 \cdot 18, \ 18 = 2 \cdot 9, \ 18 = 3 \cdot 6$
Factors: $1, 2, 3, 6, 9, 18$

3. $5 = 1 \cdot 5$ only. 5 is prime
$11 = 1 \cdot 11$ only. 11 is prime
$6 = 2 \cdot 3$. 6 is composite
$18 = 2 \cdot 9$. 18 is composite

4. $28 = 2 \cdot 2 \cdot 7$

5. $60 = 2 \cdot 2 \cdot 3 \cdot 5$

6. $297 = 3 \cdot 3 \cdot 3 \cdot 11$

7. $14 = 2 \cdot 7$
$35 = 5 \cdot 7$
$\text{LCM} = 2 \cdot 5 \cdot 7 = 70$

8. $5 = 5$
$9 = 3 \cdot 3$
$\text{LCM} = 3 \cdot 3 \cdot 5 = 45$

9. $4 = 2 \cdot 2$
$15 = 3 \cdot 5$
$10 = 2 \cdot 5$
$\text{LCM} = 2 \cdot 2 \cdot 3 \cdot 5 \cdot = 60$

Exercise Set R.1

1. $9 = 1 \cdot 9, \ 9 = 3 \cdot 3$
Factors: $1, 3, 9$

3. $24 = 1 \cdot 24, \ 24 = 2 \cdot 12, \ 24 = 3 \cdot 8, \ 24 = 4 \cdot 6$
Factors: $1, 2, 3, 4, 6, 8, 12, 24$

5. $42 = 1 \cdot 42, \ 42 = 2 \cdot 21, \ 42 = 3 \cdot 14,$
$42 = 6 \cdot 7$
Factors: $1, 2, 3, 6, 7, 14, 21, 42$

7. $80 = 1 \cdot 80, \ 80 = 2 \cdot 40, \ 80 = 4 \cdot 20,$
$80 = 5 \cdot 16, \ 80 = 8 \cdot 10$
Factors: $1, 2, 4, 5, 8, 10, 16, 20, 40, 80$

9. $19 = 1 \cdot 19$
Factors: $1, 19$

11. $13 = 1 \cdot 13$ only. 13 is prime.

13. $39 = 3 \cdot 13$. 39 is composite.

15. $37 = 1 \cdot 37$ only. 37 is prime.

17. $51 = 3 \cdot 17$.   51 is composite.

19. $2065 = 5 \cdot 413$.   2065 is composite.

21. $18 = 2 \cdot 3 \cdot 3$

23. $20 = 2 \cdot 2 \cdot 5$

25. $56 = 2 \cdot 2 \cdot 2 \cdot 7$

27. $300 = 2 \cdot 2 \cdot 3 \cdot 5 \cdot 5$

29. $81 = 3 \cdot 3 \cdot 3 \cdot 3$

31. $588 = 2 \cdot 2 \cdot 3 \cdot 7 \cdot 7$

33. c

35. $6 = 2 \cdot 3$
$14 = 2 \cdot 7$
$\text{LCM} = 2 \cdot 3 \cdot 7 = 42$

37. $3 = 3$
$4 = 2 \cdot 2$
$\text{LCM} = 2 \cdot 2 \cdot 3 = 12$

39. $20 = 2 \cdot 2 \cdot 5$
$30 = 2 \cdot 3 \cdot 5$
$\text{LCM} = 2 \cdot 2 \cdot 3 \cdot 5 = 60$

41. $5 = 5$
$7 = 7$
$\text{LCM} = 5 \cdot 7 = 35$

43. $6 = 2 \cdot 3$
$12 = 2 \cdot 2 \cdot 3$
$\text{LCM} = 2 \cdot 2 \cdot 3 = 12$

45. $12 = 2 \cdot 2 \cdot 3$
$20 = 2 \cdot 2 \cdot 5$
$\text{LCM} = 2 \cdot 2 \cdot 3 \cdot 5 = 60$

47. $50 = 2 \cdot 5 \cdot 5$
$70 = 2 \cdot 5 \cdot 7$
$\text{LCM} = 2 \cdot 5 \cdot 5 \cdot 7 = 350$

49. $24 = 2 \cdot 2 \cdot 2 \cdot 3$
$36 = 2 \cdot 2 \cdot 3 \cdot 3$
$\text{LCM} = 2 \cdot 2 \cdot 2 \cdot 3 \cdot 3 = 72$

51. $5 = 5$
$10 = 2 \cdot 5$
$12 = 2 \cdot 2 \cdot 3$
$\text{LCM} = 2 \cdot 2 \cdot 3 \cdot 5 = 60$

53. $2 = 2$
$3 = 3$
$5 = 5$
$\text{LCM} = 2 \cdot 3 \cdot 5 = 30$

55. $8 = 2 \cdot 2 \cdot 2$
$18 = 2 \cdot 3 \cdot 3$
$30 = 2 \cdot 3 \cdot 5$
$\text{LCM} = 2 \cdot 2 \cdot 2 \cdot 3 \cdot 3 \cdot 5 = 360$

57. $4 = 2 \cdot 2$
$8 = 2 \cdot 2 \cdot 2$
$24 = 2 \cdot 2 \cdot 2 \cdot 3$
$\text{LCM} = 2 \cdot 2 \cdot 2 \cdot 3 = 24$

59. $315 = 3 \cdot 3 \cdot 5 \cdot 7$
$504 = 2 \cdot 2 \cdot 2 \cdot 3 \cdot 3 \cdot 7$
$\text{LCM} = 2 \cdot 2 \cdot 2 \cdot 3 \cdot 3 \cdot 5 \cdot 7 = 2520$

61. answers may vary

63. $5 = 5$

$7 = 7$

$LCM = 5 \cdot 7 = 35$

Every 35 days

Practice Problems R.2

1. $\dfrac{1}{4} = \dfrac{1 \cdot 5}{4 \cdot 5} = \dfrac{5}{20}$

2. $\dfrac{20}{35} = \dfrac{2 \cdot 2 \cdot 5}{7 \cdot 5} = \dfrac{4}{7}$

3. $\dfrac{7}{20}$ is already in lowest terms

4. $\dfrac{12}{40} = \dfrac{2 \cdot 2 \cdot 3}{2 \cdot 2 \cdot 2 \cdot 5} = \dfrac{3}{10}$

5. $\dfrac{4}{4} = 4 \div 4 = 1$

6. $\dfrac{9}{3} = 9 \div 3 = 3$

7. $\dfrac{10}{10} = 10 \div 10 = 1$

8. $\dfrac{5}{1} = 5 \div 1 = 5$

9. $\dfrac{3}{7} \cdot \dfrac{3}{5} = \dfrac{3 \cdot 3}{7 \cdot 5} = \dfrac{9}{35}$

10. $\dfrac{2}{9} \div \dfrac{3}{4} = \dfrac{2}{9} \cdot \dfrac{4}{3} = \dfrac{2 \cdot 4}{9 \cdot 3} = \dfrac{8}{27}$

11. $\dfrac{8}{11} \div 24 = \dfrac{8}{11} \div \dfrac{24}{1} = \dfrac{8}{11} \cdot \dfrac{1}{24} = \dfrac{8 \cdot 1}{11 \cdot 3 \cdot 8} = \dfrac{1}{33}$

12. $\dfrac{5}{4} \div \dfrac{5}{8} = \dfrac{5}{4} \cdot \dfrac{8}{5} = \dfrac{5 \cdot 2 \cdot 4}{4 \cdot 5} = \dfrac{2}{1} = 2$

13. $\dfrac{2}{11} + \dfrac{5}{11} = \dfrac{2+5}{11} = \dfrac{7}{11}$

14. $\dfrac{1}{8} + \dfrac{3}{8} = \dfrac{1+3}{8} = \dfrac{4}{8} = \dfrac{4}{2 \cdot 4} = \dfrac{1}{2}$

15. $\dfrac{13}{10} - \dfrac{3}{10} = \dfrac{13-3}{10} = \dfrac{10}{10} = 1$

16. $\dfrac{7}{6} - \dfrac{2}{6} = \dfrac{7-2}{6} = \dfrac{5}{6}$

17. $\dfrac{3}{8} + \dfrac{1}{20} = \dfrac{3 \cdot 5}{8 \cdot 5} + \dfrac{1 \cdot 2}{20 \cdot 2} = \dfrac{15}{40} + \dfrac{2}{40} = \dfrac{17}{40}$

18. $\dfrac{8}{15} - \dfrac{1}{3} = \dfrac{8}{3 \cdot 5} - \dfrac{1 \cdot 5}{3 \cdot 5} = \dfrac{8-5}{3 \cdot 5} = \dfrac{3}{3 \cdot 5} = \dfrac{1}{5}$

19. $5\dfrac{1}{6} \cdot 4\dfrac{2}{5} = \dfrac{31}{6} \cdot \dfrac{22}{5} = \dfrac{31 \cdot 2 \cdot 11}{2 \cdot 3 \cdot 5} = \dfrac{341}{15} = 22\dfrac{11}{15}$

20. $7\dfrac{3}{8} - 6\dfrac{1}{4} = \dfrac{59}{8} - \dfrac{25}{4} = \dfrac{59}{8} - \dfrac{25 \cdot 2}{4 \cdot 2}$

$= \dfrac{59-50}{8} = \dfrac{9}{8} = 1\dfrac{1}{8}$

21. $76\dfrac{1}{9} = 76\dfrac{1 \cdot 4}{9 \cdot 4} = 76\dfrac{4}{36}$

$+35\dfrac{3}{4} = +35\dfrac{3 \cdot 9}{4 \cdot 9} = +35\dfrac{27}{36}$

$111\dfrac{31}{36}$

Exercise Set R.2

1. $\dfrac{7}{10} = \dfrac{7 \cdot 3}{10 \cdot 3} = \dfrac{21}{30}$

3. $\dfrac{2}{9} = \dfrac{2 \cdot 2}{9 \cdot 2} = \dfrac{4}{18}$

5. $\dfrac{4}{5} = \dfrac{4 \cdot 4}{5 \cdot 4} = \dfrac{16}{20}$

7. $\dfrac{2}{4} = \dfrac{2}{2 \cdot 2} = \dfrac{1}{2}$

9. $\dfrac{10}{15} = \dfrac{2 \cdot 5}{3 \cdot 5} = \dfrac{2}{3}$

11. $\dfrac{3}{7} = \dfrac{3}{7}$

13. $\dfrac{20}{20} = \dfrac{2 \cdot 2 \cdot 5}{2 \cdot 2 \cdot 5} = \dfrac{1}{1} = 1$

15. $\dfrac{35}{7} = \dfrac{5 \cdot 7}{7} = 5$

17. $\dfrac{18}{30} = \dfrac{2 \cdot 3 \cdot 3}{2 \cdot 3 \cdot 5} = \dfrac{3}{5}$

19. $\dfrac{16}{20} = \dfrac{2 \cdot 2 \cdot 2 \cdot 2}{2 \cdot 2 \cdot 5} = \dfrac{2 \cdot 2}{5} = \dfrac{4}{5}$

21. $\dfrac{66}{48} = \dfrac{2 \cdot 3 \cdot 11}{2 \cdot 2 \cdot 2 \cdot 2 \cdot 3} = \dfrac{11}{2 \cdot 2 \cdot 2} = \dfrac{11}{8}$

23. $\dfrac{120}{244} = \dfrac{2 \cdot 2 \cdot 2 \cdot 3 \cdot 5}{2 \cdot 2 \cdot 61} = \dfrac{2 \cdot 3 \cdot 5}{61} = \dfrac{30}{61}$

25. $\dfrac{192}{264} = \dfrac{2 \cdot 2 \cdot 2 \cdot 2 \cdot 2 \cdot 2 \cdot 3}{2 \cdot 2 \cdot 2 \cdot 3 \cdot 11} = \dfrac{2 \cdot 2 \cdot 2}{11} = \dfrac{8}{11}$

27. $\dfrac{1}{2} \cdot \dfrac{3}{4} = \dfrac{1 \cdot 3}{2 \cdot 2 \cdot 2} = \dfrac{3}{8}$

29. $\dfrac{2}{3} \cdot \dfrac{3}{4} = \dfrac{2 \cdot 3}{3 \cdot 2 \cdot 2} = \dfrac{1}{2}$

31. $5\dfrac{1}{9} \cdot 3\dfrac{2}{3} = \dfrac{46}{9} \cdot \dfrac{11}{3} = \dfrac{2 \cdot 23 \cdot 11}{3 \cdot 3 \cdot 3} = \dfrac{506}{27} = 18\dfrac{20}{27}$

33. $7\dfrac{2}{5} \div \dfrac{1}{5} = \dfrac{37}{5} \cdot \dfrac{5}{1} = \dfrac{37 \cdot 5}{5 \cdot 1} = 37$

35. $\dfrac{1}{2} \div \dfrac{7}{12} = \dfrac{1}{2} \cdot \dfrac{12}{7} = \dfrac{1 \cdot 2 \cdot 2 \cdot 3}{2 \cdot 7} = \dfrac{2 \cdot 3}{7} = \dfrac{6}{7}$

37. $\dfrac{3}{4} \div \dfrac{1}{20} = \dfrac{3}{4} \cdot \dfrac{20}{1} = \dfrac{3 \cdot 2 \cdot 2 \cdot 5}{2 \cdot 2} = \dfrac{3 \cdot 5}{1} = 15$

39. $\dfrac{7}{10} \cdot \dfrac{5}{21} = \dfrac{7 \cdot 5}{2 \cdot 5 \cdot 3 \cdot 7} = \dfrac{1}{2 \cdot 3} = \dfrac{1}{6}$

41. $\dfrac{9}{20} \div \dfrac{12}{1} = \dfrac{9}{20} \cdot \dfrac{1}{12} = \dfrac{3 \cdot 3}{2 \cdot 2 \cdot 5 \cdot 2 \cdot 2 \cdot 3}$

$= \dfrac{3}{2 \cdot 2 \cdot 2 \cdot 2 \cdot 5} = \dfrac{3}{80}$

43. $4\dfrac{2}{11} \cdot 2\dfrac{1}{2} = \dfrac{46}{11} \cdot \dfrac{5}{2} = \dfrac{2 \cdot 23 \cdot 5}{2 \cdot 11} = \dfrac{115}{11} = 10\dfrac{5}{11}$

45. $8\dfrac{3}{5} \div 2\dfrac{9}{10} = \dfrac{43}{5} \div \dfrac{29}{10} = \dfrac{43}{5} \cdot \dfrac{10}{29}$

$= \dfrac{43 \cdot 2 \cdot 5}{5 \cdot 29} = \dfrac{43 \cdot 2}{29} = \dfrac{86}{29} = 2\dfrac{28}{29}$

47. $\dfrac{4}{5} + \dfrac{1}{5} = \dfrac{4+1}{5} = \dfrac{5}{5} = 1$

49. $\dfrac{4}{5} - \dfrac{1}{5} = \dfrac{4-1}{5} = \dfrac{3}{5}$

51. $\dfrac{23}{105} + \dfrac{4}{105} = \dfrac{23+4}{105} = \dfrac{27}{105} = \dfrac{3\cdot3\cdot3}{3\cdot5\cdot7}$

$\qquad = \dfrac{3\cdot3}{5\cdot7} = \dfrac{9}{35}$

53. $\dfrac{17}{21} - \dfrac{10}{21} = \dfrac{17-10}{21} = \dfrac{7}{21} = \dfrac{7}{3\cdot7} = \dfrac{1}{3}$

55. $9\dfrac{7}{8} + 2\dfrac{3}{8} = \dfrac{79}{8} + \dfrac{19}{8} = \dfrac{98}{8} = \dfrac{2\cdot49}{4\cdot2}$

$\qquad = \dfrac{49}{4} = 12\dfrac{1}{4}$

57. $5\dfrac{2}{5} - 3\dfrac{4}{5} = \dfrac{27}{5} - \dfrac{19}{5} = \dfrac{27-19}{5} = \dfrac{8}{5} = 1\dfrac{3}{5}$

59. $\dfrac{2}{3} + \dfrac{3}{7} = \dfrac{2\cdot7}{3\cdot7} + \dfrac{3\cdot3}{7\cdot3} = \dfrac{14}{21} + \dfrac{9}{21} = \dfrac{23}{21}$

61. $\dfrac{10}{3} - \dfrac{5}{21} = \dfrac{10\cdot7}{3\cdot7} - \dfrac{5}{3\cdot7} = \dfrac{70}{21} - \dfrac{5}{21} = \dfrac{65}{21}$

63. $\dfrac{10}{21} + \dfrac{5}{21} = \dfrac{10+5}{21} = \dfrac{15}{21} = \dfrac{3\cdot5}{3\cdot7} = \dfrac{5}{7}$

65. $\dfrac{5}{22} - \dfrac{5}{33} = \dfrac{5\cdot3}{22\cdot3} - \dfrac{5\cdot2}{33\cdot2} = \dfrac{15}{66} - \dfrac{10}{66} = \dfrac{5}{66}$

67. $8\dfrac{11}{12} - 1\dfrac{5}{6} = \dfrac{107}{12} - \dfrac{11}{6} = \dfrac{107}{12} - \dfrac{11\cdot2}{6\cdot2}$

$\qquad = \dfrac{107-22}{12} = \dfrac{85}{12} = 7\dfrac{1}{12}$

69. $17\dfrac{2}{5} + 30\dfrac{2}{3} = \dfrac{87}{5} + \dfrac{92}{3} = \dfrac{87\cdot3}{5\cdot3} + \dfrac{92\cdot5}{3\cdot5}$

$\qquad = \dfrac{261}{15} + \dfrac{460}{15} = \dfrac{721}{15} = 48\dfrac{1}{15}$

71. $\dfrac{12}{5} - 1 = \dfrac{12}{5} - \dfrac{5}{5} = \dfrac{12-5}{5} = \dfrac{7}{5}$

73. $\dfrac{2}{3} - \dfrac{5}{9} + \dfrac{5}{6} = \dfrac{2\cdot2\cdot3}{3\cdot2\cdot3} - \dfrac{5\cdot2}{9\cdot2} + \dfrac{5\cdot3}{6\cdot3}$

$\qquad = \dfrac{12-10+15}{18} = \dfrac{17}{18}$

75. answers may vary

77. $1 - \dfrac{3}{10} - \dfrac{5}{10} = \dfrac{10}{10} - \dfrac{3}{10} - \dfrac{5}{10} = \dfrac{10-3-5}{10}$

$\qquad = \dfrac{2}{10} = \dfrac{2}{2\cdot5} = \dfrac{1}{5}$

The unknown part is $\dfrac{1}{5}$

79. $1 - \dfrac{1}{4} - \dfrac{3}{8} = \dfrac{8}{8} - \dfrac{1\cdot2}{4\cdot2} - \dfrac{3}{8} = \dfrac{8-2-3}{8} = \dfrac{3}{8}$

The unknown part is $\dfrac{3}{8}$

81. $237\dfrac{1}{6} = 237\dfrac{1\cdot2}{6\cdot2} = 237\dfrac{2}{12} = 236\dfrac{14}{12}$

$\qquad\qquad\qquad\quad -224\dfrac{5}{12}$

$\qquad\qquad\qquad\qquad 12\dfrac{9}{12} = 12\dfrac{3}{4}$

It was $12\dfrac{3}{4}$ feet longer.

83. a. $\dfrac{7}{50}$ are in the physical sciences

3. $7.685 = \dfrac{7685}{1000}$

b. $\dfrac{21}{100}$ are in engineering

4. a.
$$\begin{array}{r} 7.19 \\ 19.782 \\ +\ \ 1.006 \\ \hline 27.978 \end{array}$$

b.
$$\begin{array}{r} 12. \\ 0.79 \\ +\ \ 0.03 \\ \hline 12.82 \end{array}$$

c. $1 - \dfrac{4}{25} - \dfrac{7}{50} - \dfrac{7}{50} - \dfrac{7}{100} - \dfrac{21}{100} - \dfrac{3}{100}$

$= \dfrac{100}{100} - \dfrac{4 \cdot 4}{25 \cdot 4} - \dfrac{7 \cdot 2}{50 \cdot 2} - \dfrac{7 \cdot 2}{50 \cdot 2} - \dfrac{7}{100}$

$\qquad - \dfrac{21}{100} - \dfrac{3}{100}$

$= \dfrac{100 - 16 - 14 - 14 - 7 - 21 - 3}{100}$

$= \dfrac{25}{100} = \dfrac{1}{4}$

$\dfrac{1}{4}$ are in the biological and

agricultural sciences

5. a.
$$\begin{array}{r} 84.230 \\ -\ \ 26.982 \\ \hline 57.248 \end{array}$$

b.
$$\begin{array}{r} 90. \\ -\ \ 0.19 \\ \hline 89.81 \end{array}$$

6. a.
$$\begin{array}{r} 0.31 \\ \times\ \ \ 4.6 \\ \hline 186 \\ 124\ \ \\ \hline 1.426 \end{array}$$

b.
$$\begin{array}{r} 1.26 \\ \times\ 0.03 \\ \hline 0.0378 \end{array}$$

d. $\dfrac{4}{25} + \dfrac{7}{50} = \dfrac{4 \cdot 2}{25 \cdot 2} + \dfrac{7}{50} = \dfrac{15}{50} = \dfrac{3}{10}$

$\dfrac{3}{10}$ are in the social sciences

and psychology

7. a.
$$\begin{array}{r} 43.5 \\ 5\overline{)217.5} \\ \underline{20} \\ 17 \\ \underline{15} \\ 25 \\ \underline{25} \\ 0 \end{array}$$

b.
$$\begin{array}{r} 2600 \\ 6\overline{)15600} \\ \underline{12} \\ 36 \\ \underline{36} \\ 0 \end{array}$$

85. Area $= \dfrac{1}{2} \cdot \dfrac{7}{8} \cdot \dfrac{4}{9} = \dfrac{7 \cdot 4}{2 \cdot 2 \cdot 4 \cdot 9} = \dfrac{7}{36}$ sq ft

Practice Problems R.3

1. $0.27 = \dfrac{27}{100}$

2. $5.1 = \dfrac{51}{10}$

8. $12.9187 \Rightarrow 12.92$

9. $245.348 \Rightarrow 245.3$

10.
$$\begin{array}{r} 0.4 \\ 5\overline{)2.0} \\ \underline{2.0} \\ 0 \end{array}$$
$\qquad \dfrac{2}{5} = 0.4$

11.
$$\begin{array}{r} 0.833 \\ 6)\overline{5.000} \\ \underline{48} \\ 20 \\ \underline{18} \\ 20 \\ \underline{18} \\ 2 \end{array}$$

This pattern will continue

so $\dfrac{5}{6} = 0.8\bar{3}$

3. $1.86 = \dfrac{186}{100}$

5. $0.114 = \dfrac{114}{1000}$

7. $123.1 = \dfrac{1231}{10}$

12.
$$\begin{array}{r} 0.1111 \\ 9)\overline{1.0000} \\ \underline{9} \\ 10 \\ \underline{9} \\ 10 \\ \underline{9} \\ 1 \end{array}$$

This pattern will continue

so $\dfrac{1}{9} = 0.\bar{1}$

$\dfrac{1}{9} \approx 0.111$

9.
$$\begin{array}{r} 5.7 \\ +\ 1.13 \\ \hline 6.83 \end{array}$$

11.
$$\begin{array}{r} 24.6 \\ 2.39 \\ +\ \ 0.0678 \\ \hline 25.0578 \end{array}$$

13.
$$\begin{array}{r} 8.8 \\ -\ 2.3 \\ \hline 6.5 \end{array}$$

13. **a.** $20\% = 0.2$

b. $1.2\% = 0.012$

c. $465\% = 4.65$

14. **a.** $0.42 = 42\%$

b. $0.003 = 0.3\%$

c. $2.36 = 236\%$

d. $0.7 = 70\%$

15.
$$\begin{array}{r} 18. \\ -\ 2.78 \\ \hline 15.22 \end{array}$$

17.
$$\begin{array}{r} 45.02 \\ 3.006 \\ +\ \ 8.405 \\ \hline 56.431 \end{array}$$

19.
$$\begin{array}{r} 654.9 \\ -\ 56.67 \\ \hline 598.23 \end{array}$$

Exercise Set R.3

1. $0.6 = \dfrac{6}{10}$

21.
$$\begin{array}{r} 0.2 \\ \times\ 0.6 \\ \hline 0.12 \end{array}$$

23.
$$\begin{array}{r} 6.75 \\ \times\ \ \ 10 \\ \hline 000 \\ 675 \\ \hline 67.50 \end{array}$$

25.
$$\begin{array}{r} 5.62 \\ \times\ \ 7.7 \\ \hline 3934 \\ 3934 \\ \hline 43.274 \end{array}$$

27.
$$\begin{array}{r} 16.003 \\ \times\ \ \ 5.31 \\ \hline 16003 \\ 48009 \\ 80015 \\ \hline 84.97593 \end{array}$$

29.
$$\begin{array}{r} 0.094 \\ 5\overline{)0.470} \\ \underline{-45} \\ 20 \\ \underline{-20} \\ 0 \end{array}$$

31.
$$\begin{array}{r} 70 \\ 6\overline{)420} \\ \underline{-42} \\ 00 \\ \underline{-00} \end{array}$$

33.
$$\begin{array}{r} 5.8 \\ 82\overline{)475.6} \\ \underline{-410} \\ 656 \\ \underline{-656} \\ 0 \end{array}$$

35.
$$\begin{array}{r} 840 \\ 63\overline{)52920.} \\ \underline{-504} \\ 252 \\ \underline{-252} \\ 00 \\ \underline{-00} \end{array}$$

37. answers may vary

39. $0.57 \approx 0.6$

41. $0.234 \approx 0.23$

43. $0.5942 \approx 0.594$

45. $98,207.23 \approx 98,207.2$

47. $12.347 \approx 12.35$

49. $\dfrac{3}{4} = 4\overline{)3.00}^{0.75} = 0.75$

$$\begin{array}{r} 0.75 \\ 4\overline{)3.00} \\ \underline{-28} \\ 20 \\ \underline{-20} \\ 0 \end{array}$$

51. $\dfrac{1}{3} = 3\overline{)1.00} = 0.333\ldots = 0.\overline{3} \approx 0.33$

$$\begin{array}{r} 0.333 \\ 3\overline{)1.00} \\ \underline{-9} \\ 10 \\ \underline{-9} \\ 0 \end{array}$$

53. $\dfrac{7}{16} = 16\overline{)7.0000} = 0.4375$

$$\begin{array}{r} 0.4375 \\ 16\overline{)7.0000} \\ \underline{-64} \\ 60 \\ \underline{-48} \\ 120 \\ \underline{-112} \\ 80 \\ \underline{-80} \\ 0 \end{array}$$

55. $\dfrac{6}{11} = 11\overline{)6.0000} = 0.5454\ldots = 0.\overline{54} \approx 0.55$

$$\begin{array}{r} 0.5454 \\ 11\overline{)6.0000} \\ 55 \\ 50 \\ \underline{-44} \\ 60 \\ \underline{-55} \\ 50 \\ \underline{-44} \\ 6 \end{array}$$

57. $28\% = \dfrac{28}{100} = 0.28$

59. $3.1\% = \dfrac{3.1}{100} = 0.031$

61. $135\% = \dfrac{135}{100} = 1.35$

63. $96.55\% = \dfrac{96.55}{100} = 0.9655$

65. $52\% = \dfrac{52}{100} = 0.52$

67. $0.68 = 0.68 \times 100\% = 68\%$

69. $0.876 = 0.876 \times 100\% = 87.6\%$

71. $1 = 1 \times 100\% = 100\%$

73. $0.5 = 0.5 \times 100\% = 50\%$

75. $\begin{array}{r} 140.30 \\ \underline{-104.40} \\ 35.9 \end{array}$

There is 35.9 cubic feet more.

77. $\dfrac{7}{20} = 20\overline{)7.00}$

$$\begin{array}{r} 0.35 \\ 20\overline{)7.00} \\ \underline{-60} \\ 100 \\ \underline{-100} \\ 0 \end{array}$$

$\dfrac{7}{20} = 0.35 = 0.35 \times 100\% = 35\%$

is purchased in conjunction
with holidays.

Chapter R Review

1. $42 = 2 \cdot 3 \cdot 7$

2. $800 = 2 \cdot 2 \cdot 2 \cdot 2 \cdot 2 \cdot 5 \cdot 5$

3. $12 = 2 \cdot 2 \cdot 3$
$30 = 2 \cdot 3 \cdot 5$
$\text{LCM} = 2 \cdot 2 \cdot 3 \cdot 5 = 60$

4. $7 = 7$
$42 = 2 \cdot 3 \cdot 7$
$\text{LCM} = 2 \cdot 3 \cdot 7 = 42$

5. $4 = 2 \cdot 2$
$6 = 2 \cdot 3$
$10 = 2 \cdot 5$
$\text{LCM} = 2 \cdot 2 \cdot 3 \cdot 5 = 60$

6. $2 = 2$
$5 = 5$
$7 = 7$
$\text{LCM} = 2 \cdot 5 \cdot 7 = 70$

7. $\dfrac{5}{8} = \dfrac{5 \cdot 3}{2 \cdot 2 \cdot 2 \cdot 3} = \dfrac{15}{24}$

8. $\dfrac{2}{3} = \dfrac{2 \cdot 2 \cdot 2 \cdot 5}{3 \cdot 2 \cdot 2 \cdot 5} = \dfrac{40}{60}$

9. $\dfrac{8}{20} = \dfrac{2 \cdot 2 \cdot 2}{2 \cdot 2 \cdot 5} = \dfrac{2}{5}$

10. $\dfrac{15}{100} = \dfrac{3 \cdot 5}{2 \cdot 2 \cdot 5 \cdot 5} = \dfrac{3}{2 \cdot 2 \cdot 5} = \dfrac{3}{20}$

11. $\dfrac{12}{6} = \dfrac{2 \cdot 2 \cdot 3}{2 \cdot 3} = \dfrac{2}{1} = 2$

12. $\dfrac{8}{8} = \dfrac{2 \cdot 2 \cdot 2}{2 \cdot 2 \cdot 2} = \dfrac{1}{1} = 1$

13. $\dfrac{1}{7} \cdot \dfrac{8}{11} = \dfrac{1 \cdot 8}{7 \cdot 11} = \dfrac{8}{77}$

14. $\dfrac{5}{12} + \dfrac{2}{15} = \dfrac{5 \cdot 5}{12 \cdot 5} + \dfrac{2 \cdot 4}{15 \cdot 4} = \dfrac{25}{60} + \dfrac{8}{60}$
$= \dfrac{25 + 8}{60} = \dfrac{33}{60} = \dfrac{3 \cdot 11}{3 \cdot 20} = \dfrac{11}{20}$

15. $\dfrac{3}{10} \div \dfrac{6}{1} = \dfrac{3}{10} \cdot \dfrac{1}{6} = \dfrac{3 \cdot 1}{2 \cdot 5 \cdot 2 \cdot 3} = \dfrac{1}{20}$

16. $\dfrac{7}{9} - \dfrac{1}{6} = \dfrac{7 \cdot 2}{9 \cdot 2} - \dfrac{1 \cdot 3}{6 \cdot 3} = \dfrac{14}{18} - \dfrac{3}{18} = \dfrac{14 - 3}{18} = \dfrac{11}{18}$

17. $3\dfrac{3}{8} \cdot 4\dfrac{1}{4} = \dfrac{27}{8} \cdot \dfrac{17}{4} = \dfrac{27 \cdot 17}{8 \cdot 4} = \dfrac{459}{32} = 14\dfrac{11}{32}$

18. $2\dfrac{1}{3} - 1\dfrac{5}{6} = \dfrac{7}{3} - \dfrac{11}{6} = \dfrac{7 \cdot 2}{3 \cdot 2} - \dfrac{11}{6}$
$= \dfrac{14 - 11}{6} = \dfrac{3}{6} = \dfrac{3}{2 \cdot 3} = \dfrac{1}{2}$

19. $16\dfrac{9}{10} + 3\dfrac{2}{3} = \dfrac{169}{10} + \dfrac{11}{3} = \dfrac{169 \cdot 3}{10 \cdot 3} + \dfrac{11 \cdot 10}{3 \cdot 10}$
$= \dfrac{507}{30} + \dfrac{110}{30} = \dfrac{617}{30} = 20\dfrac{17}{30}$

20. $6\dfrac{2}{7} \div 2\dfrac{1}{5} = \dfrac{44}{7} \div \dfrac{11}{5} = \dfrac{44}{7} \cdot \dfrac{5}{11}$
$= \dfrac{2 \cdot 2 \cdot 5 \cdot 11}{7 \cdot 11} = \dfrac{20}{7} = 2\dfrac{6}{7}$

21. $A = lw$

$$A = \frac{11}{12} \cdot \frac{3}{5} = \frac{11 \cdot 3}{2 \cdot 2 \cdot 3 \cdot 5} = \frac{11}{2 \cdot 2 \cdot 5} = \frac{11}{20}$$

The area is $\frac{11}{20}$ sq. mile

22. $A = \frac{1}{2}bh$

$$A = \frac{1}{2} \cdot \frac{5}{4} \cdot \frac{1}{2} = \frac{1 \cdot 5 \cdot 1}{2 \cdot 4 \cdot 2} = \frac{5}{16}$$

The area is $\frac{5}{16}$ sq. meter

23. $1.81 = \frac{181}{100}$

24. $0.035 = \frac{35}{1000}$

25.
$$\begin{array}{r} 576.358 \\ + \ 18.76 \\ \hline 95.118 \end{array}$$

26.
$$\begin{array}{r} 35. \\ 0.02 \\ + \ 1.765 \\ \hline 36.785 \end{array}$$

27.
$$\begin{array}{r} 18. \\ - \ 4.62 \\ \hline 13.38 \end{array}$$

28.
$$\begin{array}{r} 804.062 \\ - \ 112.489 \\ \hline 691.573 \end{array}$$

29.
$$\begin{array}{r} 7.6 \\ \times \ 12 \\ \hline 152 \\ 76 \ \ \\ \hline 91.2 \end{array}$$

30.
$$\begin{array}{r} 14.63 \\ \times \ \ 3.2 \\ \hline 2926 \\ 4389 \ \ \\ \hline 46.816 \end{array}$$

31.
$$\begin{array}{r} 28.6 \\ 27 \overline{)\ 772.2} \\ \underline{-54} \ \ \ \ \\ 232 \ \ \\ \underline{-216} \ \ \\ 162 \\ \underline{-162} \\ 0 \end{array}$$

32.
$$\begin{array}{r} 230 \\ 6 \overline{)\ 1380} \\ \underline{-12} \ \ \ \\ 18 \ \\ \underline{-18} \ \\ 00 \end{array}$$

33. $0.7652 \approx 0.77$

34. $25.6293 \approx 25.6$

35. $\dfrac{1}{2} = 2\overline{)\begin{array}{l} 0.5 \\ 1.0 \end{array}} = 0.5$
$\phantom{\dfrac{1}{2} = 2)1.0}\underline{-10}$
$\phantom{\dfrac{1}{2} = 2)1.00}0$

36. $\dfrac{3}{8} = 8\overline{)\begin{array}{l} 0.375 \\ 3.000 \end{array}} = 0.375$
$\phantom{\dfrac{3}{8} = 8)3.0}\underline{-24}$
$\phantom{\dfrac{3}{8} = 8)3.00}60$
$\phantom{\dfrac{3}{8} = 8)3.00}\underline{-56}$
$\phantom{\dfrac{3}{8} = 8)3.000}40$
$\phantom{\dfrac{3}{8} = 8)3.000}\underline{-40}$
$\phantom{\dfrac{3}{8} = 8)3.0000}0$

37. $\dfrac{4}{11} = 11\overline{)\begin{array}{l} 0.3636 \\ 4.0000 \end{array}} = 0.3636\ldots = 0.\overline{36} \approx 0.364$
$\phantom{\dfrac{4}{11} = 11)4.0}\underline{-33}$
$\phantom{\dfrac{4}{11} = 11)4.00}70$
$\phantom{\dfrac{4}{11} = 11)4.000}\underline{-66}$
$\phantom{\dfrac{4}{11} = 11)4.000}40$
$\phantom{\dfrac{4}{11} = 11)4.0000}\underline{-33}$
$\phantom{\dfrac{4}{11} = 11)4.0000}70$
$\phantom{\dfrac{4}{11} = 11)4.00000}\underline{-66}$
$\phantom{\dfrac{4}{11} = 11)4.00000}4$

38. $\dfrac{5}{6} = 6\overline{)\begin{array}{l} 0.8333 \\ 5.0000 \end{array}} = 0.8333\ldots = 0.8\overline{3} \approx 0.833$
$\phantom{\dfrac{5}{6} = 6)5.0}\underline{-48}$
$\phantom{\dfrac{5}{6} = 6)5.00}20$
$\phantom{\dfrac{5}{6} = 6)5.000}\underline{-18}$
$\phantom{\dfrac{5}{6} = 6)5.000}20$
$\phantom{\dfrac{5}{6} = 6)5.0000}\underline{-18}$
$\phantom{\dfrac{5}{6} = 6)5.0000}20$
$\phantom{\dfrac{5}{6} = 6)5.00000}\underline{-18}$
$\phantom{\dfrac{5}{6} = 6)5.00000}2$

39. $29\% = \dfrac{29}{100} = 0.29$

40. $1.4\% = \dfrac{1.4}{100} = \dfrac{14}{1000} = 0.014$

41. $0.39 = 0.39 \cdot 100\% = 39\%$

42. $1.2 = 1.2 \cdot 100\% = 120\%$

43. $67.4\% = \dfrac{67.4}{100} = \dfrac{674}{1000} = 0.674$

44.   b. $5 = 5 \cdot 100\% = 500\%$

Chapter R Test

1. $72 = 2 \cdot 2 \cdot 2 \cdot 3 \cdot 3$

2. $5 = 5$
     $18 = 2 \cdot 3 \cdot 3$
     $20 = 2 \cdot 2 \cdot 5$
     $\text{LCM} = 2 \cdot 2 \cdot 3 \cdot 3 \cdot 5 = 180$

3. $\dfrac{5}{12} = \dfrac{5 \cdot 5}{12 \cdot 5} = \dfrac{25}{60}$

4. $\dfrac{15}{20} = \dfrac{3 \cdot 5}{2 \cdot 2 \cdot 5} = \dfrac{3}{2 \cdot 2} = \dfrac{3}{4}$

5. $\dfrac{48}{100} = \dfrac{2 \cdot 2 \cdot 2 \cdot 2 \cdot 3}{2 \cdot 2 \cdot 5 \cdot 5} = \dfrac{2 \cdot 2 \cdot 3}{5 \cdot 5} = \dfrac{12}{25}$

6. $1.3 = \dfrac{13}{10}$

7. $\dfrac{5}{8}+\dfrac{7}{10}=\dfrac{5\cdot5}{8\cdot5}+\dfrac{7\cdot4}{10\cdot4}=\dfrac{25}{40}+\dfrac{28}{40}$

$\qquad=\dfrac{25+28}{40}=\dfrac{53}{40}$

8. $\dfrac{2}{3}\cdot\dfrac{27}{49}=\dfrac{2\cdot3\cdot3\cdot3}{3\cdot7\cdot7}=\dfrac{2\cdot3\cdot3}{7\cdot7}=\dfrac{18}{49}$

9. $\dfrac{9}{10}\div\dfrac{18}{1}=\dfrac{9}{10}\cdot\dfrac{1}{18}=\dfrac{3\cdot3\cdot1}{2\cdot5\cdot2\cdot3\cdot3}=\dfrac{1}{20}$

10. $\dfrac{8}{9}-\dfrac{1}{12}=\dfrac{8\cdot4}{9\cdot4}-\dfrac{1\cdot3}{12\cdot3}=\dfrac{32}{36}-\dfrac{3}{36}=\dfrac{32-3}{36}=\dfrac{29}{36}$

11. $1\dfrac{2}{9}+3\dfrac{2}{3}=\dfrac{11}{9}+\dfrac{11}{3}=\dfrac{11}{9}+\dfrac{11\cdot3}{3\cdot3}=\dfrac{11}{9}+\dfrac{33}{9}$

$\qquad=\dfrac{11+33}{9}=\dfrac{44}{9}=4\dfrac{8}{9}$

12. $5\dfrac{6}{11}-3\dfrac{7}{22}=\dfrac{61}{11}-\dfrac{73}{22}=\dfrac{61\cdot2}{11\cdot2}-\dfrac{73}{22}$

$\qquad=\dfrac{122}{22}-\dfrac{73}{22}=\dfrac{122-73}{22}=\dfrac{49}{22}=2\dfrac{5}{22}$

13. $6\dfrac{7}{8}\div\dfrac{1}{8}=\dfrac{55}{8}\cdot\dfrac{8}{1}=\dfrac{55\cdot8}{8\cdot1}=\dfrac{55}{1}=55$

14. $2\dfrac{1}{10}\cdot6\dfrac{1}{2}=\dfrac{21}{10}\cdot\dfrac{13}{2}=\dfrac{3\cdot7\cdot13}{2\cdot2\cdot5}=\dfrac{273}{20}=13\dfrac{13}{20}$

15.
$$\begin{array}{r} 43. \\ 0.21 \\ +\ 1.9 \\ \hline 45.11 \end{array}$$

16.
$$\begin{array}{r} 123.6 \\ -\ 57.72 \\ \hline 65.88 \end{array}$$

17.
$$\begin{array}{r} 7.93 \\ \times\ 1.6 \\ \hline 4758 \\ 793 \\ \hline 12.688 \end{array}$$

18.
$$\begin{array}{r} 320 \\ 25\overline{)\ 8000} \\ \underline{-75} \\ 50 \\ \underline{-50} \\ 00 \end{array}$$

19. $23.272\approx23.73$

20. $\dfrac{7}{8}=8\overline{)\,7.000}$
$$\begin{array}{r} 0.875 \\ \underline{-64} \\ 60 \\ \underline{-56} \\ 40 \\ \underline{-40} \\ 0 \end{array}$$
$=0.875$

21. $\dfrac{1}{6}=6\overline{)\,1.0000}=0.1666\ldots=0.1\overline{6}\approx0.167$
$$\begin{array}{r} 0.1666 \\ \underline{-6} \\ 40 \\ \underline{-36} \\ 40 \\ \underline{-36} \\ 40 \\ \underline{-36} \\ 4 \end{array}$$

22. $63.2\% = \dfrac{63.2}{100} = \dfrac{632}{1000} = 0.632$

23. $0.09 = 0.09 \cdot 100\% = 9\%$

24. $\dfrac{3}{4} = 4\overline{)3.00}\;\; = 0.75 = 0.75 \cdot 100\% = 75\%$

$$
\begin{array}{r}
0.75 \\
4\overline{)3.00} \\
-28 \\
\hline
20 \\
-20 \\
\hline
0
\end{array}
$$

25. $\dfrac{3}{4}$

26. $\dfrac{1}{200}$

27. $1 - \dfrac{3}{4} - \dfrac{1}{200} = \dfrac{200}{200} - \dfrac{150}{200} - \dfrac{1}{200} = \dfrac{49}{200}$

$\dfrac{49}{200}$ of the fresh water is groundwater.

28. $\dfrac{3}{4} + \dfrac{49}{200} = \dfrac{150}{200} + \dfrac{49}{200} = \dfrac{199}{200}$

$\dfrac{199}{200}$ of the fresh water is groundwater

or icecaps and glaciers.

29. $A = \dfrac{1}{2}bh$

$A = \dfrac{1}{2} \cdot \dfrac{3}{4} \cdot \dfrac{1}{3} = \dfrac{1 \cdot 3 \cdot 1}{2 \cdot 4 \cdot 3} = \dfrac{1}{8}$

The area is $\dfrac{1}{8}$ sq. foot

30. $A = lw$

$A = \dfrac{9}{8} \cdot \dfrac{7}{8} = \dfrac{9 \cdot 7}{8 \cdot 8} = \dfrac{63}{64}$

The area is $\dfrac{63}{64}$ sq. centimeter

Chapter 1

1. $0 > -3$

2. $-10 < -8$

3. $1.7 > 1.07$

4. $|5| = 5$

5. $|-1.2| = 1.2$

6. $|0| = 0$

7. Let $x = 2$ and $y = 5$.
$$xy - x^2 = 2(5) - (2)^2 = 10 - 4 = 6$$

8. $2x - 10$

9. $4^3 = 4 \cdot 4 \cdot 4 = 64$

10. $-3^2 = -(3)(3) = -9$

11. The opposite of $-\dfrac{3}{5}$ is $\dfrac{3}{5}$

12. Reciprocal of $\dfrac{1}{8}$ is 8 since $8 \cdot \dfrac{1}{8} = 1$

13. $3 + 2(5)^2 = 3 + 2(25) = 3 + 50 = 53$

14. $-10 + 13 = 3$

15. $-6 - 21 = -6 + (-21) = -27$

16. $(-7)(-8) = 56$

17. $-2.8 \div 0.04 = -2.8 \cdot \dfrac{1}{0.04} = -70$

18. $\dfrac{-4 - 6^2}{5(-2)} = \dfrac{-4 - 36}{-10} = \dfrac{-4 + (-36)}{-10} = \dfrac{-40}{-10} = 4$

19. Let $x = -4$ and $y = -7$.
$$x^2 - 2xy = (-4)^2 - 2(-4)(-7)$$
$$= 16 - 2(-4)(-7) = 16 - (-8)(-7)$$
$$= 16 - 56 = -40$$

20. Let $x = 7$
$$x - 12 = 5$$
$$7 - 12 \overset{?}{=} 5$$
$$-5 = 5, \text{ false}$$
7 is not a solution of the equation.

21. Let $x = 40$
$$\frac{x}{8} + 2 = 7$$
$$\frac{40}{8} + 2 \overset{?}{=} 7$$
$$5 + 2 \overset{?}{=} 7$$
$$7 = 7, \text{ true}$$
40 is a solution of the equation.

22. The balance increase is
$$34 - (-21) = 34 + 21 = 55$$
The balance increased \$55

23. $2y + 5 = \underline{5 + 2y}$.

24. $4(3 + 2t) = 4(3) + 4(2t) = 12 + 8t$

25. Additive inverse property

Exercise Set 1.1

Answers will vary on Exercises 1-12.

Practice Problems 1.2

1. False, since 8 is to the right of 6 on the number line.

2. True, since 100 is to the right of 10 on the number line.

3. True, since 21=21.

4. True, since 21=21.

5. True, since 0 is to the left of 5 on the number line.

6. True, since 25 is to the right of 22 on the number line.

7. **a.** $14 \geq 14$
     b. $0 < 5$
     c. $9 \neq 10$

8. −282 represents 282 feet below sea level.

9.

10. **a.** The natural numbers are 6 and 913.
     b. The whole numbers are 0, 6 and 913.
     c. The integers are −100, 0, 6 and 913.
     d. The rational numbers are
        −11, −2/5, 0, 6 and 913.
     e. The irrational number is π.
     f. The real numbers are all
        numbers in the given set.

11. **a.** $|7| = 7$ since 7 is 7 units from 0 on the number line.
     b. $|-8| = 8$ since 8 is 8 units from 0 on the number line.
     c. $\left|-\dfrac{2}{3}\right| = \dfrac{2}{3}$ since $\dfrac{2}{3}$ is $\dfrac{2}{3}$ of a unit from 0 on the number line.

12. **a.** $|4| = 4$
     b. $-3 < |0|$ since $-3 < 0$.
     c. $|-2.7| > |2|$ since $2.7 > 2$.
     d. $|6| < |16|$ since $6 < 16$.
     e. $|-6| < |-16|$ since $6 < 16$.

Exercise Set 1.2

1. $4 < 10$

3. $7 > 3$

5. $6.26 = 6.26$

7. $0 < 7$

9. $32 < 212$

11. True, since 11=11.

13. False, since 10 is to the left of 11 on the number line.

15. False, since 11 is to the left of 24 on the number line.

17. True, since 7 is to the right of 0 on the number line.

19. $30 \le 45$

21. $20 \le 25$

23. $6 > 0$

25. $-12 < -10$

27. $7 < 11$

29. $5 \ge 4$

31. $15 \ne -2$

33. 14,494 represents an altitude of 14,494 feet. −282 represents 282 feet below sea level.

35. −34,841 represents a population decrease of 34,841.

37. 475 represents a deposit of $475. −195 represents a withdrawal of $195.

39.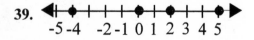

41.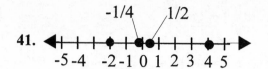

43.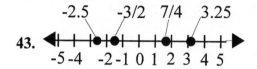

45. The number 0 belongs to the sets of: whole numbers, integers, rational numbers, and real numbers.

47. The number -2 belongs to the sets of: integers, rational numbers, and real numbers.

49. The number 2650 belongs to the sets of: natural numbers, whole numbers, integers, rational numbers, and real numbers.

51. The number 2/3 belongs to the sets of: rational numbers and real numbers.

53. False. Rational numbers may be non-integers.

55. True

57. False. Negative numbers may be irrational.

59. False. Irrational numbers are real.

61. $|-5| > -4$ since $5 > -4$

63. $|-1| = |1|$ since 1=1

65. $|-2| < |-3|$ since $2 < 3$

67. $|0| < |-8|$ since $8 < 8$

69. False, since $\dfrac{1}{2}$ is to the right of $\dfrac{1}{3}$ on the number line.

71. True, since $5.3 = 5.3$

73. False, since -9.6 is to the left of -9.1 on the number line.

75. True, since $-\dfrac{2}{3}$ is to the left of $-\dfrac{1}{5}$ on the number line.

77. Blue Ridge Parkway has the most visitors.

79. Blue Ridge Parkway had more visitors than Golden Gate National Recreation Area: $19.0 \geq 14.5$

81. $-0.04 > -26.7$

83. The sun is brighter since $-26.7 < -0.04$.

85. The sun is brighter since -26.7 is to the left of all other numbers listed.

87. Answers may vary.

Practice Problems 1.3

1. a. $4^2 = 4 \cdot 4 = 16$

   b. $2^2 = 2 \cdot 2 = 4$

   c. $3^4 = 3 \cdot 3 \cdot 3 \cdot 3 = 81$

   d. $9^1 = 9$

   e. $\left(\dfrac{2}{5}\right)^2 = \dfrac{2}{5} \cdot \dfrac{2}{5} = \dfrac{2 \cdot 2}{5 \cdot 5} = \dfrac{4}{25}$

2. $3 + 2 \cdot 4^2 = 3 + 2 \cdot 16 = 3 + 32 = 35$

3. $17 - 3 + 4 = 14 + 4 = 18$

4. $\dfrac{9}{5} \cdot \dfrac{1}{3} - \dfrac{1}{3} = \dfrac{9}{15} - \dfrac{1}{3} = \dfrac{9}{15} - \dfrac{5}{15} = \dfrac{4}{15}$

5. $8\big[2(6+3) - 9\big] = 8\big[2(9) - 9\big]$
$= 8[18 - 9] = 8[9] = 72$

6. $\dfrac{1 + |7 - 4| + 3^2}{8 - 5} = \dfrac{1 + |3| + 3^2}{8 - 5} = \dfrac{1 + 3 + 3^2}{8 - 5}$
$= \dfrac{1 + 3 + 9}{8 - 5} = \dfrac{13}{3}$

7. Let $x = 1$ and $y = 4$

   a. $2y - x = 2(4) - 1 = 8 - 1 = 7$

   b. $\dfrac{8x}{3y} = \dfrac{8(1)}{3(4)} = \dfrac{2 \cdot 4 \cdot 1}{3 \cdot 4} = \dfrac{2}{3}$

   c. $\dfrac{x}{y} + \dfrac{5}{y} = \dfrac{1}{4} + \dfrac{5}{4} = \dfrac{6}{4} = \dfrac{2 \cdot 3}{2 \cdot 2} = \dfrac{3}{2}$

   d. $y^2 - x^2 = 4^2 - 1^2 = 16 - 1 = 15$

8. Let $x = 3$.

$$5x - 10 = x + 2$$

$$5(3) - 10 \overset{?}{=} 3 + 2$$

$$15 - 10 \overset{?}{=} 3 + 2$$

$$5 = 5$$

3 is a solution of the equation.

9. **a.** $5x$

  b. $x + 7$

  c. $3x$

  d. $8 - x$

  e. $2x + 1$

10. **a.** $6x = 24$

  b. $10 - x = 18$

  c. $2x - 1 = 99$

Exercise Set 1.3

1. $3^5 = 3 \cdot 3 \cdot 3 \cdot 3 \cdot 3 = 243$

3. $3^3 = 3 \cdot 3 \cdot 3 = 27$

5. $1^5 = 1 \cdot 1 \cdot 1 \cdot 1 \cdot 1 = 1$

7. $5^1 = 5$

9. $\left(\dfrac{1}{5}\right)^3 = \left(\dfrac{1}{5}\right)\left(\dfrac{1}{5}\right)\left(\dfrac{1}{5}\right) = \dfrac{1 \cdot 1 \cdot 1}{5 \cdot 5 \cdot 5} = \dfrac{1}{125}$

11. $\left(\dfrac{2}{3}\right)^4 = \left(\dfrac{2}{3}\right)\left(\dfrac{2}{3}\right)\left(\dfrac{2}{3}\right)\left(\dfrac{2}{3}\right) = \dfrac{2 \cdot 2 \cdot 2 \cdot 2}{3 \cdot 3 \cdot 3 \cdot 3} = \dfrac{16}{81}$

13. $7^2 = 7 \cdot 7 = 49$

15. $(1.2)^2 = (1.2) \cdot (1.2) = 1.44$

17. $(5 \cdot 5)$ square meters $= 5^2$ square meters

19. $5 + 6 \cdot 2 = 5 + 12 = 17$

21. $4 \cdot 8 - 6 \cdot 2 = 32 - 12 = 20$

23. $2(8 - 3) = 2(5) = 10$

25. $2 + (5 - 2) + 4^2 = 2 + 3 + 4^2 = 2 + 3 + 16 = 21$

27. $5 \cdot 3^2 = 5 \cdot 9 = 45$

29. $\dfrac{1}{4} \cdot \dfrac{2}{3} - \dfrac{1}{6} = \dfrac{2}{12} - \dfrac{1}{6} = \dfrac{1}{6} - \dfrac{1}{6} = 0$

31. $\dfrac{6 - 4}{9 - 2} = \dfrac{2}{7}$

33. $2[5 + 2(8 - 3)] = 2[5 + 2(5)] = 2[5 + 10]$
$$= 2[15] = 30$$

35. $\dfrac{19 - 3 \cdot 5}{6 - 4} = \dfrac{19 - 15}{6 - 4} = \dfrac{4}{2} = 2$

37. $\dfrac{|6 - 2| + 3}{8 + 2 \cdot 5} = \dfrac{|4| + 3}{8 + 2 \cdot 5} = \dfrac{4 + 3}{8 + 2 \cdot 5} = \dfrac{4 + 3}{8 + 10}$
$$= \dfrac{7}{18}$$

39. $\dfrac{3 + 3(5 + 3)}{3^2 + 1} = \dfrac{3 + 3(8)}{3^2 + 1} = \dfrac{3 + 3(8)}{9 + 1}$
$$= \dfrac{3 + 24}{9 + 1} = \dfrac{27}{10}$$

41. $\dfrac{6+|8-2|+3^2}{18-3}=\dfrac{6+|6|+3^2}{18-3}=\dfrac{6+6+3^2}{18-3}$

$=\dfrac{6+6+9}{18-3}=\dfrac{21}{15}=\dfrac{3\cdot 7}{3\cdot 5}$

$=\dfrac{7}{5}$

43. No; since in the absence of grouping symbols we always perform multiplications or divisions before additions or subtractions in any expression.

45. a. $(6+2)\cdot(5+3)=8\cdot 8=64$

b. $(6+2)\cdot 5+3=8\cdot 5+3=40+3$
$=43$

c. $6+2\cdot 5+3=6+10+3=19$

d. $6+2\cdot(5+3)=6+2\cdot 8=6+16$
$=22$

47. Let $y=3$
$3y=3(3)=9$

49. Let $x=1$ and $z=5$
$\dfrac{z}{5x}=\dfrac{5}{5(1)}=\dfrac{5}{5}=1$

51. Let $x=1$
$3x-2=3(1)-2=3-2=1$

53. Let $x=1$ and $y=3$
$|2x+3y|=|2(1)+3(3)|=|2+9|=|11|=11$

55. Let $x=1$, $y=3$, and $z=5$
$xy+z=(1)(3)+5=3+5=8$

57. Let $y=3$
$5y^2=5(3)^2=5(9)=45$

59. Let $z=3$
$5z=5(3)=15$

61. Let $x=2$ and $y=6$
$\dfrac{y}{x}=\dfrac{6}{2}=\dfrac{2\cdot 3}{2}=3$

63. Let $x=2$ and $y=6$
$\dfrac{y}{x}+\dfrac{y}{x}=\dfrac{6}{2}+\dfrac{6}{2}=\dfrac{6+6}{2}=\dfrac{12}{2}=\dfrac{2\cdot 2\cdot 3}{2}=6$

65. Evaluate $2l+2w$ for each combination of values $\{l, w\}$.
$\{3, 4\}:2(3)+2(4)=6+8=14$
$\{1, 6\}:2(1)+2(6)=2+12=14$
$\{2, 5\}:2(2)+2(5)=4+10=14$
Evaluate lw for each combination of values $\{l, w\}$.
$\{3, 4\}:(3)(4)=12$
$\{1, 6\}:(1)(6)=6$
$\{2, 5\}:(2)(5)=10$

Length: l	Width: w	Perimeter $2l+2w$	Area lw
3 in.	4 in.	14 in.	12 sq.in.
1 in.	6 in.	14 in.	6 sq.in.
2 in.	5 in.	14 in.	10 sq.in.

67. Let $x = 5$

$$3x - 6 = 9$$

$$3(5) \overset{?}{-} 6 = 9$$

$$15 \overset{?}{-} 6 = 9$$

$$9 = 9, \text{ true}$$

5 is a solution of the equation.

69. Let $x = 0$

$$2x + 6 = 5x - 1$$

$$2(0) + 6 \overset{?}{=} 5(0) - 1$$

$$0 + 6 \overset{?}{=} 0 - 1$$

$$6 = -1, \text{ false}$$

0 is not a solution of the equation.

71. Let $x = 8$

$$2x - 5 = 5$$

$$2(8) \overset{?}{-} 5 = 5$$

$$16 \overset{?}{-} 5 = 5$$

$$9 = 5, \text{ false}$$

8 is not a solution of the equation.

73. Let $x = 2$

$$x + 6 = x + 6$$

$$2 + 6 \overset{?}{=} 2 + 6$$

$$8 = 8, \text{ true}$$

2 is a solution of the equation.

75. Let $x = 0$

$$x = 5x + 15$$

$$(0) \overset{?}{=} 5(0) + 15$$

$$0 \overset{?}{=} 0 + 15$$

$$0 = 15, \text{ false}$$

0 is not a solution of the equation.

77. Let $x = 27$

$$\frac{1}{3}x = 9$$

$$\frac{1}{3}(27) \overset{?}{=} 9$$

$$9 = 9, \text{ true}$$

27 is a solution of the equation.

79. $x + 15$

81. $x - 5$

83. $5 - x$

85. $3x + 22$

87. $1 + 2 = 9 \div 3$

89. $3 \neq 4 \div 2$

91. $5 + x = 20$

93. $13 - 3x = 13$

95. $\dfrac{12}{x} = \dfrac{1}{2}$

97. $(20 - 4) \cdot 4 \div 2 = (16) \cdot 4 \div 2 = 64 \div 2 = 32$

99. Answers may vary.

101. Answers may vary.

Practice Problems 1.4

1.

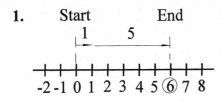

$$1+5=6$$

2.

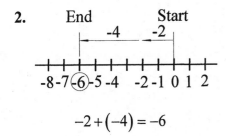

$$-2+(-4)=-6$$

3.

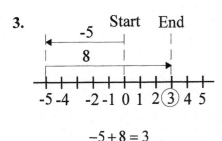

$$-5+8=3$$

4.

Start End

$$5+(-4)=1$$

5. $(-8)+(-5)=-13$

6. $(-14)+6=-8$

7. $(-17)+(-10)=-27$

8. $(-4)+12=8$

9. $1.5+(-3.2)=-1.7$

10. $-\dfrac{6}{11}+\left(-\dfrac{3}{11}\right)=-\dfrac{9}{11}$

11. $12.8+(-3.6)=9.2$

12. $-\dfrac{4}{5}+\dfrac{2}{3}=-\dfrac{4}{5}\cdot\dfrac{3}{3}+\dfrac{2}{3}\cdot\dfrac{5}{5}=-\dfrac{12}{15}+\dfrac{10}{15}=-\dfrac{2}{15}$

13. **a.** $16+(-9)+(-9)=7+(-9)=-2$

    b. $\left[3+(-13)\right]+\left[(-4)+(-7)\right]$

          $=\left[-10\right]+\left[-11\right]=-21$

14. Gains: $+3,\ +3$

      Losses: $-2,\ -1$

      Overall gain or loss:

      $(-2)+(-1)+3+3=+\$3,$ gain

15. The opposite of -35 is 35.

16. The opposite of 12 is 12.

17. The opposite of $-\dfrac{3}{11}$ is $\dfrac{3}{11}$.

18. The opposite of 1.9 is -1.9.

19. **a.** $-(-22)=22$

    b. $-\left(-\dfrac{2}{7}\right)=\dfrac{2}{7}$

    c. $-(-x)=x$

    d. $-\left|-14\right|=-14$

Exercise Set 1.4

1. $6+3=9$

3. $-6+(-8)=-14$

5. $8+(-7)=1$

7. $-14+2=-12$

9. $-2+(-3)=-5$

11. $-9+(-3)=-12$

13. $-7+3=-4$

15. $10+(-3)=7$

17. $5+(-7)=-2$

19. $-16+16=0$

21. $27+(-46)=-19$

23. $-18+49=31$

25. $-33+(-14)=-47$

27. $6.3+(-8.4)=-2.1$

29. $|-8|+(-16)=8+(-16)=-8$

31. $117+(-79)=38$

33. $-9.6+(-3.5)=-13.1$

35. $-\dfrac{3}{8}+\dfrac{5}{8}=\dfrac{2}{8}=\dfrac{1}{4}$

37. $-\dfrac{7}{16}+\dfrac{1}{4}=-\dfrac{7}{16}+\dfrac{1\cdot4}{4\cdot4}=-\dfrac{7}{16}+\dfrac{4}{16}=-\dfrac{3}{16}$

39. $-\dfrac{7}{10}+\left(-\dfrac{3}{5}\right)=-\dfrac{7}{10}+\left(-\dfrac{3\cdot2}{5\cdot2}\right)$

$=-\dfrac{7}{10}+\left(-\dfrac{6}{10}\right)=-\dfrac{13}{10}$

41. $-15+9+(-2)=-6+(-2)=-8$

43. $-21+(-16)+(-22)=-37+(-22)=-59$

45. $-23+16+(-2)=-7+(-2)=-9$

47. $|5+(-10)|=|-5|=5$

49. $6+(-4)+9=2+9=11$

51. $\left[-17+(-4)\right]+\left[-12+15\right]=\left[-21\right]+\left[3\right]$

$=-18$

53. $|9+(-12)|+|-16|=|-3|+16=3+16=19$

55. $-13+\left[5+(-3)+4\right]=-13+\left[2+4\right]$

$=-13+\left[6\right]=-7$

57. Answers may vary.

59. $-35+142=107$

The highest recorded temperature in Massachusetts was $107°$ F.

61. $-411 + 316 = -95$

You are 95 meters below sea level.

63. $-2\dfrac{1}{2} + \left(-\dfrac{7}{16}\right) = -\dfrac{5}{2} + \left(-\dfrac{7}{16}\right)$

$\quad = -\dfrac{5 \cdot 8}{2 \cdot 8} + \left(-\dfrac{7}{16}\right) = -\dfrac{40}{16} + \left(-\dfrac{7}{16}\right)$

$\quad = -\dfrac{47}{16} = -2\dfrac{15}{16}$

The change was down $2\dfrac{15}{16}$

65. $0 + (-3) + (-6) + (-5) = (-9) + (-5) = -14$

He was 14 under par.

67. $(-118) + 23 + (-30) + (-284)$

$\quad = (-95) + (-30) + (-228)$

$\quad = (-125) + (-284) = -409$

The total net income was $409 million.

69. The opposite of 6 is -6.

71. The opposite of -2 is 2.

73. The opposite of 0 is 0.

75. Since $|-6|$ is 6, the opposite of $|-6|$ is -6.

77. Answers may vary.

79. $-|-2| = -2$

81. $-|0| = -0 = 0$

83. $-\left|-\dfrac{2}{3}\right| = -\dfrac{2}{3}$

85. July

87. October

89. $\left[(-9.1) + 14.4 + 8.8\right] \div 3 = \left[5.3 + 8.8\right] \div 3$

$\quad = \left[14.1\right] \div 3 = 4.7$

The average was 4.7° F.

91. $-a$ is a <u>negative</u> number.

93. $a + a$ is a <u>positive</u> number.

Practice Problems 1.5

1. a. $-20 - 6 = -20 + (-6) = -26$

    b. $3 - (-5) = 3 + 5 = 8$

    c. $7 - 17 = 7 + (-17) = -10$

    d. $-4 - (-9) = -4 + 9 = 5$

2. $9.6 - (-5.7) = 9.6 + 5.7 = 15.3$

3. $-\dfrac{4}{9} - \dfrac{2}{9} = -\dfrac{4}{9} + \left(-\dfrac{4}{9}\right) = -\dfrac{6}{9} = -\dfrac{2 \cdot 3}{3 \cdot 3} = -\dfrac{2}{3}$

4. $-\dfrac{1}{4} - \left(-\dfrac{2}{5}\right) = -\dfrac{1}{4} + \dfrac{2}{5} = -\dfrac{1 \cdot 5}{4 \cdot 5} + \dfrac{2 \cdot 4}{5 \cdot 4}$

$\quad = -\dfrac{5}{20} + \dfrac{8}{20} = \dfrac{3}{20}$

5. $-11 - 7 = -11 + (-7) = -18$

6. a. $-20-5+12-(-3)$

$=-20+(-5)+12+3=-25+12+3$

$=-13+3=-10$

b. $5.2-(-4.4)+(-8.8)$

$=5.2+4.4+(-8.8)=9.6+(-8.8)$

$=0.8$

7. a. $-9+\left[(-4-1)-10\right]$

$=-9+\left\{\left[-4+(-1)\right]+[-10]\right\}$

$=-9+\left\{[-5]+[-10]\right\}$

$=-9+\{-15\}=-24$

b. $5^2-20+\left[-11-(-3)\right]$

$=5^2-20+[-11+3]$

$=5^2-20+[-8]=25+(-20)+[-8]$

$=5+[-8]=-3$

8. a. Let $x=1$ and $y=-4$

$\dfrac{x-y}{14+x}=\dfrac{1-(-4)}{14+1}=\dfrac{1+4}{14+1}=\dfrac{5}{15}=\dfrac{1}{3}$

b. Let $x=1$ and $y=-4$

$x^2-y=1^2-(-4)=1^1+4=1+4=5$

9. Let $x=-2$

$-1+x=1$

$-1+(-2)\overset{?}{=}1$

$-3=1$, false

-2 is not a solution to the equation.

10. The overall change is the difference of the temperatures.

$-23-14=-23+(-14)=-37$

The overall change was a drop of 37° F.

11. a. $x=180-78=180+(-78)=102$

The supplementary angle is 102°

b. $x=90-81=90+(-81)=9$

The complementary angle is 9°

Exercise Set 1.5

1. $-6-4=-6+(-4)=-10$

3. $4-9=4+(-9)=-5$

5. $16-(-3)=16+3=13$

7. $\dfrac{1}{2}-\dfrac{1}{3}=\dfrac{1}{2}+\left(-\dfrac{1}{3}\right)=\dfrac{1\cdot3}{2\cdot3}+\left(-\dfrac{1\cdot2}{3\cdot2}\right)$

$=\dfrac{3}{6}+\left(-\dfrac{2}{6}\right)=\dfrac{1}{6}$

9. $-6-(-18)=-6+18=2$

11. $-6-5=-6+(-5)=-11$

13. $7-(-4)=7+4=11$

15. $-6-(-11)=-6+11=5$

17. $16-(-21)=16+21=37$

19. $9.7-16.1=9.7+(-16.1)=-6.4$

21. $-44 - 27 = -44 + (-27) = -71$

23. $-21 - (-21) = -21 + 21 = 0$

25. $-2.6 - (-6.7) = -2.6 + 6.7 = 4.1$

27. $-\dfrac{3}{11} - \left(-\dfrac{5}{11}\right) = -\dfrac{3}{11} + \dfrac{5}{11} = \dfrac{2}{11}$

29. $-\dfrac{1}{6} - \dfrac{3}{4} = -\dfrac{1}{6} + \left(-\dfrac{3}{4}\right) = -\dfrac{1 \cdot 2}{6 \cdot 2} + \left(-\dfrac{3 \cdot 3}{4 \cdot 3}\right)$

$\qquad = -\dfrac{2}{12} + \left(-\dfrac{9}{12}\right) = -\dfrac{11}{12}$

31. $8.3 - (-0.62) = 8.3 + 0.62 = 8.92$

33. Sometimes positive and sometimes negative. If a and b are positive numbers and $a \geq b$, then $a - b \geq 0$. If a and b are positive numbers and $a \leq b$, then $a - b \leq 0$.

35. $8 - (-5) = 8 + 5 = 13$

37. $-6 - (-1) = -6 + 1 = -5$

39. $7 - 8 = 7 + (-8) = -1$

41. $-8 - 15 = -8 + (-15) = -23$

43. $-10 - (-8) + (-4) - 20$

$\qquad = -10 + 8 + (-4) + (-20)$

$\qquad = -2 + (-4) + (-20) = -6 + (-20) = -26$

45. $5 - 9 + (-4) - 8 - 8$

$\qquad = 5 + (-9) + (-4) + (-8) + (-8)$

$\qquad = -4 + (-4) + (-8) + (-8)$

$\qquad = -8 + (-8) + (-8) = -16 + (-8) = -24$

47. $-6 - (2 - 11) = -6 - (-9) = -6 + 9 = 3$

49. $3^3 - 8 \cdot 9 = 27 - 8 \cdot 9$

$\qquad = 27 - 72 = 27 + (-72) = -45$

51. $2 - 3(8 - 6) = 2 - 3(2) = 2 - 6 = 2 + (-6) = -4$

53. $(3 - 6) + 4^2 = \left[3 + (-6)\right] + 4^2 = \left[-3\right] + 4^2$

$\qquad = \left[-3\right] + 16 = 13$

55. $-2 + \left[(8 - 11) - (-2 - 9)\right]$

$\qquad = -2 + \left[(8 + (-11)) - (-2 + (-9))\right]$

$\qquad = -2 + \left[(-3) - (-11)\right] = -2 + \left[(-3) + 11\right]$

$\qquad = -2 + [8] = 6$

57. $|3| + 2^2 + \left[-4 - (-6)\right] = 3 + 2^2 + \left[-4 + 6\right]$

$\qquad = 3 + 2^2 + [2] = 3 + 4 + [2] = 7 + [2] = 9$

59. Let $x = -5$ and $y = 4$.

$\qquad x - y = -5 - 4 = -5 + (-4) = -9$

61. Let $x = -5$, $y = 4$, and $t = 10$.

$\qquad |x| + 2t - 8y = |-5| + 2(10) - 8(4)$

$\qquad = 5 + 2(10) - 8(4) = 5 + 20 - 32$

$\qquad = 25 - 32 = 25 + (-32) = -7$

63. Let $x = -5$ and $y = 4$.

$$\frac{9-x}{y+6} = \frac{9-(-5)}{4+6} = \frac{9+5}{4+6} = \frac{14}{10} = \frac{2\cdot 7}{2\cdot 5} = \frac{7}{5}$$

65. Let $x = -5$ and $y = 4$.

$$y^2 - x = 4^2 - (-5) = 16 + 5 = 21$$

67. Let $x = -5$ and $t = 10$.

$$\frac{|x-(-10)|}{2t} = \frac{|-5-(-10)|}{2(10)} = \frac{|-5+10|}{2(10)}$$

$$= \frac{|5|}{2(10)} = \frac{5}{20} = \frac{5}{4\cdot 5} = \frac{1}{4}$$

69. Let $x = -4$

$$x - 9 = 5$$

$$-4 - 9 \overset{?}{=} 5$$

$$-13 = 5, \text{ false}$$

-4 is not a solution of the equation.

71. Let $x = -2$

$$-x + 6 = -x - 1$$

$$-(-2) + 6 \overset{?}{=} -(-2) - 1$$

$$2 + 6 \overset{?}{=} 2 + (-1)$$

$$8 = 1, \text{ false}$$

-2 is not a solution of the equation.

73. Let $x = 2$

$$-x - 13 = -15$$

$$-2 - 13 \overset{?}{=} -15$$

$$-2 + (-13) \overset{?}{=} -15$$

$$-15 = -15, \text{ true}$$

2 is a solution of the equation.

75. The change in temperature is the difference between the last temperature and the first temperature.

$$-56 - 44 = -56 + (-44) = -100$$

The temperature dropped $100°$.

77. Gains: $+2$

Losses: $-5, -20$

$$2 + (-5) + (-20) = -3 + (-20) = -23$$

Total loss of 23 yards

79. $-475 - 94 = -475 + (-94) = -569$

He was born in 569 B.C.

81. Rises: $+120$

Drops: $-250, -178$

$$120 + (-250) + (-178)$$

$$= -130 + (-178) = -308$$

The overall vertical change was a drop of 308 feet.

83. $19,340 - (-512) = 19,340 + 512$

$$= 19,852$$

19,852 feet higher

85. $y = 180 - 50 = 180 + (-50) = 130$

The supplementary angle is $130°$

87. $x = 90 - 60 = 90 + (-60) = 30$

The complementary angle is $30°$

89. The change in temperature is the difference between the given month's temperature and the previous month's.

F: $-23.7-(-19.3)=-23.7+19.3=-4.4°$

Mr: $-21.1-(-23.7)=-21.1+23.7=2.6°$

Ap: $-9.1-(-21.1)=-9.1+21.1=12°$

Ma: $14.4-(-9.1)=14.4+9.1=23.5°$

Jn: $29.7-14.4=29.7+(-14.4)=15.3°$

Jy: $33.6-29.7=33.6+(-29.7)=3.9°$

Au: $33.3-33.6=33.3+(-33.6)=-0.3°$

S: $27.0-33.3=27.0+(-33.3)=-6.3°$

O: $8.8-27.0=8.8+(-27.0)=-18.2°$

N: $-6.9-8.8=-6.9+(-8.8)=-15.7°$

D: $-17.2-(-6.9)=-17.2+6.9=-10.3°$

91. October

93. True: answers may vary.

95. True: answers may vary.

97. $4.362-7.0086=-2.6466$

Practice Problems 1.6

1. $-8(3)=-24$

2. $5(-30)=-150$

3. $-4(-12)=48$

4. $-\dfrac{5}{6}\cdot\dfrac{1}{4}=-\dfrac{5\cdot1}{6\cdot4}=-\dfrac{5}{24}$

5. $6(-2.3)=-13.8$

6. $-15(-2)=30$

7. a. $5(0)(-3)=0(-3)=0$

b. $(-1)(-6)(-7)=6(-7)=-42$

c. $(-2)(4)(-8)=-8(-8)=64$

d. $-3(-9)-4(-4)=27-(-16)$
$=27+16=43$

8. a. $(-1)^2=(-1)(-1)=1$

b. $-1^2=-(1)(1)=-1$

c. $(-3)^3=(-3)(-3)(-3)=9(-3)=-27$

d. $-3^3=-(3)(3)(3)=-9(3)=-27$

9. Let $x=-1$ and $y=-5$.

a. $3x-y=3(-1)-(-5)=-3+5=2$

b. $x^2-y^3=(-1)^2-(-5)^3=1-(-125)$
$=1+125=126$

10. Let $x=-10$

$$3x+4=-26$$

$$3(-10)+4\overset{?}{=}-26$$

$$-30+4\overset{?}{=}-26$$

$$-26=-26,\ \text{true}$$

-10 is a solution of the equation.

Exercise Set 1.6

1. $-6(4)=-24$

3. $2(-1)=-2$

5. $-5(-10) = 50$

7. $-3 \cdot 4 = -12$

9. $-6(-7) = 42$

11. $2(-9) = -18$

13. $-\dfrac{1}{2}\left(-\dfrac{3}{5}\right) = \dfrac{1 \cdot 3}{2 \cdot 5} = \dfrac{3}{10}$

15. $-\dfrac{3}{4}\left(-\dfrac{8}{9}\right) = \dfrac{3 \cdot 8}{4 \cdot 9} = \dfrac{24}{36} = \dfrac{2 \cdot 12}{3 \cdot 12} = \dfrac{2}{3}$

17. $5(-1.4) = -7.0$

19. $-0.2(-0.7) = 0.14$

21. $-10(80) = -800$

23. $4(-7) = -28$

25. $(-5)(-5) = 25$

27. $\dfrac{2}{3}\left(-\dfrac{4}{9}\right) = -\dfrac{2 \cdot 4}{3 \cdot 9} = -\dfrac{8}{27}$

29. $-11(11) = -121$

31. $-\dfrac{20}{25}\left(\dfrac{5}{16}\right) = -\dfrac{20 \cdot 5}{25 \cdot 16} = -\dfrac{100}{400} = -\dfrac{1}{4}$

33. $-2.1(-0.4) = 0.84$

35. $(-1)(2)(-3)(-5)$
$= -2(-3)(-5) = 6(-5) = -30$

37. $(2)(-1)(-3)(5)(3)$
$= -2(-3)(5)(3) = 6(5)(3) = 30(3) = 90$

39. $(-4)^2 = (-4)(-4) = 16$

41. $(-6)(3)(-2)(-1)$
$= -18(-2)(-1) = 36(-1) = -36$

43. $(-5)^3 = (-5)(-5)(-5) = 25(-5) = -125$

45. $-4^2 = -(4)(4) = -16$

47. $-3(2-8) = -3\left[2+(-8)\right] = -3[-6] = 18$

49. $6(3-8) = 6\left[3+(-8)\right] = 6[-5] = -30$

51. $-3\left[(2-8)-(-6-8)\right]$
$= -3\left[(2+(-8))-(-6+(-8))\right]$
$= -3\left[-6-(-14)\right] = -3[-6+14]$
$= -3[8] = -24$

53. $\left(-\dfrac{3}{4}\right)^2 = \left(-\dfrac{3}{4}\right)\left(-\dfrac{3}{4}\right) = \dfrac{3 \cdot 3}{4 \cdot 4} = \dfrac{9}{16}$

55. $(-2)^4 = (-2)(-2)(-2)(-2) = 4(-2)(-2)$
$= -8(-2) = 16$

57. $-1^5 = -(1)(1)(1)(1)(1) = -1$
$= -8(-2) = 16$

59. $(-5)^2 = (-5)(-5) = 25$

61. $-7^2 = -(7)(7) = -49$

63. True

65. False

67. Let $x = -5$ and $y = -3$.
$$3x + 2y = 3(-5) + 2(-3) = -15 + (-6) = -21$$

69. Let $x = -5$ and $y = -3$.
$$2x^2 - y^2 = 2(-5)^2 - (-3)^2 = 2(25) - 9$$
$$= 50 + (-9) = 41$$

71. Let $x = -5$ and $y = -3$.
$$x^3 + 3y = (-5)^3 + 3(-3)$$
$$= -125 + (-9) = -134$$

73. Let $x = 7$
$$-5x = -35$$
$$-5(7) \overset{?}{=} -35$$
$$-35 = -35, \text{ true}$$
7 is a solution of the equation.

75. Let $x = 5$
$$-3x - 5 = -20$$
$$-3(5) - 5 \overset{?}{=} -20$$
$$-15 - 5 \overset{?}{=} -20$$
$$-20 = -20, \text{ true}$$
5 is a solution of the equation.

77. Let $x = -1$
$$9x + 1 = 14$$
$$9(-1) + 1 \overset{?}{=} 14$$
$$-9 + 1 \overset{?}{=} 14$$
$$-8 = 14, \text{ false}$$
-1 is not a solution of the equation.

79. Let $x = 5$
$$3x - 20 = -5$$
$$3(5) - 20 \overset{?}{=} -5$$
$$15 - 20 \overset{?}{=} -5$$
$$-5 = -5, \text{ true}$$
5 is a solution of the equation.

81. Let $x = -2$
$$17 - 4x = x + 27$$
$$17 - 4(-2) \overset{?}{=} -2 + 27$$
$$17 + 8 \overset{?}{=} 25$$
$$25 = 25, \text{ true}$$
-2 is a solution of the equation.

83. Positive

85. Can't determine

87. Negative

89. $4(-152) = -608$
The net income will be $-\$608$ million.

91. No; answers may vary

Practice Problems 1.7

1. Reciprocal of 13 is $\dfrac{1}{13}$ since $13 \cdot \dfrac{1}{13} = 1$

2. Reciprocal of $\dfrac{7}{15}$ is $\dfrac{15}{7}$ since $\dfrac{7}{15} \cdot \dfrac{15}{7} = 1$

3. Reciprocal of -5 is $-\dfrac{1}{5}$ since $-5 \cdot -\dfrac{1}{5} = 1$

4. Reciprocal of $-\dfrac{8}{11}$ is $-\dfrac{11}{8}$

  since $-\dfrac{8}{11} \cdot -\dfrac{11}{8} = 1$

5. Reciprocal of 7.9 is $\dfrac{1}{7.9}$ since $7.9 \cdot \dfrac{1}{7.9} = 1$

6. a. $-12 \div 4 = -12 \cdot \dfrac{1}{4} = -3$

  b. $\dfrac{-20}{-10} = -20 \cdot -\dfrac{1}{10} = 2$

  c. $\dfrac{36}{-4} = 36 \cdot -\dfrac{1}{4} = -9$

7. $\dfrac{-25}{5} = -5$

8. $\dfrac{-48}{6} = 8$

9. $\dfrac{50}{-2} = -25$

10. $\dfrac{-72}{0.2} = -360$

11. $-\dfrac{5}{9} \div \dfrac{2}{3} = -\dfrac{5}{9} \cdot \dfrac{3}{2} = -\dfrac{5 \cdot 3}{9 \cdot 2} = -\dfrac{15}{18} = -\dfrac{5}{6}$

12. $-\dfrac{2}{7} \div \left(-\dfrac{1}{5}\right) = -\dfrac{2}{7} \cdot \left(-\dfrac{5}{1}\right) = \dfrac{2 \cdot 5}{7 \cdot 1} = \dfrac{10}{7}$

13. $\dfrac{-7}{0}$ is undefined

14. $\dfrac{0}{-2} = 0$

15. $\dfrac{0(-5)}{3} = \dfrac{0}{3} = 0$

16. a. $\dfrac{-7(-4) + 2}{-10 - (-5)} = \dfrac{28 + 2}{-10 + 5} = \dfrac{30}{-5} = -6$

  b. $\dfrac{5(-2)^3 + 52}{-4 + 1} = \dfrac{5(-8) + 52}{-4 + 1}$

    $= \dfrac{-40 + 52}{-4 + 1} = \dfrac{12}{-3} = -4$

17. Let $x = -1$ and $y = -5$.

  $\dfrac{x + y}{3x} = \dfrac{-1 + (-5)}{3(-1)} = \dfrac{-6}{-3} = 2$

18. Let $x = -8$

  $\dfrac{x}{4} - 3 = x + 3$

  $\dfrac{-8}{4} - 3 \overset{?}{=} -8 + 3$

  $-2 - 3 \overset{?}{=} -5$

  $-5 = -5,$ true

  -8 is a solution of the equation.

Exercise Set 1.7

1. Reciprocal of 9 is $\dfrac{1}{9}$ since $9 \cdot \dfrac{1}{9} = 1$

3. Reciprocal of $\dfrac{2}{3}$ is $\dfrac{3}{2}$ since $\dfrac{2}{3} \cdot \dfrac{3}{2} = 1$

5. Reciprocal of -14 is $-\dfrac{1}{14}$

since $-14 \cdot -\dfrac{1}{14} = 1$

7. Reciprocal of $-\dfrac{3}{11}$ is $-\dfrac{11}{3}$

since $-\dfrac{3}{11} \cdot -\dfrac{11}{3} = 1$

9. Reciprocal of 0.2 is $\dfrac{1}{0.2}$

since $0.2 \cdot \dfrac{1}{0.2} = 1$

11. Reciprocal of $\dfrac{1}{-6.3}$ is -6.3

since $\dfrac{1}{-6.3} \cdot -6.3 = 1$

13. $1, -1$

15. $\dfrac{18}{-2} = 18 \cdot -\dfrac{1}{2} = -9$

17. $\dfrac{-16}{-4} = -16 \cdot -\dfrac{1}{4} = 4$

19. $\dfrac{-48}{12} = -48 \cdot \dfrac{1}{12} = -4$

21. $\dfrac{0}{-4} = 0 \cdot -\dfrac{1}{4} = 0$

23. $-\dfrac{15}{3} = -15 \cdot \dfrac{1}{3} = -5$

25. $\dfrac{5}{0}$ is undefined

27. $\dfrac{-12}{-4} = -12 \cdot -\dfrac{1}{4} = 3$

29. $\dfrac{30}{-2} = 30 \cdot -\dfrac{1}{2} = -15$

31. $\dfrac{6}{7} \div -\dfrac{1}{3} = \dfrac{6}{7} \cdot \left(-\dfrac{3}{1}\right) = -\dfrac{6 \cdot 3}{7 \cdot 1} = -\dfrac{18}{7}$

33. $-\dfrac{5}{9} \div \left(-\dfrac{3}{4}\right) = -\dfrac{5}{9} \cdot \left(-\dfrac{4}{3}\right) = \dfrac{5 \cdot 4}{9 \cdot 3} = \dfrac{20}{27}$

35. $-\dfrac{4}{9} \div \dfrac{4}{9} = -\dfrac{4}{9} \cdot \dfrac{9}{4} = -1$

37. $-\dfrac{5}{8} \div \dfrac{3}{4} = -\dfrac{5}{8} \cdot \dfrac{4}{3} = -\dfrac{20}{24} = -\dfrac{5 \cdot 4}{6 \cdot 4} = -\dfrac{5}{6}$

39. $-48 \div 1.2 = -48 \cdot \dfrac{1}{1.2} = -40$

41. $-3.2 \div -0.02 = -3.2 \cdot -\dfrac{1}{0.0.2} = 160$

43. $\dfrac{-9(-3)}{-6} = \dfrac{27}{-6} = -\dfrac{9}{2}$

45. $\dfrac{12}{9-12} = \dfrac{12}{-3} = -4$

47. $\dfrac{-6^2+4}{-2}=\dfrac{-36+4}{-2}=\dfrac{-32}{-2}=16$

49. $\dfrac{8+(-4)^2}{4-12}=\dfrac{8+16}{4-12}=\dfrac{24}{-8}=-3$

51. $\dfrac{22+(3)(-2)}{-5-2}=\dfrac{22+(-6)}{-5-2}=\dfrac{16}{-7}$

53. $\dfrac{-3-5^2}{2(-7)}=\dfrac{-3-25}{2(-7)}=\dfrac{-3+(-25)}{-14}=\dfrac{-28}{-14}=2$

55. $\dfrac{6-2(-3)}{4-3(-2)}=\dfrac{6-(-6)}{4-(-6)}=\dfrac{6+6}{4+6}=\dfrac{12}{10}=\dfrac{6}{5}$

57. $\dfrac{-3-2(-9)}{-15-3(-4)}=\dfrac{-3-(-18)}{-15-(-12)}$

$\qquad =\dfrac{-3+18}{-15+12}=\dfrac{15}{-3}=-5$

59. $\dfrac{|5-9|+|10-15|}{|2(-3)|}=\dfrac{|-4|+|-5|}{|-6|}=\dfrac{4+5}{6}=\dfrac{9}{6}=\dfrac{3}{2}$

61. $\dfrac{-7(-1)+(-3)4}{(-2)(5)+(-6)(-8)}=\dfrac{7+(-12)}{-10+48}=\dfrac{-5}{38}=-\dfrac{5}{38}$

63. Let $x=-5$ and $y=-3$.

$\dfrac{2x-5}{y-2}=\dfrac{2(-5)-5}{-3-2}=\dfrac{-10-5}{-3-2}=\dfrac{-15}{-5}=3$

65. Let $x=-5$ and $y=-3$.

$\dfrac{6-y}{x-4}=\dfrac{6-(-3)}{-5-4}=\dfrac{6+3}{-5-4}=\dfrac{9}{-9}=-1$

67. Let $x=-5$ and $y=-3$.

$\dfrac{x+y}{3y}=\dfrac{-5+(-3)}{3(-3)}=\dfrac{-5+(-3)}{-9}=\dfrac{-8}{-9}=\dfrac{8}{9}$

69. Let $x=2$

$\dfrac{10}{x}=-5$

$\dfrac{-10}{2}\overset{?}{=}-5$

$-5=-5,\ \text{true}$

2 is a solution of the equation.

71. Let $x=15$

$\dfrac{x}{5}+2=-1$

$\dfrac{15}{5}+2\overset{?}{=}-1$

$3+2\overset{?}{=}-5$

$5=-5,\ \text{false}$

15 is not a solution of the equation.

73. Let $x=-30$

$\dfrac{x+4}{5}=-6$

$\dfrac{-30+4}{5}\overset{?}{=}-6$

$\dfrac{-26}{5}\overset{?}{=}-5$

$-\dfrac{26}{5}=-5,\ \text{false}$

-30 is not a solution of the equation.

75. $\dfrac{0}{5}-7=0-7=-7$

77. $(-8)(-5)+(-1)=40+(-1)=39$

11. $\dfrac{-20}{-4}=5$

79. $\dfrac{-8}{-20}=\dfrac{4\cdot 2}{4\cdot 5}=\dfrac{2}{5}$

12. $\dfrac{30}{-6}=-5$

81. The quotient of two numbers with different signs is negative.

13. $7-(-3)=7+3=10$

83. $b+b$ is negative, $a+a$ is positive. The quotient of two numbers with different signs is negative.

14. $-8-10=-8+(-10)=-18$

15. $-14-(-12)=-14+12=-2$

85. $\dfrac{-11}{4}=-2.75$

Average net income per quarter was −$2.75 million

16. $-3-(-1)=-3+1=-2$

17. $-\dfrac{1}{2}\left(-\dfrac{3}{4}\right)=\dfrac{1\cdot 3}{2\cdot 4}=\dfrac{3}{8}$

Integrated Review 1.7

18. $-\dfrac{2}{7}\left(\dfrac{11}{12}\right)=-\dfrac{2\cdot 11}{7\cdot 12}=-\dfrac{22}{84}=-\dfrac{11}{42}$

1. positive

2. positive

19. $\dfrac{-12}{0.2}=-60$

3. negative

20. $\dfrac{-3.8}{-2}=1.9$

4. negative

5. positive

21. $-19+(-23)=-42$

6. negative

22. $18+(-25)=-7$

7. negative

23. $-15+17=2$

8. positive

24. $-2+(-37)=-39$

9. $5(-7)=-35$

25. $(-8)^{2}=(-8)(-8)=64$

10. $-3(-10)=30$

35

26. $-9^2 = -(9)(9) = -81$

27. $-3^2 = -(3)(3)(3) = -27$

28. $(-2)^4 = (-2)(-2)(-2)(-2) = 16$

29. $-1^{10} = -(1)(1)(1)(1)(1)(1)(1)(1)(1)(1) = -1$

30. $(-1)^{10} = (-1)(-1)(-1)(-1)(-1)(-1)$
$$\cdot(-1)(-1)(-1)(-1)$$
$$= 1$$

31. $(-2)^5 = (-2)(-2)(-2)(-2)(-2) = -32$

32. $-2^5 = -(2)(2)(2)(2)(2) = -32$

33. $(2)(-8)(-3) = (-16)(-3) = 48$

34. $3(-2)(5) = (-6)(5) = -30$

35. $-6(2) - 5(2) - 4 = -12 - 10 - 4$
$$= -12 + (-10) + (-4) = -22 + (-4) = -26$$

36. $-4(-3) - 9(1) - 6 = 12 - 9 - 6$
$$= 12 + (-9) + (-6) = 3 + (-6) = -3$$

37. $(7-10)(4-6) = \left[7+(-10)\right]\left[4+(-6)\right]$
$$= [-3][-2] = 6$$

38. $(9-11)(14-20)$
$$= \left[9+(-11)\right]\left[14+(-20)\right] = [-2][-6] = 12$$

39. $2(19-17)^3 - 3(7-9)^2$
$$= 2\left[19+(-17)\right]^3 - 3\left[7+(-9)\right]^2$$
$$= 2[2]^3 - 3[-2]^2 = 2[8] - 3[4]$$
$$= 16 - 12 = 16 + (-12) = 4$$

40. $3(10-9)^2 - 6(20-19)^3$
$$= 3\left[10+(-9)\right]^3 - 6\left[20+(-19)\right]^2$$
$$= 3[1]^3 - 6[1]^2 = 3[1] - 6[1]$$
$$= 3 - 6 = 3 + (-6) = -3$$

41. $\dfrac{19-25}{3(-1)} = \dfrac{19+(-25)}{-3} = \dfrac{-6}{-3} = 2$

42. $\dfrac{8(-4)}{-2} = \dfrac{-32}{-2} = 16$

43. $\dfrac{-2(3-6) - 6(10-9)}{-6-(-5)}$
$$= \dfrac{-2\left[3+(-6)\right] - 6\left[10+(-9)\right]}{-6-(-5)}$$
$$= \dfrac{-2[-3] - 6[1]}{-6-(-5)} = \dfrac{6-6}{-6-(-5)} = \dfrac{6+(-6)}{-6+5}$$
$$= \dfrac{0}{-1} = 0$$

44. $\dfrac{5(7-9)-3(100-97)}{4-5}$

$=\dfrac{5[7+(-9)]-3[100+(-97)]}{4-5}$

$=\dfrac{5[-2]-3[3]}{4-5}=\dfrac{-10-9}{4-5}=\dfrac{-10+(-9)}{4+(-5)}$

$=\dfrac{-19}{-1}=19$

45. $\dfrac{-4(8-10)^3}{-2-1-12}=\dfrac{-4[8+(-10)]^3}{-2-1-12}$

$=\dfrac{-4[-2]^3}{-2-1-12}=\dfrac{-4[-8]}{-2-1-12}$

$=\dfrac{32}{-2+(-1)+(-12)}=\dfrac{32}{-15}=-\dfrac{32}{15}$

46. $\dfrac{6(7-10)^2}{6-(-1)-2}=\dfrac{6[7+(-10)]^2}{6-(-1)-2}$

$=\dfrac{6[-3]^2}{6-(-1)-2}=\dfrac{6[9]}{6-(-1)-2}$

$=\dfrac{54}{6+1+(-2)}=\dfrac{54}{5}$

Practice Problems 1.8

1. a. $7\cdot y=y\cdot 7$

  b. $4+x=x+4$

2. a. $5\cdot(-3\cdot 6)=(5\cdot-3)\cdot 6$

  b. $(-2+7)+3=-2+(7+3)$

3. Commutative property

4. Associative property

5. $(-3+x)+17=[x+(-3)]+17$

$=x+(-3+17)=x+14$

6. $4(5x)=(4\cdot 5)x=20x$

7. $5(x+y)=5x+5y$

8. $-3(2+7x)=-3(2)+(-3)(7x)=-6-21x$

9. $4(x+6y-2z)=4(x)+4(6y)-4(2z)$

$=4x+24y-8z$

10. $-1(3-a)=-1(3)-(-1)(a)=-3+a$

11. $-(8+a-b)=-1(8+a-b)$

$=-1(8)+(-1)(a)-(-1)(b)=-8-a+b$

12. $9(2x+4)+9=9(2x)+9(4)+9$

$=18x+36+9=18x+45$

13. $9\cdot 3+9\cdot y=9(3+y)$

14. $4x+4y=4(x+y)$

15. Additive inverse property

16. Commutative property of addition

17. Associative property of addition

18. Commutative property of addition

19. Multiplicative inverse property

20. Identity element for addition

21. Commutative and associative properties of multiplication

Exercise Set 1.8

1. $x + 16 = 16 + x$

3. $-4 \cdot y = y \cdot (-4)$

5. $xy = yx$

7. $2x + 13 = 13 + 2x$

9. $(xy) \cdot z = x \cdot (yz)$

11. $2 + (a + b) = (2 + a) + b$

13. $4 \cdot (ab) = 4a \cdot (b)$

15. $(a + b) + c = a + (b + c)$

17. $8 + (9 + b) = (8 + 9) + b = 17 + b$

19. $4(6y) = (4 \cdot 6)y = 24y$

21. $\dfrac{1}{5}(5y) = \left(\dfrac{1}{5} \cdot 5\right)y = 1 \cdot y = y$

23. $(13 + a) + 13 = (a + 13) + 13 = a + (13 + 13)$
$= a + 26$

25. $-9(8x) = (-9 \cdot 8)x = -72x$

27. $\dfrac{3}{4}\left(\dfrac{4}{3}s\right) = \left(\dfrac{3}{4} \cdot \dfrac{4}{3}\right)s = 1s = s$

29. Answers may vary

31. $4(x + y) = 4x + 4y$

33. $9(x - 6) = 9x - 9 \cdot 6 = 9x - 54$

35. $2(3x + 5) = 2(3x) + 2(5) = 6x + 10$

37. $7(4x - 3) = 7(4x) - 7(3) = 28x - 21$

39. $3(6 + x) = 3(6) + 3x = 18 + 3x$

41. $-2(y - z) = -2y - (-2)z = -2y + 2z$

43. $-7(3y + 5) = -7(3y) + (-7)(5) = -21y - 35$

45. $5(x + 4m + 2) = 5x + 5(4m) + 5(2)$
$= 5x + 20m + 10$

47. $-4(1 - 2m + n) = -4(1) - (-4)(2m) + (-4)n$
$= -4 + 8m - 4n$

49. $-(5x + 2) = -1(5x + 2) = -1(5x) + (-1)(2)$
$= -5x - 2$

51. $-(r - 3 - 7p) = -1(r - 3 - 7p)$
$= -1r - (-1)(3) - (-1)(7p)$
$= -r + 3 + 7p$

53. $\dfrac{1}{2}(6x + 8) = \dfrac{1}{2}(6x) + \dfrac{1}{2}(8)$
$= \left(\dfrac{1}{2} \cdot 6\right)x + \left(\dfrac{1}{2} \cdot 8\right) = 3x + 4$

55. $-\frac{1}{3}(3x-9y)=-\frac{1}{3}(3x)-\left(-\frac{1}{3}\right)(9y)$

$=\left(-\frac{1}{3}\cdot 3\right)x-\left(-\frac{1}{3}\cdot 9\right)y=-1\cdot x+3\cdot y$

$=-x+3y$

57. $3(2r+5)-7=3(2r)+3(5)-7$

$=6r+15+(-7)=6r+8$

59. $-9(4x+8)+2=-9(4x)+(-9)(8)+2$

$=-36x-72+2=-36x-70$

61. $-4(4x+5)-5=-4(4x)+(-4)(5)-5$

$=-16x+(-20)+(-5)=-16x-25$

63. $4\cdot 1+4\cdot y=4(1+y)$

65. $11x+11y=11(x+y)$

67. $(-1)\cdot 5+(-1)\cdot x=-1(5+x)=-(5+x)$

69. $30a+30b=30(a+b)$

71. The additive inverse of 16 is -16 since $16+(-16)=0$

73. The additive inverse of -8 is 8 since $-8+8=0$

75. The additive inverse of $-(-1.2)$ is -1.2 since $-(-1.2)+(-1.2)=1.2+(-1.2)=0$

77. The additive inverse of $-|-2|$ is 2 since $-|-2|+2=-2+2=0$

79. The multiplicative inverse of $\frac{2}{3}$ is $\frac{3}{2}$ since $\frac{2}{3}\cdot\frac{3}{2}=1$

81. The multiplicative inverse of $-\frac{5}{6}$ is $-\frac{6}{5}$ since $-\frac{5}{6}\cdot -\frac{6}{5}=1$

83. The multiplicative inverse of $3\frac{5}{6}$ is $\frac{6}{23}$ since $3\frac{5}{6}\cdot\frac{6}{23}=\frac{23}{6}\cdot\frac{6}{23}=1$

85. The multiplicative inverse of -2 is $-\frac{1}{2}$ since $-2\cdot -\frac{1}{2}=1$

87. Commutative property of multiplication

89. Associative property of addition

91. Distributive property

93. Associative property of multiplication

95. Identity property of addition

97. Distributive property

99. Associative and commutative properties of multiplication

101.

Expression	Opposite	Reciprocal
8	−8	$\frac{1}{8}$

103.

Expression	Opposite	Reciprocal
x	$-x$	$\dfrac{1}{x}$

105.

Expression	Opposite	Reciprocal
$2x$	$-2x$	$\dfrac{1}{2x}$

107. a. Commutative property of addition

     b. Commutative property of addition

     c. Associative property of addition

109. Answers may vary

111. No

113. Yes

Practice Problems 1.9

1. a. 8¢ per kilowatt-hour

   b. 12¢ per kilowatt-hour

   c. $12¢ - 8¢ = 4¢$ per kilowatt-hour

2. a. Africa/Middle East with
     6 million users

   b. $105 - 16 = 89$ million users

3. a. $50

   b. 180 miles

4. a. 70 heartbeats per minute

   b. 60 heartbeats per minute

   c. 5 minutes after lighting

Exercise Set 1.9

1. approximately 15 million

3. 2002

5. Red; 23 shades

7. $20 - 11 = 9$ more shades

9. France

11. France, U.S., Spain, Italy

13. 34 million

15. Approximately 59 beats per minute

17. Approximately 26 beats per minute

19. 74,800

21. 1996; 76,400

23. 20

25. 1985

27. 1997

29. 18 million

31. 63 million

33. 1900

35. 27 million

37. Answers may vary

39. Answers may vary

41. Equator

Chapter 1 Review

1. $8 < 10$

2. $7 > 2$

3. $-4 > -5$

4. $\dfrac{12}{2} > -8$

5. $\left|-7\right| < \left|-8\right|$

6. $\left|-9\right| > -9$

7. $-\left|-1\right| \le -1$

8. $\left|-14\right| = -(-14)$

9. $1.2 > 1.02$

10. $-\dfrac{3}{2} < -\dfrac{3}{4}$

11. $4 \ge -3$

12. $6 \ne 5$

13. $0.03 < 0.3$

14. $50 > 40$

15. a. The natural numbers are 1 and 3.
    b. The whole numbers are 0, 1, and 3.
    c. The integers are -6, 0, 1, and 3.
    d. The rational numbers are $-6, 0, 1,$
        $1\dfrac{1}{2}, 3,$ and 9.62.
    e. The irrational number is π.
    f. The real numbers are all numbers
        in the given set.

16. a. The natural numbers are 2 and 5.
    b. The whole numbers are 2 and 5.
    c. The integers are -3, 2, and 5.
    d. The rational numbers are $-3, -1.6,$
       $2, 5, \dfrac{11}{2},$ and 15.1.
    e. The irrational numbers are $\sqrt{5}$ and 2π.
    f. The real numbers are all numbers
        in the given set.

17. Friday

18. Wednesday

19. c. $6 \cdot 3^2 + 2 \cdot 8 = 6 \cdot 9 + 2 \cdot 8 = 54 + 16 = 70$

20. b. $68 - 5 \cdot 2^3 = 68 - 5 \cdot 8 = 68 - 40 = 28$

21. $3(1 + 2 \cdot 5) + 4 = 3(1 + 10) + 4 = 3(11) + 4$
$$= 33 + 4 = 37$$

22. $8 + 3(2 \cdot 6 - 1) = 8 + 3(12 - 1) = 8 + 3(11)$
$$= 8 + 33 = 41$$

23. $\dfrac{4+|6-2|+8^2}{4+6\cdot4}=\dfrac{4+|4|+64}{4+24}=\dfrac{4+4+64}{4+24}$

$\qquad\qquad =\dfrac{72}{28}=\dfrac{4\cdot18}{4\cdot7}=\dfrac{18}{7}$

24. $5\big[3(2+5)-5\big]=5\big[3(7)-5\big]=5\big[21-5\big]$

$\qquad\qquad =5\big[16\big]=80$

25. $20-12=2\cdot4$

26. $\dfrac{9}{2}>-5$

27. Let $x=6$ and $y=2$.

$\quad 2x+3y=2(6)+3(2)=12+6=18$

28. Let $x=6$, $y=2$, and $z=8$.

$\quad x(y+2z)=6\big[2+2(8)\big]=6\big[2+16\big]$

$\qquad\qquad =6\big[18\big]=108$

29. Let $x=6$, $y=2$, and $z=8$.

$\quad \dfrac{x}{y}+\dfrac{z}{2y}=\dfrac{6}{2}+\dfrac{8}{2(2)}=\dfrac{6}{2}+\dfrac{8}{4}=3+2=5$

30. Let $x=6$ and $y=2$.

$\quad x^2-3y^2=(6)^2-3(2)^2=36-3(4)$

$\quad =36-12=36+(-12)=24$

31. Let $a=37$ and $b=80$.

$\quad 180-a-b=180-37-80$

$\quad =180+(-37)+(-80)=143+(-80)=63$

32. Let $x=3$.

$\quad 7x-3=18$

$\quad 7(3)-3\overset{?}{=}18$

$\quad 21-3\overset{?}{=}18$

$\quad 18=18,\ \text{true}$

$\quad$ 3 is a solution to the equation.

33. Let $x=1$.

$\quad 3x^2+4=x-1$

$\quad 3(1)^2+4\overset{?}{=}1-1$

$\quad 3+7\overset{?}{=}0$

$\quad 10=0,\ \text{false}$

$\quad$ 1 is not a solution to the equation.

34. The additive inverse of -9 is 9.

35. The additive inverse of $\dfrac{2}{3}$ is $-\dfrac{2}{3}$.

36. The additive inverse of $|-2|$ is -2 since $|-2|=2$.

37. The additive inverse of $-|-7|$ is 7 since $-|-7|=-7$.

38. $-15+4=-11$

39. $-6+(-11)=-17$

40. $\dfrac{1}{16}+\left(-\dfrac{1}{4}\right)=\dfrac{1}{16}+\left(-\dfrac{1\cdot4}{4\cdot4}\right)$

$\qquad =\dfrac{1}{16}+\left(-\dfrac{4}{16}\right)=-\dfrac{3}{16}$

41. $-8+|-3| = -8+3 = -5$

42. $-4.6+(-9.3) = -13.9$

43. $-2.8+6.7 = 3.9$

44. $6-20 = 6+(-20) = -14$

45. $-3.1-8.4 = -3.1+(-8.4) = -11.5$

46. $-6-(-11) = -6+11 = 5$

47. $4-15 = 4+(-15) = -11$

48. $-21-16+3(8-2)$
$= -21+(-16)+3\big[8+(-2)\big]$
$= -21+(-16)+3[6] = -21+(-16)+18$
$= -37+18 = -19$

49. $\dfrac{11-(-9)+6(8-2)}{2+3\cdot 4} = \dfrac{11+9+6\big[8+(-2)\big]}{2+3\cdot 4}$
$= \dfrac{11+9+6[6]}{2+3\cdot 4} = \dfrac{11+9+36}{2+12} = \dfrac{56}{14} = 4$

50. **a :** Let $x = 3$, $y = -6$, and $z = -9$.
$2x^2 - y + z = 2(3)^2 - (-6) + (-9)$
$= 2(9) + 6 + (-9) = 18 + 6 + (-9)$
$= 24 + (-9) = 15$

51. **d :** Let $x = 3$ and $y = -6$.
$\dfrac{y-4x}{2x} = \dfrac{-6-4(3)}{2(3)} = \dfrac{-6-12}{6}$
$= \dfrac{-6+(-12)}{6} = \dfrac{-18}{6} = -3$

52. Gains; $+1, +5, +1$
Losses; $-2, -4$
Overall gain or loss
$= 1+(-2)+5+1+(-4) = 1$
Price at the end of the week
$= 50+1 = \$51$

53. The multiplicative inverse of -6 is $-\dfrac{1}{6}$
since $-6\cdot -\dfrac{1}{6} = 1.$

54. The multiplicative inverse of $\dfrac{3}{5}$ is $\dfrac{5}{3}$
since $\dfrac{3}{5}\cdot\dfrac{5}{3} = 1.$

55. $6(-8) = -48$

56. $(-2)(-14) = 28$

57. $\dfrac{-18}{-6} = 3$

58. $\dfrac{42}{-3} = -14$

59. $(-2)(-14) = 28$

60. $(-4)(-3)(0)(-6) = 12(0)(-6) = (0)(-6) = 0$

61. $\dfrac{4\cdot(-3)+(-8)}{2+(-2)} = \dfrac{-12+(-8)}{2+(-2)} = \dfrac{-20}{0}$
The expression is undefined.

62. $\dfrac{3(-2)^2 - 5}{-14} = \dfrac{3(4) - 5}{-14} = \dfrac{12 - 5}{-14} = \dfrac{7}{-14} = -\dfrac{1}{2}$

63. Commutative property of addition

64. Multiplicative identity property

65. Distributive property

66. Additive inverse property

67. Associative property of addition

68. Commutative property of multiplication

69. Distributive property

70. Associative property of multiplication

71. Multiplicative inverse property

72. Additive identity property

73. Commutative property of addition

74. $2600 million

75. $200 million

76. 1998

77. Answers may vary

Chapter 1 Test

1. $|-7| > 5$

2. $(9 + 5) \geq 4$

3. $-13 + 8 = -5$

4. $-13 - (-2) = -13 + 2 = -11$

5. $6 \cdot 3 - 8 \cdot 4 = 18 - 32 = 18 + (-32) = -14$

6. $(13)(-3) = -39$

7. $(-6)(-2) = 12$

8. $\dfrac{|-16|}{-8} = \dfrac{16}{-8} = -2$

9. $\dfrac{-8}{0}$ is undefined

10. $\dfrac{|-6| + 2}{5 - 6} = \dfrac{6 + 2}{5 + (-6)} = \dfrac{8}{-1} = -8$

11. $\dfrac{1}{2} - \dfrac{5}{6} = \dfrac{1 \cdot 3}{2 \cdot 3} - \dfrac{5}{6} = \dfrac{3 - 5}{6} = \dfrac{-2}{6} = -\dfrac{1}{3}$

12. $-1\dfrac{1}{8} + 5\dfrac{3}{4} = -\dfrac{9}{8} + \dfrac{23}{4} = -\dfrac{9}{8} + \dfrac{2 \cdot 23}{2 \cdot 4}$

$\qquad = \dfrac{-9 + 46}{8} = \dfrac{37}{8} = 4\dfrac{5}{8}$

13. $-\dfrac{3}{5} + \dfrac{15}{8} = -\dfrac{3 \cdot 8}{5 \cdot 8} + \dfrac{15 \cdot 5}{8 \cdot 5} = \dfrac{-24 + 75}{40} = \dfrac{51}{40}$

14. $3(-4)^2 - 80 = 3(16) - 80 = 48 + (-80) = -32$

15. $6[5 + 2(3 - 8) - 3]$

$\qquad = 6\{5 + 2[3 + (-8)] + (-3)\}$

$\qquad = 6\{5 + 2[-5] + (-3)\}$

$\qquad = 6\{5 + (-10) + (-3)\}$

$\qquad = 6\{-5 + (-3)\} = 6\{-8\} = -48$

16. $\dfrac{-12+3\cdot 8}{4}=\dfrac{-12+24}{4}=\dfrac{12}{4}=3$

17. $\dfrac{(-2)(0)(-3)}{-6}=\dfrac{0(-3)}{-6}=\dfrac{0}{-6}=0$

18. $-3>-7$

19. $4>-8$

20. $\left|-3\right|>2$

21. $\left|-2\right|=-1-(-3)$

22. **a.** The natural numbers are 1 and 7.

    b. The whole numbers are 0, 1 and 7.

    c. The integers are $-5,\ -1,\ 0, 1,$ and 7.

    d. The rational numbers are

       $-5,\ -1,\ \dfrac{1}{4},\ 0, 1,\ 7,$ and 11.6.

    e. The irrational numbers are $\sqrt{7}$ and 3π.

    f. The real numbers are all numbers

       in the given set.

23. Let $x=6$ and $y=-2$.

$x^2+y^2=(6)^2+(-2)^2=36+4=40$

24. Let $x=6,\ y=-2$ and $z=-3$.

$x+yz=6+(-2)(-3)=6+6=12$

25. Let $x=6$ and $y=-2$.

$2+3x-y=2+3(6)-(-2)=2+18+2$

$=20+2=22$

26. Let $x=6,\ y=-2$ and $z=-3$.

$\dfrac{y+z-1}{x}=\dfrac{-2+(-3)-1}{6}=\dfrac{-5+(-1)}{6}$

$=\dfrac{-6}{6}=-1$

27. Associative property of addition

28. Commutative property of multiplication

29. Distributive property

30. Multiplicative inverse property

31. The opposite of -9 is 9.

32. The reciprocal of $-\dfrac{1}{3}$ is -3.

33. Second down

34. Gains: 5, 29

Losses: $-10,\ -2$

Total gain or loss

$=5+(-10)+(-2)+29=(-5)+(-2)+29$

$=-7+29=22$ yards gained.

Yes, they scored a touchdown.

35. Since $-14+31=17,$ the temperature

at noon was $17°$

36. Change in value per share $=-1.50$

Change in total value $=28(-1.50)=-420$

Total loss of $420

37. $380 billion

38. $1230 billion

39. $375 - 0 = 375$

The increase was $375 billion.

40. The greatest increase in revenue occurs where the line is steepest, between 2001 and 2002.

Chapter 2

Chapter 2 Pretest

1. $3c - 4 + 6c - 9 = 3c + 6c - 4 - 9$
$= (3 + 6)c - 13 = 9c - 13$

2. $-5(2y - 3) - 7y + 1 = -10y + 15 - 7y + 1$
$= -10y - 7y + 15 + 1 = (-10 - 7)y + 16$
$= -17y + 16$

3. $3 - x = -12$
$3 - x - 3 = -12 - 3$
$-x = -15$
$\dfrac{-x}{-1} = \dfrac{-15}{-1}$
$x = 15$

4. $12 - (5 - 4b) = 9 + 3b$
$12 - 5 + 4b = 9 + 3b$
$7 + 4b = 9 + 3b$
$7 + 4b - 3b = 9 + 3b - 3b$
$7 + b = 9$
$7 + b - 7 = 9 - 7$
$b = 2$

5. $\dfrac{2}{3}m = -8$
$\dfrac{3}{2}\left(\dfrac{2}{3}m\right) = \dfrac{3}{2}(-8)$
$m = -12$

6. $-7 - 3y = 17 + 5y$
$-7 - 3y - 5y = 17 + 5y - 5y$
$-7 - 8y = 17$
$-7 - 8y + 7 = 17 + 7$
$-8y = 24$
$\dfrac{-8y}{-8} = \dfrac{24}{-8}$
$y = -3$

7. $3(1 - 4x) + 2(5x) = 9$
$3 - 12x + 10x = 9$
$3 - 2x = 9$
$3 - 2x - 3 = 9 - 3$
$-2x = 6$
$\dfrac{-2x}{-2} = \dfrac{6}{-2}$
$x = -3$

8. $0.20x + 0.15(60) = 0.75(18)$
$100\big[0.20x + 0.15(60)\big] = 100\big[0.75(18)\big]$
$20x + 15(60) = 75(18)$
$20x + 900 = 1350$
$20x + 900 - 900 = 1350 - 900$
$20x = 450$
$\dfrac{20x}{20} = \dfrac{450}{20}$
$x = 22.5$

9. $2(x-1) = 2x+5$

$2x-2 = 2x+5$

$2x-2-2x = 2x+5-2x$

$-2 = 5,$ false

There is no solution

10. Let $x =$ the unknown number

$3[x+(-2)] = x+2$

$3x-6 = x+2$

$3x-x-6 = x+2-x$

$2x-6 = 2$

$2x-6+6 = 2+6$

$2x = 8$

$\dfrac{2x}{2} = \dfrac{8}{2}$

$x = 4$

The number is 4

11. Let $x =$ the smaller integer and

$x+2 =$ the next even integer

$3x = 2(x+2)+16$

$3x = 2x+4+16$

$3x = 2x+20$

$3x-2x = 2x-2x+20$

$x = 20$

$x+2 = 20+2 = 22$

The integers are 20 and 22

12. $V = \dfrac{1}{3}Ah;\ V = 60,\ h = 4$

$60 = \dfrac{1}{3}A(4)$

$\dfrac{3}{4}(60) = \dfrac{3}{4}\left(\dfrac{1}{3}\right)A(4)$

$45 = A$

13. $A = \dfrac{1}{2}bh;\ A = 18,\ h = 4$

$18 = \dfrac{1}{2}b(4)$

$18 = 2b$

$\dfrac{18}{2} = \dfrac{2b}{2}$

$9 = b$

The base is 9 feet.

14. $2x+y = 8$

$2x+y-2x = 8-2x$

$y = 8-2x$

15. Let $x =$ the unknown number

$x = (0.22)(90)$

$x = 19.8$

The number is 4

16. $\dfrac{4\text{ quarts}}{5\text{ gallons}} = \dfrac{4\text{ quarts}}{5\cdot4\text{ quarts}} = \dfrac{1}{5}$

17. $\dfrac{3x}{8} = \dfrac{9}{7}$

$21x = 72$

$\dfrac{21x}{21} = \dfrac{72}{21}$

$x = \dfrac{24}{7}$

18. $-4 + x \le 2$

$-4 + 4 + x \le 2 + 4$

$x \le 6$

19. $-\dfrac{3}{2}y > 6$

$-\dfrac{2}{3}\left(-\dfrac{3}{2}y\right) < -\dfrac{2}{3}(6)$

$y < -4$

20. $-5x + 3 \le 4(x - 6)$

$-5x + 3 \le 4x - 24$

$-5x - 4x + 3 \le 4x - 4x - 24$

$-9x + 3 \le -24$

$-9x + 3 - 3 \le -24 - 3$

$-9x \le -27$

$\dfrac{-9x}{-9} \ge \dfrac{-27}{-9}$

$x \ge 3$

Practice Problems 2.1

1. a. -4

　b. 15

　c. 1

　d. -1

　e. $\dfrac{1}{4}$

2. a. Like terms

　b. Like terms

　c. Like terms

3. a. $9y - 4y = (9 - 4)y = 5y$

　b. $11x^2 + x^2 = (11 + 1)x^2 = 12x^2$

　c. $5y - 3x + 6x = 5y + (-3 + 6) = 5y + 3x$

4. $7y + 2y + 6 + 10 = (7 + 2)y + 16 = 9y + 16$

5. $-2x + 4 + x - 11 = -2x + x + 4 - 11$
$= (-2 + 1)x - 7 = -x - 7$

6. $3z - 3z^2$ cannot be combined
because they are unlike terms.

7. $8.9y + 4.2y - 3 = (8.9 + 4.2)y - 3 = 13.1y - 3$

8. $3(y + 6) = 3(y) + 3(6) = 3y + 18$

9. $-4(x + 0.2y - 3)$
$= -4(x) + (-4)(0.2y) - (-4)(3)$
$= -4x - 0.8y + 12$

10. $-(3x + 2y + z - 1) = -3x - 2y - z + 1$

11. $4(x - 6) + 20 = 4x - 24 + 20 = 4x - 4$

12. $5-(3x+9)=5-3x-9=-3x-4$

13. $-3(7x+1)-(4x-2)=-21x-3-4x+2$
$$=-25x-1$$

14. $8+11(2y-9)=8+22y-99=22y-91$

15. $(4x-3)-(9x-19)=4x-3-9x+10$
$$=-5x+7$$

16. $10-3x$

17. $\dfrac{x+2}{5}$

18. $3x+(2x+6)==3x+2x+6=5x+6$

Mental Math 2.1

1. -7

2. 3

3. 1

4. -1

5. 17

6. 1.2

7. Like terms

8. Unlike terms

9. Unlike terms

10. Like terms

11. Like terms

12. Unlike terms

Exercise Set 2.1

1. $7y+8y=(7+8)y=15y$

3. $8w-w+6w=(8-1+6)w=13w$

5. $3b-5-10b-4=3b-10b-5-4$
$$=(3-10)b-9=-7b-9$$

7. $m-4m+2m-6=(1-4+2)m-6$
$$=-m-6$$

9. $5g-3-5-5g=5g-5g-3-5$
$$=(5-5)g-8=0g-8=-8$$

11. $6.2x-4+x-1.2=6.2x+x-4-1.2$
$$=(6.2+1)x-5.2=7.2x-5.2$$

13. $2k-k-6=(2-1)k-6=k-6$

15. $-9x+4x+18-10x=-9x+4x-10x+18$
$$=(-9+4-10)x+18=-15x+18$$

17. $6x-5x+x-3+2x=6x-5x+x+2x-3$
$$=(6-5+1+2)x-3=4x-3$$

19. $7x^2+8x^2-10x^2=(7+8-10)x^2=5x^2$

21. $3.4m-4-3.4m-7=3.4m-3.4m-4-7$
$$=(3.4-3.4)m-11=0m-11=-11$$

23. $6x + 0.5 - 4.3x - 0.4x + 3$
$$= 6x - 4.3x - 0.4x + 0.5 + 3$$
$$= (6 - 4.3 - 0.4)x + 3.5$$
$$= 1.3x + 3.5$$

25. $5(y + 4) = 5(y) + 5(4) = 5y + 20$

27. $-2(x + 2) = -2(x) + (-2)(2) = -2x - 4$

29. $-5(2x - 3y + 6)$
$$= -5(2x) - (-5)(3y) + (-5)(6)$$
$$= -10x + 15y - 30$$

31. $-(3x - 2y + 1) = -3x + 2y - 1$

33. $7(d - 3) + 10 = 7d - 21 + 10 = 7d - 11$

35. $-4(3y - 4) + 12y = -12y + 16 + 12y = 16$

37. $3(2x - 5) - 5(x - 4) = 6x - 15 - 5x + 20$
$$= x + 5$$

39. $-2(3x - 4) + 7x - 6 = -6x + 8 + 7x - 6$
$$= x + 2$$

41. $5k - (3k - 10) = 5k - 3k + 10 = 2k + 10$

43. $(3x + 4) - (6x - 1) = 3x + 4 - 6x + 1$
$$= -3x + 5$$

45. $5(x + 2) - (3x - 4) = 5x + 10 - 3x + 4$
$$= 2x + 14$$

47. $-3(7y - 1) + 4(4y + 7)$
$$= -21y + 3 + 16y + 28$$
$$= -5y + 31$$

49. $2 + 4(6x - 6) = 2 + 24x - 24 = 24x - 22$

51. $0.5(m + 2) + 0.4m = 0.5m + 1 - 0.4m$
$$= 0.9m + 1$$

53. $10 - 3(2x + 3y) = 10 - 6x - 9y$

55. $6(3x - 6) - 2(x + 1) - 17x$
$$= 18x - 36 - 2x - 2 - 17x$$
$$= -x - 38$$

57. $\frac{1}{2}(12x - 4) - (x + 5) = 6x - 2 - x - 5 = 5x - 7$

59. Answers may vary

61. $(4x - 10) + (6x + 7) = 4x - 10 + 6x + 7$
$$= 10x - 3$$

63. $(3x - 8) - (7x + 1) = 3x - 8 - 7x - 1 = -4x - 9$

65. $(m - 9) - (5m - 6) = m - 9 - 5m + 6 = -4m - 3$

67. $2x - 4$

69. $\frac{3}{4}x + 12$

71. $(5x - 2) + 7x = 5x - 2 + 7x = 12x - 2$

73. $8(x + 6) = 8x + 48$

75. $2x - (x + 10) = 2x - x - 10 = x - 10$

77. $y - x^2 = 3 - (-1)^2 = 3 - 1 = 2$

79. $a - b^2 = 2 - (-5)^2 = 2 - 25 = -23$

81. $yz - y^2 = (-5)(0) - (-5)^2 = 0 - 25 = -25$

83. 1 cone + 1 cylinder $\overset{?}{=}$ 3 cubes

1 cube + 2 cubes $\overset{?}{=}$ 3 cubes

3 cubes = 3 cubes: Balanced

85. 2 cylinders + 1 cube $\overset{?}{=}$ 3 cones + 2 cubes

$2 \cdot 2$ cubes + 1 cube $\overset{?}{=}$ 3 cubes + 2 cubes

4 cubes + 1 cube $\overset{?}{=}$ 3 cubes + 2 cubes

5 cubes = 5 cubes: Balanced

87. $5x + (4x - 1) + 5x + (4x - 1)$

$= 5x + 4x - 1 + 5x + 4x - 1$

$= 18x - 2$

89. $12(x + 2) + (3x - 1) = 12x + 24 + 3x - 1$

$= 15x + 23$

The total length is $(15x + 23)$ inches

Practice Problems 2.2

1. $x - 5 = 8$

$x - 5 + 5 = 8 + 5$

$x = 13$

2. $y + 1.7 = 0.3$

$y + 1.7 - 1.7 = 0.3 - 1.7$

$y = -1.4$

3. $\dfrac{7}{8} = y - \dfrac{1}{3}$

$\dfrac{7}{8} + \dfrac{1}{3} = y - \dfrac{1}{3} + \dfrac{1}{3}$

$\dfrac{21}{24} + \dfrac{8}{24} = y$

$\dfrac{29}{24} = y$

4. $3x + 10 = 4x$

$3x - 3x + 10 = 4x - 3x$

$10 = x$

5. $10w + 3 - 4w + 4 = -2w + 3 + 7w$

$6w + 7 = 5w + 3$

$6w - 5w + 7 = 5w - 5w + 3$

$w + 7 = 3$

$w + 7 - 7 = 3 - 7$

$w = -4$

6. $3(2w - 5) - (5w + 1) = -3$

$6w - 15 - 5w - 1 = -3$

$w - 16 = -3$

$w - 16 + 16 = -3 + 16$

$w = 13$

7. $12 - y = 9$

$12 - 12 - y = 9 - 12$

$-y = -3$

$y = 3$

8. If x is one number, then $11 - x$ is the other number.

9. $(n + 49, 489)$ votes

Mental Math 2.2

1. 2, **2.** 3, **3.** 12, **4.** 18, **5.** 17, **6.** 21

Exercise Set 2.2

1. $x + 7 = 10$

$x + 7 - 7 = 10 - 7$

$x = 3$

Check: $x + 7 = 10$

$3 + 7 \overset{?}{=} 10$

$10 = 10$

The solution is 3

3. $x - 2 = -4$

$x - 2 + 2 = -4 + 2$

$x = -2$

Check: $x - 2 = -4$

$-2 - 2 \overset{?}{=} -4$

$-4 = -4$

The solution is -2

5. $3 + x = -11$

$3 + x - 3 = -11 - 3$

$x = -14$

Check: $3 + x = -11$

$3 + (-14) \overset{?}{=} -11$

$-11 = -11$

The solution is -14

7. $r - 8.6 = -8.1$

$r - 8.6 + 8.6 = -8.1 + 8.6$

$r = 0.5$

Check: $x - 8.6 = -8.1$

$0.5 - 8.6 \overset{?}{=} -8.1$

$-8.1 = -8.1$

The solution is 0.5

9. $\dfrac{1}{3} + f = \dfrac{3}{4}$

$\dfrac{1}{3} - \dfrac{1}{3} + f = \dfrac{3}{4} - \dfrac{1}{3}$

$f = \dfrac{9}{12} - \dfrac{4}{12}$

$f = \dfrac{5}{12}$

Check: $\dfrac{1}{3} + f = \dfrac{3}{4}$

$\dfrac{1}{3} + \dfrac{5}{12} \overset{?}{=} \dfrac{3}{4}$

$\dfrac{4}{12} + \dfrac{5}{12} \overset{?}{=} \dfrac{3}{4}$

$\dfrac{9}{12} \overset{?}{=} \dfrac{3}{4}$

$\dfrac{3}{4} = \dfrac{3}{4}$

The solution is $\dfrac{5}{12}$

11. $x - \dfrac{2}{5} = -\dfrac{3}{20}$

$x - \dfrac{2}{5} + \dfrac{2}{5} = -\dfrac{3}{20} + \dfrac{2}{5}$

$x = -\dfrac{3}{20} + \dfrac{8}{20}$

$x = \dfrac{5}{20} = \dfrac{1}{4}$

Check: $x - \dfrac{2}{5} = -\dfrac{3}{20}$

$\dfrac{1}{4} - \dfrac{2}{5} \overset{?}{=} -\dfrac{3}{20}$

$\dfrac{5}{20} - \dfrac{8}{20} \overset{?}{=} -\dfrac{3}{20}$

$-\dfrac{3}{20} = -\dfrac{3}{20}$

The solution is $\dfrac{1}{4}$

13. $5b - 0.7 = 6b$

$5b - 5b - 0.7 = 6b - 5b$

$-0.7 = b$

Check: $5b - 0.7 = 6b$

$5(-0.7) - 0.7 \overset{?}{=} 6(-0.7)$

$-3.5 - 0.7 \overset{?}{=} -4.2$

$-4.2 = -4.2$

The solution is -0.7

15. $7x - 3 = 6x$

$7x - 6x - 3 = 6x - 6x$

$x - 3 = 0$

$x - 3 + 3 = 0 + 3$

$x = 3$

Check: $7x - 3 = 6x$

$7(3) - 3 \overset{?}{=} 6(3)$

$21 - 3 \overset{?}{=} 18$

$18 = 18$

The solution is 3

17. Answers may vary.

19. $7x + 2x = 8x - 3$

$9x = 8x - 3$

$9x - 8x = 8x - 8x - 3$

$x = -3$

Check: $7x + 2x = 8x - 3$

$7(-3) + 2(-3) \overset{?}{=} 8(-3) - 3$

$-21 - 6 \overset{?}{=} -24 - 3$

$-27 = -27$

The solution is -3

21. $\dfrac{5}{6}x + \dfrac{1}{6}x = -9$

$\left(\dfrac{5}{6} + \dfrac{1}{6} \right) x = -9$

$\dfrac{6}{6}x = -9$

$x = -9$

Check: $\dfrac{5}{6}x + \dfrac{1}{6}x = -9$

$\dfrac{5}{6}(-9) + \dfrac{1}{6}(-9) \overset{?}{=} -9$

$-\dfrac{45}{6} - \dfrac{9}{6} \overset{?}{=} -9$

$-\dfrac{54}{6} \overset{?}{=} -9$

$-9 = -9$

The solution is -9

23. $2y + 10 = 5y - 4y$

$2y + 10 = y$

$2y - y + 10 = y - y$

$y + 10 = 0$

$y + 10 - 10 = 0 - 10$

$y = -10$

Check: $2y + 10 = 5y - 4y$

$$2(-10) + 10 \overset{?}{=} 5(-10) - 4(-10)$$

$$-20 + 10 \overset{?}{=} -50 + 40$$

$$-10 = -10$$

The solution is -10

25.
$$3x - 6 = 2x + 5$$
$$3x - 2x - 6 = 2x - 2x + 5$$
$$x - 6 = 5$$
$$x - 6 + 6 = 5 + 6$$
$$x = 11$$

Check: $3x - 6 = 2x + 5$

$$3(11) - 6 \overset{?}{=} 2(11) + 5$$

$$33 - 6 \overset{?}{=} 22 + 5$$

$$27 = 27$$

The solution is 11

27.
$$\frac{3}{7}x + 2 = -\frac{4}{7}x - 5$$
$$\frac{3}{7}x + \frac{4}{7}x = -\frac{4}{7}x + \frac{4}{7}x - 5$$
$$\frac{7}{7}x + 2 = -5$$
$$x + 2 - 2 = -5 - 2$$
$$x = -7$$

Check: $\frac{3}{7}x + 2 = -\frac{4}{7}x - 5$

$$\frac{3}{7}(-7) + 2 \overset{?}{=} -\frac{4}{7}(-7) - 5$$

$$-3 + 2 \overset{?}{=} 4 - 5$$

$$-1 = -1$$

The solution is -7

29.
$$5x - 6 = 6x - 5$$
$$5x - 5x - 6 = 6x - 5x - 5$$
$$-6 = x - 5$$
$$-6 + 5 = x - 5 + 5$$
$$-1 = x$$

Check: $5x - 6 = 6x - 5$

$$5(-1) - 6 \overset{?}{=} 6(-1) - 5$$

$$-5 - 6 \overset{?}{=} -6 - 5$$

$$-11 = -11$$

The solution is -1

31. $8y + 2 - 6y = 3 + y - 10$
$$2y + 2 = y - 7$$
$$2y - y + 2 = y - y - 7$$
$$y + 2 = -7$$
$$y + 2 - 2 = -7 - 2$$
$$y = -9$$

Check: $8y + 2 - 6y = 3 + y - 10$

$$8(-9) + 2 - 6(-9) \overset{?}{=} 3 + (-9) - 10$$

$$-72 + 2 + 54 \overset{?}{=} -16$$

$$-16 = -16$$

The solution is -9

33. $13x - 9 + 2x - 5 = 12x - 1 + 2x$
$$15x - 14 = 14x - 1$$
$$15x - 14x - 14 = 14x - 14x - 1$$
$$x - 14 = -1$$
$$x - 14 + 14 = -1 + 14$$
$$x = 13$$

Check: $13x - 9 + 2x - 5 = 12x - 1 + 2x$

$$13(13) - 9 + 2(13) - 5 \overset{?}{=} 12(13) - 1 + 2(13)$$

$$169 - 9 + 26 - 5 \overset{?}{=} 156 - 1 + 26$$

$$181 = 181$$

The solution is 13

35. $-6.5 - 4x - 1.6 - 3x = -6x + 9.8$

$$-8.1 - 7x = -6x + 9.8$$

$$-8.1 - 7x + 7x = -6x + 7x + 9.8$$

$$-8.1 = x + 9.8$$

$$-8.1 - 9.8 = x + 9.8 - 9.8$$

$$-17.9 = x$$

Check: $-6.5 - 4x - 1.6 - 3x = -6x + 9.8$

$$-6.5 - 4(-17.9) - 1.6 - 3(-17.9)$$

$$\overset{?}{=} -6(-17.9) + 9.8$$

$$-6.5 + 71.6 - 1.6 - 3 \overset{?}{=} 107.4 + 9.8$$

$$117.2 = 117.2$$

The solution is -17.9

37. $\dfrac{3}{8}x - \dfrac{1}{6} = -\dfrac{5}{8}x - \dfrac{2}{3}$

$$\frac{3}{8}x + \frac{5}{8}x - \frac{1}{6} = -\frac{5}{8}x + \frac{5}{8}x - \frac{2}{3}$$

$$\frac{8}{8}x - \frac{1}{6} = -\frac{2}{3}$$

$$x - \frac{1}{6} + \frac{1}{6} = -\frac{2}{3} + \frac{1}{6}$$

$$x = -\frac{4}{6} + \frac{1}{6}$$

$$x = -\frac{3}{6}$$

$$x = -\frac{1}{2}$$

Check: $\dfrac{3}{8}x - \dfrac{1}{6} = -\dfrac{5}{8}x - \dfrac{2}{3}$

$$\frac{3}{8}\left(-\frac{1}{2}\right) - \frac{1}{6} \overset{?}{=} -\frac{5}{8}\left(-\frac{1}{2}\right) - \frac{2}{3}$$

$$-\frac{3}{16} - \frac{1}{6} \overset{?}{=} \frac{5}{16} - \frac{2}{3}$$

$$-\frac{9}{48} - \frac{8}{48} \overset{?}{=} \frac{15}{48} - \frac{32}{48}$$

$$-\frac{17}{48} = -\frac{17}{48}$$

The solution is $-\dfrac{1}{2}$

39. $2(x - 4) = x + 3$

$$2x - 8 = x + 3$$

$$2x - x - 8 = x - x + 3$$

$$x - 8 = 3$$

$$x - 8 + 8 = 3 + 8$$

$$x = 11$$

Check: $2(x - 4) = x + 3$

$$2(11 - 4) \overset{?}{=} 11 + 3$$

$$2(7) \overset{?}{=} 14$$

$$14 = 14$$

The solution is 11

41. $7(6 + w) = 6(2 + w)$

$$42 + 7w = 12 + 6w$$

$$42 + 7w - 6w = 12 + 6w - 6w$$

$$42 + w = 12$$

$$42 - 42 + w = 12 - 42$$

$$w = -30$$

Check: $7(6+w) = 6(2+w)$

$7(6-30) \overset{?}{=} 6(2-30)$

$7(-24) \overset{?}{=} 6(-28)$

$-168 = -168$

The solution is -30

Check: $-5(n-2) = 8-4n$

$-5(2-2) \overset{?}{=} 8-4(2)$

$-5(0) \overset{?}{=} 8-8$

$0 = 0$

The solution is 2

43. $10-(2x-4) = 7-3x$

$10-2x+4 = 7-3x$

$14-2x = 7-3x$

$14-2x+3x = 7-3x+3x$

$14+x = 7$

$14-14+x = 7-14$

$x = -7$

Check: $10-(2x-4) = 7-3x$

$10-(2(-7)-4) \overset{?}{=} 7-3(-7)$

$10-(-14-4) \overset{?}{=} 7+21$

$10-(-18) \overset{?}{=} 28$

$28 = 28$

The solution is -7

45. $-5(n-2) = 8-4n$

$-5n+10 = 8-4n$

$-5n+5n+10 = 8-4n+5n$

$10 = 8+n$

$10-8 = 8-8+n$

$2 = n$

47. $-3(x-4) = -4x$

$-3x+12 = -4x$

$-3x+4x+12 = -4x+4x$

$x+12 = 0$

$x+12-12 = 0-12$

$x = -12$

Check: $-3(x-4) = -4x$

$-3(-12-4) \overset{?}{=} -4(-12)$

$-3(-16) \overset{?}{=} 48$

$48 = 48$

The solution is -12

49. $3(n-5)-(6-2n) = 4n$

$3n-15-6+2n = 4n$

$5n-21 = 4n$

$5n-4n-21 = 4n-4n$

$n-21 = 0$

$n-21+21 = 0+21$

$n = 21$

Check: $3(n-5)-(6-2n)=4n$

$3(21-5)-(6-2(21))\overset{?}{=}4(21)$

$3(16)-(6-42)\overset{?}{=}84$

$48-(-36)\overset{?}{=}84$

$84=84$

The solution is 21

51. $-2(x+6)+3(2x-5)=3(x-4)+10$

$-2x-12+6x-15=3x-12+10$

$4x-27=3x-2$

$4x-3x-27=3x-3x-2$

$x-27=-2$

$x-27+27=-2+27$

$x=25$

Check:

$-2(x+6)+3(2x-5)=3(x-4)+10$

$-2(25+6)+3(2(25)-5)\overset{?}{=}3(25-4)+10$

$-2(31)+3(50-5)\overset{?}{=}3(21)+10$

$-62+3(45)\overset{?}{=}63+10$

$-62+135\overset{?}{=}63+10$

$73=73$

The solution is 25

53. The other number is $20-p$.

55. The length of the other piece is $(10-x)$ feet

57. The supplement of the angle $x°$ is $(180-x)°$.

59. Ortiz received $(n+47,628)$ votes.

61. The area of the Sahara Desert is $7x$ square miles.

63. The reciprocal of $\dfrac{5}{8}$ is $\dfrac{8}{5}$ since $\dfrac{5}{8}\cdot\dfrac{8}{5}=1$

65. The reciprocal of 2 is $\dfrac{1}{2}$ since $2\cdot\dfrac{1}{2}=1$

67. The reciprocal of $-\dfrac{1}{9}$ is -9

since $-\dfrac{1}{9}\cdot-9=1$

69. $\dfrac{3x}{3}=x$

71. $-5\left(-\dfrac{1}{5}y\right)=y$

73. $\dfrac{3}{5}\left(\dfrac{5}{3}x\right)=x$

75. $\qquad 36.766+x=-108.712$

$36.766-36.766+x=-108.712-36.766$

$x=-145.478$

77. $180-\left[x+(2x+7)\right]=180-\left[x+2x+7\right]$

$=180-\left[3x+7\right]=180-3x-7=173-3x$

The third angle is $(173-3x)°$.

Practice Problems 2.3

1. $\dfrac{3}{7}x = 9$

$$\dfrac{7}{3}\left(\dfrac{3}{7}x\right) = \dfrac{7}{3}(9)$$

$$1x = 21$$

$$x = 21$$

2. $7x = 42$

$$\dfrac{7x}{7} = \dfrac{42}{7}$$

$$1x = 6$$

$$x = 6$$

3. $-4x = 52$

$$\dfrac{-4x}{-4} = \dfrac{52}{-4}$$

$$1x = -13$$

$$x = -13$$

4. $\dfrac{y}{5} = 13$

$$5\left(\dfrac{y}{5}\right) = 5(13)$$

$$1y = 65$$

$$y = 65$$

5. $2.6x = 13.52$

$$\dfrac{2.6x}{2.6} = \dfrac{13.52}{2.6}$$

$$1x = 5.2$$

$$x = 5.2$$

6. $-\dfrac{5}{6}y = -\dfrac{3}{5}$

$$-\dfrac{6}{5}\left(-\dfrac{5}{6}y\right) = -\dfrac{6}{5}\left(-\dfrac{3}{5}\right)$$

$$1y = \dfrac{18}{25}$$

$$y = \dfrac{18}{25}$$

7. $-x + 7 = -12$

$$-x + 7 - 7 = -12 - 7$$

$$-x = -19$$

$$\dfrac{-x}{-1} = \dfrac{-19}{-1}$$

$$1x = 19$$

$$x = 19$$

8. $-7x + 2x + 3 - 20 = -2$

$$-5x - 17 = -2$$

$$-5x - 17 + 17 = -2 + 17$$

$$-5x = 15$$

$$\dfrac{-5x}{-5} = \dfrac{15}{-5}$$

$$1x = -3$$

$$x = -3$$

9. Sum = first integer + second integer.

$$\text{Sum} = x + (x+1)$$

$$= x + x + 1 = 2x + 1$$

Mental Math 2.3

1. $3a = 27$

$$a = 9$$

2. $9c = 54$

   $c = 6$

3. $5b = 10$

   $b = 2$

4. $7t = 14$

   $t = 2$

5. $6x = -30$

   $x = -5$

6. $8r = -64$

   $r = -8$

Exercise Set 2.3

1. $-5x = 20$

   $\dfrac{-5x}{-5} = \dfrac{20}{-5}$

   $x = -4$

   Check: $-5x = 20$

   $-5(-4) \overset{?}{=} 20$

   $20 = 20$

   The solution is -4

3. $3x = 0$

   $\dfrac{3x}{3} = \dfrac{0}{3}$

   $x = 0$

   Check: $3x = 0$

   $3(0) \overset{?}{=} 0$

   $0 = 0$

   The solution is 0

5. $-x = -12$

   $\dfrac{-x}{-1} = \dfrac{-12}{-1}$

   $x = 12$

   Check: $-x = -12$

   $-(12) \overset{?}{=} -12$

   $-12 = -12$

   The solution is 12

7. $\dfrac{2}{3}x = -8$

   $\dfrac{3}{2}\left(\dfrac{2}{3}x\right) = \dfrac{3}{2}(-8)$

   $x = -12$

   Check: $\dfrac{2}{3}x = -8$

   $\dfrac{2}{3}(-12) \overset{?}{=} -8$

   $-8 = -8$

   The solution is -12

9. $\dfrac{1}{6}d = \dfrac{1}{2}$

   $6\left(\dfrac{1}{6}d\right) = 6\left(\dfrac{1}{2}\right)$

   $d = 3$

   Check: $\dfrac{1}{6}d = \dfrac{1}{2}$

   $\dfrac{1}{6}(3) \overset{?}{=} \dfrac{1}{2}$

   $\dfrac{1}{2} = \dfrac{1}{2}$

   The solution is 3

11. $\dfrac{a}{2} = 1$

$$2\left(\dfrac{a}{2}\right) = 2(1)$$

$$a = 2$$

Check: $\dfrac{a}{2} = 1$

$$\dfrac{2}{2} \overset{?}{=} 1$$

$$1 = 1$$

The solution is 2

13. $\dfrac{k}{-7} = 0$

$$-7\left(\dfrac{k}{-7}\right) = -7(0)$$

$$k = 0$$

Check: $\dfrac{k}{-7} = 0$

$$\dfrac{0}{-7} \overset{?}{=} 0$$

$$0 = 0$$

The solution is 0

15. $1.7x = 10.71$

$$\dfrac{1.7x}{1.7} = \dfrac{10.71}{1.7}$$

$$x = 6.3$$

Check: $1.7x = 10.71$

$$1.7(6.3) \overset{?}{=} 10.71$$

$$10.71 = 10.71$$

The solution is 6.3

17. $42 = 7x$

$$\dfrac{42}{7} = \dfrac{7x}{7}$$

$$6 = x$$

Check: $42 = 7x$

$$42 \overset{?}{=} 7(6)$$

$$42 = 42$$

The solution is 6

19. $4.4 = -0.8x$

$$\dfrac{4.4}{-0.8} = \dfrac{-0.8x}{-0.8}$$

$$-5.5 = x$$

Check: $4.4 = -0.8x$

$$4.4 \overset{?}{=} -0.8(-5.5)$$

$$4.4 = 4.4$$

The solution is -5.5

21. $-\dfrac{3}{7}p = -2$

$$-\dfrac{7}{3}\left(-\dfrac{3}{7}p\right) = -\dfrac{7}{3}(-2)$$

$$p = \dfrac{14}{3}$$

Check: $-\dfrac{3}{7}p = -2$

$$-\dfrac{3}{7}\left(\dfrac{14}{3}\right) \overset{?}{=} -2$$

$$-2 = -2$$

The solution is $\dfrac{14}{3}$

23.
$$-\frac{4}{3}x = 12$$
$$-\frac{3}{4}\left(-\frac{4}{3}x\right) = -\frac{3}{4}(12)$$
$$x = -9$$

Check: $-\frac{4}{3}x = 12$

$$-\frac{4}{3}(-9)\overset{?}{=}12$$
$$12 = 12$$

The solution is -9

25.
$$2x - 4 = 16$$
$$2x - 4 + 4 = 16 + 4$$
$$2x = 20$$
$$\frac{2x}{2} = \frac{20}{2}$$
$$x = 10$$

Check: $2x - 4 = 16$

$$2(10) - 4 \overset{?}{=} 16$$
$$20 - 4 \overset{?}{=} 16$$
$$16 = 16$$

The solution is 10

27.
$$-x + 2 = 22$$
$$-x + 2 - 2 = 22 - 2$$
$$-x = 20$$
$$x = -20$$

Check: $-x + 2 = 22$

$$-(-20) + 2 \overset{?}{=} 22$$
$$20 + 2 \overset{?}{=} 22$$
$$22 = 22$$

The solution is -20

29.
$$6a + 3 = 3$$
$$6a + 3 - 3 = 3 - 3$$
$$6a = 0$$
$$\frac{6a}{6} = \frac{0}{6}$$
$$a = 0$$

Check: $6a + 3 = 3$

$$6(0) + 3 \overset{?}{=} 3$$
$$0 + 3 \overset{?}{=} 3$$
$$3 = 3$$

The solution is 0

31.
$$6x + 10 = -20$$
$$6x + 10 - 10 = -20 - 10$$
$$6x = -30$$
$$\frac{6x}{6} = \frac{-30}{6}$$
$$x = -5$$

Check: $6x + 10 = -20$

$$6(-5) + 10 \overset{?}{=} -20$$
$$-30 + 10 \overset{?}{=} -20$$
$$-20 = -20$$

The solution is -5

33.
$$5 - 0.3k = 5$$
$$5 - 5 - 0.3k = 5 - 5$$
$$-0.3k = 0$$
$$\frac{-0.3k}{-0.3} = \frac{0}{-0.3}$$
$$k = 0$$

Check: $5 - 0.3k = 5$

$5 - 0.3(0) \stackrel{?}{=} 5$

$5 - 0 \stackrel{?}{=} 5$

$5 = 5$

The solution is 0

35. $-2x + \dfrac{1}{2} = \dfrac{7}{2}$

$-2x + \dfrac{1}{2} - \dfrac{1}{2} = \dfrac{7}{2} - \dfrac{1}{2}$

$-2x = \dfrac{6}{2}$

$-2x = 3$

$\dfrac{-2x}{-2} = \dfrac{3}{-2}$

$x = -\dfrac{3}{2}$

Check: $-2x + \dfrac{1}{2} = \dfrac{7}{2}$

$-2\left(-\dfrac{3}{2}\right) + \dfrac{1}{2} \stackrel{?}{=} \dfrac{7}{2}$

$3 + \dfrac{1}{2} \stackrel{?}{=} \dfrac{7}{2}$

$\dfrac{6}{2} + \dfrac{1}{2} \stackrel{?}{=} \dfrac{7}{2}$

$\dfrac{7}{2} = \dfrac{7}{2}$

The solution is $-\dfrac{3}{2}$

37. $\dfrac{x}{3} + 2 = -5$

$\dfrac{x}{3} + 2 - 2 = -5 - 2$

$\dfrac{x}{3} = -7$

$3\left(\dfrac{x}{3}\right) = 3(-7)$

$x = -21$

Check: $\dfrac{x}{3} + 2 = -5$

$\dfrac{-21}{3} + 2 \stackrel{?}{=} -5$

$-7 + 2 \stackrel{?}{=} -5$

$-5 = -5$

The solution is -21

39. $10 = 2x - 1$

$10 + 1 = 2x - 1 + 1$

$11 = 2x$

$\dfrac{11}{2} = \dfrac{2x}{2}$

$\dfrac{11}{2} = x$

Check: $10 = 2x - 1$

$10 \stackrel{?}{=} 2\left(\dfrac{11}{2}\right) - 1$

$10 \stackrel{?}{=} 11 - 1$

$10 = 10$

The solution is $\dfrac{11}{2}$

63

41. $6z - 8 - z + 3 = 0$

$$5z - 5 = 0$$

$$5z - 5 + 5 = 0 + 5$$

$$5z = 5$$

$$\frac{5z}{5} = \frac{5}{5}$$

$$z = 1$$

Check: $6z - 8 - z + 3 = 0$

$$6(1) - 8 - (1) + 3 \overset{?}{=} 0$$

$$6 - 8 - 1 + 3 \overset{?}{=} 0$$

$$0 = 0$$

The solution is 1

43. $10 - 3x - 6 - 9x = 7$

$$4 - 12x = 7$$

$$4 - 4 - 12x = 7 - 4$$

$$-12x = 3$$

$$\frac{-12x}{-12} = \frac{3}{-12}$$

$$x = -\frac{1}{4}$$

Check: $10 - 3x - 6 - 9x = 7$

$$10 - 3\left(-\frac{1}{4}\right) - 6 - 9\left(-\frac{1}{4}\right) \overset{?}{=} 7$$

$$10 + \frac{3}{4} - 6 + \frac{9}{4} \overset{?}{=} 7$$

$$4 + \frac{12}{4} \overset{?}{=} 7$$

$$4 + 3 \overset{?}{=} 7$$

$$7 = 7$$

The solution is $-\frac{1}{4}$

45. $1 = 0.4x - 0.6x - 5$

$$1 = -0.2x - 5$$

$$1 + 5 = -0.2x - 5 + 5$$

$$6 = -0.2x$$

$$\frac{6}{-0.2} = \frac{-0.2x}{-0.2}$$

$$-30 = x$$

Check: $1 = 0.4x - 0.6x - 5$

$$1 \overset{?}{=} 0.4(-30) - 0.6(-30) - 5$$

$$1 \overset{?}{=} -12 + 18 - 5$$

$$1 = 1$$

The solution is -30

47. $z - 5z = 7z - 9 - z$

$$-4z = 6z - 9$$

$$-4z - 6z = 6z - 6z - 9$$

$$-10z = -9$$

$$\frac{-10z}{-10} = \frac{-9}{-10}$$

$$z = \frac{9}{10}$$

Check: $z - 5z = 7z - 9 - z$

$$\frac{9}{10} - 5\left(\frac{9}{10}\right) \overset{?}{=} 7\left(\frac{9}{10}\right) - 9 - \frac{9}{10}$$

$$\frac{9}{10} - \frac{45}{10} \overset{?}{=} \frac{63}{10} - 9 - \frac{9}{10}$$

$$-\frac{36}{10} \overset{?}{=} \frac{54}{10} - \frac{90}{10}$$

$$-\frac{36}{10} = -\frac{36}{10}$$

The solution is $\frac{9}{10}$

49. Sum = first integer + second integer.

$$\text{Sum} = x + (x+2)$$
$$= x + x + 2 = 2x + 2$$

51. Sum = first integer + third integer.

$$\text{Sum} = x + (x+2)$$
$$= x + x + 2 = 2x + 2$$

53. $5x + 2(x-6) = 5x + 2x - 12 = 7x - 12$

55. $6(2z+4) + 20 = 12z + 24 + 20 = 12z + 44$

57. $-(x-1) + x = -x + 1 + x = 1$

59.
$$0.07x - 5.06 = -4.92$$
$$0.07x - 5.06 + 5.06 = -4.92 + 5.06$$
$$0.07x = 0.14$$
$$\frac{0.07x}{0.07} = \frac{0.14}{0.07}$$
$$x = 2$$

61. Answers may vary

63. Answers may vary

Practice Problems 2.4

1. $5(3x-1) + 2 = 12x + 6$
$$15x - 5 + 2 = 12x + 6$$
$$15x - 3 = 12x + 6$$
$$15x - 12x - 3 = 12x - 12x + 6$$
$$3x - 3 = 6$$
$$3x - 3 + 3 = 6 + 3$$
$$3x = 9$$
$$\frac{3x}{3} = \frac{9}{3}$$
$$x = 3$$

2. $9(5-x) = -3x$
$$45 - 9x = -3x$$
$$45 - 9x + 9x = -3x + 9x$$
$$45 = 6x$$
$$\frac{45}{6} = \frac{6x}{6}$$
$$\frac{15}{2} = x$$

3. $\dfrac{5}{2}x - 1 = \dfrac{3}{2}x - 4$
$$2\left(\frac{5}{2}x - 1\right) = 2\left(\frac{3}{2}x - 4\right)$$
$$5x - 2 = 3x - 8$$
$$5x - 3x - 2 = 3x - 3x - 8$$
$$2x - 2 = -8$$
$$2x - 2 + 2 = -8 + 2$$
$$2x = -6$$
$$\frac{2x}{2} = \frac{-6}{2}$$
$$x = -3$$

4.
$$\frac{3(x-2)}{5} = 3x+6$$

$$5\left(\frac{3(x-2)}{5}\right) = 5(3x+6)$$

$$3(x-2) = 15x+30$$

$$3x-6 = 15x+30$$

$$3x-15x-6 = 15x-15x+30$$

$$-12x-6 = 30$$

$$-12x-6+6 = 30+6$$

$$-12x = 36$$

$$\frac{-12x}{-12} = \frac{36}{-12}$$

$$x = -3$$

5.
$$0.06x-0.10(x-2) = -0.02(8)$$

$$100\left[0.06x-0.10(x-2)\right] = 100\left[-0.02(8)\right]$$

$$6x-10(x-2) = -2(8)$$

$$6x-10x+20 = -16$$

$$-4x+20 = -16$$

$$-4x+20-20 = -16-20$$

$$-4x = -36$$

$$\frac{-4x}{-4} = \frac{-36}{-4}$$

$$x = 9$$

6. $5(2-x)+8x = 3(x-6)$

$$10-5x+8x = 3x-18$$

$$10+3x = 3x-18$$

$$10+3x-3x = 3x-3x-18$$

$$10 = -18$$

There is no solution

7. $-6(2x+1)-14 = -10(x+2)-2x$

$$-12x-6-14 = -10x-20-2x$$

$$-12x-20 = -12x-20$$

$$-12x+12x-20 = -12x+12x-20$$

$$-20 = -20$$

Every real number is a solution

Exercise Set 2.4

1. $-4y+10 = -2(3y+1)$

$$-4y+10 = -6y-2$$

$$-4y+6y+10 = -6y+6y-2$$

$$2y+10 = -2$$

$$2y+10-10 = -2-10$$

$$2y = -12$$

$$\frac{2y}{2} = \frac{-12}{2}$$

$$y = -6$$

3. $9x-8 = 10+15x$

$$9x-15x-8 = 10+15x-15x$$

$$-6x-8 = 10$$

$$-6x-8+8 = 10+8$$

$$-6x = 18$$

$$\frac{-6x}{-6} = \frac{18}{-6}$$

$$x = -3$$

5. $-2(3x-4) = 2x$

$$-6x+8 = 2x$$

$$-6x+6x+8 = 2x+6x$$

$$8 = 8x$$

$$\frac{8}{8} = \frac{8x}{8}$$

$$1 = x$$

7. $4(2n-1)=(6n+4)+1$

$$8n-4=6n+4+1$$
$$8n-4=6n+5$$
$$8n-6n-4=6n-6n+5$$
$$2n-4=5$$
$$2n-4+4=5+4$$
$$2n=9$$
$$\frac{2n}{2}=\frac{9}{2}$$
$$n=\frac{9}{2}$$

9. $5(2x-1)-2(3x)=1$

$$10x-5-6x=1$$
$$4x-5=1$$
$$4x-5+5=1+5$$
$$4x=6$$
$$\frac{4x}{4}=\frac{6}{4}$$
$$x=\frac{3}{2}$$

11. $6(x-3)+10=-8$

$$6x-18+10=-8$$
$$6x-8=-8$$
$$6x-8+8=-8+8$$
$$6x=0$$
$$\frac{6x}{6}=\frac{0}{6}$$
$$x=0$$

13. $8-2(a-1)=7+a$

$$8-2a+2=7+a$$
$$-2a+10=7+a$$
$$-2a+2a+10=7+a+2a$$
$$10=7+3a$$
$$10-7=7-7+3a$$
$$3=3a$$
$$\frac{3}{3}=\frac{3a}{3}$$
$$1=a$$

15. $4x+3=2x+11$

$$4x-2x+3=2x-2x+11$$
$$2x+3=11$$
$$2x+3-3=11-3$$
$$2x=8$$
$$\frac{2x}{2}=\frac{8}{2}$$
$$x=4$$

17. $-2y-10=5y+18$

$$-2y-5y-10=5y-5y+18$$
$$-7y-10=18$$
$$-7y-10+10=18+10$$
$$-7y=28$$
$$\frac{-7y}{-7}=\frac{28}{-7}$$
$$y=-4$$

19. $-3(t-5)+2t=5t-4$

$-3t+15+2t=5t-4$

$-t+15=5t-4$

$-t-5t+15=5t-5t-4$

$-6t+15=-4$

$-6t+15-15=-4-15$

$-6t=-19$

$\dfrac{-6t}{-6}=\dfrac{-19}{-6}$

$t=\dfrac{19}{6}$

21. $5y+2(y-6)=4(y+1)-2$

$5y+2y-12=4y+4-2$

$7y-12=4y+2$

$7y-4y-12=4y-4y+2$

$3y-12=2$

$3y-12+12=2+12$

$3y=14$

$\dfrac{3y}{3}=\dfrac{14}{3}$

$y=\dfrac{14}{3}$

23. $\dfrac{3}{4}x-\dfrac{1}{2}=1$

$4\left(\dfrac{3}{4}x-\dfrac{1}{2}\right)=4(1)$

$3x-2=4$

$3x-2+2=4+2$

$3x=6$

$\dfrac{3x}{3}=\dfrac{6}{3}$

$x=2$

25. $x+\dfrac{5}{4}=\dfrac{3}{4}x$

$4\left(x+\dfrac{5}{4}\right)=4\left(\dfrac{3}{4}x\right)$

$4x+5=3x$

$4x-3x+5=3x-3x$

$x+5=0$

$x+5-5=0-5$

$x=-5$

27. $\dfrac{x}{2}-1=\dfrac{x}{5}+2$

$10\left(\dfrac{x}{2}-1\right)=10\left(\dfrac{x}{5}+2\right)$

$5x-10=2x+20$

$5x-2x-10=2x-2x+20$

$3x-10=20$

$3x-10+10=20+10$

$3x=30$

$\dfrac{3x}{3}=\dfrac{30}{3}$

$x=10$

29. $\dfrac{6(3-z)}{5}=-z$

$5\left[\dfrac{6(3-z)}{5}\right]=5(-z)$

$6(3-z)=-5z$

$18-6z=-5z$

$18-6z+6z=-5z+6z$

$18=z$

31.
$$0.06 - 0.01(x+1) = -0.02(2-x)$$
$$100\big[0.06 - 0.01(x+1)\big] = 100\big[-0.02(2-x)\big]$$
$$6 - (x+1) = -2(2-x)$$
$$6 - x - 1 = -4 + 2x$$
$$5 - x = -4 + 2x$$
$$5 - x - 2x = -4 + 2x - 2x$$
$$5 - 3x = -4$$
$$5 - 5 - 3x = -4 - 5$$
$$-3x = -9$$
$$\frac{-3x}{-3} = \frac{-9}{-3}$$
$$x = 3$$

33.
$$\frac{3(x-5)}{2} = \frac{2(x+5)}{3}$$
$$6\left[\frac{3(x-5)}{2}\right] = 6\left[\frac{2(x+5)}{3}\right]$$
$$9(x-5) = 4(x+5)$$
$$9x - 45 = 4x + 20$$
$$9x - 4x - 45 = 4x - 4x + 20$$
$$5x - 45 = 20$$
$$5x - 45 + 45 = 20 + 45$$
$$5x = 65$$
$$\frac{5x}{5} = \frac{65}{5}$$
$$x = 13$$

35.
$$0.50x + 0.15(70) = 0.25(142)$$
$$100\big[0.50x + 0.15(70)\big] = 100\big[0.25(142)\big]$$
$$50x + 15(70) = 25(142)$$
$$50x + 1050 = 3550$$

$$50x + 1050 - 1050 = 3550 - 1050$$
$$50x = 2500$$
$$\frac{50x}{50} = \frac{2500}{50}$$
$$x = 50$$

37.
$$0.12(y-6) + 0.06y = 0.08y - 0.07(10)$$
$$100\big[0.12(y-6) + 0.06y\big] = 100\big[0.08y - 0.07(10)\big]$$
$$12(y-6) + 6y = 8y - 7(10)$$
$$12y - 72 + 6y = 8y - 70$$
$$18y - 72 = 8y - 70$$
$$18y - 8y - 72 = 8y - 8y - 70$$
$$10y - 72 = -70$$
$$10y - 72 + 72 = -70 + 72$$
$$10y = 2$$
$$\frac{10y}{10} = \frac{2}{10}$$
$$y = \frac{1}{5} = 0.2$$

39.
$$\frac{2(x+1)}{4} = 3x - 2$$
$$4\left[\frac{2(x+1)}{4}\right] = 4(3x-2)$$
$$2(x+1) = 12x - 8$$
$$2x + 2 = 12x - 8$$
$$2x - 12x + 2 = 12x - 12x - 8$$
$$-10x + 2 = -8$$
$$-10x + 2 - 2 = -8 - 2$$
$$-10x = -10$$
$$\frac{-10x}{-10} = \frac{-10}{-10}$$
$$x = 1$$

41.
$$x + \frac{7}{6} = 2x - \frac{7}{6}$$
$$6\left(x + \frac{7}{6}\right) = 6\left(2x - \frac{7}{6}\right)$$
$$6x + 7 = 12x - 7$$
$$6x - 12x + 7 = 12x - 12x - 7$$
$$-6x + 7 = -7$$
$$-6x + 7 - 7 = -7 - 7$$
$$-6x = -14$$
$$\frac{-6x}{-6} = \frac{-14}{-6}$$
$$x = \frac{14}{6}$$
$$x = \frac{7}{3}$$

43.
$$\frac{9}{2} + \frac{5}{2}y = 2y - 4$$
$$2\left(\frac{9}{2} + \frac{5}{2}y\right) = 2(2y - 4)$$
$$9 + 5y = 4y - 8$$
$$9 + 5y - 4y = 4y - 4y - 8$$
$$9 + y = -8$$
$$9 - 9 + y = -8 - 9$$
$$y = -17$$

45. Answers may vary

47.
$$5x - 5 = 2(x + 1) + 3x - 7$$
$$5x - 5 = 2x + 2 + 3x - 7$$
$$5x - 5 = 5x - 5$$
$$5x - 5x - 5 = 5x - 5x - 5$$
$$-5 = -5$$
Every real number is a solution.

49.
$$\frac{x}{4} + 1 = \frac{x}{4}$$
$$4\left(\frac{x}{4} + 1\right) = 4\left(\frac{x}{4}\right)$$
$$x + 4 = x$$
$$x - x + 4 = x - x$$
$$4 = 0$$
There is no solution.

51.
$$3x - 7 = 3(x + 1)$$
$$3x - 7 = 3x + 3$$
$$3x - 3x - 7 = 3x - 3x + 3$$
$$-7 = 3$$
There is no solution.

53.
$$2(x + 3) - 5 = 5x - 3(1 + x)$$
$$2x + 6 - 5 = 5x - 3 - 3x$$
$$2x + 1 = 2x - 3$$
$$2x - 2x + 1 = 2x - 2x - 3$$
$$1 = -3$$
There is no solution.

55. Answers may vary

57.
$$x + (2x - 3) + (3x - 5) = x + 2x - 3 + 3x - 5$$
$$= 6x - 8$$
The perimeter is $(6x - 8)$ meters

59. $-8 - x$

61. $-3 + 2x$

63. $9(x + 20)$

65. $1000(7x-10)=50(412+100x)$

$7000x-10,000=20,600+5000x$

$7000x-5000x-10,000$

$\qquad =20,600+5000x-5000x$

$2000x-10,000=20,600$

$2000x-10,000+10,000$

$\qquad =20,600+10,000$

$2000x=30,600$

$\dfrac{2000x}{2000}=\dfrac{30,600}{2000}$

$x=15.3$

67. $0.035x+5.112=0.010x+5.107$

$1000(0.035x+5.112)=1000(0.010x+5.107)$

$35x+5112=10x+5107$

$35x-10x+5112=10x-10x+5107$

$25x+5112=5107$

$25x+5112-5112=5107-5112$

$25x=-5$

$\dfrac{25x}{25}=\dfrac{-5}{25}$

$x=-\dfrac{1}{5}=-0.2$

69. Since the perimeter is the sum of the lengths of the sides,

$x+x+x+2x+2x=28$

$7x=28$

$\dfrac{7x}{7}=\dfrac{28}{7}$

$x=4$

$2x=2(4)=8$

The lengths are 4 cm and 8 cm.

Integrated Review 2.4

1. $x-10=-4$

$x-10+10=-4+10$

$x=6$

2. $y+14=-3$

$y+14-14=-3-14$

$y=-17$

3. $9y=108$

$\dfrac{9y}{9}=\dfrac{108}{9}$

$y=12$

4. $-3x=78$

$\dfrac{-3x}{-3}=\dfrac{78}{-3}$

$x=-26$

5. $-6x+7=25$

$-6x+7-7=25-7$

$-6x=18$

$\dfrac{-6x}{-6}=\dfrac{18}{-6}$

$x=-3$

6. $5y-42=-47$

$5y-42+42=-47+42$

$5y=-5$

$\dfrac{5y}{5}=\dfrac{-5}{5}$

$y=-1$

7. $\dfrac{2}{3}x = 9$

$$\dfrac{3}{2}\left(\dfrac{2}{3}x\right) = \dfrac{3}{2}(9)$$

$$x = \dfrac{27}{2} = 13.5$$

8. $\dfrac{4}{5}z = 10$

$$\dfrac{5}{4}\left(\dfrac{4}{5}z\right) = \dfrac{5}{4}(10)$$

$$z = \dfrac{25}{2} = 12.5$$

9. $\dfrac{r}{-4} = -2$

$$-4\left(\dfrac{r}{-4}\right) = -4(-2)$$

$$r = 8$$

10. $\dfrac{y}{-8} = 8$

$$-8\left(\dfrac{y}{-8}\right) = -8(8)$$

$$y = -64$$

11. $6 - 2x + 8 = 10$

$$-2x + 14 = 10$$

$$-2x + 14 - 14 = 10 - 14$$

$$-2x = -4$$

$$\dfrac{-2x}{-2} = \dfrac{-4}{-2}$$

$$x = 2$$

12. $-5 - 6y + 6 = 19$

$$-6y + 1 = 19$$

$$-6y + 1 - 1 = 19 - 1$$

$$-6y = 18$$

$$\dfrac{-6y}{-6} = \dfrac{18}{-6}$$

$$y = -3$$

13. $2x - 7 = 6x - 27$

$$2x - 6x - 7 = 6x - 6x - 27$$

$$-4x - 7 = -27$$

$$-4x - 7 + 7 = -27 + 7$$

$$-4x = -20$$

$$\dfrac{-4x}{-4} = \dfrac{-20}{-4}$$

$$x = 5$$

14. $3 + 8y = 3y - 2$

$$3 + 8y - 3y = 3y - 3y - 2$$

$$3 + 5y = -2$$

$$3 - 3 + 5y = -2 - 3$$

$$5y = -5$$

$$\dfrac{5y}{5} = \dfrac{-5}{5}$$

$$y = -1$$

15. $-3a + 6 + 5a = 7a - 8a$

$$2a + 6 = -a$$

$$2a - 2a + 6 = -a - 2a$$

$$6 = -3a$$

$$\dfrac{6}{-3} = \dfrac{-3a}{-3}$$

$$-2 = a$$

16.
$$4b - 8 - b = 10b - 3b$$
$$3b - 8 = 7b$$
$$3b - 3b - 8 = 7b - 3b$$
$$-8 = 4b$$
$$\frac{-8}{4} = \frac{4b}{4}$$
$$-2 = b$$

17.
$$-\frac{2}{3}x = \frac{5}{9}$$
$$-\frac{3}{2}\left(-\frac{2}{3}x\right) = -\frac{3}{2}\left(\frac{5}{9}\right)$$
$$x = -\frac{5}{6}$$

18.
$$-\frac{3}{8}y = -\frac{1}{16}$$
$$-\frac{8}{3}\left(-\frac{3}{8}y\right) = -\frac{8}{3}\left(-\frac{1}{16}\right)$$
$$y = \frac{1}{6}$$

19.
$$10 = -6n + 16$$
$$10 - 16 = -6n + 16 - 16$$
$$-6 = -6n$$
$$\frac{-6}{-6} = \frac{-6n}{-6}$$
$$1 = n$$

20.
$$-5 = -2m + 7$$
$$-5 - 7 = -2m + 7 - 7$$
$$-12 = -2m$$
$$\frac{-12}{-2} = \frac{-2m}{-2}$$
$$6 = m$$

21.
$$3(5c - 1) - 2 = 13c + 3$$
$$15c - 3 - 2 = 13c + 3$$
$$15c - 5 = 13c + 3$$
$$15c - 13c - 5 = 13c - 13c + 3$$
$$2c - 5 = 3$$
$$2c - 5 + 5 = 3 + 5$$
$$2c = 8$$
$$\frac{2c}{2} = \frac{8}{2}$$
$$c = 4$$

22.
$$4(3t + 4) - 20 = 3 + 5t$$
$$12t + 16 - 20 = 3 + 5t$$
$$12t - 4 = 3 + 5t$$
$$12t - 5t - 4 = 3 + 5t - 5t$$
$$7t - 4 = 3$$
$$7t - 4 + 4 = 3 + 4$$
$$7t = 7$$
$$\frac{7t}{7} = \frac{7}{7}$$
$$t = 1$$

23.
$$\frac{2(z + 3)}{3} = 5 - z$$
$$3\left[\frac{2(z + 3)}{3}\right] = 3(5 - z)$$
$$2z + 6 = 15 - 3z$$
$$2z + 3z + 6 = 15 - 3z + 3z$$
$$5z + 6 = 15$$
$$5z + 6 - 6 = 15 - 6$$
$$5z = 9$$
$$\frac{5z}{5} = \frac{9}{5}$$
$$z = \frac{9}{5}$$

24. $\dfrac{3(w+2)}{4} = 2w+3$

$4\left[\dfrac{3(w+2)}{4}\right] = 4(2w+3)$

$3w+6 = 8w+12$

$3w-8w+6 = 8w-8w+12$

$-5w+6 = 12$

$-5w+6-6 = 12-6$

$-5w = 6$

$\dfrac{-5w}{-5} = \dfrac{6}{-5}$

$w = -\dfrac{6}{5}$

25. $-2(2x-5) = -3x+7-x+3$

$-4x+10 = -4x+10$

$-4x+4x+10 = -4x+4x+10$

$10 = 10$

Every real number is a solution

26. $-4(5x-2) = -12x+4-8x+4$

$-20x+8 = -20x+8$

$-20x+20x+8 = -20x+20x+8$

$8 = 8$

Every real number is a solution

27. $0.02(6t-3) = 0.04(t-2)+0.02$

$100\left[0.02(6t-3)\right] = 100\left[0.04(t-2)+0.02\right]$

$2(6t-3) = 4(t-2)+2$

$12t-6 = 4t-8+2$

$12t-6 = 4t-6$

$12t-4t-6 = 4t-4t-6$

$8t-6 = -6$

$8t-6+6 = -6+6$

$8t = 0$

$\dfrac{8t}{8} = \dfrac{0}{8}$

$t = 0$

28. $0.03(m+7) = 0.02(5-m)+0.03$

$100\left[0.03(m+7)\right] = 100\left[0.02(5-m)+0.03\right]$

$3(m+7) = 2(5-m)+3$

$3m+21 = 10-2m+3$

$3m+21 = 13-2m$

$3m+2m+21 = 13-2m+2m$

$5m+21 = 13$

$5m+21-21 = 13-21$

$5m = -8$

$\dfrac{5m}{5} = \dfrac{-8}{5}$

$m = -\dfrac{8}{5} = -1.6$

29. $-3y = \dfrac{4(y-1)}{5}$

$5(-3y) = 5\left[\dfrac{4(y-1)}{5}\right]$

$-15y = 4y-4$

$-15y-4y = 4y-4y-4$

$-19y = -4$

$\dfrac{-19y}{-19} = \dfrac{-4}{-19}$

$y = \dfrac{4}{19}$

30. $\qquad -4x = \dfrac{5(1-x)}{6}$

$$6(-4x) = 6\left[\dfrac{5(1-x)}{6}\right]$$

$$-24x = 5 - 5x$$

$$-24x + 5x = 5 - 5x + 5x$$

$$-19x = 5$$

$$\dfrac{-19x}{-19} = \dfrac{5}{-19}$$

$$x = -\dfrac{5}{19}$$

31. $\qquad \dfrac{5}{3}x - \dfrac{7}{3} = x$

$$3\left(\dfrac{5}{3}x - \dfrac{7}{3}\right) = 3(x)$$

$$5x - 7 = 3x$$

$$5x - 5x - 7 = 3x - 5x$$

$$-7 = -2x$$

$$\dfrac{-7}{-2} = \dfrac{-2x}{-2}$$

$$\dfrac{7}{2} = x$$

32. $\qquad \dfrac{7}{5}n + \dfrac{3}{5} = -n$

$$5\left(\dfrac{7}{5}n + \dfrac{3}{5}\right) = 5(-n)$$

$$7n + 3 = -5n$$

$$7n - 7n + 3 = -5n - 7n$$

$$3 = -12n$$

$$\dfrac{3}{-12} = \dfrac{-12n}{-12}$$

$$-\dfrac{1}{4} = n$$

Practice Problems 2.5

1. $\qquad$ Let x = the number.

$$3(x - 5) = 2x - 3$$

$$3x - 15 = 2x - 3$$

$$3x - 2x - 15 = 2x - 2x - 3$$

$$x - 15 = -3$$

$$x - 15 + 15 = -3 + 15$$

$$x = 12$$

The number $= 12$

2. Let x = length of the shorter piece and $5x$ = length of the longer piece.

$$x + 5x = 18$$

$$6x = 18$$

$$\dfrac{6x}{6} = \dfrac{18}{6}$$

$$x = 3$$

$$5x = 5(3) = 15$$

The shorter piece $= 3$ ft. and the longer piece $= 15$ ft

3. Let x = the number of electoral votes for Texas and $x + 22$ = the number for California.

$$x + x + 22 = 86$$

$$2x + 22 = 86$$

$$2x + 22 - 22 = 86 - 22$$

$$2x = 64$$

$$\dfrac{2x}{2} = \dfrac{64}{2}$$

$$x = 32$$

$$x + 22 = 32 + 22 = 54$$

Texas had 32 votes

California had 54 votes.

4. Let x = the number of miles driven
and 0.20 = the charge per mile.

$$34 + 0.20x = 104$$
$$34 - 34 + 0.20x = 104 - 34$$
$$0.20x = 70$$
$$\frac{0.20x}{0.20} = \frac{70}{0.20}$$
$$x = 350$$

350 miles were driven

5. Let x = the measure of the smallest
angle, $2x$ = the measure of the second
angle, and $3x$ = the measure of the third.

$$x + 2x + 3x = 180$$
$$6x = 180$$
$$\frac{6x}{6} = \frac{180}{6}$$
$$x = 30$$
$$2x = 2(30) = 60$$
$$3x = 3(30) = 90$$

The 3 angles are $30°$, $60°$, $90°$

Exercise Set 2.5

1.   Let x = the number.

$$5\left(2x + \frac{1}{5}\right) = 5\left(3x - \frac{4}{5}\right)$$
$$10x + 1 = 15x - 4$$
$$10x - 15x + 1 = 15x - 15x - 4$$
$$-5x + 1 = -4$$
$$-5x + 1 - 1 = -4 - 1$$
$$-5x = -5$$
$$\frac{-5x}{-5} = \frac{-5}{-5}$$
$$x = 1$$

The number $= 1$

3.   Let x = the number.

$$2(x - 8) = 3(x + 3)$$
$$2x - 16 = 3x + 9$$
$$2x - 2x - 16 = 3x - 2x + 9$$
$$-16 = x + 9$$
$$-16 - 9 = x + 9 - 9$$
$$-25 = x$$

The number $= -25$

5.   Let x = the number.

$$2x(3) = 5x - \frac{3}{4}$$
$$6x = 5x - \frac{3}{4}$$
$$6x - 5x = 5x - 5x - \frac{3}{4}$$
$$x = -\frac{3}{4}$$

The number $= -\frac{3}{4}$

7.   Let x = the number.

$$3(x+5) = 2x - 1$$
$$3x + 15 = 2x - 1$$
$$3x - 2x + 15 = 2x - 2x - 1$$
$$x + 15 = -1$$
$$x + 15 - 15 = -1 - 15$$
$$x = -16$$

The number $= -16$

9. Let x = the salary of the govenor of Oregon and $x + 39,000$ = the salary of the govenor of Michigan.

$$x + x + 39,000 = 215,600$$
$$2x + 39,000 = 215,600$$
$$2x + 39,000 - 39,000 = 215,600 - 39,000$$
$$2x = 176,600$$
$$\frac{2x}{2} = \frac{176,600}{2}$$
$$x = 88,300$$

$x + 39,000 = 88,300 + 39,000 = 127,300$
The govenor of Oregon makes $88,300 and the govenor of Michigan makes 127,300.

11. Let x = length of the first piece, $2x$ = length of the second piece, and $5x$ = length of the third piece.

$$x + 2x + 5x = 40$$
$$8x = 40$$
$$\frac{8x}{8} = \frac{40}{8}$$
$$x = 5$$

$$2x = 2(5) = 10$$
$$5x = 5(5) = 25$$

The lengths are 5, 10, and 25 inches

13. Let x = the number of miles driven, 0.29 = the charge per mile, and 24.95 = the charge per day.

$$2(24.95) + 0.29x = 100$$
$$49.90 + 0.29x = 100$$
$$49.90 - 49.90 + 0.29x = 100 - 49.90$$
$$0.29x = 50.10$$
$$\frac{0.29x}{0.29} = \frac{50.10}{0.29}$$
$$x = 172$$

172 miles were driven

15. Let x = the measure of each of the two equal angle, and $2x + 30$ = the measure of the third.

$$x + x + 2x + 30 = 180$$
$$4x + 30 = 180$$
$$4x + 30 - 30 = 180 - 30$$
$$4x = 150$$
$$\frac{4x}{4} = \frac{150}{4}$$
$$x = 37.5$$

$$2x + 30 = 2(37.5) + 30 = 105$$

The 3 angles are $37.5°$, $37.5°$, $105°$

17. Let $x =$ the number of votes for cerulean and $x + 3366 =$ the number for blue.

$$x + x + 3366 = 19,278$$
$$2x + 3366 = 19,278$$
$$2x + 3366 - 3366 = 19,278 - 3366$$
$$2x = 15,912$$
$$\frac{2x}{2} = \frac{15,912}{2}$$
$$x = 7956$$
$$x + 3366 = 7956 + 3366 = 11,322$$

Cerulean had 7956 votes.
Blue had 11,322 votes.

19. Let $x =$ the measure of the smaller angle and $3x =$ the measure of the other.

$$x + 3x = 180$$
$$4x = 180$$
$$\frac{4x}{4} = \frac{180}{4}$$
$$x = 45$$
$$3x = 3(45) = 135$$

The 2 angles are $45°, 135°$.

21. Let $x =$ length of the shorter piece and $2x + 2 =$ length of the longer piece.

$$x + 2x + 2 = 17$$
$$3x + 2 = 17$$
$$3x + 2 - 2 = 17 - 2$$
$$3x = 15$$
$$\frac{3x}{3} = \frac{15}{3}$$
$$x = 5$$

$$2x + 2 = 2(5) + 2 = 12$$

The shorter piece $= 5$ ft. and the longer piece $= 12$ ft

23. Let $x =$ diameter and $5x + 8 =$ height.

$$x + 5x + 8 = 14$$
$$6x + 8 = 14$$
$$6x + 8 - 8 = 14 - 8$$
$$6x = 6$$
$$\frac{6x}{6} = \frac{6}{6}$$
$$x = 1$$

$$5x + 8 = 5(1) + 8 = 13$$

The diameter $= 1$ meter. and the height $= 13$ meters.

25. Let $x =$ the area of the Gobi Desert and $7x =$ the area of the Sahara Desert.

$$x + 7x = 4,000,000$$
$$8x = 4,000,000$$
$$\frac{8x}{8} = \frac{4,000,000}{8}$$
$$x = 500,000$$

$$7x = 7(500,000) = 3,500,000$$

Gobi Desert: 500,000 sq mi.
Sahara Desert: 3,500,000 sq mi.

27. Answers may vary

29. Texas and Florida

31. Let $x =$ the amount spent by Pennsylvania and $2x - 8.1 =$ the amount spent by Hawaii.

$$x + 2x - 8.1 = 60.9$$
$$3x - 8.1 = 60.9$$
$$3x - 8.1 + 8.1 = 60.9 + 8.1$$
$$3x = 69$$
$$\frac{3x}{3} = \frac{69}{3}$$
$$x = 23$$
$$2x - 8.1 = 2(23) - 8.1 = 37.9$$

Pennsylvania spent $23 million.
Hawaii spends $37.9 million.

33. Let $x =$ the floor area of the Empire State Building.

$$3x = 6.5$$
$$\frac{3x}{3} = \frac{6.5}{3}$$
$$x = \frac{6.5}{3} \approx 2.2$$

The floor area of the Empire State Building is about 2.2 million sq ft.

35. Let $x =$ Purdue's score and $x + 2 =$ NotreDame's score.

$$x + x + 2 = 134$$
$$2x + 2 = 134$$
$$2x + 2 - 2 = 134 - 2$$
$$2x = 132$$
$$\frac{2x}{2} = \frac{132}{2}$$
$$x = 66$$

$$x + 2 = 66 + 2 = 68$$

Purdue's score was 66 and NotreDame's score was 68.

37. Let $x =$ number of medals won by Germany, $x + 1 =$ number of medals won by Australia, and $x + 2 =$ number of medals won by China.

$$x + x + 1 + x + 2 = 174$$
$$3x + 3 = 174$$
$$3x + 3 - 3 = 174 - 3$$
$$3x = 171$$
$$\frac{3x}{3} = \frac{171}{3}$$
$$x = 57$$

$$x + 1 = 57 + 1 = 58, \; x + 2 = 57 + 2 = 59$$

Germany won 57 medals.
Australia won 58 medals.
Chaina won 59 medals.

39. Let $x =$ the measure of the smallest angle, $x + 2 =$ the measure of the second, and $x + 4 =$ the measure of the third.

$$x + x + 2 + x + 4 = 180$$
$$3x + 6 = 180$$
$$3x + 6 - 6 = 180 - 6$$
$$3x = 174$$
$$\frac{3x}{3} = \frac{174}{3}$$
$$x = 58$$

$$x + 2 = 58 + 2 = 60$$
$$x + 4 = 58 + 4 = 62$$

The 3 angles are 58°, 60°, 62°

41. $\dfrac{1}{2}(x-1) = 37$

43. $\dfrac{3(x+2)}{5} = 0$

45. Let $W = 7$ and $L = 10$

$2W + 2L = 2(7) + 2(10) = 14 + 20 = 34$

47. Let $r = 15$

$\pi r^2 = \pi(15)^2 = 225\pi$

49. Answers may vary

51. Let $L = 1.6W$

$P = 2W + 2L$

$78 = 2W + 2(1.6W)$

$78 = 2W + 3.2W$

$78 = 5.2W$

$\dfrac{78}{5.2} = \dfrac{5.2W}{5.2}$

$15 = W$

$1.6W = 1.6(15) = 24$

Width = 15 ft, Length = 24 ft

53. Answers may vary

Practice Problems 2.6

1. Let $d = 1175$ and $r = 50$

$d = rt$

$1175 = 50t$

$\dfrac{1175}{50} = \dfrac{50t}{50}$

$23.5 = t$

They will drive $23\dfrac{1}{2}$ hours

2. Let $A = 450$ and $w = 18$

$A = lw$

$450 = l(18)$

$\dfrac{450}{18} = \dfrac{18l}{18}$

$l = 25$

The length of the deck is 25 ft

3. $C = 2\pi r$

$\dfrac{C}{2\pi} = \dfrac{2\pi r}{2\pi}$

$\dfrac{C}{2\pi} = r$

4. $P = 2l + 2w$

$P - 2l = 2l - 2l + 2w$

$P - 2l = 2w$

$\dfrac{P - 2l}{2} = \dfrac{2w}{2}$

$\dfrac{P - 2l}{2} = w$

5.
$$A = \frac{a+b}{2}$$
$$2A = 2\left(\frac{a+b}{2}\right)$$
$$2A = a+b$$
$$2A-a = a-a+b$$
$$2A-a = b$$

Exercise Set 2.6

1. Let $A = 45$ and $b = 15$
$$A = bh$$
$$45 = 15h$$
$$\frac{45}{15} = \frac{15h}{15}$$
$$3 = h$$

3. Let $S = 102,\ l = 7,$ and $w = 3$
$$S = 4lw + 2wh$$
$$102 = 4(7)(3) + 2(3)h$$
$$102 = 84 + 6h$$
$$102 - 84 = 84 - 84 + 6h$$
$$18 = 6h$$
$$\frac{18}{6} = \frac{6h}{6}$$
$$3 = h$$

5. Let $A = 180,\ B = 11,$ and $b = 7$
$$A = \frac{1}{2}(B+b)h$$
$$180 = \frac{1}{2}(11+7)h$$
$$2(180) = 2\left[\frac{1}{2}(18)h\right]$$

$$360 = 18h$$
$$\frac{360}{18} = \frac{18h}{18}$$
$$20 = h$$

7. Let $P = 30,\ a = 8,$ and $b = 10$
$$P = a+b+c$$
$$30 = 8+10+c$$
$$30 = 18+c$$
$$30-18 = 18-18+c$$
$$12 = c$$

9. Let $C = 15.7,$ and $\pi = 3.14$
$$C = 2\pi r$$
$$15.7 = 2(3.14)r$$
$$15.7 = 6.28r$$
$$\frac{15.7}{6.28} = \frac{6.28r}{6.28}$$
$$2.5 = r$$

11. Let $I = 3750,\ P = 25,000,$ and $R = 0.05$
$$I = PRT$$
$$3750 = 25,000(0.05)T$$
$$3750 = 1250T$$
$$\frac{3750}{1250} = \frac{1250T}{1250}$$
$$3 = T$$

13. Let $V = 565.2$, $r = 6$, and $\pi = 3.14$

$$V = \frac{1}{3}\pi r^2 h$$

$$565.2 = \frac{1}{3}(3.14)(6)^2 h$$

$$565.2 = 37.68h$$

$$\frac{565.2}{37.68} = \frac{37.68h}{37.68}$$

$$15 = h$$

15. Let $A = 52,400$ and $l = 400$

$$A = lw$$

$$52,400 = 400w$$

$$\frac{52,400}{400} = \frac{400w}{400}$$

$$131 = w$$

The width is 131 ft

17. Let $t = 2.5$ and $r = 55$

$$d = rt$$

$$d = 55(2.5)$$

$$d = 137.5$$

They are 137.5 miles apart.

19. Let $F = 122$

$$C = \frac{5}{9}(F - 32)$$

$$C = \frac{5}{9}(122 - 32)$$

$$C = \frac{5}{9}(90)$$

$$C = 50° C$$

21. Let $l = 8$, $w = 3$, and $h = 6$

$$V = lwh$$

$$V = 8(3)(6) = 144$$

Let x = number of fish and volume
per fish $= 1.5$

$$144 = 1.5x$$

$$\frac{144}{1.5} = \frac{1.5x}{1.5}$$

$$96 = x$$

96 fish can be placed in the tank.

23. Let $A = 1,813,500$ and $w = 150$

$$A = lw$$

$$1,813,500 = l(150)$$

$$\frac{1,813,500}{150} = \frac{150l}{150}$$

$$12,090 = l$$

The length is 12,090 ft

25. Let $d = 25,000$ and $r = 4000$

$$d = rt$$

$$25,000 = 4000t$$

$$\frac{25,000}{4000} = \frac{4000t}{4000}$$

$$6.25 = t$$

It will take 6.25 hours

27. Let $h = 60$, $B = 130$, and $b = 70$

$$A = \frac{1}{2}(B + b)h$$

$$A = \frac{1}{2}(130 + 70)60 = \frac{1}{2}(200)(60) = 6000$$

Let x = number of bags of fertilizer
and the area per bag = 4000.

$$4000x = 6000$$

$$\frac{4000x}{4000} = \frac{6000}{4000}$$

$$x = 1.5$$

Two bags must be purchased.

29. Let $l = 199$, $w = 78.5$, and $h = 33$

$$V = lwh$$

$$V = 199(78.5)(33) = 515,509.5$$

The volume must be 515,509.5 cu in.

31. Let $d = 16$, so $r = 8$

$$A = \pi r^2 = \pi(8)^2 = 64\pi$$

Let $d = 10$, so $r = 5$

$$A = 2\pi r^2 = 2\pi(5)^2 = 50\pi$$

One 16 inch pizza has more area and
therefore gives more pizza for the price.

33. Let $C = -78.5$

$$F = \frac{9}{5}C + 32 = \frac{9}{5}(-78.5) + 32$$

$$= -141.3 + 32 = -109.3$$

The equivalent temperature is $-109°\,\text{F}$.

35. Let $d = 93,000,000$ and $r = 186,000$

$$d = rt$$

$$93,000,000 = 186,000t$$

$$\frac{93,000,000}{186,000} = \frac{186,000t}{186,000}$$

$$500 = t$$

It will take 500 seconds or $8\frac{1}{3}$ minutes.

37. Let $\pi = 3.14$ and $d = 9.5$ so $r = 4.75$

$$V = \frac{4}{3}\pi r^3 = \frac{4}{3}(3.14)(4.75)^3 = 449$$

The volume is 449 cu in.

39. Let $C = 167$

$$F = \frac{9}{5}C + 32 = \frac{9}{5}(167) + 32$$

$$= 300.6 + 32 = 332.6$$

The equivalent temperature is $332.6°\,\text{F}$.

41. Let $t = 1$ and $r = 270,000$

$$d = rt = 270,000(1) = 270,000 \text{ miles}$$

Let x = number of times around when
it is 25,120 miles per time.

$$25,120x = 270,000$$

$$\frac{25,120x}{25,120} = \frac{270,000}{25,120}$$

$$x = 10.7$$

It can circle the world about 10.7 times.

43. $20\dfrac{\text{miles}}{\text{hour}}$

$= 20\dfrac{\text{miles}}{\text{hour}}\left(\dfrac{5280\text{ feet}}{1\text{ mile}}\right)\left(\dfrac{1\text{ hour}}{3600\text{ seconds}}\right)$

$= \dfrac{88}{3}$ feet/second

Let $d = 1300$ and $r = \dfrac{88}{3}$

$d = rt$

$1300 = \dfrac{88}{3}t$

$\dfrac{3}{88}(1300) = \dfrac{3}{88}\left(\dfrac{88}{3}t\right)$

$44.3 = t$

It will take about 44.3 seconds.

45. Let $d = 42.8$ and $r = 552$

$d = rt$

$42.8 = 552t$

$\dfrac{42.8}{552} = \dfrac{552t}{552}$

$\dfrac{42.8}{552} = t$

$\dfrac{42.8\text{ hour}}{552}\left(\dfrac{60\text{ min}}{1\text{ hour}}\right) = 4.65$ min

It will last about 4.65 minutes.

47. $f = 5gh$

$\dfrac{f}{5g} = \dfrac{5gh}{5g}$

$\dfrac{f}{5g} = h$

49. $V = LWH$

$\dfrac{V}{LH} = \dfrac{LWH}{LH}$

$\dfrac{V}{LH} = W$

51. $3x + y = 7$

$3x - 3x + y = 7 - 3x$

$y = 7 - 3x$

53. $A = P + PRT$

$A - P = P - P + PRT$

$A - P = PRT$

$\dfrac{A-P}{PT} = \dfrac{PRT}{PT}$

$\dfrac{A-P}{PT} = R$

55. $V = \dfrac{1}{3}Ah$

$3V = 3\left(\dfrac{1}{3}Ah\right)$

$3V = Ah$

$\dfrac{3V}{h} = \dfrac{Ah}{h}$

$\dfrac{3V}{h} = A$

57. $P = a + b + c$

$P - b - c = a + b - b + c - c$

$P - b - c = a$

59.
$$S = 2\pi rh + 2\pi r^2$$
$$S - 2\pi r^2 = 2\pi rh + 2\pi r^2 - 2\pi r^2$$
$$S - 2\pi r^2 = 2\pi rh$$
$$\frac{S - 2\pi r^2}{2\pi r} = \frac{2\pi rh}{2\pi r}$$
$$\frac{S - 2\pi r^2}{2\pi r} = h$$

61. $32\% = 32(0.01) = 0.32$

63. $200\% = 200(0.01) = 2$

65. $0.17 = 0.17(100\%) = 17\%$

67. $7.2 = 7.2(100\%) = 720\%$

69.
$$N = R + \frac{V}{G}$$
$$N - R = R - R + \frac{V}{G}$$
$$N - R = \frac{V}{G}$$
$$G(N - R) = G\frac{V}{G}$$
$$G(N - R) = V$$

71. The original box has a volume
$V = LWH$
The altered box, has a length $2L$,
a width $2W$, a height $2H$ and
a new volume
$V = 2L(2W)(2H) = 8LWH.$
The volume is multiplied by 8.

73. Let $C = F$
$$F = \frac{9}{5}C + 32$$
$$F = \frac{9}{5}F + 32$$
$$F - \frac{9}{5}F = \frac{9}{5}F - \frac{9}{5}F + 32$$
$$-\frac{4}{5}F = 32$$
$$-\frac{5}{4}\left(-\frac{4}{5}F\right) = -\frac{5}{4}(32)$$
$$F = -40$$
The measurements are the same
number at $-40°$.

Practice Problems 2.7

1. Let $x =$ the unknown percent.
$22 = x \cdot 40$
$0.55 = x$
$55\% = x$
22 is 55% of 40.

2. Let $x =$ the unknown number.
$150 = 0.40x$
$375 = x$
150 is 40% of 375.

3. a. 66%
   b. $66\% + 4\% = 70\%$
   c. Let $x =$ the unknown number
$x = 0.66(250) = 165$
165 are traveling soley for pleasure.

4. a. $\dfrac{3}{7}$

   b. $\dfrac{40 \text{ min}}{3 \text{ hr}} = \dfrac{40 \text{ min}}{3\left(60 \text{ min}\right)} = \dfrac{40}{180} = \dfrac{2}{9}$

5. $\dfrac{3}{8} = \dfrac{63}{x}$

   $3x = 8\left(63\right)$

   $x = 168$

6. $\dfrac{2x+1}{7} = \dfrac{x-3}{5}$

   $5\left(2x+1\right) = 7\left(x-3\right)$

   $10x + 5 = 7x - 21$

   $3x + 5 = -21$

   $3x = -26$

   $x = -\dfrac{26}{3}$

7. Let x = the number uninsured

   $\dfrac{39}{250} = \dfrac{x}{50,000}$

   $39\left(50,000\right) = 250x$

   $1,950,000 = 250x$

   $7800 = x$

   Expect 7800 to be uninsured.

8.

Size	Price	Unit Price
8 ounce	$2.59	$\dfrac{2.59}{8} \approx \$0.324$
10 ounce	$3.11	$\dfrac{3.11}{10} \approx \$0.311$

The 10 ounce size is the better buy.

Mental Math 2.7

1. No. $25\% + 25\% + 40\% = 90\%$

2. No. $30\% + 30\% + 30\% = 90\%$

3. Yes. $25\% + 25\% + 25\% + 25\% = 100\%$

4. Yes. $10\% + 40\% + 50\% = 100\%$

Exercise Set 2.7

1. Let x = the unknown number.

   $x = 0.16\left(70\right) = 11.2$

   11.2 is 16% of 70.

3. Let x = the unknown percent.

   $28.6 = x \cdot 52$

   $0.55 = x$

   $55\% = x$

   28.6 is 55% of 52.

5. Let x = the unknown number.

   $45 = 0.25x$

   $180 = x$

   45 is 25% of 180.

7. Let x = the unknown number.

   $x = 0.23\left(20\right) = 4.6$

   4.6 is 23% of 20.

9. Let x = the unknown number.

   $40 = 0.80x$

   $50 = x$

   40 is 80% of 50.

11. Let x = the unknown percent.

$144 = x \cdot 480$

$0.30 = x$

$30\% = x$

144 is 30% of 480.

13. Let x = the decrease in price.

$x = 0.25(256) = 64$

The decrease in price is \$64.

The sale price is $256 - 64 = \$192$.

15. Let x = the increase in hotness.

$x = 0.48(577) = 277$

The hotness of the Naga Jolokia pepper

is $577 + 277 = 854$ thousand units

17. 81%

19. Let x = the number of catalog shoppers

in Anchorage.

$x = 0.65(260,283) = 169,184$

There are 169,184 catalog shoppers

in Anchorage.

21. No. Answers may vary

23. 4%

25. Let x = the number who talk 16-60

minutes each day..

$x = 0.37(135,000) = 49,950$

Expect 49,950 to talk 16-60

minutes each day..

27. Let x = the number who ranked flexible

hours as their top priority.

$x = 0.42(860) = 361$

Expect 361 to rank flexible hours as

their top priority.

29.

Ford Motor Company

Year 2000 Vehicle Sales in North America

	Thousands of Vehicles	Percent of Total
U.S.	4486	$\dfrac{4486}{4933} \approx 91\%$
Canada	300	$\dfrac{300}{4933} \approx 6\%$
Mexico	147	$\dfrac{147}{4933} \approx 3\%$
Total	4933	

31. $\dfrac{2}{15}$

33. $\dfrac{10}{12} = \dfrac{5}{6}$

35. $\dfrac{5 \text{ quarts}}{3 \text{ gallons}} = \dfrac{5 \text{ quarts}}{3(4 \text{ quarts})} = \dfrac{5}{12}$

37. $\dfrac{4 \text{ nickles}}{2 \text{ dollars}} = \dfrac{4 \text{ nickles}}{2(20 \text{ nickles})} = \dfrac{4}{40} = \dfrac{1}{10}$

39. $\dfrac{175 \text{ centimeters}}{5 \text{ meters}} = \dfrac{175 \text{ centimeters}}{5(100 \text{ centimeters})}$

$= \dfrac{175}{500} = \dfrac{7}{20}$

41. $\dfrac{190 \text{ minutes}}{3 \text{ hours}} = \dfrac{190 \text{ minutes}}{3(60 \text{ minutes})} = \dfrac{190}{180} = \dfrac{19}{18}$

43. Answers may vary

45. $\dfrac{2}{3} = \dfrac{x}{6}$

$12 = 3x$

$4 = x$

47. $\dfrac{x}{10} = \dfrac{5}{9}$

$9x = 50$

$x = \dfrac{50}{9}$

49. $\dfrac{4x}{6} = \dfrac{7}{2}$

$8x = 42$

$x = \dfrac{42}{8} = \dfrac{21}{4}$

51. $\dfrac{x-3}{x} = \dfrac{4}{7}$

$7(x-3) = 4x$

$7x - 21 = 4x$

$-21 = -3x$

$7 = x$

53. $\dfrac{x+1}{2x+3} = \dfrac{2}{3}$

$3(x+1) = 2(2x+3)$

$3x + 3 = 4x + 6$

$3 = x + 6$

$-3 = x$

55. $\dfrac{9}{5} = \dfrac{12}{3x+2}$

$9(3x+2) = 5(12)$

$27x + 18 = 60$

$27x = 42$

$x = \dfrac{42}{27} = \dfrac{14}{9}$

57. $\dfrac{3}{x+1} = \dfrac{5}{2x}$

$3(2x) = 5(x+1)$

$6x = 5x + 5$

$x = 5$

59. $\dfrac{15}{3x-4} = \dfrac{5}{x}$

$15x = 5(3x-4)$

$15x = 15x - 20$

$0 = -20$

There is no solution.

61. Let x = the elephant's weight on Pluto.

$\dfrac{100}{3} = \dfrac{4100}{x}$

$100x = 3(4100)$

$100x = 12,300$

$x = 123$

The elephant's weight is 123 pounds.

63. Let x = the number of calories in 42.6 grams.

$$\frac{110}{28.4} = \frac{x}{42.6}$$

$$110(42.6) = 28.4x$$

$$4686 = 28.4x$$

$$165 = x.$$

There are 165 calories in 42.6 grams.

65. Let x = the number of women earning bigger paychecks.

$$\frac{1}{6} = \frac{x}{23,000}$$

$$23,000 = 6x$$

$$3833 = x$$

Expect 3833 women to earn bigger paychecks.

67. Let x = the number of gallons of water needed.

$$\frac{8}{2} = \frac{36}{x}$$

$$8x = 2(36)$$

$$8x = 72$$

$$x = 9$$

Need to mix 9 gallons of water with the entire box.

69.

Size	Price	Unit Price
110 ounce	$5.79	$\frac{5.79}{110} \approx \$0.053$
240 ounce	$13.99	$\frac{13.99}{240} \approx \$0.058$

The 110 ounce size is the better buy.

71.

Size	Price	Unit Price
6 ounce	$0.69	$\frac{0.69}{6} \approx \$0.115$
8 ounce	$0.90	$\frac{0.90}{8} \approx \$0.113$
16 ounce	$1.89	$\frac{1.89}{16} \approx \$0.118$

The 8 ounce size is the better buy.

73. $-5 > -7$

75. $|-5| = -(-5)$

77. $(-3)^2 > -3^2$

79. $x(2400) = 230$

$$x = \frac{230}{2400} \approx 0.096 = 9.6\%$$

This is about 9.6% of the daily value.

81. Let x = percent of calories from fat.

$$x(130) = 35$$

$$x = \frac{35}{130} \approx 0.269 = 26.9\%$$

This is less than 30% so it satisfies the recommendation.

83. Let x = percent of calories from protein.

$$x(280) = 4(12)$$

$$x = \frac{48}{280} \approx 0.171 = 17.1\%$$

About 17.1% of calories comes from protein.

Practice Problems 2.8

1. $x \geq -2$

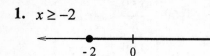

2. $5 > x$

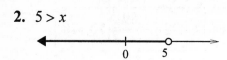

3. $x - 6 \geq -11$

$x \geq -5$

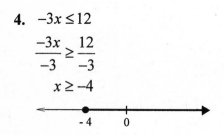

4. $-3x \leq 12$

$\dfrac{-3x}{-3} \geq \dfrac{12}{-3}$

$x \geq -4$

5. $5x > -20$

$x > -4$

6. $-3x + 11 \leq -13$

$-3x \leq -24$

$\dfrac{-3x}{-3} \geq \dfrac{-24}{-3}$

$x \geq 8$

$\left\{ x \mid x \geq 8 \right\}$

7. $-6x - 3 > -4(x + 1)$

$-6x - 3 > -4x - 4$

$-2x - 3 > -4$

$-2x > -1$

$\dfrac{-2x}{-2} < \dfrac{-1}{-2}$

$x < \dfrac{1}{2}$

$\left\{ x \mid x < \dfrac{1}{2} \right\}$

8. $3(x + 5) - 1 \geq 5(x - 1) + 7$

$3x + 15 - 1 \geq 5x - 5 + 7$

$3x + 14 \geq 5x + 2$

$-2x + 14 \geq 2$

$-2 \geq -12$

$\dfrac{-2x}{-2} \leq \dfrac{-12}{-2}$

$x \leq 6$

$\left\{ x \mid x \leq 6 \right\}$

9. Let x = the amount of sales and
$0.04x$ = the amount earned from sales.

$600 + 0.04x \geq 3000$

$0.04x \geq 2400$

$x \geq 60,000$

He must sell at least $60,000.

Mental Math 2.8

1. $5x > 10$

$x > 2$

2. $4x < 20$

$x < 5$

3. $2x \geq 6$

$x \geq 8$

4. $9x \leq 63$

$x \leq 7$

5. -5 is not a solution to $x \geq -3$.

6. $|-6|$ is not a solution to $x < 6$.

7. 4.1 is not a solution to $x < 4.01$.

8. -4 is not a solution to $x \geq -3$.

Exercise Set 2.8

1. $x \leq -1$

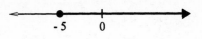

3. $x > \dfrac{1}{2}$

5. $y < 4$

7. $-2 \leq m$

9. $x - 2 \geq -7$

$x \geq -5$

$\{x \mid x \geq -5\}$

11. $-9 + y < 0$

$y < 9$

$\{y \mid y < 9\}$

13. $3x - 5 > 2x - 8$

$x - 5 > -8$

$x > -3$

$\{x \mid x > -3\}$

15. $4x - 1 \leq 5x - 2x$

$4x - 1 \leq 3x$

$x - 1 \leq 0$

$x \leq 1$

$\{x \mid x \leq 1\}$

17. $2x < -6$

$x < -3$

$\{x \mid x < -3\}$

19. $-8x \leq 16$

$\dfrac{-8x}{-8} \geq \dfrac{16}{-8}$

$x \geq -2$

$\{x \mid x \geq -2\}$

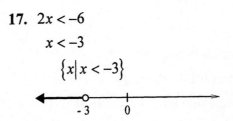

21. $-x > 0$

$$\frac{-x}{-1} < \frac{0}{-1}$$

$$x < 0$$

$$\{x | x < 0\}$$

23. $\frac{3}{4}y \geq -2$

$$y \geq -\frac{8}{3}$$

$$\left\{y \mid y \geq -\frac{8}{3}\right\}$$

25. $-0.6y < -1.8$

$$\frac{-0.6y}{-0.6} > \frac{-1.8}{-0.6}$$

$$y > 3$$

$$\{y | y > 3\}$$

27. When multiplying or dividing by a negative number, the direction of the inequality sign must be reversed.

29. $3x - 7 < 6x + 2$

$$-3x - 7 < 2$$

$$-3x < 9$$

$$\frac{-3x}{-3} > \frac{9}{-3}$$

$$x > -3$$

$$\{x | x > -3\}$$

31. $5x - 7x \leq x + 2$

$$-2x \leq x + 2$$

$$-3x \leq 2$$

$$\frac{-3x}{-3} \leq \frac{2}{-3}$$

$$x \leq -\frac{2}{3}$$

$$\left\{x \mid x \leq -\frac{2}{3}\right\}$$

33. $-6x + 2 \geq 2(5 - x)$

$$-6x + 2 \geq 10 - 2x$$

$$-4x + 2 \geq 10$$

$$-4x \geq 8$$

$$\frac{-4x}{-4} \leq \frac{8}{-4}$$

$$x \leq -2$$

$$\{x | x \leq -2\}$$

35. $4(3x - 1) \leq 5(2x - 4)$

$$12x - 4 \leq 10x - 20$$

$$2x - 4 \leq -20$$

$$2x \leq -16$$

$$x \leq -8$$

$$\{x | x \leq -8\}$$

37. $3(x + 2) - 6 > -2(x - 3) + 14$

$$3x + 6 - 6 > -2x + 6 + 14$$

$$3x > -2x + 20$$

$$5x > 20$$

$$x > 4$$

$$\{x | x > 4\}$$

39. $-2(x-4)-3x < -(4x+1)+2x$

$$-2x+8-3x < -4x-1+2x$$
$$-5x+8 < -2x-1$$
$$-3x+8 < -1$$
$$-3x < -9$$
$$\frac{-3x}{-3} > \frac{-9}{-3}$$
$$x > 3$$
$$\{x \mid x > 3\}$$

41. $\frac{1}{2}(x-5) < \frac{1}{3}(2x-1)$

$$6\left[\frac{1}{2}(x-5)\right] < 6\left[\frac{1}{3}(2x-1)\right]$$
$$3x-15 < 4x-2$$
$$-x-15 < -2$$
$$-x < 13$$
$$\frac{-x}{-1} > \frac{13}{-1}$$
$$x > -13$$
$$\{x \mid x > -13\}$$

43. $-5x+4 \le -4(x-1)$

$$-5x+4 \le -4x+4$$
$$-x+4 \le 4$$
$$-x \le 0$$
$$\frac{-x}{-1} \ge \frac{0}{-1}$$
$$x \ge 0$$
$$\{x \mid x \ge 0\}$$

45. Let x = the unknown number.

$$2x+6 > -14$$
$$2x > -20$$
$$x > -10$$

All numbers greater than -10.

47. Let x = the length and 15 = the width.

$$P = 2l + 2w$$
$$2x + 2(15) \le 100$$
$$2x + 30 \le 100$$
$$2x \le 70$$
$$x \le 35$$

The maximum length is 35 cm.

49. Let x = his score on the third game.

$$\frac{146+201+x}{3} \ge 180$$
$$3\left(\frac{146+201+x}{3}\right) \ge 3(180)$$
$$347 + x \ge 540$$
$$x \ge 193$$

He must score at least 193.

51. $3^4 = (3)(3)(3)(3) = 81$

53. $1^8 = (1)(1)(1)(1)(1)(1)(1)(1) = 1$

55. $\left(\frac{7}{8}\right)^2 = \left(\frac{7}{8}\right)\left(\frac{7}{8}\right) = \frac{49}{64}$

57. Approximately 1000

59. The greatest increase is between 1999 and 2000, where the graph is the steepest.

61. 1997

63. Let x = his score on the final exam.

$$\frac{75+83+85+2x}{5} \geq 80$$

$$5\left(\frac{243+2x}{5}\right) \geq 5(80)$$

$$243+2x \geq 400$$

$$2x \geq 157$$

$$x \geq 78.5$$

He must score at least 78.5.

Chapter 2 Review

1. $5x - x + 2x = 6x$

2. $0.2z - 4.6z - 7.4z = -11.8z$

3. $\frac{1}{2}x + 3 + \frac{7}{2}x - 5 = \frac{8}{2}x - 2 = 4x - 2$

4. $\frac{4}{5}y + 1 + \frac{6}{5}y + 2 = \frac{10}{5}y + 3 = 2y + 3$

5. $2(n-4) + n - 10 = 2n - 8 + n - 10 = 3n - 18$

6. $3(w+2) - (12-w) = 3w + 6 - 12 + w$
$$= 4w - 6$$

7. $(x+5) - (7x-2) = x + 5 - 7x + 2 = -6x + 7$

8. $(y-0.7) - (1.4y-3) = y - 0.7 - 1.4y + 3$
$$= -0.4y + 2.3$$

9. $3x - 7$

10. $3x + 2(x+2.8) = 3x + 2x + 5.6 = 5x + 5.6$

11. $8x + 4 = 9x$
$$4 = x$$

12. $5y - 3 = 6y$
$$-3 = y$$

13. $\frac{2}{7}x + \frac{5}{7}x = 6$
$$\frac{7}{7}x = 6$$
$$x = 6$$

14. $3x - 5 = 4x + 1$
$$-5 = x + 1$$
$$-6 = x$$

15. $2x - 6 = x - 6$
$$x - 6 = -6$$
$$x = 0$$

16. $4(x+3) = 3(1+x)$
$$4x + 12 = 3 + 3x$$
$$x + 12 = 3$$
$$x = -9$$

17. $6(3+n) = 5(n-1)$
$$18 + 6n = 5n - 5$$
$$18 + n = -5$$
$$n = -23$$

18. $5(2+x) - 3(3x+2) = -5(x-6) + 2$
$$10 + 5x - 9x - 6 = -5x + 30 + 2$$
$$4 - 4x = -5x + 32$$
$$4 + x = 32$$
$$x = 28$$

19. b. $10 - x$

20. a. $x - 5$

21. c. $180 - (x + 5) = 180 - x - 5 = (175 - x)^\circ$

22. $\dfrac{3}{4}x = -9$

$$\dfrac{4}{3}\left(\dfrac{3}{4}x\right) = \dfrac{4}{3}(-9)$$

$$x = -12$$

23. $\dfrac{x}{6} = \dfrac{2}{3}$

$$x = 4$$

24. $-5x = 0$

$$x = 0$$

25. $-y = 7$

$$y = -7$$

26. $0.2x = 0.15$

$$x = \dfrac{0.15}{0.2}$$

$$x = 0.75$$

27. $\dfrac{-x}{3} = 1$

$$-x = 3$$

$$x = -3$$

28. $-3x + 1 = 19$

$$-3x = 18$$

$$x = -6$$

29. $5x + 25 = 20$

$$5x = -5$$

$$x = -1$$

30. $5x - 6 + x = 4x$

$$6x - 6 = 4x$$

$$-6 = -2x$$

$$3 = x$$

31. $-y + 4y = -y$

$$3y = -y$$

$$4y = 0$$

$$y = 0$$

32. $-5x + \dfrac{3}{7} = \dfrac{10}{7}$

$$-5x = \dfrac{7}{7}$$

$$-5x = 1$$

$$x = -\dfrac{1}{5}$$

33. Let x = the first even integer.

Sum $= x + (x + 2) + (x + 4) = 3x + 6$

34. $\dfrac{5}{3}x + 4 = \dfrac{2}{3}x$

$$\dfrac{3}{3}x + 4 = 0$$

$$x = -4$$

35. $-(5x + 1) = -7x + 3$

$$-5x - 1 = -7x + 3$$

$$2x - 1 = 3$$

$$2x = 4$$

$$x = 2$$

36. $-4(2x+1) = -5x+5$

$$-8x-4 = -5x+5$$
$$-3x-4 = 5$$
$$-3x = 9$$
$$x = -3$$

37. $-6(2x-5) = -3(9+4x)$

$$-12x+30 = -27-12x$$
$$30 = -27$$

There is no solution.

38. $3(8y-1) = 6(5+4y)$

$$24y-3 = 30+24y$$
$$-3 = 30$$

There is no solution.

39. $\dfrac{3(2-z)}{5} = z$

$$3(2-z) = 5z$$
$$6-3z = 5z$$
$$6 = 8z$$
$$\dfrac{6}{8} = z$$
$$\dfrac{3}{4} = z$$

40. $\dfrac{4(n+2)}{5} = -n$

$$4(n+2) = -5n$$
$$4n+8 = -5n$$
$$8 = -9n$$
$$-\dfrac{8}{9} = n$$

41. $0.5(2n-3)-0.1 = 0.4(6+2n)$

$$10\big[0.5(2n-3)-0.1\big] = 10\big[0.4(6+2n)\big]$$
$$5(2n-3)-1 = 4(6+2n)$$
$$10n-15-1 = 24+8n$$
$$10n-16 = 24+8n$$
$$2n-16 = 24$$
$$2n = 40$$
$$n = 20$$

42. $-9-5a = 3(6a-1)$

$$-9-5a = 18a-3$$
$$-9 = 23a-3$$
$$-6 = 23a$$
$$-\dfrac{6}{23} = a$$

43. $\dfrac{5(c+1)}{6} = 2c-3$

$$5(c+1) = 6(2c-3)$$
$$5c+5 = 12c-18$$
$$-7c+5 = -18$$
$$-7c = -23$$
$$c = \dfrac{23}{7}$$

44. $\dfrac{2(8-a)}{3} = 4-4a$

$$2(8-a) = 3(4-4a)$$
$$16-2a = 12-12a$$
$$10a+16 = 12$$
$$10a = -4$$
$$a = \dfrac{-4}{10}$$
$$a = -\dfrac{2}{5}$$

45. $200(70x - 3560) = -179(150x - 19,300)$

$14,000x - 712,000 = -26,850x + 3,454,700$

$40,850x - 712,000 = 3,454,700$

$40,850x = 4,166,700$

$x = 102$

47. Let $x =$ the length and

$10x + 50.5 =$ the height.

$x + 10x + 50.5 = 7327$

$11x + 50.5 = 7327$

$11x = 7276.5$

$x = 661.5$

$10x + 50.5 = 10(661.5) + 50.5 = 6665.5$

The height is 6665.5 inches.

48. Let $x =$ the length of the shorter piece

and $2x =$ the length of the other.

$x + 2x = 12$

$3x = 12$

$x = 4$

$2x = 8$

The lengths are 4 feet and 8 feet.

49. Let $x =$ the number of Keebler plants

and $2x - 1 =$ the number of Kellogg plants.

$x + 2x - 1 = 53$

$3x - 1 = 53$

$3x = 54$

$x = 18$

$2x - 1 = 2(18) - 1 = 35$

There were 18 Keebler plants

and 35 Kellogg plants.

50. Let $x =$ the first integer, $x + 1 =$ the

second integer, and $x + 2 =$ the third.

$x + x + 1 + x + 2 = -114$

$3x + 3 = -114$

$3x = -117$

$x = -39$

$x + 1 = -38$, and $x + 2 = -37$

The integers are -39, -38, -37.

51. Let $x =$ the unknown number.

$\dfrac{x}{3} = x - 2$

$x = 3(x - 2)$

$x = 3x - 6$

$-2x = -6$

$x = 3$

The number is 3.

52. Let $x =$ the unknown number.

$2(x + 6) = -x$

$2x + 12 = -x$

$12 = -3x$

$-4 = x$

The number is -4.

53. Let $P = 46$ and $l = 14$.

$P = 2l + 2w$

$46 = 2(14) + 2w$

$46 = 28 + 2w$

$18 = 2w$

$9 = w$

54. Let $V = 192$, $l = 8$, and $w = 6$.

$$V = lwh$$
$$192 = 8(6)h$$
$$192 = 48h$$
$$4 = h$$

55.
$$y = mx + b$$
$$y - b = mx$$
$$\frac{y-b}{x} = m$$

56.
$$r = vst - 5$$
$$r + 5 = vst$$
$$\frac{r+5}{vt} = s$$

57. $2y - 5x = 7$
$$-5x = -2y + 7$$
$$x = \frac{-2y+7}{-5} = \frac{2y-7}{5}$$

58. $3x - 6y = -2$
$$-6y = -3x - 2$$
$$y = \frac{-3x-2}{-6} = \frac{3x+2}{6}$$

59. $C = \pi D$
$$\frac{C}{D} = \pi$$

60. $C = 2\pi r$
$$\frac{C}{2r} = \pi$$

61. Let $V = 900$, $l = 20$, and $h = 3$.

$$V = lwh$$
$$900 = 20w(3)$$
$$900 = 60w$$
$$15 = w$$

Width $= 15$ meters

62. Let $F = 104$

$$C = \frac{5}{9}(F - 32) = \frac{5}{9}(104 - 32) = \frac{5}{9}(72)$$
$$= 40$$

The temperature was $40°$ C.

63. Let $d = 10,000$ and $r = 125$

$$d = rt$$
$$10,000 = 125t$$
$$80 = t$$

It will take 80 minutes.

64. Let $x =$ the unknown percent.

$$9 = x \cdot 45$$
$$\frac{1}{5} = x$$
$$x = \frac{1}{5} = 0.20 = 20\%$$

9 is 20% of 45.

65. Let $x =$ the unknown percent.

$$59.5 = x \cdot 85$$
$$\frac{59.5}{585} = x$$
$$x = \frac{59.5}{85} = 0.70 = 70\%$$

59.5 is 70% of 85.

66. Let x = the unknown number.

$137.5 = 1.25 \cdot x$

$110 = x$

137.5 is 125% of 110.

67. Let x = the unknown number.

$768 = 0.60 \cdot x$

$1280 = x$

768 is 60% of 1280.

68. Let x = the number who use the internet.

$x = 0.669(76,000) = 50,844$

Expect 50,844 to use the internet.

69. 18%

70. Swerving into another lane

71. Let x = the number who cut off someone.

$x = 0.21(4600) = 966$

Expect 966 to cut off someone.

72. No: Answers may vary

73. $\dfrac{20 \text{ cents}}{1 \text{ dollars}} = \dfrac{20 \text{ cents}}{1(100 \text{ cents})} = \dfrac{20}{100} = \dfrac{1}{5}$

74. $\dfrac{4 \text{ parts}}{6 \text{ parts}} = \dfrac{2}{3}$

75. $\dfrac{x}{2} = \dfrac{12}{4}$

$4x = 24$

$x = 6$

76. $\dfrac{20}{1} = \dfrac{x}{25}$

$500 = x$

77. $\dfrac{32}{100} = \dfrac{100}{x}$

$32x = 10,000$

$x = 312.5$

78. $\dfrac{20}{2} = \dfrac{c}{5}$

$100 = 2c$

$50 = c$

79. $\dfrac{2}{x-1} = \dfrac{3}{x+3}$

$2(x+3) = 3(x-1)$

$2x + 6 = 3x - 3$

$6 = x - 3$

$9 = x$

80. $\dfrac{4}{y-3} = \dfrac{2}{y-3}$

$4(y-3) = 2(y-3)$

$4y - 12 = 2y - 6$

$2y - 12 = -6$

$2y = 6$

$y = 3$

$y = 3$ doesn't check.

No solution

81.
$$\frac{y+2}{y} = \frac{5}{3}$$
$$3(y+2) = 5y$$
$$3y+6 = 5y$$
$$6 = 2y$$
$$3 = y$$

82.
$$\frac{x-3}{3x+2} = \frac{2}{6}$$
$$6(x-3) = 2(3x+2)$$
$$6x-18 = 6x+4$$
$$-18 = 4$$

No solution

83.

Size	Price	Unit Price
10 ounce	$1.29	$\frac{1.29}{10} \approx \$0.129$
16 ounce	$2.15	$\frac{2.15}{16} \approx \$0.134$

The 10 ounce size is the better buy.

84.

Size	Price	Unit Price
8 ounce	$0.89	$\frac{0.89}{8} \approx \$0.111$
15 ounce	$1.63	$\frac{1.63}{15} \approx \$0.109$
20 ounce	$2.36	$\frac{2.36}{20} \approx \$0.118$

The 15 ounce size is the better buy.

85. Let x = the number of parts processed in 45 minutes.
$$\frac{300}{20} = \frac{x}{45}$$
$$13,500 = 20x$$
$$675 = x$$

675 parts can be processed in 45 minutes.

86. Let x = the charge for 3 hours.
$$\frac{90.00}{8} = \frac{x}{3}$$
$$270.00 = 8x$$
$$33.75 = x$$

He charges $33.75 for 3 hours.

87. Let x = the number of letters addressed in 55 minutes.
$$\frac{100}{35} = \frac{x}{55}$$
$$5500 = 35x$$
$$157 \approx x$$

He can address 157 letters in 55 minutes.

88. $x \le -2$

89. $x > 0$

90. $x - 5 \le -4$
$$x \le 1$$
$$\{x \mid x \le 1\}$$

91. $x + 7 > 2$

$x > -5$

$\{x \mid x > -5\}$

92. $-2x \geq -20$

$\dfrac{-2x}{-2} \leq \dfrac{-20}{-2}$

$x \leq 10$

$\{x \mid x \leq 10\}$

93. $-3x > 12$

$\dfrac{-3x}{-3} < \dfrac{12}{-3}$

$x < -4$

$\{x \mid x < -4\}$

94. $5x - 7 > 8x + 5$

$-3x - 7 > 5$

$-3x > 12$

$\dfrac{-3x}{-3} < \dfrac{12}{-3}$

$x < -4$

$\{x \mid x < -4\}$

95. $x + 4 \geq 6x - 16$

$-5x + 4 \geq -16$

$-5x \geq -20$

$\dfrac{-5x}{-5} \leq \dfrac{-20}{-5}$

$x \leq 4$

$\{x \mid x \leq 4\}$

96. $\dfrac{2}{3}y > 6$

$y > 9$

$\{y \mid y > 9\}$

97. $-0.5y \leq 7.5$

$\dfrac{-0.5y}{-0.5} \geq \dfrac{7.5}{-0.5}$

$y \geq -15$

$\{y \mid y \geq -15\}$

98. $-2(x - 5) > 2(3x - 2)$

$-2x + 10 > 6x - 4$

$-8x + 10 > -4$

$-8x > -14$

$\dfrac{-8x}{-8} < \dfrac{-14}{-8}$

$x < \dfrac{7}{4}$

$\left\{x \mid x < \dfrac{7}{4}\right\}$

99. $4(2x - 5) \leq 5x - 1$

$8x - 20 \leq 5x - 1$

$3x - 20 \leq -1$

$3x \leq 19$

$x \leq \dfrac{19}{3}$

$\left\{x \mid x \leq \dfrac{19}{3}\right\}$

100. Let x = the amount of sales then

$0.05x$ = her commission.

$$175 + 0.05x \geq 300$$
$$0.05x \geq 125$$
$$x \geq 2500$$

Sales must be at least $2500.

101. Let x = his score on the fourth round.

$$\frac{76 + 82 + 79 + x}{4} < 80$$
$$237 + x < 320$$
$$x < 83$$

His score must be less than 83.

Chapter 2 Test

1. $2y - 6 - y - 4 = y - 10$

2. $2.7x + 6.1 + 3.2x - 4.9 = 5.9x + 1.2$

3. $4(x-2) - 3(2x-6) = 4x - 8 - 6x + 18$
$$= -2x + 10$$

4. $-5(y+1) + 2(3-5y) = -5y - 5 + 6 - 10y$
$$= -15y + 1$$

5. $-\dfrac{4}{5}x = 4$
$$x = -5$$

6. $4(n-5) = -(4-2n)$
$$4n - 20 = -4 + 2n$$
$$2n - 20 = -4$$
$$2n = 16$$
$$n = 8$$

7. $5y - 7 + y = -(y + 3y)$
$$6y - 7 = -4y$$
$$-7 = -10y$$
$$\frac{7}{10} = y$$

8. $4z + 1 - z = 1 + z$
$$3z + 1 = 1 + z$$
$$2z + 1 = 1$$
$$2z = 0$$
$$z = 0$$

9. $\dfrac{2(x+6)}{3} = x - 5$
$$2(x+6) = 3(x-5)$$
$$2x + 12 = 3x - 15$$
$$12 = x - 15$$
$$27 = x$$

10. $\dfrac{4(y-1)}{5} = 2y + 3$
$$4(y-1) = 5(2y+3)$$
$$4y - 4 = 10y + 15$$
$$-6y - 4 = 15$$
$$-6y = 19$$
$$y = \frac{19}{6}$$

11. $\dfrac{1}{2} - x + \dfrac{3}{2} = x - 4$

$$2\left(\dfrac{1}{2} - x + \dfrac{3}{2}\right) = 2(x - 4)$$

$$1 - 2x + 3 = 2x - 8$$

$$-2x + 4 = 2x - 8$$

$$-4x + 4 = -8$$

$$-4x = -12$$

$$x = 3$$

12. $\dfrac{5}{y+1} = \dfrac{4}{y+2}$

$$5(y+2) = 4(y+1)$$

$$5y + 10 = 4y + 4$$

$$y + 10 = 4$$

$$y = -6$$

13. $\dfrac{1}{3}(y+3) = 4y$

$$y + 3 = 12y$$

$$3 = 11y$$

$$\dfrac{3}{11} = y$$

14. $-0.3(x-4) + x = 0.5(3-x)$

$$10\big[-0.3(x-4) + x\big] = 10\big[0.5(3-x)\big]$$

$$-3(x-4) + 10x = 5(3-x)$$

$$-3x + 12 + 10x = 15 - 5x$$

$$7x + 12 = 15 - 5x$$

$$12x + 12 = 15$$

$$12x = 3$$

$$x = \dfrac{3}{12} = \dfrac{1}{4} = 0.25$$

15. $-4(a+1) - 3a = -7(2a-3)$

$$-4a - 4 - 3a = -14a + 21$$

$$-7a - 4 = -14a + 21$$

$$7a - 4 = 21$$

$$7a = 25$$

$$a = \dfrac{25}{7}$$

16. Let $x =$ the number.

$$x + \dfrac{2}{3}x = 35$$

$$3x + 2x = 105$$

$$5x = 105$$

$$x = 21$$

The number is 21.

17. Let $l = 35,$ and $w = 20.$

$$2A = 2lw = 2(35)(20) = 1400$$

Let $x =$ the number of gallons needed
at 200 square feet per gallon.

$$1400 = 200x$$

$$7 = x$$

7 gallons are needed.

18.

Size	Price	Unit Price
6 ounce	$1.19	$\dfrac{1.19}{6} \approx \$0.198$
10 ounce	$2.15	$\dfrac{2.15}{10} \approx \$0.215$
16 ounce	$3.25	$\dfrac{3.25}{16} \approx \$0.203$

The 6 ounce size is the better buy.

19. Let $x =$ the number of defective bulbs.

$$\frac{85}{3} = \frac{510}{x}$$

$$85x = 1530$$

$$x = 18$$

Expect to find 18 defective bulbs.

20. Let $y = -14$, $m = -2$, and $b = -2$.

$$y = mx + b$$

$$-14 = -2x - 2$$

$$-12 = -2x$$

$$6 = x$$

21. $\quad V = \pi r^2 h$

$$\frac{V}{\pi r^2} = \frac{\pi r^2 h}{\pi r^2}$$

$$\frac{V}{\pi r^2} = h$$

22. $3x - 4y = 10$

$$-4y = -3x + 10$$

$$y = \frac{-3x + 10}{-4}$$

$$= \frac{3x - 10}{4}$$

23. $\quad 3x - 5 > 7x + 3$

$$-4x - 5 > 3$$

$$-4x > 8$$

$$\frac{-4x}{-4} < \frac{8}{-4}$$

$$x < -2$$

$$\{x \mid x < -2\}$$

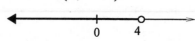

24. $\quad x + 6 > 4x - 6$

$$-3x + 6 > -6$$

$$-3x > -12$$

$$\frac{-3x}{-3} < \frac{-12}{-3}$$

$$x < 4$$

$$\{x \mid x < 4\}$$

25. $\quad -0.3x \geq 2.4$

$$\frac{-0.3x}{-0.3} \leq \frac{2.4}{-0.3}$$

$$x \leq -8$$

$$\{x \mid x \leq -8\}$$

26. $\quad -5(x - 1) + 6 \leq -3(x + 4) + 1$

$$-5x + 5 + 6 \leq -3x - 12 + 1$$

$$-5x + 11 \leq -3x - 11$$

$$-2x + 11 \leq -11$$

$$-2x \leq -22$$

$$\frac{-2x}{-2} \geq \frac{-22}{-2}$$

$$x \geq 11$$

$$\{x \mid x \geq 11\}$$

27.
$$\frac{2(5x+1)}{3} > 2$$
$$2(5x+1) > 6$$
$$10x+2 > 6$$
$$10x > 4$$
$$x > \frac{4}{10} = \frac{2}{5}$$
$$\left\{ x \mid x > \frac{2}{5} \right\}$$

28. 29% are strong

29. Let x = the number of weak tornadoes.
$$x = 0.69(800) = 552$$
Expect 552 weak tornadoes.

30. Let x = the unknown percent.
$$72 = x \cdot 180$$
$$\frac{72}{180} = x$$
$$\frac{72}{180} = \frac{2}{5} = 0.40 = 40\%$$
$$72 = 40\% \text{ of } 180.$$

31. Let x = the number of public libraries in Indiana and $x + 650$ = the number in New York.
$$x + x + 650 = 1504$$
$$2x + 650 = 1504$$
$$2x = 854$$
$$x = 427$$
$$x + 650 = 427 + 650 = 1077$$
There are 427 public libraries in Indiana and 1077 in New York.

32. Let x = the number of NBA basketball teams and $x + 3$ = the number of NFL football teams.
$$x + x + 3 = 61$$
$$2x + 3 = 61$$
$$2x = 58$$
$$x = 29$$
$$x + 3 = 29 + 3 = 32$$
There are 29 NBA basketball teams and 32 NFL football teams.

Chapter 2 Cumulative Review

1. $8 \geq 8$, True since $8 = 8$.

2. $8 \leq 8$, True since $8 = 8$.

3. $23 \leq 0$, False since 23 is to the right of 0 on the number line.

4. $0 \leq 23$, True since 23 is to the right of 0 on the number line.

5. a. $|0| < 2$ since $0 < 2$.
    b. $|-5| = 5$
    c. $|-3| > |-2|$ since $3 > 2$.
    d. $|5| < |6|$ since $5 < 6$.
    e. $|-7| > |6|$ since $7 > 6$.

6. $\dfrac{3 + |4 - 3| + 2^2}{6 - 3} = \dfrac{3 + |1| + 2^2}{6 - 3} = \dfrac{3 + 1 + 4}{6 - 3}$
$$= \frac{8}{3}$$

7. $(-8) + (-11) = -19$

8. $(-2)+10=8$

9. $0.2+(-0.5)=-0.3$

10. a. $-3+\left[(-2-5)-2\right]=-3+\left[(-7)-2\right]$

$=-3+\left[(-7)+(-2)\right]=-3+\left[-9\right]=-12$

    b. $2^3-10+\left[-6-(-5)\right]$

$=2^3-10+\left[-6+5\right]=2^3-10+\left[-1\right]$

$=8+(-10)+\left[-1\right]=-3$

11. a. $7(0)(-6)=(0)(-6)=0$

    b. $(-2)(-3)(-4)=6(-4)=-24$

    c. $(-1)(5)(-9)=(-5)(-9)=45$

    d. $-4(-11)-5(-2)=44-(-10)$

$=44+10=54$

12. a. $-18\div 3=-18\cdot\dfrac{1}{3}=-6$

    b. $\dfrac{-14}{-2}=-14\cdot-\dfrac{1}{2}=7$

    c. $\dfrac{20}{-4}=20\cdot-\dfrac{1}{4}=-5$

13. $-5(-3+2z)=15-10z$

14. $4(3x+7)+10=12x+28+10=12x+38$

15. a. $70

    b. 280 miles

16. a. unlike

    b. like

    c. like

    d. like

17. $(2x-3)-(4x-2)=2x-3-4x+2$

$=-2x-1$

18. $x-7=10$

$x=17$

19. $-z-4=6$

$-z=10$

$z=-10$

20. $\dfrac{2(a+3)}{3}=6a+2$

$2(a+3)=3(6a+2)$

$2a+6=18a+6$

$-16a+6=6$

$-16a=0$

$a=0$

21. Let x = the number of Democratic representatives and $x+10$ = the number of Republican representatives.

$x+x+10=430$

$2x+10=430$

$2x=420$

$x=210$

$x+10=210+10=220$

There are 210 Democratic representatives and 220 Republican.

22. Let $d=31,680$ and $r=400$.

$d=rt$

$31,680=400t$

$79.2=t$

It takes 79.2 years.

23. Let x = the unknown percent.

$$63 = x \cdot 72$$

$$\frac{63}{72} = x$$

$$\frac{63}{72} = \frac{7}{8} = 0.875 = 87.5\%$$

63 is 87.5% of 72.

24. $\dfrac{45}{x} = \dfrac{5}{7}$

$$315 = 5x$$

$$63 = x$$

25. $-1 > x$

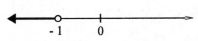

26. $2(x-3)-5 \le 3(x+2)-18$

$$2x-6-5 \le 3x+6-18$$

$$2x-11 \le 3x-12$$

$$-x-11 \le -12$$

$$-x \le -1$$

$$\frac{-x}{-1} \ge \frac{-1}{-1}$$

$$x \ge 1$$

$$\{x \mid x \ge 1\}$$

Chapter 3

1. $\left(-\dfrac{3}{4}\right)^2 = \left(-\dfrac{3}{4}\right)\left(-\dfrac{3}{4}\right) = \dfrac{9}{16}$

2. $\left(4y^6\right)\left(2y^7\right) = 4 \cdot 2 \cdot y^6 \cdot y^7 = 8y^{13}$

3. $\dfrac{a^9 b^{16}}{a^{12} b^5} = \left(a^{9-12}\right)\left(b^{16-5}\right) = a^{-3}b^{11} = \dfrac{b^{11}}{a^3}$

4. $4^0 + 2x^0 = 1 + 2 \cdot 1 = 1 + 2 = 3$

5. $\left(-\dfrac{1}{6}\right)^{-3} = \left(-\dfrac{1}{6}\right)^{-3} = \dfrac{(-1)^{-3}}{6^{-3}} = \dfrac{6^3}{(-1)^3}$

$= \dfrac{216}{-1} = -216$

6. $\left(\dfrac{m^{-2}n}{m^6 n^{-8}}\right)^{-2} = \dfrac{m^4 n^{-2}}{m^{-12} n^{16}} = \left(m^{4-(-12)}\right)\left(n^{-2-16}\right)$

$= m^{16} n^{-18} = \dfrac{m^{16}}{n^{18}}$

7. $12x^2 + 3x - 5 - 8x^2 + 7x$

$= 12x^2 - 8x^2 + 3x + 7x - 5$

$= 4x^2 + 10x - 5$

8. $0.000000814 = 8.14 \times 10^{-7}$

9. The degree of $8x - 4x^5 + 6x^3 + 10$ is 5.

10. $-3x^3 + 2x^2 - 4 = -3(-1)^3 + 2(-1)^2 - 4$

$= -3(-1) + 2(1) - 4 = 3 + 2 - 4 = 1$

11. $\left(4x^2 - 3x + 9\right) + \left(6x^2 + 3x - 8\right)$

$= 4x^2 - 3x + 9 + 6x^2 + 3x - 8$

$= 4x^2 + 6x^2 - 3x + 3x + 9 - 8$

$= 10x^2 + 1$

12. $\left(6y^2 - 4\right) - \left(-3y^2 + 5y - 1\right)$

$= 6y^2 - 4 + 3y^2 - 5y + 1$

$= 6y^2 + 3y^2 - 5y - 4 + 1$

$= 9y^2 - 5y - 4 + 1$

$= 9y^2 - 5y - 3$

13. $\left(2a^2 + 3ab - 7b^2\right) - \left(-3a^2 + 3ab + 9b^2\right)$

$= 2a^2 + 3ab - 7b^2 - 3a^2 - 3ab - 9b^2$

$= 2a^2 - 3a^2 + 3ab - 3ab - 7b^2 - 9b^2$

$= -a^2 - 16b^2$

14. $\left(-\dfrac{2}{7}n^6\right)\left(\dfrac{21}{16}n^3\right) = -\dfrac{2}{7} \cdot \dfrac{21}{16} \cdot n^6 \cdot n^3$

$= -\dfrac{42}{112}n^9 = -\dfrac{3}{8}n^9$

15. $-2t^2\left(3t^5 + 4t^3 - 8\right)$

$= -2t^2\left(3t^5\right) + \left(-2t^2\right)\left(4t^3\right) - \left(-2t^2\right)(8)$

$= -6t^7 - 8t^5 + 16t^2$

16. $(2y - 1)(5y + 6)$

$= 2y(5y) + 5y(-1) + 2y(6) + (-1)(6)$

$= 10y^2 - 5y + 12y - 6$

$= 10y^2 + 7y - 6$

17. $(7a-5)^2 = (7a-5)(7a-5)$

$= (7a)(7a) + (7a)(-5) + (-5)(7a) + (-5)(-5)$

$= 49a^2 - 35a - 35a + 25$

$= 49a^2 - 70a + 25$

18. $(4b+9)(4b-9)$

$= (4b)(4b) + (4b)(-9) + (9)(4b) + (9)(-9)$

$= 16b^2 - 36b + 36b - 81 = 16b^2 - 81$

19. $\dfrac{16p^4 - 8p^3 + 20p^2}{4p} = \dfrac{16p^4}{4p} - \dfrac{8p3}{4p} + \dfrac{20p^2}{4p}$

$\qquad\qquad\qquad = 4p - 2p^2 + 5p$

20.
$$
\begin{array}{r}
5x+2 \\
x-6\overline{)5x^2 - 28x - 12} \\
\underline{5x^2 - 30x} \\
2x - 12 \\
\underline{2x - 12} \\
0
\end{array}
$$

Thus, $\dfrac{5x^2 - 28x - 12}{x - 6} = 5x + 2.$

Practice Problems 3.1

1. $3^4 = 3 \cdot 3 \cdot 3 \cdot 3 = 81$

2. $7^1 = 7$

3. $(-2)^3 = (-2)(-2)(-2) = -8$

4. $-2^3 = -(2 \cdot 2 \cdot 2) = -8$

5. $\left(\dfrac{2}{3}\right)^2 = \left(\dfrac{2}{3}\right)\left(\dfrac{2}{3}\right) = \dfrac{4}{9}$

6. $5 \cdot 6^2 = 5 \cdot 6 \cdot 6 = 180$

7. a. $3x^2 = 3(4)^2 = 3 \cdot 4 \cdot 4 = 48$

     b. $\dfrac{x^4}{-8} = \dfrac{(-2)^4}{-8} = \dfrac{(-2)(-2)(-2)(-2)}{-8}$

$\qquad = \dfrac{16}{-8} = -2$

8. $7^3 \cdot 7^2 = 7^{3+2} = 7^5$

9. $x^4 \cdot x^9 = x^{4+9} = x^{13}$

10. $r^5 \cdot r = r^5 \cdot r^1 = r^{5+1} = r^6$

11. $s^6 \cdot s^2 \cdot s^3 = s^{6+2+3} = s^{11}$

12. $(-3)^9(-3) - (-3)^9(-3)^1 = (-3)^{9+1} = (-3)^{10}$

13. $(6x^3)(-2x^9) = 6 \cdot (-2) \cdot x^3 \cdot x^9 = -12x^{12}$

14. $(9^4)^{10} = 9^{4 \cdot 10} = 9^{40}$

15. $(z^6)^3 = z^{6 \cdot 3} = z^{18}$

16. $(xy)^7 = x^7 y^7$

17. $(3y)^4 = 3^4 y^4 = 81 y^4$

18. $(-2p^4 q^2 r)^3 = (-2)^3 (p^4)^3 (q^2)^3 r^3$

$\qquad\qquad\qquad = -8p^{12} q^6 r^3$

19. $\left(\dfrac{r}{s}\right)^6 = \dfrac{r^6}{s^6}, \; s \neq 0$

20. $\left(\dfrac{5x^6}{9y^3}\right)^2 = \dfrac{5^2 (x^6)^2}{9^2 (y^3)^2} = \dfrac{25x^{12}}{81y^6}, \; y \neq 0$

21. $\dfrac{y^7}{y^3} = y^{7-3} = y^4$

22. $\dfrac{5^9}{5^6} = 5^{9-6} = 5^3 = 125$

23. $\dfrac{(-2)^{14}}{(-2)^{10}} = (-2)^{14-10} = (-2)^4 = 16$

24. $\dfrac{7a^4b^{11}}{ab} = 7 \cdot \dfrac{a^4}{a^1} \cdot \dfrac{b^{11}}{b^1} = 7a^{4-1}b^{11-1} = 7a^3b^{10}$

25. $8^0 = 1$

26. $(2r^2s)^0 = 1$

27. $(-5)^0 = 1$

28. $-5^0 = -1 \cdot 5^0 = -1 \cdot 1 = -1$

29. a. $\dfrac{x^7}{x^4} = x^{7-4} = x^3$

b. $(3y^4)^4 = 3^4(y^4)^4 = 81y^{16}$

c. $\left(\dfrac{x}{4}\right)^3 = \dfrac{x^3}{4^3} = \dfrac{x^3}{64}$

Mental Math 3.1

1. 3^2
base: 3
exponent: 2

2. 5^4
base: 5
exponent: 4

3. $(-3)^6$
base: -3
exponent: 6

4. -3^7
base: 3
exponent: 7

5. -4^2
base: 4
exponent: 2

6. $(-4)^3$
base: -4
exponent: 3

7. $5 \cdot 3^4$
base: 5; exponent: 1
base: 3; exponent: 4

8. $9 \cdot 7^6$
base: 9; exponent: 1
base: 7; exponent: 6

9. $5x^2$
base: 5; exponent: 1
base: x; exponent: 2

10. $(5x)^2$
base: $5x$
exponent: 2

Exercise Set 3.1

1. $7^2 = 7 \cdot 7 = 49$

3. $(-5)^1 = -5$

5. $-2^4 = -2 \cdot 2 \cdot 2 \cdot 2 = -16$

7. $(-2)^4 = (-2)(-2)(-2)(-2) = 16$

9. $\left(\dfrac{1}{3}\right)^3 = \left(\dfrac{1}{3}\right)\left(\dfrac{1}{3}\right)\left(\dfrac{1}{3}\right) = \dfrac{1}{27}$

11. $7 \cdot 2^4 = 7 \cdot 2 \cdot 2 \cdot 2 \cdot 2 = 112$

13. Answers may vary.

15. $x^2 = (-2)^2 = (-2)(-2) = 4$

17. $5x^3 = 5(3)^3 = 5 \cdot 3 \cdot 3 \cdot 3 = 135$

19. $2xy^2 = 2(3)(5)^2 = 2(3)(5)(5) = 150$

21. $\dfrac{2z^4}{5} = \dfrac{2(-2)^4}{5} = \dfrac{2(-2)(-2)(-2)(-2)}{5} = \dfrac{32}{5}$

23. $x^2 \cdot x^5 = x^{2+5} = x^7$

25. $(-3)^3 \cdot (-3)^9 = (-3)^{3+9} = (-3)^{12}$

27. $(5y^4)(3y) = 5(3)y^{4+1} = 15y^5$

29. $(4z^{10})(-6z^7)(z^3) = 4(-6)z^{10+7+3} = -24z^{20}$

31. $(4x^2)(5x^3) = 4(5)x^{2+3} = 20x^5$ sq ft

33. $(x^9)^4 = x^{9 \cdot 4} = x^{36}$

35. $(pq)^7 = p^7 q^7$

37. $(2a^5)^3 = 2^3 a^{5 \cdot 3} = 8a^{15}$

39. $\left(\dfrac{m}{n}\right)^9 = \dfrac{m^9}{n^9}$

41. $(x^2 y^3) = x^{2 \cdot 5} y^{3 \cdot 5} = x^{10} y^{15}$

43. $\left(\dfrac{-2xz}{y^5}\right)^2 = \dfrac{(-2)^2 x^2 z^2}{y^{5 \cdot 2}} = \dfrac{4x^2 z^2}{y^{10}}$

45. $\left(8z^5\right)^2 = 8^2 z^{5 \cdot 2} = 64z^{10}$

The area is $64z^{10}$ sq. decimeters.

47. $\left(3y^4\right)^3 = 3^3 y^{4 \cdot 3} = 27y^{11}$

The volume is $27y^{12}$ cubic feet.

49. $\dfrac{x^3}{x} = \dfrac{x^3}{x^1} = x^{3-1} = x^2$

51. $\dfrac{(-2)^5}{(-2)^3} = (-2)^{5-3} = (-2)^2 = 4$

53. $\dfrac{p^7 q^{20}}{pq^{15}} = p^{7-1} q^{20-15} = p^6 q^5$

55. $\dfrac{7x^2 y^6}{14x^2 y^3} = \dfrac{7}{14} x^{2-2} y^{6-3} = \dfrac{1}{2} x^0 y^3 = \dfrac{y^3}{2}$

57. $(2x)^0 = 1$

59. $-2x^0 = -2(1) = -2$

61. $5^0 + y^0 = 1 + 1 = 2$

63. Answers may vary.

65. $-5^2 = -5 \cdot 5 = -25$

67. $\left(\dfrac{1}{4}\right)^3 = \dfrac{1^3}{4^3} = \dfrac{1}{64}$

69. $\dfrac{z^{12}}{z^4} = z^{12-4} = z^8$

71. $(9xy)^2 = 9^2 x^2 y^2 = 81x^2 y^2$

73. $(6b)^0 = 1$

75. $2^3 + 2^5 = 8 + 32 = 40$

77. $b^4 b^2 = b^{4+2} = b^6$

79. $a^2 a^3 a^4 = a^{2+3+4} = a^9$

81. $(2x^3)(-8x^4) = 2(-8)x^{3+4} = -16x^7$

83. $(4a)^3 = 4^3 a^3 = 64a^3$

85. $(-6xyz^3)^2 = (-6)^2 x^2 y^2 z^{3\cdot 2} = 36x^2 y^2 z^6$

87. $\left(\dfrac{3y^5}{6x^4}\right)^3 = \dfrac{3^3 y^{5\cdot 3}}{6^3 x^{4\cdot 3}} = \dfrac{27y^{15}}{216x^{12}} = \dfrac{y^{15}}{8x^{12}}$

89. $\dfrac{3x^5}{x^4} = 3x^{5-4} = 3x$

91. $\dfrac{2x^3 y^2 z}{x^4} = 2x^{3-1} y^{2-1} z^{1-1} = 2x^2 y$

93. $5 - 7 = 5 + (-7) = -2$

95. $3 - (-2) = 3 + 2 = 5$

97. $-11 - (-4) = -11 + 4 = -7$

99. $V = x^3 = 7^3 = 7 \cdot 7 \cdot 7 = 343$

The volume is 343 cubic meters.

101. We use the volume formula.

103. $x^{5a} x^{4a} = x^{5a+4a} = x^{9a}$

105. $(a^b)^5 = a^{b\cdot 5} = a^{5b}$

107. $\dfrac{x^{9a}}{x^{4a}} = x^{9a-4a} = x^{5a}$

109. $A = P\left(1 + \dfrac{r}{12}\right)^6$

$A = 1000\left(1 + \dfrac{0.09}{12}\right)^6$

$A = 1000(1.0075)^6$

$A = 1045.85$

You need \$1045.85 to pay off the loan.

Practice Problems 3.2

1. $5^{-3} = \dfrac{1}{5^3} = \dfrac{1}{125}$

2. $7x^{-4} = 7 \cdot \dfrac{1}{x^4} = \dfrac{7}{x^4}$

3. $5^{-1} + 3^{-1} = \dfrac{1}{5^1} + \dfrac{1}{3^1} = \dfrac{3}{15} + \dfrac{5}{15} = \dfrac{8}{15}$

4. $(-3)^{-4} = \dfrac{1}{(-3)^4} = \dfrac{1}{81}$

5. $\left(\dfrac{6}{7}\right)^{-2} = \dfrac{6^{-2}}{7^{-2}} = \dfrac{7^2}{6^2} = \dfrac{49}{36}$

6. $\dfrac{x}{x^{-4}} = \dfrac{x^1}{x^{-4}} = x^{1-(-4)} = x^5$

7. $\dfrac{y^{-9}}{z^{-5}} = \dfrac{z^5}{y^9}$

8. $\dfrac{y^{-4}}{y^6} = y^{-4-6} = y^{-10} = \dfrac{1}{y^{10}}$

9. $\dfrac{\left(x^5\right)^3 x}{x^4} = \dfrac{x^{15}x^1}{x^4} = x^{15+1-4} = x^{12}$

10. $\left(\dfrac{9x^3}{y}\right)^{-2} = \dfrac{9^{-2}x^{-6}}{y^{-2}} = \dfrac{y^2}{9^2 x^6} = \dfrac{y^2}{81x^6}$

11. $\left(a^{-4}b^7\right)^{-5} = a^{20}b^{-35} = \dfrac{a^{20}}{b^{35}}$

12. $\dfrac{(2x)^4}{x^8} = \dfrac{2^4 x^4}{x^8} = 2^4 x^{4-8} = 16x^{-4} = \dfrac{16}{x^4}$

13. $\dfrac{y^{-10}}{\left(y^5\right)^4} = \dfrac{y^{-10}}{y^{20}} = y^{-10-20} = y^{-30} = \dfrac{1}{y^{30}}$

14. $\left(4a^2\right)^{-3} = 4^{-3}a^{-6} = \dfrac{1}{4^3 a^6} = \dfrac{1}{64a^6}$

15. $\dfrac{\left(3x^{-2}y\right)^{-2}}{4x^7 y} = \dfrac{3^{-2}x^4 y^{-2}}{4x^7 y} = \dfrac{x^{4-7}y^{-2-1}}{3^2(4)}$

$= \dfrac{x^{-3}y^{-3}}{36} = \dfrac{1}{36x^3 y^3}$

16. a. $420,000 = 4.2 \times 10^5$
   b. $0.00017 = 1.7 \times 10^{-4}$
   c. $9,060,000,000 = 9.06 \times 10^9$
   d. $0.000007 = 7 \times 10^{-6}$

17. a. $3.062 \times 10^{-4} = 40.0003062$
   b. $5.21 \times 10^4 = 52,100$
   c. $9.6 \times 10^{-5} = 0.000096$
   d. $6.002 \times 10^6 = 6,002,000$

18. a. $\left(9 \times 10^7\right)\left(4 \times 10^{-9}\right) = 9 \cdot 4 \cdot 10^7 \cdot 10^{-9}$
$= 36 \times 10^{-2} = 0.36$

   b. $\dfrac{8 \times 10^4}{2 \times 10^{-3}} = \dfrac{8}{2} \times 10^{4-(-3)} = 4 \times 10^7$
$= 40,000,000$

Mental Math 3.2

1. $5x^{-2} = \dfrac{5}{x^2}$

2. $3x^{-3} = \dfrac{3}{x^3}$

3. $\dfrac{1}{y^{-6}} = y^6$

4. $\dfrac{1}{x^{-3}} = x^3$

5. $\dfrac{4}{y^{-3}} = 4y^3$

6. $\dfrac{16}{y^{-7}} = 16y^7$

Exercise Set 3.2

1. $4^{-3} = \dfrac{1}{4^3} = \dfrac{1}{64}$

3. $7x^{-3} = 7 \cdot \dfrac{1}{x^3} = \dfrac{7}{x^3}$

5. $\left(-\dfrac{1}{4}\right)^{-3} = \dfrac{(-1)^{-3}}{(4)^{-3}} = \dfrac{4^3}{(-1)^3} = \dfrac{64}{-1} = -64$

7. $3^{-1} + 2^{-1} = \dfrac{1}{3} + \dfrac{1}{2} = \dfrac{2}{6} + \dfrac{3}{6} = \dfrac{5}{6}$

9. $\dfrac{1}{p^{-3}} = p^3$

11. $\dfrac{p^{-5}}{q^{-4}} = \dfrac{q^4}{p^5}$

13. $\dfrac{x^{-2}}{x} = x^{-2-1} = x^{-3} = \dfrac{1}{x^3}$

15. $\dfrac{z^{-4}}{a^{-7}} = z^{-4-(-7)} = z^3$

17. $2^0 + 3^{-1} = 1 + \dfrac{1}{3} = \dfrac{3}{3} + \dfrac{1}{3} = \dfrac{4}{3}$

19. $(-3)^{-2} = \dfrac{1}{(-3)^2} = \dfrac{1}{9}$

21. $\dfrac{-1}{p^{-4}} = 1\left(p^4\right) = -p^4$

23. $-2^0 - 3^0 = -1(1) - 1 = -2$

25. $\dfrac{x^2 x^5}{x^3} = x^{2+5-3} = x^4$

27. $\dfrac{p^2 p}{p^{-1}} = p^{2+1-(-1)} = p^{2+1+1} = p^4$

29. $\dfrac{\left(m^5\right)^4 m}{m^{10}} = m^{5(4)+1-10} = m^{20+1-10} = m^{11}$

31. $\dfrac{r}{r^{-3}r^{-2}} = r^{1-(-3)-(-2)} = r^{1+3+2} = r^6$

33. $\left(x^5 y^3\right)^{-3} = x^{5(-3)} y^{3(-3)} = x^{-15} y^{-9} = \dfrac{1}{x^{15} y^9}$

35. $\dfrac{\left(x^2\right)^3}{x^{10}} = \dfrac{x^6}{x^{10}} = x^{6-10} = x^{-4} = \dfrac{1}{x^4}$

37. $\dfrac{\left(a^5\right)^2}{\left(a^3\right)^4} = \dfrac{a^{10}}{a^{12}} = a^{10-12} = a^{-2} = \dfrac{1}{a^2}$

39. $\dfrac{8k^4}{2k} = \dfrac{8}{2} \cdot k^{4-1} = 4k^3$

41. $\dfrac{-6m^4}{-2m^3} = \dfrac{-6}{-2} \cdot m^{4-3} = 3m$

43. $\dfrac{-24a^6 b}{6ab^2} = \dfrac{-24}{6} \cdot a^{6-1} b^{1-2} = -4a^5 b^{-1}$

$= -\dfrac{4a^5}{b}$

45. $\dfrac{6x^2 y^3}{-7xy^5} = -\dfrac{6}{7} x^{2-1} y^{3-5} = -\dfrac{6}{7} x^1 y^{-2}$

$= -\dfrac{6x}{7y^2}$

47. $\left(a^{-5}b^2\right)^{-6} = a^{-5(-6)}b^{2(-6)} = a^{30}b^{-12} = \dfrac{a^{30}}{b^{12}}$

49. $\left(\dfrac{x^{-2}y^4}{x^3y^7}\right) = \dfrac{x^{-2(2)}y^{4(2)}}{x^{3(2)}y^{7(2)}} = \dfrac{x^{-4}y^8}{x^6y^{14}}$

     $= x^{-4-6}y^{8-14} = x^{-10}y^{-6} = \dfrac{1}{x^{10}y^6}$

51. $\dfrac{4^2z^{-3}}{4^3z^{-5}} = 4^{2-3}z^{-3-(-5)} = 4^{-1}z^2 = \dfrac{z^2}{4}$

53. $\dfrac{2^{-3}x^{-4}}{2^2x} = 2^{-3-2}x^{-4-1} = 2^{-5}x^{-5} = \dfrac{1}{2^5x^5} = \dfrac{1}{32x^5}$

55. $\dfrac{7ab^{-4}}{7^{-1}a^{-3}b^2} = 7^{1-(-1)}a^{1-(-3)}b^{-4-2}$

     $= 7^2a^4b^{-6}$

     $= \dfrac{49a^4}{b^6}$

57. $\left(\dfrac{a^{-5}b}{ab^3}\right)^{-4} = \dfrac{a^{-5(-4)}b^{-4}}{a^{-4}b^{3(-4)}} = \dfrac{a^{20}b^{-4}}{a^{-4}b^{-12}}$

     $= a^{20-(-4)}b^{-4-(-12)}$

     $= a^{24}b^8$

59. $\dfrac{\left(xy^3\right)^5}{\left(xy\right)^{-4}} = \dfrac{x^5y^{3(5)}}{x^{-4}y^{-4}} = \dfrac{x^5y^{15}}{x^{-4}y^{-4}}$

     $= x^{5-(-4)}y^{15-(-4)}$

     $= x^9y^{19}$

61. $\dfrac{\left(-2xy^{-3}\right)^{-3}}{\left(xy^{-1}\right)^{-1}} = \dfrac{(-2)^{-3}x^{-3}y^9}{x^{-1}y^1}$

     $= (-2)^{-3}x^{-3-(-1)}y^{9-1}$

     $= -\dfrac{y^8}{8x^2}$

63. $\dfrac{\left(a^4b^{-7}\right)}{\left(5a^2b^{-1}\right)} = \dfrac{a^{-20}b^{35}}{5^{-2}a^{-4}b^2}$

     $= 5^2a^{-20-(-4)}b^{35-2}$

     $= 25a^{-16}b^{33}$

     $= \dfrac{25b^{33}}{a^{16}}$

65. $\left(\dfrac{3x^{-2}}{z}\right)^3 = \dfrac{3^3x^{-6}}{z^3} = \dfrac{27}{x^6z^3}$

The volume is $\dfrac{27}{x^6z^3}$ cubic inches.

67. $78,000 = 7.8 \times 10^4$

69. $0.00000167 = 1.67 \times 10^{-6}$

71. $0.00635 = 6.35 \times 10^{-3}$

73. $1,160,000 = 1.16 \times 10^6$

75. $15,600,000 = 1.56 \times 10^7$

77. $13,600 = 1.36 \times 10^4$

79. $284,000,000 = 2.84 \times 10^8$

81. $8.673 \times 10^{-10} = 0.0000000008673$

83. $3.3 \times 10^{-2} = 0.033$

85. $2.032 \times 10^4 = 20,320$

87. $3.97 \times 10^{-24} = 0.00000000000000000000000397$

89. $7.0 \times 10^8 = 700,000,000$

91. $(1.2 \times 10^{-3})(3 \times 10^{-2}) = 1.2 \cdot 3 \cdot 10^{-3} \cdot 10^{-2}$
$$= 3.6 \times 10^{-5}$$
$$= 0.000036$$

93. $(4 \times 10^{-10})(7 \times 10^{-9}) = 4 \cdot 7 \cdot 10^{-10} \cdot 10^{-9}$
$$= 28 \times 10^{-19}$$
$$= 0.0000000000000000028$$

95. $\dfrac{8 \times 10^{-1}}{16 \times 10^{5}} = \dfrac{8}{16} \times 10^{-1-5}$
$$= 0.5 \times 10^{-6}$$
$$= 0.0000005$$

97. $\dfrac{1.4 \times 10^{-2}}{7 \times 10^{-8}} = \dfrac{1.4}{7} \times 10^{-2-(-8)}$
$$= 0.2 \times 10^{6}$$
$$= 200,000$$

99. $7.5 \times 10^{5} \dfrac{\text{gallons}}{\text{second}} \left(\dfrac{3600 \text{ seconds}}{1 \text{ hour}} \right) = 27,000 \times 10^{5}$
$$= 2.7 \times 10^{4} \times 10^{5} = 2.7 \times 10^{9}$$
2.7×10^{9} gallons flows over Niagra Falls in one hour.

101. $3x - 5x + 7 = (3 - 5)x + 7 = -2x + 7$

103. $y - 10 + y = (1 + 1)y - 10 = 2y - 10$

105. $7x + 2 - 8x - 6 = (7 - 8)x + (2 - 6) = -x - 4$

107. $(2.63 \times 10^{12})(-1.5 \times 10^{-10})$
$$= 2.63 \cdot (-1.5) \cdot 10^{12} \cdot 10^{-10}$$
$$= -3.945 \times 10^{2} = -394.5$$

109.
$$d = r \cdot t$$
$$238,857 = (1.86 \times 10^{5})t$$
$$t = \frac{238,857}{1.86 \times 10^{5}}$$
$$t = \frac{2.38857}{1.86} \times 10^{5-5}$$
$$t = 1.3 \text{ seconds}$$

111. $a^{-4m} \cdot a^{5m} = a^{-4m+5m} = a^{m}$

113. $(3y^{2z})^{3} = 3^{3}y^{2z \cdot 3} = 27y^{6z}$

115. Answers may vary.

Practice Problems 3.3

1. $-6x^{6} + 4x^{5} + 7x3 - 9x^{2} - 1$

Term	Coefficient
$7x^{3}$	7
$-9x^{2}$	-9
$-6x^{6}$	-6
$4x^{5}$	4
-1	-1

2. $-15x^{3} + 2x^{2} - 5$
The term $-15x^{3}$ has degree 3.
The term $2x^{2}$ has degree 2.
The term -5 has degree 0 because -5 is $-5x^{0}$.

3. a. The degree of the binomial $-6x+14$ is
  1 because $-6x$ is $-6x^1$.

  b. The degree of the polynomial $9x-3x^6+2$
  is 6, the greatest degree of any of its terms.
  It is not a monomial, binomial, or trinomial.

  c. The degree of the trinomial $10x^2-6x-6$ is
  2, the greatest degree of any of its terms.

4. a. $-2x+10=-2(-1)+10=2+10=12$

  b. $6x^2+11x-20=6(-1)^2+11(-1)-20$
  $=6-11-20=-25$

5. $-16t^2+1821=-16(3)^2+1821$
  $=-16(9)+1821=-144+1821=1677$
  The height of the object at 3 seconds is
  16,777 feet.
  $-16t^2+1821=-16(7)^2+1821$
  $=-16(49)+1821$
  $=1037$
  The height of the object at 7 seconds is
  1037 feet.

6. $-6y+8y=(-6+8)y=2y$

7. $14y^2+3-10y^2-9=14y^2-10y^2+3-9=4y^2-6$

8. $7x^3+x^3=7x^3+1x^3=8x^3$

9. $23x^2-6x-x-15=23x^2-7x-15$

10. $\dfrac{2}{7}x^3-\dfrac{1}{4}x+2-\dfrac{1}{2}x^3+\dfrac{3}{8}x$
$=\left(\dfrac{2}{7}-\dfrac{1}{2}\right)x^3+\left(-\dfrac{1}{4}+\dfrac{3}{8}\right)x+2$
$=\left(\dfrac{4}{14}-\dfrac{7}{14}\right)x^3+\left(-\dfrac{2}{8}+\dfrac{3}{8}\right)x+2$
$=-\dfrac{3}{14}x^3+\dfrac{1}{8}x+2$

11. Area $=5\cdot x+x\cdot x+4\cdot5+x\cdot x+8\cdot x$
$=5x+x^2+20+x^2+8x$
$=2x^2+13x+20$

12. $-2x^3y^2+4-8xy+3x^3y+5xy^2$

Terms	Degree	Degree of Polynomial
$-2x^3y^2$	3+2 or 5	5(highest degree)
4	0	
$-8xy$	1+1=2	
$3x^3y$	3+1 or 4	
$5xy^2$	1+2 or 3	

13. $11ab-6a^2-ba+8b^2$
$=(11-1)ab-6a^2+8b^2$
$=10ab-6a^2+8b^2$

14. $7x^2y^2+2y^2-4y^2x^2+x^2-y^2+5x^2$
$=(7-4)x^2y^2+(2-1)y^2+(1+5)x^2$
$=3x^2y^2+y^2+6x^2$

Exercise Set 3.3

1. $x^2 - 3x + 5$

Term	Coefficient
x^2	1
$-3x$	-3
5	5

3. $-5x^4 + 3.2x^2 + x - 5$

Term	Coefficient
$-5x^4$	-5
$3.2x^2$	3.2
x	1
-5	-5

5. $x + 2$

The degree is 1 since x is x^1. It is a binomial because it has two terms.

7. $9m^3 - 5m^2 + 4m - 8$

The degree is 3, the greatest degree of any of its terms. It is none of these because it has more than three terms.

9. $12x^4 - x^2 - 12x^2 = 12x^4 - 13x^2$

The degree is 4, the greatest degree of any of its terms. It is a binomial because the simplified form has two terms.

11. $3z - 5$

The degree is 1 because $3z$ is $3z^1$. It is a binomial because it has two terms.

13. Answers may vary.

15. Answers may vary.

17. a. $x + 6 = 0 + 6 = 6$

b. $x + 6 = -1 + 6 = 5$

19. a. $x^2 - 5x - 2 = 0^2 - 5(0) - 2 = -2$

b. $x^2 - 5x - 2 = (-1)^2 - 5(-1) - 2$

$= 1 + 5 - 2 = 4$

21. a. $x^3 - 15 = 0^3 - 15 = -15$

b. $x^3 - 15 = (-1)^3 - 15 = -1 - 15 = -16$

23. $-16t^2 + 200t = -16(1)^2 + 200(1)$

$= -16 + 200 = 184$ feet

25. $-16t^2 + 200t = -16(7.6)^2 + 200(7.6)$

$= -924.16 + 1520 = 595.84$ feet

27. Let $x = 15$

$0.97x^2 - 0.91x + 7.46$

$= 0.97(15)^2 - 0.91(15) + 7.46$

$= 218.25 - 13.65 + 7.46$

$= 212.06$

Expect 212.06 wireless telephone subscribers in 2005.

29. $14x^2 + 9x^2 = (14 + 9)x^2 = 23x^2$

31. $15x^2 - 3x^2 - y$

$(15 - 3)x^2 - y = 12x^2 - y$

33. $8s - 5s + 4s = (8 - 5 + 4)s = 7s$

35. $0.1y^2 - 1.2y^2 + 6.7 - 1.9$

$= (0.1 - 1.2)y^2 + (6.7 - 1.9)$

$= -1.1y^2 + 4.8$

37. $5x + 3 + 4x + 3 + 2x + 6 + 3x + 7x$

$= (5x + 4x + 2x + 3x + 7x) + (3 + 3 + 6)$

$= 21x + 12$

39. $(2x)^2 + 7x + x^2 + 5x = 4x^2 + x^2 + 7x + 5x$

$= 5x^2 + 12x$

41. $9ab - 6a + 5b - 3$

Terms	Degree	Degree of Polynomial
$9ab$	$1+1$ or 2	2(highest degree)
$-6a$	1	
$5b$	1	
-3	0	

43. $x^3y - 6 + 2x^2y^2 + 5y^3$

Terms	Degree	Degree of Polynomial
x^3y	$3+1$ or 4	4
-6	0	
$2x^2y^2$	$2+2$ or 4	
$5y^3$	3	

45. $3ab - 4a + 6ab - 7a = (3+6)ab + (-4-7)a$

$= 9ab - 11a$

47. $4x^2 - 6xy + 3y^2 - xy$

$= 4x^2 + (-6-1)xy + 3y^2$

$= 4x^2 - 7xy + 3y^2$

49. $5x^2y + 6xy^2 - 5yx^2 + 4 - 9y^2x$

$= (5-5)x^2y + (6-9)xy^2 + 4$

$= -3xy^2 + 4$

51. $14y^3 - 9 + 3a^2b^2 - 10 - 19b^2a^2$

$= 14y^3 + (-9-10) + (3-19)a^2b^2$

$= 14y^3 - 19 - 16a^2b^2$

53. $4 + 5(2x + 3) = 4 + 10x + 15 = 10x + 19$

55. $2(x-5) + 3(5-x) = 2x - 10 + 15 - 3x = -x + 5$

57. Answers may vary.

59. $1.85x^2 - 3.76x + 9.25x^2 + 10.76 - 4.21x$

$= (1.85 + 9.25)x^2(-3.76 - 4.21)x + 10.76$

$= 11.1x^2 - 7.97x + 10.76$

Practice Problems 3.4

1. $(3x^5 - 7x^3 + 2x - 1) + (3x^3 - 2x)$

$= 3x^5 - 7x^3 + 2x - 1 + 3x^3 - 2x$

$= 3x^5 + (-7x^3 + 3x^3) + (2x - 2x) - 1$

$= 3x^5 - 4x^3 - 1$

2. $(5x^2 - 2x + 1) + (-6x^2 + x - 1)$

$= 5x^2 - 2x + 1 - 6x^2 + x - 1$

$= (5x^2 - 6x^2) + (-2x + x) + (1 - 1)$

$= -x^2 - x$

3. $9y^2 - 6y + 55$

$ \underline{4y + 3}$

$9y^2 - 2y + 8$

4. $(9x+5)-(4x-3)=(9x+5)+\left[-(4x-3)\right]$

$=(9x+5)+(-4x+3)=5x+8$

5. $\left(4x^3-10x^2+1\right)-\left(-4x^3+x^2-11\right)$

$=\left(4x^3-10x^2+1\right)+\left(4x^3-x^2+11\right)$

$=4x^3+4x^3-10x^2-x^2+1+11$

$=8x^3-11x^2+12$

6. $2y^2-2y+7$

  $-\left(6y^2-3y+2\right)$

  $\overline{}$

  $2y^2-2y+7$

  $-6y^2+3y-2$

  $\overline{}$

  $-4y^2+y+5$

7. $\left[(4x-3)+(12x-5)\right]-(3x+1)$

$=4x-3+12x-5-3x-1$

$=4x+12x-3x-3-5-1$

$=13x-9$

8. $\left(2a^2-ab+6b^2\right)-\left(-3a^2+ab-7b^2\right)$

$=2a^2-ab+6b^2+3a^2-ab+7b^2$

$=5a^2-2ab+13b^2$

9. $\left(5x^2y^2+3-9x^2y+y^2\right)$

$\qquad\qquad -\left(-x^2y^2+7-8xy^2+2y^2\right)$

$=5x^2y^2+3-9x^2y+y^2$

$\qquad\qquad +x^2y^2-7+8xy^2-2y^2$

$=6x^2y^2-4-9x^2y-y^2+8xy^2$

Exercise Set 3.4

1. $(3x+7)+(9x+5)=3x+7+9x+5$

$=(3x+9x)+(7+5)=12x+12$

3. $(-7x+5)+\left(-3x^2+7x+5\right)$

$=-7x+5+\left(-3x^2\right)+7x+5$

$=-3x^2+(-7x+7x)+(5+5)$

$=-3x^2+10$

5. $\left(-5x^2+3\right)+\left(2x^2+1\right)$

$=-5x^2+3+2x^2+1$

$=\left(-5x^2+2x^2\right)+(3+1)$

$=-3x^2+4$

7. $\left(-3y^2-4y\right)+\left(2y^2+y-1\right)$

$=-3y^2-4y+2y^2+y-1$

$=\left(-3y^2+2y^2\right)+(-4y+y)-1$

$=-y^2-3y-1$

9. $3t^2+4$

  $+5t^2-8$

  $\overline{}$

  $8t^2-4$

11. $10a^3-8a^2+9$

  $+5a^3+9a^2+7$

  $\overline{}$

  $15a^3+a^2+16$

13. $(2x+5)-(3x-9)=(2x+5)+(-3x+9)$

$=2x+5+(-3x)+9=(2x-3x)+(5+9)$

$=-x+14$

15. $3x - (5x - 9) = 3x + (-5x + 9)$

$\quad = 3x + (-5x) + 9 = -2x + 9$

17. $(2x^2 + 3x - 9) - (-4x + 7)$

$\quad = (2x^2 + 3x - 9) + (4x - 7)$

$\quad = 2x^2 + 3x - 9 + 4x - 7$

$\quad = 2x^2 + (3x + 4x) + (-9 - 7)$

$\quad = 2x^2 + 7x - 16$

19. $(-7y^2 + 5) - (-8y^2 + 12)$

$\quad = (-7y^2 + 5) + (8y^2 - 12)$

$\quad = -7y^2 + 5 + 8y^2 - 12$

$\quad = (-7y^2 + 8y^2) + (5 - 12)$

$\quad = y^2 - 7$

21. $(5x + 8) - (-2x^2 - 6x + 8)$

$\quad = (5x + 8) + (2x^2 + 6x - 8)$

$\quad = 5x + 8 + 2x^2 + 6x - 8$

$\quad = 2x^2 + (5x + 6x) + (8 - 8)$

$\quad = 2x^2 + 11x$

23. $\quad 4z^2 - 8z + 3$

$\quad \underline{-(6z^2 + 8z - 3)}$

$\quad\quad 4z^2 - 8z + 3$

$\quad \underline{+(-6z^2 - 8z + 3)}$

$\quad\; -2z^2 - 16z + 6$

25. $\quad 5u^5 - 4u^2 + 3u - 7$

$\quad \underline{-(3u^5 + 6u^2 - 8u + 2)}$

$\quad\quad 5u^5 - 4u^2 + 3u - 7$

$\quad \underline{+(-3u^5 - 6u^2 + 8u - 2)}$

$\quad\; 2u^5 - 10u^2 + 11u - 9$

27. $(3x + 5) + (2x - 14)\,3x + 5 + 2x - 14$

$\quad = 5x - 9$

29. $(7y + 7) - (y - 6) = 7y + 7 - y + 6$

$\quad = 6y + 13$

31. $(x^2 + 2x + 1) - (3x^2 - 6x + 2)$

$\quad = x^2 + 2x + 1 - 3x^2 + 6x - 2$

$\quad = -2x^2 + 8x - 1$

33. $(3x^2 + 5x - 8) + (5x^2 + 9x + 12) - (x^2 - 14)$

$\quad = 3x^2 + 5x - 8 + 5x^2 + 9x + 12 - x^2 + 14$

$\quad = 7x^2 + 14x + 18$

35. $(7x - 3) - 4x = 7x - 3 - 4x = 3x - 3$

37. $(4x^2 - 6x + 1) + (3x^2 + 2x + 1)$

$\quad = 4x^2 - 6x + 1 + 3x^2 + 2x + 1$

$\quad = 7x^2 - 4x + 2$

39. $(7x^2 + 3x + 9) - (5x + 7)$

$\quad = 7x^2 + 3x + 9 - 5x - 7$

$\quad = 7x^2 - 2x + 2$

41. $\left[(8y^2 + 7) + (6y + 9)\right] - (4y^2 - 6y - 3)$

$\quad = 8y^2 + 7 + 6y + 9 - 4y^2 + 6y + 3$

$\quad = 4y^2 + 12y + 19$

43. $\left(x^2 - 9x + 2\right) + \left(2x^2 - 6x + 1\right) - \left(3x^2 - 4\right)$

$= x^2 - 9x + 2 + 2x^2 - 6x + 1 - 3x^2 + 4$

$= -15x + 7$

45. $\left(9a + 6b - 5\right) + \left(-11a - 7b + 6\right)$

$= 9a + 6b - 5 - 11a - 7b + 6$

$= -2a - b + 1$

47. $\left(4x^2 + y^2 + 3\right) - \left(x^2 + y^2 - 2\right)$

$= 4x^2 + y^2 + 3 - x^2 - y^2 + 2$

$= 3y^4 + 5$

49. $\left(x^2 + 2xy - y^2\right) + \left(5x^2 - 4xy + 20y^2\right)$

$= x^2 + 2xy - y^2 + 5x^2 - 4xy + 20y^2$

$= 6x^2 - 2xy + 19y^2$

51. $\left(11r^rs + 16rs - 3 - 2r^2s^2\right) - \left(3sr^2 + 5 - 9r^2s^2\right)$

$= 11r^2s + 16rs - 3 - 2r^2s^2 - 3sr^2 - 5 + 9r^2s^2$

$= 8r^2s + 16rs + 7r^2s^2 - 8$

53. $3x(2x) = 3 \cdot 2 \cdot x \cdot x = 6x^2$

55. $\left(12x^3\right)\left(-x^5\right) = \left(12x^3\right)\left(-1x^5\right)$

$= (12)(-1)\left(x^3\right)\left(x^5\right) = -12x^8$

57. $10x^2(20xy^2) = 10 \cdot 20x^2 \cdot x \cdot y^2 = 200x^3y^2$

59. $\left(-x^2 + 3x\right) + \left(2x^2 + 5\right) + \left(4x - 1\right)$

$= -x^2 + 3x + 2x^2 + 5 + 4x - 1$

$= \left(x^2 + 7x + 4\right)$ feet

61. $\left(4y^2 + 4y + 1\right) - \left(y^2 - 10\right)$

$= 4y^2 + 4y + 1 - y^2 + 10$

$= \left(3y^2 + 4y + 11\right)$ meters

63. $\left[\left(1.2x^2 - 3x + 9.1\right) - \left(7.8x^2 - 3.1 + 8\right)\right] + \left(1.2x - 6\right)$

$= 1.2x^2 - 3x + 9.1 - 7.8x^2 + 3.1 - 8 + 1.2x - 6$

$= -6.6x^2 - 1.8x - 1.8$

65. $\left(-2.85x^2 + 8.75x + 26.7\right) + \left(0.35x^2 + 3.55x + 40\right)$

$= -2.50x^2 + 12.3x + 66.7$

67. a. $2x$

b. x^2

c. $-2x$

d. x^2; answers may vary

Practice Problems 3.5

1. $10x \cdot 9x = (10 \cdot 9)(x \cdot x) = 90x^2$

2. $8x^3(-11x^7) = 8 \cdot (-11)(x^3 \cdot x^7) = -88x^{10}$

3. $\left(-5x^4\right)\left(-x\right) = \left(-5x^4\right)\left(-1x\right)$

$= (-5)(-1)\left(x^4 \cdot x\right) = 5x^5$

4. $4x\left(x^2 + 4x + 3\right) = 4x\left(x^2\right) + 4x\left(4x\right) + 4x\left(3\right)$

$= 4x^3 + 16x^2 + 12x$

5. $8x\left(7x^4 + 1\right) = 8x\left(7x^4\right) + 8x\left(1\right)$

$= 56x^5 + 8x$

6. $-2x^3\left(3x^2 - x + 2\right)$

$= -2x^3\left(3x^2\right) - 2x^3\left(-x\right) - 2x^3\left(2\right)$

$= -6x^5 + 2x^4 - 4x^3$

7. $\left(4x + 5\right)\left(3x - 4\right)$

$= 4x\left(3x\right) + 4x\left(-4\right) + 5\left(3x\right) + 5\left(-4\right)$

$= 12x^2 - 16x + 15x - 20$

$= 12x^2 - x - 20$

8. $(3x-2y)^2 = (3x-2y)(3x-2y)$

$\quad = 3x(3x) + 3x(-2y) - 2y(3x) - 2y(-2y)$

$\quad = 9x^2 - 6xy - 6xy + 4y^2$

$\quad = 9x^2 - 12xy + 4y^2$

9. $(x+3)(2x^2-5x+4)$

$\quad = x(2x^2) + x(-5x) + x(4) + 3(2x^2) + 3(-5x) + 3(4)$

$\quad = 2x^3 - 5x^2 + 4x + 6x^2 - 15x + 12$

$\quad = 2x^3 + x^2 - 11x + 12$

10.

$$\begin{array}{r} y^2 - 4y + 5 \\ 3y^2 \qquad\quad +1 \\ \hline y^2 - 4y + 5 \\ 3y^4 - 12y^3 + 15y^2 \\ \hline 3y^4 - 12y^3 + 16y^2 - 4y + 5 \end{array}$$

11.

$$\begin{array}{r} 4x^2 \quad -x-1 \\ 3x^2 + 6x - 2 \\ \hline -8x^2 + 2x + 2 \\ 24x^3 - 6x^2 - 6x \\ 12x^4 - \quad 3x^3 - 3x^2 \\ \hline 12x^4 + \quad 21x^3 - 17x^2 - 4x + 2 \end{array}$$

Mental Math 3.5

1. $x^3 \cdot x^5 = x^8$

2. $x^2 \cdot x^6 = x^8$

3. $y^4 y = y^{10}$

4. $y^9 \cdot y = y^{10}$

5. $x^7 \cdot x^7 = x^{14}$

6. $x^{11} \cdot x^{11} = x^{22}$

Exercise Set 3.5

1. $8x^2 \cdot 3x = (8 \cdot 3)(x^2 \cdot x) = 24x^3$

3. $(-3.1x^3)(4x^9) = (-3.1 \cdot 4)(x^3 \cdot x^9)$

$\quad = -12.4x^{12}$

5. $(-x^3)(x) = (-1)(-1)(x^3 \cdot x) = x^4$

7. $\left(-\dfrac{1}{3}y^2\right)\left(\dfrac{2}{5}y\right) = \left(-\dfrac{1}{3} \cdot \dfrac{2}{5}\right)(y^2 \cdot y) = -\dfrac{2}{15}y^3$

9. $(2x)(-3x^2)(4x^5) = (2)(-3)(4)(x \cdot x^2 \cdot x^5) = -24x^8$

11. $3x(2x+5) = 3x(2x) + 3x(5) = 6x^2 + 15x$

13. $7x(x^2 + 2x - 1)$

$\quad = 7x(x^2) + 7x(2x) + 7x(-1)$

$\quad = 7x^3 + 14x^2 - 7x$

15. $-2a(a+4) = -2a(a) + (-2a)(4) = -2a^2 - 8a$

17. $3x(2x^2 - 3x + 4)$

$\quad = 3x(2x^2) + 3x(-3x) + 3x(4)$

$\quad = 6x^3 - 9x^2 + 12x$

19. $3a(a^2 + 2) = 3a(a^2) + 3a(2) = 3a^3 + 6a$

21. $-2a^2(3a^2 - 2a + 3)$

$\quad = -2a^2(3a^2) - 2a^2(-2a) - 2a^2(3)$

$\quad = -6a^4 + 4a^3 - 6a^2$

23. $3x^2 y(2x^3 - x^2 y^2 + 8y^3)$

$\quad = 3x^2 y(2x^3) + 3x^2 y(-x^2 y^2) + 3x^2 y(8y^3)$

$\quad = 6x^5 y - 3x^4 y^3 + 24x^2 y^4$

25. $x^2 + 3x = x(x + 3)$

27. $(x + 4)(x + 3) = x(x) + x(3)x + 4(x) + 4(3)$
$= x^2 + 3x + 4x + 12 = x^2 + 7x + 12$

29. $(a + 7)(a - 2) = a(a)a(-2) + 7(a) + 7(-2)$
$= a^2 - 2a + 7a - 14$
$= a^2 + 5a - 14$

31. $\left(x + \dfrac{2}{3}\right)\left(x - \dfrac{1}{3}\right)$
$= x(x) + x\left(-\dfrac{1}{3}\right) + \dfrac{2}{3}(x) + \dfrac{2}{3}\left(-\dfrac{1}{3}\right)$
$= x^2 - \dfrac{1}{3}x + \dfrac{2}{3}x - \dfrac{2}{9}$
$= x^2 + \dfrac{1}{3}x - \dfrac{2}{9}$

33. $\left(3x^2 + 1\right)\left(4x^2 + 7\right)$
$= 3x^2\left(4x^2\right) + 3x^2(7) + 1\left(4x^2\right) + 1(7)$
$= 12x^4 + 21x^2 + 4x^2 + 7$
$= 12x^4 + 25x^2 + 7$

35. $(4x - 3)(3x - 5)$
$= 4x(3x) + 4x(-5) - 3(3x) - 3(-5)$
$= 12x^2 - 20x - 9x + 15$
$= 12x^2 - 29x + 15$

37. $(1 - 3a)(1 - 4a)$
$= 1(1) + 1(-4a) - 3a(1) - 3a(-4a)$
$= 1 - 4a - 3a + 12a^2$
$= 1 - 7a + 12a^2$

39. $(2y - 4)^2 = (2y - 4)(2y - 4)$
$= 2y(2y) + 2y(-4) - 4(2y) - 4(-4)$
$= 4y^2 - 8y - 8y + 16$
$= 4y^2 - 16y + 16$

41. $(x - 2)\left(x^2 - 3x + 7\right)$
$= x\left(x^2\right) + x(-3x) + x(7)$
$\qquad - 2\left(x^2\right) - 2(-3x) - 2(7)$
$= x^3 - 3x^2 + 7x - 2x^2 + 6x - 14$
$= x^3 - 5x^2 + 13x - 14$

43. $(x + 5)\left(x^3 - 3x + 4\right) = x\left(x^3\right) + x(-3x)$
$\qquad + x(4) + 5\left(x^3\right) + 5(-3x) + 5(4)$
$= x^4 - 3x^2 + 4x + 5x^3 - 15x + 20$
$= x^4 + 5x^3 - 3x^2 - 11x + 20$

45. $(2a - 3)\left(5a^2 - 6a + 4\right) = 2a\left(5a^2\right) + 2a(-6a)$
$\qquad + 2a(4) - 3\left(5a^2\right) - 3(-6a) - 3(4)$
$= 10a^3 - 12a^2 + 8a - 15a^2 + 18a - 12$
$= 10a^3 - 27a^2 + 26a - 12$

47. $(7xy - y)^2 = (7xy - y)(7xy - y)$
$= 7xy(7xy) + 7xy(-y) - y(7xy) - y(-y)$
$= 49x^2y^2 - 7xy^2 - 7xy^2 + y^2$
$= 49x^2y^2 - 14xy^2 + y^2$

49. $x^2 + 2x + 3x + 2(3) = x^2 + 5x + 6$

51.

$$
\begin{array}{r}
2x - 11 \\
6x + 1 \\
\hline
2x - 11 \\
12x^2 - 66x \\
\hline
12x^2 - 64x - 11
\end{array}
$$

53.

$$
\begin{array}{r}
2x^2 + 4x - 1 \\
x + 3 \\
\hline
6x^2 + 12x - 3 \\
2x^3 + 4x^2 - x \\
\hline
2x^3 + 10x^2 + 11x - 3
\end{array}
$$

55.

$$
\begin{array}{r}
x^2 + 5x - 7 \\
x^2 - 7x - 9 \\
\hline
9x^2 - 45x + 63 \\
-7x^3 - 35x^2 + 49x \\
x^4 + 5x^3 - 7x^2 \\
\hline
x^4 - 2x^3 - 51x^2 + 4x + 63
\end{array}
$$

57. $(5x)^2 = 5^2 x^2 = 25x^2$

59. $(-3y^3)^2 = (-3)^2 y^{3 \cdot 2} = 9y^6$

61. At $t = 0$, value = \$7000

63. At $t = 0$, value $= \$7000$

At $t = 1$, value $= \$6500$

$\$7000 - \$6500 = \$500$

65. Answers may vary.

67. $(2x - 5)(2x + 5)$

$= 2x(2x) + 2x(5) - 5(2x) - 5(5)$

$= 4x^2 + 10x - 10x - 25 = 4x^2 - 25$

$(4x^2 - 25)$ square yards

69. $\dfrac{1}{2}(3x - 2)(4x) = 2x(3x - 2)$

$= 2x(3x) + 2x(-2) = 6x^2 - 4x$

$(6x^2 - 4x)$ square inches

71. a. $(3x + 5) + (3x + 7) = 3x + 5 + 3x + 7$

$= 6x + 12$

Answers may vary.

b. $(3x + 5)(3x + 7)$

$= 3x(3x) + 3x(7) + 5(3x) + 5(7)$

$= 9x^2 + 21x + 15x + 35$

$= 9x^2 + 36x + 35$

Answers may vary.

73. a. $(a + b)(a - b) = a^2 - ab + ab - b^2$

$= a^2 - b^2$

b. $(2x + 3y)(2x - 3y)$

$= (2x)^2 - 6xy + 6xy - (3y)^2$

$= 4x^2 - 9y^2$

c. $(4x + 7)(4x - 7)$

$= (4x)^2 - 28x + 28x - 7^2$

$= 16x^2 - 49$

d. Answers may vary.

Practice Problems 3.6

1. $(x + 7)(x - 5)$

$= (x)(x) + (x)(-5) + (7)(x) + (7)(-5)$

$= x^2 - 5x + 7x - 35 = x^2 + 2x - 35$

2. $(6x-1)(x-4)$

$= 6x(x) + 6x(-4) + (-1)(x) + (-1)(-4)$

$= 6x^2 - 24x - x + 4$

$= 6x^2 - 25x + 4$

3. $(2y^2 + 3)(y-4)$

$= (2y^2)(y) + (2y^2)(-4) + (3)(y) + (3)(-4)$

$= 2y^3 - 8y^2 + 3y - 12$

4. $(2x+9)^2 = (2x+9)(2x+9)$

$= 2x(2x) + 2x(9) + 9(2x) + 9(9)$

$= 4x^2 + 18x + 18x + 81$

$= 4x^2 + 36x + 81$

5. $(y+3)^2 = y^2 + 2(3) + 3^2$

$= y^2 + 6y + 9$

6. $(r-s)^2 = r^2 - 2rs + s^2$

7. $(6x+5)^2 = (6x)^2 + 2(6x)(5) + 5^2$

$= 36x^2 + 60x + 25$

8. $(x^2 - 3y)^2 = (x^2)^2 - 2(x^2)(3y) + (3y)^2$

$= x^4 - 6x^2 y + 9y^2$

9. $(x+7)(x-7) = x^2 - 7^2 = x^2 - 49$

10. $(4y+5)(4y-5) = (4y)^2 - 5^2$

$= 16y^2 - 25$

11. $\left(x - \dfrac{1}{3}\right)\left(x + \dfrac{1}{3}\right) = x^2 - \left(\dfrac{1}{3}\right)^2 = x^2 - \dfrac{1}{9}$

12. $(3a-b)(3a+b) - (3a)^2 - b^2 = 9a^2 - b^2$

13. $(2x^2 - 6y)(2x^2 + 6y) = (2x^2)^2 - (6y)^2$

$= 4x^4 - 36y^2$

14. $(7x-1)^2 = (7x)^2 - 2(7x)(1) + 1^2$

$= 49x^2 - 14x + 1$

15. $(5y+3)(2y-5)$

$= 5y(2y) + 5y(-5) + 3(2y) + 3(-5)$

$= 10y^2 - 25y + 6y - 15$

$= 10y^2 - 19y - 15$

16. $(2a-1)(2a+1) = (2a)^2 - 1^2 = 4a^2 - 1$

Exercise Set 3.6

1. $(x+3)(x+4) = x^2 + 4x + 3x + 12$

$= x^2 + 7x + 12$

3. $(x-5)(x+10) = x^2 + 10x - 5x - 50$

$= x^2 + 5x - 50$

5. $(5x-6)(x+2) = 5x^2 + 10x - 6x - 12$

$= 5x^2 + 4x - 12$

7. $(y-6)(4y-1) = 4y^2 - 1y - 24y + 6$

$= 4y^2 - 25y + 6$

9. $(2x+5)(3x-1) = 6x^2 - 2x + 15x - 5$

$= 6x^2 + 13x - 5$

11. $(y^2 + 7)(6y+4) = 6y^3 + 4y^2 + 42y + 28$

13. $\left(x - \dfrac{1}{3}\right)\left(x + \dfrac{2}{3}\right) = x^2 + \dfrac{2}{3}x - \dfrac{1}{3}x - \dfrac{2}{9}$

$$= x^2 + \dfrac{1}{3}x - \dfrac{2}{9}$$

15. $(4 - 3a)(2 - 5a) = 8 - 20a - 6a + 15a^2$

$$= 8 - 26a + 15a^2$$

17. $(x + 5y)(2x - y) = 2x^2 - xy + 10xy - 5y^2$

$$= 2x^2 + 9xy - 5y^2$$

19. $(x + 2)^2 = x^2 + 2(x)(2) + 2^2$

$$= x^2 + 4x + 4$$

21. $(2x - 1)^2 = (2x)^2 - 2(2x)(1) + (1)^2$

$$= 4x^2 - 4x + 1$$

23. $(3a - 5)^2 = (3a)^2 - 2(3a)(5) + 5^2$

$$= 9a^2 - 30a + 25$$

25. $(x^2 + 5)^2 = (x^2)^2 + 2(x^2)(5) + 5^2$

$$= x^4 + 10x^2 + 25$$

27. $\left(y - \dfrac{2}{7}\right)^2 = y^2 - 2(y)\left(\dfrac{2}{7}\right) + \left(\dfrac{2}{7}\right)^2$

$$= y^2 - \dfrac{4}{7}y + \dfrac{4}{49}$$

29. $(2a - 3)^2 = (2a)^2 - 2(2a)(3) + 3^2$

$$= 4a^2 - 12a + 9$$

31. $(5x + 9)^2 = (5x)^2 + 2(5x)(9) + 9^2$

$$= 25x^2 + 90x + 81$$

33. $(3x - 7y)^2 = (3x)^2 - 2(3x)(7y) + (7y)^2$

$$= 9x^2 - 42xy + 49y^2$$

35. $(4m + 5n)^2 = (4m)^2 + 2(4m)(5n) + (5n)^2$

$$= 16m^2 + 40mn + 25n^2$$

37. Answers may vary.

39. $(a - 7)(a + 7) = a^2 - 7^2 = a^2 - 49$

41. $(x + 6)(x - 6) = x^2 - 6^2 = x^2 - 36$

43. $(3x - 1)(3x - 1) = (3x)^2 - 1^2 = 9x^2 - 1$

45. $(x^2 + 5)(x^2 - 5) = (x^2)^2 - 5^2 = x^4 - 25$

47. $(2y^2 - 1)(2y^2 + 1) = (2y^2)^2 - 1^2 = 4y^4 - 1$

49. $(4 - 7x)(4 + 7x) = 4^2 - (7x)^2 = 16 - 49x^2$

51. $\left(3x - \dfrac{12}{2}\right)\left(3x + \dfrac{1}{2}\right) = (3x)^2 - \left(\dfrac{1}{2}\right)^2$

$$= 9x^2 - \dfrac{1}{4}$$

53. $(9x + y)(9x - y) = (9x)^2 - y^2 = 81x^2 - y^2$

55. $(2m + 5n)(2m - 5n) = (2m)^2 - (5n)^2$

$$= 4m^2 - 25n^2$$

57. $(a + 5)(a + 4) = a^2 + 4a + 5a + 20$

$$= a^2 + 9a + 20$$

59. $(a - 7)^2 = a^2 - 2(a)(7) + 7^2$

$$= a^2 - 14a + 49$$

61. $(4a+1)(3a-1) = 12a^2 - 4a + 3a - 1$
$$= 12a^2 - a - 1$$

63. $(x+2)(x-2) = x^2 - 2^2 = x^2 - 4$

65. $(3a+1)^2 = (3a)^2 + 2(3a)(1) + 1^2$
$$= 9a^2 + 6a + 1$$

67. $(x+y)(4x-y) = 4x^2 - xy + 4xy - y^2$
$$= 4x^2 + 3xy - y^2$$

69. $\left(a - \frac{1}{2}y\right)\left(a + \frac{1}{2}y\right) = a^2 - \left(\frac{1}{2}y\right)^2$
$$= a^2 - \frac{1}{4}y^2$$

71. $(3b+7)(2b-5) = 6b^2 - 15b + 14b - 35$
$$= 6b^2 - b - 35$$

73. $(x^2+10)(x^2-10) = (x^2)^2 - (10)^2$
$$= x^4 - 100$$

75. $(4x+5)(4x-5) = (4x)^2 - 5^2$
$$= 16x^2 - 25$$

77. $(5x-6y)^2 = (5x)^2 - 2(5x)(6y) + (6y)^2$
$$= 25x^2 - 60xy + 36y^2$$

79. $(2r-3s)(2r+3s) = (2r)^2 - (3s)^2$
$$= 4r^2 - 9s^2$$

81. $\dfrac{50b^{10}}{70b^5} = \dfrac{10 \cdot 5 \cdot b^5 \cdot b^5}{10 \cdot 7 \cdot b^5} = \dfrac{5b^5}{7}$

83. $\dfrac{8a^{17}b^5}{-4a^7b^{10}} = \dfrac{4 \cdot 2 \cdot a^7 \cdot a^{10} \cdot b^5}{4 \cdot (-1) \cdot a^7 \cdot b^5 \cdot b^5} = -\dfrac{2a^{10}}{b^5}$

85. $\dfrac{2x^4y^{12}}{3x^4y^4} = \dfrac{2 \cdot x^4 \cdot y^4 \cdot y^8}{3 \cdot x^4 \cdot y^4} = \dfrac{2y^8}{3}$

87. $(2x+1)^2 = (2x)^2 + 2(2x)(1) + 1^2$
$$= 4x^2 + 4x + 1$$
$\left(4x^2 + 4x + 1\right)$ square feet

89. $(5x-3)^2 - (x+1)^2$
$$= \left[(5x)^2 - 2(5x)(3) + 3^2\right] - \left[x^2 + 2(x)(1) + 1^2\right]$$
$$= (25x^2 - 30x + 9) - (x^2 + 2x + 1)$$
$$= 25x^2 - 30x + 9 - x^2 - 2x - 1$$
$$= \left(224x^2 - 32x + 8\right) \text{ square meters}$$

Integrated Review 3.6

1. $(5x^2)(7x^3) = (5 \cdot 7)(x^2 \cdot x^3)$
$$= 35x^5$$

2. $(4y^2)(8y^7) = (4 \cdot 8)(y^2 \cdot y^7)$
$$= 32y^9$$

3. $-4^2 = -(4 \cdot 4) = -16$

4. $(-4)^2 = (-4)(-4) = 16$

5. $(x-5) + (2x+1) = x - 5 + 2x + 1$
$$= 3x - 4$$

6. $(3x-2) + (x+5) = 3x - 2 + x + 5$
$$= 4x + 3$$

7. $(4y-3)(4y+3) = (4y)^2 - 3^2$
$$= 16y^2 - 9$$

8. $(7x-1)(7x+1) = (7x)^2 - 1^2$
$$= 49x^2 - 1$$

9. $\dfrac{7x^9 y^{12}}{x^3 y^{10}} = 7x^{9-3} y^{12-10}$
$$= 7x^6 y^2$$

10. $\dfrac{20a^2 b^8}{14a^2 b^2} = \dfrac{10a^{2-2} b^{8-2}}{7}$
$$= \dfrac{10b^6}{7}$$

11. $\left(12m^7 n^6\right)^2 = 12^2 m^{7\cdot 2} n^{6\cdot 2}$
$$= 144m^{14} n^{12}$$

12. $\left(4y^9 z^{10}\right)^3 = 4^3 y^{9\cdot 3} z^{10\cdot 3}$
$$= 64y^{27} z^{30}$$

13. $(4y-3)(4y+3) = (4y)^2 - 3^2$
$$= 16y^2 - 9$$

14. $(7x-1)(7x+1) = (7x)^2 - 1^2$
$$= 49x^2 - 1$$

15. $\left(x^{-7} y^5\right)^9 = x^{-63} y^{45}$
$$= \dfrac{y^{45}}{x^{63}}$$

16. $\left(3^{-1} x^9\right)^3 = 3^{-3} x^{27}$
$$= \dfrac{x^{27}}{3^3}$$
$$= \dfrac{x^{27}}{27}$$

17. $\left(7x^2 - 2x + 3\right) - \left(5x^2 + 9\right)$
$$= 7x^2 - 2x + 3 - 5x^2 - 9$$
$$= 2x^2 - 2x - 6$$

18. $\left(10x^2 + 7x - 9\right) - \left(4x^2 - 6x + 2\right)$
$$= 10x^2 + 7x - 9 - 4x^2 + 6x - 2$$
$$= 6x^2 + 13x - 11$$

19. $0.7y^2 - 1.2 + 1.8y^2 - 6y + 1$
$$= 2.5y^2 - 6y - 0.2$$

20. $7.8x^2 - 6.8x - 3.3 + 0.6x^2 - 9$
$$= 8.4x^2 - 6.8x - 12.3$$

21. $(x+4)^2 = (x+4)(x+4)$
$$= x^2 + 2(x)(4) + 4^2$$
$$= x^2 + 8x + 16$$

22. $(y-9)^2 = (y-9)(y-9)$
$$= y^2 - 2(y)(9) + 9^2$$
$$= y^2 - 18y + 81$$

23. $(x+4)(x+4) = x + 4 + x + 4$
$$= 2x + 8$$

24. $(y-9)(y-9) = y - 9 + y - 9$
$$= 2y - 18$$

25. $7x^2 - 6xy + 4\left(y^2 - xy\right)$

$= 7x^2 - 6xy + 4y^2 - 4xy$

$= 7x^2 - 10xy + 4y^2$

26. $5a^2 - 3ab + 6\left(6^2 - a^2\right)$

$= 5a^2 - 3ab + 6b^2 - 6a^2$

$= -a^2 - 3ab + 6b^2$

27. $(x-3)\left(x^2 + 5x - 1\right)$

$= x\left(x^2\right) + x(5x) + x(-1) - 3\left(x^2\right)$

$\quad - 3(5x) - 3(-1)$

$= x^3 + 5x^2 - x - 3x^2 - 15x + 3$

$= x^3 + 2x^2 - 16x + 3$

28. $(x+1)\left(x^2 - 3x - 2\right)$

$= x\left(x^2\right) + x(-3x) + x(-2) + 1\left(x^2\right)$

$\quad + 1(-3x) + 1(-2)$

$= x^3 - 3x^2 - 2x + x^2 - 3x - 2$

$= x^3 - 2x^2 - 5x - 2$

29. $(2x-7)(3x+10)$

$= 2x(3x) + 2x(10) - 7(3x) - 7(10)$

$= 6x^2 + 20x - 21x - 70$

$= 6x^2 - x - 70$

30. $(5x-1)(4x+5)$

$= 5x(4x) + 5x(5) - 1(4x) - 1(5)$

$= 20x^2 + 25x - 4x - 5$

$= 20x^2 + 21x - 5$

31. $(2x-7)\left(x^2 - 6x + 1\right)$

$= 2x\left(x^2\right) - 2x(6x) + 2x(1) - 7\left(x^2\right)$

$\quad - 7(-6x) - 7(1)$

$= 2x^3 - 12x^2 + 2x - 7x^2 + 42x - 7$

$= 2x^3 - 19x^2 + 44x - 7$

32. $(5x-1)\left(x^2 + 2x - 3\right)$

$= 5x\left(x^2\right) + 5x(2x) + 5x(-3) - 1\left(x^2\right)$

$\quad - 1(2x) - 1(-3)$

$= 5x^3 + 10x^2 - 15x - x^2 - 2x + 3$

$= 5x^3 + 9x^2 - 17x + 3$

Practice Problems 3.7

1. $\dfrac{25x^3 + 5x^2}{5x^2} = \dfrac{25x^3}{5x^2} + \dfrac{5x^2}{5x^2} = 5x + 1$

2. $\dfrac{30x^7 + 10x^2 - 5x}{5x^2} = \dfrac{30x^7}{5x^2} + \dfrac{10x^2}{5x^2} - \dfrac{5x}{5x^2}$

$= 6x^5 + 2 - \dfrac{1}{x}$

3. $\dfrac{12x^3y^3 - 18xy + 6y}{3xy} = \dfrac{12x^3y^3}{3xy} - \dfrac{18xy}{3xy} + \dfrac{6y}{3xy}$

$= 4x^2y^2 - 6 + \dfrac{2}{x}$

4.
$$\begin{array}{r} x+7 \\ x+5\overline{\smash{\big)}\,x^2 +12x+35} \\ \underline{x^2 + 5x} \\ 7x+35 \\ \underline{7x+35} \\ 0 \end{array}$$

The quotient is $x + 7$.

5.

$$
\begin{array}{r}
3x+5 \\
2x-1\overline{\smash{\big)}\,6x^2+7x-5} \\
\underline{6x^2-3x} \\
10x-5 \\
\underline{10x-5} \\
0
\end{array}
$$

The quotient is $3x+5$.

6.

$$
\begin{array}{r}
3x^2-2x+1 \\
3x+2\overline{\smash{\big)}\,9x^3+0x^2-x+5} \\
\underline{9x^3+6x^2} \\
-6x^2-\ x \\
\underline{-6x^2-4x} \\
3x+5 \\
\underline{3x+2} \\
3
\end{array}
$$

$$\frac{5-x+9x^3}{3x+2}=3x^2-2x+1+\frac{3}{3x+2}$$

7.

$$
\begin{array}{r}
x^2+x+1 \\
x-1\overline{\smash{\big)}\,x^3+0x^2+0x-1} \\
\underline{x^3-x^2} \\
x^2+0x \\
\underline{x^2-\ x} \\
x-1 \\
\underline{x-1} \\
0
\end{array}
$$

$$\frac{x^3-1}{x-1}=x^2+x+1$$

Mental Math 3.7

1. $\dfrac{a^6}{a^4}=a^2$

2. $\dfrac{y^2}{y}=y$

3. $\dfrac{a^3}{a}=a^2$

4. $\dfrac{p^8}{p^3}=p^5$

5. $\dfrac{k^5}{k^2}=k^3$

6. $\dfrac{k^7}{k^5}=k^2$

Exercise Set 3.7

1. $\dfrac{20x^2+5x+9}{5}=\dfrac{20x^2}{5}+\dfrac{5x}{5}+\dfrac{9}{5}$

$$=4x^2+x+\frac{9}{5}$$

3. $\dfrac{12x^4+3x^2}{x}=\dfrac{12x^4}{x}+\dfrac{3x^2}{x}=12x^3+3x$

5. $\dfrac{15p^3+18p^2}{3p}=\dfrac{15p^3}{3p}+\dfrac{18p^2}{3p}=5p^2+6p$

7. $\dfrac{-9x^4+18x^5}{6x^5}=\dfrac{-9x^4}{6x^5}+\dfrac{18x^5}{6x^5}=-\dfrac{3}{2x}+3$

9. $\dfrac{-9x^5+3x^4-12}{3x^3}=\dfrac{-9x^5}{3x^3}+\dfrac{3x^4}{3x^3}-\dfrac{12}{3x^3}$

$$=-3x^2+x-\frac{4}{x^3}$$

11. $\dfrac{4x^4-6x^3+7}{-4x^4}=\dfrac{4x^4}{-4x^4}-\dfrac{6x^3}{-4x^4}+\dfrac{7}{-4x^4}$

$$=-1+\frac{3}{2x}-\frac{7}{4x^4}$$

13. $\dfrac{a^2b^2 - ab^3}{ab} = \dfrac{a^2b^2}{ab} - \dfrac{ab^3}{ab} = ab - b^2$

15. $\dfrac{2x^2y + 8x^2y^2 - xy^2}{2xy} = \dfrac{2x^2y}{2xy} + \dfrac{8x^2y^2}{2xy} - \dfrac{xy^2}{2xy}$

$$= x + 4xy - \dfrac{y}{2}$$

17.
$$
\begin{array}{r}
x + 1 \\
x+3\overline{)x^2 + 4x + 3} \\
\underline{x^2 + 3x} \\
x + 3 \\
\underline{x + 3} \\
0
\end{array}
$$

$$\dfrac{x^2 + 4x + 3}{x + 3} = x + 1$$

19.
$$
\begin{array}{r}
2x + 3 \\
x+5\overline{)2x^2 + 13x + 15} \\
\underline{2x^2 + 10x} \\
3x + 15 \\
\underline{3x + 15} \\
0
\end{array}
$$

$$\dfrac{2x^2 + 13x + 15}{x + 5} = 2x + 3$$

21.
$$
\begin{array}{r}
2x + 1 \\
x-4\overline{)2x^2 - 7x + 3} \\
\underline{2x^2 - 8x} \\
x + 3 \\
\underline{x - 4} \\
7
\end{array}
$$

$$\dfrac{2x^2 - 7x + 3}{x - 4} = 2x + 1 + \dfrac{7}{x - 4}$$

23.
$$
\begin{array}{r}
4x + 9 \\
2x-3\overline{)8x^2 + 6x - 27} \\
\underline{8x^2 - 12x} \\
18x - 27 \\
\underline{18x - 27} \\
0
\end{array}
$$

$$\dfrac{8x^2 + 6x - 27}{2x - 3} = 4x + 9$$

25.
$$
\begin{array}{r}
3a^2 - 3a + 1 \\
3a+2\overline{)9a^3 - 3a^2 - 3a + 4} \\
\underline{9a^3 + 6a^2} \\
-9a^2 - 3a \\
\underline{-9a^2 - 6a} \\
3a + 4 \\
\underline{3a + 2} \\
2
\end{array}
$$

$$\dfrac{9a^3 - 3a^2 - 3a + 4}{3a + 2} = 3a^2 - 3a + 1 + \dfrac{2}{3a + 2}$$

27.
$$
\begin{array}{r}
2b^2 + b + 2 \\
b+4\overline{)2b^3 + 9b^2 + 6b - 4} \\
\underline{2b^3 + 8b^2} \\
b^2 + 6b \\
\underline{b^2 + 4b} \\
2b - 4 \\
\underline{2b + 8} \\
-12
\end{array}
$$

$$\dfrac{2b^3 + 9b^2 + 6b - 4}{b + 4} = 2b^2 + b + 2 - \dfrac{12}{b + 4}$$

29.

$$2x+1\overline{\smash{\big)}\,8x^2+10x+1}$$ (quotient $4x+3$)

$$\underline{8x^2+\ 4x}$$
$$6x+1$$
$$\underline{6x+3}$$
$$-2$$

$$\frac{8x^2+10x+1}{2x+1}=4x+3-\frac{2}{2x+1}$$

31.

$$x-2\overline{\smash{\big)}\,2x^3+2x^2-17x+8}$$ (quotient $2x^2+6x-5$)

$$\underline{2x^3-4x^2}$$
$$6x^2-17x$$
$$\underline{6x^2-12x}$$
$$-5x+\ 8$$
$$\underline{-5x+10}$$
$$-\ 2$$

$$\frac{2x^3+2x^2-17x+8}{x-2}=2x^2+6x-5-\frac{2}{x-2}$$

33.

$$x-3\overline{\smash{\big)}\,x^3+0x^2+0x-27}$$ (quotient x^2+3x+9)

$$\underline{x^3-3x^2}$$
$$3x^2+0x$$
$$\underline{3x^2-9x}$$
$$9x-27$$
$$\underline{9x-27}$$
$$0$$

$$\frac{x^3-27}{x-3}=x^2+3x+9$$

35.

$$x+2\overline{\smash{\big)}\,-3x^2+0x+1}$$ (quotient $-3x+6$)

$$\underline{-3x^2-6x}$$
$$6x+\ 1$$
$$\underline{6x+12}$$
$$-11$$

$$\frac{1-3x^2}{x+2}=-3x+6-\frac{11}{x+2}$$

37.

$$2b-1\overline{\smash{\big)}\,4b^2-4b-5}$$ (quotient $2b-1$)

$$\underline{4b^2-2b}$$
$$-2b-5$$
$$\underline{-2b+1}$$
$$-6$$

$$\frac{-4b+4b^2-5}{2b-1}=2b-1-\frac{6}{2b-1}$$

39. $12=4\cdot3$

41. $20=-5\cdot(-4)$

43. $9x^2=3x\cdot3x$

45. $36x^2=4x\cdot9x$

47.

$$x^2+x\overline{\smash{\big)}\,x^5+0x^4+0x^3+x^2}$$ (quotient x^3-x^2+x)

$$\underline{x^5+\ x^4}$$
$$-x^4+0x^3$$
$$\underline{-x^4-\ x^3}$$
$$x^3+x^2$$
$$\underline{x^3+x^2}$$
$$0$$

$$\frac{x^5+x^2}{x^2+x}=x^3-x^2+x$$

49. $\dfrac{12x^3 + 4x - 16}{4} = \dfrac{12x^3}{4} + \dfrac{4x}{x} - \dfrac{16}{4}$

$= 3x^3 + x - 4$

Each side is $\left(3x^2 + x - 4\right)$ feet.

51.

$$\begin{array}{r} 2x + 5 \\ 5x+3\overline{)10x^2 + 31x + 15} \\ \underline{10x^2 + 6x} \\ 25 + 15 \\ \underline{25 + 15} \\ 0 \end{array}$$

The height is $(2x + 5)$ meters.

53. Answers may vary.

Chapter 3 Review

1. 3^2

base: 3

exponent: 2

2. $(-5)^4$

base: -5

exponent: 4

3. -5^4

base: 5

exponent: 4

4. x^2

base: x

exponent: 6

5. $8^3 = 8 \cdot 8 \cdot 8 = 512$

6. $(-6)^2 = (-6)(-6) = 36$

7. $-6^2 = -6 \cdot 6 = -36$

8. $-4^3 - 4^0 = -4 \cdot 4 \cdot 4 - 1 = -65$

9. $(3b)^0 = 1$

10. $\dfrac{8b}{8b} = 1$

11. $y^2 \cdot y^2 = y^{2+7} = y^9$

12. $x^9 \cdot x^5 = x^{9+5} = x^{14}$

13. $(2x^5)(-3x^6) = 2(-3) \cdot (x^5 \cdot x^6) = -6x^{11}$

14. $(-5y^3)(4y^4) = (-5 \cdot 4)(y^3 \cdot y^4) = -20y^7$

15. $(x^4)^2 = x^{4 \cdot 2} = x^8$

16. $(y^3)^5 = y^{3 \cdot 5} = y^{15}$

17. $(3y^6)^4 = 3^4 y^{6 \cdot 4} = 81y^{24}$

18. $(2x^3)^3 = 2^3 x^{3 \cdot 3} = 8x^9$

19. $\dfrac{x^9}{x^4} = x^{9-4} = x^5$

20. $\dfrac{z^{12}}{z^5} = z^{12-5} = z^7$

21. $\dfrac{a^5 b^4}{ab} = a^{5-1} b^{4-1} = a^4 b^3$

22. $\dfrac{x^4 y^6}{xy} = x^{4-1} y^{6-1} = x^3 y^5$

23. $\dfrac{12xy^6}{3x^4y^{10}} = \dfrac{12}{3} \cdot x^{1-4} \cdot y^{6-10}$

$\qquad = 4x^{-3}y^{-4}$

$\qquad = \dfrac{4}{x^3y^4}$

24. $\dfrac{2x^7y^8}{8xy^2} = \dfrac{2}{8} \cdot x^{7-1}y^{8-2}$

$\qquad = \dfrac{x^6y^6}{4}$

25. $5a^7\left(2a^4\right)^3$

$\qquad = 5a^7\left(2^3a^{4\cdot3}\right)$

$\qquad = 5a^7\left(8a^{12}\right)$

$\qquad = 5 \cdot 8a^{7+12}$

$\qquad = 40a^{19}$

26. $\left(2x\right)^2\left(9x\right)$

$\qquad = \left(2^2 \cdot x^2\right)\left(9x\right)$

$\qquad = 4x^2 \cdot 9x$

$\qquad = 4 \cdot 9 \cdot x^{2+1}$

$\qquad = 36x^3$

27. $\left(-5a\right)^0 + 7^0 + 8^0$

$\qquad = 1 + 1 + 1$

$\qquad = 3$

28. $8x^0 + 9x^0$

$\qquad = 8 \cdot 1 + 1$

$\qquad = 9$

29. $\left(\dfrac{3x^4}{4y}\right)^3$

$\qquad = \dfrac{3^3 \, x^{4\cdot3}}{4^3 \, y^3}$

$\qquad = \dfrac{27x^{12}}{64y^3}$

Answer: b

30. $\left(\dfrac{5a^6}{b^3}\right) = \dfrac{5^2 \, a^{6\cdot2}}{b^{3\cdot2}} = \dfrac{25a^{12}}{b^6}$

Answer: c

31. $7^{-2} = \dfrac{1}{7^2} = \dfrac{1}{49}$

32. $-7^{-2} = -\dfrac{1}{7^2} = -\dfrac{1}{49}$

33. $2x^{-4} = \dfrac{2}{x^4}$

34. $\left(2x\right)^{-4} = \dfrac{1}{\left(2x\right)^4} = \dfrac{1}{16x^4}$

35. $\left(\dfrac{1}{5}\right)^{-3} = \dfrac{1^{-3}}{5^{-3}} = \dfrac{5^3}{1^3} = 125$

36. $\left(\dfrac{-2}{3}\right)^{-2} = \dfrac{\left(-2\right)^{-2}}{3^{-2}} = \dfrac{3}{\left(-2\right)^2} = \dfrac{9}{4}$

37. $2^0 + 2^{-4} = 1 + \dfrac{1}{2^4} = \dfrac{16}{16} + \dfrac{1}{16} = \dfrac{17}{16}$

38. $6^{-1} - 7^{-1} = \dfrac{1}{6} - \dfrac{1}{7} = \dfrac{7}{42} - \dfrac{6}{42} = \dfrac{1}{42}$

39. $\dfrac{x^5}{x^{-3}} = x^{5-(-3)} = x^8$

40. $\dfrac{z^4}{z^{-4}} = z^{4-(-4)} = z^8$

41. $\dfrac{r^{-3}}{r^{-4}} = r^{-3-(-4)} = r^1 = r$

42. $\dfrac{y^{-2}}{y^{-5}} = y^{-2-(-5)} = y^3$

43. $\left(\dfrac{bc^{-2}}{bc^{-3}}\right)^4 = \dfrac{b^4 c^{-8}}{b^4 c^{-12}} = b^{4-4}c^{-8-(-12)} = c^4$

44. $\left(\dfrac{x^{-3}y^{-4}}{x^{-2}y^{-5}}\right)^{-3} = \dfrac{x^9 y^{12}}{x^6 y^{15}} = x^{9-6}y^{12-15} = \dfrac{x^3}{y^3}$

45. $\dfrac{x^{-4}y^{-6}}{x^2 y^7} = x^{-4-2}y^{-6-7} = x^{-6}y^{-13} = \dfrac{1}{x^6 y^{13}}$

46. $\dfrac{a^5 b^{-5}}{a^{-5}b^5} = a^{5-(-5)}b^{-5-5}$
$= a^{10}b^{-10}$
$= \dfrac{a^{10}}{b^{10}}$

47. $0.00027 = 2.7 \times 10^{-4}$

48. $0.8868 = 8.868 \times 10^{-1}$

49. $80,800,000 = 8.08 \times 10^7$

50. $-868,000 = -8.68 \times 10^5$

51. $109,379,000 = 1.09379 \times 10^8$ kg

52. $150,000 = 1.5 \times 10^5$ light years

53. $8.67 \times 10^5 = 867,000$

54. $3.86 \times 10^{-3} = 0.00386$

55. $8.6 \times 10^{-4} = 0.00086$

56. $8.936 \times 10^5 = 893,600$

57. $1.43128 \times 10^{15} = 1,431,280,000,000,000$ cu. km

58. $1 \times 10^{-10} = 0.0000000001$ m

59. $\left(8 \times 10^4\right)\left(2 \times 10^{-7}\right)$
$= (8 \times 2) \times \left(10^4 \times 10^{-7}\right)$
$= 16 \times 10^{-3}$
$= 0.016$

60. $\dfrac{8 \times 10^4}{2 \times 10^{-7}}$
$= \dfrac{8}{2} \times \left(10^{4-(-7)}\right)$
$= 4 \times 10^{11}$
$= 400,000,000,000$

61. The degree is 5 because y^5 is the term with the highest degree.

62. The degree is 2 because $9y^2$ is the term with the highest degree.

63. The degree is 5 because $-28x^2 y^3$ is the term with the highest degree.

64. The degree is 5 because $6x^2 y^2 z^2$ is the term with the highest degree.

65. $2(1)^2 + 20(1) = 22$

$2(3)^2 + 20(3) = 78$

$2(5.1)^2 + 20(5.1) = 154.02$

$2(10)^2 + 20(10) = 400$

x	1	3	5.1	10
$2x^2 + 20x$	22	78	154.02	400

66. $7a^2 - 4a^2 - a^2 = (7 - 4 - 1)a^2$

$\qquad\qquad = 2a^2$

67. $9y + y - 14y = (9 + 1 - 14)y$

$\qquad\qquad = -4y$

68. $6a^2 - 4a + 9a^2 = (6 + 9)a^2 + 4a$

$\qquad\qquad = 15a^2 + 4a$

69. $21x^2 + 3x + x^2 + 6$

$= (21 + 1)x^2 + 3x + 6$

$= 22x^2 + 3x + 6$

70. $4a^2b - 3b^2 - 8q^2 - 10a^2b + 7q^2$

$= (4a^2b - 10a^2b) - 3b^2 + (-8q^2 + 7q^2)$

$= -6a^2b - 3b^2 - q^2$

71. $2s^{14} + 3s^{13} + 12s^{12} - s^{10}$

Cannot be combined.

72. $(3x^2 + 2x + 6) + (5x^2 + x)$

$= 3x^2 + 2x + 6 + 5x^2 + x$

$= 8x^2 + 3x + 6$

73. $(2x^5 + 3x^4 + 4x^3 + 5x^2) + (4x^2 + 7x + 6)$

$= 2x^5 + 3x^4 + 4x^3 + 5x^2 + 4x^2 + 7x + 6$

$= 2x^5 + 3x^4 + 4x^3 + 9x^2 + 7x + 6$

74. $(-5y^2 + 3) - (2y^2 + 4)$

$= -5y^2 + 3 - 2y^2 - 4$

$= -7y^2 - 1$

75. $(2m^7 + 3x^4 + 7m^6) - (8m^7 + 4m^2 + 6x^4)$

$= 2m^7 + 3x^4 + 7m^6 - 8m^7 - 4m^2 - 6x^4$

$= -6m^7 - 3x^4 + 7m^6 - 4m^2$

76. $(3x^2 - 7xy + 7y^2) - (4x^2 - xy + 9y^2)$

$= 3x^2 - 7xy + 7y^2 - 4x^2 + xy - 9y^2$

$= -x^2 - 6xy - 2y^2$

77. $(-9x^2 + 6x + 2) + (4x^2 - x - 1)$

$= -9x^2 + 6x + 2 + 4x^2 - x - 1$

$= -5x^2 + 5x + 1$

78. $\left[(x^2 + 7x + 9) + (x^2 + 4)\right] - (4x^2 + 8x - 7)$

$= x^2 + 7x + 9 + x^2 + 4 - 4x^2 - 8x + 7$

$= -2x^2 - x + 20$

79. $6(x + 5) = 6x + 6(5)$

$\qquad\qquad = 6x + 30$

80. $9(x - 7) = 9x - 9(7)$

$\qquad\qquad = 9x - 63$

81. $4(2a + 7) = 4(2a) + 4(7)$

$\qquad\qquad = 8a + 28$

82. $9(6a-3) = 9(6a) - 9(3)$
$$= 54a - 27$$

83. $-7x(x^2+5) = -7(x^2) - 7x(5)$
$$= -7x^3 - 35x$$

84. $-8y(4y^2-6) = -8y(4y^2) - 8y(-6)$
$$= -32y^3 + 48y$$

85. $-2(x^3 - 9x^2 + x) = -2(x^3) - 2(-9x^2) - 2(x)$
$$= -2x^3 + 18x^2 - 2x$$

86. $-3a(a^2b + ab + b^2)$
$$= -3a(a^2b) - 3a(ab) - 3a(b^2)$$
$$= -3a^3b - 3a^2b - 3ab^2$$

87. $(3a^3 - 4a + 1)(-2a)$
$$= 3a^3(-2a) - 4a(-2a) + 1(-2a)$$
$$= -6a^4 + 8a^2 - 2a$$

88. $(6b^3 - 4b + 2)(7b)$
$$= 6b^3(7b) - 4b(7b) + 2(7b)$$
$$= 42b^4 - 28b^2 + 14b$$

89. $(2x+2)(x-7)$
$$= 2x(x) + 2x(-7) + 2(x) + 2(-7)$$
$$= 2x^2 - 12x - 14$$

90. $(2x-5)(3x+2)$
$$= 2x(3x) + 2x(2) - 5(3x) - 5(2)$$
$$= 6x^2 + 4x - 15x - 10$$
$$= 6x^2 - 11x - 10$$

91. $(4a-1)(a+7) = 4a^2 + 28a - a - 7$
$$= 4a^2 + 27a - 7$$

92. $(6a-1)(7a+3) = 42a^2 + 18a - 7a - 3$
$$= 42a^2 + 11a - 3$$

93. $(x+7)(x^3 + 4x - 5)$
$$= x^4 + 4x^2 - 5x + 7x^3 + 28x - 35$$
$$= x^4 + 7x^3 + 4x^2 + 23x - 35$$

94. $(x+2)(x^5 + x + 1)$
$$= x^6 + x^2 + x + 2x^5 + 2x + 2$$
$$= x^6 + 2x^5 + x^2 + 3x + 2$$

95. $(x^2 + 2x + 4)(x^2 + 2x - 4)$
$$= x^4 + 2x^3 - 4x^2 + 2x^3 + 4x^2 - 8x$$
$$+ 4x^2 + 8x - 16$$
$$= x^4 + 4x^3 + 4x^2 - 16$$

96. $(x^3 + 4x + 4)(x^3 + 4x - 4)$
$$= x^6 + 4x^4 - 4x^3 + 4x^4 + 16x^2 - 16x$$
$$+ 4x^3 + 16x - 16$$
$$= x^6 + 8x^4 + 16x^2 - 16$$

97. $(x+7)^3$
$$= (x+7)(x+7)(x+7)$$
$$= (x^2 + 7x + 7x + 49)(x+7)$$
$$= (x^2 + 14x + 49)(x+7)$$
$$= x^3 + 7x^2 + 14x^2 + 98x + 49x + 343$$
$$= x^3 + 21x^2 + 147x + 343$$

98. $(2x-5)^3$

$\quad = (2x-5)(2x-5)(2x-5)$

$\quad = (4x^2-10x-10x+25)(2x-5)$

$\quad = (4x^2-20x+25)(2x-5)$

$\quad = 8x^3-20x^2-40x^2+100x+50x-125$

$\quad = 8x^3-60x^2+150x-125$

99. $(x+7)^2 = x^2+2(x)(7)+7^2$

$\quad\quad = x^2+14x+49$

100. $(x-5)^2 = x^2-2(x)(5)+5^2$

$\quad\quad = x^2-10x+25$

101. $(3x-7)^2 = (3x)^2-2(3x)(7)+7^2$

$\quad\quad = 9x^2-42x+49$

102. $(4x+2)^2 = (4x)^2+2(4x)(2)+2^2$

$\quad\quad = 16x^2+16x+4$

103. $(5x-9)^2 = (5x)^2-2(5x)(9)+9^2$

$\quad\quad = 25x^2-90x+81$

104. $(5x+1)(5x-1) = (5x)^2-1^2$

$\quad\quad = 25x^2-1$

105. $(7x+4)(7x-4) = (7x)^2-4^2$

$\quad\quad = 49x^2-16$

106. $(a+2b)(a-2b) = a^2-(2b)^2$

$\quad\quad = a^2-4b^2$

107. $(2x-6)(2x+6) = (2x)^2-6^2$

$\quad\quad = 4x^2-36$

108. $(4a^2-2b)(4a^2+2b) = (4a^2)^2-(2b)^2$

$\quad\quad = 16a^4-4b^2$

109. $(3x-1)(3x-1) = 9x^2-2(3x)+1$

$\quad\quad = (9x^2-6x+1)$ sq m

110. $(5x+2)(x-1) = 5x^2-5x+2x-2$

$\quad\quad = (5x^2-3x-2)$ sq mi

111. $\dfrac{x^2+21x+49}{7x^2} = \dfrac{x^2}{7x^2}+\dfrac{21x}{7x^2}+\dfrac{49}{7x^2}$

$\quad\quad = \dfrac{1}{7}+\dfrac{3}{x}+\dfrac{7}{x^2}$

112. $\dfrac{5a^3-15ab^2+20ab}{-5ab}$

$\quad = \dfrac{5a^3b}{-5ab}-\dfrac{15ab^2}{-5ab}+\dfrac{20ab}{-5ab}$

$\quad = -a^2+3b-4$

113.
$$
\begin{array}{r}
a+1 \\
a-2\overline{\smash{)}a^2-a+4} \\
\underline{a^2-2a} \\
a+4 \\
\underline{a-2} \\
6
\end{array}
$$

$\quad (a^2-a+4)\div(a-2) = a+1+\dfrac{6}{a-2}$

114.
$$
\begin{array}{r}
4x \\
x+5\overline{\smash{)}4x^2+20x+7} \\
\underline{4x^2+20x} \\
7
\end{array}
$$

$\quad (4x^2+20x+7)\div(x+5) = 4x+\dfrac{7}{x+5}$

115.
$$\require{enclose}
\begin{array}{r}
a^2 + 3a + 8 \\
a - 2 \enclose{longdiv}{a^3 + a^2 + 2a + 6} \\
\underline{a^3 - 2a^2} \\
3a^2 + 2a \\
\underline{3a^2 - 6a} \\
8a + 6 \\
\underline{8a - 16} \\
22
\end{array}$$

$$\frac{a^3 + a^2 + 2a + 6}{a - 2} = a^2 + 3a + 8 + \frac{22}{a - 2}$$

116.
$$\begin{array}{r}
3b^2 - 4b \\
3b - 2 \enclose{longdiv}{9b^3 - 18b^2 + 8b - 1} \\
\underline{9b^3 - 6b^2} \\
-12b^2 + 8b \\
\underline{-12b^2 + 8b} \\
-1
\end{array}$$

$$\frac{9b^3 - 18b^2 + 8b - 1}{3b - 2} = 3b^2 - 4b - \frac{1}{3b - 2}$$

117.
$$\begin{array}{r}
2x^3 - x^2 + 2 \\
2x - 1 \enclose{longdiv}{4x^4 - 4x^3 + x^2 + 4x - 3} \\
\underline{4x^4 - 2x^3} \\
-2x^3 + x^2 \\
\underline{-2x^2 + x^2} \\
4x - 3 \\
\underline{4x - 2} \\
-1
\end{array}$$

$$\frac{4x^4 - 4x^3 + x^2 + 4x - 3}{2x - 1}$$
$$= 2x^3 - x^2 + 2 - \frac{1}{2x - 1}$$

118.
$$\begin{array}{r}
-x^2 - 16x - 117 \\
x - 6 \enclose{longdiv}{-4x^3 - 10x^2 - 21x + 18} \\
\underline{-x^3 + 10x^2} \\
-16x^2 - 21x \\
\underline{-16x^2 + 96x} \\
-117x + 18 \\
\underline{-117x + 702} \\
-684
\end{array}$$

$$\frac{-10x^2 - x^3 - 21x + 18}{x - 6}$$
$$= -x^2 - 16x - 117 - \frac{684}{x - 6}$$

119. Width $= \dfrac{15x^3 - 3x^2 + 60}{3x^2}$

$$= \left(5x - 1 + \frac{20}{x^2}\right) \text{ ft}$$

120. Length $= \dfrac{21a^3b^6 + 3a - 3}{3}$

$$= \left(7a^2b^2 + a - 1\right) \text{ units}$$

Chapter 3 Test

1. $2^5 = 2 \cdot 2 \cdot 2 \cdot 2 \cdot 2 = 32$

2. $(-3)^4 = (-3)(-3)(-3)(-3) = 81$

3. $-3^4 = -3 \cdot 3 \cdot 3 \cdot 3 = -81$

4. $4^{-3} = \dfrac{1}{4^3} = \dfrac{1}{64}$

5. $(3x^2)(-5x^9) = (3)(-5)(x^2 \cdot x^9)$
$$= -15x^{11}$$

6. $\dfrac{y^7}{y^2} = y^{7-2} = y^5$

7. $\dfrac{r^{-8}}{r^{-3}} = r^{-8-(-3)} = r^{-5} = \dfrac{1}{r^5}$

8. $\left(\dfrac{x^2 y^3}{x^3 y^{-4}}\right)^2 = \dfrac{x^4 y^6}{x^6 y^{-8}}$

$\qquad = x^{4-6} y^{6-(-8)}$

$\qquad = x^{-2} y^{14}$

$\qquad = \dfrac{y^{14}}{x^2}$

9. $\left(\dfrac{6^2 x^{-4} y^{-1}}{6^3 x^{-3} y^7}\right) = 6^{2-3} x^{-4-(-3)} y^{-1-7}$

$\qquad = 6^{2-3} x^{-4-(-3)} y^{-1-7}$

$\qquad = 6^{-1} x^{-1} y^{-8}$

$\qquad = \dfrac{1}{6xy^8}$

10. $563,000 = 5.63 \times 10^5$

11. $0.0000863 = 8.63 \times 10^{-5}$

12. $1.5 \times 10^{-3} = 0.0015$

13. $6.23 \times 10^4 = 62,300$

14. $\left(1.2 \times 10^5\right)\left(3 \times 10^{-7}\right)$

$\qquad = (1.2)(3) \times 10^{5-7}$

$\qquad = 3.6 \times 10^{-2}$

$\qquad = 0.036$

15. The degree is 5 because $9x^3 yz$ or $9x^3 y^1 z^1$ is the term with the highest degree.

16. $5x^2 + 4x - 7x^2 + 11 + 8x$

$\qquad = \left(5x^2 - 7x^2\right) + (4x + 8x) + 11$

$\qquad = -2x^2 + 12x + 11$

17. $\left(8x^3 + 7x^2 + 4x - 7\right) + \left(8x^3 - 7x - 6\right)$

$\qquad = 8x^3 + 7x^2 + 4x - 7 + 8x^3 - 7x - 6$

$\qquad = 16x^3 + 7x^2 - 3x - 13$

18.
$$\begin{array}{r} 5x^3 + x^2 + 5x - 2 \\ -\left(8x^3 - 4x^2 + x - 7\right) \\ \hline \end{array}$$

$$\begin{array}{r} 5x^3 + x^2 + 5x - 2 \\ -8x^3 + 4x^2 - x + 7 \\ \hline -3x^3 + 5x^2 + 4x + 5 \end{array}$$

19. $\left[\left(8x^2 + 7x + 5\right) + \left(x^3 - 8\right)\right] - (4x + 2)$

$\qquad = 8x^2 + 7x + 5 + x^3 - 8 - 4x - 2$

$\qquad = x^3 + 8x^2 + 3x - 5$

20. $(3x + 7)\left(x^2 + 5x + 2\right)$

$\qquad = 3x^3 + 15x^2 + 6x + 7x^2 + 35x + 14$

$\qquad = 3x^3 + 22x^2 + 41x + 14$

21.
$$\begin{array}{r} x^3 - x^2 + x + 1 \\ 2x^2 - 3x + 7 \\ \hline 7x^3 - 7x^2 + 7x + 7 \\ -3x^4 + 3x^3 - 3x^2 - 3x \\ 2x^5 - 2x^4 + 2x^3 + 2x^2 \\ \hline 2x^5 - 5x^4 + 12x^3 - 8x^2 + 4x + 7 \end{array}$$

22. $(x + 7)(3x - 5) = 3x^2 - 5x + 21x - 35$

$\qquad\qquad\qquad\qquad = 3x^2 + 16x - 35$

23. $(3x-7)(3x+7) = (3x)^2 - 7^2$

$\qquad = 9x^2 - 49$

24. $(4x-2)^2 = (4x)^2 - 2(4x)(2) + 2^2$

$\qquad = 16x^2 - 16x + 4$

25. $(8x+3)^2 = (8x)^2 + 2(8x)(3) + 3^2$

$\qquad = 64x^2 + 48x + 9$

26. $(x^2 - 9b)(x^2 + 9b) = (x^2)^2 - (9b)^2$

$\qquad = x^4 - 81b^2$

27. $-16t^2 + 1516$

$t = 0: \ 16(0)^2 + 1516 = 1516 \text{ ft}$

$t = 3: \ -16(3)^2 + 1516 = 1372 \text{ ft}$

$t = 6: \ -16(6)^2 + 1516 = 940 \text{ ft}$

$t = 9: \ -16(9)^2 + 1516 = 220 \text{ ft}$

28. $A = lw$

$\qquad = (2x+3)(2x-3)$

$\qquad = (4x^2 - 9) \text{ sq in.}$

29. $\dfrac{4x^2 + 2xy - 7x}{8xy} = \dfrac{4x^2}{8xy} + \dfrac{2xy}{8xy} - \dfrac{7x}{8xy}$

$\qquad = \dfrac{x}{2y} + \dfrac{1}{4} - \dfrac{7}{8y}$

30.

$$x+5 \overline{)\, x^2 + 7x + 10} \quad \begin{array}{r} x+2 \end{array}$$

$\qquad \dfrac{x^2 + 5x}{}$

$\qquad\qquad 2x + 10$

$\qquad\qquad \dfrac{2x + 10}{}$

$\qquad\qquad\qquad 0$

$\dfrac{x^2 + 7x + 10}{x + 5} = x + 2$

31.

$$3x+2 \overline{)\, 27x^3 + 0x^2 + 0x - 8} \quad \begin{array}{r} 9x^2 - 6x + 4 \end{array}$$

$\qquad \dfrac{27x^3 + 18x^2}{}$

$\qquad\qquad -18x^2 + 0x$

$\qquad\qquad \dfrac{-18x^2 - 12x}{}$

$\qquad\qquad\qquad 12x - 8$

$\qquad\qquad\qquad \dfrac{12x + 8}{}$

$\qquad\qquad\qquad\qquad -16$

$\dfrac{27x^3 - 8}{3x + 2} = 9x^2 - 6x + 4 - \dfrac{16}{3x + 2}$

Cumulative Review Chapter 3

1. a. The natural numbers are 11 and 112.

b. The whole numbers are 0, 11, and 112.

c. The integers are $-3, -2, 0, 11,$ and 112.

d. The rational numbers are $-3, -2, 0, \dfrac{1}{4},$

11 and 112.

e. The irrational number is $\sqrt{2}$.

f. The real numbers are all the numbers in the given set.

2. a. $3^2 = 3 \cdot 3 = 9$

b. $5^3 = 5 \cdot 5 \cdot 5 = 125$

c. $2^4 = 2 \cdot 2 \cdot 2 \cdot 2 = 16$

d. $7^1 = 7$

e. $\left(\dfrac{3}{7}\right)^2 = \left(\dfrac{3}{7}\right)\left(\dfrac{3}{7}\right) = \dfrac{9}{49}$

3. $\dfrac{3}{2} \cdot \dfrac{1}{2} - \dfrac{1}{2} = \dfrac{3 \cdot 1}{2 \cdot 2} - \dfrac{1}{2} = \dfrac{3}{4} - \dfrac{1}{2}$

$= \dfrac{3}{4} - \dfrac{1 \cdot 2}{2 \cdot 2} = \dfrac{3}{4} - \dfrac{2}{4} = \dfrac{3-2}{4} = \dfrac{1}{4}$

4. a. $x + 3$

    b. $3x$

    c. $2x$

    d. $10 - x$

    e. $5x + 7$

5. $11.4 + (-4.7) = 6.7$

6. a. $\dfrac{x-y}{12+x} = \dfrac{2-(-5)}{12+2} = \dfrac{2+5}{12+2}$

      $= \dfrac{7}{14} = \dfrac{7}{2 \cdot 7} = \dfrac{1}{2}$

    b. $x^2 - y = 2^2 - (-5) = 4 - (-5)$

      $= 4 + 5 = 9$

7. $\dfrac{-30}{10} = \dfrac{-3 \cdot 2 \cdot 5}{-2 \cdot 5} = 3$

8. $\dfrac{42}{= 0.6} = -70$

9. $5(x+2) = 5(x) + 5(2) = 5x + 10$

10. $-2(y + 0.3z - 1)$

    $= -2(y) + (-2)(0.3z) - (-2)(1)$

    $= -2y - 0.6z + 2$

11. $-(x + y - 2z + 6) = -1(x + y - 2z + 6)$

    $= -1(x) + (-1)(y) - (-1)(2z) + (-1)(6)$

    $= -x - y + 2z - 6$

12. $6(2a - 1) - (11a + 6) = 7$

    $12a - 6 - 11a - 6 = 7$

    $12a - 11a - 6 - 6 = 7$

    $a - 12 = 7$

    $a - 12 + 12 = 7 + 12$

    $a = 19$

13. $\dfrac{y}{7} = 20$

      $7\left(\dfrac{y}{7}\right) = 7(20)$

         $y = 140$

14. $0.25x + 0.10(x - 3) = 0.05(22)$

   $100\left[0.25x + 0.10(x - 3)\right] = 100\left[0.05(22)\right]$

       $25x + 10(x - 3) = 5(22)$

        $25x + 10x - 30 = 110$

           $35x - 30 = 110$

      $35x - 30 + 30 = 110 + 30$

              $35x = 140$

           $\dfrac{35x}{35} = \dfrac{140}{35}$

               $x = 4$

15. Let x = the unknown number

    $2(x + 4) = 4x - 12$

    $2x + 8 = 4x - 12$

    $2x + 8 - 2x = 4x - 12 = 2x$

    $8 = 2x - 12$

    $8 + 12 = 2x - 12 + 12$

    $20 = 2x$

    $\dfrac{20}{2} = \dfrac{2x}{2}$

    $10 = x$

The number is 10.

16. The perimeter of a rectangle is given by the formula $P = 2l + 2w$. Let l = the length of the garden. $P = 2l + 2w$

$140 = 2l + 2w$

$140 = 2l + 2(30)$

$140 = 2l + 60$

$140 - 60 = 2l + 60 - 60$

$80 = 2l$

$\dfrac{80}{2} = \dfrac{2l}{2}$

$40 = l$

The length of the garden is 40 feet.

17. Let x = the unknown number.

$120 = (0.15)(x)$

$\dfrac{120}{0.15} = \dfrac{0.15x}{0.15}$

$800 = x$

18. $-4x + 7 \geq -9$

$-4x + 7 - 7 \geq -9 - 7$

$-4x \geq -16$

$\dfrac{-4x}{-4} \leq \dfrac{-16}{-4}$

$x \leq 4$

$\{x \mid x \leq 4\}$

19. a. $x^7 \cdot x^4 = x^{7+4} = x^{11}$

b. $\left(\dfrac{1}{2}\right)^4 = \dfrac{1^4}{2^4} = \dfrac{1}{16}$

c. $\left(9y^5\right)^2 = 9^2\left(y^5\right)^2 = 81y^{10}$

20. $\left(\dfrac{3a^2}{b}\right)^{-3} = \dfrac{3^{-3}a^{-6}}{b^{-3}} = \dfrac{b^3}{3^3 a^6} = \dfrac{b^3}{27a^6}$

21. $\left(5y^3\right)^{-2} = 5^{-2}\left(y^3\right)^{-2} = 5^{-2}y^{-6}$

$= \dfrac{1}{5^2 y^6} = \dfrac{1}{25y^6}$

22. $9x^3 + x^3 = 9x^3 + 1x^3 = 10x^3$

23. $5x^2 + 6x - 9x = 5x^2 - 3x - 3$

24. $7x\left(x^2 + 2x + 5\right) = 7x\left(x^2\right) + 7x\left(2x\right) + 7x\left(5\right)$

$= 7x^3 + 14x^2 + 35x$

25. $\dfrac{9x^5 - 12x^2 + 3x}{3x^2} = \dfrac{9x^5}{3x^2} - \dfrac{12x^2}{3x^2} + \dfrac{3x}{3x^2}$

$= 3x^3 - 4 + \dfrac{1}{x}$

Chapter 4

1. $2x^3y - 6x^2y^2 = 2x^2y(x - 3y)$

2. $xy + 6x - 4y - 24 = (xy + 6x) + (-4y - 24)$
$= x(y + 6) - 4(y + 6) = (y + 6)(x - 4)$

3. $a^2 + 8a + 12 = (a + 6)(a + 2)$

4. $m^2 + 4m - 3$ is a prime polynomial.

5. $3x^3 - 18x^2 + 15x = 3x(x^2 - 6x + 5)$
$= 3x(x - 5)(x - 1)$

6. $2x^2 + 5x - 12 = (2x - 3)(x + 4)$

7. $14x^2 + 63x + 70 = 7(2x^2 + 9x + 10)$
$= 7(2x + 5)(x + 2)$

8. $24b^2 - 25b + 6 = 24b^2 - 16b - 9b + 6$
$= 8b(3b - 2) - 3(3b - 2) = (3b - 2)(8b - 3)$

9. $15y^2 + 38y + 7 = 15y^2 + 35y + 3y + 7$
$= 5y(3y + 7) + 1(3y + 7) = (3y + 7)(5y + 1)$

10. $x^2 + 24x + 144 = (x^2) + 2(x)(12) + (12)^2$
$= (x + 12)(x + 12) = (x + 12)^2$

11. $4x^2 - 12xy + 9y^2$
$= (2x)^2 - 2(2x)(3y) + (3y)^2$
$= (2x - 3y)(2x - 3y) = (2x - 3y)^2$

12. $a^2 - 49b^2 = a^2 - (7b)^2 = (a + 7b)(a - 7b)$

13. $1 - 64t^2 = 1^2 - (8t)^2 = (1 + 8t)(1 - 8t)$

14. $25b^2 + 4$ is a prime polynomial.

15. $x^2 + 18x + 81$ is a perfect square trinomial.

16. $(x - 12)(x + 5) = 0$
$x - 12 = 0$ or $x + 5 = 0$
$x = 12$ $x = -5$
The solutions are 12 and -5.

17. $y^2 - 13y = 0$
$y(y - 13) = 0$
$y = 0$ or $y - 13 = 0$
                        $y = 13$
The solutions are 0 and 13.

18. $2m^3 - 2m^2 - 24m = 0$
$2m(m^2 - m - 12) = 0$
$2m(m - 4)(m + 3) = 0$

$2m = 0$ or $m - 4 = 0$ or $m + 3 = 0$
$m = 0$ $m = 4$ $m = -3$
The solutoins are 0, 4, and -3.

19. Let x = the width. Then $x + 7$ = the length.

$A = lw$

$120 = (x + 7)(x)$

$120 = x^2 + 7x$

$0 = x^2 + 7x - 120$

$0 = (x + 15)(x - 8)$

$x + 15 = 0$ or $x - 8 = 0$

     $x = -15$ $x = 8$

Since the width cannot be negative, we discard the result -15. The width is 8 inches and the length is $8 + 7 = 15$ inches.

20. Let x = the number

$x + x^2 = 240$

$x^2 + x - 240 = 0$

$(x + 16)(x - 15) = 0$

$x + 16 = 0$ or $x - 15 = 0$

     $x = -16$ $x = 15$

The number is -16 or 15.

Practice Problems 4.1

1. a. $6x^2 = 2 \cdot 3 \cdot x^2$

     $9x^4 = 3 \cdot 3 \cdot x^4$

     $-12x^5 = -2 \cdot 2 \cdot 3 \cdot x^5$

     GCF $= 3 \cdot x^2 = 3x^2$

   b. $-16y = -2 \cdot 2 \cdot 2 \cdot 2 \cdot y$

     $-20y^6 = -2 \cdot 2 \cdot 5 \cdot y^6$

     $40y^4 = 2 \cdot 2 \cdot 2 \cdot 5 \cdot y^4$

     GCF $= 2 \cdot 2 \cdot y = 4y$

   c. The GCF of a^5, a and a^3 is a.

     The GCF of b^4, b^3 and b^2 is b^2.

     The GCF of a^5b^4, ab^3, and a^3b^2 is ab^2.

2. a. $10y + 25 = 5(2y + 5)$

   b. $x^4 - x^9 = x^4(1 - x^5)$

3. $-10x^3 + 8x^2 - 2x = -2x(5x^2 - 4x + 1)$

4. $4x^3 + 12x = 4x(x^2 + 3)$

5. $\dfrac{2}{5}a^5 - \dfrac{4}{5}a^3 + \dfrac{1}{5}a^2 = \dfrac{1}{5}a^2(2a^3 - 4a + 1)$

6. $6a^3b + 3a^3b^2 + 9a^2b^4$

   $= 3a^2b(2a + ab + 3b^3)$

7. $7(p + 2) + q(p + 2) = (p + 2)(7 + q)$

8. $ab + 7a + 2b + 14 = a(b + 7) + 2(b + 7)$

   $= (b + 7)(a + 2)$

9. $28x^3 - 7x^2 + 12x - 3$

   $= 7x^2(4x - 1) + 3(4x - 1)$

   $= (4x - 1)(7x^2 + 3)$

10. $2xy + 5y^2 - 4x - 10y$

   $= y(2x + 5y) - 2(2x + 5y)$

   $= (2x + 5y)(y - 2)$

11. $4x^3 + x - 20x^2 - 5$

   $= x(4x^2 + 1) - 5(4x^2 + 1)$

   $= (4x^2 + 1)(x - 5)$

12. $2x - 2 + x^3 - 3x^2 = 2(x - 1) + x^2(x - 3)$

The polynomial is not factorable by grouping.

13. $3xy - 4 + x - 12y = 3xy + x - 4 - 12y$

       $= x(3y + 1) - 4(1 + 3y)$

       $= (3y + 1)(x - 4)$

Mental Math 4.1

1. $2 = 2$

    $16 = 2 \cdot 2 \cdot 2 \cdot 2$

    $GCF = 2$

2. $3 = 3$

    $18 = 2 \cdot 3 \cdot 3$

    $GCF = 3$

3. $6 = 2 \cdot 3$

    $15 = 3 \cdot 5$

    $GCF = 3$

4. $20 = 2 \cdot 2 \cdot 5$

    $15 = 3 \cdot 5$

    $GCF = 5$

5. $14 = 2 \cdot 7$

    $35 = 5 \cdot 7$

    $GCF = 7$

6. $27 = 3 \cdot 3 \cdot 3$

    $36 = 2 \cdot 2 \cdot 3 \cdot 3$

    $GCF = 3 \cdot 3 = 9$

Exercise Set 4.1

1. y^2

3. xy^2

5. $8x = 2 \cdot 2 \cdot 2 \cdot x$

    $4 = 2 \cdot 2$

    $GCF = 2 \cdot 2 = 4$

7. $12y^4 = 2 \cdot 2 \cdot 3 \cdot y^4$

    $20y^3 = 2 \cdot 2 \cdot 5 \cdot y^3$

    $GCF = 2 \cdot 2 \cdot y^3 = 4y^3$

9. $-10x^2 = -2 \cdot 5 \cdot x^2$

    $15x^3 = 3 \cdot 5 \cdot x^3$

    $GCF = 5 \cdot x^2 = 5x^2$

11. $12x^3 = 2 \cdot 2 \cdot 3 \cdot x^3$

    $-6x^4 = -2 \cdot 3 \cdot x^4$

    $3x^5 = 3 \cdot x^5$

    $GCF = 3 \cdot x^3 = 3x^3$

13. $-18x^2y = -2 \cdot 3 \cdot 3 \cdot x^2 \cdot y$

     $9x^3y^3 = 3 \cdot 3 \cdot x^3 \cdot y^3$

     $36x^3y = 2 \cdot 2 \cdot 3 \cdot 3 \cdot x^3 \cdot y$

     $GCF = 3 \cdot 3 \cdot x^2 \cdot y = 9x^2y$

15. $3a + 6 = 3(a + 2)$

17. $30x - 15 = 15(2x - 1)$

19. $x^3 + 5x^2 = x^2(x + 5)$

21. $6y^4 - 2y = 2y(3y^3 - 1)$

23. $32xy - 18x^2 = 2x(16y - 9x)$

25. $4x - 8y + 4 = 4(x - 2y + 1)$

27. $6x^3 - 9x^2 + 12x = 3x\left(2x^2 - 3x + 4\right)$

29. $a^7b^6 - a^3b^2 + a^2b^5 - a^2b^2$
$= a^2b^2\left(a^5b^4 - a + b^3 - 1\right)$

31. $5x^3y - 15x^2y + 10xy = 5xy\left(x^2 - 3x + 2\right)$

33. $8x^5 + 16x^4 - 20x^3 + 12$
$= 4\left(2x^5 + 4x^4 - 5x^3 + 3\right)$

35. $\dfrac{1}{3}x^4 + \dfrac{2}{3}x^3 - \dfrac{4}{3}x^5 + \dfrac{1}{3}x$
$= \dfrac{1}{3}x\left(x^3 + 2x^2 - 4x^4 + 1\right)$

37. $y\left(x+2\right) + 3\left(x+2\right) = \left(x+2\right)\left(y+3\right)$

39. $8\left(x+2\right) - y\left(x+2\right) = \left(x+2\right)\left(8-y\right)$

41. Answers may vary.

43. $x^3 + 2x^2 + 5x + 10 = x^2\left(x+2\right) + 5\left(x+2\right)$
$= \left(x^2 + 5\right)\left(x+2\right)$

45. $5x + 15 + xy + 3y = 5\left(x+3\right) + y\left(x+3\right)$
$= \left(x+3\right)\left(5+y\right)$

47. $6x^3 - 4x^2 + 15x - 10$
$= 2x^2\left(3x-2\right) + 5\left(3x-2\right)$
$= \left(2x^2 + 5\right)\left(3x-2\right)$

49. $2y - 8 + xy - 4x = 2\left(y-4\right) + x\left(y-4\right)$
$= \left(y-4\right)\left(2+x\right)$

51. $2x^3 + x^2 + 8x + 4 = x^2\left(2x+1\right) + 4\left(2x+1\right)$
$= \left(2x+1\right)\left(x^2 + 4\right)$

53. $4x^2 - 8xy - 3x + 6y$
$= 4x\left(x-2y\right) - 3\left(x-2y\right)$
$= \left(x-2y\right)\left(4x-3\right)$

55. Answers may vary

57. $\left(x+2\right)\left(x+5\right) = x^2 + 2x + 5x + 10$
$= x^2 + 7x + 10$

59. $\left(b+1\right)\left(b-4\right) = b^2 + b - 4b - 4$
$= b^2 - 3b - 4$

61. The two numbers are 2 and 6.
$2 \cdot 6 = 12;\ 2 + 6 = 8$

63. The two numbers are -1 and -8.
$-1 \cdot \left(-8\right) = 8;\ -1 + \left(-8\right) = -9$

65. The two numbers are -2 and 5.
$-2 \cdot 5 = -10;\ -2 + 5 = 3$

67. The two numbers are -8 and 3.
$-8 \cdot 3 = -24;\ -8 + 3 = -5$

69. $12x^2y - 42x^2 - 4y + 14$
$= 2\left(6x^2y - 21x^2 - 2y + 7\right)$
$= 2\left(3x^2\left(2y-7\right) - 1\left(2y-7\right)\right)$
$= 2\left(3x^2 - 1\right)\left(2y-7\right)$

71. Subtract the area of the innter rectangle from the area of the outer rectangle.

Outer rectangle: $A = l \cdot w$

$$A = 12x \cdot x^2 = 12x^3$$

Inner rectangle: $A = l \cdot w$

$$A = 2 \cdot x = 2x$$

The area of the shaded region is given by the expression $12x^3 - 2x = 2x\left(6x^2 - 1\right)$.

73. Let l = length of the rectangle.

$$A = l \cdot w$$

$$4n^4 - 24n = 4n \cdot l$$

$$4n\left(n^3 - 6\right) = 4n \cdot l$$

$$\frac{4n\left(n^3 - 6\right)}{4n} = \frac{4n \cdot l}{4n}$$

$$n^3 - 6 = l$$

The length is $\left(n^3 - 6\right)$ units.

75. a. When $x = 0$

$$-8x^2 + 60x + 2000$$

$$= 8(0)^2 + 60(0) + 2000$$

$$= 2000 \text{ billion kilowatt hours}$$

   b. When $x = 2$

$$-8x^2 + 60x + 2000$$

$$= -8(2)^2 + 60(2) + 2000$$

$$= 2088 \text{ billion kilowatt hours}$$

   c. $-8x^2 + 60x + 2000$

$$= -4\left(2x^2 - 15x - 500\right)$$

Practice Problems 4.2

1. $x^2 + 9x + 20 = (x + 4)(x + 5)$

2. a. $x^2 - 13x + 22 = (x - 11)(x - 2)$

   b. $x^2 - 27x + 50 = (x - 25)(x - 2)$

3. $x^2 + 5x - 36 = (x + 9)(x - 4)$

4. a. $q^2 - 3q - 40 = (q - 8)(q + 5)$

   b. $y^2 + 2y - 48 = (y + 8)(y - 6)$

5. $x^2 + 6x + 15$ is a prime polynomial.

6. a. $x^2 + 6xy + 8y^2 = (x + 4y)(x + 2y)$

   b. $a^2 - 13ab + 30b^2 = (a - 10b)(a - 3b)$

7. $x^4 + 9x^2 + 12 = \left(x^2 + 6\right)\left(x^2 + 2\right)$

8. a. $x^3 + 3x^2 - 4x = x\left(x^2 + 3x - 4\right)$

$$= x(x + 4)(x - 1)$$

   b. $4x^2 - 24x + 36 = 4\left(x^2 - 6x + 9\right)$

$$= 4(x - 3)(x - 3)$$

9. $5x^5 - 25x^4 - 30x^3 = 5x^3\left(x^2 - 5x - 6\right)$

$$= 5x^3(x - 6)(x + 1)$$

Mental Math 4.2

1. $x^2 + 9x + 20 = (x + 4)(x + 5)$

2. $x^2 + 12x + 35 = (x + 5)(x + 7)$

3. $x^2 - 7x + 12 = (x - 4)(x - 3)$

4. $x^2 - 13x + 22 = (x - 2)(x - 11)$

5. $x^2 + 4x + 4 = (x + 2)(x + 2)$

6. $x^2 + 10x + 24 = (x + 6)(x + 4)$

Exercise Set 4.2

1. $x^2 + 7x + 6 = (x + 6)(x + 1)$

3. $x^2 - 10x + 9 = (x - 9)(x - 1)$

5. $x^2 - 3x - 18 = (x - 6)(x + 3)$

7. $x^2 + 3x - 70 = (x + 10)(x - 7)$

9. $x^2 + 5x + 2$ is a prime polynomial.

11. $x^2 + 8xy + 15y^2 = (x + 5y)(x + 3y)$

13. $a^4 - 2a^2 - 15 = (a^2 - 5)(a^2 + 3)$

15. $(x - 3)(x + 8) = x^2 - 3x + 8x - 24$
$$= x^2 + 5x - 24$$

17. Answers may vary.

19. $2z^2 + 20z + 32 = (z^2 + 10z + 16)$
$$= 2(z + 8)(z + 2)$$

21. $2x^3 - 18x^2 + 40x = 2x(x^2 - 9x + 20)$
$$= 2x(x - 5)(x - 4)$$

23. $x^2 - 3xy - 4y^2 = (x - 4y)(x + y)$

25. $x^2 + 15x + 36 = (x + 12)(x + 3)$

27. $x^2 - x - 2 = (x - 2)(x + 1)$

29. $r^2 - 16r + 48 = (r - 12)(r - 4)$

31. $x^2 + xy - 2y^2 = (x + 2)(x - y)$

33. $3x^2 + 9x - 30 = 3(x^2 + 3x - 10)$
$$= 3(x + 5)(x - 2)$$

35. $3x^2 - 60x + 108 = 3(x^2 - 20x + 36)$
$$= 3(x - 18)(x - 2)$$

37. $x^2 - 18x - 144 = (x - 24)(x + 6)$

39. $r^2 - 3r + 6$ is a prime polynomial.

41. $x^2 - 8x + 15 = (x - 5)(x - 3)$

43. $6x^3 + 54x^2 + 120 = 6x(x^2 + 9x + 20)$
$$= 6x(x + 4)(x + 5)$$

45. $4x^2 y + 4xy - 12y = 4y(x^2 + x - 3)$

47. $x^2 - 4x - 21 = (x - 7)(x + 3)$

49. $x^2 + 7xy + 10y^2 = (x + 5y)(x + 2y)$

51. $64 + 24t + 2t^2 = 2t^2 + 24t + 64$
$$= 2(t^2 + 12t + 32)$$
$$= 2(t + 8)(t + 4)$$

53. $x^3 - 2x^2 - 24x = x(x^2 - 2x - 24)$
$$= x(x - 6)(x + 4)$$

55. $2t^5 - 14t^4 + 24t^3 = 2t^3\left(t^2 - 7t + 12\right)$
$$= 2t^3\left(t - 4\right)\left(t - 3\right)$$

57. $5x^3y - 25x^2y^2 - 120xy^3$
$$= 5xy\left(x^2 - 5xy - 24y^2\right)$$
$$= 5xy\left(x - 8y\right)\left(x + 3y\right)$$

59. $\left(2x + 1\right)\left(x + 5\right) = 2x^2 + x + 10x + 5$
$$= 2x^2 + 11x + 5$$

61. $\left(5y - 4\right)\left(3y - 1\right) = 15y^2 - 12y - 5y + 4$
$$= 15y^2 - 17y + 4$$

63. $\left(a + 3\right)\left(9a - 4\right) = 9a^2 + 27a - 4a - 12$
$$= 9a^2 + 23a - 12$$

65. $P = 2l + 2w$
$l = x^2 + 10x$ and $w = 4x + 33$, so
$P = 2\left(x^2 + 10x\right) + 2\left(4x + 33\right)$
$$= 2x^2 + 20x + 8x + 66$$
$$= 2x^2 + 28x + 66 = \left(x^2 + 14x + 33\right)$$
$$= 2\left(x + 11\right)\left(x + 3\right)$$

The perimeter of the rectangle is given by the polynomial $2x^2 + 28x + 66$ which factors as $2\left(x + 11\right)\left(x + 3\right)$.

67. $y^2\left(x + 1\right) - 2y\left(x + 1\right) - 15\left(x + 1\right)$
$$= \left(x + 1\right)\left(y^2 - 2y - 15\right)$$
$$= \left(x + 1\right)\left(y - 5\right)\left(y + 3\right)$$

69. $y^2 - 4y + c$ if factorable when c is 3 or 4.

71. $x^2 + bx + 15$ is factorable when b is 8 or 16.

73. $x^{2n} + 5x^n + 6 = \left(x^n + 2\right)\left(x^n + 3\right)$

Practice Problems 4.3

1. a. $4x^2 + 12x + 5 = \left(2x + 5\right)\left(2x + 1\right)$
     b. $5x^2 + 27x + 10 = \left(5x + 2\right)\left(x + 5\right)$

2. a. $6x^2 - 5x + 1 = \left(3x - 1\right)\left(2x - 1\right)$
     b. $2x^2 - 11x + 12 = \left(2x - 3\right)\left(x - 4\right)$

3. a. $35x^2 + 4x - 4 = \left(5x + 2\right)\left(7x - 2\right)$
     b. $4x^2 + 3x - 7 = \left(4x + 7\right)\left(x - 1\right)$

4. a. $14x^2 - 3xy - 2y^2 = \left(7x + 2y\right)\left(2x - y\right)$
     b. $12a^2 - 16ab - 3b^2 = \left(6a + b\right)\left(2a - 3b\right)$

5. a. $3x^3 + 17x^2 + 10x = \left(3x^2 + 17x + 10\right)$
$$= x\left(3x + 2\right)\left(x + 5\right)$$
     b. $6xy^2 + 33xy - 18x = 3x\left(2y^2 + 11y - 6\right)$
$$= 3x\left(2y - 1\right)\left(y + 6\right)$$

6. $-5x^2 - 19x + 4 = -1\left(5x^2 + 19x - 4\right)$
$$= -1\left(5x - 1\right)\left(x + 4\right)$$

Exercise Set 4.3

1. $5x^2 + 22x + 8 = \left(5x + 2\right)\left(x + 4\right)$

3. $50x^2 + 15x - 2 = \left(5x + 2\right)\left(10x - 1\right)$

5. $20x^2 - 7x - 6 = \left(5x + 2\right)\left(4x - 3\right)$

7. $2x^2 + 13x + 15 = \left(2x + 3\right)\left(x + 5\right)$

9. $8y^2 - 17y + 9 = (y-1)(8y-9)$

11. $2x^2 - 9x - 5 = (2x+1)(x-5)$

13. $20r^2 + 27r - 8 = (4r-1)(5r+8)$

15. $10x^2 + 17x + 3 = (5x+1)(2x+3)$

17. $3x^2 + x - 2 = (3x-2)(x+1)$

19. $6x^2 - 13xy + 5y^2 = (3x-5y)(2x-y)$

21. $15x^2 - 16x - 15 = (3x-5)(5x+3)$

23. $x^2 - 9x + 20 = (x-4)(x-5)$

25. $2x^2 - 7x - 99 = (2x+11)(x-9)$

27. $-27t + 7t^2 - 4 = 7t^2 - 27t - 4$
$$= (7t+1)(t-4)$$

29. $3a^2 + 10ab + 3b^2 = (3a+b)(a+3b)$

31. $49x^2 - 7x - 2 = (7x+1)(7x-2)$

33. $18x^2 - 9x - 14 = (6x-7)(3x+2)$

35. $12x^3 + 11x^2 + 2x = x(12x^2 + 11x + 2)$
$$= x(3x+2)(4x+1)$$

37. $21x^2 - 48x - 45 = 3(7x^2 - 16x - 15)$
$$= 3(7x+5)(x-3)$$

39. $12x^2 + 7x - 12 = (3x+4)(4x-3)$

41. $6x^2y^2 - 2xy^2 - 60y^2 = 2y^2(3x^2 - x - 30)$
$$= 2y^2(3x-10)(x+3)$$

43. $4x^2 - 8x - 21 = (2x-7)(2x+3)$

45. $3x^2 - 42x + 63 = 3(x^2 - 14x + 21)$

47. $8x^2 + 6x - 27 = (4x+9)(2x-3)$

49. $-x^2 + 2x + 24 = -1(x^2 - 2x - 24)$
$$= -1(x+4)(x-6)$$

51. $4x^3 - 9x^2 - 9x = x(4x^2 - 9x - 9)$
$$= x(4x+3)(x-3)$$

53. $24x^2 - 58x + 9 = (4x-9)(6x-1)$

55. $40a^2b + 9ab - 9b = b(40a^2 + 9a - 9)$
$$= b(8a-3)(5a+3)$$

57. $15x^4 + 19x^2 + 6 = (3x^2+2)(5x^2+3)$

59. $6y^3 - 8y^2 - 30y = 2y(3y^2 - 4y - 15)$
$$= 2y(3y+5)(y-3)$$

61. $10x^3 + 25x^2y - 15xy^2 = 5x(2x^2 + 5xy - 3y^2)$
$$= 5x(2x-y)(x+3y)$$

63. $-14x^2 + 39x - 10 = -1(14x^2 - 39x + 10)$
$$= -1(2x-5)(7x-2)$$

65. January 2001 and February 2001

67. Increased 0.5%

69. $4x^2(y-1)^2 + 10x(y-1)^2 + 25(y-1)^2$

$\qquad = (y-1)^2(4x^2 + 10x + 25)$

71. $-12x^3y^2 + 3x^2y^2 + 15xy^2$

$\qquad = -3xy^2(4x^2 - x - 5)$

$\qquad = -3xy^2(4x-5)(x+1)$

73. $2z^2 + bz - 7$ is factorable when b is 5 or 13.

75. $3x^2 - 8x + c$ is factorable when c is 4 or 5.

Practice Problems 4.4

1. a. $3x^2 + 14x + 8 = 3x^2 + 12x + 2x + 8$

$\qquad = 3x(x+4) + 2(x+4)$

$\qquad = (x+4)(3x+2)$

    b. $12x^2 + 19x + 5 = 12x^2 + 15x + 4x + 5$

$\qquad = 3x(4x+5) + 1(4x+5)$

$\qquad = (4x+5)(3x+1)$

2. a. $6x^2y - 7xy - 5y = y(x^2 - 7x - 5)$

$\qquad = y(6x^2 - 10x + 3x - 5)$

$\qquad = y\left[2x(3x-5) + 1(3x-5)\right]$

$\qquad = y(3x-5)(2x+1)$

    b. $30x^2 - 26x + 4 = 2(15x^2 - 13x + 2)$

$\qquad = 2(15x^2 - 10x - 3x + 2)$

$\qquad = 2\left[5x(3x-2) - 1(3x-2)\right]$

$\qquad = 2(3x-2)(5x-1)$

Exercise Set 4.4

1. $x^2 + 3x + 2x + 6 = x(x+3) + 2(x+3)$

$\qquad = (x+3)(x+2)$

3. $x^2 - 4x + 7x - 28 = x(x-4) + 7(x-4)$

$\qquad = (x-4)(x+7)$

5. $y^2 + 8y - 2y - 16 = y(y+8) - 2(y+8)$

$\qquad = (y+8)(y-2)$

7. $3x^2 + 4x + 12x + 16 = x(3x+4) + 4(3x+4)$

$\qquad = (3x+4)(x+4)$

9. $8x^2 - 5x - 24x + 15 = x(8x-5) - 3(8x-5)$

$\qquad = (8x-5)(x-3)$

11. $5x^4 - 3x^2 + 25x^2 - 15$

$\qquad = x^2(5x^2 - 3) + 5(5x^2 - 3)$

$\qquad = (5x^2 - 3)(x^2 + 5)$

13. a. The numbers are 9 and 2.

$\qquad 9 \cdot 2 = 18$

$\qquad 9 + 2 = 11$

    b. $9x + 2x = 11x$

    c. $6x^2 + 11x + 3 = 6x^2 + 9x + 2x + 3$

$\qquad = 3x(2x+3) + 1(2x+3)$

$\qquad = (2x+3)(3x+1)$

15. a. The numbers are -20 and -3.

$\qquad -20 \cdot (-3) = 60$

$\qquad -20 + (-3) = -23$

    b. $-20x - 3x = -23x$

    c. $15x^2 - 23x + 4 = 15x^2 - 20x - 3x + 4$

$\qquad = 5x(3x-4) - (3x-4)$

$\qquad = (3x-4)(5x-1)$

17. $21y^2 + 17y + 2 = 21y^2 + 3y + 14y + 2$
$$= 3y(7y+1) + 2(7y+1)$$
$$= (3y+2)(7y+1)$$

19. $7x^2 - 4x - 11 = 7x^2 - 11x + 7x - 11$
$$= x(7x-11) + 1(7x-11)$$
$$= (7x-11)(x+1)$$

21. $10x^2 - 9x + 2 = 10x^2 - 5x - 4x + 2$
$$= 5x(2x-1) - 2(2x-1)$$
$$= (2x-1)(5x-2)$$

23. $2x^2 - 7x + 5 = 2x^2 - 5x - 2x + 5$
$$= x(2x-5) - 1(2x-5) = (2x-5)(x-1)$$

25. $4x^2 + 12x + 9 = 4x^2 + 6x + 6x + 9$
$$= 2x(2x+3) + 3(2x+3)$$
$$= (2x+3)(2x+3)$$
$$= (2x+3)^2$$

27. $4x^2 - 8x - 21 = 4x^2 - 14x + 6x - 21$
$$= 2x(2x-7) + 3(2x-7)$$
$$= (2x-7)(2x+3)$$

29. $10x^2 - 23x + 12 = 10x^2 - 15x - 8x + 12$
$$= 5x(2x-3) - 4(2x-3)$$
$$= (2x-3)(5x-4)$$

31. $2x^3 + 13x^2 + 15x = x(2x^2 + 13x + 15)$
$$= x(2x^2 + 10x + 3x + 15)$$
$$= x[2x(x+5) + 3(x+5)] = x(x+5)(2x+3)$$

33. $16y^2 - 34y + 18 = 2(8y^2 - 17y + 9)$
$$= 2(8y^2 - 8y - 9y + 9)$$
$$= 2[8y(y-1) - 9(y-1)] = 2(y-1)(8y-9)$$

35. $6x^2 - 13x + 6 = 6x^2 - 9x - 4x + 6$
$$= 3x(2x-3) - 2(2x-3)$$
$$= (2x-3)(3x-2)$$

37. $54a^2 - 9a - 30 = 3(18a^2 - 3a - 10)$
$$= 3(18a^2 - 15a + 12a - 10)$$
$$= 3[3a(6a-5) + 2(6a-5)]$$
$$= 3(6a-5)(3a+2)$$

39. $20a^3 + 37a^2 + 8a = a(20a^2 + 37a + 8)$
$$= a(20a^2 + 5a + 32a + 8)$$
$$= a[5a(4a+1) + 8(4a+1)]$$
$$= a(4a+1)(5a+8)$$

41. $12x^3 - 27x^2 - 27x = 3x(4x^2 - 9x - 9)$
$$= 3x(4x^2 - 12x + 3x - 9)$$
$$= 3x[4x(x-3) + 3(x-3)] = 3x(x-3)(4x+3)$$

43. $(x-2)(x+2) = x^2 - 2x + 2x - 4$
$$= x^2 - 4$$

45. $(y+4)(y+4) = y^2 + 4y + 4y + 16$
$$= y^2 + 8y + 16$$

47. $(9z+5)(9z-5) = 81z^2 + 45z - 45a - 25$
$$= 81z^2 - 25$$

49. $(4x-3)^2 = 16x^2 + 2(4x)(-3) + 9$
$$= 16x^2 - 24x + 9$$

51. $x^{2n} + 2x^n + 3x^n + 6 = x^n(x^n + 2) + 3(x^n + 2)$
$$= (x^n + 2)(x^n + 3)$$

53. $3x^{2n} + 16x^n - 35 = 3x^n - 5x^n + 21x^n - 35$
$$= x^n(3x^n - 5) + 7(3x^n - 5)$$
$$= (3x^n - 5)(x^n + 7)$$

55. Answers may vary.

Practice Problems 4.5

1. a. Yes; two terms, x^2 and 36, are squares
   $(36 = 6^2)$ and the third term of the trinomial,
   12x, is twice the product of x and $6 (2 \cdot x \cdot 6 = 12)$.

   b. Yes; two terms, x^2 and 100, are squares $(100 = 10^2)$,
   and the third term of the trinomial, 20x, is twice the
   product of x and $10 (2 \cdot x \cdot 10 = 20x)$.

2. a. No; the two terms, $9x^2$ and 25,
   $\left(9x^2 = (3x)^2 \text{ and } 25 = 5^2\right)$ are squares, but the
   third term, 20x, is not twice the product of 3x
   and 5, or its opposite.

   b. No; only one of the terms, $4x^2$, is a square.

3. a. Yes; two terms, $25x^2$ and 1, are squares
   $\left(25x^2 = (5x)^2 \text{ and } 1 = 1^2\right)$, and the third term of
   the trinomial, $-10x$, is the opposite of twice the
   product of 5x and $1 (-2 \cdot 5x \cdot 1 = -10x)$.

   b. Yes; two terms, $9x^2$ and 49, are squares
   $\left(9x^2 = (3x)^2, \text{and } 49 = 7^2\right)$, and the third
   term of the trinomial, $- 42x$, is the opposite
   of twice the product of 3x and
   $7 (-2 \cdot 3x \cdot 7 = -42x)$.

4. $x^2 + 16x + 64 = x^2 + 2 \cdot x \cdot 8 + 8^2$
$$= (x + 8)^2$$

5. $9r^2 + 24rs + 16s^2 = (3r)^2 + 2 \cdot 3r \cdot 4s + (4s)^2$
$$= (3r + 4s)^2$$

6. $9n^2 - 6n + 1 = (3n)^2 - 2 \cdot 3n \cdot 1 + 1^2$
$$= (3n - 1)^2$$

7. $9x^2 + 15x + 4 = 9x^2 + 12x + 3x + 4$
$$= 3x(3x + 4) + 1(3x + 4)$$
$$= (3x + 4)(3x + 1)$$

8. $12x^3 - 84x^2 + 147x = 3x(4x^2 - 28x + 49)$
$$= 3x(3x + 4) + 1(3x + 4)$$
$$= (3x + 4)(3x + 1)$$

9. $x^2 - 9 = x^2 - 3^2 = (x + 3)(x - 3)$

10. $a^2 - 16 = a^2 - 4^2 = (a + 4)(a - 4)$

11. $c^2 - \dfrac{9}{25} = c^2 - \left(\dfrac{3}{5}\right)^2 = \left(c + \dfrac{3}{5}\right)\left(c - \dfrac{3}{5}\right)$

12. $s^2 + 9 = s^2 + 3^2$
   This is not a difference of squares, it is
   a prime polynomial.

13. $9s^2 - 1 = (3s)^2 - 1^2 = (3s + 1)(3s - 1)$

14. $16x^2 - 49y^2 = (4x)^2 - (7y)^2$
$$= (4x + 7y)(4x - 7y)$$

15. $p^4 - 81 = (p^2)^2 - 9^2 = (p^2 + 9)(p^2 - 9)$
$$= (p^2 + 9)(p^2 - 3^2)$$
$$= (p^2 + 9)(p + 3)(p - 3)$$

16. $9x^3 - 25x = x(9x^2 - 25)$

$$= x\left[(3x)^2 - 5^2\right] = x(3x+5)(3x-5)$$

17. $48x^4 - 3 = 3(16x^4 - 1) = 3\left[(4x^2)^2 - 1^2\right]$

$$= 3(4x^2 + 1)(4x^2 - 1)$$

$$= 3(4x^2 + 1)\left[(2x)^2 - 1^2\right]$$

$$= 3(4x^2 + 1)(2x + 1)(2x - 1)$$

18. $-9x^2 + 100 = -1(9x^2 - 100)$

$$= -1\left[(3x)^2 - 10^2\right]$$

$$= -1(3x + 10)(3x - 10)$$

Mental Math 4.5

1. $1 = 1^2$

2. $25 = 5^2$

3. $81 = 9^2$

4. $64 = 8^2$

5. $9 = 3^2$

6. $100 = 10^2$

7. $9x^2 = (3x)^2$

8. $16y^2 = (4y)^2$

9. $25a^2 = (5a)^2$

10. $81b^2 = (9b)^2$

11. $36p^4 = (6p^2)^2$

12. $4q^4 = (2q^2)^2$

Exercise Set 4.5

1. Yes; two terms, x^2 and 64, are squares $(64 = 8^2)$, and the third term of the trinomial, $16x$, is twice the product of x and $8(2 \cdot x \cdot 8 = 16x)$.

3. No; the two terms, y^2 and 25, are squares $(25 = 5^2)$, but the third term of the trinomial, $5y$, is not twice the product of y and 5, or its opposite.

5. Yes; two terms, m^2 and 1, are squares $(1 = 1^2)$, and the third term of the trinomial, $-2m$, is the opposite of twice the product of m and $1(-(2 \cdot m \cdot 1) = -2m)$.

7. No; the two terms, a^2 and 49, are squares $(49 = 7^2)$, but the third term of the trinomial, $-16a$, is not twice the product of a and 7, or its opposite.

9. No; if we first factor out the GCF, 4, we find that only one of the terms, x^2, is a square.

11. Yes; two terms, $25a^2$ and $16b^2$, are squares $(25a^2 = (5a)^2$ and $16b^2 = (4b)^2)$, and the third term of the trinomial, $-40ab$, is the opposite of twice the product of $5a$ and $4b(-(2 \cdot 5a \cdot 4b = -40ab)$.

Exercise Set 4.5

1. Yes; two terms, x^2 and 64, are squares $(64 = 8^2)$, and the third term of the trinomial, $16x$, is twice the product of x and $8\,(2 \cdot x \cdot 8 = 16x)$.

3. No; the two terms, y^2 and 25, are squares $(25 = 5^2)$, but the third term of the trinomial, $5y$, is not twice the product of y and 5, or its opposite.

5. Yes; two terms, m^2 and 1, are squares $(1 = 1^2)$, and the third term of the trinomial, $-2m$, is the opposite of twice the product of m and $1\,(-(2 \cdot m \cdot 1) = -2m)$.

7. No; the two terms, a^2 and 49, are squares $(49 = 7^2)$, but the third term of the trinomial, $-16a$, is not twice the product of a and 7, or its opposite.

9. No; if we first factor out the GCF, 4, we find that only one of the terms, x^2, is a square.

11. Yes; two terms, $25a^2$ and $16b^2$, are squares $(25a^2 = (5a)^2$ and $16b^2 = (4b)^2)$, and the third term of the trinomial, $-40ab$, is the opposite of twice the product of $5a$ and $4b\,(-(2 \cdot 5a \cdot 4b = -40ab)$.

13. $x^2 + 8x + 16$ is a perfect square trinomial because, x^2 and 16 are squares $(16 = 4^2)$, and $8x$ is twice the product of x and 4 $(2 \cdot x \cdot 4 = 8x)$.

15. $x^2 + 22x + 121 = x^2 + 2 \cdot x \cdot 11 + 11^2$
$$= (x + 11)^2$$

17. $x^2 - 16x + 64 = x^2 - 2 \cdot x \cdot 8 + 8^2$
$$= (x - 8)^2$$

19. $16a^2 - 24a + 9 = (4a)^2 - 2 \cdot 4a \cdot 3 + 3^2$
$$= (4a - 3)^2$$

21. $x^4 + 4x^2 + 4 = (x^2)^2 + 2 \cdot x^2 \cdot 2 + 2^2$
$$= (x^2 + 2)^2$$

23. $2n^2 - 28n + 98 = 2(n^2 - 14x + 49)$
$$= 2(n^2 - 2 \cdot n \cdot 7 + 7^2) = 2(n - 7)^2$$

25. $16y^2 + 40y + 25 = (4y)^2 + 2 \cdot 4y \cdot 5 + 5^2$
$$= (4y + 5)^2$$

27. $x^2 y^2 - 10xy + 25 = (xy)^2 - 2 \cdot xy \cdot 5 + 5^2$
$$= (xy - 5)^2$$

29. $m^2 + 18m^2 + 81m = m(m^2 + 18m + 81)$
$$= m(m^2 + 2 \cdot m \cdot 9 + 9^2)$$
$$= m(m + 9)^2$$

31. The trinomial $1 + 6x^2 + x^4 = x^4 + 6x^2 + 1$ is not factorable with integers, and is, therefore, a prime polynomial.

33. $9x^2 - 24xy + 16y^2 = (3x)^2 - 2 \cdot 3x \cdot 4y + (4y)^2$
$$= (3x - 4y)^2$$

35. $x^2 + 14xy + 49y^2 = x^2 + 2 \cdot x \cdot 7y + (7y)^2$
$$= (x + 7y)^2$$

37. Answers may vary.

39. $x^2 - 4 = x^2 - 2^2 = (x + 2)(x - 2)$

41. $81 - p^2 = 9^2 - p^2 = (9 + p)(9 - p)$

43. $4r^2 - 1 = (2r)^2 - 1^2 = (2r + 1)(2r - 1)$

45. $9x^2 - 16 = (3x)^2 - 4^2 = (3x + 4)(3x - 4)$

47. $16r^2 + 1$ is the sum of two squares, $(4r)^2 + 1^2$, not the difference of two squares. $16r^2 + 1$ is a prime polynomial.

49. $-36 + x^2 = -(6)^2 + x^2 = (-6 + x)(6 + x)$

51. $m^4 - 1 = (m^2)^2 - 1^1$
$$= (m^2 + 1)(m^2 - 1)$$
$$= (m^2 + 1)(m^2 - 1^2)$$
$$= (m^2 + 1)(m + 1)(m - 1)$$

53. $x^2 - 169y^2 = x^2 - (13y)^2$
$$= (x + 13y)(x - 13y)$$

55. $18r^2 - 8 = 2(9r^2 - 4)$
$$= 2((3r)^2 - 2^2)$$
$$= 2(3r + 2)(3r - 2)$$

57. $9xy^2 - 4x = x(9y^2 - 4)$
$$= x((3y)^2 - 2^2)$$
$$= x(3y + 2)(3y - 2)$$

59. $25y^4 - 100y^2 = 25y^2(y^2 - 4)$
$$= 25y^2(y^2 - 2^2)$$
$$= 25y^2(y + 2)(y - 2)$$

61. $x^3y - 4xy^3 = xy(x^2 - 4y^2)$
$$= xy(x^2 - (2y)^2)$$
$$= xy(x + 2y)(x - 2y)$$

63. $225a^2 - 81b^2 = 9(25a^2 - 9b^2)$
$$= 9((5a)^2 - (3b)^2)$$
$$= 9(5a + 3b)(5a - 3b)$$

65. $12x^2 - 27 = 3(4x^2 - 9) = 3((2x)^2 - 3^2)$
$$= 3(2x + 3)(2x - 3)$$

67. $49a^2 - 16 = (7a)^2 - 4^2$
$$= (7a + 4)(7a - 4)$$

69. $169a^2 - 49b^2 = (13a)^2 - (7b)^2$
$$= (13a + 7b)(13a - 7b)$$

71. $16 - a^2b^2 = 4^2 - (ab)^2$
$$= (4 + ab)(4 - ab)$$

73. $y^2 - \dfrac{1}{16} = y^2 - \left(\dfrac{1}{4}\right)^2$

$\qquad = \left(y + \dfrac{1}{4}\right)\left(y - \dfrac{1}{4}\right)$

75. $100 - \dfrac{4}{81}n^2 = 10^2 - \left(\dfrac{2}{9}n\right)^2$

$\qquad = \left(10 + \dfrac{2}{9}n\right)\left(10 - \dfrac{2}{9}n\right)$

77. $5 - y$, since

$\qquad (5-y)(5+y) = 25 - 5y + 5y - y^2$

$\qquad = 25 - y^2 = 5^2 - y^2$

79. $\qquad y + 5 = 0$

$\qquad y + 5 - 5 = 0 - 5$

$\qquad\qquad y = -5$

81. $\qquad 3x - 9 = 0$

$\qquad 3x - 9 + 9 = 0 + 9$

$\qquad\qquad 3x = 9$

$\qquad\qquad \dfrac{3x}{3} = \dfrac{9}{3}$

$\qquad\qquad x = 3$

83. $\qquad 4a + 2 = 0$

$\qquad 4a + 2 - 2 = 0 - 2$

$\qquad\qquad 4a = -2$

$\qquad\qquad \dfrac{4a}{4} = \dfrac{-2}{4}$

$\qquad\qquad a = -\dfrac{1}{2}$

85. The sail is shaped like a triangle. The area of a triangle is given by $A = \dfrac{1}{2}bh$. Use $b = 10$ feet and $h = x$ feet. Then,

$A = \dfrac{1}{2}bh$

$25 = \dfrac{1}{2} \cdot 10 \cdot x$

$25 = 5x$

$\dfrac{25}{5} = \dfrac{5x}{5}$

$5 = x$

The height, x, is 5 feet.

87. $(y-6)^2 - z^2 = (y - 6 + z)(y - 6 - z)$

89. $m^2(n+8) - 9(n+8) = (n+8)(m^2 - 9)$

$\qquad = (n+8)(m^2 - 3^2) = (n+8)(m+3)(m-3)$

91. $(x^2 + 2x + 1) - 36y^2$

$\qquad = [(x+1)(x+1)] - 36y^2$

$\qquad = (x+1)^2 - (6y)^2$

$\qquad = (x+1+6y)(x+1-6y)$

93. $x^{2n} - 81 = (x^n)^2 - 9^2 = (x^n + 9)(x^n - 9)$

95. The formula for factoring a perfect square trinomial.

97. a. Let $t = 1$.

$$529 - 16t^2 = 529 - 16(1)^2$$
$$= 529 - 16(1) = 529 - 16 = 513$$

After 1 second the height of the bolt is 513 feet.

b. Let $t = 4$.

$$529 - 16t^2 = 529 - 16(4)^2$$
$$= 529 - 16(16)$$
$$529 - 256 = 273$$

After 4 seconds the height of the bolt is 273 feet.

c. When the object hits the ground, its height is zero feet. Thus, to find the time, t, when the object's height is zero feet above the ground, we set the expression $529 - 16t^2$ equal to 0 and solve for t.

$$529 - 16t^2 = 0$$
$$529 - 16t^2 + 16t^2 = 0 + 16t^2$$
$$529 = 16t^2$$
$$\frac{529}{16} = \frac{16t^2}{16}$$
$$33.0625 = t^2$$
$$\sqrt{33.0625} = \sqrt{t^2}$$
$$5.75 = t$$

Thus, the object will hit the ground after approximately 6 seconds.

d. $529 - 16t^2 = 23^2 - (4t)^2$
$$= (23 + 4t)(23 - 4t)$$

99. a. Let $t = 2$

$$784 - 16t^2 = 784 - 16(2)^2 = 720$$

After 2 seconds the height is 720 feet.

b. Let $t = 5$

$$784 - 16t^2 = 784 - 16(5)^2$$
$$= 384$$

After 5 seconds the height is 384 feet.

c. When he reaches ground level, the height is 0.

$$0 = 784 - 16t^2$$
$$16t^2 = 784$$
$$t^2 = 49$$
$$t = \sqrt{49}$$
$$t = 7$$

He reaches ground level after 7 seconds.

d. $784 - 16t^2 = 16(49 - t^2)$
$$= 16(7^2 - t^2)$$
$$= 16(7 + t)(7 - t)$$

Integrated Review 4.5

1. $x^2 + x - 12 = (x + 4)(x - 3)$

2. $x^2 - 10x + 16 = (x - 2)(x - 8)$

3. $x^2 - x - 6 = (x + 2)(x - 3)$

4. $x^2 + 2x + 1 = (x + 1)(x + 1) = (x + 1)^2$

5. $x^2 - 6x + 9 = (x - 3)(x - 3) = (x - 3)^2$

6. $x^2 + x - 2 = (x+2)(x-1)$

7. $x^2 + x - 6 = (x+3)(x-2)$

8. $x^2 + 7x + 12 = (x+4)(x+3)$

9. $x^2 - 7x + 10 = (x-5)(x-2)$

10. $x^2 - x - 30 = (x-6)(x+5)$

11. $2x^2 - 98 = (x^2 - 49)$
$$= 2(x^2 - 7^2)$$
$$= 2(x+7)(x-7)$$

12. $3x^2 - 75 = 3(x^2 - 25)$
$$= 3(x^2 - 5^2)$$
$$= 3(x+5)(x-5)$$

13. $x^2 + 3x + 5x + 15 = x(x+3) + 5(x+3)$
$$= (x+3)(x+5)$$

14. $3y - 21 + xy - 7x = 3(y-7) + x(y-7)$
$$= (y-7)(3+x)$$

15. $x^2 + 6x - 16 = (x+8)(x-2)$

16. $x^2 - 3x - 28 = (x-7)(x+4)$

17. $4x^3 + 20x^2 - 56x = 4x(x^2 + 5x - 14)$
$$= 4x(x+7)(x-2)$$

18. $6x^3 - 6x^2 - 120x = 6x(x^2 - x - 20)$
$$= 6x(x-5)(x+4)$$

19. $12x^2 + 34x + 24 = 2(6x^2 + 17x + 12)$
$$= 2(6x^2 + 9x + 8x + 12)$$
$$= 2[3x(2x+3) + 4(2x+3)]$$
$$= 2(2x+3)(3x+4)$$

20. $8a^2 + 6ab - 5b^2 = 8a^2 + 10ab - 4ab - 5b^2$
$$= 2a(4a+5b) - b(4a+5b)$$
$$= (4a+5b)(2a-b)$$

21. $4a^2 - b^2 = (2a)^2 - b^2 = (2a+b)(2a-b)$

22. $x^2 - 25y^2 = x^2 - (5y)^2 = (x+5y)(x-5y)$

23. $28 - 13x - 6x^2 = 28 - 21x + 8x - 6x^2$
$$= 7(4-3x) + 2x(4-3x) = (4-3x)(7+2x)$$

24. $20 - 3x - 2x^2 = 20 - 8x + 5x - 2x^2$
$$= 4(5-2x) + x(5-2x)$$
$$= (5-2x)(4+x)$$

25. $x^2 - 2x + 4$ is a prime polynomial.

26. $a^2 + a - 3$ is a prime polynomial.

27. $6y^2 + y - 15 = 6y^2 + 10y - 9y - 15$
$$= 2y(3y+5) - 3(3y+5)$$
$$= (3y+5)(2y-3)$$

28. $4x^2 - x - 5 = 4x^2 - 5x + 4x - 5$
$$= x(4x-5) + 1(4x-5)$$
$$= (4x-5)(x+1)$$

29. $18x^3 - 63x^2 + 9x = 9x(2x^2 - 7x + 1)$

30. $12a^3 - 24a^2 + 4a = 4a(3a^2 - 6a + 1)$

31. $16a^2 - 56a + 49 = (4a)^2 - 2 \cdot 4a \cdot 7 + 7^2$
$$= (4a - 7)^2$$

32. $25p^2 - 70p + 49 = (5p)^2 - 2 \cdot 5p \cdot 7 + 7^2$
$$= (4a - 7)^2$$

33. $14 + 5x - x^2 = (7 - x)(2 + x)$

34. $3 - 2x - x^2 = (3 + x)(1 - x)$

35. $3x^4 y + 6x^3 y - 72x^2 y = 3x^2 y(x^2 + 2x - 24)$
$$= 3x^2 y(x + 6)(x - 4)$$

36. $2x^3 y + 8x^2 y^2 - 10xy^3 = 2xy(x^2 + 4xy - 5y^2)$
$$= 2xy(x + 5y)(x - y)$$

37. $12x^3 y + 243xy = 3xy(4x^2 + 81)$

38. $6x^3 y^2 + 8xy^2 = 2xy^2(3x^2 + 4)$

39. $2xy - 72x^3 = 2xy(1 - 36x^2)$
$$= 2xy(1^2 - (6x)^2) - 2xy(1 + 6x)(1 - 6x)$$

40. $2x^3 - 18x = 2x(x^2 - 9)$
$$= 2x(x^2 - 3^2)$$
$$= 2x(x + 3)(x - 3)$$

41. $x^3 + 6x^2 - 4x - 24 = x^2(x + 6) - 4(x + 6)$
$$= (x + 6)(x^2 - 4) = (x + 6)(x^2 - 2^2)$$
$$= (x + 6)(x + 2)(x - 2)$$

42. $x^3 - 2x^2 - 36x + 72$
$$= x^2(x - 2) - 36(x - 2)$$
$$= (x - 2)(x^2 - 36) = (x - 2)(x^2 - 6^2)$$
$$= (x - 2)(x + 6)(x - 6)$$

43. $6a^3 + 10a^2 = 2a^2(3a + 5)$

44. $4n^2 - 6n = 2n(2n - 3)$

45. $3x^3 - x^2 + 12x - 4 = x^2(3x - 1) + 4(3x - 1)$
$$= (3x - 1)(x^2 + 4)$$

46. $x^3 - 2x^2 + 3x - 6 = x^2(x - 2) + 3(x - 2)$
$$= (x - 2)(x^2 + 3)$$

47. $6x^2 + 18xy + 12y^2 = 6(x^2 + 3xy + 2y^2)$
$$= 6(x + 2)(x + y)$$

48. $12x^2 + 46xy - 8y^2 = 2(6x^2 + 23xy - 4y^2)$
$$= 2(6x^2 + 24xy - xy - 4y^2)$$
$$= 2[6x(x + 4y) - y(x + 4y)]$$
$$= 2(x + 4y)(6x - y)$$

49. $5(x + y) + x(x + y) = (x + y)(5 + x)$

50. $7(x - y) + y(x - y) = (x - y)(7 + y)$

51. $14t^2 - 9t + 1 = 14t^2 - 7t - 2t + 1$
$$= 7t(2t - 1) - 1(2t - 1)$$
$$= (2t - 1)(t - 1)$$

52. $3t^2 - 5t + 1$ is a prime polynomial.

53. $3x^2 + 2x - 5 = 3x^2 + 5x - 3x - 5$
$$= x(3x+5) - 1(3x+5)$$
$$= (3x+5)(x-1)$$

54. $7x^2 + 19x - 6 = 7x^2 + 21x - 2x - 6$
$$= 7x(x+3) - 2(x+3)$$
$$= (x+3)(7x-2)$$

55. $1 - 8a - 20a^2 = 1 - 10a + 2a - 20a^2$
$$= 1(1-10a) + 2a(1-10a)$$
$$= (1-10a)(1+2a)$$

56. $1 - 7a - 60a^2 = 1 - 12a + 5a - 60a^2$
$$= 1(1-12a) + 5a(1-12a)$$
$$= (1-12a)(1+5a)$$

57. $x^4 - 10x^2 + 9 = (x^2 - 9)(x^2 - 1)$
$$= (x^2 - 3^2)(x^2 - 1^2)$$
$$= (x+3)(x-3)(x+1)(x-1)$$

58. $x^4 - 13x^2 + 36 = (x^2 - 9)(x^2 - 4)$
$$= (x^2 - 3^2)(x^2 - 2^2)$$
$$= (x+3)(x-3)(x+2)(x-2)$$

59. $x^2 - 23x + 120 = (x-15)(x-8)$

60. $y^2 + 22y + 96 = (y+16)(y+6)$

61. $x^2 - 14x - 48$ is prime.

62. $16a^2 - 56ab + 49b^2$
$$= (4a)^2 - 2(4a)(7b) + (7b)^2$$
$$= (4a - 7b)^2$$

63. $25p^2 - 70pq + 49q^2$
$$= (5p)^2 - 2(5p)(7q) + (7q)^2$$
$$= (5p - 7q)^2$$

64. $7x^2 + 24xy + 9y = 7x^2 + 3xy + 21xy + 9y^2$
$$= x(7x+3y) + 3y(7x+3y)$$
$$= (7x+3y)(x+3y)$$

65. $-x^2 - x + 30 = -1(x^2 + x - 30)$
$$= -1(x+6)(x+5)$$

66. $-x^2 + 6x - 8 = -1(x^2 - 6x + 8)$
$$= -1(x-2)(x+-4)$$

67. $3rs - s + 12r - 4 = s(3r-1) + 4(3r-1)$
$$= (3r-1)(s+4)$$

68. $x^3 - 2x^2 + 3x - 6 = x^2(x-2) + 3(x-2)$
$$= (x-2)(x^2+3)$$

69. $4x^2 - 8xy - 3x + 6y = 4x(x-2y) - 3(x-2y)$
$$= (x-2y)(4x-3)$$

70. $4x^2 - 2xy - 7yz + 14xz$
$$= 2x(2x-y) + 7z(-y+2x)$$
$$= (2x-y)(2x+7z)$$

71. $x^2 + 9xy - 36y^2 = (x+12y)(x-3y)$

72. $3x^2 + 10xy - 8y^2 = 3x^2 - 2xy + 12xy - 8y^2$
$$= x(3x-2y) + 4y(3x-2y)$$

73. $x^4 - 14x^2 - 32 = (x^2 + 2)(x^2 - 16)$

$\qquad = (x^2 + 2)(x + 4)(x - 4)$

74. $x^4 - 22x^2 - 75 = (x^2 + 3)(x^2 - 25)$

$\qquad = (x^2 + 3)(x + 5)(x - 5)$

75. Answers may vary.

Practice Problems 4.6

1. $(x - 7)(x + 2) = 0$

$x - 7 = 0 \quad$ or $\quad x + 2 = 0$

$x = 7 \qquad\qquad x = -2$

The solutions are 7 and -2.

2. $(x - 10)(3x + 1) = 0$

$x - 10 = 0 \quad$ or $\quad 3x + 1 = 0$

$x = 10 \qquad\qquad 3x = -1$

$\qquad\qquad\qquad\qquad x = -\dfrac{1}{3}$

The solutions are 10 and $-\dfrac{1}{3}$.

3. a. $y(y + 3) = 0$

$y = 0 \quad$ or $\quad y + 3 = 0$

$\qquad\qquad\qquad y = -3$

The solutions are 0 and -3.

b. $x(4x - 3) = 0$

$x = 0 \quad$ or $\quad 4x - 3 = 0$

$\qquad\qquad\qquad 4x = 3$

$\qquad\qquad\qquad x = \dfrac{3}{4}$

The solutions are 0 and $\dfrac{3}{4}$.

4. $x^2 - 3x - 18 = 0$

$(x - 6)(x + 3) = 0$

$x - 6 = 0 \quad$ or $\quad x + 3 = 0$

$x = 6 \qquad\qquad x = -3$

The solutions are 6 and -3.

5. $x^2 - 14x = -24$

$x^2 - 14x + 24 = 0$

$(x - 12)(x - 2) = 0$

$x - 12 = 0 \quad$ or $\quad x - 2 = 0$

$x = 12 \qquad\qquad x = 2$

The solutions are 12 and 2.

6. a. $x(x - 4) = 5$

$x^2 - 4x = 5$

$x^2 - 4x - 5 = 0$

$(x - 5)(x + 1) = 0$

$x - 5 = 0 \quad$ or $\quad x + 1 = 0$

$x = 5 \qquad\qquad x = -1$

The solutions are 5 and -1.

b. $x(3x + 7) = 6$

$3x^2 + 7x = 6$

$3x^2 + 7x - 6 = 0$

$(3x - 2)(x + 3) = 0$

$3x - 2 = 0 \quad$ or $\quad x + 3 = 0$

$3x = 2 \qquad\qquad x = -3$

$x = \dfrac{2}{3}$

The solutions are $\dfrac{2}{3}$ and -3.

7. $2x^3 - 18x = 0$

$2x(x^2 - 9) = 0$

$2x(x+3)(x-3) = 0$

$2x = 0$ or $x+3 = 0$ or $x-3 = 0$

$x = 0$ $x = -3$ $x = 3$

The solutions are 0, -3, and 3.

8. $(x+3)(3x^2 - 20x - 7) = 0$

$(x+3)(3x+1)(x-7) = 0$

$x+3 = 0$ or $3x+1 = 0$ or $x-7 = 0$

$x = -3$ $x = -1$ $x = 7$

$x = -\dfrac{1}{3}$

The solutions are -3, $-\dfrac{1}{3}$, and 7.

Mental Math 4.6

1. $(a-3)(a-7) = 0$

$a-3 = 0$ or $a-7 = 0$

$a = 3$ $a = 7$

The solutions are 3 and 7.

2. $(a-5)(a-2) = 0$

$a-5 = 0$ or $a-2 = 0$

$a = 5$ $a = 2$

The solutions are 5 and 2.

3. $(x+8)(x+6) = 0$

$x+8 = 0$ or $x+6 = 0$

$x = -8$ $x = -6$

The solutions are -8 and -6.

4. $(x+2)(x+3) = 0$

$x+2 = 0$ or $x+3 = 0$

$x = -2$ $x = -3$

The solutions are -2 and -3.

5. $(x+1)(x-3) = 0$

$x+1 = 0$ or $x-3 = 0$

$x = -1$ $x = 3$

The solutions are -1 and 3.

6. $(x-1)(x+2) = 0$

$x-1 = 0$ or $x+2 = 0$

$x = 1$ $x = -2$

The solutions are 1 and -2.

Exercise Set 4.6

1. $(x-2)(x+1) = 0$

$x-2 = 0$ or $x+1 = 0$

$x = 2$ $x = -1$

The solutions are 2 and -1.

3. $(x-6)(x-7) = 0$

$x-6 = 0$ or $x-7 = 0$

$x = 6$ $x = 7$

The solutions are 6 and 7.

5. $(x+9)(x+17) = 0$

$x+9 = 0$ or $x+17 = 0$

$x = -9$ $x = -17$

The solutions are -9 and -17.

7. $x(x+6)=0$

   $x=0$ or $x+6=0$

                      $x=-6$

   The solutions are 0 and -6.

9. $3x(x-8)=0$

   $3x=0$ or $x-8=0$

   $x=0$ $x=8$

   The solutions are 0 and 8.

11. $(2x+3)(4x-5)=0$

   $2x+3=0$ or $4x-5=0$

   $2x=-3$ $4x=5$

   $x=-\dfrac{3}{2}$ $x=\dfrac{5}{4}$

   The solutions are $-\dfrac{3}{2}$ and $\dfrac{5}{4}$.

13. $(2x-7)(x+2)=0$

   $2x-7=0$ or $7x+2=0$

   $2x=7$ $7x=-2$

   $x=\dfrac{7}{2}$ $x=-\dfrac{2}{7}$

   The solutions are $\dfrac{7}{2}$ and $-\dfrac{2}{7}$.

15. $\left(x-\dfrac{1}{2}\right)\left(x+\dfrac{1}{3}\right)=0$

   $x-\dfrac{1}{2}=0$ or $x+\dfrac{1}{3}=0$

   $x=\dfrac{1}{2}$ $x=-\dfrac{1}{3}$

   The solutions are $\dfrac{1}{2}$ and $-\dfrac{1}{3}$.

17. $(x+0.2)(x+1.5)=0$

   $x+0.2=0$ or $x+1.5=0$

   $x=-0.2$ $x=-1.5$

   The solutions are 0.2 and -1.5.

19. If $x=6$ and $x=-1$ are the solutions, then

   $x=6$ or $x=-1$

   $x-6=0$ $x+1=0$

   $(x-6)(x+1)=0$

21. $x^2-13x+36=0$

   $(x-9)(x-4)=0$

   $x-9=0$ or $x-4=0$

   $x=9$ $x=4$

   The solutions are 9 and 4.

23. $x^2+2x-8=0$

   $(x+4)(x-2)=0$

   $x+4=0$ or $x-2=0$

   $x=-4$ $x=2$

   The solutions are -4 and 2.

25. $x^2-7x=0$

   $x(x-7)=0$

   $x=0$ or $x-7=0$

                      $x=7$

   The solutions are 0 and 7.

27. $x^2+20x=0$

   $x(x+20)=0$

   $x=0$ or $x+20=0$

                      $x=-20$

   The solutions are 0 and -20.

29. $x^2 = 16$

$x^2 - 16 = 0$

$x^2 - 4^2 = 0$

$(x+4)(x-4) = 0$

$x + 4 = 0$ or $x - 4 = 0$

    $x = -4$ $x = 4$

The solutions are -4 and 4.

31. $x^2 - 4x = 32$

$x^2 - 4x - 32 = 0$

$(x-8)(x+4) = 0$

$x - 8 = 0$ or $x + 4 = 0$

    $x = 8$ $x = -4$

The solutions are 8 and -4.

33. $x(3x-1) = 14$

$3x^2 - x = 14$

$3x^2 - x - 14 = 0$

$(3x-7)(x+2) = 0$

$3x - 7 = 0$ or $x + 2 = 0$

    $3x = 7$ $x = -2$

     $x = \dfrac{7}{3}$

The solutions are $\dfrac{7}{3}$ and -2.

35. $3x^2 + 19x - 72 = 0$

$(3x-8)(x+9) = 0$

$3x - 8 = 0$ or $x + 9 = 0$

    $3x = 9$ $x = -9$

     $x = \dfrac{8}{3}$

The solutions are $\dfrac{8}{3}$ and -9.

37. $4x^3 - x = 0$

$x(4x^2 - 1) = 0$

$x(2x+1)(2x-1) = 0$

$x = 0$ or $2x + 1 = 0$ or $2x - 1 = 0$

              $x = -\dfrac{1}{2}$ $x = \dfrac{1}{2}$

The solutions are 0, $-\dfrac{1}{2}$, and $\dfrac{1}{2}$.

39. $4(x-7) = 6$

$4x - 28 = 6$

$4x = 34$

$x = \dfrac{34}{4}$

$x = \dfrac{17}{2}$

The solution is $\dfrac{17}{2}$.

41. $(4x-3)(16x^2 - 24x + 9) = 0$

$(4x-3)(4x-3)^2 = 0$

$(4x-3)^3 = 0$

$4x - 3 = 0$

$4x = 3$

$x = \dfrac{3}{4}$

The solution is $\dfrac{3}{4}$.

43. $4y^2 - 1 = 0$

$(2y+1)(2y-1) = 0$

$2y+1 = 0$ or $2y-1 = 0$

$2y = -1$ $2y = 1$

$y = -\dfrac{1}{2}$ $y = \dfrac{1}{2}$

The solutions are $-\dfrac{1}{2}$ and $\dfrac{1}{2}$.

45. $(2x+3)(2x^2-5x-3) = 0$

$(2x+3)(2x+1)(x-3) = 0$

$2x+3 = 0$ or $2x+1 = 0$ or $x-3 = 0$

$2x = -3$ $2x = -1$ $x = 3$

$x = -\dfrac{3}{2}$ $x = -\dfrac{1}{2}$

The solutions are $-\dfrac{3}{2}$, $-\dfrac{1}{2}$, and 3.

47. $x^2 - 15 = -2x$

$x^2 + 2x - 15 = 0$

$(x+5)(x-3) = 0$

$x+5 = 0$ or $x-3 = 0$

$x = -5$ $x = 3$

The solutions are -5 and 3.

49. $x^2 - 16x = 0$

$x(x-16) = 0$

$x = 0$ or $x-16 = 0$

$x = 16$

The solutions are 0 and 16.

51. $x^2 - x = 30$

$x^2 - x - 30 = 0$

$(x-6)(x+5) = 0$

$x-6 = 0$ or $x+5 = 0$

$x = 6$ $x = -5$

The solutions are 6 and -5.

53. $6y^2 - 22y - 40 = 0$

$2(3y^2 - 11y - 20) = 0$

$2(3y+4)(y-5) = 0$

$3y+4 = 0$ or $y-5 = 0$

$3y = -4$ $y = 5$

$y = -\dfrac{4}{3}$

The solutions are $-\dfrac{4}{3}$ and 5.

55. $(y-2)(y+3) = 6$

$y^2 - 2y + 3y - 6 = 6$

$y^2 + y - 12 = 0$

$(y+4)(y-3) = 0$

$y+4 = 0$ or $y-1 = 0$

$y = -4$ $y = 3$

The solutions are -4 and 3.

57. $x^3 - 12x^2 + 32x = 0$

$x(x^2 - 12x + 32) = 0$

$x(x-8)(x-4) = 0$

$x = 0$ or $x-8 = 0$ or $x-4 = 0$

$x = 8$ $x = 4$

The solutions are 0, 8, and 4.

59. If the solutions are $x = 5$ and $x = 7$, then, by the zero factor property,

$$x = 5 \quad \text{or} \quad x = 7$$
$$x - 5 = 0 \qquad x - 7 = 0$$
$$(x - 5)(x - 7) = 0$$
$$x^2 - 5x - 7x + 35 = 0$$
$$x^2 - 12x + 35 = 0$$

61. $\dfrac{3}{5} + \dfrac{4}{9} = \dfrac{3 \cdot 9}{5 \cdot 9} + \dfrac{4 \cdot 5}{9 \cdot 5}$

$$= \dfrac{27}{45} + \dfrac{20}{45}$$

$$= \dfrac{27 + 20}{45} = \dfrac{47}{45}$$

63. $\dfrac{7}{10} - \dfrac{5}{12} = \dfrac{7 \cdot 6}{10 \cdot 6} - \dfrac{5 \cdot 5}{12 \cdot 5}$

$$= \dfrac{42}{60} - \dfrac{25}{60}$$

$$= \dfrac{42 - 25}{60}$$

$$= \dfrac{17}{60}$$

65. $\dfrac{4}{5} \cdot \dfrac{7}{8} = \dfrac{4 \cdot 7}{5 \cdot 8}$

$$= \dfrac{4 \cdot 7}{5 \cdot 2 \cdot 4}$$

$$= \dfrac{7}{10}$$

67. The equation is not written in standard form.

69. a. When $x = 0$;

$$y = -16x^2 + 20x + 300$$
$$y = -16(0^2) + 20(0) + 300$$
$$= -16(0) + 20(0) + 300$$
$$= 0 + 0 + 300 = 300$$

When $x = 1$:

$$y = -16x^2 + 20x + 300$$
$$y = -16(1)^2 + 20(1) + 300$$
$$= -16(1) + 20(1) + 300$$
$$= -16 + 20 + 300 + 304$$

When $x = 2$:

$$y = -16x^2 + 20x + 300$$
$$y = -16(2)^2 + 20(2) + 300$$
$$= -16(4) + 20(2) + 300$$
$$= -64 + 40 + 300$$
$$= 276$$

When $x = 3$:

$$y = -16x^2 + 20x + 300$$
$$y = -16(3^2) + 20(3) + 300$$
$$= -16(9) + 20(3) + 300$$
$$= -144 + 60 + 300$$
$$= 216$$

When $x = 4$:

$$y = -16x^2 + 20x + 300$$
$$y = -16(4^2) + 20(4) + 300$$
$$= -16(16) + 20(4) + 300$$
$$= -256 + 80 + 300$$
$$= 124$$

When $x = 5$:

$y = -16x^2 + 20x + 300$

$y = -16(5^2) + 20(5) + 300$

$\quad = -16(25) + 20(5) + 300$

$\quad = -400 + 100 + 300$

$\quad = 0$

When $x = 6$:

$y = -16x^2 + 20x + 300$

$y = -16(6^2) + 20(6) + 300$

$\quad = -16(36) + 20(6) + 300$

$\quad = -576 + 120 + 300$

$\quad = -156$

b. The compass strikes the ground after 5 seconds, when the height, y, is zero feet.

c. The maximum height was approximately 304 feet.

71. $(x-3)(3x+4) = (x+2)(x-6)$

$3x^2 - 9x + 4x - 12 = x^2 + 2x - 6x - 12$

$3x^2 - 5x - 12 = x^2 - 4x - 12$

$2x^2 - x = 0$

$x(2x-1) = 0$

$x = 0 \quad$ or $\quad 2x - 1 = 0$

$\qquad\qquad\qquad\quad 2x = 1$

$\qquad\qquad\qquad\quad x = \dfrac{1}{2}$

The solutions are 0 and $\dfrac{1}{2}$.

73. $(2x-3)(x+8) = (x-6)(x+4)$

$2x^2 - 3x + 16x - 24 = x^2 - 6x + 4x - 24$

$2x^2 + 13x - 24 = x^2 - 2x - 24$

$x^2 + 15x = 0$

$x(x+15) = 0$

$x = 0 \quad$ or $\quad x + 15 = 0$

$\qquad\qquad\qquad\qquad x = -15$

The solutions are 0 and -15.

Practice Problems 4.7

1. Find t when $h = 0$.

$h = -16t^2 + 144$

$0 = -16t^2 + 144$

$0 = -16(t^2 - 9)$

$0 = -16(t+3)(t-3)$

$t + 3 = 0 \quad$ or $\quad t - 3 = 0$

$\quad t = -3 \qquad\qquad\quad t = 3$

Since the time cannot be negative, the solution is 3 seconds.

2. Let x = the unknown number.

$x^2 - 2x = 63$

$x^2 - 2x - 63 = 0$

$(x-9)(x+7) = 0$

$x - 9 = 0 \quad$ or $\quad x + 7 = 0$

$\quad x = 9 \qquad\qquad\quad x = -7$

The two numbers are 9 and -7.

3. Let x = the width of the rectangle. Then $x + 5$ = the length of the rectangle.

$A = lw$

$176 = (x+5)(x)$

$176 = x^2 + 5x$

$0 = x^2 + 5x - 176$

$0 = (x+16)(x-11)$

$x + 16 = 0$ or $x - 11 = 0$

      $x = -16$ $x = 11$

Since the dimensions cannot be negative, we discard $x = -16$. The width is 11 feet and the length is $11 + 5 = 16$ feet.

4. a. Let x = the first integer. Then $x + 2$ = the next consecutive odd integer.

$x(x+2) - 23 = x + (x+2)$

$x^2 + 2x - 23 = 2x + 2$

$x^2 - 25 = 0$

$(x+5)(x-5) = 0$

$x + 5 = 0$ or $x - 5 = 0$

    $x = -5$ $x = 5$

The integers are -5 and -3 or 5 and 7.

b. Let x = length of the shorter leg. Then $x + 7$ = length of the longer leg. By the Pythagorean theorem

$x^2 + (x+7)^2 = 13^2$

$x^2 + x^2 + 14x + 49 = 169$

$2x^2 + 14x + 49 = 169$

$2x^2 + 14x - 120 = 0$

$2(x^2 + 7x - 60) = 0$

$2(x+12)(x-5) = 0$

$x + 12 = 0$ or $x - 5 = 0$

    $x = -12$ $x = 5$

Since the length cannot be negative, we discard $x = -12$. The legs are 5 meters and $5 + 7 = 12$ meters.

Exercise Set 4.7

1. Let x = the width, then $x + 4$ = the length.

3. Let x = the first odd integer, then $x + 2$ = the next consecutive odd integer.

5. Let x = the base, then $4x + 1$ = the height.

7. Let x = the length of one side.

$A = x^2$

$121 = x^2$

$0 = x^2 - 121$

$0 = x^2 - 11^2$

$0 = (x+11)(x-11)$

$x + 11 = 0$ or $x - 11 = 0$

    $x = -11$ $x = 11$

Since the length cannot be negative, the sides are 11 units long.

9. The perimeter is the sum of the lengths of the sides.

$120 = (x+5) + (x^2 - 3x) + (3x-8)(x+3)$

$120 = x + 5 + x^2 - 3x + 3x - 8 + x + 3$

$120 = x^2 + 2x$

$0 = x^2 + 2x - 120$

$x^2 + 2x - 120 = 0$

$(x+12)(x-10) = 0$

$x + 12 = 0$ or $x - 10 = 0$

$\quad\quad x = -12 \quad\quad\quad\quad x = 10$

Since the dimensions cannot be negative, the lengths of the sides are:

$10 + 5 = 15$ cm, $10^2 - 3(10) = 70$ cm,

$3(10) - 8 = 22$ cm, and $10 + 3 = 13$ cm.

11. $x + 5 =$ the base and $x - 5 =$ the height.

$A = bh$

$96 = (x+5)(x-5)$

$96 = x^2 + 5x - 5x - 25$

$96 = x^2 - 25$

$0 = x^2 - 121$

$x^2 - 121 = 0$

$(x+11)(x-11) = 0$

$x + 11 = 0$ or $x - 11 = 0$

$\quad\quad x = -11 \quad\quad\quad\quad x = 11$

Since the dimensions cannot be negative, $x = 11$. The base is $11 + 5 = 16$ miles, and the height is $11 - 5 = 6$ miles.

13. Find t when $h = 0$.

$h = -16t^2 + 64t + 80$

$0 = -16t^2 + 64t + 80$

$0 = -16(t^2 - 4t - 5)$

$0 = -16(t-5)(t+1)$

$t - 5 = 0$ or $t + 1 = 0$

$\quad t = 5 \quad\quad\quad\quad t = -1$

Since the time t cannot be negative, the object hits the ground after 5 seconds.

15. Let $x =$ the width then $2x - 7 =$ the length.

$A = lw$

$30 = (2x-7)(x)$

$30 = 2x^2 - 7x$

$0 = 2x^2 - 7x - 30$

$0 = (2x+5)(x-6)$

$2x + 5 = 0$ or $x - 6 = 0$

$\quad x = -\dfrac{5}{2} \quad\quad\quad\quad x = 6$

Since the dimensions cannot be negative, the width is 6 cm and the length is $2(6) - 7 = 5$ cm.

17. Let n = 12.

$D = \dfrac{1}{2}n(n-3)$

$D = \dfrac{1}{2} \cdot 12(12-3) = 6(9) = 54$

A polygon with 12 sides has 54 diagonals.

19. Let D = 35 and solve for n.

$$D = \frac{1}{2}n(n-3)$$

$$35 = \frac{1}{2}n(n-3)$$

$$35 = \frac{1}{2}n^2 - \frac{3}{2}n$$

$$0 = \frac{1}{2}n^2 - \frac{3}{2}n - 35$$

$$0 = \frac{1}{2}\left(n^2 - 3n - 70\right)$$

$$0 = \frac{1}{2}(n-10)(n+7)$$

$$n - 10 = 0 \quad \text{or} \quad n + 7 = 0$$
$$n = 10 \qquad\qquad n = -7$$

The polygon has 10 sides.

21. Let x = the unknown number.

$$x + x^2 = 132$$
$$x^2 + x - 132 = 0$$
$$(x+12)(x-11) = 0$$
$$x + 12 = 0 \quad \text{or} \quad x - 11 = 0$$
$$x = -12 \qquad\qquad x = 11$$

The two numbers are -12 and 11.

23. Let x = the rate (in mph) of the slower boat, then $x + 7$ = the rate (in mph) of the faster boat. After one hour, the slower boat has traveled x miles and the faster boat has traveled $x + 7$ miles. By the Pythagorean theorem,

$$x^2 + (x+7)^2 = 17^2$$
$$x^2 + x^2 + 14x + 49 = 289$$
$$2x^2 + 14x + 49 = 289$$
$$2x^2 + 14x - 240 = 0$$

$$2\left(x^2 + 7x - 120\right) = 0$$
$$2(x+15)(x-8) = 0$$
$$x + 15 = 0 \quad \text{or} \quad x - 8 = 0$$
$$x = -15 \qquad\qquad x = 8$$

Since the rate cannot be negative, the slower boat travels at 8 mph. The faster boat travels at $8 + 7 = 15$ mph.

25. Let x = the first number, then $20 - x$ = the other number.

$$x^2 + (20-x)^2 = 218$$
$$x^2 + 400 - 40x + x^2 = 218$$
$$2x^2 - 40x + 400 = 218$$
$$2x^2 - 40x + 182 = 0$$
$$2\left(x^2 - 20x + 91\right) = 0$$
$$2(x-13)(x-7) = 0$$
$$x - 13 = 0 \quad \text{or} \quad x - 7 = 0$$
$$x = 13 \qquad\qquad x = 7$$

The numbers are 13 and 7.

27. Let x = the length of a side of the original square. Then $x + 3$ = the length of a side of the larger square.

$$64 = (x+3)^2$$
$$64 = x^2 + 6x + 9$$
$$0 = x^2 + 6x - 55$$
$$0 = (x+11)(x-5)$$
$$x + 11 = 0 \quad \text{or} \quad x - 5 = 0$$
$$x = -11 \qquad\qquad x = -5$$

Since the length cannot be negative, the sides of the original square are 5 inches long.

29. Let x = the length of the shorter leg. Then $x + 4$ = the length of the longer leg and $x + 8$ = the length of the hypotenuse. By the Pythagorean theorem,

$$x^2 + (x+4)^2 = (x+8)^2$$
$$x^2 + x^2 + 8x + 16 = x^2 + 16x + 64$$
$$x^2 - 8x - 48 = 0$$
$$(x - 12)(x + 4) = 0$$
$$x - 12 = 0 \quad \text{or} \quad x + 4 = 0$$
$$x = 12 \qquad\qquad x = -4$$

Since the length cannot be negative, the sides of the triangle are 12 mm, $12 + 4 = 16$ mm, and $12 + 8 = 20$ mm.

31. Let x = the height of the triangle, then $2x$ = the base.

$$A = \frac{1}{2}bh$$
$$100 = \frac{1}{2}(2x)(x)$$
$$100 = x^2$$
$$0 = x^2 - 100$$
$$0 = (x + 10)(x - 10)$$
$$x + 10 = 0 \quad \text{or} \quad x - 10 = 0$$
$$x = -10 \qquad\qquad x = 10$$

Since the altitude cannot be negative, the height of the triangle is 10 km.

33. Let x = the length of the shorter leg, then $x + 12$ = the length of the longer leg and $2x - 12$ = the length of the hypotenuse. By the Pythagorean theorem,

$$x^2 + (x+12)^2 = (2x-12)^2$$
$$x^2 + x^2 + 24x + 144 = 4x^2 - 48x + 144$$
$$0 = 2x^2 - 72x$$
$$0 = 2x(x - 36)$$
$$2x = 0 \quad \text{or} \quad x - 36 = 0$$
$$x = 0 \qquad\qquad x = 36$$

Since the length cannot be zero feet, the shorter leg is 36 feet long.

35. Find t when $h = 0$.

$$h = -16t^2 + 1444$$
$$0 = -16t^2 + 1444$$
$$0 = -4(4t^2 - 361)$$
$$0 = -4(2t + 19)(2t - 19)$$
$$2t + 19 = 0 \quad \text{or} \quad 2t - 19 = 0$$
$$2t = -19 \qquad\qquad 2t = 19$$
$$t = -9.5 \qquad\qquad t = 9.5$$

Since the time cannot be negative, the solution is 9.5 seconds.

37. Let $P = 100$ and $A = 144$

$$A = P(1+r)^2$$
$$144 = 100(1+r)^2$$
$$1.2 = 1 + r$$
$$0.2 = r$$

The interest rate is 20%.

39. Let x = the length and $x - 7$ = the width.

$A = lw$

$120 = (x-7)(x)$

$120 = x^2 - 7x$

$0 = x^2 - 7x - 120$

$0 = (x+8)(x-15)$

$x + 8 = 0 \quad$ or $\quad x - 15 = 0$

$\quad\quad x = -8 \quad\quad\quad\quad x = 15$

Since the length cannot be negative, the length is 15 miles. The width is $15 - 7 = 8$ miles.

41. Let C = 9500

$C = x^2 - 15x + 50$

$9500 = x^2 - 15x + 50$

$0 = x^2 - 15x - 9450$

$0 = (x+90)(x-105)$

$x + 90 = 0 \quad$ or $\quad x - 105 = 0$

$\quad\quad x = -90 \quad\quad\quad\quad x = 105$

Since the number of units cannot be negative the solution is 105 units.

43. 9600 thousand acres

45. 9500 thousand acres

47. end of 1998

49. Answers may vary

51. Pool: x = length and $x + 6$ = width.

Total: $x + 8$ = length and $x + 14$ = width.

$A_{\text{Total}} = l_{\text{Total}} w_{\text{Total}} - l_{\text{Pool}} w_{\text{Pool}}$

$576 = (x+14)(x+8) - (x+6)(x)$

$576 = x^2 + 22x + 112 - x^2 - 6x$

$576 = 16x + 112$

$464 = 16x$

$29 = x$

$x + 6 = 29 + 6 = 35$

The length is 35 meters. The width is 29 meters.

Chapter 4 Review

1. $6x^2 - 15x = 3x(2x - 5)$

2. $4x^5 + 2x - 10x^4 = 2x(2x^4 + 1 - 5x^3)$

3. $5m + 30 = 5(m + 6)$

4. $20x^3 + 12x^2 + 24x = 4x(5x^2 + 3x + 6)$

5. $3x(2x+3) - 5(2x+3) = (2x+3)(3x-5)$

6. $5x(x+1) - (x+1) = (x+1)(3x-5)$

7. $3x^2 - 3x + 2x - 2 = 3x(x-1) + 2(x-1)$
$\quad\quad\quad\quad\quad\quad\quad\quad = (x-1)(3x+2)$

8. $6x^2 + 10x - 3x - 5 = 2x(3x+5) - 1(3x+5)$
$\quad\quad\quad\quad\quad\quad\quad\quad = (3x+5)(2x-1)$

9. $3a^2 + 9ab + 3b^2 + ab$
$= 3a(a+3b) + b(3b+a)$
$= 3a(a+3b) + b(a+3b)$
$= (a+3b)(3a+b)$

10. $x^2 + 6x + 8 = (x+4)(x+2)$

11. $x^2 - 11x + 24 = (x-8)(x-3)$

12. $x^2 + x + 2$ is a prime polynomial.

13. $x^2 - 5x - 6 = (x-6)(x+1)$

14. $x^2 + 2x - 8 = (x+4)(x-2)$

15. $x^2 + 4xy - 12xy^2 = (x+6y)(x-2y)$

16. $x^2 + 8xy + 15y^2 = (x+5y)(x+3y)$

17. $72 - 18x - 2x^2 = 2(36 - 9x - x^2)$
$$= 2(3-x)(12+x)$$

18. $32 + 12x - 4x^2 = 4(8 + 3x - x^2)$

19. $5y^3 - 50y^2 + 120y = 5y(y^2 - 10y + 24)$
$$= 5y(y-6)(y-4)$$

20. To factor $x^2 + 2x - 48$, think of two numbers whose product is -48 and whose sum is 2.

21. Factor out the GCF, which is 3.

22. $2x^2 + 13x + 6 = 2x^2 + 12x + x + 6$
$$= 2x(x+6) + 1(x+6)$$
$$= (x+6)(2x+1)$$

23. $4x^2 + 4x - 3 = 4x^2 + 6x - 2x - 3$
$$= 2x(2x+3) - 1(2x+3)$$
$$= (2x+3)(2x-1)$$

24. $6x^2 + 5xy - 4y^2 = 6x^2 + 8xy - 3xy - 4y^2$
$$= 2x(3x+4y) - y(3x+4y)$$
$$= (3x+4y)(2x-y)$$

25. $x^2 - x + 2$ is a prime polynomial.

26. $2x^2 - 23x - 39 = 2x^2 - 26x + 3x - 39$
$$= 2x(x-13)(x-13)$$
$$= (x-13)(2x+3)$$

27. $18x^2 - 9xy - 20y^2$
$$= 18x^2 - 24xy + 15xy - 20y^2$$
$$= 6x(3x-4y) + 5y(3x-4y)$$
$$= (3x-4y)(6x+5y)$$

28. $10y^3 + 25y^2 - 60y$
$$= 5y(2y^2 + 5y - 12)$$
$$= 5y(2y^2 + 8y - 3y - 12)$$
$$= 5y[2y(y+4) - 3(y+4)]$$
$$= 5y(y+4)(2y-3)$$

29. The perimeter is the sum of the lengths of the sides.
$$P = (x^2 - 2) + (x^2 - 4x) + (3x^2 - 5x)$$
$$= x^2 - 2 + x^2 - 4x + 3x^2 - 5x$$
$$= 5x^2 - 9x - 2$$
$$= (5x+1)(x-2)$$

30. $l = 6x^2 - 14x$ and $w = 2x^2 + 3$.

$P = 2l + 2w$

$P = 2(6x^2 - 14x) + 2(2x^2 + 3)$

$= 12x^2 - 28x + 4x^2 + 6$

$= 16x^2 - 28x + 6$

$= 2(8x^2 - 14x + 3)$

$= 2(4x - 1)(2x - 3)$

31. Yes; two terms, x^2 and 9, are squares $(9 = 3^2)$, and the third term of the trinomial, $6x$, is twice the product of x and $3 (2 \cdot x \cdot 3 = 6x)$.

32. No; the two terms, x^2 and 64, are squares $(64 = 8^2)$, but the third term of the trinomial, $8x$, is not twice the product of x and 8, or its opposite.

33. No; the two terms, $9m^2$ and 16, are squares $\left(9m^2 = (3m)^2 \text{ and } 16 = 4^2\right)$, but the third term of the trinomial, $-12m$, is not twice the product of $3m$ and 4, or its opposite.

34. Yes; two terms, $4y^2$ and 49, are squares $\left(4y^2 = (2y)^2 \text{ and } 49 = 7^2\right)$, and the third term of the trinomial, $-28y$, is the opposite of twice the product of $2y$ and 7.

35. Yes; $x^2 - 9 = x^2 - 3^2$ is the difference of squares.

36. No; $x^2 + 16$ is the sum of two squares, $x^2 + 16 = x^2 + 4^2$.

37. Yes; $4x^2 - 25y^2 = (2x)^2 - (5y)^2$ is the difference of two squares.

38. No; only one of the terms, 1, is a square.

39. $x^2 - 81 = x^2 - 9^2 = (x+9)(x-9)$

40. $x^2 + 12x + 36 = (x+6)(x+6) = (x+6)^2$

41. $4x^2 - 9 = (2x)^2 - 3^2 = (2x+3)(2x-3)$

42. $9t^2 - 25s^2 = (3t)^2 - (5s)^2 = (3t+5s)(3t-5s)$

43. $16x^2 + y^2$ is a prime polynomial.

44. $n^2 - 18n + 81 = (n-9)(n-9) = (n-9)^2$

45. $3r^2 + 36 + 108 = 3(r^2 + 12r + 36)$

$= 3(r+6)(r+6) = 3(r+6)^2$

46. $9y^2 - 42y + 49 = (3y-7)(3y-7)$

$= (3y-7)^2$

47. $5m^8 - 5m^6 = 5m^6(m^2 - 1) = 5m^6(m^2 - 1^2)$

$= 5m^6(m+1)(m-1)$

48. $4x^2 - 28xy + 49y^2 = (2x-7y)(2x-7y)$

$= (2x-7y)^2$

49. $3x^2 y + 6xy^2 + 3y^3 = 3y\left(x^2 + 2xy + y^2\right)$
$$= 3y(x+y)(x+y)$$
$$= 3y(x+y)^2$$

50. $16x^4 - 1 = \left(4x^2\right)^2 - 1^2$
$$= \left(4x^2 + 1\right)\left(4x^2 - 1\right)$$
$$= \left(4x^2 + 1\right)\left((2x)^2 - 1^2\right)$$
$$= \left(4x^2 + 1\right)(2x+1)(2x-1)$$

51. $(x+6)(x-2) = 0$
$$x + 6 = 0 \quad \text{or} \quad x - 2 = 0$$
$$x = -6 \qquad\qquad x = 2$$
The solutions are -6 and 2.

52. $(x+6)(x-2) = 0$
$$3x = 0 \quad \text{or} \quad x + 1 = 0 \quad \text{or} \quad 7x - 2 = 0$$
$$x = 0 \qquad\qquad x = -1 \qquad\qquad 7x = 2$$
$$x = \frac{2}{7}$$
The solutions are 0, -1, and $\frac{2}{7}$.

53. $4(5x+1)(x+3) = 0$
$$5x + 1 = 0 \quad \text{or} \quad x + 3 = 0$$
$$5x = -1 \qquad\qquad x = -3$$
$$x = -\frac{1}{5}$$
The solutions are $-\frac{1}{5}$ and -3.

54. $x^2 + 8x + 7 = 0$
$$(x+7)(x+1) = 0$$
$$x + 7 = 0 \quad \text{or} \quad x + 1 = 0$$
$$x = -7 \qquad\qquad x = -1$$
The solutions are -7 and -1.

55. $x^2 - 2x - 24 = 0$
$$(x-6)(x+4) = 0$$
$$x - 6 = 0 \quad \text{or} \quad x + 4 = 0$$
$$x = 6 \qquad\qquad x = -4$$
The solutions are 6 and -4.

56. $x^2 + 10x = -25$
$$x^2 + 10x + 25 = 0$$
$$(x+5)(x+5) = 0$$
$$x + 5 = 0 \quad \text{or} \quad x + 5 = 0$$
$$x = -5 \qquad\qquad x = -5$$
The solution is -5.

57. $x(x-10) = -16$
$$x^2 - 10x = -16$$
$$x^2 - 10x + 16 = 0$$
$$(x-8)(x-2) = 0$$
$$x - 8 = 0 \quad \text{or} \quad x - 2 = 0$$
$$x = 8 \qquad\qquad x = 2$$
The solutions are 8 and 2.

58. $(3x-1)(9x^2+3x+1)=0$

$3x-1=0$ or $9x^2+3x+1=0$

$9x^2+3x+1$ is a prime polynomial.

$3x-1=0$

$\quad 3x=1$

$\quad\quad x=\dfrac{1}{3}$

59. $56x^2-5x-6=0$

$56x^2+16x-21x-6=0$

$8x(7x+2)(8x-3)=0$

$(7x+2)(8x-3)=0$

$7x+2=0$ or $8x-3=0$

$\quad 7x=-2 \quad\quad\quad\quad 8x=3$

$\quad\quad x=-\dfrac{2}{7} \quad\quad\quad x=\dfrac{3}{8}$

The solutions are $-\dfrac{2}{7}$ and $\dfrac{3}{8}$.

60. $m^2=6m$

$m^2-6m=0$

$m(m-6)=0$

$m=0$ or $m-6=0$

$\quad\quad\quad\quad\quad\quad\quad m=6$

The solutions are 0 and 6.

61. $r^2=25$

$r^2-25=0$

$r^2-5^2=0$

$(r+5)(r-5)=0$

$x+5=0$ or $x-5=0$

$\quad x=-5 \quad\quad\quad\quad x=5$

The solutions are -5 and 5.

62. If $x=4$ and $x=5$ are the solutions, then by the zero factor property

$\quad x=4$ or $x=5$

$x-4=0 \quad\quad\quad\quad x-5=0$

$(x-4)(x-5)=0$

$x^2-4x-5x+20=0$

$x^2-9x+20=0$

63. Let $x=$ the width, then $2x=$ the length.

$P=2l+2w$

$24=2(2x)+2x$

$24=4x+2x$

$24=6x$

$4=x$

The width is 4 inches and the length is $2\cdot4=8$ inches. Thus, (c) is the correct answer.

64. Let $x=$ the width, then $3x+1=$ the length.

$A=lw$

$80=(3x+1)(x)$

$80=3x^2+x$

$0=3x^2+x-80$

$0=(3x+16)(x-5)$

$3x+16=0$ or $x-5=0$

$\quad 3x=-16 \quad\quad\quad\quad x=5$

$\quad\quad x=-\dfrac{16}{3}$

Since the width cannot be negative, the width is 5 meters and the length is $3(5)+1=16$ meters. Thus (d) is the correct answer.

65. $x^2 = 81$

$x^2 - 81 = 0$

$(x+9)(x-9) = 0$

$x+9 = 0$　or　$x-9 = 0$

$x = -9$　　　　　$x = 9$

Since the length cannot be negative, the sides are 9 units long.

66. The perimeter is the sum of the lengths of the sides.

$47 = (2x+3)+(3x+1)+(x^2-3x)+(x+3)$

$47 = 2x+3+3x+1+x^2-3x+x+3$

$47 = x^2+3x+7$

$0 = x^2+3x-40$

$0 = (x+8)(x-5)$

$x+8 = 0$　or　$x-5 = 0$

$x = -8$　　　　　$x = 5$

Since the lengths cannot be negative, $x = 5$. The lengths of the sides are $2(5)+3 = 13$ units, $3(5)+1 = 16$ units, $5^2-3(5) = 10$ units, and $5+3 = 8$ units.

67. Let x = the width of the flag. Then $2x-15$ = the length of the flag.

$A = lw$

$500 = (2x-15)(x)$

$500 = 2x^2-15x$

$0 = 2x^2-15x-500$

$0 = (2x+25)(x-20)$

$2x+25 = 0$　or　$x-20 = 0$

$2x = -25$　　　　　$x = 20$

$x = -\dfrac{25}{2}$

Since the dimensions cannot be negative, the width is 20 inches and the length is $2(20)-15 = 25$ inches.

68. Let x = the height of the sail, then $4x$ = the base of the sail.

$A = \dfrac{1}{2}bh$

$162 = \dfrac{1}{2}(4x)(x)$

$162 = 2x^2$

$0 = 2x^2-162$

$0 = 2(x^2-81)$

$0 = 2(x+9)(x-9)$

$x+9 = 0$　or　$x-9 = 0$

$x = -9$　　　　　$x = 9$

Since the dimensions cannot be negative, the height is 9 yards and the base is $4 \cdot 9 = 36$ yards.

69. Let x = the first integer. Then $x+1$ = the next consecutive integer.

$x(x+1)380$

$x^2+x = 380$

$x^2+x-380 = 0$

$(x+20)(x-19) = 0$

$x+20 = 0$　or　$x-19 = 0$

$x = -21$　　　　　$x = 19$

The integers are 19 and 20.

70. a. Let h = 2800 and solve for t.

$$h = -16t^2 + 440t$$
$$2800 = -16t^2 + 440t$$
$$0 = -16t^2 + 440t - 2800$$
$$0 = -8(2t^2 - 55t + 350)$$
$$0 = -8(2t - 35)(t - 10)$$

$$2t - 35 = 0 \quad \text{or} \quad t - 10 = 0$$
$$2t = 35 \qquad\qquad t = 10$$
$$t = \frac{35}{2}$$
$$t = 17.5$$

The solutions are 17.5 and 10.
Answers may vary.

b. Find t when $h = 0$.

$$h = -16t^2 + 440t$$
$$0 = 16t^2 + 440t$$
$$0 = -8t(2t - 55)$$

$$-8t = 0 \quad \text{or} \quad 2t - 55 = 0$$
$$t = 0 \qquad\qquad 2t = 55$$
$$t = \frac{55}{2}$$
$$t = 27.5$$

27.5 seconds after being fired, the rocket will reach the ground again.

71. Let x = the length of the longer leg, then $x - 8$ = the length of the shorter leg and $x + 8$ = the length of the hypotenuse. By the Pythagorean theorem,

$$x^2 + (x - 8)^2 = (x + 8)^2$$
$$x^2 + x^2 - 16x + 64 = x^2 + 16x + 64$$

$$x^2 - 32x = 0$$
$$x(x - 32) = 0$$
$$x = 0 \quad \text{or} \quad x = 32$$

Since the length cannot be zero cm, the length of the longer leg is 32 cm.

Chapter 4 Test

1. $9x^2 - 3x = 3x(3x - 1)$

2. $x^2 + 11x + 28 = (x + 7)(x + 4)$

3. $49 - m^2 = 7^2 - m^2 = (7 + m)(7 - m)$

4. $y^2 + 22y + 121 = (y + 11)(y + 11)$
$$= (y + 11)^2$$

5. $x^4 - 16 = (x^2)^2 - 4^2$
$$= (x^2 + 4)(x^2 - 4)$$
$$= (x^2 + 4)(x^2 - 2^2)$$
$$= (x^2 + 4)(x + 2)(x - 2)$$

6. $4(a + 3) - y(a + 3) = (a + 3)(4 - y)$

7. $x^2 + 4$ is a prime polynomial.

8. $y^2 - 8y - 48 = (y - 12)(y + 4)$

9. $3a^2 + 3ab - 7a - 7b = 3a(a + b) - 7(a + b)$
$$= (a + b)(3a - 7)$$

10. $3x^2 - 5x + 2 = (3x - 2)(x - 1)$

11. $180 - 5x^2 = 5(36 - x^2)$

$\qquad = 5(6^2 - x^2)$

$\qquad = 5(6 + x)(6 - x)$

12. $3x^3 - 12x^2 + 30x = 3x(x^2 - 7x + 10)$

$\qquad\qquad\qquad = 3x(x - 5)(x - 2)$

13. $6t^2 - t - 5 = (6t + 5)(t - 1)$

14. $xy^2 - 7y^2 - 4x + 28$

$\qquad = y^2(x - 7) - 4(x - 7)$

$\qquad = (x - 7)(y^2 - 4)$

$\qquad = (x - 7)(y^2 - 2^2)$

$\qquad = (x - 7)(y + 2)(y - 2)$

15. $x - x^5 = x(1 - x^4)$

$\qquad = x\left(1 - (x^2)^2\right)$

$\qquad = x(1 + x^2)(1 - x^2)$

$\qquad = x(1 + x^2)(1 + x)(1 - x)$

16. $x^2 + 14xy + 24y^2 = (x + 12y)(x + 2y)$

17. $(x - 3)(x + 9) = 0$

$x - 3 = 0 \quad$ or $\quad x + 9 = 0$

$\qquad x = 3 \qquad\qquad\quad x = -9$

The solutions are 3 and -9.

18. $x^2 + 10x + 24 = 0$

$(x + 6)(x + 4) = 0$

$x + 6 = 0 \quad$ or $\quad x + 4 = 0$

$\quad x = -6 \qquad\qquad\quad x = -4$

The solutions are -6 and -4.

19. $x^2 + 5x = 14$

$x^2 + 5x - 14 = 0$

$(x + 7)(x - 2) = 0$

$x + 7 = 0 \quad$ or $\quad x - 2 = 0$

$\quad x = -7 \qquad\qquad\quad x = 2$

The solutions are -7 and 2.

20. $3x(2x - 3)(3x + 4) = 0$

$3x = 0 \quad$ or $\quad 2x - 3 = 0 \quad$ or $\quad 3x + 4 = 0$

$\;x = 0 \qquad\qquad 2x = 3 \qquad\qquad 3x = -4$

$\qquad\qquad\qquad\quad x = \dfrac{3}{2} \qquad\qquad x = -\dfrac{4}{3}$

The solutions are 0, $\dfrac{3}{2}$, and $-\dfrac{4}{3}$.

21. $5t^3 - 45t = 0$

$5t(t^2 - 0) = 0$

$5t(t + 3)(t - 3) = 0$

$5t = 0 \quad$ or $\quad t + 3 = 0 \quad$ or $\quad t - 3 = 0$

$\;t = 0 \qquad\qquad\quad t = -3 \qquad\qquad t = 3$

The solutions are 0, -3, and 3.

22. $3x^2 = -12x$

$3x^2 + 12x = 0$

$3x(x + 4) = 0$

$3x = 0 \quad$ or $\quad x + 4 = 0$

$\;x = 0 \qquad\qquad\quad x = -4$

The solutions are 0 and -4.

23. $t^2 - 2t - 15 = 0$

$(t-5)(t+3) = 0$

$x - 5 = 0$ or $t + 3 = 0$

$t = 5$ $t = -3$

The solutions are 5 and -3.

24. $(x-1)(3x^2 - x - 2) = 0$

$(x-1)(3x+2)(x-1) = 0$

$(x-1)^2(3x+2) = 0$

$x - 1 = 0$ or $3x + 2 = 0$

$x = 1$ $3x = -2$

$x = -\dfrac{2}{3}$

The solutions are 1 and $-\dfrac{2}{3}$.

25. Let $x + 2 =$ the length of the rectangle and $x - 1 =$ the width of the rectangle.

$A = lw$

$54 = (x+2)(x-1)$

$54 = x^2 + x - 2$

$0 = x^2 + x - 56$

$0 = (x+8)(x-7)$

$x + 8 = 0$ or $x - 7 = 0$

$x = -8$ $x = 7$

Since the dimensions cannot be negative, the length of the rectangle is $7 + 2 = 9$ units, and the width is $7 - 1 = 6$ units.

$2(20) - 15 = 25$ inches.

26. Let $x =$ the height of the triangle, then $x + 9 =$ the base.

$A = \dfrac{1}{2}bh$

$68 = \dfrac{1}{2}(x+9)(x)$

$68 = \dfrac{1}{2}x^2 + \dfrac{9}{2}x$

$0 = \dfrac{1}{2}x^2 + \dfrac{9}{2}x - 68$

$0 = \dfrac{1}{2}(x^2 + 9x - 136)$

$0 = \dfrac{1}{2}(x+17)(x-8)$

$x + 17 = 0$ or $x - 8 = 0$

$x = -17$ $x = 8$

Since the length of the base cannot be negative, the base is $8 + 9 = 17$ feet.

27. Let $x =$ the first number, then $17 - x =$ the other number.

$x^2 + (17 - x)^2 = 145$

$x^2 + 289 - 34x + x^2 = 145$

$2x^2 - 34x + 144 = 0$

$2(x^2 - 17x + 72) = 0$

$2(x-9)(x-8) = 0$

$x - 9 = 0$ or $x - 8 = 0$

$x = 9$ $x = 8$

The numbers are 8 and 9.

28. Find t when $h = 0$.

$h = -16t^2 + 1089$

$0 = -16t^2 + 1089$

$16t^2 = 1089$

$t^2 = 68.0625$

$t = 8.25$

It reaches the ground after 8.25 seconds.

29. Let x = the length of the shorter leg, then $x + 5$ = the length of the longer leg and $x + 10$ = the length of the hypotenuse. By the Pythagorean theorem,

$x^2 + (x+5)^2 = (x+10)^2$

$x^2 + x^2 + 10x + 25 = x^2 + 20x + 100$

$x^2 - 10x - 75 = 0$

$(x-15)(x+5) = 0$

$x - 15 = 0 \quad$ or $\quad x + 5 = 0$

$\qquad x = 15 \qquad\qquad x = -5$

Since the lengths cannot be negative, the length of the shorter leg is 15 cm, the longer let is $15 + 5 = 20$ cm, and the hypotenuse is $15 + 10 = 25$ cm.

Cumulative Review Chapter 4

1. a. $9 \le 11$

   b. $8 > 1$

   c. $3 \ne 4$

2. Replace x with 2 and see if a true statement results.

$3x + 10 = 8x$

$3(2) + 10 \overset{?}{=} 8(2)$

$6 + 10 \overset{?}{=} 16$

$16 = 16$

Since $16 = 16$ is a true statement, 2 is a solution of the equation $3x + 10 = 8x$.

3. $-4 - 8 = -4 + (-8) = -12$

4. a. $5x - y = 5(-2) - (-4) = -10 + 4 = -6$

   b. $x^3 - y^2 = (-2)^3 - (-4)^2 = -8 - 16 = -24$

5. $2x + 3x + 5 + 2 = (2+3)x + (5+2)$
$$= 5x + 7$$

6. $-5a - 3 + a + 2 = -5a + a + (-3 + 2)$
$$= -4a - 1$$

7. $2.3x + 5x - 6 = (2.3 + 5)x - 6 = 7.3x - 6$

8. $-3x = 33$

$\dfrac{-3x}{-3} = \dfrac{33}{-3}$

$x = -11$

9. $\quad 3(x-4) = 3x - 12$

$3x - 12 = 3x - 12$

$3x - 12 + 12 = 3x - 12 + 12$

$3x = 3x$

$3x - 3x = 3x - 3x$

$0 = 0$

Since $0 = 0$ is true for every value of x, every real number is a solution.

10. $V = lwh$

$$\frac{V}{wh} = \frac{lwh}{wh}$$

$$\frac{V}{wh} = 1$$

11. $\dfrac{x-5}{3} = \dfrac{x+2}{5}$

$$5(x-5) = 3(x+2)$$

$$5x - 25 = 3x + 6$$

$$5x = 3x + 31$$

$$2x = 31$$

$$\frac{2x}{2} = \frac{31}{2}$$

$$x = \frac{31}{2}$$

12. $\left(5^3\right)^6 = 5^{3 \cdot 6} = 5^{18}$

13. $\left(y^8\right)^2 = y^{8 \cdot 2} = y^{16}$

14. $\dfrac{\left(x^3\right)^4 x}{7} = \dfrac{x^{12} \cdot x}{7}$

$$= \frac{x^{12+1}}{x^7} = \frac{x^{13}}{x^7}$$

$$= x^{13-7} = x^6$$

15. $\left(y^{-3} z^6\right)^{-6} = \left(y^{-3}\right)^6 \left(z^6\right)^{-6}$

$$= y^{18} z^{-36} = \frac{y^{18}}{z^{36}}$$

16. $\dfrac{x^{-7}}{\left(x^4\right)^3} = \dfrac{x^{-7}}{x^{12}} = x^{-7-12} = x^{-19} = \dfrac{1}{x^{19}}$

17. $-3x + 7x = (-3 + 7)x = 4x$

18. $11x^2 + 5 + 2x^2 - 7 = 11x^2 + 2x^2 + 5 - 7$

$$= 13x^2 - 2$$

19. $(2x - y)^2 = (2x - y)(2x - y)$

$$= 2x(2x) + 2x(-y) + (-y)(2x) + (-y)(-y)$$

$$= 4x^2 - 2xy - 2xy + y^2 = 4x^2 - 4xy + y^2$$

20. $(t + 2)^2 = t^2 + 2(t)(2) + 2^2$

$$= t^2 + 4t + 4$$

21. $\left(x^2 - 7y\right)^2 = \left(x^2\right)^2 - 2\left(x^2\right)(7y) + (7y)^2$

$$= x^4 - 14x^2 y + 49y^2$$

22. $\dfrac{8x^2 y^2 - 16xy + 2x}{4xy} = \dfrac{8x^2 y^2}{4xy} - \dfrac{16xy}{4xy} + \dfrac{2x}{4xy}$

$$= 2xy - 4 + \frac{1}{2y}$$

23. $5(x + 3) + y(x + 3) = (x + 3)(5 + y)$

24. $x^4 + 5x^2 + 6 = \left(x^2 + 2\right)\left(x^2 + 3\right)$

25. $6x^2 - 2x - 20 = 2\left(3x^2 - x - 10\right)$

$$= 2\left(3x^2 - 6x + 5x - 10\right)$$

$$= 2\left[3x(x - 2) + 5(x - 2)\right]$$

$$= 2(x - 2)(3x + 5)$$

26. Find t when $h = 0$.

$h = -16t^2 + 256$

$0 = -16t^2 + 256$

$16t^2 = 256$

$t^2 = 16$

$t = 4$

It hits the ground after 4 seconds.

Chapter 5

Chapter 5 Pretest

1. Find the values for x that make the denominator 0.

$$x^2 - 9x - 10 = 0$$
$$(x - 10)(x + 1) = 0$$
$$x - 10 = 0 \quad \text{or} \quad x + 1 = 0$$
$$x = 10 \qquad\qquad x = -1$$

The rational expression $\dfrac{x + 2}{x^2 - 9x - 10}$ is undefined when $x = 10$ or when $x = -1$.

2. $\dfrac{4x + 32}{x^2 + 10x + 16} = \dfrac{4(x + 8)}{(x + 8)(x + 2)} = \dfrac{4}{x + 2}$

3. Factor each denominator.

$$5x + 10 = 5(x + 2)$$
$$2x^2 + 10x + 12 = 2(x^2 + 5x + 6)$$
$$= 2(x + 3)(x + 2)$$
$$\text{LCD} = 2 \cdot 5(x + 2)(x + 3)$$
$$= 10(x + 2)(x + 3)$$

4. $\dfrac{y^2 - 8y + 7}{2y - 14} \cdot \dfrac{6y + 18}{y^2 + 2y - 3}$

$= \dfrac{(y - 7)(y - 1)}{2(y - 7)} \cdot \dfrac{2 \cdot 3(y + 3)}{(y + 3)(y - 1)}$

$= \dfrac{(y - 7)(y - 1) \cdot 2 \cdot 3(x + 3)}{2(y - 7) \cdot (y + 3)(y - 1)}$

5. $\dfrac{5x^3}{x^2 - 25} \div \dfrac{x^6}{(x + 5)^2} = \dfrac{5x^3}{x^2 - 25} \cdot \dfrac{(x + 5)^2}{x^6}$

$= \dfrac{5x^3}{(x + 5)(x - 5)} \cdot \dfrac{(x + 5)^2}{x^3 \cdot x^3}$

$= \dfrac{5x^3 \cdot (x + 5)^2}{(x + 5)(x - 5) \cdot x^3 \cdot x^3} = \dfrac{5(x + 5)}{x^3(x - 5)}$

6. $\dfrac{b}{b^2 - 9b - 22} + \dfrac{2}{b^2 - 9b - 22}$

$= \dfrac{b + 2}{b^2 - 9b - 22} = \dfrac{b + 2}{(b - 11)(b + 2)}$

$= \dfrac{1}{b - 11}$

7. $\dfrac{3}{x - 1} - 4 = \dfrac{3}{x - 1} - \dfrac{4(x - 1)}{1(x - 1)} = \dfrac{3 - 4(x - 1)}{x - 1}$

$= \dfrac{3 - 4x + 4}{x - 1} = \dfrac{7 - 4x}{x - 1}$

8. $\dfrac{2}{x - 5} - \dfrac{7}{5 - x} = \dfrac{2}{x - 5} - \dfrac{7}{-(x - 5)}$

$= \dfrac{2}{x - 5} - \dfrac{-7}{x - 5} = \dfrac{2 - (-7)}{x - 5} = \dfrac{9}{x - 5}$

9. $\dfrac{x}{x^2-16}+\dfrac{3}{x^2-7x+12}$

$=\dfrac{x}{(x+4)(x-4)}+\dfrac{3}{(x-4)(x-3)}$

$=\dfrac{x(x-3)}{(x+4)(x-4)(x-3)}$

$\qquad +\dfrac{3(x+4)}{(x+4)(x-4)(x-3)}$

$=\dfrac{x(x-3)+3(x+4)}{(x+4)(x-4)(x-3)}$

$=\dfrac{x^2-3x+3x+12}{(x+4)(x-4)(x-3)}$

$=\dfrac{x^2+12}{(x+4)(x-4)(x-3)}$

10.

$\dfrac{5}{b}+\dfrac{3}{5}=\dfrac{4}{5b}$

$5b\left(\dfrac{5}{b}+\dfrac{3}{5}\right)=5b\left(\dfrac{4}{5b}\right)$

$5b\left(\dfrac{5}{b}\right)+5b\left(\dfrac{3}{5}\right)=4$

$25+3b=4$

$3b=-21$

$b=-=7$

11. $9+\dfrac{7}{d-7}=\dfrac{d}{d-7}$

$(d-7)\left(9+\dfrac{7}{d-7}\right)=(d-7)\left(\dfrac{d}{d-7}\right)$

$(d-7)(9)+(d-7)\left(\dfrac{7}{d-7}\right)=d$

$9d-63+7=d$

$-56=-8d.$

$d=7$

However, $d=7$ makes the denominators 0 in the original equation. The equation has no solution.

12. $\dfrac{4y+5}{y^2+5y+6}+\dfrac{3}{y+3}=\dfrac{2}{y+2}$

$y^2+5y+6=(y+3)(y+2)$

$(y+3)(y+2)\left(\dfrac{4y+5}{(y+3)(y+2)}+\dfrac{3}{y+3}\right)$

$=(y+3)(y+2)\left(\dfrac{2}{y+2}\right)$

$(y+3)(y+2)\left(\dfrac{4y+5}{(y+3)(y+2)}\right)$

$+(y+3)(y+2)\left(\dfrac{3}{y+3}\right)=2(y+3)$

$4y+5+3(y+2)=2(y+3)$

$4y+5+3y+6=2y+6$

$5y=-5$

$y=-1$

13. $\dfrac{2A}{b}=h$

$b\left(\dfrac{2A}{b}\right)=b(h)$

$2A=bh$

$\dfrac{2A}{h}=\dfrac{bh}{h}$

$\dfrac{2A}{h}=b$

14.

$$\frac{\frac{12m^3}{5n^2}}{\frac{4m^6}{25n^8}} = \frac{12m^3}{5n^2} \cdot \frac{25n^8}{4m^6}$$

$$= \frac{12m^3 \cdot 25n^8}{5n^2 \cdot 4m^6}$$

$$= \frac{3 \cdot 4 \cdot 5 \cdot 5m^3 \cdot n^6 \cdot n^2}{5 \cdot 4m^3 \cdot m^3 \cdot n^2}$$

$$= \frac{3 \cdot 5n^6}{m^3}$$

$$= \frac{15n^6}{m^3}$$

15.

$$\frac{16 - \frac{1}{a^2}}{\frac{4}{a} + \frac{1}{a^2}} = \frac{a^2\left(16 - \frac{1}{a^2}\right)}{a^2\left(\frac{4}{a} + \frac{1}{a^2}\right)} = \frac{16a^2 - 1}{4a + 1}$$

$$= \frac{(4a+1)(4a-1)}{(4a+1)} = 4a - 1$$

16.

$$\frac{3}{x} = \frac{9}{15}$$

$$45 = 9x$$

$$5 = x$$

17. Let x = the unknown number.

$$\left(10 \cdot \frac{1}{x}\right) + x = 7$$

$$\frac{10}{x} + x = 7$$

$$x\left(\frac{10}{x} + x\right) = x(7)$$

$$10 + x^2 = 7x$$

$$x^2 - 7x + 10 = 0$$

$$(x-5)(x-2) = 0$$

$$x - 5 = 0 \quad \text{or} \quad x - 2 = 0$$

$$x = 5 \qquad\qquad x = 2$$

The number is 2 or 5.

18. Let x = the time in hours it takes if they work together. Then $\frac{1}{x}$ = the part of the job they complete is 1 hour. Since Sonya completes $\frac{1}{5}$ of the job in 1 hour, and her daughter completes $\frac{1}{8}$ of the job in one hour,

$$\frac{1}{5} + \frac{1}{8} = \frac{1}{x}$$

$$40x\left(\frac{1}{5}\right) + 40x\left(\frac{1}{8}\right) = 40x\left(\frac{1}{x}\right)$$

$$8x + 5x = 40$$

$$13x = 40$$

$$x = \frac{40}{13}$$

$$x = 3\frac{1}{13}$$

It will take $3\frac{1}{3}$ hrs if they work together.

19. Let r = the rate of the plane in still air. Then r + 25 = the rate with a tail wind and r − 25 = the rate against the wind. Since

$$d = rt, \ t = \frac{d}{r}.$$

With a tail wind:

$$\frac{495}{r+25} = t$$

Against the wind:

$$\frac{405}{r-25} = t$$

$$\frac{495}{r+25} = \frac{405}{r-25}$$

$$(r+25)(r-25)\left(\frac{495}{r+25}\right)$$

$$=(r+25)(r-25)\left(\frac{405}{r-25}\right)$$

$$495(r-25) = 405(r+25)$$

$$495r - 12,375 = 405r + 10,125$$

$$90r = 22,500$$

$$r = 250$$

The rate of the plane in still air is 250 mph.

Practice Problems 5.1

1. a. $\dfrac{x-3}{5x+1} = \dfrac{4-3}{5(4)+1} = \dfrac{1}{20+1} = \dfrac{1}{21}$

b. $\dfrac{x-3}{5x+1} = \dfrac{-3-3}{5(-3)+1} = \dfrac{-6}{-15+1} = \dfrac{-6}{-14}$

$= \dfrac{-2\cdot3}{-2\cdot7} = \dfrac{3}{7}$

2. a. $x+2 = 0$

$x = -2$

The expression is undefined when $x = -2$.

b. $x^2 + 5x + 4 = 0$

$(x+4)(x+1) = 0$

$x + 4 = 0$ or $x + 1 = 0$

$x = -4$ $x = -1$

The expression is undefined when $x = -4$ or $x = -1$.

c. The denominator of $\dfrac{x^2 - 3x + 2}{5}$ is never zero, so there are no values of x for which the expression is undefined.

3. $\dfrac{x^4 + x^3}{5x+5} = \dfrac{x^3(x+1)}{5(x+1)} = \dfrac{x^3}{5}$

4. $\dfrac{x^2 + 11x + 18}{x^2 + x - 2} = \dfrac{(x+2)(x+9)}{(x+2)(x-1)} = \dfrac{x+9}{x-1}$

5. $\dfrac{x^2 + 10x + 25}{x^2 + 5x} = \dfrac{(x+5)(x+5)}{x(x+5)} = \dfrac{x+5}{x}$

6. $\dfrac{x+5}{x^2 - 25} = \dfrac{x+5}{(x-5)(x+5)} = \dfrac{1}{x-5}$

7. a. $\dfrac{x+4}{4+x} = \dfrac{x+4}{x+4} = 1$

b. $\dfrac{x-4}{4-x} = \dfrac{x-4}{(-1)(x-4)} = \dfrac{1}{-1} = -1$

Mental Math 5.1

1. $x = 0$

2. $x = 3$

3. $x = 0,\ x = 1$

4. $x = 5,\ x = 6$

Exercise Set 5.1

1. $\dfrac{x+5}{x+2} = \dfrac{2+5}{2+2} = \dfrac{7}{4}$

3. $\dfrac{y^3}{y^2-1} = \dfrac{(-2)^3}{(-2)^2-1} = \dfrac{-8}{4-1} = \dfrac{-8}{3} = -\dfrac{8}{3}$

5. $\dfrac{x^2+8x+2}{x^2-x-6} = \dfrac{2^2+8(2)+2}{2^2-2-6}$

$\qquad = \dfrac{4+16+2}{4-8}$

$\qquad = \dfrac{22}{-4}$

$\qquad = \dfrac{11\cdot 2}{-2\cdot 2}$

$\qquad = -\dfrac{11}{2}$

7. a. $\dfrac{150x^2}{x^2+3} = \dfrac{150(1)^2}{1^2+3} = \dfrac{150}{4} = 37.5$

The revenue is approximately \$37.5 million at the end of the first year.

b. $\dfrac{150x^2}{x^2+3} = \dfrac{150(2)^2}{2^2+3} = \dfrac{150(4)}{4+3} = \dfrac{600}{7}$

$\qquad = 85.7$

The revenue is approximately \$85.7 million at the end of the second year.

c. $\$85.7 - \$37.5 = \$48.2$ million

9. $2x = 0$

$x = 0$

The expression is undefined when $x = 0$.

11. $x + 2 = 0$

$x = -2$

The expression is undefined when $x = -2$.

13. $2x - 8 = 0$

$2x = 8$

$x = 4$

The expression is undefined when $x = 4$.

15. $15x + 30 = 0$

$15x = -30$

$x = -2$

The expression is undefined when $x = -2$.

17. The denominator is never zero so there are no values for which

$\dfrac{x^2-5x-2}{4}$ is undefined.

19. Answers may vary.

21. $\dfrac{2}{8x+16} = \dfrac{2}{8(x+2)} = \dfrac{2}{2\cdot 4(x+2)} = \dfrac{1}{4(x+2)}$

23. $\dfrac{x-2}{x^2-4} = \dfrac{x-2}{(x+2)(x-2)} = \dfrac{1}{x+2}$

25. $\dfrac{2x-10}{3x-30} = \dfrac{2(x-5)}{3(x-10)}$; does not simplify

27. $\dfrac{x+7}{7+x} = \dfrac{x+7}{x+7} = 1$

29. $\dfrac{x-7}{7-x} = \dfrac{x-7}{-1(x-7)} = \dfrac{1}{-1} = -1$

31. $\dfrac{-5a-5b}{a+b} = \dfrac{-5(a+b)}{a+b} = -5$

33. $\dfrac{x+5}{x^2-4x-45} = \dfrac{x+5}{(x-9)(x+5)} = \dfrac{1}{x-9}$

35. $\dfrac{5x^2+11x+2}{x+2} = \dfrac{(5x+1)(x+2)}{x+2} = 5x+1$

37. $\dfrac{x+7}{x^2+5x-14} = \dfrac{x+7}{(x-2)(x+7)} = \dfrac{1}{x-2}$

39. $\dfrac{2x^2+3x-2}{2x-1} = \dfrac{(2x-1)(x+2)}{2x-1} = x+2$

41. $\dfrac{x^2+7x+10}{x^2-3x-10} = \dfrac{(x+5)(x+2)}{(x-5)(x+2)} = \dfrac{x+5}{x-5}$

43. $\dfrac{3x^2+7x+2}{3x^2+13x+4} = \dfrac{(x+2)(3x+1)}{(x+4)(3x+1)} = \dfrac{x+2}{x+4}$

45. $\dfrac{2x^2-8}{4x-8} = \dfrac{2(x^2-4)}{4(x-2)}$

$\qquad = \dfrac{2(x+2)(x-2)}{2\cdot 2(x-2)}$

$\qquad = \dfrac{x+2}{2}$

47. $\dfrac{11x^2-22x^3}{6x-12x^2} = \dfrac{11x^2(1-2x)}{6x(1-2x)}$

$\qquad = \dfrac{11x\cdot x(1-2x)}{6\cdot x(1-2x)}$

$\qquad = \dfrac{11x}{6}$

49. $\dfrac{2-x}{x-2} = \dfrac{-1(x-2)}{x-2} = -1$

51. $\dfrac{x^2-1}{x^2-2x+1} = \dfrac{(x-1)(x+1)}{(x-1)(x-1)}$

$\qquad = \dfrac{x+1}{x-1}$

53. $\dfrac{m^2-6m+9}{m^2-9} = \dfrac{(m-3)(m-3)}{(m+3)(m-3)}$

$\qquad = \dfrac{m-3}{m+3}$

55. $\dfrac{1}{3}\cdot\dfrac{9}{11} = \dfrac{1\cdot 9}{3\cdot 11} = \dfrac{3\cdot 3}{3\cdot 11} = \dfrac{3}{11}$

57. $\dfrac{5}{6}\cdot\dfrac{10}{11}\cdot\dfrac{2}{3} = \dfrac{5\cdot 10\cdot 2}{6\cdot 11\cdot 3}$

$\qquad = \dfrac{5\cdot 2\cdot 5\cdot 2}{3\cdot 2\cdot 11\cdot 3}$

$\qquad = \dfrac{5\cdot 5\cdot 2}{3\cdot 11\cdot 3} = \dfrac{50}{99}$

59. $\dfrac{1}{3}\div\dfrac{1}{4} = \dfrac{1}{3}\cdot\dfrac{4}{1} = \dfrac{4}{3}$

61. $\dfrac{13}{20}\div\dfrac{2}{9} = \dfrac{13}{20}\cdot\dfrac{9}{2} = \dfrac{13\cdot 9}{20\cdot 2} = \dfrac{117}{40}$

63. $\dfrac{x^2+xy+2x+2y}{x+2} = \dfrac{x(x+y)+2(x+y)}{x+2}$

$\qquad = \dfrac{(x+y)(x+2)}{x+2}$

$\qquad = x+y$

65. $\dfrac{5x+15-xy-3y}{2x+6} = \dfrac{5(x+3)-y(x+3)}{2(x+3)}$

$\qquad = \dfrac{(x+3)(5-y)}{2(x+3)}$

$\qquad = \dfrac{5-y}{2}$

67. Answers may vary.

Let $R = 15.3$ and $C = 12.3$

69. $P = \dfrac{R-C}{R}$

$P = \dfrac{15.3-12.3}{15.3}$

$\quad = \dfrac{3}{15.3}$

$\quad = 0.196$

The gross profit margin was 19.6%.

71. Let $h = 154$, $d = 34$, $t = 2$, $r = 38$, $b = 439$

$S = \dfrac{h+d+2t+3r}{b}$

$S = \dfrac{154+34+2(2)+3(38)}{439}$

$\quad = \dfrac{306}{439}$

$\quad = 0.697$

The slugging percentage is 69.7%.

Practice Problems 5.2

1. a. $\dfrac{16y}{3} \cdot \dfrac{1}{x^2} = \dfrac{16y \cdot 1}{3 \cdot x^2} = \dfrac{16y}{3x^2}$

b. $\dfrac{-5a^3}{3b^3} \cdot \dfrac{2b^2}{15a} = \dfrac{-5a^3 \cdot 2b^2}{3b^3 \cdot 15a}$

$\qquad = \dfrac{-1 \cdot 5 \cdot 2 \cdot a \cdot a^2 \cdot b^2}{3 \cdot 3 \cdot 5 \cdot a \cdot b \cdot b^2} = -\dfrac{2a^2}{9b}$

2. $\dfrac{6x+6}{7} \cdot \dfrac{14}{x^2-1} = \dfrac{6(x+1)}{7} \cdot \dfrac{2 \cdot 7}{(x-1)(x+1)}$

$\qquad = \dfrac{6(x+1) \cdot 2 \cdot 7}{7 \cdot (x-1)(x+1)} = \dfrac{12}{x-1}$

3. $\dfrac{4x+8}{7x^2-14x} \cdot \dfrac{3x^2-5x-2}{9x^2-1}$

$\qquad = \dfrac{4(x+2)}{7x(x-2)} \cdot \dfrac{(3x+1)(x-2)}{(3x+1)(3x-1)}$

$\qquad = \dfrac{4(x+2)(3x+1)(x-2)}{7x(x-2)(3x+1)(3x-1)}$

$\qquad = \dfrac{4(x+2)}{7x(3x-1)}$

4. $\dfrac{7x^2}{6} \div \dfrac{x}{2y} = \dfrac{7x^2}{6} \cdot \dfrac{2y}{x} = \dfrac{7x \cdot x \cdot 2y}{2 \cdot 3 \cdot x} = \dfrac{7xy}{3}$

5. $\dfrac{(2x+3)(x-4)}{6} \div \dfrac{3x-12}{2}$

$\qquad = \dfrac{(2x+3)(x-4)}{6} \cdot \dfrac{2}{3x-12}$

$\qquad = \dfrac{(2x+3)(x-4)}{2 \cdot 3 \cdot 3(x-4)} = \dfrac{2x+3}{9}$

6. $\dfrac{10x+4}{x^2-4} \div \dfrac{5x^3+2x^2}{x+2} = \dfrac{10x+4}{x^2-4} \cdot \dfrac{x+2}{5x^3+2x^2}$

$\qquad = \dfrac{2(5x+2) \cdot (x+2)}{(x-2)(x+2) \cdot x^2(5x+2)} = \dfrac{2}{x^2(x-2)}$

7. $\dfrac{3x^2-10x+8}{7x-14} \div \dfrac{9x-12}{21}$

$\qquad = \dfrac{3x^2-10x+8}{7x-14} \cdot \dfrac{21}{9x-12}$

$\qquad = \dfrac{(3x-4)(x-2) \cdot 3 \cdot 7}{7(x-2) \cdot 3(3x-4)} = \dfrac{1}{1} = 1$

8. a. $\dfrac{x+3}{x} \cdot \dfrac{7}{x+3} = \dfrac{(x+3)\cdot 7}{x\cdot(x+3)} = \dfrac{7}{x}$

b. $\dfrac{x+3}{x} \div \dfrac{7}{x+3} = \dfrac{x+3}{x} \cdot \dfrac{x+3}{7}$

$= \dfrac{(x+3)\cdot(x+3)}{x\cdot 7} = \dfrac{(x+3)^2}{7x}$

c. $\dfrac{3-x}{x^2+6x+5} \cdot \dfrac{2x+10}{x^2-7x+12}$

$= \dfrac{-1(x-3)(2)(x+5)}{(x+1)(x+5)(x-3)(x-4)}$

$= -\dfrac{2}{(x+1)(x-4)}$

9. $21,444 \text{ sq yd} = 21,444 \text{ sq yd} \cdot \dfrac{9 \text{ sq ft}}{1 \text{ sq yd}}$

$= 192,996 \text{ sq ft}$

10. 40.9 ft/sec

$= \dfrac{40.9 \text{ feet}}{1 \text{ second}} \cdot \dfrac{3600 \text{ seconds}}{1 \text{ hour}} \cdot \dfrac{1 \text{ mile}}{5280 \text{ feet}}$

≈ 27.9 miles/hour

Mental Math 5.2

1. $\dfrac{2}{y} \cdot \dfrac{x}{3} = \dfrac{2x}{3y}$

2. $\dfrac{3x}{4} \cdot \dfrac{1}{y} = \dfrac{3x}{4y}$

3. $\dfrac{5}{7} \cdot \dfrac{y^2}{x^2} = \dfrac{5y^2}{7x^2}$

4. $\dfrac{x^5}{11} \cdot \dfrac{4}{z^3} = \dfrac{4x^5}{11z^3}$

5. $\dfrac{9}{x} \cdot \dfrac{x}{5} = \dfrac{9x}{5x} = \dfrac{9}{5}$

6. $\dfrac{y}{7} \cdot \dfrac{3}{y} = \dfrac{3y}{7y} = \dfrac{3}{7}$

Exercise Set 5.2

1. $\dfrac{3x}{y^2} \cdot \dfrac{7y}{4x} = \dfrac{3x\cdot 7y}{y^2\cdot 4x} = \dfrac{3\cdot 7\cdot x\cdot y}{4\cdot x\cdot y\cdot y} = \dfrac{3\cdot 7}{4\cdot y} = \dfrac{21}{4y}$

3. $\dfrac{8x}{2} \cdot \dfrac{x^5}{4x^2} = \dfrac{8x\cdot x^5}{2\cdot 4x^2} = \dfrac{2\cdot 4\cdot x\cdot x\cdot x^4}{2\cdot 4\cdot x\cdot x} = x^4$

5. $-\dfrac{5a^2b}{30a^2b^2} \cdot b^3 = \dfrac{5a^2b\cdot b^3}{30a^2b^2}$

$= -\dfrac{5\cdot a^2\cdot b\cdot b\cdot b^2}{5\cdot 6\cdot a^2\cdot b^2} = -\dfrac{b\cdot b}{6} = -\dfrac{b^2}{6}$

7. $\dfrac{x}{2x-14} \cdot \dfrac{x^2-7x}{5} = \dfrac{x\cdot(x^2-7x)}{(2x-14)\cdot 5}$

$= \dfrac{x\cdot x(x-7)}{2(x-7)\cdot 5} = \dfrac{x\cdot x}{2\cdot 5} = \dfrac{x^2}{10}$

9. $\dfrac{6x+6}{5} \cdot \dfrac{10}{36x+36} = \dfrac{(6x+6)\cdot 10}{5\cdot(36x+36)}$

$= \dfrac{6(x+1)\cdot 2\cdot 5}{5\cdot 36(x+1)} = \dfrac{6\cdot 5\cdot 2\cdot(x+1)}{6\cdot 5\cdot 2\cdot 3\cdot(x+1)}$

$= \dfrac{1}{3}$

11. $\dfrac{m^2-n^2}{m+n} \cdot \dfrac{m}{m^2-mn} = \dfrac{(m^2-n^2)\cdot m}{(m+n)\cdot(m^2-mn)}$

$= \dfrac{(m-n)(m+n)\cdot m}{(m+n)\cdot m\cdot(m-n)} = 1$

13. $\dfrac{x^2-25}{x^2-3x-10}\cdot\dfrac{x+2}{x}=\dfrac{\left(x^2-25\right)\cdot(x+2)}{\left(x^2-3x-10\right)\cdot x}$

$=\dfrac{(x-5)(x+5)\cdot(x+2)}{(x-5)(x+2)\cdot x}=\dfrac{x+5}{x}$

15. $A=\dfrac{2x}{x^2-25}\cdot\dfrac{x+5}{9x}=\dfrac{2x\cdot(x+5)}{\left(x^2-25\right)\cdot 9x}$

$=\dfrac{2\cdot x\cdot(x+5)}{9\cdot x\cdot(x+5)(x-5)}=\dfrac{2}{9(x-5)}$

17. $\dfrac{5x^7}{2x^5}\div\dfrac{10x}{4x^3}=\dfrac{5x^7}{2x^5}\cdot\dfrac{4x^3}{10x}$

$=\dfrac{5\cdot x^2\cdot x^5\cdot 2\cdot 2x\cdot x^2}{2x^5\cdot 2\cdot 5\cdot x}$

$=x^4$

19. $\dfrac{8x^2}{y^3}\div\dfrac{4x^2y^3}{6}=\dfrac{8x^2}{y^3}\cdot\dfrac{6}{4x^2y^3}$

$=\dfrac{2\cdot 4\cdot x^2\cdot 6}{y^3\cdot 4x^2y^3}$

$=\dfrac{12}{y^6}$

21. $\dfrac{(x-6)(x+4)}{4x}\div\dfrac{2x-12}{8x^2}$

$=\dfrac{(x-6)(x+4)}{4x}\cdot\dfrac{8x^2}{2x-12}$

$=\dfrac{(x-6)(x+4)\cdot 2\cdot 4\cdot x\cdot x}{4x\cdot 2(x-6)}$

$=x(x+4)$

23. $\dfrac{3x^2}{x^2-1}\div\dfrac{x^5}{(x+1)^2}=\dfrac{3x^2}{x^2-1}\cdot\dfrac{(x+1)^2}{x^5}$

$=\dfrac{3x^2\cdot(x+1)(x+1)}{(x-1)(x+1)\cdot x^2\cdot x^3}$

$=\dfrac{3(x+1)}{x^3(x-1)}$

25. $\dfrac{m^2-n^2}{m+n}\div\dfrac{m}{m^2+nm}$

$=\dfrac{m^2-n^2}{m+n}\cdot\dfrac{m^2+nm}{m}$

$=\dfrac{(m-n)(m+n)\cdot m(m+n)}{(m+n)\cdot m}$

$=(m-n)(m+n)=m^2-n^2$

27. $\dfrac{x+2}{7-x}\div\dfrac{x^2-5x+6}{x^2-9x+14}=\dfrac{x+2}{7-x}\cdot\dfrac{x^2-9x+14}{x^2-5x+6}$

$=\dfrac{(x+2)\cdot(x-7)(x-2)}{-1(x-7)\cdot(x-3)(x-2)}$

$=-\dfrac{x+2}{x-3}$

29. $\dfrac{x^2+7x+10}{x-1}\div\dfrac{x^2+2x-15}{x-1}$

$=\dfrac{x^2+7x+10}{x-1}\cdot\dfrac{x-1}{x^2+2x-15}$

$=\dfrac{(x+5)(x+2)\cdot(x-1)}{(x-1)\cdot(x+5)(x-3)}=\dfrac{x+2}{x-3}$

31. $\dfrac{5x-10}{12}\div\dfrac{4x-8}{8}=\dfrac{5x-10}{12}\cdot\dfrac{8}{4x-8}$

$=\dfrac{5(x-2)\cdot 2\cdot 4}{6\cdot 2\cdot 4(x-2)}=\dfrac{5}{6}$

33. $\dfrac{x^2+5x}{8} \cdot \dfrac{9}{3x+15} = \dfrac{x(x+5)\cdot 3 \cdot 3}{8 \cdot 3(x+5)} \cdot \dfrac{3x}{8}$

35. $\dfrac{7}{6p^2+q} \div \dfrac{14}{18p^2+3q}$

$= \dfrac{7}{6p^2+q} \cdot \dfrac{18p^2+3q}{14}$

$= \dfrac{7 \cdot 3\left(6p^2+q\right)}{\left(6p^2+q\right)\cdot 7 \cdot 2} = \dfrac{3}{2}$

37. $\dfrac{3x+4y}{x^2+4xy+4y^2} \cdot \dfrac{x+2y}{2}$

$= \dfrac{(3x+4y)\cdot(x+2y)}{(x+2y)(x+2y)\cdot 2}$

$= \dfrac{3x+4y}{2(x+2y)}$

39. $\dfrac{(x+2)^2}{x-2} \div \dfrac{x^2-4}{2x-4} = \dfrac{(x+2)^2}{x-2} \cdot \dfrac{2x-4}{x^2-4}$

$= \dfrac{(x+2)(x+2)\cdot 2(x-2)}{(x-2)\cdot(x+2)(x-2)} = \dfrac{2(x+2)}{x-2}$

41. $\dfrac{3y}{3-x} \div \dfrac{12xy}{x^2-9} = \dfrac{3y}{3-x} \cdot \dfrac{x^2-9}{12xy}$

$= \dfrac{3y(x+3)(x-3)}{-(x-3)(12xy)}$

$= -\dfrac{x+3}{4x}$

43. $\dfrac{a^2+7a+12}{a^2+5a+6} \cdot \dfrac{a^2+8a+15}{a^2+5a+4}$

$= \dfrac{(a+3)(a+4)\cdot(a+5)(a+3)}{(a+3)(a+2)\cdot(a+4)(a+1)}$

$= \dfrac{(a+5)(a+3)}{(a+2)(a+1)}$

45. 1 square foot is 12 inches by 12 inches or 144 square inches.

10 sq ft $\cdot \dfrac{144 \text{ sq in}}{1 \text{ sq ft}} = 1440$ sq in.

47. 90,000 cu in = 90,000 cu in

$\left(\dfrac{1 \text{ cu ft}}{1728 \text{ cu in}}\right)\left(\dfrac{1 \text{ cu yd}}{27 \text{ cu ft}}\right) = 1.93$ cu yd

49. $\dfrac{50 \text{ miles}}{1 \text{ hour}} \cdot \dfrac{1 \text{ hour}}{3600 \text{ seconds}} = \dfrac{5280 \text{ feet}}{1 \text{ mile}}$

$= \dfrac{50 \cdot 5280}{3600}$ feet/sec ≈ 73 feet/sec

51. 3,705,793 sq ft

$= 3,705,793$ sq ft $\left(\dfrac{1 \text{ sq yd}}{9 \text{ sq ft}}\right)$

$\approx 411,755$ sq yd

53. $763\dfrac{\text{mi}}{\text{hr}} = 763\dfrac{\text{mi}}{\text{hr}}\left(\dfrac{1 \text{ hr}}{3600 \text{ sec}}\right)\left(\dfrac{5280 \text{ ft}}{\text{mi}}\right)$

$\approx 1119\dfrac{\text{ft}}{\text{sec}}$

55. $\dfrac{1}{5}+\dfrac{4}{5} = \dfrac{5}{5} = 1$

57. $\dfrac{9}{9}-\dfrac{19}{9} = -\dfrac{10}{9}$

59. $\dfrac{6}{5} + \left(\dfrac{1}{5} - \dfrac{8}{5} \right) = \dfrac{6}{5} + \left(-\dfrac{7}{5} \right) = -\dfrac{1}{5}$

61. $\left(\dfrac{x^2 - y^2}{x^2 + y^2} \div \dfrac{x^2 - y^2}{3x} \right) \cdot \dfrac{x^2 + y^2}{6}$

$= \dfrac{x^2 - y^2}{x^2 + y^2} \cdot \dfrac{3x}{x^2 - y^2} \cdot \dfrac{x^2 + y^2}{6}$

$= \dfrac{\left(x^2 - y^2 \right) \cdot 3x \cdot \left(x^2 + y^2 \right)}{\left(x^2 + y^2 \right) \cdot \left(x^2 - y^2 \right) \cdot 2 \cdot 3} = \dfrac{x}{2}$

63. $\left(\dfrac{2a + b}{b^2} \cdot \dfrac{3a^2 - 2ab}{ab + 2b^2} \right) \div \dfrac{a^2 - 3ab + 2b^2}{5ab - 10b^2}$

$= \dfrac{2a + b}{b^2} \cdot \dfrac{3a^2 - 2ab}{ab + 2b^2} \cdot \dfrac{5ab - 10b^2}{a^2 - 3ab + 2b^2}$

$= \dfrac{\left(2a + b \right) \cdot \left(3a^2 - 2ab \right) \cdot \left(5ab - 10b^2 \right)}{b^2 \cdot \left(ab + 2b^2 \right) \cdot \left(a^2 - 3ab + 2b^2 \right)}$

$= \dfrac{\left(2a + b \right) \cdot a \left(3a - 2b \right) \cdot 5b \left(a - 2b \right)}{b^2 \cdot b \left(a + 2b \right) \cdot \left(a - 2b \right) \left(a - b \right)}$

$= \dfrac{5a \left(2a + b \right) \left(3a - 2b \right)}{b^2 \left(a + 2b \right) \left(a - b \right)}$

65. Answers may vary.

67. $\$2000 = \$2000 \left(\dfrac{1 \text{ euro}}{0.85 \text{ dollars}} \right)$

$\approx 2352.94 \text{ euros}$

Practice Problems 5.3

1. $\dfrac{8x}{3y} + \dfrac{x}{3y} = \dfrac{8x + x}{3y} = \dfrac{9x}{3y} = \dfrac{3x}{y}$

2. $\dfrac{3x}{3x - 7} - \dfrac{7}{3x - 7} = \dfrac{3x - 7}{3x - 7} = \dfrac{1}{1} = 1$

3. $\dfrac{2x^2 + 5x}{x + 2} - \dfrac{4x + 6}{x + 2} = \dfrac{2x^2 + 5x - \left(4x + 6 \right)}{x + 2}$

$= \dfrac{2x^2 + 5x - 4x - 6}{x + 2} = \dfrac{2x^2 + x - 6}{x + 2}$

$= \dfrac{\left(2x - 3 \right) \left(x + 2 \right)}{x + 2} = 2x - 3$

4. a. $9 = 3 \cdot 3 = 3^2$ and $15 = 3 \cdot 5$

       $\text{LCD} = 3^2 \cdot 5 = 9 \cdot 5 = 45$

  b. $6x^3 = 2 \cdot 3 \cdot x^3$ and $8x^5 = 2^3 \cdot x^5$

       $\text{LCD} = 2^3 \cdot 3 \cdot x^5 = 8 \cdot 3 \cdot x^5 = 24x^5$

5. Since $a + 5$ and $a - 5$ are completely factored and each factor appears once, the $\text{LCD} = \left(a + 5 \right) \left(a - 5 \right)$.

6. $\left(x - 4 \right)^2 = \left(x - 4 \right)^2$

     $3x - 12 = 3 \left(x - 4 \right)$

     $\text{LCD} = 3 \left(x - 4 \right)^2$

7. $y^2 + 2y - 3 = \left(y + 3 \right) \left(y - 1 \right)$

    $y^2 - 3y + 2 = \left(y - 2 \right) \left(y - 1 \right)$

       $\text{LCD} = \left(y + 3 \right) \left(y - 1 \right) \left(y - 2 \right)$

8. Since $x - 4$ and $4 - x$ are opposites, $\text{LCD} = x - 4$ or $\text{LCD} = 4 - x$.

9. $\dfrac{2x}{5y} = \dfrac{2x \left(4x^2 y \right)}{5y \left(4x^2 y \right)} = \dfrac{8x^3 y}{20x^2 y^2}$

10. $\dfrac{3}{x^2 - 25} = \dfrac{3}{(x+5)(x-5)}$

$= \dfrac{3(x-3)}{(x+5)(x-5)(x-3)}$

$= \dfrac{3x-9}{(x+5)(x-5)(x-3)}$

Mental Math 5.3

1. $\dfrac{2}{3} + \dfrac{1}{3} = \dfrac{3}{3} = 1$

2. $\dfrac{5}{11} + \dfrac{1}{11} = \dfrac{6}{1}$

3. $\dfrac{3x}{9} + \dfrac{4x}{9} = \dfrac{7x}{9}$

4. $\dfrac{3y}{8} + \dfrac{2y}{8} = \dfrac{5y}{8}$

5. $\dfrac{8}{9} - \dfrac{7}{9} = \dfrac{1}{9}$

6. $\dfrac{14}{12} - \dfrac{3}{12} = \dfrac{11}{12}$

7. $\dfrac{7y}{5} + \dfrac{10y}{5} = \dfrac{17y}{5}$

8. $\dfrac{12x}{7} - \dfrac{4x}{7} = \dfrac{8x}{7}$

Exercise Set 5.3

1. $\dfrac{a}{13} + \dfrac{9}{13} = \dfrac{a+9}{13}$

3. $\dfrac{4m}{3n} + \dfrac{5m}{3n} = \dfrac{4m+5m}{3n} = \dfrac{9m}{3n} = \dfrac{3m}{n}$

5. $\dfrac{4m}{m-6} - \dfrac{24}{m-6} = \dfrac{4m-24}{m-6} = \dfrac{4(m-6)}{m-6} = 4$

7. $\dfrac{9}{3+y} + \dfrac{y+1}{3+y} = \dfrac{9+y+1}{3+y} = \dfrac{y+10}{3+y}$

9. $\dfrac{5x+4}{x-1} - \dfrac{2x+7}{x-1} = \dfrac{5x+4-(2x+7)}{x-1}$

$= \dfrac{5x+4-2x-7}{x-1} = \dfrac{3x-3}{x-1} = \dfrac{3(x-1)}{x-1} = 3$

11. $\dfrac{a}{a^2+2a-15} - \dfrac{3}{a^2+2x-15} = \dfrac{a-3}{a^2+2a-15}$

$= \dfrac{a-3}{(a+5)(a-3)} = \dfrac{1}{a+5}$

13. $\dfrac{2x+3}{x^2-x-30} - \dfrac{x-2}{x^2-x-30}$

$= \dfrac{2x+3-(x-2)}{x^2-x-30}$

$= \dfrac{2x+3-x+2}{x^2-x-30} = \dfrac{x+5}{x^2-x-30}$

$= \dfrac{x+5}{(x-6)(x+5)} = \dfrac{1}{x-6}$

15. $P = \dfrac{5}{x-2} + \dfrac{5}{x-2} + \dfrac{5}{x-2} + \dfrac{5}{x-2}$

$= \dfrac{5+5+5+5}{x-2} = \dfrac{20}{x-2}$

The perimeter is $\dfrac{20}{x-2}$ meters.

17. Answers may vary.

19.　$2x = 2 \cdot x$

　　　$4x^3 = 2^2 \cdot x^3$

　　　$\text{LCD} = 2^2 \cdot x^3 = 4x^3$

21.　$8x = 2^{} \cdot x$

　　　$2x + 4 = 2(x+2)$

　　　$\text{LCD} = 2^3 \cdot x \cdot (x+2) = 8x(x+2)$

23.　$x + 3 = x + 3$

　　　$x - 2 = x - 2$

　　　$\text{LCD} = (x+3)(x-2)$

25.　$x + 6 = x + 6$

　　　$3x + 18 = 3 \cdot (x+6)$

　　　$\text{LCD} = 3(x+6)$

27.　$3x + 3 = 3 \cdot (x+1)$

　　　$2x^2 + 4x + 2 = 2(x^2 + 2x + 1) = 2 \cdot (x+1)^2$

　　　$\text{LCD} = 2 \cdot 3(x+1)^2$

　　　　　　$= 6(x+1)^2$

29.　$x - 8 = x - 8$

　　　$8 - x = -(x-8)$

　　　$\text{LCD} = x - 8 \text{ or } 8 - x$

31.　$x^2 + 3x - 4 = (x+4)(x-1)$

　　　$x^2 + 2x - 3 = (x+3)(x-1)$

　　　$\text{LCD} = (x+4)(x+3)(x-1)$

33. Answers may vary

35.　$\dfrac{3}{2x} = \dfrac{3(2x)}{2x(2x)} = \dfrac{6x}{4x^2}$

37.　$\dfrac{6}{3a} = \dfrac{6(4b^2)}{3a(4b^2)} = \dfrac{24b^2}{12ab^2}$

39.　$\dfrac{9}{x+3} = \dfrac{9(2)}{(x+3)(2)} = \dfrac{18}{2(x+3)}$

41.　$\dfrac{9a+2}{5a+10} = \dfrac{9a+2}{5(a+2)}$

　　　　　$= \dfrac{(9a+2)(b)}{5(a+2)(b)}$

　　　　　$= \dfrac{9ab+2b}{5b(a+2)}$

43.　$\dfrac{x}{x^3 + 6x^2 + 8x} = \dfrac{x}{x(x^2 + 6x + 8)}$

　　　　　$= \dfrac{x}{x(x+4)(x+2)(x+1)}$

　　　　　$= \dfrac{x(x+1)}{x(x+4)(x+2)(x+1)}$

　　　　　$= \dfrac{x^2 + x}{x(x+4)(x+2)(x+1)}$

45.　$\dfrac{9y-1}{15x^2 - 30} = \dfrac{(9y-1)(2)}{(15x^2 - 30)2} = \dfrac{18y-2}{30x^2 - 60}$

47.　$\text{LCD} = 21$

　　　$\dfrac{2}{3} + \dfrac{5}{7} = \dfrac{2(7)}{3(7)} + \dfrac{5(3)}{7(3)} = \dfrac{14}{21} + \dfrac{15}{21} = \dfrac{29}{21}$

49. Since $6 = 2 \cdot 3$ and $4 = 2^2$,

LCD $= 2^2 \cdot 3 = 12$.

$$\frac{2}{6} - \frac{3}{4} = \frac{2(2)}{6(2)} - \frac{3(3)}{4(3)} = \frac{4}{12} - \frac{9}{12} = \frac{4-9}{12}$$

$$= -\frac{5}{12}$$

51. Since $12 = 2^2 \cdot 3$ and $20 = 2^2 \cdot 5$,

LCD $= 2^2 \cdot 3 \cdot 5 = 60$.

$$\frac{1}{12} + \frac{3}{20} = \frac{1(5)}{12(5)} + \frac{3(3)}{20(3)} = \frac{5}{60} + \frac{9}{60} = \frac{14}{60}$$

$$= \frac{7(2)}{30(2)} = \frac{7}{30}$$

53. Since $8 = 2^3$ and $12 = 2^2 \cdot 3$, the least common multiple of 8 and 12 is $2^2 \cdot 3 = 24$. Since $8 \cdot 3 = 24$ and $12 \cdot 2 = 24$, buy three packages of hot dogs and two packages of buns.

55. Answers may vary.

Practice Problems 5.4

1. a. LCD $= 5 \cdot 3 = 15$

$$\frac{y}{5} - \frac{3y}{15} = \frac{y(3)}{5(3)} - \frac{3y}{15} = \frac{3y}{15} - \frac{3y}{15}$$

$$= \frac{3y - 3y}{15} = \frac{0}{15} = 0$$

b. $8x = 2^3 \cdot x$

$10x^2 = 2 \cdot 5 \cdot x^2$

LCD $= 2^3 \cdot \cdot x^2 = 8 \cdot 5 \cdot x^2 = 40x^2$

$$\frac{5}{8x} + \frac{11}{10x^2} = \frac{5(5x)}{8x(5x)} + \frac{11(4)}{10x^2(4)}$$

$$= \frac{25x}{40x^2} + \frac{44}{40x^2} = \frac{25x + 44}{40x^2}$$

2. Since $x^2 - 9 = (x+3)(x-3)$, the LCD $= (x+3)(x-3)$.

$$\frac{10x}{x^2 - 9} - \frac{5}{x+3}$$

$$= \frac{10x}{(x+3)(x-3)} - \frac{5(x-3)}{(x+3)(x-3)}$$

$$= \frac{10x - 5(x-3)}{(x+3)(x-3)} = \frac{10x - 5x + 15}{(x+3)(x-3)}$$

$$= \frac{5x + 15}{(x+3)(x-3)} = \frac{5(x+3)}{(x+3)(x-3)}$$

$$= \frac{5}{x-3}$$

3. $\dfrac{5}{7x} + \dfrac{2}{x+1} = \dfrac{5(x+1)}{7x(x+1)} + \dfrac{2(7x)}{7x(x+1)}$

$$= \frac{5(x+1) + 2(7x)}{7x(x+1)} = \frac{5x + 5 + 14x}{7x(x+1)}$$

$$= \frac{19x + 5}{7x(x+1)}$$

4. $\dfrac{10}{x-6} - \dfrac{15}{6-x} = \dfrac{10}{x-6} - \dfrac{15}{-(x-6)}$

$$= \frac{10}{x-6} - \frac{-15}{x-6} = \frac{10 - (-15)}{x-6} = \frac{25}{x-6}$$

5. $2 + \dfrac{x}{x+5} = \dfrac{2}{1} + \dfrac{x}{x+5} = \dfrac{2(x+5)}{1(x+5)} + \dfrac{x}{x+5}$

$$= \frac{2x + 10 + x}{x+5} = \frac{3x + 10}{x+5}$$

6. $\dfrac{4}{3x^2 + 2x} - \dfrac{3x}{12x + 8} = \dfrac{4}{x(3x+2)} - \dfrac{3x}{4(3x+2)}$

$$= \frac{4(4)}{x(3x+2)(4)} - \frac{3x(x)}{4(3x+2)(x)} = \frac{16 - 3x^2}{4x(3x+2)}$$

7. $\dfrac{6x}{x^2+4x+4}+\dfrac{x}{x^2-4}$

$=\dfrac{6x}{(x+2)^2}+\dfrac{x}{(x+2)(x-2)}$

$=\dfrac{6x(x-2)}{(x+2)^2(x-2)}+\dfrac{x(x+2)}{(x+2)(x-2)(x+2)}$

$=\dfrac{6x^2-12x+x^2+2x}{(x+2)^2(x-2)}$

$=\dfrac{7x^2-10x}{(x+2)^2(x-2)}=\dfrac{x(7x-10)}{(x+2)^2(x-2)}$

Exercise Set 5.4

1. $\text{LCD}=2\cdot3\cdot x=6x$

$\dfrac{4}{2x}+\dfrac{9}{3x}=\dfrac{4(3)}{2x(3)}+\dfrac{9(2)}{3x(2)}=\dfrac{12}{6x}+\dfrac{18}{6x}$

$=\dfrac{30}{6x}=\dfrac{5(6)}{6x}=\dfrac{5}{x}$

3. $\text{LCD}=5b$

$\dfrac{15a}{b}+\dfrac{6b}{5}=\dfrac{15a(5)}{b(5)}+\dfrac{6b(b)}{5(b)}=\dfrac{75a}{5b}+\dfrac{6b^2}{5b}$

$=\dfrac{75a+6b^2}{5b}$

5. $\text{LCD}=2x^2$

$\dfrac{3}{x}+\dfrac{5}{2x^2}=\dfrac{3(2x)}{x(2x)}+\dfrac{5}{2x^2}=\dfrac{6x}{2x^2}+\dfrac{5}{2x^2}$

$=\dfrac{6x+5}{2x^2}$

7. $2x+2=2(x+1)$

$\text{LCD}=2(x+1)$

$\dfrac{6}{x+1}+\dfrac{10}{2x+2}=\dfrac{6}{x+1}+\dfrac{10}{2(x+1)}$

$=\dfrac{6(2)}{(x+1)2}+\dfrac{10}{2(x+1)}=\dfrac{12}{2(x+1)}+\dfrac{10}{2(x+1)}$

$=\dfrac{12+10}{2(x+1)}=\dfrac{22}{2(x+1)}=\dfrac{2\cdot11}{2(x+1)}=\dfrac{11}{x+1}$

9. $2x-4=2(x-2)$

$x^2-4=(x-2)(x+2)$

$\text{LCD}=2(x-2)(x+2)$

$\dfrac{15}{2x-4}+\dfrac{x}{x^2-4}=\dfrac{15}{2(x-2)}+\dfrac{x}{(x-2)(x+2)}$

$=\dfrac{15(x+2)}{2(x-2)(x+2)}+\dfrac{x(2)}{(x-2)(x+2)(x)}$

$=\dfrac{15x+30}{2(x-2)(x+2)}+\dfrac{2x}{2(x-2)(x+2)}$

$=\dfrac{15x+30+2x}{2(x-2)(x+2)}=\dfrac{17x+30}{2(x-2)(x+2)}$

11. $\text{LCD}=4x(x-2)$

$\dfrac{3}{4x}+\dfrac{8}{x-2}=\dfrac{3(x-2)}{4x(x-2)}+\dfrac{8(4x)}{(x-2)(4x)}$

$=\dfrac{3x-6}{4x(x-2)}+\dfrac{32x}{4x(x-2)}=\dfrac{3x-6+32x}{4x(x-2)}$

$=\dfrac{35x-6}{4x(x-2)}$

13. $\dfrac{6}{x-3}+\dfrac{8}{3-x}=\dfrac{6}{x-3}+\dfrac{8}{-(x-3)}$

$=\dfrac{6}{x-3}+\dfrac{-8}{x-3}=\dfrac{6+(-8)}{x-3}=-\dfrac{2}{x-3}$

15. $\dfrac{-8}{x^2-1} - \dfrac{7}{1-x^2} = \dfrac{8}{-\left(x^2-1\right)} - \dfrac{7}{1-x^2}$

$= \dfrac{8}{1-x^2} - \dfrac{7}{1-x^2} = \dfrac{8-7}{1-x^2}$

$= \dfrac{1}{1-x^2}$ or $\dfrac{1}{x^2-1}$

17. $\dfrac{5}{x} + 2 = \dfrac{5}{x} + \dfrac{2}{1} = \dfrac{5}{x} + \dfrac{2(x)}{1(x)} = \dfrac{5+2x}{x}$

19. $\dfrac{5}{x-2} + 6 = \dfrac{5}{x-2} + \dfrac{6}{1} = \dfrac{5}{x-2} + \dfrac{6(x-2)}{1(x-2)}$

$= \dfrac{5}{x-2} + \dfrac{6x-12}{x-2} = \dfrac{5+6x-12}{x-2} = \dfrac{6x-7}{x-2}$

21. $\dfrac{y+2}{y+3} - 2 = \dfrac{y+2}{y+3} - \dfrac{2}{1} = \dfrac{y+2}{y+3} - \dfrac{2(y+3)}{y+3}$

$= \dfrac{y+2}{y+3} - \dfrac{2y+6}{y+3} = \dfrac{y+2-(2y+6)}{y+3}$

$= \dfrac{y+2-2y-6}{y+3} = \dfrac{-y-4}{y+3} = \dfrac{-(y+4)}{y+3}$

$= -\dfrac{y+4}{y+3}$

23. $\dfrac{-x+2}{x} - \dfrac{x-6}{4x} = \dfrac{(-x+2)}{x(4)} - \dfrac{(x-6)}{4x}$

$= \dfrac{-4x+8-(x-6)}{4x}$

$= \dfrac{-4x+8-x+6}{4x}$

$= \dfrac{-5x+14}{4x}$

25. $\dfrac{5x}{x+2} - \dfrac{3x-4}{x+2} = \dfrac{5x-(3x-4)}{x+2}$

$= \dfrac{5x-3x+4}{x+2} = \dfrac{2x+4}{x+2} = \dfrac{2(x+2)}{x+2} = 2$

27. $\dfrac{3x^4}{x} - \dfrac{4x^2}{x^2} = \dfrac{3x^4(x)}{x(x)} - \dfrac{4x^2}{x^2} = \dfrac{3x^5}{x^2} - \dfrac{4x^2}{x^2}$

$= \dfrac{3x^5-4x^2}{x^2} = \dfrac{x^2(3x^3-4)}{x^2} = 3x^3-4$

29. $\dfrac{1}{x+3} - \dfrac{1}{(x+3)^2} = \dfrac{1(x+3)}{(x+3)(x+3)} - \dfrac{1}{(x+3)^2}$

$= \dfrac{x+3}{(x+3)^2} - \dfrac{1}{(x+3)^2} = \dfrac{x+3-1}{(x+3)^2} = \dfrac{x+2}{(x+3)^2}$

31. $\dfrac{4}{5b} + \dfrac{1}{b-1} = \dfrac{4(b-1)}{5b(b-1)} + \dfrac{1(5b)}{(b-1)(5b)}$

$= \dfrac{4b-4}{5b(b-1)} + \dfrac{5b}{5b(b-1)} = \dfrac{4b-4+5b}{5b(b-1)}$

$= \dfrac{9b-4}{5b(b-1)}$

33. $\dfrac{2}{m} + 1 = \dfrac{2}{m} + \dfrac{1}{1} = \dfrac{2}{m} + \dfrac{1(m)}{1(m)} = \dfrac{2+m}{m}$

35. $\dfrac{6}{1-2x} - \dfrac{4}{2x-1} = \dfrac{6}{1-2x} - \dfrac{4}{-(1-2x)}$

$= \dfrac{6}{1-2x} - \dfrac{-4}{1-2x} = \dfrac{6-(-4)}{1-2x} = \dfrac{10}{1-2x}$

37. $\dfrac{7}{(x+1)(x-1)}+\dfrac{8}{(x+1)^2}$

$$=\frac{7(x+1)}{(x+1)(x-1)(x+1)}+\frac{8(x-1)}{(x+1)^2(x-1)}$$

$$=\frac{7x+7}{(x+1)^2(x-1)}+\frac{8x-8}{(x+1)^2(x-1)}$$

$$=\frac{7x+7+8x-8}{(x+1)^2(x-1)}=\frac{15x-1}{(x+1)^2(x-1)}$$

39. $\dfrac{x}{x^2-1}-\dfrac{2}{x^2-2x+1}$

$$=\frac{x}{(x-1)(x+1)}-\frac{2}{(x-1)^2}$$

$$=\frac{x(x-1)}{(x-1)(x+1)(x-1)}-\frac{2(x+1)}{(x-1)^2(x+1)}$$

$$=\frac{x^2-x}{(x-1)^2(x+1)}-\frac{2x+2}{(x-1)^2(x+1)}$$

$$=\frac{x^2-x-(2x+2)}{(x-1)^2(x+1)}=\frac{x^2-x-2x-2}{(x-1)^2(x+1)}$$

$$=\frac{x^2-3x-2}{(x-1)^2(x+1)}$$

41. $\dfrac{3a}{2a+6}-\dfrac{a-1}{a+3}=\dfrac{3a}{2(a+3)}-\dfrac{a-1}{a+3}$

$$=\frac{3a}{2(a+3)}-\frac{(a-1)(2)}{(a+3)(2)}$$

$$=\frac{3a}{2(a+3)}-\frac{2a-2}{2(a+3)}$$

$$=\frac{3a-(2a-2)}{2(a+3)}=\frac{3a-2a+2}{2(a+3)}=\frac{a+2}{2(a+3)}$$

43. $\dfrac{y-1}{2y+3}+\dfrac{3}{(2y+3)^2}$

$$=\frac{(y-1)(2y+3)}{(2y+3)(2y+3)}+\frac{3}{(2y+3)^2}$$

$$=\frac{2y^2+y-3+3}{(2y+3)^2}$$

$$=\frac{2y^2+y}{(2y+3)^2}$$

$$=\frac{y(2y+1)}{(2y+3)^2}$$

45. $\dfrac{5}{2-x}+\dfrac{x}{2x-4}=\dfrac{5}{-(x-2)}+\dfrac{x}{2(x-2)}$

$$=\frac{-5}{x-2}+\frac{x}{2(x-2)}$$

$$=\frac{-5(2)}{(x-2)(2)}+\frac{x}{2(x-2)}$$

$$=\frac{-10}{2(x-2)}+\frac{x}{2(x-2)}=\frac{x-10}{2(x-2)}$$

47. $\dfrac{-7}{y^2-3y+2}-\dfrac{2}{y-1}=\dfrac{-7}{(y-1)(y-2)}-\dfrac{2}{y-1}$

$$=\frac{-7}{(y-1)(y-2)}-\frac{2(y-2)}{(y-1)(y-2)}$$

$$=\frac{-7-(2y-4)}{(y-1)(y-2)}=\frac{-7-2y+4}{(y-1)(y-2)}$$

$$=\frac{-3-2y}{(y-2)(y-1)}$$

49. $\dfrac{13}{x^2-5x+6}-\dfrac{5}{x-3}=\dfrac{13}{(x-3)(x-2)}-\dfrac{5}{x-3}$

$=\dfrac{13}{(x-3)(x-2)}-\dfrac{5(x-2)}{(x-3)(x-2)}$

$=\dfrac{13-(5x-10)}{(x-3)(x-2)}=\dfrac{213-5x+10}{(x-3)(x-2)}$

$=\dfrac{-5x+23}{(x-3)(x-2)}$

51. $\dfrac{x+1}{x^2-5x-6}+\dfrac{x+1}{x^2-4x-5}$

$=\dfrac{x+8}{(x-6)(x+1)}+\dfrac{x+1}{(x-5)(x+1)}$

$=\dfrac{(x+8)(x-5)}{(x-6)(x+1)(x-5)}+\dfrac{(x+1)(x-6)}{(x-5)(x+1)(x-6)}$

$=\dfrac{x^2+3x-40+x^2-5x-6}{(x-6)(x+1)(x-5)}$

$=\dfrac{2x^2-2x-46}{(x-6)(x+1)(x-5)}$

53. Answers may vary.

55. $\qquad 3x+5=7$

$3x+5-5=7-5$

$\qquad\qquad 3x=2$

$\qquad\qquad \dfrac{3x}{3}=\dfrac{2}{3}$

$\qquad\qquad\quad x=\dfrac{2}{3}$

57. $2x^2-x-1=0$

$(2x+1)(x-1)=0$

$2x+1=0 \quad \text{or} \quad x-1=0$

$2x=-1 \qquad\qquad\qquad x=1$

$x=-\dfrac{1}{2}$

The solutions are $x=-\dfrac{1}{2}$ and $x=1$.

59. $4(x+6)+3=-3$

$4x+24+3=-3$

$4x+27=-3$

$4x+27-27=-3-27$

$4x=-30$

$\dfrac{4x}{4}=-\dfrac{30}{4}$

$x=-\dfrac{30}{4}=\dfrac{-15\cdot2}{2\cdot2}$

$=-\dfrac{15}{2}$

61. $\dfrac{3}{x}-\dfrac{2x(x)}{(x^2-1)(x)}+\dfrac{5}{x+1}$

$=\dfrac{3(x^2-1)}{x(x^2-1)}-\dfrac{2x^2}{x(x^2-1)}+\dfrac{5(x-1)x}{(x+1)(x-1)x}$

$=\dfrac{3x^2-3-2x^2+5x^2-5x}{x(x+1)(x-1)}$

$=\dfrac{6x^2-5x-3}{x(x+1)(x-1)}$

63. $\dfrac{5}{x^2-4}+\dfrac{2}{x^2-4x+4}-\dfrac{3}{x^2-x-6}$

$=\dfrac{5}{(x-2)(x+2)}+\dfrac{2}{(x-2)^2}$

$\qquad -\dfrac{3}{(x-3)(x+2)}$

$=\dfrac{5(x-2)(x-3)}{(x-2)(x+2)(x-2)(x-3)}$

$\qquad +\dfrac{2(x+2)(x-3)}{(x-2)^2(x+2)(x-3)}$

$\qquad -\dfrac{3(x-2)^2}{(x-3)(x+2)(x-2)^2}$

$=\dfrac{5\left(x^2-5x+6\right)}{(x-2)^2(x+2)(x-3)}$

$\qquad +\dfrac{2\left(x^2-x-6\right)}{(x-2)^2(x+2)(x-3)}$

$\qquad -\dfrac{3\left(x^2-4x+4\right)}{(x-2)^2(x+2)(x-3)}$

$=\dfrac{5x^2-25x+30}{(x-2)^2(x+2)(x-3)}$

$\qquad +\dfrac{2x^2-2x-12}{(x-2)^2(x+2)(x-3)}$

$\qquad -\dfrac{3x^2-12x+12}{(x-2)^2(x+2)(x-3)}$

$=\dfrac{4x^2-15x+6}{(x-2)^2(x+2)(x-3)}$

65. $\dfrac{9}{x^2+9x+14}-\dfrac{3x}{x^2+10x+21}+\dfrac{4}{x^2+5x+6}$

$=\dfrac{9}{(x+7)(x+2)}-\dfrac{3x}{(x+7)(x+3)}$

$\qquad +\dfrac{4}{(x+2)(x+3)}$

$=\dfrac{9(x+3)-3x(x+2)+4(x+7)}{(x+7)(x+2)(x+3)}$

$=\dfrac{9x+27-3x^2-6x+4x+28}{(x+7)(x+2)(x+3)}$

$=\dfrac{-3x^2+7x+55}{(x+7)(x+2)(x+3)}$

67. $\dfrac{3}{x+4}-\dfrac{1}{x-4}$

$=\dfrac{3(x-4)}{(x+4)(x-4)}-\dfrac{1(x+4)}{(x+4)(x-4)}$

$=\dfrac{3x-12}{(x+4)(x-4)}-\dfrac{x+4}{(x+4)(x-4)}$

$=\dfrac{3x-12-(x+4)}{(x+4)(x-4)}=\dfrac{3x-12-x-4}{(x+4)(x-4)}$

$=\dfrac{2x-16}{(x+4)(x-4)}$

The length of the other board is

$\dfrac{2x-16}{(x+4)(x-4)}$ inches.

69. $1-\dfrac{G}{P}=\dfrac{1(P)}{P}-\dfrac{G}{P}=\dfrac{P-G}{P}$

71. Answers may vary.

Practice Problems 5.5

1. $\dfrac{x}{4}+\dfrac{4}{5}=\dfrac{1}{20}$

$20\left(\dfrac{x}{4}+\dfrac{4}{5}\right)=20\left(\dfrac{1}{20}\right)$

$20\left(\dfrac{x}{4}\right)+20\left(\dfrac{4}{5}\right)=20\left(\dfrac{1}{20}\right)$

$5x+16=1$

$5x=-15$

$x=-3$

Check:

$\dfrac{x}{4}+\dfrac{4}{5}=\dfrac{1}{20}$

$\dfrac{-3}{4}+\dfrac{4}{5}\overset{?}{=}\dfrac{1}{20}$

$\dfrac{-15}{20}+\dfrac{16}{20}\overset{?}{=}\dfrac{1}{20}$

$\dfrac{1}{20}=\dfrac{1}{20}$ True

The solution is -3.

2. $\dfrac{x+2}{3}+\dfrac{x-1}{5}=\dfrac{1}{15}$

$15\left(\dfrac{x+2}{3}-\dfrac{x-1}{5}\right)=15\left(\dfrac{1}{15}\right)$

$15\left(\dfrac{x+2}{3}\right)-15\left(\dfrac{x-1}{5}\right)=15\left(\dfrac{1}{15}\right)$

$5(x+2)-3(x-1)=1$

$5x+10-3x+3=1$

$2x+13=1$

$2x=-12$

$x=-6$

Check:

$\dfrac{x+2}{3}+\dfrac{x-1}{5}=\dfrac{1}{15}$

$\dfrac{-3+2}{3}-\dfrac{-6-1}{5}\overset{?}{=}\dfrac{1}{15}$

$\dfrac{-4}{3}-\dfrac{-7}{5}\overset{?}{=}\dfrac{1}{15}$

$\dfrac{-20}{15}-\dfrac{-21}{15}\overset{?}{=}\dfrac{1}{15}$

$\dfrac{-20+21}{15}\overset{?}{=}\dfrac{1}{15}$

$\dfrac{1}{15}=\dfrac{1}{15}$ True

The solution is -6.

3. $2+\dfrac{6}{x}=x+7$

$x\left(2+\dfrac{6}{x}\right)=x(x+7)$

$x(2)+x\left(\dfrac{6}{x}\right)=x^2+7x$

$2x+6=x^2+7x$

$0=x^2+5x-6$

$0=(x+6)(x-1)$

$x+6=0$ or $x-1=0$

$x=-6$ $x=1$

Check:

$x=-6$ or $x=1$

$2+\dfrac{6}{x}=x+7$ $2+\dfrac{6}{x}=x+7$

$2+\dfrac{6}{-6}\overset{?}{=}-6+7$ $2+\dfrac{6}{1}\overset{?}{=}1+7$

$1+(-1)\overset{?}{=}1$ $2+6\overset{?}{=}8$

$1=1$ $8=8$ True

Both -6 and 1 are solutions.

4. $\dfrac{2}{x+3} + \dfrac{3}{x-3} = \dfrac{-2}{x^2-9}$

$\qquad (x+3)(x-3)\left(\dfrac{2}{x+3} + \dfrac{3}{x-3}\right)$

$\qquad = (x+3)(x-3)\left(\dfrac{-2}{x^2-9}\right)$

$\qquad (x+3)(x-3)\left(\dfrac{2}{x+3}\right)$

$\qquad\qquad + (x+3)(x-3)\left(\dfrac{3}{x-3}\right)$

$\qquad = (x+3)(x-3)\left(\dfrac{-2}{x^2-9}\right)$

$\qquad 2(x-3) + 3(x+3) = -2$

$\qquad 2x-6+3x+9 = -2$

$\qquad 5x+3 = -2$

$\qquad 5x = -5$

$\qquad x = -1$

Check:

$\qquad \dfrac{2}{x+3} + \dfrac{3}{x-3} = \dfrac{-2}{x^2-9}$

$\qquad \dfrac{2}{-1+3} + \dfrac{3}{-1-3} \stackrel{?}{=} \dfrac{-2}{(-1)^2-9}$

$\qquad \dfrac{2}{2} + \dfrac{3}{-4} \stackrel{?}{=} \dfrac{-2}{1-9}$

$\qquad 1 - \dfrac{3}{4} \stackrel{?}{=} \dfrac{-2}{-8}$

$\qquad \dfrac{1}{4} = \dfrac{1}{4}$ True

The solution is -1.

5. $\dfrac{5x}{x-1} = \dfrac{5}{x-1} + 3$

$\qquad (x-1)\left(\dfrac{5x}{x-1}\right) = (x-1)\left(\dfrac{5}{x-1} + 3\right)$

$\qquad (x-1)\left(\dfrac{5x}{x-1}\right) = (x-1)\left(\dfrac{5}{x-1} + \right.$

$\qquad\qquad\qquad\qquad\qquad + (x-1)(3)$

$\qquad 5x = 5 + 3x - 3$

$\qquad 5x = 3x + 2$

$\qquad 2x = 2$

$\qquad x = 1$

Notice that 1 makes the denominator 0 in the original equation. This equation has no solution.

6. $x - \dfrac{6}{x+3} = \dfrac{2x}{x+3} + 2$

$\qquad (x+3)\left(x - \dfrac{6}{x+3}\right) = (x+3)\left(\dfrac{2x}{x+3} + 2\right)$

$\qquad (x+3)(x) - (x+3)\left(\dfrac{6}{x+3}\right)$

$\qquad = (x+3)\left(\dfrac{2x}{x+3}\right) + (x+3)(2)$

$\qquad x^2 + 3x - 6 = 2x + 2x + 6$

$\qquad x^2 + 3x - 6 = 4x + 6$

$\qquad x^2 - x - 12 = 0$

$\qquad (x-4)(x+3) = 0$

$\qquad x-4 = 0$ or $x+3 = 0$

$\qquad\qquad x = 4$ $x = -3$

Since -3 would make a denominator 0, -3 cannot be a solution. The only solution is 4.

7.

$$\frac{1}{a} + \frac{1}{b} = \frac{1}{x}$$

$$abx\left(\frac{1}{a} + \frac{1}{b}\right) = abx\left(\frac{1}{x}\right)$$

$$abx\left(\frac{1}{a}\right) + abx\left(\frac{1}{b}\right) = abx\left(\frac{1}{x}\right)$$

$$bx + ax = ab$$

$$bx = ab - ax$$

$$bx = a(b - x)$$

$$\frac{bx}{b - x} = a$$

Mental Math 5.5

1. $\frac{x}{5} = 2$

$\quad x = 10$

2. $\frac{x}{8} = 4$

$\quad x = 32$

3. $\frac{z}{6} = 6$

$\quad z = 36$

4. $\frac{y}{7} = 8$

$\quad y = 56$

Exercise Set 5.5

1. $\frac{x}{5} + 3 = 9$

$$5\left(\frac{x}{5} + 3\right) = 5(9)$$

$$5\left(\frac{x}{5}\right) + 5(3) = 5(9)$$

$$x + 15 = 45$$

$$x = 30$$

Check:

$$\frac{x}{5} + 3 = 9$$

$$\frac{30}{5} + 3 \overset{?}{=} 9$$

$$6 + 3 \overset{?}{=} 9$$

$$9 = 9 \quad \text{True}$$

The solution is 30.

3. $\frac{x}{2} + \frac{5x}{4} = \frac{x}{12}$

$$12\left(\frac{x}{2} + \frac{5x}{4}\right) = 12\left(\frac{x}{12}\right)$$

$$12\left(\frac{x}{2}\right) + 12\left(\frac{5x}{4}\right) = 12\left(\frac{x}{12}\right)$$

$$6x + 15x = x$$

$$21x = x$$

$$20x = 0$$

$$x = 0$$

Check:

$$\frac{x}{2}+\frac{5x}{4}=\frac{x}{12}$$

$$\frac{0}{2}+\frac{5\cdot 0}{4}\overset{?}{=}\frac{0}{12}$$

$$0+\frac{0}{4}\overset{?}{=}0$$

$$0=0 \quad \text{True}$$

The solution is 0.

5. $2-\dfrac{8}{x}=6$

$$x\left(2-\frac{8}{x}\right)=x(6)$$

$$x(2)-x\left(\frac{8}{x}\right)=x(6)$$

$$2x-8=6x$$

$$-8=4x$$

$$-2=x$$

Check:

$$2-\frac{8}{x}=6$$

$$2-\frac{8}{-2}\overset{?}{=}6$$

$$2-(-4)\overset{?}{=}6$$

$$2+4\overset{?}{=}6$$

$$6=6 \quad \text{True}$$

The solution is -2.

7. $2+\dfrac{10}{x}=x+5$

$$x\left(2+\frac{10}{x}\right)=x(x+5)$$

$$x(2)+x\left(\frac{10}{x}\right)=x(x+5)$$

$$2x+10=x^2+5x$$

$$0=x^2+3x-10$$

$$0=(x+5)(x-2)$$

$$x+5=0 \quad \text{or} \quad x-2=0$$

$$x=-5 \qquad\qquad x=2$$

Check:

$x=-5:$

$$2+\frac{10}{x}=x+5$$

$$2+\frac{10}{-5}\overset{?}{=}-5+5$$

$$2+(-2)\overset{?}{=}-5+5$$

$$0=0 \quad \text{True}$$

$x=2:$

$$2+\frac{10}{x}=x+5$$

$$2+\frac{10}{2}\overset{?}{=}2+5$$

$$2+5\overset{?}{=}2+5$$

$$7=7 \quad \text{True}$$

Both -5 and 2 are solutions.

9. $\dfrac{a}{5}=\dfrac{a-3}{2}$

$$10\left(\frac{a}{5}\right)=10\left(\frac{a-3}{2}\right)$$

$$2a=5(a-3)$$

$$2a=5a-15$$

$$-3a=-15$$

$$a=5$$

Check:

$$\frac{a}{5} = \frac{a-3}{2}$$

$$\frac{5}{5} \overset{?}{=} \frac{5-3}{2}$$

$$\frac{5}{5} \overset{?}{=} \frac{2}{2}$$

$$1 = 1 \quad \text{True}$$

The solution is 5.

11. $\dfrac{x-3}{5} + \dfrac{x-2}{2} = \dfrac{1}{2}$

$$10\left(\frac{x-3}{5} + \frac{x-2}{2}\right) = 10\left(\frac{1}{2}\right)$$

$$10\left(\frac{x-3}{5}\right) + 10\left(\frac{x-2}{2}\right) = 10\left(\frac{1}{2}\right)$$

$$2(x-3) + 5(x-2) = 5$$

$$2x - 6 + 5x - 10 = 5$$

$$7x - 16 = 5$$

$$7x = 21$$

$$x = 3$$

Check:

$$\frac{x-3}{5} + \frac{x-2}{2} = \frac{1}{2}$$

$$\frac{3-3}{5} + \frac{3-2}{2} \overset{?}{=} \frac{1}{2}$$

$$\frac{0}{5} + \frac{1}{2} \overset{?}{=} \frac{1}{2}$$

$$0 + \frac{1}{2} \overset{?}{=} \frac{1}{2}$$

$$\frac{1}{2} = \frac{1}{2} \quad \text{True}$$

The solution is 3.

13. $\dfrac{2}{y} + \dfrac{1}{2} = \dfrac{5}{2y}$

$$2y\left(\frac{2}{y} + \frac{1}{2}\right) = 2y\left(\frac{5}{2y}\right)$$

$$2y\left(\frac{2}{y}\right) + 2y\left(\frac{1}{2}\right) = 2y\left(\frac{5}{2y}\right)$$

$$4 + y = 5$$

$$y = 1$$

Check:

$$\frac{2}{y} + \frac{1}{2} = \frac{5}{2y}$$

$$\frac{2}{1} + \frac{1}{2} \overset{?}{=} \frac{5}{2(1)}$$

$$\frac{4}{2} + \frac{1}{2} \overset{?}{=} \frac{5}{2}$$

$$\frac{5}{2} = \frac{5}{2} \quad \text{True}$$

The solution is 1.

15. $\dfrac{11}{2x} + \dfrac{2}{3} = \dfrac{7}{2x}$

$$6x\left(\frac{11}{2x} + \frac{2}{3}\right) = 6x\left(\frac{7}{2x}\right)$$

$$6x\left(\frac{11}{2x}\right) + 6x\left(\frac{2}{3}\right) = 6x\left(\frac{7}{2x}\right)$$

$$33 + 4x = 21$$

$$4x = -12$$

$$x = -3$$

Check:

$$\frac{11}{2x} + \frac{2}{3} = \frac{7}{2x}$$

$$\frac{11}{2(-3)} + \frac{2}{3} \overset{?}{=} \frac{7}{2(-3)}$$

$$\frac{11}{-6} + \frac{2}{3} \overset{?}{=} \frac{7}{-6}$$

$$\frac{-11}{6} + \frac{4}{6} \overset{?}{=} -\frac{7}{6}$$

$$\frac{-11+4}{6} \overset{?}{=} -\frac{7}{6}$$

$$-\frac{7}{6} = -\frac{7}{6} \quad \text{True}$$

The solution is -3.

17. $2 + \dfrac{3}{a-3} = \dfrac{a}{a-3}$

$$(a-3)\left(2 + \frac{3}{a-3}\right) = (a-3)\left(\frac{a}{a-3}\right)$$

$$(a-3)(2) + (a-3)\left(\frac{3}{a-3}\right)$$

$$= (a-3)\left(\frac{a}{a-3}\right)$$

$$2a - 6 + 3 = a$$

$$2a - 3 = a$$

$$-3 = -a$$

$$3 = a$$

In the original equation, 3 makes a denominator 0. This equation has no solution.

19. $\dfrac{3}{2a-5} = -1$

$$(2a-5)\left(\frac{3}{2a-5}\right) = (2a-5)(-1)$$

$$3 = -2a + 5$$

$$-2 = -2a$$

$$1 = a$$

Check:

$$\frac{3}{2a-5} = -1$$

$$\frac{3}{2(1)-5} \overset{?}{=} -1$$

$$\frac{3}{2-5} \overset{?}{=} -1$$

$$\frac{3}{-3} \overset{?}{=} -1$$

$$-1 = -1 \quad \text{True}$$

The solution is 1.

21. $\dfrac{y}{y+4} + \dfrac{4}{y+4} = 3$

$$(y+4)\left(\frac{y}{y+4} + \frac{4}{y+4}\right) = (y+4)(3)$$

$$(y+4)\left(\frac{y}{y+4}\right) + (y+4)\left(\frac{4}{y+4}\right)$$

$$= (y+4)(3)$$

$$y + 4 = 3y + 12$$

$$4 = 2y + 12$$

$$-8 = 2y$$

$$-\frac{8}{2} = y$$

$$-4 = y$$

In the original equation, -4 makes a denominator 0. This equation has no solution.

23. $\dfrac{a}{a-6}=\dfrac{-2}{a-1}$

$(a-6)(a-1)\left(\dfrac{a}{a-6}\right)$

$\qquad =(a-6)(a-1)\left(\dfrac{-2}{a-1}\right)$

$a(a-1)=-2(a-6)$

$a^2-a=-2a+12$

$a^2+a-12=0$

$(a+4)(a-3)=0$

$a+4=0 \quad$ or $\quad a-3=0$

$\qquad a=-4 \qquad\qquad a=3$

Check:

$a=-4: \qquad\qquad a=3:$

$\dfrac{a}{a-6}=\dfrac{-2}{a-1} \qquad \dfrac{a}{a-6}=\dfrac{-2}{a-1}$

$\dfrac{-4}{-4-6}\overset{?}{=}\dfrac{-2}{-4-1} \qquad \dfrac{3}{3-6}\overset{?}{=}\dfrac{-2}{a-1}$

$\dfrac{-4}{-10}\overset{?}{=}\dfrac{-2}{-5} \qquad\quad \dfrac{3}{3-6}\overset{?}{=}\dfrac{-2}{3-1}$

$\dfrac{2}{5}=\dfrac{2}{5} \quad$ True $\qquad \dfrac{3}{3-6}\overset{?}{=}\dfrac{-2}{3-1}$

$\qquad\qquad\qquad\qquad \dfrac{3}{-3}\overset{?}{=}\dfrac{-2}{2}$

$\qquad\qquad\qquad\qquad -1=-1 \quad$ True

The solutions are -4 and 3

25. $\dfrac{2x}{x+2}-2=\dfrac{x-8}{x-2}$

$(x+2)(x-2)\left(\dfrac{2x}{x+2}\right)$

$\qquad =(x+2)(x-2)\left(\dfrac{x-8}{x-2}\right)$

$(x+2)(x-2)\left(\dfrac{2x}{x+2}\right)-(x+2)(x-2)(2)$

$\qquad =(x+2)(x-2)\left(\dfrac{x-8}{x-2}\right)$

$2x(x-2)-2(x^2-4)=(x+2)(x-8)$

$2x^2-4x-2x^2+8=x^2-6x-16$

$-4x+8=x^2-6x-16$

$0=x^2-2x-24$

$0=(x-6)(x+4)$

$x-6=0 \quad$ or $\quad x+4=0$

$\qquad x=6 \qquad\qquad x=-4$

Check:

$x=6: \qquad\qquad x=-4:$

$\dfrac{2x}{x+2}-2=\dfrac{x-8}{x-2} \qquad \dfrac{2x}{x+2}-2=\dfrac{x-8}{x-2}$

$\dfrac{2(6)}{6+2}-2\overset{?}{=}\dfrac{6-8}{6-2} \qquad \dfrac{2(-4)}{-4+2}-2\overset{?}{=}\dfrac{-4-8}{-4-2}$

$\dfrac{12}{8}-2\overset{?}{=}-\dfrac{2}{4} \qquad\quad \dfrac{-8}{-2}-2\overset{?}{=}\dfrac{-12}{-6}$

$\dfrac{3}{2}-\dfrac{4}{2}\overset{?}{=}-\dfrac{1}{2} \qquad\quad 4-2\overset{?}{=}2$

$\dfrac{3-4}{2}\overset{?}{=}-\dfrac{1}{2} \qquad\qquad 2=2 \quad$ True

$-\dfrac{1}{2}=-\dfrac{1}{2} \quad$ True

The solutions are 6 and -4.

27. $\dfrac{4y}{y-4}+5=\dfrac{5y}{y-4}$

$(y-4)\left(\dfrac{4y}{y-4}+5\right)=(y-4)\left(\dfrac{5y}{y-4}\right)$

$(y-4)\left(\dfrac{4y}{y-4}\right)+(y-4)(5)=(y-4)\left(\dfrac{5y}{y-4}\right)$

$4y+5y-20=5y$

$9y-20=5y$

$4y-20=0$

$4y=20$

$y=5$

Check:

$$\frac{4y}{y-4}+5=\frac{5y}{y-4}$$

$$\frac{4(5)}{5-4}+5\overset{?}{=}\frac{5(5)}{5-4}$$

$$\frac{20}{1}+5\overset{?}{=}\frac{25}{1}$$

$25=25$ True

The solution is 5.

29. $\dfrac{2}{x-2}+1=\dfrac{x}{x+2}$

$$(x-2)(x+2)\left(\frac{2}{x-2}+1\right)$$

$$=(x-2)(x+2)\left(\frac{x}{x+2}\right)$$

$$(x-2)(x+2)\left(\frac{2}{x-2}\right)+(x-2)(x+2)$$

$$=(x-2)(x+2)\left(\frac{x}{x+2}\right)$$

$$2(x+2)+(x-2)(x+2)=x(x-2)$$

$$2x+4+x^2-4=x^2-2x$$

$$2x+x^2=x^2-2x$$

$$2x=-2x$$

$$4x=0$$

$$x=0$$

Check:

$$\frac{2}{x-2}+1=\frac{x}{x+2}$$

$$\frac{2}{0-2}+1\overset{?}{=}\frac{0}{0+2}$$

$$\frac{2}{-2}+1\overset{?}{=}0$$

$$-1+1\overset{?}{=}0$$

$0=0$ True   The solution is 0.

31. $\dfrac{t}{t-4}=\dfrac{t+4}{6}$

$$6(t-4)\left(\frac{t}{t-4}\right)=6(t-4)\left(\frac{t+4}{6}\right)$$

$$6t=t^2-6t-16$$

$$0=t^2-6t-16$$

$$0=(t-8)(t+2)$$

$$t-8=0 \quad \text{or} \quad t+2=0$$

$$t=8 \qquad\qquad t=-2$$

Check:

$t=8:$ $t=-2:$

$$\frac{t}{t-4}=\frac{t+4}{6} \qquad \frac{t}{t-4}=\frac{t+4}{6}$$

$$\frac{8}{8-4}\overset{?}{=}\frac{8+4}{6} \qquad \frac{-2}{-2-4}\overset{?}{=}\frac{-2+4}{6}$$

$$\frac{8}{4}\overset{?}{=}\frac{12}{6} \qquad\qquad \frac{-2}{-6}\overset{?}{=}\frac{2}{6}$$

$$2=2 \quad \text{True} \qquad \frac{1}{3}=\frac{1}{3} \quad \text{True}$$

The solutions are 8 and -2.

33. $\dfrac{x+1}{3} - \dfrac{x-1}{6} = \dfrac{1}{6}$

$6\left(\dfrac{x+1}{3} - \dfrac{x-1}{6}\right) = 6\left(\dfrac{1}{6}\right)$

$6\left(\dfrac{x+1}{3}\right) - 6\left(\dfrac{x-1}{6}\right) = 6\left(\dfrac{1}{6}\right)$

$2(x+1) - (x-1) = 1$

$2x + 2 - x + 1 = 1$

$x + 3 = 1$

$x = -2$

Check:

$\dfrac{x+1}{3} - \dfrac{x-1}{6} = \dfrac{1}{6}$

$\dfrac{-2+1}{3} - \dfrac{-2-1}{6} \overset{?}{=} \dfrac{1}{6}$

$-\dfrac{1}{3} - \dfrac{-3}{6} \overset{?}{=} \dfrac{1}{6}$

$-\dfrac{2}{6} - \dfrac{-3}{6} \overset{?}{=} \dfrac{1}{6}$

$\dfrac{-2-(-3)}{6} \overset{?}{=} \dfrac{1}{6}$

$\dfrac{-2-(-3)}{6} \overset{?}{=} \dfrac{1}{6}$

$\dfrac{1}{6} = \dfrac{1}{6}$ True

The solution is -2.

35. $\dfrac{y}{2y+2} + \dfrac{2y-16}{4y+4} = \dfrac{2y-3}{y+1}$

$\dfrac{y}{2(y+1)} + \dfrac{2y-16}{4(y+1)} = \dfrac{2y-3}{y+1}$

$4(y+1)\left(\dfrac{y}{2(y+1)} + \dfrac{2y-16}{4(y+1)}\right)$

$\qquad = 4(y+1)\left(\dfrac{2y-3}{y+1}\right)$

$4(y+1)\left(\dfrac{y}{2(y+1)}\right) + 4(y+1)\left(\dfrac{2y-16}{4(y+1)}\right)$

$\qquad = 4(y+1)\left(\dfrac{2y-3}{y+1}\right)$

$2y + 2y - 16 = 4(2y-3)$

$4y - 16 = 8y - 12$

$-4y = 4$

$y = -1$

In the original equation, -1 makes a denominator 0.

This equation has no solution.

37. $\dfrac{4r-4}{r^2+5r-14} + \dfrac{2}{r+7} = \dfrac{1}{r-2}$

$\dfrac{4r-4}{(r+7)(r-2)} + \dfrac{2}{r+7} = \dfrac{1}{r-2}$

$(r+7)(r-2)\left(\dfrac{4r-4}{(r+7)(r-2)} + \dfrac{2}{r+7}\right)$

$= (r+7)(r-2)\left(\dfrac{1}{r-2}\right)$

$(r+7)(r-2)\left(\dfrac{4r-4}{(r+7)(r-2)}\right)$

$\qquad + (r+7)(r-2)\left(\dfrac{2}{r+7}\right)$

$\qquad = (r+7)(r-2)\left(\dfrac{1}{r-2}\right)$

$4r - 4 + 2(r-2) = (r+7)(1)$

$4r - 4 + 2r - 4 = r + 7$

$6r - 8 = r + 7$

$5r = 15$

$r = 3$

Check:

$$\frac{4r-4}{r^2+5r-14}+\frac{2}{r+7}=\frac{1}{r-2}$$

$$\frac{4(3)-4}{3^2+5(3)-14}+\frac{2}{3+7}\overset{?}{=}\frac{1}{3-2}$$

$$\frac{12-4}{9+15-14}+\frac{2}{10}\overset{?}{=}\frac{1}{1}$$

$$\frac{8}{10}+\frac{2}{10}\overset{?}{=}1$$

$$\frac{8+2}{10}\overset{?}{=}1$$

$$\frac{10}{10}\overset{?}{=}1$$

$$1=1 \quad \text{True}$$

The solution is 3.

39. $\dfrac{x+1}{x+3}=\dfrac{x^2-11x}{x^2+x-6}-\dfrac{x-3}{x-2}$

$$\frac{x+1}{x+3}=\frac{x^2-11x}{(x+3)(x-2)}-\frac{x-3}{x-2}$$

$$(x+3)(x-2)\left(\frac{x+1}{x+3}\right)$$

$$=(x+3)(x-2)\left(\frac{x^2-11x}{(x+3)(x-2)}-\frac{x-3}{x-2}\right)$$

$$(x+3)(x-2)\left(\frac{x+1}{x+3}\right)$$

$$=(x+3)(x-2)\left(\frac{x^2-11x}{(x+3)(x-2)}\right)$$

$$-(x+3)(x-2)\left(\frac{x-3}{x-2}\right)$$

$$(x-2)(x+1)=x^2-11x-(x+3)(x-3)$$

$$x^2-x-2=x^2-11x-\left(x^2-9\right)$$

$$x^2-x-2=x^2-11x-x^2+9$$

$$x^2-x-2=-11x+9$$

$$x^2+10x-11=0$$

$$(x+11)(x-1)=0$$

$$x+11=0 \quad \text{or} \quad x-1=0$$

$$x=-11 \qquad\qquad x=1$$

Check:

$x=-11$:

$$\frac{x+1}{x+3}=\frac{x^2-11x}{x^2+x-6}-\frac{x-3}{x-2}$$

$$\frac{-11+1}{-11+3}\overset{?}{=}\frac{(-11)^2-11(11)}{(-11)^2+(-11)-6}-\frac{-11-3}{-11-2}$$

$$\frac{-10}{-8}\overset{?}{=}\frac{121+121}{121-17}-\frac{-14}{-13}$$

$$\frac{5}{4}\overset{?}{=}\frac{242}{104}-\frac{14}{13}$$

$$\frac{5}{4}\overset{?}{=}\frac{121}{52}-\frac{14}{13}$$

$$\frac{65}{52}\overset{?}{=}\frac{121}{52}-\frac{56}{52}$$

$$\frac{65}{52}\overset{?}{=}\frac{121-56}{52}$$

$$\frac{65}{52}=\frac{65}{52} \quad \text{True}$$

$x=1$:

$$\frac{x+1}{x+3}=\frac{x^2-11x}{x^2+x-6}-\frac{x-3}{x-2}$$

$$\frac{1+1}{1+3}\overset{?}{=}\frac{(1)^2-11(1)}{(1)^2+1-6}-\frac{1-3}{1-2}$$

$$\frac{2}{4}\overset{?}{=}\frac{1-11}{1+1-6}-\frac{-2}{-1}$$

$$\frac{1}{2} \stackrel{?}{=} \frac{-10}{-4} - 2$$

$$\frac{1}{2} \stackrel{?}{=} \frac{5}{2} - \frac{4}{2}$$

$$\frac{1}{2} = \frac{1}{2} \quad \text{True}$$

The solutions are -11 and 1.

41. $R = \frac{E}{I}$

$$IR = I\left(\frac{E}{I}\right)$$

$$IR = E$$

$$\frac{IR}{R} = \frac{E}{R}$$

$$I = \frac{E}{R}$$

43. $T = \frac{V}{Q}$

$$Q(T) = Q\left(\frac{V}{Q}\right)$$

$$QT = V$$

$$\frac{QT}{T} = \frac{V}{T}$$

$$Q = \frac{V}{T}$$

45. $i = \frac{A}{t + B}$

$$(t + B)(i) = (t + B)\left(\frac{A}{t + B}\right)$$

$$ti + Bi = A$$

$$ti = A - Bi$$

$$\frac{ti}{i} = \frac{A - Bi}{i}$$

$$t = \frac{A - Bi}{i}$$

47. $N = R + \frac{V}{G}$

$$N - R = \frac{V}{G}$$

$$G(N - R) = G\left(\frac{V}{G}\right)$$

$$G(N - R) = V$$

$$\frac{G(N - R)}{N - R} = \frac{V}{N - R}$$

$$G = \frac{V}{N - R}$$

49. $\frac{C}{\pi r} = 2$

$$\pi r\left(\frac{C}{\pi r}\right) = \pi r(2)$$

$$C = 2\pi r$$

$$\frac{C}{2\pi} = \frac{2\pi r}{2\pi}$$

$$\frac{C}{2\pi} = r$$

51. $\frac{1}{y} + \frac{1}{3} = \frac{1}{x}$

$$3xy\left(\frac{1}{y}\right) + 3xy\left(\frac{1}{3}\right) = 3xy\left(\frac{1}{x}\right)$$

$$3x + xy = 3y$$

$$x(3 + y) = 3y$$

$$\frac{x(3 + y)}{3 + y} = \frac{3y}{3 + y}$$

$$x = \frac{3y}{y + 3}$$

53. The reciprocal of x is $\frac{1}{x}$.

55. The reciprocal of x added to the reciprocal of 2 is $\dfrac{1}{x}+\dfrac{1}{2}$.

57. If a tank is filled in 3 hours, the part of the tank filled in 1 hour is $\dfrac{1}{3}$.

59. $\dfrac{20x}{3}+\dfrac{32x}{6}=180$

$6\left(\dfrac{180}{3}+\dfrac{32x}{6}\right)=6(180)$

$6\left(\dfrac{20x}{3}\right)+6\left(\dfrac{32x}{6}\right)=6(180)$

$40x+32x=1080$

$72x=1080$

$\dfrac{72x}{72}=\dfrac{1080}{72}$

$x=15$

$\dfrac{20x}{3}=\dfrac{20(15)}{3}=100$

$\dfrac{32x}{6}=\dfrac{32(15)}{6}=80$

The angles are $100°$ and $80°$.

61. $\dfrac{150}{x}+\dfrac{450}{x}=90$

$x\left(\dfrac{150}{x}+\dfrac{450}{x}\right)=x(90)$

$x\left(\dfrac{150}{x}\right)+x\left(\dfrac{450}{x}\right)=x(90)$

$150+450=90x$

$600=90x$

$\dfrac{600}{90}=x$

$\dfrac{20}{3}=x$

$\dfrac{150}{x}=\dfrac{150}{\frac{20}{3}}=150\left(\dfrac{3}{20}\right)=\dfrac{45}{2}=22.5$

$\dfrac{450}{x}=\dfrac{450}{\frac{20}{3}}=450\left(\dfrac{3}{20}\right)=\dfrac{135}{2}=67.5$

The angles are $22.5°$ and $67.5°$.

63. $\dfrac{4}{a^2+4a+3}+\dfrac{2}{a^2+a-6}-\dfrac{3}{a^2-a-2}=0$

$\dfrac{4}{(a+3)(a+1)}+\dfrac{2}{(a+3)(a-2)}$
$\qquad\qquad\qquad -\dfrac{3}{(a-2)(a+1)}=0$

$(a+3)(a+1)(a-2)\left(\dfrac{\dfrac{4}{(a+3)(a+1)}}{+\dfrac{2}{(a+3)(a-2)}}\right)$

$\qquad\qquad =(a+3)(a+1)(a-2)(0)$

$(a+3)(a+1)(a-2)\left(\dfrac{4}{(a+3)(a+1)}\right)$

$+(a+3)(a+1)(a-2)\left(\dfrac{2}{(a+3)(a-2)}\right)$

$-(a+3)(a+1)(a-2)\left(\dfrac{3}{(a-2)(a+1)}\right)$

$\qquad\qquad\qquad\qquad\qquad =0$

$4(a-2)+2(a+1)-3(a+3)=0$

$4a-8+2a+2-3a-9=0$

$3a-15=0$

$3a=15$

$a=5$

65. No, multiplying both terms in the expression by 4 changes the value of the original expression.

Integrated Review 5.5

1. expression

$$\frac{1}{2}+\frac{2}{3}=\frac{1(3)}{x(3)}+\frac{2(x)}{3(x)}=\frac{3}{3x}+\frac{2x}{3x}=\frac{3+2x}{3x}$$

2. expression

$$\frac{3}{a}+\frac{5}{6}=\frac{3(6)}{a(6)}+\frac{5(a)}{6(a)}=\frac{18}{6a}+\frac{5a}{6a}=\frac{18+5a}{6a}$$

3. equation

$$\frac{1}{x}+\frac{2}{3}=\frac{3}{x}$$

$$3x\left(\frac{1}{x}+\frac{2}{3}\right)=3x\left(\frac{3}{x}\right)$$

$$3x\left(\frac{1}{x}\right)+3x\left(\frac{2}{3}\right)=3x\left(\frac{3}{x}\right)$$

$$3+2x=9$$

$$2x=6$$

$$x=3$$

The solution is 3.

4. equation

$$\frac{3}{a}+\frac{5}{6}=1$$

$$6a\left(\frac{3}{a}+\frac{5}{6}\right)=6a(1)$$

$$6a\left(\frac{3}{a}\right)+6a\left(\frac{5}{6}\right)=6a$$

$$18+5a=6a$$

$$18=a$$

The solution is 18.

5. expression

$$\frac{2}{x+1}-\frac{1}{x}=\frac{2(x)}{(x+1)(x)}-\frac{1(x+1)}{x(x+1)}$$

$$=\frac{2x-(x+1)}{x(x+1)}=\frac{x-1}{x(x+1)}$$

6. expression

$$\frac{4}{x-3}-\frac{1}{x}=\frac{4(x)}{(x-3)(x)}-\frac{1(x-3)}{x(x-3)}$$

$$=\frac{4x-(x-3)}{x(x-3)}=\frac{4x-x+3}{x(x-3)}=\frac{3x+3}{x(x-3)}$$

$$=\frac{3(x+1)}{x(x-3)}$$

7. equation

$$\frac{2}{x+1}-\frac{1}{x}=1$$

$$x(x+1)\left(\frac{2}{x+1}-\frac{1}{x}\right)=x(x+1)(1)$$

$$x(x+1)\left(\frac{2}{x+1}\right)-x(x+1)\left(\frac{1}{x}\right)=x(x+1)$$

$$2x-(x+1)=x(x+1)$$

$$2x-x-1=x^2+x$$

$$x-1=x^2+x$$

$$-1=x^2$$

There is no real number solution.

8. equation

$$\frac{4}{x-3}-\frac{1}{x}=\frac{6}{x(x-3)}$$

$$x(x-3)\left(\frac{4}{x-3}-\frac{1}{x}\right)=x(x-3)\left(\frac{6}{x(x-3)}\right)$$

$$x(x-3)\left(\frac{4}{x-3}\right)-x(x-3)\left(\frac{1}{x}\right)=6$$

$$4x-(x-3)=6$$

$$4x-x+3=6$$

$$3x+3=6$$

$$3x=3$$

$$x=1$$

The solution is 1.

9. expression

$$\frac{15x}{x+8}\cdot\frac{2x+16}{3x}=\frac{15x\cdot(2x+16)}{(x+8)\cdot 3x}$$

$$=\frac{3\cdot 5\cdot x\cdot 2\cdot(x+8)}{(x+8)\cdot 3\cdot x}=5\cdot 2=10$$

10. expression

$$\frac{9z+5}{15}\cdot\frac{5z}{81z^2-25}=\frac{(9z+5)\cdot 5z}{15\cdot(81z^2-25)}$$

$$=\frac{(9z+5)\cdot 5\cdot z}{5\cdot 3\cdot(9z+5)(9z-5)}=\frac{z}{3(9z-5)}$$

11. expression

$$\frac{2x+1}{x-3}+\frac{3x+6}{x-3}=\frac{2x+1+3x+6}{x-3}$$

$$=\frac{5x+7}{x-3}$$

12. expression

$$\frac{4p-3}{2p+7}+\frac{3p+8}{2p+7}=\frac{4p-3+3p+8}{2p+7}$$

$$=\frac{7p+5}{2p+7}$$

13. equation

$$\frac{x+5}{7}=\frac{8}{2}$$

$$14\left(\frac{x+5}{7}\right)=14\left(\frac{8}{2}\right)$$

$$2(x+5)=56$$

$$2x+10=56$$

$$2x=46$$

$$x=23$$

The solution is 23.

14. equation

$$\frac{1}{2}=\frac{x+1}{8}$$

$$8\left(\frac{1}{2}\right)=8\left(\frac{x+1}{8}\right)$$

$$4=x+1$$

$$3=x$$

The solution is 3.

15. expression

$$\frac{5a+10}{18}\div\frac{a^2-4}{10a}=\frac{5a+10}{18}\cdot\frac{10a}{a^2-4}$$

$$=\frac{5(a+2)\cdot 2\cdot 5\cdot a}{2\cdot 9(a+2)(a-2)}$$

$$=\frac{5\cdot 5\cdot a}{9(a-2)}=\frac{25a}{9(a-2)}$$

16. expression

$$\frac{9}{x^2-1} \div \frac{12}{3x+3} = \frac{9}{x^2-1} \cdot \frac{3x+3}{12}$$

$$= \frac{3\cdot3\cdot3(x+1)}{(x-1)(x+1)\cdot3\cdot4} = \frac{3\cdot3}{(x-1)\cdot4} = \frac{9}{4(x-1)}$$

17. expression

$$\frac{x+2}{3x-1} + \frac{5}{(3x-1)^2}$$

$$= \frac{(x+2)(3x-1)}{(3x-1)(3x-1)} + \frac{5}{(3x-1)^2}$$

$$= \frac{3x^2+5x-2+5}{(3x-1)^2}$$

$$= \frac{3x^2+5x+3}{(3x-1)^2}$$

18. expression

$$\frac{4}{(2x-5)^2} + \frac{x+1}{2x-5}$$

$$= \frac{4}{(2x-5)^2} + \frac{(x+1)(2x-5)}{(2x-5)(2x-5)}$$

$$= \frac{4+2x^2-3x-5}{(2x-5)^2}$$

$$= \frac{2x^2-3x-1}{(2x-5)^2}$$

19. expression

$$\frac{x-7}{x} - \frac{x+2}{5x} = \frac{(x-7)(5)}{x(5)} - \frac{x+2}{5x}$$

$$= \frac{5x-25-x-2}{5x}$$

$$= \frac{4x-37}{5x}$$

20. equation

$$\frac{9}{x^2-4} + \frac{2}{x+2} = \frac{-1}{x-2}$$

$$(x^2-4)\left(\frac{9}{x^2-4}\right) + (x^2-4)\left(\frac{2}{x+2}\right)$$

$$= (x^2-4)\left(\frac{-1}{x-2}\right)$$

$$9 + (x-2)(2) = (x+2)(-1)$$

$$9 + 2x - 4 = -x - 2$$

$$2x + 5 = -x - 2$$

$$3x + 5 = -2$$

$$3x = -7$$

$$x = -\frac{7}{3}$$

The solution is $-\dfrac{7}{3}$.

21. equation

$$\frac{3}{x+3} = \frac{5}{x^2-9} - \frac{2}{x-3}$$

$$(x^2-9)\left(\frac{3}{x+3}\right)$$

$$= (x^2-9)\left(\frac{5}{x^2-9}\right) - (x^2-9)\left(\frac{2}{x-3}\right)$$

$$(x-3)(3) = 5 - (x+3)(2)$$

$$3x - 9 = 5 - 2x - 6$$

$$3x - 9 = -2x - 1$$

$$5x - 9 = -1$$

$$5x = 8$$

$$x = \frac{8}{5}$$

The solution is $\dfrac{8}{5}$.

22. expression

$$\frac{10x-9}{x} - \frac{x-4}{3x} = \frac{(10x-9)(3)}{x(3)} - \frac{x-4}{3x}$$

$$= \frac{30x-27-x+4}{3x}$$

$$= \frac{29x-23}{3x}$$

23. Answers may vary.

24. Answers may vary.

Practice Problems 5.6

Let x = the unknown number.

1. $\dfrac{x}{2} - \dfrac{1}{3} = \dfrac{x}{6}$

$$6\left(\frac{x}{2} - \frac{1}{3}\right) = 6\left(\frac{x}{6}\right)$$

$$6\left(\frac{x}{2}\right) - 6\left(\frac{1}{3}\right) = 6\left(\frac{x}{6}\right)$$

$$3x - 2 = x$$

$$-2 = -2x$$

$$x = 1$$

The unknown number is 1.

2.

	Hours to Complete Total Job	Part of Job Completed in 1 Hour
Andrew	2	$1/2$
Timothy	3	$1/3$
Together	x	$1/x$

$$\frac{1}{2} + \frac{1}{3} = \frac{1}{x}$$

$$6x\left(\frac{1}{2}\right) + 6x\left(\frac{1}{3}\right) = 6x\left(\frac{1}{x}\right)$$

$$3x + 2x = 6$$

$$5x = 6$$

$$x = \frac{6}{5} \text{ or } 1\frac{1}{5}$$

Andrew and Timothy can recycle a batch in $1\frac{1}{5}$ hour.

3. Let r = the motorcycle's speed

	Distance =	rate	time
car	280	$r+10$	$280/r+10$
motorcycle	240	r	$240/r$

$$\frac{280}{r+10} = \frac{240}{r}$$

$$280r = 240(r+10)$$

$$280r = 240r + 2400$$

$$40r = 2400$$

$$r = 60$$

$$r + 10 = 70$$

The speed of the car is 70 miles per hour and the speed of the motorcycle is 60 miles per hour.

4. Since the triangles are similar, their corresponding sides are in proportion.

$$\frac{x}{12} = \frac{15}{9}$$

$$9x = 180$$

$$x = 20$$

The side has length of 20 units.

Mental Math 5.6

1. c

2. a

Exercise Set 5.6

1. $3 \cdot \dfrac{1}{x} = 9 \cdot \dfrac{1}{6}$

$\dfrac{3}{x} = \dfrac{9}{6}$

$6x\left(\dfrac{3}{x}\right) = 6x\left(\dfrac{9}{6}\right)$

$18 = 9x$

$x = 2$

The unknown number is 2.

3. $\dfrac{3+2x}{x+1} = \dfrac{3}{2}$

$2(x+1)\left(\dfrac{3+2x}{x+1}\right) = 2(x+1)\left(\dfrac{3}{2}\right)$

$2(3+2x) = 3(x+1)$

$6 + 4x = 3x + 3$

$x = -3$

The unknown number is -3.

5. $\dfrac{2}{x-3} - \dfrac{4}{x+3} = 8 \cdot \dfrac{1}{x^2-9}$

$(x-3)(x+3)\left(\dfrac{2}{x-3} - \dfrac{4}{x+3}\right)$

$\qquad = (x-3)(x+3)\left(\dfrac{8}{x^2-9}\right)$

$(x-3)(x+3)\left(\dfrac{2}{x-3}\right)$

$\qquad - (x-3)(x+3)\left(\dfrac{4}{x+3}\right) = 8$

$2(x+3) - 4(x-3) = 8$

$2x + 6 - 4x + 12 = 8$

$-2x = -10$

$x = 5$

The unknown number is 5.

7. $\dfrac{1}{4} = \dfrac{x}{8}$

$8\left(\dfrac{1}{4}\right) = 8\left(\dfrac{x}{8}\right)$

$2 = x$

The unknown number is 2.

9.

	Hours to Complete Total Job	Part of Job Completed in 1 Hour
Experienced	4	1/4
Apprentice	5	1/5
Together	x	1/x

$\dfrac{1}{4} + \dfrac{1}{5} = \dfrac{1}{x}$

$20x\left(\dfrac{1}{4}\right) + 20x\left(\dfrac{1}{5}\right) = 20x\left(\dfrac{1}{x}\right)$

$5x + 4x = 20$

$9x = 20$

$x = \dfrac{20}{9} \text{ or } 2\dfrac{2}{9}$

The experienced surveyor and apprentice surveyor, working together, can survey the road in $2\dfrac{2}{9}$ hours.

11.

	Minutes to Complete Total Job	Part of Job Completed in 1 Minute
Larger belt	2	1/2
Smaller belt	6	1/6
Both belts	x	1/x

$$\frac{1}{2} + \frac{1}{6} = \frac{1}{x}$$

$$6x\left(\frac{1}{2}\right) + 6x\left(\frac{1}{6}\right) = 6x\left(\frac{1}{x}\right)$$

$$3x + x = 6$$

$$4x = 6$$

$$x = \frac{6}{4} = \frac{3}{2} = 1\frac{1}{2}$$

Both belts together can move the cans

to the storage area in $1\frac{1}{2}$ minute.

13.

	Hours to Complete Total Job	Part of Job Completed in 1 Hour
Marcus	6	1/6
Tony	4	1/4
Together	x	$1/x$

$$\frac{1}{6} + \frac{1}{4} = \frac{1}{x}$$

$$12x\left(\frac{1}{6}\right) + 12x\left(\frac{1}{4}\right) = 12x\left(\frac{1}{x}\right)$$

$$2x + 3x = 12$$

$$5x = 12$$

$$x = \frac{12}{5} = 2\frac{2}{5}$$

$$45\left(\frac{12}{5}\right) = 108$$

Together Marcus and Tony work for

$2\frac{2}{5}$ hours at \$45 per hour. The labor

estimate should be \$108.

15.

	Hours to Complete Total Job	Part of Job Completed in 1 Hour
Custodian	3	1/3
2nd Worker	x	$1/x$
Together	$1\frac{1}{2}$ or $\frac{3}{2}$	2/3

$$\frac{1}{3} + \frac{1}{x} = \frac{2}{3}$$

$$3x\left(\frac{1}{3}\right) + 3x\left(\frac{1}{x}\right) = 3x\left(\frac{2}{3}\right)$$

$$x + 3 = 2x$$

$$3 = x$$

It takes the second worker 3 hours

to do the job alone.

17.

	Hours to Complete Total Job	Part of Job Completed in 1 Hour
1st Pipe	20	1/20
2nd Pipe	15	1/15
3rd Pipe	x	$1/x$
3 Pipes Together	6	1/6

$$\frac{1}{20} + \frac{1}{15} + \frac{1}{x} = \frac{1}{6}$$

$$60x\left(\frac{1}{20}\right) + 60x\left(\frac{1}{15}\right) + 60x\left(\frac{1}{x}\right)$$

$$= 60x\left(\frac{1}{6}\right)$$

$$3x + 4x + 60 = 10x$$

$$7x + 60 = 10x$$

$$60 = 3x$$

$$20 = x$$

It takes the third pipe 20 hours to fill

the pond.

19.

Distance =	rate ·	time
Trip to Park	3	$3/x$	x
Return Trip	9	$9/x+1$	$x+1$

$$\frac{3}{x} = \frac{9}{x+1}$$
$$3(x+1) = 9x$$
$$3x + 3 = 9x$$
$$3 = 6x$$
$$\frac{1}{2} = x$$

The jogger spends $\frac{1}{2}$ hour on her trip to

the park, so her rate is $\frac{3}{\frac{1}{2}} = \frac{3}{1} \cdot \frac{2}{1} = 6$ miles

per hour.

21.

Distance =	rate ·	time
1st portion	20	r	$20/r$
Cooldown portion	16	$r-2$	$16/r-2$

$$\frac{20}{r} = \frac{16}{r-2}$$
$$20(r-2) = 16r$$
$$20r - 40 = 16r$$
$$-40 = -4r$$
$$r = 10 \text{ and } r - 2 = 10 - 2 = 8$$

His speed was 10 miles per hour
during the first portion and 8 miles per
hour during the cooldown portion.

23.

Distance =	rate ·	time
Upstream	9	$r-3$	$9/r-3$
Downstream	11	$r+3$	$11/r+3$

$$\frac{9}{r-3} = \frac{11}{r+3}$$
$$9(r+3) = 11(r-3)$$
$$9r + 27 = 11r - 33$$
$$60 = 2r$$
$$r = 30$$

The speed of the boat in still water is
30 miles per hour.

25. Let w = the rate of the wind.

	Distance =	rate	time
With the wind	48	$16+w$	$48/16+w$
Into the wind	16	$16-w$	$16/16-w$

$$\frac{48}{16+w} = \frac{16}{16-w}$$
$$48(16-w) = 16(16+w)$$
$$768 - 48w = 256 + 16w$$
$$512 = 64w$$
$$w = 8$$

The rate of the wind is 8 miles per hour.

27. Let r = the speed of the car in still air.

	Distance =	rate ·	time
Into the wind	10	$r-3$	$10/r-3$
With the wind	11	$r+3$	$11/r+3$

$$\frac{10}{r-3} = \frac{11}{r+3}$$
$$10(r+3) = 11(r-3)$$
$$10r + 30 = 11r - 33$$
$$63 = r$$

The speed of the car in still air is 63 miles
per hour.

29. $\dfrac{12}{4} = \dfrac{18}{x}$

$12x = 72$

$x = 6$

31. $\dfrac{x}{3.75} = \dfrac{12}{9}$

$9x = 45$

$x = 5$

33. $\dfrac{16}{10} = \dfrac{34}{y}$

$16y = 340$

$y = 21.25$

35. $\dfrac{y}{30} = \dfrac{3}{5}$

$y = \dfrac{90}{5}$

$y = 18$ feet

37. $\dfrac{x}{8} = \dfrac{20}{6}$

$x = \dfrac{160}{6}$

$x = \dfrac{80}{3} = 26\dfrac{2}{3}$

The side is $26\dfrac{2}{3}$ feet long.

39. $\dfrac{\frac{3}{4} + \frac{1}{4}}{\frac{3}{8} + \frac{13}{8}} = \dfrac{\frac{3+1}{4}}{\frac{3+13}{8}} = \dfrac{\frac{4}{4}}{\frac{16}{8}} = \dfrac{1}{2}$

41. $\dfrac{\frac{2}{5} + \frac{1}{5}}{\frac{7}{10} + \frac{7}{10}} = \dfrac{\frac{2+1}{5}}{\frac{7+7}{10}} = \dfrac{\frac{3}{5}}{\frac{14}{10}} = \dfrac{3}{5} \div \dfrac{14}{10} = \dfrac{3}{5} \cdot \dfrac{10}{14}$

$= \dfrac{3 \cdot 2 \cdot 5}{5 \cdot 2 \cdot 7} = \dfrac{3}{7}$

43.

	Distance =	rate	time
J	2.459	x	$2.459/x$
C	2.5	$x+3.6$	$2.5/x+3.6$

$\dfrac{2.5}{x+3.6} = \dfrac{2.459}{x}$

$2.5x = 2.459x + 8.8524$

$0.041x = 8.8524$

$x \approx 215.9$

$x + 3.6 \approx 219.5$

Junqueira's speed was 215.9 miles per hour. Castroneves' speed was 219.5 miles per hour.

45. It would take them less than 3 hours but more than $1\dfrac{1}{2}$ hours.

Practice Problems 5.7

1. $\dfrac{\frac{3}{7}}{\frac{5}{9}} = \dfrac{3}{7} \cdot \dfrac{9}{5} = \dfrac{27}{35}$

2. $\dfrac{\frac{3}{4} - \frac{2}{3}}{\frac{1}{2} + \frac{3}{8}} = \dfrac{\frac{3(3)}{4(3)} - \frac{2(4)}{3(4)}}{\frac{1(4)}{2(4)} + \frac{3}{8}} = \dfrac{\frac{9}{12} - \frac{8}{12}}{\frac{4}{8} + \frac{3}{8}} = \dfrac{\frac{1}{12}}{\frac{7}{8}}$

$= \dfrac{1}{12} \cdot \dfrac{8}{7} = \dfrac{1 \cdot 4 \cdot 2}{3 \cdot 4 \cdot 7} = \dfrac{2}{21}$

3. $\dfrac{\frac{2}{5} - \frac{1}{x}}{\frac{x}{10} - \frac{1}{3}} = \dfrac{\frac{2x}{5x} - \frac{5}{5x}}{\frac{3x}{30} - \frac{10}{30}} = \dfrac{\frac{2x-5}{5x}}{\frac{3x-10}{30}}$

$= \dfrac{2x-5}{5x} \cdot \dfrac{30}{3x-10} = \dfrac{5 \cdot 6(2x-5)}{5 \cdot x(3x-10)}$

$= \dfrac{6(2x-5)}{x(3x-10)}$

4. $\dfrac{\frac{3}{4}-\frac{2}{3}}{\frac{1}{2}+\frac{3}{8}} = \dfrac{24\left(\frac{3}{4}-\frac{2}{3}\right)}{24\left(\frac{1}{2}+\frac{3}{8}\right)} = \dfrac{24\left(\frac{3}{4}\right)-24\left(\frac{2}{3}\right)}{24\left(\frac{1}{2}\right)+24\left(\frac{3}{8}\right)}$

$= \dfrac{18-16}{12+9} = \dfrac{2}{21}$

5. $\dfrac{1+\frac{x}{y}}{\frac{2x+1}{y}} = \dfrac{y\left(1+\frac{x}{y}\right)}{y\left(\frac{2x+1}{y}\right)} = \dfrac{y(1)+y\left(\frac{x}{y}\right)}{y\left(\frac{2x+1}{y}\right)} = \dfrac{y+x}{2x+1}$

6. $\dfrac{\frac{5}{6y}+\frac{y}{x}}{\frac{y}{x}-x} = \dfrac{6xy\left(\frac{5}{6y}+\frac{y}{x}\right)}{6xy\left(\frac{y}{3}-x\right)} = \dfrac{6xy\left(\frac{5}{6y}\right)+6xy\left(\frac{y}{x}\right)}{6xy\left(\frac{y}{3}\right)-6xy(x)}$

$= \dfrac{5x+6y^2}{2xy^2-6x^2y} = \dfrac{5x+6y^2}{2xy(y-3x)}$

Exercise Set 5.7

1. $\dfrac{\frac{1}{2}}{\frac{3}{4}} = \dfrac{1}{2}\cdot\dfrac{4}{3} = \dfrac{1\cdot 2\cdot 2}{2\cdot 3} = \dfrac{2}{3}$

3. $\dfrac{-\frac{4x}{9}}{-\frac{2x}{3}} = -\dfrac{4x}{9}\cdot -\dfrac{3}{2x} = \dfrac{2\cdot 2\cdot 3\cdot x}{3\cdot 3\cdot 2\cdot x} = \dfrac{2}{3}$

5. $\dfrac{\frac{-5}{12x^2}}{\frac{25}{16x^3}} = -\dfrac{5}{12x^2}\cdot\dfrac{16x^3}{25} = -\dfrac{5\cdot 4\cdot 4\cdot x^2\cdot x}{4\cdot 3\cdot x^2\cdot 5\cdot 5}$

$= -\dfrac{4x}{15}$

7. $\dfrac{\frac{1}{3}}{\frac{1}{2}-\frac{1}{4}} = \dfrac{12\left(\frac{1}{3}\right)}{12\left(\frac{1}{2}-\frac{1}{4}\right)} = \dfrac{12\left(\frac{1}{3}\right)}{12\left(\frac{1}{2}\right)-12\left(\frac{1}{4}\right)}$

$= \dfrac{4}{6-3} = \dfrac{4}{3}$

9. $\dfrac{2+\frac{7}{10}}{1+\frac{3}{5}} = \dfrac{10\left(2+\frac{7}{10}\right)}{10\left(1+\frac{3}{5}\right)}$

$= \dfrac{10(2)+10\left(\frac{7}{10}\right)}{10(1)+10\left(\frac{3}{5}\right)} = \dfrac{20+7}{10+6} = \dfrac{27}{16}$

11. $\dfrac{\frac{m}{n}-1}{\frac{m}{n}+1} = \dfrac{n\left(\frac{m}{n}-1\right)}{n\left(\frac{m}{n}+1\right)} = \dfrac{n\left(\frac{m}{n}\right)-n(1)}{n\left(\frac{m}{n}\right)+n(1)} = \dfrac{m-n}{m+n}$

13. $\dfrac{\frac{1}{5}-\frac{1}{x}}{\frac{7}{10}+\frac{1}{x^2}} = \dfrac{10x^2\left(\frac{1}{5}-\frac{1}{x}\right)}{10x^2\left(\frac{7}{10}+\frac{1}{x^2}\right)}$

$= \dfrac{10x^2\left(\frac{1}{5}\right)-10x^2\left(\frac{1}{x}\right)}{10x^2\left(\frac{7}{10}\right)+10x^2\left(\frac{1}{x^2}\right)} = \dfrac{2x^2-10x}{7x^2+10}$

$= \dfrac{2x(x-5)}{7x^2+10}$

15. $\dfrac{1+\frac{1}{y-2}}{y+\frac{1}{y-2}} = \dfrac{(y-2)\left(1+\frac{1}{y-2}\right)}{(y-2)\left(y+\frac{1}{y-2}\right)}$

$= \dfrac{(y-2)(1)+(y-2)\left(\frac{1}{y-2}\right)}{(y-2)(y)+(y-2)\left(\frac{1}{y-2}\right)}$

$= \dfrac{y-2+1}{y^2-2y+1} = \dfrac{y-1}{(y-1)^2} = \dfrac{1}{y-1}$

17. $\dfrac{\frac{4y-8}{16}}{\frac{6y-12}{4}} = \dfrac{4y-8}{16}\cdot\dfrac{4}{6y-12} = \dfrac{4(y-2)\cdot 4}{4\cdot 4\cdot 6(y-2)}$

$= \dfrac{1}{6}$

19. $\dfrac{\frac{x}{y}+1}{\frac{x}{y}-1} = \dfrac{y\left(\frac{x}{y}+1\right)}{n\left(\frac{x}{y}-1\right)} = \dfrac{y\left(\frac{x}{y}\right)+y(1)}{y\left(\frac{x}{y}\right)-y(1)} = \dfrac{x+y}{x-y}$

21. $\dfrac{1}{2+\frac{1}{3}} = \dfrac{3(1)}{3\left(2+\frac{1}{3}\right)} = \dfrac{3(1)}{3(2)+3\left(\frac{1}{3}\right)}$

$= \dfrac{3}{6+1} = \dfrac{3}{7}$

23. $\dfrac{\frac{ax+ab}{x^2-b^2}}{\frac{x+b}{x-b}} = \dfrac{ax+ab}{x^2-b^2} \cdot \dfrac{x-b}{x+b}$

$= \dfrac{a(x+b)\cdot(x-b)}{(x+b)(x-b)\cdot(x+b)} = \dfrac{a}{x+b}$

25. $\dfrac{\frac{8}{x+4}+2}{\frac{12}{x+4}-2} = \dfrac{(x+4)\left(\frac{8}{x+4}+2\right)}{(x+4)\left(\frac{12}{x+4}-2\right)}$

$= \dfrac{(x+4)\left(\frac{8}{x+4}\right)+(x+4)(2)}{(x+4)\left(\frac{12}{x+4}\right)-(x+4)(2)}$

$= \dfrac{8+2x+8}{12-2x-8} = \dfrac{16+2x}{4-2x} = \dfrac{2(8+x)}{2(2-x)}$

$= \dfrac{8+x}{2-x}$

27. $\dfrac{\frac{s}{r}+\frac{r}{s}}{\frac{s}{r}-\frac{r}{s}} = \dfrac{rs\left(\frac{s}{r}+\frac{r}{s}\right)}{rs\left(\frac{s}{r}-\frac{r}{s}\right)} = \dfrac{rs\left(\frac{s}{r}\right)+rs\left(\frac{r}{s}\right)}{rs\left(\frac{s}{r}\right)-rs\left(\frac{r}{s}\right)}$

$= \dfrac{s^2+r^2}{s^2-r^2}$

29. Answers may vary.

31. Steffi Graf

33. Monica Seles, Martina Hingis, Arantxa Sanchez-Vicario

35. $\dfrac{\frac{1}{3}+\frac{3}{4}}{2} = \dfrac{12\left(\frac{1}{3}+\frac{3}{4}\right)}{12(2)} = \dfrac{12\left(\frac{1}{3}\right)+12\left(\frac{3}{4}\right)}{12(2)}$

$= \dfrac{4+9}{24} = \dfrac{13}{24}$

37. $\dfrac{1}{\frac{1}{R_1}+\frac{1}{R_2}} = \dfrac{R_1R_2(1)}{R_1R_2\left(\frac{1}{R_1}+\frac{1}{R_2}\right)}$

$= \dfrac{R_1R_2}{R_1R_2\left(\frac{1}{R_1}\right)+R_1R_2\left(\frac{1}{R_2}\right)} = \dfrac{R_1R_2}{R_2+R_1}$

39. $\dfrac{x^{-1}+2^{-1}}{x^{-2}-4^{-1}} = \dfrac{\frac{1}{x}+\frac{1}{2}}{\frac{1}{x^2}-\frac{1}{4}} = \dfrac{4x^2\left(\frac{1}{x}+\frac{1}{2}\right)}{4x^2\left(\frac{1}{x^2}-\frac{1}{4}\right)}$

$= \dfrac{4x^2\left(\frac{1}{x}\right)+4x^2\left(\frac{1}{2}\right)}{4x^2\left(\frac{1}{x^2}\right)-4x^2\left(\frac{1}{4}\right)} = \dfrac{4x+2x^2}{4-x^2}$

$= \dfrac{2x(2+x)}{(2-x)(2+x)} = \dfrac{2x}{2-x}$

41. $\dfrac{y^{-2}}{1-y^{-2}} = \dfrac{\frac{1}{y^2}}{1-\frac{1}{y^2}} = \dfrac{y^2\left(\frac{1}{y^2}\right)}{y^2\left(1-\frac{1}{y^2}\right)}$

$= \dfrac{y^2\left(\frac{1}{y^2}\right)}{y^2(1)-y^2\left(\frac{1}{y^2}\right)} = \dfrac{1}{y^2-1}$

Chapter 5 Review

1. The rational expression is undefined when

$x^2-4=0$

$(x-2)(x+2)=0$

$x-2=0 \quad \text{or} \quad x+2=0$

$\phantom{x-2=0 \quad \text{or} \quad} x=2 x=-2$

2. The rational expression is undefined when

$$4x^2 - 4x - 15 = 0$$

$$(2x+3)(2x-5) = 0$$

$$2x+3 = 0 \quad \text{or} \quad 2x-5 = 0$$

$$2x = -3 \qquad\qquad 2x = 5$$

$$x = -\frac{3}{2} \qquad\qquad x = \frac{5}{2}$$

3. $\dfrac{2-z}{z+5} = \dfrac{2-(-2)}{-2+5} = \dfrac{2+2}{3} = \dfrac{4}{3}$

4. $\dfrac{x^2 + xy - y^2}{x+y} = \dfrac{5^2 + 5 \cdot 7 - 7^2}{5+7}$

$= \dfrac{25 + 35 - 49}{12} = \dfrac{11}{12}$

5. $\dfrac{2x+6}{x^2+3x} = \dfrac{2(x+3)}{x(x+3)} = \dfrac{2}{x}$

6. $\dfrac{3x-12}{x^2-4x} = \dfrac{3(x-4)}{x(x-4)} = \dfrac{3}{x}$

7. $\dfrac{x+2}{x^2-3x-10} = \dfrac{x+2}{(x-5)(x+2)} = \dfrac{1}{x-5}$

8. $\dfrac{x+4}{x^2+5x+4} = \dfrac{x+4}{(x+1)(x+4)} = \dfrac{1}{x+1}$

9. $\dfrac{x^3-4x}{x^2+3x+2} = \dfrac{x(x^2-4)}{(x+2)(x+1)}$

$= \dfrac{x(x-2)(x+2)}{(x+2)(x+1)} = \dfrac{x(x-2)}{x+1}$

10. $\dfrac{5x^2-125}{x^2+2x-15} = \dfrac{5(x^2-25)}{(x-3)(x+5)}$

$= \dfrac{5(x-5)(x+5)}{(x-3)(x+5)} = \dfrac{5(x-5)}{x-3}$

11. $\dfrac{x^2-x-6}{x^2-3x-10} = \dfrac{(x-3)(x+2)}{(x-5)(x+2)} = \dfrac{x-3}{x-5}$

12. $\dfrac{x^2-2x}{x^2+2x-8} = \dfrac{x(x-2)}{(x+4)(x-2)} = \dfrac{x}{x+4}$

13. $\dfrac{x^2+xa+xb+ab}{x^2-xc+bx-bc} = \dfrac{x(x+a)+b(x+a)}{x(x-c)+b(x-c)}$

$= \dfrac{(x+a)(x+b)}{(x-c)(x+b)} = \dfrac{x+a}{x-c}$

14. $\dfrac{x^2+5x-2x-10}{x^2-3x-2x+6} = \dfrac{x(x+5)-2(x+5)}{x(x-3)-2(x-3)}$

$= \dfrac{(x+5)(x-2)}{(x-3)(x-2)} = \dfrac{x+5}{x-3}$

15. $\dfrac{15x^3 y^2}{z} \cdot \dfrac{z}{5xy^3} = \dfrac{15x^3 y^2 \cdot z}{z \cdot 5xy^3}$

$= \dfrac{3 \cdot 5 \cdot x^2 \cdot x \cdot y^2 \cdot z}{z \cdot 5 \cdot x \cdot y^2 \cdot y} = \dfrac{3x^2}{y}$

16. $\dfrac{-y^3}{8} \cdot \dfrac{9x^2}{y^3} = \dfrac{y^3 \cdot 9x^2}{8 \cdot y^3} = -\dfrac{9x^2}{8}$

17. $\dfrac{x^2-9}{x^2-4} \cdot \dfrac{x-2}{x+3} = \dfrac{(x^2-9) \cdot (x-2)}{(x^2-4) \cdot (x+3)}$

$= \dfrac{(x-3)(x+3)(x-2)}{(x+2)(x-2)(x+3)} = \dfrac{x-3}{x+2}$

18. $\dfrac{2x+5}{x-6} \cdot \dfrac{2x}{-x+6} = \dfrac{2x+5}{x-6} \cdot \dfrac{2x}{-(x-6)}$

$= \dfrac{2x+5}{x-6} \cdot \dfrac{-2x}{x-6} = \dfrac{(2x+5)\cdot(-2x)}{(x-6)\cdot(x-6)}$

$= \dfrac{-2x(2x+5)}{(x-6)^2}$

19. $\dfrac{x^2-5x-24}{x^2-x-12} \div \dfrac{x^2-10x+16}{x^2+x-6}$

$= \dfrac{x^2-5x-24}{x^2-x-12} \cdot \dfrac{x^2+x-6}{x^2-10x+16}$

$= \dfrac{(x-8)(x+3)\cdot(x+3)(x-2)}{(x-4)(x+3)\cdot(x-8)(x-2)}$

$= \dfrac{x+3}{x-4}$

20. $\dfrac{4x+4y}{xy^2} \div \dfrac{3x+3y}{x^2y} = \dfrac{4x+4y}{xy^2} \cdot \dfrac{x^2y}{3x+3y}$

$= \dfrac{4(x+y)\cdot x\cdot x\cdot y}{x\cdot y\cdot y\cdot 3(x+y)} = \dfrac{4x}{3y}$

21. $\dfrac{x^2+x-42}{x-3} \cdot \dfrac{(x-3)^2}{x+7}$

$= \dfrac{(x+7)(x-6)\cdot(x-3)(x-3)}{(x-3)\cdot(x+7)}$

$= (x-6)(x-3)$

22. $\dfrac{2a+2b}{3} \cdot \dfrac{a-b}{a^2-b^2} = \dfrac{2(a+b)\cdot(a-b)}{3\cdot(a+b)(a-b)} = \dfrac{2}{3}$

23. $\dfrac{x^2-9x+14}{x^2-5x+6} \cdot \dfrac{x+2}{x^2-5x-14}$

$= \dfrac{(x-7)(x-2)\cdot(x+2)}{(x-3)(x-2)\cdot(x-7)(x+2)} = \dfrac{1}{x-3}$

24. $(x-3)\cdot \dfrac{x}{x^2+3x-18}$

$= \dfrac{(x-3)\cdot x}{(x-3)(x+6)} = \dfrac{x}{x+6}$

25. $\dfrac{2x^2-9x+9}{8x-12} \div \dfrac{x^2-3x}{2x}$

$= \dfrac{2x^2-9x+9}{9x-12} \cdot \dfrac{2x}{x^2-3x}$

$= \dfrac{(2x-3)(x-3)\cdot 2x}{4(2x-3)\cdot x(x-3)}$

$= \dfrac{2}{4} = \dfrac{1}{2}$

26. $\dfrac{x^2-y^2}{x^2+xy} \div \dfrac{3x^2-2xy-y^2}{3x^2+6x}$

$= \dfrac{x^2-y^2}{x^2+xy} \cdot \dfrac{3x^2+6x}{3x^2-2xy-y^2}$

$= \dfrac{(x-y)(x+y)\cdot 3x(x+2)}{x(x+y)\cdot(3x+y)(x-y)}$

$= \dfrac{3(x+2)}{3x+y}$

27. $\dfrac{x}{x^2+9x+14} + \dfrac{7}{x^2+9x+14}$

$= \dfrac{x+7}{x^2+9x+14} = \dfrac{x+7}{(x+2)(x+7)} = \dfrac{1}{x+2}$

28. $\dfrac{x}{x^2+2x-15} + \dfrac{5}{x^2+2x-15} = \dfrac{x+5}{x^2+2x-15}$

$= \dfrac{x+5}{(x-3)(x+5)} = \dfrac{1}{x-3}$

29. $\dfrac{4x-5}{3x^2} - \dfrac{2x+5}{3x^2} = \dfrac{4x-5-(2x+5)}{3x^2}$

$= \dfrac{4x-5-2x-5}{3x^2} = \dfrac{2x-10}{3x^2}$

30. $\dfrac{9x+7}{6x^2} - \dfrac{3x+4}{6x^2} = \dfrac{9x+7-(3x+4)}{6x^2}$

$= \dfrac{9x+7-3x-4}{6x^2} = \dfrac{6x+3}{6x^2} = \dfrac{3(2x+1)}{3\cdot 2x^2}$

$= \dfrac{2x+1}{2x^2}$

31. $2x = 2\cdot x$

$7x = 7\cdot x$

$\text{LCD} = 2\cdot 7\cdot x = 14x$

32. $x^2 - 5x - 24 = (x-8)(x+3)$

$x^2 + 11x + 24 = (x+8)(x+3)$

$\text{LCD} = (x-8)(x+3)(x+8)$

33. $\dfrac{5}{7x} = \dfrac{5(2x^2y)}{7x(2x^2y)} = \dfrac{10x^2y}{14x^3y}$

34. $\dfrac{9}{4y} = \dfrac{9(4y^2x)}{4y(4y^2x)} = \dfrac{36y^2x}{16y^3x}$

35. $\dfrac{x+2}{x^2+11x+18} = \dfrac{x+2}{(x+9)(x+2)}$

$= \dfrac{(x+2)(x-5)}{(x+9)(x+2)(x-5)}$

$= \dfrac{x^2-3x-10}{(x+2)(x-5)(x+9)}$

36. $\dfrac{3x-5}{x^2+4x+4} = \dfrac{3x-5}{(x+2)^2}$

$= \dfrac{(3x-5)(x+3)}{(x+2)^2(x+3)} = \dfrac{3x^2+4x-15}{(x+2)^2(x+3)}$

$= \dfrac{x^2-3x-10}{(x+2)(x-5)(x+9)}$

37. $\dfrac{4}{5x^2} - \dfrac{6}{y} = \dfrac{4(y)}{5x^2(y)} - \dfrac{6(5x^2)}{y(5x^2)} = \dfrac{4y-30x^2}{5x^2y}$

38. $\dfrac{2}{x-3} - \dfrac{4}{x-1}$

$= \dfrac{2(x-1)}{(x-3)(x-1)} - \dfrac{4(x-3)}{(x-1)(x-3)}$

$= \dfrac{2(x-1)-4(x-3)}{(x-3)(x-1)} = \dfrac{2x-2-4x+12}{(x-3)(x-1)}$

$= \dfrac{-2x+10}{(x-3)(x-1)}$

39. $\dfrac{x+7}{x+3} - \dfrac{x-3}{x+7}$

$= \dfrac{(x+7)(x+7)}{(x+3)(x+7)} - \dfrac{(x-3)(x+3)}{(x+7)(x+3)}$

$= \dfrac{x^2+14x+49-(x^2-9)}{(x+3)(x+7)}$

$= \dfrac{x^2+14x+49-x^2+9}{(x+3)(x+7)} = \dfrac{14x+58}{(x+3)(x+7)}$

40. $\dfrac{4}{x+3} - 2 = \dfrac{4}{x+3} - \dfrac{2(x+3)}{x+3}$

$= \dfrac{4-2(x+3)}{x+3} = \dfrac{4-2x-6}{x+3} = \dfrac{-2x-2}{x+3}$

41. $\dfrac{3}{x^2 + 2x - 8} + \dfrac{2}{x^2 - 3x + 2}$

$= \dfrac{3}{(x+4)(x-2)} + \dfrac{2}{(x-1)(x-2)}$

$= \dfrac{3(x-1)}{(x+4)(x-2)(x-1)}$

$\qquad + \dfrac{2(x+4)}{(x-1)(x-2)(x+4)}$

$= \dfrac{3(x-1) + 2(x+4)}{(x+4)(x-2)(x-1)}$

$= \dfrac{3x - 3 + 2x + 8}{(x+4)(x-2)(x-1)}$

$= \dfrac{5x + 5}{(x+4)(x-2)(x-1)}$

42. $\dfrac{2x - 5}{6x + 9} - \dfrac{4}{2x^2 + 3x}$

$= \dfrac{2x - 5}{3(2x + 3)} - \dfrac{4}{x(2x + 3)}$

$= \dfrac{(2x - 5)(x)}{3(2x + 3)(x)} - \dfrac{4(3)}{x(2x + 3)(3)}$

$= \dfrac{2x^2 - 5x - 12}{3x(2x + 3)} = \dfrac{(2x + 3)(x - 4)}{3x(2x + 3)}$

$= \dfrac{x - 4}{3x}$

43. $\dfrac{x - 1}{x^2 - 2x + 1} - \dfrac{x + 1}{x - 1} = \dfrac{x - 1}{(x - 1)^2} - \dfrac{x + 1}{x - 1}$

$= \dfrac{1}{x - 1} = \dfrac{x + 1}{x - 1} = \dfrac{1 - (x + 1)}{x - 1}$

$= \dfrac{1 - x - 1}{x - 1} = \dfrac{-x}{x - 1} = -\dfrac{x}{x - 1}$

44. $\dfrac{x - 1}{x^2 + 4x + 4} + \dfrac{x - 1}{x + 2}$

$= \dfrac{x - 1}{(x + 2)^2} + \dfrac{(x - 1)(x + 2)}{(x + 2)(x + 2)}$

$= \dfrac{x - 1 + (x - 1)(x + 2)}{(x + 2)^2}$

$= \dfrac{x - 1 + x^2 + x - 2}{(x + 2)^2}$

$= \dfrac{x^2 + 2x - 3}{(x + 2)^2}$

45. $P = 2l + 2w$

$P = 2\left(\dfrac{2}{8}\right) + 2\left(\dfrac{x + 2}{4x}\right)$

$= \dfrac{x}{4} + \dfrac{2(x + 2)}{4x}$

$= \dfrac{x \cdot x}{4 \cdot x} + \dfrac{2x + 4}{4x}$

$= \dfrac{x^2 + 2x + 4}{4x}$

$A = l \cdot w$

$A = \dfrac{x}{8} \cdot \dfrac{x + 2}{4x} = \dfrac{x \cdot (x + 2)}{8 \cdot 4x} = \dfrac{x + 2}{32}$

The perimeter is $\dfrac{x^2 + 2x + 4}{4x}$ units

and the area is $\dfrac{x + 2}{32}$ square units.

46. $P = \dfrac{3x}{4x-4} + \dfrac{2x}{3x-3} + \dfrac{x}{x-1}$

$= \dfrac{3x}{4(x-1)} + \dfrac{2x}{3(x-1)} + \dfrac{x}{x-1}$

$= \dfrac{3x(3)}{4(x-1)(3)} + \dfrac{2x(4)}{3(x-1)(4)} + \dfrac{x(12)}{(x-1)(12)}$

$= \dfrac{9x+8x+12x}{12(x-1)} = \dfrac{29x}{12(x-1)}$

$A = \dfrac{1}{2} \cdot b \cdot h$

$A = \dfrac{1}{2} \cdot \dfrac{x}{x-1} \cdot \dfrac{6y}{5}$

$= \dfrac{1 \cdot x \cdot 2 \cdot 3y}{2 \cdot (x-1) \cdot 5}$

$= \dfrac{3xy}{5(x-1)}$

The perimeter is $\dfrac{29x}{12(x-1)}$ units and the

area is $\dfrac{3xy}{5(x-1)}$ square units.

47. $\dfrac{x+4}{9} = \dfrac{5}{9}$

$9\left(\dfrac{x+4}{9}\right) = 9\left(\dfrac{5}{9}\right)$

$x+4 = 5$

$x = 1$

48. $\dfrac{n}{10} = 9 - \dfrac{n}{5}$

$10\left(\dfrac{n}{10}\right) = 10\left(9 - \dfrac{n}{5}\right)$

$10\left(\dfrac{n}{10}\right) = 10(9) - 10\left(\dfrac{n}{5}\right)$

$n = 90 - 2n$

$3n = 90$

$n = 30$

49. $\dfrac{5y-3}{7} = \dfrac{15y-2}{28}$

$28\left(\dfrac{5y-3}{7}\right) = 28\left(\dfrac{15y-2}{28}\right)$

$4(5y-3) = 15y-2$

$20y-12 = 15y-2$

$5y = 10$

$y = 2$

50. $\dfrac{2}{x+1} - \dfrac{1}{x-2} = -\dfrac{1}{2}$

$2(x+1)(x-2)\left(\dfrac{2}{x+1} - \dfrac{1}{x-2}\right)$

$= 2(x+1)(x-2)\left(-\dfrac{1}{2}\right)$

$2(x+1)(x-2)\left(\dfrac{2}{x+1}\right)$

$-2(x+1)(x-2)\left(\dfrac{1}{x-2}\right)$

$= 2(x+1)(x-2)\left(-\dfrac{1}{2}\right)$

$4(x-2) - 2(x+1) = -(x+1)(x-2)$

$4x-8-2x-2 = -\left(x^2 - x - 2\right)$

$2x-10 = -x^2 + x + 2$

$x^2 + x - 12 = 0$

$(x+4)(x-3) = 0$

$x+4 = 0 \quad \text{or} \quad x-3 = 0$

$x = -4 \qquad\qquad x = 3$

51. $\dfrac{1}{a+3}+\dfrac{1}{a-3}=-\dfrac{5}{a^2-9}$

$(a-3)(a+3)\left(\dfrac{1}{a+3}+\dfrac{1}{a-3}\right)$

$\qquad =(a-3)(a+3)\left(-\dfrac{5}{(a-3)(a+3)}\right)$

$(a-3)(a+3)\left(\dfrac{1}{a+3}\right)$

$\qquad +(a-3)(a+3)\left(\dfrac{1}{a-3}\right)=-5$

$a-3+a+3=-5$

$2a=-5$

$a=-\dfrac{5}{2}$

52. $\dfrac{y}{2y+2}+\dfrac{2y-16}{4y+4}=\dfrac{y-3}{y+1}$

$\dfrac{y}{2(y+1)}+\dfrac{2y-16}{4(y+1)}=\dfrac{y-3}{y+1}$

$4(y+1)\left(\dfrac{y}{2(y+1)}+\dfrac{2y-16}{4(y+1)}\right)$

$\qquad =4(y+1)\left(\dfrac{y-3}{y+1}\right)$

$4(y+1)\left(\dfrac{y}{2(y+1)}\right)+4(y+1)\left(\dfrac{2y-16}{4(y+1)}\right)$

$\qquad =4(y+1)\left(\dfrac{y-3}{y+1}\right)$

$2y+2y-16=4(y-3)$

$4y-16=4y-12$

$-16=-12$ False

This equation has no solution.

53. $\dfrac{4}{x+3}+\dfrac{8}{x^2-9}=0$

$(x-3)(x+3)\left(\dfrac{4}{x+3}+\dfrac{8}{(x-3)(x+3)}\right)$

$\qquad =(x-3)(x+3)(0)$

$(x-3)(x+3)\left(\dfrac{4}{x+3}\right)$

$\qquad +(x-3)(x+3)\left(\dfrac{8}{(x-3)(x+3)}\right)=0$

$4(x-3)+8=0$

$4x-12+8=0$

$4x-4=0$

$4x=4$

$x=1$

54. $\dfrac{2}{x-3}-\dfrac{4}{x+3}=\dfrac{8}{x^2-9}$

$(x-3)(x+3)\left(\dfrac{2}{x-3}-\dfrac{4}{x+3}\right)$

$\qquad =(x-3)(x+3)\left(\dfrac{8}{(x-3)(x+3)}\right)$

$(x-3)(x+3)\left(\dfrac{2}{x-3}\right)$

$\qquad -(x-3)(x+3)\left(\dfrac{4}{x+3}\right)=8$

$2(x+3)-4(x-3)=8$

$2x+6-4x+12=8$

$-2x+18=8$

$-2x=-10$

$x=5$

55. $\dfrac{x-3}{x+1}-\dfrac{x-6}{x+5}=0$

$(x+1)(x+5)\left(\dfrac{x-3}{x+1}-\dfrac{x-6}{x+5}\right)$

$=(x+1)(x+5)(0)$

$(x+1)(x+5)\left(\dfrac{x-3}{x+1}\right)$

$-(x+1)(x+5)\left(\dfrac{x-6}{x+5}\right)=0$

$(x+5)(x-3)-(x+1)(x-6)=0$

$x^2+2x-15-\left(x^2-5x-6\right)=0$

$x^2+2x-15-x^2+5x+6=0$

$7x-9=0$

$7x=9$

$x=\dfrac{9}{7}$

56. $x+5=\dfrac{6}{x}$

$x(x+5)=x\left(\dfrac{6}{x}\right)$

$x^2+5x=6$

$x^2+5x-6=0$

$(x+6)(x-1)=0$

$x+6=0 \quad\text{or}\quad x-1=0$

$x=-6 x=1$

57. $\dfrac{4A}{5b}=x^2$

$4A=5bx^2$

$\dfrac{4A}{5x^2}=\dfrac{5bx^2}{5x^2}$

$\dfrac{4A}{5x^2}=b$

58. $\dfrac{x}{7}+\dfrac{y}{8}=10$

$56\left(\dfrac{x}{7}\right)+56\left(\dfrac{y}{8}\right)=56(10)$

$8x+7y=560$

$7y=560-8x$

$y=\dfrac{560-8x}{7}$

59. $5\cdot\dfrac{1}{x}=\dfrac{3}{2}\cdot\dfrac{1}{x}+\dfrac{7}{6}$

$\dfrac{5}{x}=\dfrac{3}{2x}+\dfrac{7}{6}$

$6x\left(\dfrac{5}{x}\right)=6x\left(\dfrac{3}{2x}\right)+6x\left(\dfrac{7}{6}\right)$

$30=9+7x$

$21=7x$

$x=3$

The unknown number is 3.

60. $\dfrac{1}{x}=\dfrac{1}{4-x}$

$4-x=x$

$4=2x$

$2=x$

The unknown number is 2.

61.

	Distance	=	rate	·	time
1st car	90		r		$90/r$
2nd car	60		$r-10$		$60/r-10$

$\dfrac{90}{r}=\dfrac{60}{r-10}$

$90(r-10)=60r$

$90r-900=60r$

$-900=-30r$

$30 = r$

$r - 10 = 30 - 10 = 20$

The rate of the first car is 30 miles per hour and the rate of the second car is 20 miles per hour.

62.

	Distance =	rate	time
Upstream	48	$r - 4$	$48/r - 4$
Downstream	72	$r + 4$	$72/r + 4$

$\dfrac{48}{r - 4} = \dfrac{72}{r + 4}$

$48(r + 4) = 72(r - 4)$

$48r + 192 = 72r - 288$

$480 = 24r$

$r = 20$

The speed of the boat in still water is 20 miles per hour.

63.

	Hours to Complete Total Job	Part of Job Completed in 1 Hour
Mark	7	$1/7$
Maria	x	$1/x$
Together	5	$1/5$

$\dfrac{1}{7} + \dfrac{1}{x} = \dfrac{1}{5}$

$35x\left(\dfrac{1}{7}\right) + 35x\left(\dfrac{1}{x}\right) = 35x\left(\dfrac{1}{5}\right)$

$5x + 35 = 7x$

$35 = 2x$

$x = \dfrac{35}{2}$ or $17\dfrac{1}{2}$

It takes Maria $17\dfrac{1}{2}$ hours to complete the job alone.

64.

	Days to Complete Total Job	Part of Job Completed in 1 Day
Pipe A	20	$1/20$
Pipe B	15	$1/15$
Together	x	$1/x$

$\dfrac{1}{20} + \dfrac{1}{25} = \dfrac{1}{x}$

$60x\left(\dfrac{1}{20}\right) + 60x\left(\dfrac{1}{15}\right) = 60x\left(\dfrac{1}{x}\right)$

$3x + 4x = 60$

$7x = 60$

$x = \dfrac{60}{7} = 8\dfrac{4}{7}$

Both pipes fill the pond in $8\dfrac{4}{7}$ days.

65. $\dfrac{2}{3} = \dfrac{10}{x}$

$2x = 30$

$x = 15$

The missing length is 15.

66. $\dfrac{12}{4} = \dfrac{18}{x}$

$12x = 72$

$x = 6$

The missing length is 6.

67. $\dfrac{9}{7\frac{1}{5}} = \dfrac{x}{12}$

$108 = 7\dfrac{1}{5}x$

$108 = \dfrac{36}{5}x$

$540 = 36x$

$15 = x$

The missing length is 15.

68. $\dfrac{x}{5} = \dfrac{30}{2.5}$

$2.5x = 150$

$x = 60$

The missing length is 60.

69. $\dfrac{\frac{5x}{27}}{-\frac{10xy}{21}} = \dfrac{5x}{27} \cdot -\dfrac{21}{10xy} = -\dfrac{5x \cdot 3 \cdot 7}{3 \cdot 9 \cdot 5 \cdot 2 \cdot x \cdot y}$

$= -\dfrac{7}{18y}$

70. $\dfrac{\frac{8x}{x^2-9}}{\frac{4}{x+3}} = \dfrac{8x}{x^2-9} \cdot \dfrac{x+3}{4}$

$= \dfrac{2 \cdot 4 \cdot x(x+3)}{(x-3)(x+3) \cdot 4} = \dfrac{2x}{x-3}$

71. $\dfrac{\frac{3}{5}+\frac{2}{7}}{\frac{1}{5}+\frac{5}{6}} = \dfrac{\frac{21}{35}+\frac{10}{35}}{\frac{6}{30}+\frac{25}{30}} = \dfrac{\frac{31}{35}}{\frac{31}{30}} = \dfrac{31}{35} \cdot \dfrac{30}{31}$

$= \dfrac{31 \cdot 5 \cdot 6}{5 \cdot 7 \cdot 31} = \dfrac{6}{7}$

72. $\dfrac{2+\frac{1}{x^2}}{\frac{1}{x}+\frac{2}{x^2}} = \dfrac{x^2\left(2+\frac{1}{x^2}\right)}{x^2\left(\frac{1}{x}+\frac{2}{x^2}\right)} = \dfrac{x^2(2)+x^2\left(\frac{1}{x^2}\right)}{x^2\left(\frac{1}{x}\right)+x^2\left(\frac{2}{x^2}\right)}$

$= \dfrac{2x^2+1}{x+2}$

73. $\dfrac{3-\frac{1}{y}}{2-\frac{1}{y}} = \dfrac{y\left(3-\frac{1}{y}\right)}{y\left(2-\frac{1}{y}\right)} = \dfrac{y(3)-y\left(\frac{1}{y}\right)}{y(2)-y\left(\frac{1}{y}\right)}$

$= \dfrac{3y-1}{2y-1}$

74. $\dfrac{\frac{6}{x+2}+4}{\frac{8}{x+2}-4} = \dfrac{(x+2)\left(\frac{6}{x+2}+4\right)}{(x+2)\left(\frac{8}{x+2}-4\right)}$

$= \dfrac{(x+2)\left(\frac{6}{x+2}\right)+(x+2)(4)}{(x+2)\left(\frac{8}{x+2}\right)-(x+2)(4)}$

$= \dfrac{6+4x+8}{8-4x-8} = \dfrac{4x+14}{-4x} = -\dfrac{2(2x+7)}{2 \cdot 2x}$

$= -\dfrac{2x+7}{2x}$

Chapter 5 Test

1. The rational expression is undefined when

$x^2+4x+3=0$

$(x+3)(x+1)=0$

$x+3=0 \quad \text{or} \quad x+1=0$

$x=-3 \qquad\qquad x=-1$

2. a. $C = \dfrac{100x+3000}{x}$

$= \dfrac{100(200)+3000}{200}$

$= \dfrac{20,000+3000}{200}$

$$= \frac{23,000}{200} = 115$$

The average cost/desk is $115.

b. $C = \dfrac{100x + 3000}{x}$

$$= \frac{100(1000) + 3000}{1000}$$

$$= \frac{100,000 + 3000}{1000}$$

$$= \frac{103,000}{1000} = 103$$

The average cost/desk is $103.

3. $\dfrac{3x - 6}{5x - 10} = \dfrac{3(x - 2)}{5(x - 2)} = \dfrac{3}{5}$

4. $\dfrac{x + 10}{x^2 - 100} = \dfrac{x + 10}{(x - 10)(x + 10)} = \dfrac{1}{x - 10}$

5. $\dfrac{x + 6}{x^2 + 12x + 36} = \dfrac{x + 6}{(x + 6)^2} = \dfrac{1}{x + 6}$

6. $\dfrac{7 - x}{x - 7} = \dfrac{-(x - 7)}{x - 7} = -1$

7. $\dfrac{2m^3 - 2m^2 - 12m}{m^2 - 5m + 6} = \dfrac{2m(m^2 - m - 6)}{(m - 3)(m - 2)}$

$$= \frac{2m(m - 3)(m + 2)}{(m - 3)(m - 2)} = \frac{2m(m + 2)}{m - 2}$$

8. $\dfrac{y - x}{x^2 - y^2} = \dfrac{-(x - y)}{(x - y)(x + y)} = -\dfrac{1}{x + y}$

9. $\dfrac{x^2 - 13x + 42}{x^2 + 10x + 21} \div \dfrac{x^2 - 4}{x^2 + x - 6}$

$$= \frac{x^2 - 13x + 42}{x^2 + 10x + 21} \cdot \frac{x^2 + x - 6}{x^2 - 4}$$

$$= \frac{(x - 6)(x - 7) \cdot (x + 3)(x - 2)}{(x + 7)(x + 3) \cdot (x + 2)(x - 2)}$$

$$= \frac{(x - 6)(x - 7)}{(x + 7)(x + 2)}$$

10. $\dfrac{3}{x - 1} \cdot (5x - 5) = \dfrac{3}{x - 1} \cdot 5(x - 1)$

$$= \frac{3 \cdot 5(x - 1)}{x - 1} = 15$$

11. $\dfrac{y^2 - 5y + 6}{2y + 4} \cdot \dfrac{y + 2}{2y - 6}$

$$= \frac{(y - 3)(y - 2) \cdot (y + 2)}{2(y + 2) \cdot 2(y - 3)} = \frac{y - 2}{4}$$

12. $\dfrac{5}{2x + 5} - \dfrac{6}{2x + 5} = \dfrac{5 - 6}{2x + 5} = \dfrac{-1}{2x + 5}$

13. $\dfrac{5a}{a^2 - a - 6} - \dfrac{2}{a - 3}$

$$= \frac{5a}{(a - 3)(a + 2)} - \frac{2(a + 2)}{(a - 3)(a + 2)}$$

$$= \frac{5a - 2(a + 2)}{(a - 3)(a + 2)} = \frac{5a - 2a - 4}{(a - 3)(a + 2)}$$

$$= \frac{3a - 4}{(a - 3)(a + 2)}$$

14. $\dfrac{6}{x^2-1}+\dfrac{3}{x+1}$

$$=\dfrac{6}{(x+1)(x-1)}+\dfrac{3(x-1)}{(x+1)(x-1)}$$

$$=\dfrac{6+3x-3}{(x+1)(x-1)}=\dfrac{3x+3}{(x+1)(x-1)}$$

$$=\dfrac{3(x+1)}{(x+1)(x-1)}=\dfrac{3}{x-1}$$

15. $\dfrac{x^2-9}{x^2-3x}\div\dfrac{x^2+4x+1}{2x+10}$

$$=\dfrac{x^2-9}{x^2-3x}\cdot\dfrac{2x+10}{y^4+4x+1}$$

$$=\dfrac{(x-3)(x+3)\cdot 2(x+5)}{x(x-3)\cdot\left(x^2+4x+1\right)}$$

$$=\dfrac{2(x+3)(x+5)}{x\left(x^2+4x+1\right)}$$

16. $\dfrac{x+2}{x^2+11x+18}+\dfrac{5}{x^2-3x-10}$

$$=\dfrac{x+2}{(x+9)(x+2)}+\dfrac{5}{(x-5)(x+2)}$$

$$=\dfrac{(x+2)(x-5)}{(x+9)(x+2)(x-5)}$$

$$+\dfrac{5(x+9)}{(x-5)(x+2)(x+9)}$$

$$=\dfrac{(x+2)(x-5)+5(x+9)}{(x+9)(x+2)(x-5)}$$

$$=\dfrac{x^2-3x-10+5x+45}{(x+9)(x+2)(x-5)}$$

$$=\dfrac{x^2+2x+35}{(x+9)(x+2)(x-5)}$$

17. $\dfrac{4y}{x^2+6y+5}-\dfrac{3}{y^2+5y+4}$

$$=\dfrac{4y}{(y+5)(y+1)}-\dfrac{3}{(y+4)(y+1)}$$

$$=\dfrac{4y(y+4)}{(y+5)(y+1)(y+4)}$$

$$-\dfrac{3(y+5)}{(y+4)(y+1)(y+5)}$$

$$=\dfrac{4y(y+4)-3(y+5)}{(y+5)(y+1)(y+4)}$$

$$=\dfrac{4y^2+16y-3y-15}{(y+5)(y+1)(y+4)}$$

$$=\dfrac{4y^2+13y-15}{(y+5)(y+1)(y+4)}$$

18. $\dfrac{4}{y}-\dfrac{5}{3}=-\dfrac{1}{5}$

$$15y\left(\dfrac{4}{y}-\dfrac{5}{3}\right)=15y\left(-\dfrac{1}{5}\right)$$

$$15y\left(\dfrac{4}{y}\right)-15y\left(\dfrac{5}{3}\right)=15y\left(-\dfrac{1}{5}\right)$$

$$60-25y=-3y$$

$$60=22y$$

$$\dfrac{60}{22}=y$$

$$y=\dfrac{30}{11}$$

19. $\dfrac{5}{y+1} = \dfrac{4}{y+2}$

$5(y+2) = 4(y+1)$

$5y + 10 = 4y + 4$

$\qquad y = -6$

20. $\dfrac{a}{a-3} = \dfrac{3}{a-3} - \dfrac{3}{2}$

$2(a-3)\left(\dfrac{a}{a-3}\right) = 2(a-3)\left(\dfrac{3}{a-3} - \dfrac{3}{2}\right)$

$2a = 2(a-3)\left(\dfrac{3}{a-3}\right) - 2(a-3)\left(\dfrac{3}{2}\right)$

$2a = 6 - 3(a-3)$

$2a = 6 - 3a + 9$

$2a = 15 - 3a$

$5a = 15$

$a = 3$

In the original equation, 3 makes a denominator 0. This equation has no solution.

21. $\dfrac{10}{x^2 - 25} = \dfrac{3}{x+5} + \dfrac{1}{x-5}$

$(x+5)(x-5)\left(\dfrac{10}{(x+5)(x-5)}\right)$

$\qquad = (x+5)(x-5)\left(\dfrac{3}{x+5} + \dfrac{1}{x-5}\right)$

$10 = (x+5)(x-5)\left(\dfrac{3}{x+5}\right)$

$\qquad\qquad + (x+5)(x-5)\left(\dfrac{1}{x-5}\right)$

$10 = 3(x-5) + x + 5$

$10 = 3x - 15 + x + 5$

$10 = 4x - 10$

$20 = 4x$

$x = 5$

In the original equation, 5 makes the denominator 0. This equation has no solution.

22. $\dfrac{\frac{5x^2}{yz^2}}{\frac{10x}{z^3}} = \dfrac{5x^2}{yz^2} \cdot \dfrac{z^3}{10x} = -\dfrac{5 \cdot x \cdot x \cdot z \cdot z^2}{y \cdot z^2 \cdot 2 \cdot 5 \cdot x}$

$\qquad = \dfrac{xz}{2y}$

23. $\dfrac{\frac{b}{a} - \frac{a}{b}}{\frac{1}{b} + \frac{1}{a}} = \dfrac{ab\left(\frac{b}{a} - \frac{a}{b}\right)}{ab\left(\frac{1}{b} + \frac{1}{a}\right)} = \dfrac{ab\left(\frac{b}{a}\right) - ab\left(\frac{b}{a}\right)}{ab\left(\frac{1}{b}\right) + ab\left(\frac{1}{a}\right)}$

$\qquad = \dfrac{b^2 - a^2}{a+b} = \dfrac{(b+a)(b-a)}{b+a} = b - a$

24. $\dfrac{5 - \frac{1}{y^2}}{\frac{1}{y} + \frac{2}{y^2}} = \dfrac{y^2\left(5 - \frac{1}{y^2}\right)}{y^2\left(\frac{1}{y} + \frac{2}{y^2}\right)} = \dfrac{y^2(5) - y^2\left(\frac{1}{y^2}\right)}{y^2\left(\frac{1}{y}\right) + y^2\left(\frac{2}{y^2}\right)}$

$\qquad = \dfrac{5y^2 - 1}{y+2}$

25. $\dfrac{8}{x} = \dfrac{10}{15}$

$8(15) = 10x$

$120 = 10x$

$12 = x$

26. $x + 5 \cdot \dfrac{1}{x} = 6$

$x + \dfrac{5}{x} = 6$

$x\left(x + \dfrac{5}{x}\right) = x(6)$

$x(x) + x\left(\dfrac{5}{x}\right) = x(6)$

$x^2 + 5 = 6x$

$x^2 - 6x + 5 = 0$

$(x - 5)(x - 1) = 0$

$x - 5 = 0$ or $x - 1 = 0$

$x = 5$ $x = 1$

The unknown number is 5 or 1.

27.

	Distance =	rate ·	time
Upstream	14	$r - 2$	$14/r - 2$
Downstream	16	$r + 2$	$16/r + 2$

$\dfrac{14}{r - 2} = \dfrac{16}{r + 2}$

$14(r + 2) = 16(r - 2)$

$14r + 28 = 16r - 32$

$60 = 2r$

$r = 30$

The speed of the boat in still water is 30 miles per hour.

28.

	Hours to Complete Total Job	Part of Job Completed in 1 Hour
1st pipe	12	1/12
2nd pipe	15	1/15
Together	x	$1/x$

$\dfrac{1}{12} + \dfrac{1}{15} = \dfrac{1}{x}$

$60x\left(\dfrac{1}{12}\right) + 60x\left(\dfrac{1}{15}\right) = 60x\left(\dfrac{1}{x}\right)$

$5x + 4x = 60$

$9x = 60$

$x = \dfrac{60}{9} = \dfrac{20}{3} = 6\dfrac{2}{3}$

Together, the pipes can fill the tank in

$6\dfrac{2}{3}$ hours.

Cumulative Review Chapter 5

1. a. $\dfrac{15}{x} = 4$

   b. $12 - 3 = x$

   c. $4x + 17 = 21$

2. a. $3 + (-7) + (-8) = -4 + (-8) = -12$

   b. $[7 + (-10)] + [-2 + (-4)]$

       $= [-3] + [-6] = -9$

3. commutative property of multiplication

4. associative property of addition.

5. $3 - x = 7$

      $3 - x - 3 = 7 - 3$

         $-x = 4$

         $\dfrac{-x}{-1} = \dfrac{4}{-1}$

         $x = -4$

6. Let x = the length of the shorter piece.
Then $4x$ = the length of the longer piece.

$x + 4x = 10$

$5x = 10$

$x = 2$

The shorter piece is 2 feet long; the longer
piece is $4 \cdot 2 = 8$ feet long.

7.
$$y = mx + b$$
$$y - b = mx + b - b$$
$$y - b = mx$$
$$\frac{y - b}{m} = \frac{mx}{m}$$
$$\frac{y - b}{m} = x$$

8. $x + 4 \le -6$

$x + 4 - 4 \le -6 - 4$

$x \le -10$

$\{x \mid x \le 10\}$

9. $\dfrac{x^5}{x^2} = x^{5-2} = x^3$

10. $\dfrac{4^7}{4^3} = 4^{7-3} = 4^4 = 256$

11. $\dfrac{(-3)^5}{(-3)^2} = (-3)^{5-2} = (-3)^3 = -27$

12. $\dfrac{2x^5 y^2}{xy} = 2x^{5-1} y^{2-1} = 2x^4 y$

13. $2x^{-3} = \dfrac{2}{x^3}$

14. $(-2)^{-4} = \dfrac{1}{(-2)^4} = \dfrac{1}{16}$

15. $5x\left(2x^3 + 6\right) = 5x\left(2x^3\right) + 5(6)$
$$= 10x^4 + 30x$$

16. $-3x^2\left(5x^2 + 6x - 1\right)$
$$= -3x^2\left(5x^2\right) + \left(-3x^2\right)(6x) - \left(-3x^2\right)(1)$$
$$= -15x^4 - 18x^3 + 3x^2$$

17. Write $4x^2 + 7 + 8x^3$ as $8x^3 + 4x^2 + 0x + 7$
before beginning long division.

$$
\begin{array}{r}
4x^2 - 4x + 6 \\
2x+3 \overline{)\ 8x^3 + 4x^2 + 0x + 7} \\
\underline{8x^3 + 12x^2} \\
-8x^2 + \ 0x \\
\underline{-8x^2 - 12x} \\
12x + \ 7 \\
\underline{12x + 18} \\
-11
\end{array}
$$

$$\frac{4x^2 + 7 + 8x^3}{2x + 3} = 4x^2 - 4x + 6 + \frac{-11}{2x + 3}.$$

18. $x^2 + 7x + 12 = (x + 3)(x + 4)$

19. $25x^2 + 20xy + 4y^2$
$$= (5x)^2 + 2 \cdot 5x \cdot 2y + (2y)^2$$
$$= (5x + 2y)^2$$

20. $x^2 - 9x - 22 = 0$

$(x-11)(x+2) = 0$

$x - 11 = 0$ or $x + 2 = 0$

     $x = 11$ $x = -2$

The solutions are 11 and -2.

21. $\dfrac{x^2 + x}{3x} \cdot \dfrac{6}{5x+5} = \dfrac{x(x+1) \cdot 2 \cdot 3}{3x \cdot 5(x+1)} = \dfrac{2}{5}$

22. $\dfrac{3x^2 + 2x}{3x} - \dfrac{10x - 5}{x - 1}$

$= \dfrac{3x^2 + 2x - (10x - 5)}{x - 1}$

$= \dfrac{3x^2 + 2x - 10x + 5}{x - 1}$

$= \dfrac{3x^2 - 8x + 5}{x - 1} = \dfrac{(x-1)(3x-5)}{x-1}$

$= 3x - 5$

23. $\dfrac{6x}{x^2 - 4} - \dfrac{3}{x+2} = \dfrac{6x}{(x+2)(x-2)} - \dfrac{3}{x+2}$

$= \dfrac{6x}{(x+2)(x-2)} - \dfrac{3(x-2)}{(x+2)(x-2)}$

$= \dfrac{6x - 3(x-2)}{(x+2)(x-2)} = \dfrac{6x - 3x + 6}{(x+2)(x-2)}$

$= \dfrac{3x + 6}{(x+2)(x-2)} = \dfrac{3(x+2)}{(x+2)(x-2)}$

$= \dfrac{3}{x - 2}$

24. $\dfrac{t-4}{2} - \dfrac{t-3}{9} = \dfrac{5}{18}$

$18\left(\dfrac{t-4}{2} - \dfrac{t-3}{9}\right) = 18\left(\dfrac{5}{18}\right)$

$9(t-4) - 2(t-3) = 5$

$9t - 36 - 2t + 6 = 5$

$7t - 30 = 5$

$7t = 35$

$t = 5$

25. Let $x =$ the time in hours it takes Sam and Frank to complete the job together.

Then $\dfrac{1}{x} =$ the part of the job they complete in 1 hour. Since Sam completes $\dfrac{1}{3}$ of the job in 1 hour, and Frank completes $\dfrac{1}{7}$ of the job in 1 hour, we have

$\dfrac{1}{3} + \dfrac{1}{7} = \dfrac{1}{x}$

$21x\left(\dfrac{1}{3} + \dfrac{1}{7}\right) = 21x\left(\dfrac{1}{x}\right)$

$7x + 3x = 21$

$10x = 21$

$x = \dfrac{21}{10}$

$x = 2\dfrac{1}{10}$

Sam and Frank, working together can complete the quality control tour in $2\dfrac{1}{10}$ hours.

26. $\dfrac{\frac{2}{5} - \frac{1}{x}}{\frac{x}{10} - \frac{1}{3}} = \dfrac{\frac{2x}{5x} - \frac{5}{5x}}{\frac{3x}{30} - \frac{10}{30}} = \dfrac{\frac{2x-5}{5x}}{\frac{3x-10}{30}}$

$\quad = \dfrac{2x-5}{5x} \cdot \dfrac{30}{3x-10} = \dfrac{5 \cdot 6(2x-5)}{5 \cdot x(3x-10)}$

$\quad = \dfrac{6(2x-5)}{x(3x-10)}$

Chapter 6

Chapter 6 Pretest

1. $(-4,3), (0,-2), (5,0)$

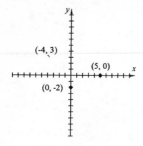

2. $8x - 3y = 2$

If $x = -2$

$8(-2) - 3y = 2$

$-16 - 3x = 2$

$-3x = 18$

$x = -6$

$(-2,-6)$

3. $3x - y = 6$

x	y
0	-6
2	0

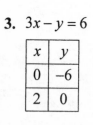

4.

x	y
0	4
-1	0

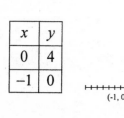

5. $3x + 2y \leq 6$

x	y
0	3
2	0

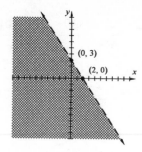

6. $(-7,8)$ and $(3,5)$

$$m = \frac{y_2 - y_1}{x_2 - x_1} = \frac{5-8}{3-(-7)} = \frac{-3}{10}$$

7. $4x - 5y = 20$

$-5y = -4x + 20$

$y = \frac{4}{5}x - 4$

$m = \frac{4}{5}$

8. $x = 10$ is a vertical line therefore the slope is undefined.

9. $m = -\frac{1}{3}; \ (3,-6)$

$$y - y_1 = m(x - x_1)$$

$$y - (-6) = -\frac{1}{3}(x - 3)$$

$$3(y + 6) = -(x - 3)$$

$$3y + 18 = -x + 3$$

$$x + 3y + 18 = 3$$

$$x + 3y = -15$$

10. $(0,0)$ and $(-8,1)$

$$m = \frac{y_2 - y_1}{x_2 - x_1} = \frac{1-0}{-8-0} = -\frac{1}{8}$$

Use $m = -\frac{1}{8}$; $(0,0)$

$$y - y_1 = m(x - x_1)$$

$$y - 0 = -\frac{1}{8}(x - 0)$$

$$8y = -x$$

$$x + 8y = 0$$

11. $m = \frac{2}{7}$; $b = 14$

$$y = mx + b$$

$$y = \frac{2}{7}x + 98$$

$$7y = 2x + 98$$

$$2x - 7y = -98$$

12. $\{(-3,8),(7,-1),(0,6),(2,-1)\}$

domain: $\{-3,0,2,7\}$

range: $\{-1,6,8\}$

13. $\{(1,7),(-8,7),(6,3),(9,2)\}$

It is a function.

14. $\{(0,4),(1,3),(2,-5),(1,10),(-2,-8)\}$

It is not a function because two pair have the same x value.

15. $f(x) = -3x + 8$

a. $f(-1) = -3(-1) + 8 = 3 + 8 = 11$

b. $f(0) = -3(0) + 8 = 0 + 8 = 8$

c. $f(10) = -3(10) + 8 = -30 + 8 = -22$

Practice Problems 6.1

1.

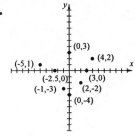

Point $(4,2)$ lies in quadrant I.

Point $(-5,1)$ lies in quadrant II.

Point $(-1,-3)$ lies in quadrant III.

Point $(2,-2)$ lies in quadrant IV.

Points $(0,3),\left(-2\tfrac{1}{2},0\right),(3,0)$, and $(0,-4)$ lies on axes, so they are not in any quadrant.

2.a. $(1995,1234),(1996,1173),(1997,1148),$
$(1998,1424),(1999,1343),(2000,997)$

b.

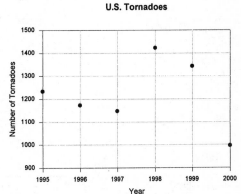

c. The number of tornadoes varies greatly from year to year.

3. $x + 2y = 8$

   a. $x = 0,\ 0 + 2y = 8$

$$y = 4;\ (0, 4)$$

   b. $y = 3,\ x + 2(3) = 8$

$$x + 6 = 8$$

$$x = 2;\ (2, 3)$$

   c. $x = -4,\ -4 + 2y = 8$

$$2y = 12$$

$$y = 6;\ (-4, 6)$$

4. $y = -2x$

   a. $x = -3,\ y = -2(-3) = 6;\ (-3, 6)$

   b. $y = 0,\ 0 = -2x,\ x = 0;\ (0, 0)$

   c. $y = 10,\ 10 = -2x,\ x = -5;\ (-5, 10)$

x	y
-3	6
0	0
-5	10

5. $x = 5$

x	y
5	-2
5	0
5	4

6. $y = -50x$

x	1	2	3	4	5	6	7
y	350	300	250	200	150	100	50

Mental Math 6.1

1. $x + y = 10$

   Answers may vary; Ex. $(5, 5), (7, 3)$

2. $x + y = 6$

   Answers may vary; Ex. $(0, 6), (6, 0)$

Exercise Set 6.1

1.

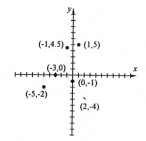

Point $(1, 5)$ lies in quadrant I.

Point $\left(-1, 4\frac{1}{2}\right)$ lies in quadrant II.

Point $(-5, -2)$ lies in quadrant III.

Point $(2, -4)$ lies in quadrant IV.

Point $(-3, 0)$ lies on the x-axis.

Point $(0, -1)$ lies on the y-axis.

3. When $a = b$.

5. $A : (0, 0)$

7. $C : (3, 2)$

9. $E : (-2, -2)$

11. $G : (2, -1)$

13. $B : (0, -3)$

15. $D:(1,3)$

17. $F:(-3,-1)$

19.a. $(1995,438),(1996,438),(1997,436),$
$(1998,435),(1999,432),(2000,434)$

b.

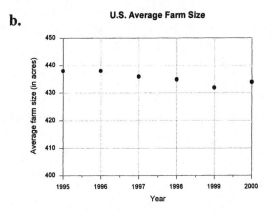

U.S. Average Farm Size

c. The number of tornadoes varies greatly from year to year.

21.a. $(2313,2),(2085,1),(2711,21),(2869,39),$
$(2920,42),(4038,99),(1783,0),(2493,9)$

b.

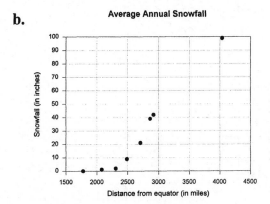

Average Annual Snowfall

c. The farther from the equator, the more snowfall.

23.a. $(0.50,10),(0.75,12),(1.00,15),(1.25,16),$
$(1.50,18),(1.50,19),(1.75,19),(2.00,20)$

b.

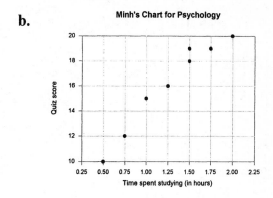

Minh's Chart for Psychology

c. Answers may vary.

25. $x-4y=4$
$y=-2,\ x-4(-2)=4$
$x+8=4$
$x=-4;\ (-4,-2)$
$x=4,\ 4-4y=4$
$-4y=0$
$y=0;\ (4,0)$

27. $3x+y=9$
$x=0,\ 3(0)+y=9$
$0+y=9$
$y=9;\ (0,9)$
$y=0,\ 3x+0=9$
$3x=9$
$x=3;\ (3,0)$

29. $y=-7$
$x=11,\ y=-7;\ (11,-7)$
$y=-7,\ x=$ any value

31. $x + 3y = 6$

$x = 0,\ 0 + 3y = 6,\ y = 2;\ (0, 2)$

$y = 0,\ x + 3(0) = 6,\ x = 6;\ (6, 0)$

$y = 1,\ x + 3(1) = 6,\ x = 3;\ (3, 1)$

x	y
0	2
6	0
3	1

33. $2x - y = 12$

$x = 0,\ 2(0) - y = 12,\ y = -12;\ (0, -12)$

$y = -2,\ 2x - (-2) = 12$

$\qquad 2x + 2 = 12$

$\qquad\quad 2x = 10$

$\qquad\quad x = 5;\ (5, -2)$

$x = 3,\ 2(3) - y = 12,$

$\qquad 6 - y = 12$

$\qquad\ -y = 6$

$\qquad\quad y = -6;\ (3, -6)$

x	y
0	-12
5	-2
3	-6

35. $2x + 7y = 5$

$x = 0,\ 2(0) + 7y = 5,$

$\qquad\quad 7y = 5$

$\qquad\quad y = \dfrac{5}{7};\ \left(0, \dfrac{5}{7}\right)$

$y = 0,\ 2x + 7(0) = 5$

$\qquad\quad 2x = 5$

$\qquad\quad x = \dfrac{5}{2};\ \left(\dfrac{5}{2}, 0\right)$

$y = 1,\ 2x + 7(1) = 5,$

$\qquad\quad 2x + 7 = 5$

$\qquad\quad 2x = -2$

$\qquad\quad x = -1;\ (-1, 1)$

x	y
0	$\frac{5}{7}$
$\frac{5}{2}$	0
-1	1

37. $x = 3$

x	y
3	0
3	-0.5
3	$\frac{1}{4}$

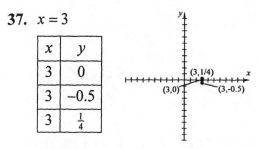

39. $x = -5y$

$y = 0,\ x = -5(0) = 0$

$y = 1,\ x = -5(1) = -5$

$x = 10,\ 10 = -5y,\ y = -2$

x	y
0	0
-5	1
10	-2

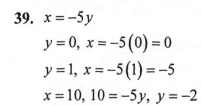

41.a. $y = 80x + 5000$

$x = 100, \ y = 80(100) + 5000 = 13,000$

$x = 200, \ y = 80(200) + 5000 = 21,000$

$x = 300, \ y = 80(300) + 5000 = 29,000$

x	100	200	300
y	13,000	21,000	29,000

b. Let $y = 8600$

$8600 = 80x + 5000$

$3600 = 80x$

$45 = x$

45 desks can be produced

43. $x + y = 5$

$y = 5 - x$

45. $2x + 4y = 5$

$4y = 5 - 2x$

$y = \dfrac{5 - 2x}{4}$

47. $10x = -5y$

$-2x = y$

49.

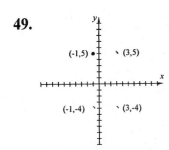

Rectangle is 9 units by 4 units.

Perimeter is $9 + 4 + 9 + 4 = 26$ units.

51. Years 0 to 1: $21 million

Years 1 to 2: $23 million

Years 2 to 3: $24 million

Years 3 to 4: $25 million

53. Answers may vary.

55.a. $y = -4.22x + 985.02$

$x = 4, \ y = -4.22(4) + 985.02 = 968.14$

$x = 7, \ y = -4.22(7) + 985.02 = 955.48$

$x = 10, \ y = -4.22(10) + 985.02 = 942.82$

x	4	7	10
y	968.14	955.48	942.82

b. Let $y = 947$

$947 = -4.22x + 985.02$

$-38.02 = -4.22x$

$9 \approx x$

The year 1999

Practice Problems 6.2

1. $x + 3y = 6$

$x = 0, \ 0 + 3y = 6, \ y = 2; \ (0, 2)$

$x = 3, \ 3 + 3y = 6,$

$3y = 3$

$y = 1; \ (3, 1)$

$x = 6, \ 6 + 3y = 6,$

$3y = 0$

$y = 0; \ (6, 0)$

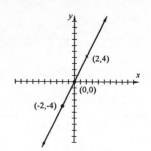

x	y
0	2
3	1
6	0

x	y
−2	−4
0	0
2	4

2. $-2x + 4y = 8$

$x = -2, \ -2(-2) + 4y = 8$

$4 + 4y = 8$

$4y = 4$

$y = 1$

$x = 0, \ -2(0) + 4y = 8$

$4y = 8$

$y = 2$

$x = 2, \ -2(2) + 4y = 8$

$-4 + 4y = 8$

$4y = 12$

$y = 3$

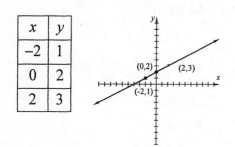

x	y
−2	1
0	2
2	3

3. $y = 2x$

$x = -2, \ y = 2(-2) = -4$

$x = 0, \ y = 2(0) = 0$

$x = 2, \ y = 2(2) = 4$

4. $y = -\dfrac{1}{2}x$

$x = -4, \ y = -\dfrac{1}{2}(-4) = 2$

$x = 0, \ y = -\dfrac{1}{2}(0) = 0$

$x = 4, \ y = -\dfrac{1}{2}(4) = -2$

x	y
−4	2
0	0
4	−2

5. $y = 2x + 3$

$x = -2, \ y = 2(-2) + 3 = -4 + 3 = -1$

$x = 0, \ y = 2(0) + 3 = 0 + 3 = 3$

$x = 2, \ y = 2(2) + 3 = 4 + 3 = 7$

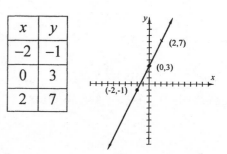

x	y
−2	−1
0	3
2	7

6. $x = 3$

x	y
3	4
3	0
3	-4

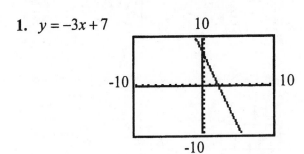

4. $y = -1.3x + 5.2$

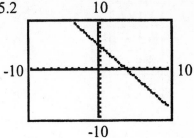

Graphing Calculator Explorations

1. $y = -3x + 7$

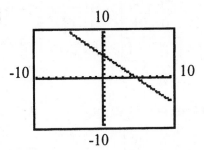

5. $y = -\dfrac{3}{10}x + \dfrac{32}{5}$

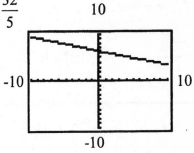

2. $y = -x + 5$

6. $y = \dfrac{2}{9}x - \dfrac{22}{3}$

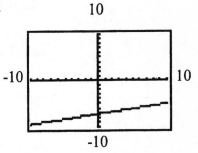

3. $y = 2.5x - 7.9$

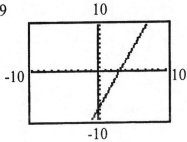

Exercise Set 6.2

1, $x - y = 6$

$y = 0,\ x - 0 = 6$

$x = 6$

$x = 4,\ 4 - y = 6$

$-y = 2$

$y = -2$

$y = -1,\ x - (-1) = 6$

$x + 1 = 6$

$x = 5$

x	y
6	0
4	-2
5	-1

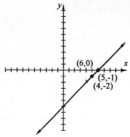

7. $y = -4x + 3$

$x = 0, \ y = -4(0) + 3 = 0 + 3 = 3$

$x = 1, \ y = -4(1) + 3 = -4 + 3 = -1$

$x = 2, \ y = -4(2) + 3 = -8 + 3 = -5$

x	y
0	3
1	-1
2	-5

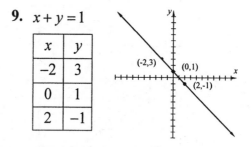

3. $y = -4x$

$x = 1, \ y = -4(1) = -4$

$x = 0, \ y = -4(0) = 0$

$x = -1, \ y = -4(-1) = 4$

x	y
1	-4
0	0
-1	4

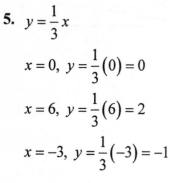

9. $x + y = 1$

x	y
-2	3
0	1
2	-1

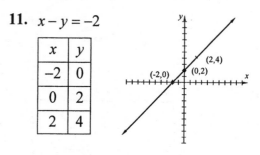

5. $y = \dfrac{1}{3}x$

$x = 0, \ y = \dfrac{1}{3}(0) = 0$

$x = 6, \ y = \dfrac{1}{3}(6) = 2$

$x = -3, \ y = \dfrac{1}{3}(-3) = -1$

x	y
0	0
6	2
-3	-1

11. $x - y = -2$

x	y
-2	0
0	2
2	4

13. $x - 2y = 6$

x	y
-4	-5
0	-3
4	-1

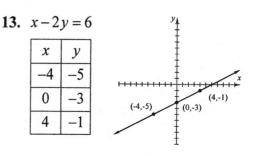

15. $y = 6x + 3$

x	y
-1	-3
0	3
1	9

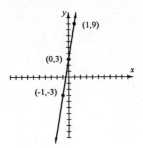

17. $x = -4$

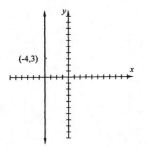

19. $y = 3$

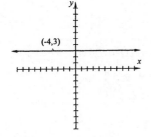

21. $y = x$

x	y
-4	-4
0	0
4	4

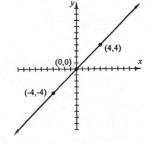

23. $y = 5x$

x	y
-1	-5
0	0
1	5

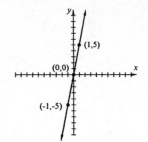

25. $x - 3y = 9$

x	y
-3	4
0	3
3	2

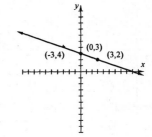

27. $y = \dfrac{1}{2}x - 1$

x	y
-4	-3
0	-1
4	1

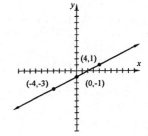

29. $3x - 2y = 12$

x	y
4	0
2	-3
0	-6

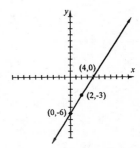

31. $y = 5x$ $y = 5x + 4$

x	y
-1	-5
0	0
1	5

x	y
-1	-1
0	4
1	9

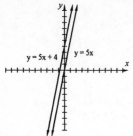

39. $y = 2x$

$y = 0,\ 0 = 2x,\ 0 = x$

$x = 0,\ y = 2(0) = 0$

x	y
0	0
0	0

33. $y = -2x$ $y = -2x - 3$

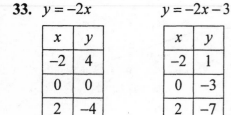

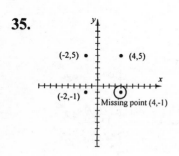

41. $y = x^2$

x	y
0	0
1	1
-1	1
2	4
-2	4

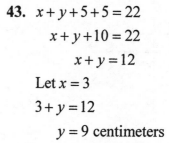

43. $x + y + 5 + 5 = 22$

$x + y + 10 = 22$

$x + y = 12$

Let $x = 3$

$3 + y = 12$

$y = 9$ centimeters

35.

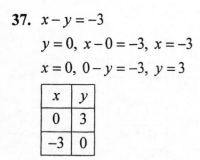

45. $y = 45x + 2214$

a.

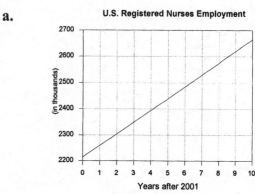

37. $x - y = -3$

$y = 0,\ x - 0 = -3,\ x = -3$

$x = 0,\ 0 - y = -3,\ y = 3$

x	y
0	3
-3	0

b. Yes. Answers may vary.

47. $y = 1.43x + 95$

a.

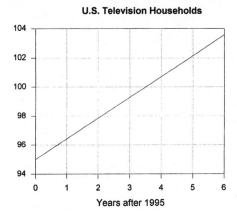

b. $y = 1.43x + 95$

Let $x = 5$

$y = 1.43(5) + 95 = 7.15 + 95 = 102.15$

$(5, 102.15)$

c. In 2000, there were 102.15 million households in the United States with at least one television.

Practice Problems 6.3

1. x-intercept: $(2, 0)$; y-intercept: $(0, -4)$

2. x-intercepts: $(-4, 0)$, $(2, 0)$

y-intercept: $(0, 2)$

3. x-intercept: none; y-intercept: $(0, 3)$

4. $2x - y = 4$

$y = 0,\ 2x - 0 = 4,\ x = 2$

$x = 0,\ 2(0) - y = 4,\ y = -4$

x-intercept: $(2, 0)$; y-intercept: $(0, -4)$

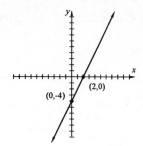

x	y
2	0
0	-4

5. $y = 3x$

$y = 0,\ 0 = 3x,\ x = 0$

$x = 0,\ y = 3(0) = 0$

x-intercept: $(0, 0)$; y-intercept: $(0, 0)$

$x = 2,\ y = 3(2) = 6$

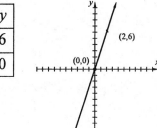

x	y
2	6
0	0

6. $x = -3$

$y = 0,\ x = -3$

x-intercept: $(-3, 0)$

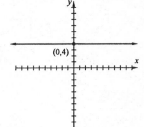

7. $y = 4$

$x = 0,\ y = 4$

y-intercept: $(0, 4)$

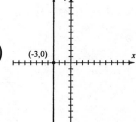

Graphing Calculator Explorations 6.3

1. $x = 3.78y$

$$y = \frac{x}{3.78}$$

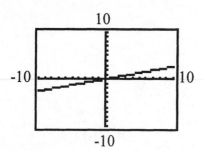

2. $-2.61y = x$

$$y = \frac{x}{-2.61}$$

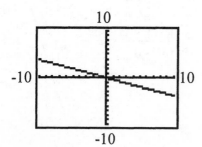

3. $-2.2x + 6.8y = 15.5$

$$6.8y = 2.2x + 15.5$$

$$y = \frac{2.2}{6.8}x + \frac{15.5}{6.8}$$

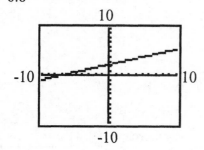

4. $5.9x - 0.8y = -10.4$

$$-0.8y = -5.9x - 10.4$$

$$y = \frac{5.9}{0.8}x + \frac{10.4}{0.8}$$

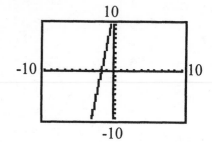

Mental Math 6.3

1. False

2. False

3. True

4. True

Exercise Set 6.3

1. x-intercept: $(-1, 0)$; y-intercept: $(0, 1)$

3. x-intercepts: $(-2, 0), (1, 0), (3, 0)$
  y-intercept: $(0, 3)$

5. Infinite

7. 0

9. $x - y = 3$
  $y = 0,\ x - 0 = 3,\ x = 3$
  $x = 0,\ 0 - y = 3,\ y = -3$
  x-intercept: $(3, 0)$; y-intercept: $(0, -3)$

x	y
3	0
0	-3

11. $x = 5y$

$y = 0,\ x = 5(0) = 0$

$x = 0,\ 0 = 5y,\ y = 0$

x-intercept: $(0,0)$; y-intercept: $(0,0)$

$y = 1,\ x = 5(1) = 5$

x	y
0	0
5	1

13. $-x + 2y = 6$

$y = 0,\ -x + 2(0) = 6,\ x = -6$

$x = 0,\ -0 + 2y = 6,\ y = 3$

x-intercept: $(-6,0)$; y-intercept: $(0,3)$

x	y
-6	0
0	3

15. $2x - 4y = 8$

$y = 0,\ 2x - 4(0) = 8,\ x = 4$

$x = 0,\ 2(0) - 4y = 8,\ y = -2$

x-intercept: $(4,0)$; y-intercept: $(0,-2)$

x	y
4	0
0	-2

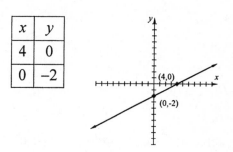

17. $x = 2y$

$y = 0,\ x = 2(0) = 0$

$x = 0,\ 0 = 2y,\ y = 0$

x-intercept: $(0,0)$; y-intercept: $(0,0)$

$y = 4,\ x = 2(4) = 8$

x	y
4	8
0	0

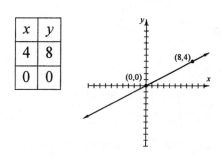

19. $y = 3x + 6$

$y = 0,\ 0 = 3x + 6,\ x = -2$

$x = 0,\ y = 3(0) + 6 = 6$

x-intercept: $(-2,0)$; y-intercept: $(0,6)$

x	y
-2	0
0	6

25. $5 = 6x - y$

$y = 0,\ 5 = 6x - 0,\ x = \dfrac{5}{6}$

$x = 0,\ 5 = 6(0) - y,\ y = -5$

x-intercept: $\left(\dfrac{5}{6}, 0\right)$; y-intercept: $(0, -5)$

x	y
$\dfrac{5}{6}$	0
0	-5

21. $x = y$

$y = 0,\ x = 0$

$x = 0,\ 0 = y$

x-intercept: $(0,0)$; y-intercept: $(0,0)$

$y = 4,\ x = 4$

x	y
4	4
0	0

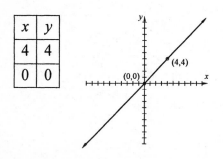

27. $-x + 10y = 11$

$y = 0,\ -x + 10(0) = 11,\ x = -11$

$x = 0,\ -0 + 10y = 11,\ y = \dfrac{11}{10}$

x-intercept: $(-11, 0)$; y-intercept: $\left(0, \dfrac{11}{10}\right)$

23. $x + 8y = 8$

$y = 0,\ x + 8(0) = 8,\ x = 8$

$x = 0,\ 0 + 8y = 8,\ y = 1$

x-intercept: $(8, 0)$; y-intercept: $(0, 1)$

x	y
-11	0
0	$\dfrac{11}{10}$

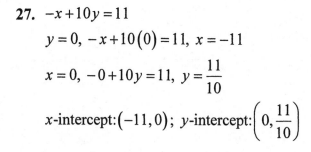

x	y
8	0
0	1

29. $x = -1$
for all values of y.

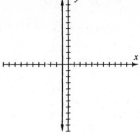

31. $y = 0$
for all values of x.

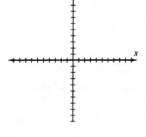

33. $y + 7 = 0$
$y = -7$
for all values of x.

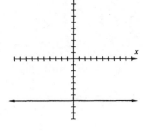

35. $x + 3 = 0$
$x = -3$
for all values of y.

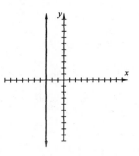

37. $\dfrac{-6 - 3}{2 - 8} = \dfrac{-9}{-6} = \dfrac{3}{2}$

39. $\dfrac{-8 - (-2)}{-3 - (-2)} = \dfrac{-6}{-1} = 6$

41. $\dfrac{0 - 6}{5 - 0} = \dfrac{-6}{5} = -\dfrac{6}{5}$

43. $y = 3$
C

45. $x = 3$
A

47. Answers may vary.

49. $3x + 6y = 1200$

   a. $x = 0$, $3(0) + 6y = 1200$, $y = 200$
     $(0, 200)$ corresponds to no chairs
     and 200 desks being manufactured.

   b. $y = 0$, $3x + 6(0) = 1200$, $x = 400$
     $(400, 0)$ corresponds to 400 chairs
     and no desks being manufactured.

   c. $y = 50$, $3x + 6(50) = 1200$
$$3x + 300 = 1200$$
$$3x = 900$$
$$x = 300$$
     300 chairs can be made.

51. Parallel to $y = -1$ is horizontal.
y-intercept is $(0, -4)$, so $y = -4$
for all values of x. $y = -4$

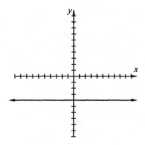

259

53. $y = 51.6x + 560.2$

    a. $x = 0,\ y = 51.6(0) + 560.2 = 560.2$

    $(0, 560.2)$.

    b. In 1996, the number of Disney

        Stores was about 560.2

Practice Problems 6.4

1. $(-2, 3)$ and $(4, -1)$

$$m = \frac{y_2 - y_1}{x_2 - x_1} = \frac{-1 - 3}{4 - (-2)} = \frac{-4}{6} = -\frac{2}{3}$$

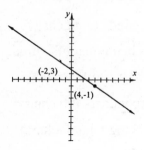

2. $(-2, 1)$ and $(3, 5)$

$$m = \frac{y_2 - y_1}{x_2 - x_1} = \frac{5 - 1}{3 - (-2)} = \frac{4}{5}$$

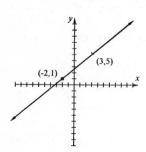

3. $5x + 4y = 10$

    $4y = -5x + 10$

$$y = -\frac{5}{4}x + \frac{5}{2}$$

$$m = -\frac{5}{4}$$

4. $y = 3$

    $y = 0x + 3$

    $m = 0$

5. $x = -2$ for all values of y. Pick two

    points; $(-2, 0)$ and $(-2, 4)$

$$m = \frac{y_2 - y_1}{x_2 - x_1} = \frac{4 - 0}{-2 - (-2)} = \frac{4}{0} \text{ is undefined}$$

6. **a.** $x + y = 5,\ y = -x + 5,\ m_1 = -1$

        $2x + y = 5,\ y = -2x + 5,\ m_2 = -2$

        $m_1 \neq m_2$ and $m_1 m_2 \neq -1$, neither

    b. $5y = 2x - 3,\ y = \frac{2}{5}x - \frac{3}{5},\ m_1 = \frac{2}{5}$

        $5x + 2y = 1,\ 2y = -5x + 1,\ y = -\frac{5}{2}x + \frac{1}{2}$

        $m_2 = -\frac{5}{2}$

        $m_1 m_2 = \left(\frac{2}{5}\right)\left(-\frac{5}{2}\right) = -1$, perpendicular

    c. $y = 2x + 1,\ m_1 = 2$

        $4x - 2y = 8,\ -2y = -4x + 8,$

        $y = 2x - 4,\ m_2 = 2$

        $m_1 = m_2$, parallel

7. grade $= \dfrac{\text{rise}}{\text{run}} = \dfrac{3}{20} = 0.15 = 15\%$

8. $(1980,120)$ and $(1990,240)$

$$m = \frac{y_2 - y_1}{x_2 - x_1} = \frac{240 - 120}{1990 - 1980} = \frac{120}{10} = 12$$

Each year the sales of food and drink from restaurants increases by $12 billion.

Graphing Calculator Explorations 6.4

1. $y_1 = 3.8x,\ y_2 = 3.8x - 3,\ y_3 = 3.8x + 6$

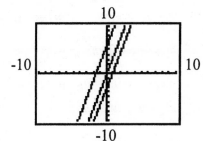

2. $y_1 = -4.9x,\ y_2 = -4.9x + 2,\ y_3 = -4.9x + 9$

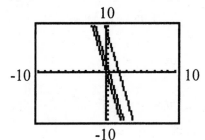

3. $y_1 = \frac{1}{4}x,\ y_2 = \frac{1}{4}x + 5,\ y_3 = \frac{1}{4}x - 8$

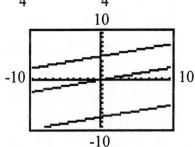

4. $y_1 = -\frac{3}{4}x,\ y_2 = -\frac{3}{4}x - 5,\ y_3 = -\frac{3}{4}x + 6$

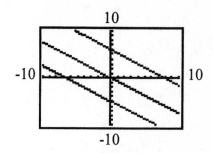

Mental Math 6.4

1. Upward

2. Downward

3. Horizontal

4. Vertical

Exercise Set 6.4

1. $(-1,2)$ and $(2,-2)$

$$m = \frac{y_2 - y_1}{x_2 - x_1} = \frac{-2 - 2}{2 - (-1)} = -\frac{4}{3}$$

3. $(1,-2)$ and $(3,3)$

$$m = \frac{y_2 - y_1}{x_2 - x_1} = \frac{3 - (-2)}{3 - 1} = \frac{5}{2}$$

5. $(0,0)$ and $(7,8)$

$$m = \frac{y_2 - y_1}{x_2 - x_1} = \frac{8 - 0}{7 - 0} = \frac{8}{7}$$

7. $(-1,5)$ and $(6,-2)$

$$m = \frac{y_2 - y_1}{x_2 - x_1} = \frac{-2-5}{6-(-1)} = -\frac{7}{7} = -1$$

9. $(1,4)$ and $(5,3)$

$$m = \frac{y_2 - y_1}{x_2 - x_1} = \frac{3-4}{5-1} = -\frac{1}{4}$$

11. $(-2,8)$ and $(1,6)$

$$m = \frac{y_2 - y_1}{x_2 - x_1} = \frac{6-8}{1-(-2)} = -\frac{2}{3}$$

13. $(5,1)$ and $(-2,1)$

$$m = \frac{y_2 - y_1}{x_2 - x_1} = \frac{1-1}{-2-5} = \frac{0}{-7} = 0$$

15. Line 1

17. Line 2

19. $y = 5x - 2$, $m = 5$

21. $2x + y = 7$

$$y = -2x + 7, \; m = -2$$

23. $2x - 3y = 10$

$$-3y = -2x + 10$$
$$y = \frac{2}{3}x - \frac{10}{3}, \; m = \frac{2}{3}$$

25. $x = 2y$

$$2y = x$$
$$y = \frac{1}{2}x, \; m = \frac{1}{2}$$

27. $(2,-1)$ and $(2,3)$

$$m = \frac{y_2 - y_1}{x_2 - x_1} = \frac{3-(-1)}{2-2} = \frac{4}{0} \text{ is undefined}$$

29. $x = 1$ is a vertical line, so it has an undefined slope.

31. $y = -3$ is a horizontal line, so it has a slope $m = 0$.

33. $x - 3y = -6$, $-3y = -x - 6$,

$$y = \frac{1}{3}x + 2, \; m_1 = \frac{1}{3}$$
$$3x - y = 0, \; -y = -3x, \; y = 3x, \; m_2 = 3$$
$$m_1 \neq m_2 \text{ and } m_1 m_2 \neq -1, \text{ neither}$$

35. $10 + 3x = 5y$, $2 + \frac{3}{5}x = y$, $m_1 = \frac{3}{5}$

$$5x + 3y = 1, \; 3y = -5x + 1, \; y = -\frac{5}{3}x + \frac{1}{3}$$

$$m_2 = -\frac{5}{3}$$

$$m_1 m_2 = \left(\frac{3}{5}\right)\left(-\frac{5}{3}\right) = -1, \text{ perpendicular}$$

37. $6x = 5y + 1$, $6x - 1 = 5y$, $\frac{6}{5}x - \frac{1}{5} = y$,

$$m_1 = \frac{6}{5}$$
$$-12x + 10y = 1, \; 10y = 12x + 1,$$
$$y = \frac{12}{10}x + \frac{1}{10}, \; y = \frac{6}{5}x + \frac{1}{10}, \; m_2 = \frac{6}{5}$$
$$m_1 = m_2, \text{ parallel}$$

39. $(-3,-3)$ and $(0,0)$

$$m = \frac{y_2 - y_1}{x_2 - x_1} = \frac{0-(-3)}{0-(-3)} = \frac{3}{3} = 1$$

a. $m = 1$

b. $m = -1$

41. $(-8,-4)$ and $(3,5)$

$$m = \frac{y_2 - y_1}{x_2 - x_1} = \frac{5-(-4)}{3-(-8)} = \frac{9}{11}$$

a. $m = \dfrac{9}{11}$

b. $m = -\dfrac{11}{9}$

43. pitch $= \dfrac{6}{10} = \dfrac{3}{5}$

45. grade $= \dfrac{\text{rise}}{\text{run}} = \dfrac{2}{16} = 0.125 = 12.5\%$

47. grade $= \dfrac{\text{rise}}{\text{run}} = \dfrac{2580}{6450} = 0.40 = 40\%$

49. slope $= \dfrac{\text{rise}}{\text{run}} = \dfrac{0.25}{12} = 0.02$

51. $(1999,99)$ and $(2002,144)$

$$m = \frac{y_2 - y_1}{x_2 - x_1} = \frac{144-99}{2002-1999} = \frac{45}{3}$$

$= 15$ million users per year.
Every year there will be 15 million more Internet users.

53. $(5000,1800)$ and $(20,000,7200)$

$$m = \frac{y_2 - y_1}{x_2 - x_1} = \frac{7200-1800}{20,000-5000} = \frac{5400}{15,000}$$

$= 0.36$ dollars per mile
It costs \$0.36 per mile to own and operate a compact car.

55. $y-(-6) = 2(x-4)$

$$y+6 = 2x-8$$
$$y = 2x-14$$

57. $y-1 = -6(x-(-2))$

$$y-1 = -6(x+2)$$
$$y-1 = -6x-12$$
$$y = -6x-11$$

59. $(0,0)$ and $(1,1)$

$$m = \frac{y_2 - y_1}{x_2 - x_1} = \frac{1-0}{1-0} = 1$$

D

61. A vertical line has undefined slope.

B

63. $(2,0)$ and $(4,-1)$

$$m = \frac{y_2 - y_1}{x_2 - x_1} = \frac{-1-0}{4-2} = -\frac{1}{2}$$

E

65. 28.3 miles per gallon

67. 1992 the average was 27.6 miles per gallon.

69. The greatest slope was from 1992 to 1993.

71. pitch $= \dfrac{\text{rise}}{\text{run}}$

$\dfrac{1}{3} = \dfrac{x}{18}$

$3x = 18$

$x = 6$

73. a. $(1994, 782)$ and $(2001, 1132)$

b. $m = \dfrac{y_2 - y_1}{x_2 - x_1} = \dfrac{1132 - 782}{2001 - 1994} = \dfrac{350}{7} = 50$

c. For the years 1994 through 2001, the price per acre of U.S. farmland rose $50 every year.

75. $y = -30x + 1485$

a. $(0, 1485)$

b. In 1998, there were 1585 million admissions to movie theatres in the U.S. and Canada

c. $m = -30$

d. For the years 1998 through 2000, the number of movie theater admissions has decreased at a rate of 30 million per year.

77. $(1, 1)$, $(-4, 4)$ and $(-3, 0)$

$m_1 = \dfrac{0 - 1}{-3 - 1} = \dfrac{1}{4}$, $m_2 = \dfrac{0 - 4}{-3 - (-4)} = -4$

$m_1 m_2 = -1$, so the sides are perpendicular.

79. $(2.1, 6.7)$ and $(-8.3, 9.3)$

$m = \dfrac{y_2 - y_1}{x_2 - x_1} = \dfrac{9.3 - 6.7}{-8.3 - 2.1} = \dfrac{2.6}{-10.4} = -0.25$

81. $(2.3, 0.2)$ and $(7.9, 5.1)$

$m = \dfrac{y_2 - y_1}{x_2 - x_1} = \dfrac{5.1 - 0.2}{7.9 - 2.3} = \dfrac{4.9}{5.6} = 0.875$

83. $y = -\dfrac{1}{3}x + 2$

$y = -2x + 2$

$y = -4x + 2$

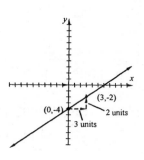

The line becomes steeper.

Practice Problems 6.5

1. $m = \dfrac{3}{5}$, $b = -2$

$y = mx + b$

$y = \dfrac{3}{5}x - 2$

2. $y = \dfrac{2}{3}x - 4$

$m = \dfrac{2}{3}$, $b = -4$

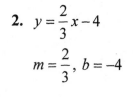

3. $3x + y = 2$

$y = -3x + 2$

$m = \dfrac{-3}{1}$, $b = 2$

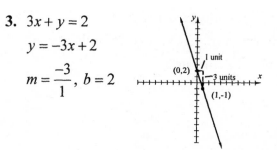

4. $\quad m = -3;\ (2, -4)$

$$y - y_1 = m(x - x_1)$$
$$y - (-4) = -3(x - 2)$$
$$y + 4 = -3x + 6$$
$$3x + y + 4 = 6$$
$$3x + y = 2$$

5. $(1, 3)$ and $(5, -2)$

$$m = \frac{y_2 - y_1}{x_2 - x_1} = \frac{-2 - 3}{5 - 1} = -\frac{5}{4}$$

$$m = -\frac{5}{4};\ (1, 3)$$

$$y - y_1 = m(x - x_1)$$
$$y - 3 = -\frac{5}{4}(x - 1)$$
$$4(y - 3) = -5(x - 1)$$
$$4y - 12 = -5x + 5$$
$$5x + 4y = 17$$

6. a. $(10, 200)$ and $(9, 250)$

$$m = \frac{y_2 - y_1}{x_2 - x_1} = \frac{250 - 200}{9 - 10} = -50$$

$$m = -50;\ (10, 200)$$
$$y - y_1 = m(x - x_1)$$
$$y - 200 = -50(x - 10)$$
$$y - 200 = -50x + 500$$
$$y = -50x + 700$$

b. Let $x = 7.50$

$$y = -50(7.50) + 700$$
$$= -375 + 700$$
$$= 325$$

Expect to sell 325 toys

Graphing Calculator Explorations 6.5

1. $y_1 = x,\ y_2 = 6x,\ y_3 = -6x$

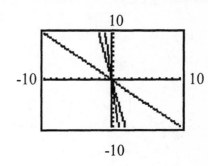

2. $y_1 = -x,\ y_2 = -5x,\ y_3 = -10x$

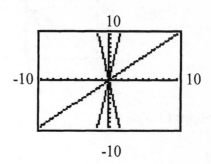

3. $y_1 = \frac{1}{2}x + 2,\ y_2 = \frac{3}{4}x + 2,\ y_3 = x + 2$

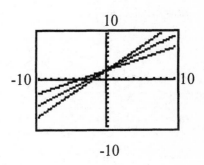

4. $y_1 = x + 1,\ y_2 = \frac{5}{4}x + 1,\ y_3 = \frac{5}{2}x + 1$

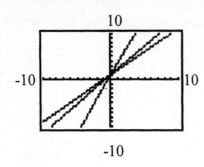

Mental Math 6.5

1. $y = 2x - 1$

   $m = 2,\ (0, -1)$

2. $y = -7x + 3$

   $m = -7,\ (0, 3)$

3. $y = x + \dfrac{1}{3}$

   $m = 1,\ \left(0, \dfrac{1}{3}\right)$

4. $y = -x - \dfrac{2}{9}$

   $m = -1,\ \left(0, -\dfrac{2}{9}\right)$

5. $y = \dfrac{5}{7}x - 4$

   $m = \dfrac{5}{7},\ (0, -4)$

6. $y = -\dfrac{1}{4}x + \dfrac{3}{5}$

   $m = -\dfrac{1}{4},\ \left(0, \dfrac{3}{5}\right)$

7. $y - 8 = 3(x - 4)$

   $m = 3$

   Answers may vary. Example: $(4, 8)$

8. $y - 1 = 5(x - 2)$

   $m = 5$

   Answers may vary. Example: $(2, 1)$

9. $y + 3 = -2(x - 10)$

   $m = -2$

   Answers may vary. Example: $(10, -3)$

10. $y + 6 = -7(x - 2)$

    $m = -7$

    Answers may vary. Example: $(2, -6)$

11. $y = \dfrac{2}{5}(x + 1)$

    $m = \dfrac{2}{5}$

    Answers may vary. Example: $(-1, 0)$

12. $y = \dfrac{3}{7}(x + 4)$

    $m = \dfrac{3}{7}$

    Answers may vary. Example: $(-4, 0)$

Exercise Set 6.5

1. $m = 5,\ b = 3$

   $y = mx + b$

   $y = 5x + 3$

266

3. $m = \dfrac{2}{3}, \ b = 0$

$y = mx + b$

$y = \dfrac{2}{3}x$

5. $m = -\dfrac{1}{5}, \ b = \dfrac{1}{9}$

$y = mx + b$

$y = -\dfrac{1}{5}x + \dfrac{1}{9}$

7. $y = 2x + 1$

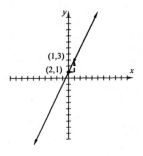

9. $y = \dfrac{2}{3}x + 5$

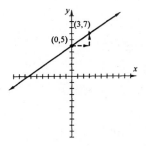

11. $y = -5x$

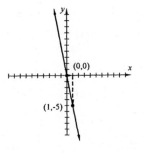

13. $4x + y = 6$

$\qquad y = -4x + 6$

15. $4x - 7y = -14$

$\qquad -7y = -4x - 14$

$\qquad y = \dfrac{4}{7}x + 2$

17. $\qquad m = 6; \ (2, 2)$

$y - y_1 = m(x - x_1)$

$y - 2 = 6(x - 2)$

$y - 2 = 6x - 12$

$-6x + y = 10$

19. $\qquad m = -8; \ (-1, -5)$

$y - y_1 = m(x - x_1)$

$y - (-5) = -8(x - (-1))$

$y + 5 = -8x - 8$

$8x + y = -13$

21.
$$m=\frac{1}{2};\ (5,-6)$$
$$y-y_1=m(x-x_1)$$
$$y-(-6)=\frac{1}{2}(x-5)$$
$$2(y+6)=x-5$$
$$2y+12=x-5$$
$$-x+2y=-17$$
$$x-2y=17$$

23.
$$m=-\frac{1}{2};\ (-3,0)$$
$$y-y_1=m(x-x_1)$$
$$y-0=-\frac{1}{2}(x-(-3))$$
$$2y=-x-3$$
$$x+2y=-3$$

25. $(3,2)$ and $(5,6)$
$$m=\frac{y_2-y_1}{x_2-x_1}=\frac{6-2}{5-3}=\frac{4}{2}=2$$
$$m=2;\ (3,2)$$
$$y-y_1=m(x-x_1)$$
$$y-2=2(x-3)$$
$$y-2=2x-6$$
$$-2x+y=-4$$
$$2x-y=4$$

27. $(-1,3)$ and $(-2,-5)$
$$m=\frac{y_2-y_1}{x_2-x_1}=\frac{-5-3}{-2-(-1)}=\frac{-8}{-1}=8$$
$$m=8;\ (-1,3)$$
$$y-y_1=m(x-x_1)$$
$$y-3=8(x-(-1))$$
$$y-3=8x+8$$
$$-8x+y=11$$
$$8x-y=-11$$

29. $(2,3)$ and $(-1,-1)$
$$m=\frac{y_2-y_1}{x_2-x_1}=\frac{-1-3}{-1-2}=\frac{-4}{-3}=\frac{4}{3}$$
$$m=\frac{4}{3};\ (2,3)$$
$$y-y_1=m(x-x_1)$$
$$y-3=\frac{4}{3}(x-2)$$
$$3(y-3)=4(x-2)$$
$$3y-9=4x-8$$
$$-4x+3y=1$$
$$4x-3y=-1$$

31. $(10,7)$ and $(7,10)$
$$m=\frac{y_2-y_1}{x_2-x_1}=\frac{10-7}{7-10}=\frac{3}{-3}=-1$$
$$m=-1;\ (10,7)$$
$$y-y_1=m(x-x_1)$$
$$y-7=-1(x-10)$$
$$y-7=-x+10$$
$$x+y=17$$

33. $(10,7)$ and $(7,10)$

$$m = \frac{y_2 - y_1}{x_2 - x_1} = \frac{10-7}{7-10} = \frac{3}{-3} = -1$$

$m = -1; \ (10,7)$

$y - y_1 = m(x - x_1)$

$y - 7 = -1(x - 10)$

$y - 7 = -x + 10$

$x + y = 17$

35. $(-8,1)$ and $(0,0)$

$$m = \frac{y_2 - y_1}{x_2 - x_1} = \frac{0-1}{0-(-8)} = -\frac{1}{8}$$

$m = -\frac{1}{8}; \ (0,0)$

$y - y_1 = m(x - x_1)$

$y - 0 = -\frac{1}{8}(x - 0)$

$8y = -x$

$x + 8y = 0$

37. a. $(1,32)$ and $(3,96)$

$$m = \frac{y_2 - y_1}{x_2 - x_1} = \frac{96-32}{3-1} = \frac{64}{2} = 32$$

$m = 32; \ (1,32)$

$s - s_1 = m(t - t_1)$

$s - 32 = 32(t - 1)$

$s - 32 = 32t - 32$

$s = 32t$

b. If $t = 4$, then $s = 32(4) = 128$ ft/sec.

39. a. $(0,5242)$ and $(2,7590)$

$$m = \frac{y_2 - y_1}{x_2 - x_1} = \frac{7590-5242}{2-0} = \frac{2348}{2} = 1174$$

$m = 1174; \ (0,5242)$

$y - y_1 = m(x - x_1)$

$y - 5242 = 1174(x - 0)$

$y - 5242 = 1174x$

$y = 1174x + 5242$

b. If $x = 7$,

then $y = 1174(7) + 5242 = 13,460$

Expect 13,460 vehicles.

41. a. $(0,70.3)$ and $(10,79.6)$

$$m = \frac{y_2 - y_1}{x_2 - x_1} = \frac{79.6-70.3}{10-0} = \frac{9.3}{10} = 0.93$$

$m = 0.93; \ (0,70.3)$

$y - y_1 = m(x - x_1)$

$y - 70.3 = 0.93(x - 0)$

$y - 70.3 = 0.93x$

$y = 0.93x + 70.3.$

b. If $x = 17$,

then $y = 0.93(17) + 70.3 = 86.11$

Expect 86.11 person per square mile.

43. a. $(0,191)$ and $(5,260)$

b. $m = \dfrac{y_2 - y_1}{x_2 - x_1} = \dfrac{260-191}{5-0} = \dfrac{69}{5} = 13.8$

$m = 13.8; \ (0,191)$

$y - y_1 = m(x - x_1)$

$y - 191 = 13.8(x - 0)$

$y - 191 = 13.8x$

$y = 13.8x + 191$

c. If $x = 4$,

then $y = 13.8(4) + 191 = 246.2$

Expect $246.2 million in sales.

45. a. $(3, 10, 000)$ and $(5, 8000)$

$$m = \frac{y_2 - y_1}{x_2 - x_1} = \frac{8000 - 10,000}{5 - 3}$$

$$= \frac{-2000}{2} = -1000$$

$m = -1000;\ (5, 8000)$

$$s - s_1 = m(p - p_1)$$

$$s - 8000 = -1000(p - 5)$$

$$s - 8000 = -1000p + 5000$$

$$s = -1000p + 13,000$$

b. If $p = 3.50$,

then $s = -1000(3.5) + 13,000 = 9500$

Expect $9500 in daily sales.

47. If $x = 2$, then

$$x^2 - 3x + 1 = (2)^2 - 3(2) + 1 = 4 - 6 + 1 = -1$$

49. If $x = -1$, then

$$x^2 - 3x + 1 = (-1)^2 - 3(-1) + 1 = 1 + 3 + 1 = 5$$

51. No

53. Yes

55. $y = 2x + 1$

$m = 2, b = 1$

B

57. $y = -3x - 2$

$m = -3, b = -2$

D

59. $y = 3x - 1,\ m_1 = 3$

Same slope: $m_2 = m_1 = 3;\ (-1, 2)$

$$y - y_1 = m_2(x - x_1)$$

$$y - 2 = 3(x - (-1))$$

$$y - 2 = 3x + 3$$

$$-3x + y = 5$$

$$3x - y = -5$$

61. $y = 3x - 1,\ m_1 = 3$

a. Parallel: $m_2 = m_1 = 3;\ (-1, 2)$

$$y - y_1 = m_2(x - x_1)$$

$$y - 2 = 3(x - (-1))$$

$$y - 2 = 3x + 3$$

$$-3x + y = 5$$

$$3x - y = -5$$

b. Perpendicular: $m_2 = -\dfrac{1}{m_1} = -\dfrac{1}{3}$;

$(-1, 2)$

$$y - y_1 = m_2(x - x_1)$$

$$y - 2 = -\frac{1}{3}(x - (-1))$$

$$3(y - 2) = -1(x + 1)$$

$$3y - 6 = -x - 1$$

$$x + 3y = 5$$

Integrated Review 6.5

1. $(0,0)$ and $(2,4)$

$$m = \frac{y_2 - y_1}{x_2 - x_1} = \frac{4-0}{2-0} = \frac{4}{2} = 2$$

2. Horizontal line, $m = 0$

3. $(0,1)$ and $(3,-1)$

$$m = \frac{y_2 - y_1}{x_2 - x_1} = \frac{-1-1}{3-0} = -\frac{2}{3}$$

4. Vertical line, slope is undefined.

5. $y = 2x$

$m = 2, b = 0$

6. $x + y = 3$

$y = -x + 3$

$m = -1, b = 3$

7. $x = -1$ for
all values of y.
Vertical line
Slope is undefined.

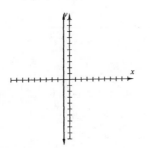

8. $y = 4$ for all
values of x
Horizontal line
$m = 0$

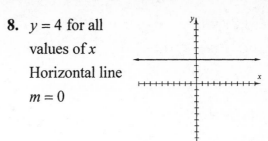

9. $x - 2y = 6$

$-2y = -x + 6$

$y = \frac{1}{2}x - 3$

$m = \frac{1}{2}, b = -3$

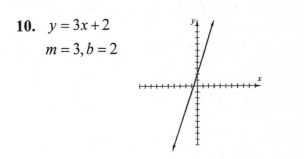

10. $y = 3x + 2$

$m = 3, b = 2$

11. $y = 3x - 1$

$y = mx + b$

$m = 3$

12. $y = -6x + 2$

$y = mx + b$

$m = -6$

13. $7x + 2y = 11$

$$2y = -7x + 11$$

$$y = -\frac{7}{2}x + \frac{11}{2}$$

$$y = mx + b$$

$$m = -\frac{7}{2}$$

14. $2x - y = 0$

$$-y = -2x$$

$$y = 2x$$

$$y = mx + b$$

$$m = 2$$

15. $x = 2$, vertical line, slope is undefined.

16. $y = -4$, horizontal line, $m = 0$

17. $m = 2$, $b = -\frac{1}{3}$

$$y = mx + b$$

$$y = 2x - \frac{1}{3}$$

18. $m = -4$; $(-1, 3)$

$$y - y_1 = m(x - x_1)$$

$$y - 3 = -4(x - (-1))$$

$$y - 3 = -4x - 4$$

$$4x + y = -1$$

19. $(2, 0)$ and $(-1, -3)$

$$m = \frac{y_2 - y_1}{x_2 - x_1} = \frac{-3 - 0}{-1 - 2} = \frac{-3}{-3} = 1$$

$$m = 1; (2, 0)$$

$$y - y_1 = m(x - x_1)$$

$$y - 0 = 1(x - 2)$$

$$y = x - 2$$

$$-x + y = -2$$

20. $6x - y = 7$, $-y = -6x + 7$,

$$y = 6x + 7, \ m_1 = 6$$

$$2x + 3y = 4, \ 3y = -2x + 4,$$

$$y = -\frac{2}{3}x + \frac{4}{3}, \ m_2 = -\frac{2}{3}$$

$m_1 \neq m_2$ and $m_1 m_2 \neq -1$, neither

21. $3x - 6y = 4$, $-6y = -3x + 4$,

$$y = \frac{1}{2}x - \frac{2}{3}, \ m_1 = \frac{1}{2}$$

$$y = -2x, \ m_2 = -2$$

$$m_1 m_2 = \left(\frac{1}{2}\right)(-2) = -1, \text{ perpendicular}$$

22. **a.** $(1997, 11.6)$ and $(2001, 15.4)$

b. $m = \dfrac{y_2 - y_1}{x_2 - x_1} = \dfrac{15.4 - 11.6}{2001 - 1997} = \dfrac{3.8}{4} = 0.95$

c. For the years 1997 through 2001, the number of grill units shipped increased at a rate of 0.95 million per year.

Practice Problems 6.6

1. $\{(-3, 5), (-3, 1), (4, 6), (7, 0)\}$

Domain: $\{-3, 4, 7\}$

Range: $\{0, 1, 5, 6\}$

2. **a.** Every point has a unique x-value: it is a function.

  b. Two points have the same x-value: it is not a function.

3. **a.** This is the graph of the relation
$\{(-3,-2),(-1,-1),(0,0),(1,1)\}$
  Every point has a unique x-value: it is a function.

  b. This is the graph of the relation
$\{(-1,-1),(-1,2),(1,0),(3,1)\}$
  Two points have the same x-value: it is not a function.

4. (a) and (b) pass the vertical line test- they are functions. (c) and (d) do not pass the vertical line test- they are not functions.

5. **a.** 6:30 A.M.

  b. middle of March and middle of September

6. $f(x) = x^2 + 1$

  a. $f(1) = (1)^2 + 1 = 2; (1,2)$

  b. $f(-3) = (-3)^2 + 1 = 9 + 1 = 10; (-3,10)$

  c. $f(0) = (0)^2 + 1 = 1; (0,1)$

Exercise Set 6.6

1. $\{(2,4),(0,0),(-7,10),(10,-7)\}$
  Domain: $\{-7,0,2,10\}$
  Range: $\{-7,0,4,10\}$

3. $\{(0,-2),(1,-2),(5,-2),\}$
  Domain: $\{0,1,5\}$
  Range: $\{-2\}$

5. Every point has a unique x-value: it is a function.

7. Two points have the same x-value: it is not a function.

9. No

11. Yes

13. Yes

15. No

17. 5:20 A.M.

19. Answers may vary

21. 9:30 A.M.

23. January 1 and December 1

25. Yes: it passes the vertical line test.

27. $4.75 per hour

29. 2002

31. Yes; answers may vary

33. $f(x) = 2x - 5$
  $f(-2) = 2(-2) - 5 = -4 - 5 = -9$
  $f(0) = 2(0) - 5 = -5$
  $f(3) = 2(3) - 5 = 6 - 5 = 1$

35. $f(x) = x^2 + 2$

$f(-2) = (-2)^2 + 2 = 4 + 2 = 6$

$f(0) = (0)^2 + 2 = 2$

$f(3) = (3)^2 + 2 = 9 + 2 = 11$

37. $f(x) = 3x$

$f(-2) = 3(-2) = -6$

$f(0) = 3(0) = 0$

$f(3) = 3(3) = 9$

39. $f(x) = |x|$

$f(-2) = |-2| = 2$

$f(0) = |0| = 0$

$f(3) = |3| = 3$

41. $h(x) = -5x$

$h(-1) = -5(-1) = 5$

$h(0) = -5(0) = 0$

$h(4) = -5(4) = -20$

43. $h(x) = 2x^2 + 3$

$h(-1) = 2(-1)^2 + 3 = 2 + 3 = 5$

$h(0) = 2(0)^2 + 3 = 3$

$h(4) = 2(4)^2 + 3 = 2 \cdot 16 + 3 = 32 + 3 = 35$

45. $2x + 5 < 7$

$2x < 2$

$x < 1$

47. $-x + 6 \le 9$

$-x \le 3$

$\dfrac{-x}{-1} \ge \dfrac{3}{-1}$

$x \ge -3$

49. $P = \dfrac{3}{x} + \dfrac{3}{2x} + \dfrac{5}{x} = \dfrac{6}{2x} + \dfrac{3}{2x} + \dfrac{10}{2x} = \dfrac{19}{2x}$ m

51. $f(x) = 2.59x + 47.24$

a. $f(46) = 2.59(46) + 47.24 = 166.38$ cm

b. $f(39) = 2.59(39) + 47.24 = 148.25$ cm

53. Answers may vary

55. $y = x + 7$

$f(x) = x + 7$

Practice Problems 6.7

1. $x - 4y > 8$

a. $(-3, 2)$, $-3 - 4(2) \overset{?}{>} 8$

$-3 - 8 \overset{?}{>} 8$

$-11 > 8$, False

$(-3, 2)$ is not a solution

b. $(9, 0)$, $9 - 4(0) \overset{?}{>} 8$

$9 - 0 \overset{?}{>} 8$

$9 > 8$, True

$(9, 0)$ is a solution

2. $x - y > 3$

Test $(0, 0)$

$0 - 0 \overset{?}{>} 3$, False

Shade below.

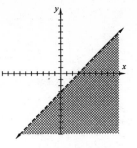

3. $x - 4y \le 4$

Test $(0, 0)$

$0 - 4(0) \overset{?}{\le} 4$, True

Shade above.

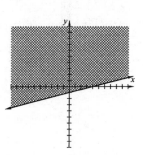

4. $y < 3x$

Test $(0, 1)$

$1 \overset{?}{<} 3(0)$, False

Shade below.

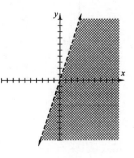

5. $3x + 2y \ge 12$

Test $(0, 0)$

$3(0) + 2(0) \overset{?}{\ge} 12$,

False

Shade above.

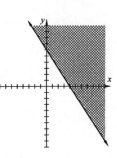

6. $x < 2$

Test $(0, 0)$

$0 \overset{?}{<} 2$, True

Shade to the left.

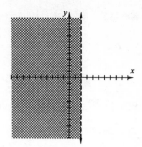

7. $y \ge \dfrac{1}{4}x + 3$

Test $(0, 0)$

$0 \overset{?}{\ge} \dfrac{1}{4}(0) + 3$,

False

Shade above.

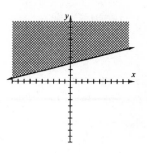

Mental Math 6.7

1. Yes

2. No

3. Yes

4. No

5. $x + y > -5$, $(0, 0)$

$0 + 0 \overset{?}{>} -5$

$0 \overset{?}{>} -5$

Yes

6. $2x + 3y < 10$, $(0, 0)$

$2(0) + 3(0) \overset{?}{<} 10$

$0 \overset{?}{<} 10$

Yes

7. $x-y\le-1,\ (0,0)$

$$0-0\overset{?}{\le}-1$$

$$0\le-1$$

No

8. $\dfrac{2}{3}x+\dfrac{5}{6}y>4,\ (0,0)$

$$\dfrac{2}{3}(0)+\dfrac{5}{6}(0)\overset{?}{>}4$$

$$0>4$$

No

Exercise Set 6.7

1. $x-y>3$

$(0,3),\ 0-3\overset{?}{>}3$

$$-3\overset{?}{>}3,\ \text{False}$$

$(0,3)$ is not a solution

$(2,-1),\ 2-(-1)\overset{?}{>}3$

$$2+1\overset{?}{>}3$$

$$3\overset{?}{>}3,\ \text{False}$$

$(2,-1)$ is not a solution

3. $3x-5y\le-4$

$(2,3),\ 3(2)-5(3)\overset{?}{\le}-4$

$$6-15\overset{?}{\le}-4$$

$$-9\overset{?}{\le}-4,\ \text{True}$$

$(2,3)$ is a solution

$(-1,-1),\ 3(-1)-5(-1)\overset{?}{\le}-4$

$$-3+5\overset{?}{\le}-4$$

$$2\overset{?}{\le}-4,\ \text{False}$$

$(-1,-1)$ is not a solution

5. $x<-y$

$(0,2),\ 0\overset{?}{<}-2,\ \text{False}$

$(0,2)$ is not a solution

$(-5,1),\ -5\overset{?}{<}-1,\ \text{True}$

$(-5,1)$ is a solution

7. $x+y\le1$

Test $(0,0)$

$0+0\overset{?}{\le}1,\ \text{True}$

Shade below.

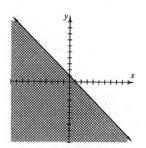

9. $2x-y>-4$

Test $(0,0)$

$2(0)-0\overset{?}{>}-4$

True

Shade below.

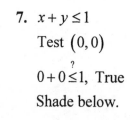

11. $y>2x$

Test $(0,1)$

$1\overset{?}{>}2(0)$

True

Shade above.

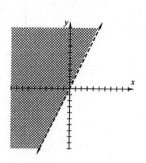

13. $x \le -3y$

Test $(0,1)$

$0 \overset{?}{\le} -3(1)$

False

Shade below.

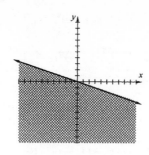

15. $y \ge x + 5$

Test $(0,0)$

$0 \overset{?}{\ge} 0 + 5$

False

Shade above.

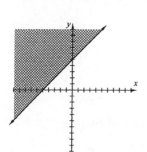

17. $y < 4$

Test $(0,0)$

$0 \overset{?}{<} 4$

True

Shade below.

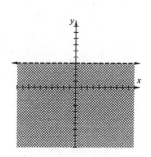

19. $x \ge -3$

Test $(0,0)$

$0 \overset{?}{\ge} -3$

True

Shade right.

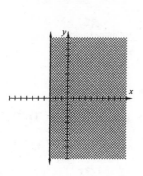

21. $5x + 2y \le 10$

Test $(0,0)$

$5(0) + 2(0) \overset{?}{\le} 10$

True

Shade below.

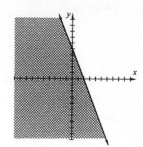

23. $x > y$

Test $(0,1)$

$0 \overset{?}{>} 1$

False

Shade below.

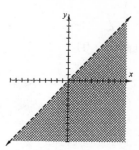

25. $x - y \le 6$

Test $(0,0)$

$0 - 0 \overset{?}{\le} 6$

True

Shade above.

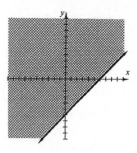

27. $x \ge 0$

Test $(1,0)$

$1 \overset{?}{\ge} 0$

True

Shade right.

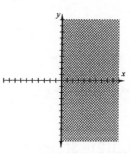

29. $2x + 7y > 5$

Test $(0,0)$

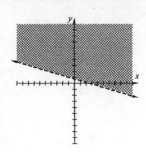

$2(0) + 7(0) \overset{?}{>} 5$

False

Shade above.

31. $y \geq \dfrac{1}{2}x - 4$

Test $(0,0)$

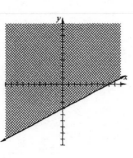

$0 \overset{?}{\geq} \dfrac{1}{2}(0) - 4$

True

Shade above.

33. $(-2,1)$

35. $(-3,-1)$

37. $x > 2$

a

39. $y \leq 2x$

b

41. Answers may vary

43.a. $30x + 0.15y \leq 500$

b.

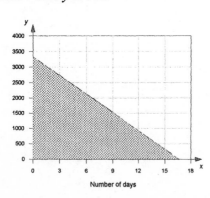

Number of days

c. Answers may vary

Chapter 6 Review

1.-6.

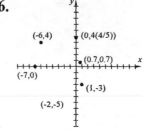

7. $-2 + y = 6x, \quad x = 7$

$-2 + y = 6(7)$

$-2 + y = 42$

$y = 44$

$(7, 44)$

8. $y = 3x + 5, \quad y = -8$

$-8 = 3x + 5$

$-13 = 3x$

$-\dfrac{13}{3} = x$

$\left(-\dfrac{13}{3}, -8 \right)$

9. $9 = -3x + 4y$

$y = 0, \; 9 = -3x + 4(0), \; 9 = -3x, \; -3 = x$

$y = 3, \; 9 = -3x + 4(3), \; 9 = -3x + 12$

$-3 = -3x, \; 1 = x$

$x = 9, \; 9 = -3(9) + 4y, \; 9 = -27 + 4y$

$36 = 4y, \; 9 = y$

x	y
−3	0
1	3
9	9

10. $y = 5$ for all values of x.

x	y
7	5
−7	5
0	5

11. $x = 2y$

$y = 0, \; x = 2(0) = 0$

$y = 5, \; x = 2(5) = 10$

$y = -5, \; x = 2(-5) = -10$

x	y
0	0
10	5
−10	−5

12.a. $y = 5x + 2000$

$x = 1, \; y = 5(1) + 2000 = 2005$

$x = 100, \; y = 5(100) + 2000 = 2500$

$x = 1000, \; y = 5(1000) + 2000 = 7000$

x	1	100	1000
y	2005	2500	7000

b. Let $y = 6430$

$6430 = 5x + 2000$

$4430 = 5x$

$886 = x$

886 disk holders can be produced

13. $x - y = 1$

x	y
1	0
0	−1

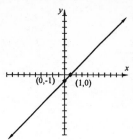

14. $x + y = 6$

x	y
6	0
0	6

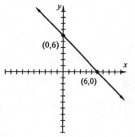

15. $x - 3y = 12$

x	y
12	0
0	−4

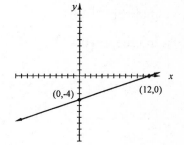

16. $5x - y = -8$

x	y
−2	−2
0	8

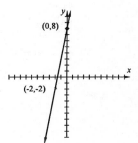

17. $x = 3y$

x	y
0	0
6	2

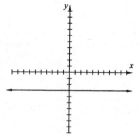

18. $y = -2x$

x	y
0	0
4	-8

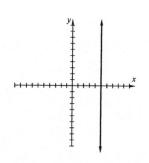

19. x-intercept: $(4, 0)$

y-intercept: $(0, -2)$

20. x-intercepts: $(-2, 0), (2, 0)$

y-intercepts: $(0, 2), (0, -2)$

21. $y = -3$ for all values of x.

22. $x = 5$ for all values of y.

23. $x - 3y = 12$

$y = 0,\ x - 3(0) = 12.\ x = 12$

$x = 0,\ 0 - 3y = 12,\ y = -4$

x-intercept: $(12, 0)$

y-intercept: $(0, -4)$

24. $-4x + y = 8$

$y = 0,\ -4x + 0 = 8.\ x = -2$

$x = 0,\ -4(0) + y = 8,\ y = 8$

x-intercept: $(-2, 0)$

y-intercept: $(0, 8)$

25. $(-1, 2)$, and $(3, -1)$

$$m = \frac{y_2 - y_1}{x_2 - x_1} = \frac{-1 - 2}{3 - (-1)} = -\frac{3}{4}$$

26. $(-2, -2)$, and $(3, -1)$

$$m = \frac{y_2 - y_1}{x_2 - x_1} = \frac{-1 - (-2)}{3 - (-2)} = \frac{1}{5}$$

27. $m = 0$

D

28. $m = -1$

B

29. Slope is undefined.

C

30. $m = 4$

A

31. $(2, 5)$, and $(6, 8)$

$$m = \frac{y_2 - y_1}{x_2 - x_1} = \frac{8 - 5}{6 - 2} = \frac{3}{4}$$

280

32. $(4,7)$, and $(1,2)$

$$m = \frac{y_2 - y_1}{x_2 - x_1} = \frac{2-7}{1-4} = \frac{-5}{-3} = \frac{5}{3}$$

33. $(1,3)$, and $(-2,-9)$

$$m = \frac{y_2 - y_1}{x_2 - x_1} = \frac{-9-3}{-2-1} = \frac{-12}{-3} = 4$$

34. $(-4,1)$, and $(3,-6)$

$$m = \frac{y_2 - y_1}{x_2 - x_1} = \frac{-6-1}{3-(-4)} = \frac{-7}{7} = -1$$

35. $y = 3x + 7$

$y = mx + b$

$m = 3$

36. $x - 2y = 4$

$-2y = -x + 2$

$y = \frac{1}{2}x - 1$

$y = mx + b$

$m = \frac{1}{2}$

37. $y = -2$

$y = 0x - 2$

$y = mx + b$

$m = 0$

38. $x = 0$

Undefined slope

39. $x - y = -6, \; -y = -x - 6,$

$y = x + 6, \; m_1 = 1$

$x + y = 3, \; y = -x + 3, \; m_2 = -1$

$m_1 m_2 = (1)(-1) = -1$, perpendicular

40. $3x + y = 7, \; y = -3x + 7, \; m_1 = -3$

$-3x - y = 10, \; -y = 3x + 10,$

$y = -3x - 10, \; m_2 = -3$

$m_1 = m_2$, parallel

41. $y = 4x + \frac{1}{2}, \; m_1 = 4$

$4x + 2y = 1, \; 2y = -4x + 1,$

$y = -2x + \frac{1}{2}, \; m_2 = -2$

$m_1 \neq m_2$ and $m_1 m_2 \neq -1$, neither

42. $(1995, 39.2)$ and $(1998, 42.92)$

$$m = \frac{y_2 - y_1}{x_2 - x_1} = \frac{42.92 - 39.2}{1998 - 1995} = \frac{3.72}{3}$$

$$= 1.24 \text{ million } \frac{\text{persons with degrees}}{\text{year}}$$

Each year 1.24 million more persons have a bachelor's degree or higher.

43. $(1995, 805)$ and $(1997, 859)$

$$m = \frac{y_2 - y_1}{x_2 - x_1} = \frac{859 - 805}{1997 - 1995} = \frac{54}{2}$$

$$= 27 \text{ million } \frac{\text{travelers}}{\text{year}}$$

Each year 27 million more people go on vacations.

44. $3x + y = 7$

$y = -3x + 7$

$y = mx + b$

$m = -3$, y-intercept $= (0,7)$

45. $x - 6y = -1$

$$-6y = -x - 1$$

$$y = \frac{1}{6}x + \frac{1}{6}$$

$$y = mx + b$$

$$m = \frac{1}{6}, \; y\text{-intercept} = \left(0, \frac{1}{6}\right)$$

46. $m = -5, \; y\text{-intercept} = \left(0, \frac{1}{2}\right)$

$$y = mx + b$$

$$y = -5x + \frac{1}{2}$$

47. $m = \frac{2}{3}, \; y\text{-intercept} = (0,6)$

$$y = mx + b$$

$$y = \frac{2}{3}x + 6$$

48. $y = 2x + 1$

$m = 2, \; b = 1$

D

49. $y = -4x$

$m = -4, \; b = 0$

C

50. $y = 2x$

$m = 2, \; b = 0$

A

51. $y = 2x - 1$

$m = 2, \; b = -1$

B

52. $m = 4; \; (2,0)$

$$y - y_1 = m(x - x_1)$$

$$y - 0 = 4(x - 2)$$

$$y = 4x - 8$$

$$-4x + y = -8$$

53. $m = -3; \; (0, -5)$

$$y - y_1 = m(x - x_1)$$

$$y - (-5) = -3(x - 0)$$

$$y + 5 = -3x$$

$$3x + y = -5$$

54. $m = \frac{3}{5}; \; (1,4)$

$$y - y_1 = m(x - x_1)$$

$$y - 4 = \frac{3}{5}(x - 1)$$

$$5(y - 4) = 3(x - 1)$$

$$5y - 20 = 3x - 3$$

$$-3x + 5y = 17$$

$$y = 4x - 8$$

$$-4x + y = -8$$

55. $m = -\frac{1}{3}; \; (-3,3)$

$$y - y_1 = m(x - x_1)$$

$$y - 3 = -\frac{1}{3}(x - (-3))$$

$$3(y - 3) = -(x + 3)$$

$$3y - 9 = -x - 3$$

$$x + 3y = 6$$

56. $(1,7)$ and $(2,-7)$

$$m = \frac{y_2 - y_1}{x_2 - x_1} = \frac{-7-7}{2-1} = \frac{-14}{1} = -14$$

$$m = -14; \ (1,7)$$

$$y - y_1 = m(x - x_1)$$

$$y - 7 = -14(x-1)$$

$$y - 7 = -14x + 14$$

$$14x + y = 21$$

57. $(-2,5)$ and $(-4,6)$

$$m = \frac{y_2 - y_1}{x_2 - x_1} = \frac{6-5}{-4-(-2)} = \frac{1}{-2} = -\frac{1}{2}$$

$$m = -\frac{1}{2}; \ (-2,5)$$

$$y - y_1 = m(x - x_1)$$

$$y - 5 = -\frac{1}{2}(x-(-2))$$

$$2(y-5) = -(x+2)$$

$$2y - 10 = -x - 2$$

$$x + 2y = 8$$

58. Two points have the same *x*-value: it is not a function.

59. Every point has a unique *x*-value: it is a function.

60. Yes

61. Yes

62. No

63. Yes

64. $f(x) = -2x + 6$

  a. $f(0) = -2(0) + 6 = 6$

  b. $f(-2) = -2(-2) + 6 = 4 + 6 = 10$

  c. $f\left(\frac{1}{2}\right) = -2\left(\frac{1}{2}\right) + 6 = -1 + 6 = 5$

65. $x + 6y < 6$

Test $(0,0)$

$$0 + 6(0) \overset{?}{<} 6$$

True

Shade below.

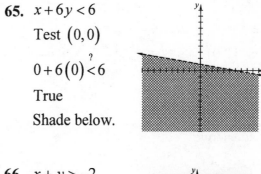

66. $x + y > -2$

Test $(0,0)$

$$0 + 0 \overset{?}{>} -2$$

True

Shade above.

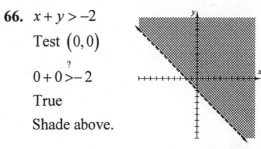

67. $y \geq -7$

Test $(0,0)$

$$0 \overset{?}{\geq} -7$$

True

Shade above.

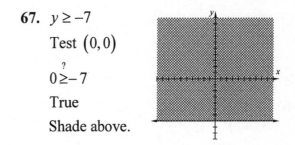

68. $y \leq -4$

Test $(0,0)$

$$0 \overset{?}{\leq} -4$$

False

Shade below.

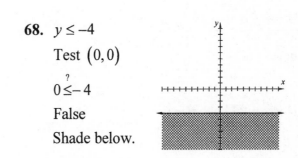

69. $-x \le y$

Test $(1,0)$

$-1 \overset{?}{\le} 0$

True

Shade above.

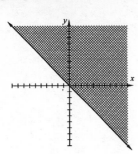

70. $x \ge -y$

Test $(1,0)$

$1 \overset{?}{\ge} 0$

True

Shade above.

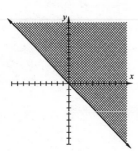

Chapter 6 Test

1. $12y - 7x = 5, \quad x = 1$

$12y - 7(1) = 5$

$12y - 7 = 5$

$12y = 12$

$y = 1$

$(1,1)$

2. $y = 17, \quad x = -4$

$y = 17$ for all values of x.

$(-4, 17)$

3. $(-1, -1)$, and $(4, 1)$

$m = \dfrac{y_2 - y_1}{x_2 - x_1} = \dfrac{1 - (-1)}{4 - (-1)} = \dfrac{2}{5}$

4. Horizontal line: $m = 0$

5. $(6, -5)$, and $(-1, 2)$

$m = \dfrac{y_2 - y_1}{x_2 - x_1} = \dfrac{2 - (-5)}{-1 - 6} = \dfrac{7}{-7} = -1$

6. $(0, -8)$, and $(-1, -1)$

$m = \dfrac{y_2 - y_1}{x_2 - x_1} = \dfrac{-1 - (-8)}{-1 - 0} = \dfrac{7}{-1} = -7$

7. $-3x + y = 5$

$y = 3x + 5$

$y = mx + b$

$m = 3$

8. $x = 6$ is a vertical line.

The slope is undefined.

9. $2x + y = 8$

x	y
4	0
0	8

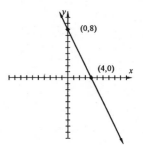

10. $-x + 4y = 5$

x	y
-5	0
-1	1

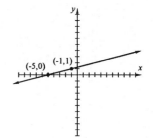

284

11. $x - y \geq -2$

Test $(0,0)$

$0 - 0 \overset{?}{\geq} -2$

True

Shade below.

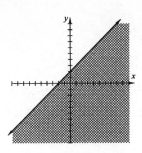

15. $6x + y > -1$

Test $(0,0)$

$6(0) + 0 \overset{?}{>} -1$

True

Shade above.

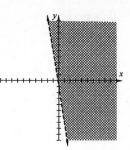

12. $y \geq -4x$

Test $(1,0)$

$0 \overset{?}{\geq} -4(1)$

True

Shade above.

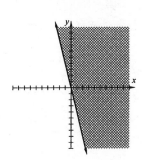

16. $y = -1$

for all values of x

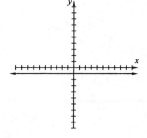

13. $5x - 7y = 10$

x	y
2	0
−5	−5

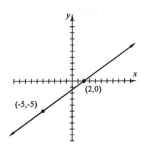

14. $2x - 3y > -6$

Test $(0,0)$

$2(0) - 3(0) \overset{?}{>} -6$

True

Shade below.

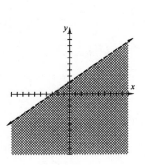

17. $y = 2x - 6, \ m_1 = 2$

$-4x = 2y, \ -2x = y,$

$y = -2x, \ m_2 = -2$

$m_1 \neq m_2$ and $m_1 m_2 \neq -1$, neither

18. $m = -\dfrac{1}{4}; \ (2,2)$

$y - y_1 = m(x - x_1)$

$y - 2 = -\dfrac{1}{4}(x - 2)$

$4(y - 2) = -(x - 2)$

$4y - 8 = -x + 2$

$x + 4y = 10$

19. $(0,0)$ and $(6,-7)$

$$m = \frac{y_2 - y_1}{x_2 - x_1} = \frac{-7-0}{6-0} = -\frac{7}{6}$$

$$m = -\frac{7}{6}; \ (0,0)$$

$$y - y_1 = m(x - x_1)$$

$$y - 0 = -\frac{7}{6}(x - 0)$$

$$6y = -7x$$

$$7x + 6y = 0$$

20. $(2,-5)$ and $(1,3)$

$$m = \frac{y_2 - y_1}{x_2 - x_1} = \frac{3-(-5)}{1-2} = \frac{8}{-1} = -8$$

$$m = -8; \ (1,3)$$

$$y - y_1 = m(x - x_1)$$

$$y - 3 = -8(x - 1)$$

$$y - 3 = -8x + 8$$

$$8x + y = 11$$

21. $m = \frac{1}{8}, \ b = 12$

$$y = mx + b$$

$$y = \frac{1}{8}x + 12$$

$$8y = x + 96$$

$$-x + 8y = 96$$

22. Every point has a unique x-value: it is a function.

23. Two points have the same x-value: it is not a function.

24. Yes

25. Yes

26. $f(x) = 2x - 4$

   a. $f(-2) = 2(-2) - 4 = -4 - 4 = -8$

   b. $f(0.2) = 2(0.2) - 4 = 0.4 - 4 = -3.6$

   c. $f(0) = 2(0) - 4 = -4$

27. $f(x) = x^3 - x$

   a. $f(-1) = (-1)^3 - (-1) = -1 + 1 = 0$

   b. $f(0) = (0)^3 - (0) = 0$

   c. $f(4) = (4)^3 - (4) = 64 - 4 = 60$

28. $2x + 2(2y) = P$

$$2x + 4y = 42$$

$$x + 2y = 21$$

Let $y = 8$

$$x + 2(8) = 21$$

$$x + 16 = 21$$

$$x = 5 \text{ meters}$$

29.a. $\{(1986, 38), (1988, 44), (1990, 50), (1992, 53),$
$(1994, 57), (1996, 62), (1998, 67), (2000, 69)\}$

b.

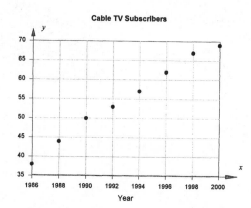

30. $(1998, 1480)$ and $(2000, 1420)$

$$m = \frac{y_2 - y_1}{x_2 - x_1} = \frac{1420 - 1480}{2000 - 1998} = \frac{-60}{2}$$

$$= -30 \; \frac{\text{million dollars in ticket sales}}{\text{year}}$$

Cumulative Review Chapter 6

1. $6 \div 3 + 5^2 = 6 \div 3 + 25 = 2 + 25 = 27$

2. $3\left[4(5+2) - 10\right] = 3\left[4(7) - 10\right]$

$$= 3\left[28 - 10\right]$$

$$= 3\left[18\right] = 54$$

3.a. US/Canada region; 167 million users

  b. $167 - 113 = 154$ million more users

4. $2x + 6$

5. $(x - 4) \div 7$

6. $5 + (x + 1) = x + 6$

7. $\dfrac{5}{2}x = 15$

$$\frac{2}{5}\left(\frac{5}{2}x\right) = \frac{2}{5}(15)$$

$$x = 6$$

8. $2x < -4$

    $x < -2$

    $\{x \mid x < -2\}$

9.a. Degree 2, trinomial

  b. Degree 1, binomial

  c. Degree 3, none of these

10. $\left(-2x^2 + 5x - 1\right) + \left(-2x^2 + x + 3\right)$

$$= -2x^2 + 5x - 1 + -2x^2 + x + 3$$

$$= -4x^2 + 6x + 2$$

11. $(3y + 1)^2 = (3y + 1)(3y + 1)$

$$= (3y)^2 + 2(3y) + (1)^2$$

$$= 9y^2 + 6y + 1$$

12. $-9a^5 + 18a^2 - 3a = -3a\left(3a^4 - 6a + 1\right)$

13. $x^2 + 4x - 12 = (x + 6)(x - 2)$

14. $8x^2 - 22x + 5 = (4x - 1)(2x - 5)$

15. $x^2 - 9x = -20$

$$x^2 - 9x + 20 = 0$$

$$(x - 5)(x - 4) = 0$$

$$x - 5 = 0 \quad \text{or} \quad x - 4 = 0$$

$$x = 5 \quad \text{or} \quad\quad x = 4$$

16. $\dfrac{2x^2 - 11x + 5}{5x - 25} \div \dfrac{4x - 2}{10}$

$$= \frac{2x^2 - 11x + 5}{5x - 25} \cdot \frac{10}{4x - 2}$$

$$= \frac{(2x - 1)(x - 5)(2)(5)}{5(x - 5)(2)(2x - 1)}$$

$$= 1$$

17. $\dfrac{4b}{9a} \cdot \dfrac{3ab}{3ab} = \dfrac{12ab^2}{27a^2 b}$

18. $1 + \dfrac{m}{m+1} = 1 \cdot \dfrac{m+1}{m+1} + \dfrac{m}{m+1} = \dfrac{2m+1}{m+1}$

19. $\qquad 3 - \dfrac{6}{x} = x + 8$

$\qquad 3x - x\left(\dfrac{6}{x}\right) = x^2 + 8x$

$\qquad\quad 3x - 6 = x^2 + 8x$

$\qquad\qquad\quad 0 = x^2 + 5x + 6$

$\qquad\qquad\quad 0 = (x+3)(x+2)$

$\qquad\quad x+3 = 0 \quad$ or $\quad x+2 = 0$

$\qquad\qquad x = -3 \quad$ or $\qquad x = -2$

20. $\dfrac{\frac{x+1}{y}}{\frac{x}{y}+2} = \dfrac{\frac{x+1}{y}}{\frac{x+2y}{y}} = \dfrac{x+1}{y} \cdot \dfrac{y}{x+2y} = \dfrac{x+1}{x+2y}$

21. $3x + y = 12$

    a. $x = 0, \; 3(0) + y = 12, \; y = 12, \; (0,12)$

    b. $y = 6, \; 3x + (6) = 12, \; 3x = 6,$

        $x = 2, \; (2,6)$

    c. $x = -1, \; 3(-1) + y = 12, \; y = 15, \; (-1,15)$

22. $2x + y = 5$

x	y
4	-3
0	5

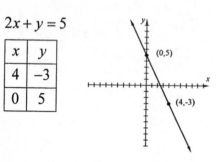

23. $-2x + 3y = 11$

$\qquad\quad 3y = 2x + 11$

$\qquad\quad\; y = \dfrac{2}{3}x + \dfrac{11}{3}$

$\qquad\quad\; y = mx + b$

$\qquad\quad\; m = \dfrac{2}{3}$

24. $\qquad m = -2; \; (-1,5)$

$\qquad y - y_1 = m(x - x_1)$

$\qquad\; y - 5 = -2(x - (-1))$

$\qquad\; y - 5 = -2x - 2$

$\qquad 2x + y = 3$

25. $g(x) = x^2 - 3$

    a. $g(2) = (2)^2 - 3 = 4 - 3 = 1; \; (2,1)$

    b. $g(-2) = (-2)^2 - 3 = 4 - 3 = 1; \; (-2,1)$

    c. $g(0) = (0)^2 - 3 = 0 - 3 = -3; \; (0,-3)$

Chapter 7

1. $\begin{cases} x+y=5 \\ x-y=7 \end{cases}$

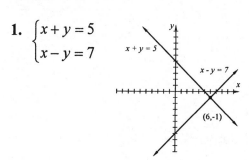

The solution of the system is $(6,-1)$.

2. $\begin{cases} y=4x \\ x=1 \end{cases}$

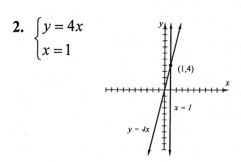

The solution of the system is $(1,4)$.

3. $\begin{cases} x+y=6 \\ x=3y-2 \end{cases}$

Substitute $3y-2$ for x in the first equation.

$3y-2+y=6$

$\qquad 4y=8$

$\qquad\; y=2$

Let $y=2$ in the second equation.

$x=3(2)-2$

$x=4$

The solution is $(4,2)$.

4. $\begin{cases} 5x+y=13 \\ 4x-5y=22 \end{cases}$

Solve the first equation for y.

$y=13-5x$

Substitute $13-5x$ for y in the second equation.

$4x-5(13-5x)=22$

$\quad 4x-65+25x=22$

$\qquad\qquad\; 29x=87$

$\qquad\qquad\quad x=3$

Let $x=3$ in $y=13-5x$.

$y=13-5(3)$

$y=-2$

The solution is $(3,-2)$.

5. $\begin{cases} 7y=x-6 \\ 2x+3y=-5 \end{cases}$

Solve the first equation for x.

$x=7y+6$

Substitute $7y+6$ for x in the second equation.

$2(7y+6)+3y=-5$

$\quad 14y+12+3y=-5$

$\qquad\qquad\; 17y=-17$

$\qquad\qquad\quad y=-1$

Let $y=-1$ in $x=7y+6$.

$x=7(-1)+6$

$x=-1$

The solution is $(-1,-1)$.

6. $\begin{cases} 4x = y + 6 \\ 8x - 2y = 12 \end{cases}$

Solve the first equation for y.

$y = 4x - 6$

Substitute $4x - 6$ for y in the second equation.

$8x - 2(4x - 6) = 12$

$8x - 8x + 12 = 12$

$12 = 12$

The equations in the original system are equivalent and there are an infinite number of solutions.

7. $\begin{cases} x - 5 = 3y \\ 6y - 2x = 10 \end{cases}$

Solve the first equation for x.

$x = 3y + 5$

Substitute $3y + 5$ for x in the second equation.

$6y - 2(3y + 5) = 10$

$6y - 6y - 10 = 10$

$-10 = 10$

The system has no solution.

8. $\begin{cases} 4x + 6y = -14 \\ 6x + y = -1 \end{cases}$

Solve the second equation for y.

$y = -1 - 6x$

Substitute $-1 - 6x$ for y in the first equation.

$4x + 6(-1 - 6x) = -14$

$4x - 6 - 36x = -14$

$-32x = -8$

$x = \dfrac{1}{4}$

Let $x = \dfrac{1}{4}$ in $y = -1 - 6x$.

$y = -1 - 6\left(\dfrac{1}{4}\right)$

$y = -\dfrac{5}{2}$

The solution is $\left(\dfrac{1}{4}, -\dfrac{5}{2}\right)$.

9. $\begin{cases} \dfrac{1}{5}x - y = 3 \\ x - 5y = 15 \end{cases}$

Solve the second equation for x.

$x = 15 + 5y$

Substitute $15 + 5y$ for x in the first equation.

$\dfrac{1}{5}(15 + 5y) - y = 3$

$3 + y - y = 3$

$3 = 3$

The equations in the original system are equivalent and there are an infinite number of solutions.

10. $\begin{cases} y = 3x + 7 \\ y = 10x + 21 \end{cases}$

Substitute $3x + 7$ for y in the second equation.

$3x + 7 = 10x + 21$

$-14 = 7x$

$-2 = x$

Let $x = -2$ in the first equation.

$y = 3(-2) + 7$

$y = 1$

The solution is $(-2, 1)$.

11. $\begin{cases} 2x + y = 11 \\ 3x - y = 29 \end{cases}$

$2x + y = 11$

$\underline{3x - y = 29}$

$5x \quad = 40$

$x \quad = 8$

Substitute 8 for x in the first equation.

$2(8) + y = 11$

$\quad 16 + y = 11$

$\qquad y = -5$

The solution of the system is $(8, -5)$

12. $\begin{cases} 4x - 3y = 13 \\ 5x - 9y = 53 \end{cases}$

Multiply the first equation by -3.

$-12x + 9y = -39$

$\underline{\quad 5x - 9y = \ 53}$

$-7x \qquad = 14$

$\quad x \qquad = -2$

Let $x = -2$ in the first equation.

$4(-2) - 3y = 13$

$\quad -8 - 3y = 13$

$\qquad -3y = 21$

$\qquad\quad y = -7$

The solution of the system is $(-2, -7)$.

13. $\begin{cases} 6x + 8y = 92 \\ 5x - 3y = 9 \end{cases}$

Multiply the first equation by 3 and the second equation by 8.

$18x + 24y = 276$

$\underline{40x - 24y = \ 72}$

$58x \qquad\quad = 348$

$\quad x \qquad\quad = 6$

Let $x = 6$ in the first equation.

$6(6) + 8y = 92$

$\quad 36 + 8y = 92$

$\qquad\quad 8y = 56$

$\qquad\quad y = 7$

The solution of the system is $(6, 7)$.

14. $\begin{cases} 3x - 4y = 7 \\ -9x + 12y = 21 \end{cases}$

Multiply the first equation by 3.

$\quad 9x - 12y = 21$

$\underline{-9x + 12y = 21}$

$\qquad\qquad 0 = 42$

Since this is a false statement, the system has no solution.

15. $\begin{cases} \dfrac{x}{2} + \dfrac{y}{3} = 2 \\ \dfrac{x}{6} - \dfrac{y}{4} = 5 \end{cases}$

Multiply the first equation by 18 and the second equation by 24.

$9x + 6y = \ 36$

$\underline{4x - 6y = 120}$

$13x \qquad = 156$

$\quad x \qquad = 12$

Let $x = 12$ in the first equation.

$$\frac{12}{2} + \frac{y}{3} = 2$$

$$6 + \frac{y}{3} = 2$$

$$\frac{y}{3} = -4$$

$$y = -12$$

The solution of the system is $(12, -12)$.

16. $\begin{cases} 6x + 10y = -4 \\ -x + y = -1 \end{cases}$

Multiply the second equation by 6.

$$6x + 10y = -4$$
$$\underline{-6x + 6y = -6}$$
$$16y = -10$$

$$y = -\frac{10}{16}$$

$$y = -\frac{5}{8}$$

Let $y = -\frac{5}{8}$ in the second equation.

$$-x - \frac{5}{8} = -1$$

$$-8x - 5 = -8$$

$$-8x = -3$$

$$x = \frac{3}{8}$$

The solution of the system is $\left(\frac{3}{8}, -\frac{5}{8}\right)$.

17. $\begin{cases} 2x = 8 - 3y \\ 9y = 24 - 6x \end{cases}$

Put in standard form.

$$\begin{cases} 2x + 3y = 8 \\ 6x + 9y = 24 \end{cases}$$

Multiply the first equation by -3.

$$-6x - 9y = -24$$
$$\underline{6x + 9y = 24}$$
$$0 = 0$$

The equations in the original system are equivalent and there are an infinite number of solutions.

18. $\begin{cases} 11x = 5y + 30 \\ 3x + 4y = -24 \end{cases}$

Put in standard form.

$$\begin{cases} 11x - 5y = 30 \\ 3x + 4y = -24 \end{cases}$$

Multiply the first equation by 4 and the second equation by 5.

$$44x - 20y = 120$$
$$\underline{15x + 20y = -120}$$
$$59x \quad\quad = 0$$
$$x \quad\quad = 0$$

Let $x = 0$ in the first equation.

$$11(0) = 5y + 30$$

$$-30 = 5y$$

$$-6 = y$$

The solution of the system is $(0, -6)$.

19. Let x = the first number and y = the second number.

$$\begin{cases} x + y = 97 \\ x - y = 65 \end{cases}$$

$$\begin{array}{l} x + y = 97 \\ \underline{x - y = 65} \\ 2x \quad\;\; = 162 \\ \;\;x \quad\;\; = 81 \end{array}$$

Let $x = 81$ in the first equation.

$$81 + y = 97$$
$$\quad y = 16$$

The numbers are 81 and 16.

20. Let x = the measure of the first angle and y = the measure of the second angle.

$$\begin{cases} x + y = 90 \\ x = 2y - 6 \end{cases}$$

Re write in standard form.

$$\begin{cases} x + y = 90 \\ x - 2y = -6 \end{cases}$$

Multiply the first equation by -1.

$$\begin{array}{l} -x - \;\; y = -90 \\ \underline{\;\;x - 2y = -6} \\ \quad -3y = -96 \\ \qquad y = 32 \end{array}$$

Let $y = 32$ in the first equation.

$$x + 32 = 90$$
$$\quad x = 58$$

The measures of the angles are $32°$ and $58°$.

Practice Problems 7.1

1. Let $x = 3$ and $y = 9$.

$$5(3) - 2(9) \overset{?}{=} -3 \qquad\qquad 9 \overset{?}{=} 3(3)$$
$$15 - 18 \overset{?}{=} -3 \qquad\qquad 9 = 9$$
$$-3 = -3 \qquad\qquad\qquad \text{True}$$

True

$(3, 9)$ is a solution of the system.

2. Let $x = 3$ and $y = -2$.

$$2(3) - (-2) \overset{?}{=} 8 \qquad\qquad 3 + 3(-2) \overset{?}{=} 4$$
$$6 + 2 \overset{?}{=} 8 \qquad\qquad\qquad 3 - 6 \overset{?}{=} 4$$
$$8 = 8 \qquad\qquad\qquad\qquad -3 = 4$$

True   False

$(3, -2)$ is not a solution of the system.

3. $\begin{cases} -3x + y = -10 \\ x - y = 6 \end{cases}$

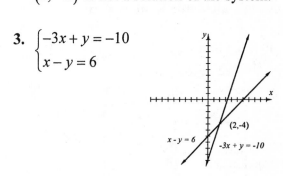

The solution of the system is $(2, -4)$.

4. $\begin{cases} x + 3y = -1 \\ y = 1 \end{cases}$

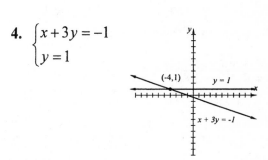

The solution of the system is $(-4, 1)$.

5. $\begin{cases} 3x - y = 6 \\ 6x = 2y \end{cases}$

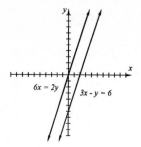

There is no solution.

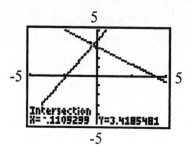

The solution of the system is $(-0.11, 3.42)$.

6. $\begin{cases} 3x + 4y = 12 \\ 9x + 12y = 36 \end{cases}$

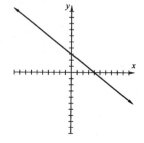

There are an infinite number of solutions.

3. $\begin{cases} 4.3x - 2.9y = 5.6 \\ 8.1x + 7.6y = -14.1 \end{cases}$

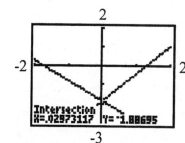

The solution of the system is $(0.03, -1.89)$.

Graphing Calculator Explorations 7.1

1. $\begin{cases} y = -2.68x + 1.21 \\ y = 5.22x - 1.68 \end{cases}$

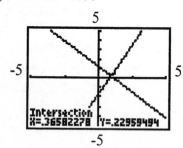

The solution of the system is $(0.37, 0.23)$.

4. $\begin{cases} -3.6x - 8.6y = 10 \\ -4.5x + 9.6y = -7.7 \end{cases}$

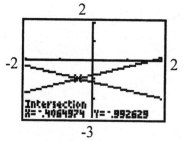

The solution of the system is $(-0.41, -0.99)$.

2. $\begin{cases} y = 4.25x + 3.89 \\ y = -1.88x + 3.21 \end{cases}$

Mental Math 7.1

1. One solution, $(-1, 3)$

2. No solution

3. Infinite number of solutions.

4. One solution, $(3, 4)$

5. No solution

6. Infinite number of solutions.

7. One solution, $(3, 2)$

8. One solution, $(0, -3)$

Exercise Set 7.1

1. a. Let $x = 2$ and $y = 4$.

$$x + y = 8 \qquad\qquad 3x + 2y = 21$$
$$2 + 4 \overset{?}{=} 8 \qquad\quad 3(2) + 2(4) \overset{?}{=} 21$$
$$6 = 8 \qquad\qquad\qquad 6 + 8 \overset{?}{=} 21$$
$$\text{False} \qquad\qquad\qquad 14 = 21$$
$$\qquad\qquad\qquad\qquad \text{False}$$

$(2, 4)$ is not a solution of the system.

b. Let $x = 5$ and $y = 3$.

$$x + y = 8 \qquad\qquad 3x + 2y = 21$$
$$5 + 3 \overset{?}{=} 8 \qquad\quad 3(5) + 2(3) \overset{?}{=} 21$$
$$8 = 8 \qquad\qquad\qquad 15 + 6 \overset{?}{=} 21$$
$$\text{True} \qquad\qquad\qquad 21 = 21$$
$$\qquad\qquad\qquad\qquad \text{True}$$

$(5, 3)$ is a solution of the system

3. a. Let $x = 3$ and $y = 4$.

$$3x - y = 5 \qquad\qquad x + 2y = 11$$
$$3(3) - 4 \overset{?}{=} 5 \qquad 3 + 2(4) \overset{?}{=} 11$$
$$9 - 4 \overset{?}{=} 5 \qquad\qquad 3 + 8 \overset{?}{=} 11$$
$$5 = 5 \qquad\qquad\qquad 11 = 11$$
$$\text{True} \qquad\qquad\qquad \text{True}$$

$(3, 4)$ is a solution of the system.

b. Let $x = 0$ and $y = -5$.

$$3x - y = 5 \qquad\qquad x + 2y = 11$$
$$3(0) - (-5) \overset{?}{=} 5 \qquad 0 + 2(-5) \overset{?}{=} 11$$
$$0 + 5 \overset{?}{=} 5 \qquad\qquad 0 - 10 \overset{?}{=} 11$$
$$5 = 5 \qquad\qquad\qquad -10 = 11$$
$$\text{True} \qquad\qquad\qquad \text{False}$$

$(0, -5)$ is not a solution of the system

5. a. Let $x = -3$ and $y = -6$.

$$2y = 4x \qquad\qquad 2x - y = 0$$
$$2(-6) \overset{?}{=} 4(-3) \qquad 2(-3) - (-6) \overset{?}{=} 0$$
$$-12 = -12 \qquad\qquad -6 + 6 \overset{?}{=} 0$$
$$\text{True} \qquad\qquad\qquad 0 = 0$$
$$\qquad\qquad\qquad\qquad \text{True}$$

$(-3, -6)$ is a solution of the system

b. Let $x = 0$ and $y = 0$.

$$2y = 4x \qquad\qquad 2x - y = 0$$
$$2(0) \overset{?}{=} 4(0) \qquad 2(0) - (0) \overset{?}{=} 0$$
$$0 = 0 \qquad\qquad\qquad 0 - 0 \overset{?}{=} 0$$
$$\text{True} \qquad\qquad\qquad 0 = 0$$
$$\qquad\qquad\qquad\qquad \text{True}$$

$(0, 0)$ is a solution of the system.

7. $\begin{cases} x+y=4 \\ x-y=2 \end{cases}$

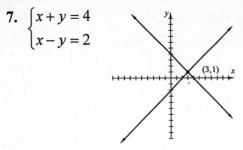

The solution of the system is $(3,1)$.

15. $\begin{cases} 2x+y=0 \\ 3x+y=1 \end{cases}$

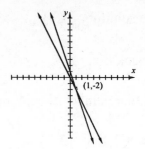

The solution of the system is $(1,-2)$.

9. $\begin{cases} x+y=6 \\ -x+y=-6 \end{cases}$

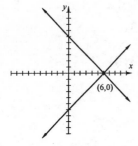

The solution of the system is $(6,0)$.

17. $\begin{cases} y=-x-1 \\ y=2x+5 \end{cases}$

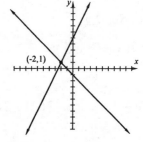

The solution of the system is $(-2,1)$.

11. $\begin{cases} y=2x \\ 3x-y=-2 \end{cases}$

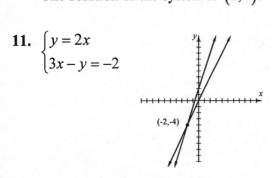

The solution of the system is $(-2,-4)$.

19. $\begin{cases} 2x-y=6 \\ y=2 \end{cases}$

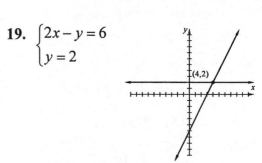

The solution of the system is $(4,2)$.

13. $\begin{cases} y=x+1 \\ y=2x-1 \end{cases}$

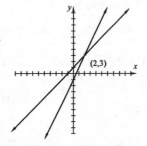

The solution of the system is $(2,3)$.

21. $\begin{cases} x+y=5 \\ x+y=6 \end{cases}$

There is no solution.

23. $\begin{cases} 2x + y = 4 \\ x + y = 2 \end{cases}$

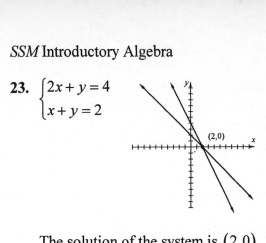

The solution of the system is $(2,0)$.

25. $\begin{cases} x - 2y = 2 \\ 3x + 2y = -2 \end{cases}$

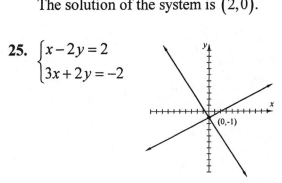

The solution of the system is $(0,-1)$.

27. $\begin{cases} y - 3x = -2 \\ 6x - 2y = 4 \end{cases}$

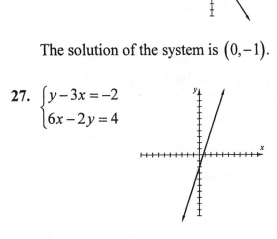

There are an infinite number of solutions.

29. $\begin{cases} x = 3 \\ y = -1 \end{cases}$

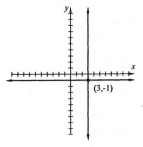

The solution of the system is $(3,-1)$.

31. $\begin{cases} y = x - 2 \\ y = 2x + 3 \end{cases}$

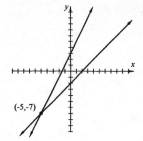

The solution of the system is $(-5,-7)$.

33. $\begin{cases} 2x - 3y = -2 \\ -3x + 5y = 5 \end{cases}$

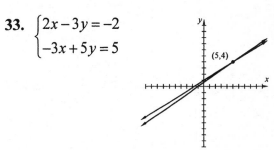

The solution of the system is $(5,4)$.

35. Possible answer

$\begin{cases} y = x + 5 \\ y = 4x + 8 \end{cases}$

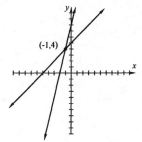

37. Possible answer

$\begin{cases} y = -x + 3 \\ y = -x - 2 \end{cases}$

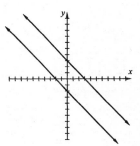

39. 1984, 1988

41. 1996

43.a. Each table includes the point $(4,9)$. Therefore $(4,9)$ is a solution of the system.

b.

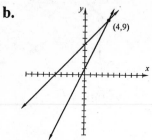

c. Yes

45. $-2x + 3(x+6) = 17$

$-2x + 3x + 18 = 17$

$x + 18 = 17$

$x = -1$

The solution is -1.

47. $-y + 12\left(\dfrac{y-1}{4}\right) = 3$

$-y + 3(y-1) = 3$

$-y + 3y - 3 = 3$

$2y - 3 = 3$

$2y = 6$

$y = 3$

The solution is 3.

49. $3z - (4z - 2) = 9$

$3z - 4z + 2 = 9$

$-z + 2 = 9$

$-z = 7$

$z = -7$

The solution is -7.

51. Answers may vary.
Possible answer

$$\begin{cases} 3x - 2y = -2 \\ 6x + 4y = 4 \end{cases}$$

53. Answers may vary.

Practice Problems 7.2

1. $\begin{cases} 2x + 3y = 13 \\ x = y + 4 \end{cases}$

Substitute $y + 4$ for x in the first equation.

$2(y+4) + 3y = 13$

$2y + 8 + 3y = 13$

$5y = 5$

$y = 1$

Let $y = 1$ in the second equation.

$x = 1 + 4$

$x = 5$

The solution is $(5,1)$.

2. $\begin{cases} 4x - y = 2 \\ y = 5x \end{cases}$

Substitute $5x$ for y in the first equation.

$4x - (5x) = 2$

$-x = 2$

$x = -2$

Let $x = -2$ in the second equation.

$y = 5(-2)$

$y = -10$

The solution is $(-2, -10)$.

3. $\begin{cases} 3x + y = 5 \\ 3x - 2y = -7 \end{cases}$

Solve the first equation for y.

$y = 5 - 3x$

Substitute $5 - 3x$ for y in the second equation.

$3x - 2(5 - 3x) = -7$

$3x - 10 + 6x = -7$

$9x = 3$

$x = \dfrac{1}{3}$

Let $x = \dfrac{1}{3}$ in $y = 5 - 3x$.

$y = 5 - 3\left(\dfrac{1}{3}\right)$

$y = 4$

The solution is $\left(\dfrac{1}{3}, 4\right)$.

4. $\begin{cases} 5x - 2y = 6 \\ -3x + y = -3 \end{cases}$

Solve the second equation for y.

$y = -3 + 3x$

Substitute $-3 + 3x$ for y in the first equation.

$5x - 2(-3 + 3x) = 6$

$5x + 6 - 6x = 6$

$-x = 0$

$x = 0$

Let $x = 0$ in $y = -3 + 3x$.

$y = -3 + 3(0)$

$y = -3$

The solution is $(0, -3)$.

5. $\begin{cases} -x + 3y = 6 \\ y = \dfrac{1}{3}x + 2 \end{cases}$

Substitute $\dfrac{1}{3}x + 2$ for y in the first equation.

$-x + 3\left(\dfrac{1}{3}x + 2\right) = 6$

$-x + x + 6 = 6$

$6 = 6$

The equations in the original system are equivalent and there are an infinite number of solutions.

6. $\begin{cases} 2x - 3y = 6 \\ -4x + 6y = -12 \end{cases}$

Solve the first equation for x.

$2x = 3y + 6$

$x = \dfrac{3}{2}y + 3$

Substitute $\dfrac{3}{2}y + 3$ for x in the second equation.

$-4\left(\dfrac{3}{2}y + 3\right) + 6y = -12$

$-6y - 12 + 6y = -12$

$-12 = -12$

The equations in the original system are equivalent and there are an infinite number of solutions..

Exercise Set 7.2

1. $\begin{cases} x+y=3 \\ x=2y \end{cases}$

Substitute $2y$ for x in the first equation.

$2y+y=3$

$\quad 3y=3$

$\qquad y=1$

Let $y=1$ in the second equation.

$x=2(1)$

$x=2$

The solution is $(2,1)$.

3. $\begin{cases} x+y=6 \\ y=-3x \end{cases}$

Substitute $-3x$ for y in the first equation.

$x+(-3x)=6$

$\quad -2x=6$

$\qquad x=-3$

Let $x=-3$ in the second equation.

$y=-3(-3)$

$y=9$

The solution is $(-3,9)$.

5. $\begin{cases} 3x+2y=16 \\ x=3y-2 \end{cases}$

Substitute $3y-2$ for x in the first equation.

$3(3y-2)+2y=16$

$\quad 9y-6+2y=16$

$\qquad 11y=22$

$\qquad\quad y=2$

Let $y=2$ in the second equation.

$x=3(2)-2$

$x=4$

The solution is $(4,2)$.

7. $\begin{cases} 3x-4y=10 \\ x=2y \end{cases}$

Substitute $2y$ for x in the first equation.

$3(2y)-4y=10$

$\quad 6y-4y=10$

$\qquad 2y=10$

$\qquad\; y=5$

Let $y=5$ in the second equation.

$x=2(5)$

$x=10$

The solution is $(10,5)$.

9. $\begin{cases} y=3x+1 \\ 4y-8x=12 \end{cases}$

Substitute $3x+1$ for y in the second equation.

$4(3x+1)-8x=12$

$\quad 12x+4-8x=12$

$\qquad 4x=8$

$\qquad\; x=2$

Let $x=2$ in the first equation.

$y=3(2)+1$

$y=7$

The solution is $(2,7)$.

11. $\begin{cases} y = 2x + 9 \\ y = 7x + 10 \end{cases}$

Substitute $2x + 9$ for y in the second equation.

$2x + 9 = 7x + 10$

$-5x = 1$

$x = -\dfrac{1}{5}$

Let $x = -\dfrac{1}{5}$ in the first equation.

$y = 2\left(-\dfrac{1}{5}\right) + 9$

$y = \dfrac{43}{5}$

The solution is $\left(-\dfrac{1}{5}, \dfrac{43}{5}\right)$.

13. $\begin{cases} x + 2y = 6 \\ 2x + 3y = 8 \end{cases}$

Solve the first equation for x.

$x = 6 - 2y$

Substitute $6 - 2y$ for x in the second equation.

$2(6 - 2y) + 3y = 8$

$12 - 4y + 3y = 8$

$-y = -4$

$y = 4$

Let $y = 4$ in $x = 6 - 2y$.

$x = 6 - 2(4)$

$y = -2$

The solution is $(-2, 4)$.

15. $\begin{cases} 2x - 5y = 1 \\ 3x + y = -7 \end{cases}$

Solve the second equation for y.

$y = -7 - 3x$

Substitute $-7 - 3x$ for y in the first equation.

$2x - 5(-7 - 3x) = 1$

$2x + 35 + 15x = 1$

$17x = -34$

$x = -2$

Let $x = -2$ in $y = -7 - 3x$.

$y = -7 - 3(-2)$

$y = -1$

The solution is $(-2, -1)$.

17. $\begin{cases} 2y = x + 2 \\ 6x - 12y = 0 \end{cases}$

Solve the first equation for x.

$x = 2y - 2$

Substitute $2y - 2$ for x in the second equation.

$6(2y - 2) - 12y = 0$

$12y - 12 - 12y = 0$

$-12 = 0$

The system has no solution.

19. $\begin{cases} 4x + y = 11 \\ 2x + 5y = 1 \end{cases}$

Solve the first equation for y.

$y = 11 - 4x$

Substitute $11 - 4x$ for y in the second equation.

$$2x + 5(11 - 4x) = 1$$
$$2x + 55 - 20x = 1$$
$$-18x = -54$$
$$x = 3$$

Let $x = 3$ in $y = 11 - 4x$.

$$y = 11 - 4(3)$$
$$y = -1$$

The solution is $(3, -1)$.

21. $\begin{cases} 2x - 3y = -9 \\ 3x = y + 4 \end{cases}$

Solve the second equation for y.

$$y = 3x - 4$$

Substitute $3x - 4$ for y in the first equation.

$$2x - 3(3x - 4) = -9$$
$$2x - 9x + 12 = -9$$
$$-7x = -21$$
$$x = 3$$

Let $x = 3$ in $y = 3x - 4$.

$$y = 3(3) - 4$$
$$y = 5$$

The solution is $(3, 5)$.

23. $\begin{cases} 6x - 3y = 5 \\ x + 2y = 0 \end{cases}$

Solve the second equation for x.

$$x = -2y$$

Substitute $-2y$ for x in the first equation.

$$6(-2y) - 3y = 5$$
$$-12y - 3y = 5$$

$$-15y = 5$$
$$y = -\frac{1}{3}$$

Let $y = -\frac{1}{3}$ in $x = -2y$.

$$x = -2\left(-\frac{1}{3}\right)$$
$$x = \frac{2}{3}$$

The solution is $\left(\frac{2}{3}, -\frac{1}{3}\right)$.

25. $\begin{cases} 3x - y = 1 \\ 2x - 3y = 10 \end{cases}$

Solve the first equation for y.

$$y = 3x - 1$$

Substitute $3x - 1$ for y in the second equation.

$$2x - 3(3x - 1) = 10$$
$$2x - 9x + 3 = 10$$
$$-7x = 7$$
$$x = -1$$

Let $x = -1$ in $y = 3x - 1$.

$$y = 3(-1) - 1$$
$$y = -4$$

The solution is $(-1, -4)$.

27. $\begin{cases} -x + 2y = 10 \\ -2x + 3y = 18 \end{cases}$

Solve the first equation for x.

$$x = 2y - 10$$

Substitute $2y - 10$ for x in the second equation.

$$-2(2y-10)+3y=18$$
$$-4y+20+3y=18$$
$$-y=-2$$
$$y=2$$

Let $y=2$ in $x=2y-10$.

$$x=2(2)-10$$
$$x=-6$$

The solution is $(-6,2)$.

29. $\begin{cases} 5x+10y=20 \\ 2x+6y=10 \end{cases}$

Solve the first equation for x.

$$x+2y=4$$
$$x=4-2y$$

Substitute $4-2y$ for x in the second equation.

$$2(4-2y)+6y=10$$
$$8-4y+6y=10$$
$$2y=2$$
$$y=1$$

Let $y=1$ in $x=4-2y$.

$$x=4-2(1)$$
$$x=2$$

The solution is $(2,1)$.

31. $\begin{cases} 3x+6y=9 \\ 4x+8y=16 \end{cases}$

Solve the first equation for x.

$$x+2y=3$$
$$x=3-2y$$

Substitute $3-2y$ for x in the second equation.

$$4(3-2y)+8y=16$$
$$12-8y+8y=16$$
$$12=16$$

The system has no solution.

33. $\begin{cases} \dfrac{1}{3}x-y=2 \\ x-3y=6 \end{cases}$

Solve the second equation for x.

$$x=6+3y$$

Substitute $6+3y$ for x in the first equation.

$$\frac{1}{3}(6+3y)-y=2$$
$$2+y-y=2$$
$$2=2$$

The equations in the original system are equivalent and there are an infinite number of solutions.

35. Answers may vary.

37.
$$3x+2y=6$$
$$-2(3x+2y)=-2(6)$$
$$-6x-4y=-12$$

39.
$$-4x+y=3$$
$$3(-4x+y)=3(3)$$
$$-12x+3y=9$$

41. $3n+6m$

$\underline{2n-6m}$

$5n$

43.

$$-5a - 7b$$
$$\underline{5a - 8b}$$
$$-15b$$

45.

$$
\begin{cases}
\begin{aligned}
-5y + 6y &= 3x + 2(x-5) - 3x + 5 \\
y &= 3x + 2x - 10 - 3x + 5 \\
y &= 2x - 5
\end{aligned} \\
\\
\begin{aligned}
4(x+y) - x + y &= -12 \\
4x + 4y - x + y &= -12 \\
3x + 5y &= -12
\end{aligned}
\end{cases}
$$

Substitute $2x - 5$ for y in the second equation.

$$3x + 5(2x - 5) = -12$$
$$3x + 10x - 25 = -12$$
$$13x = 13$$
$$x = 1$$

Let $x = 1$ in $y = 2x - 5$.

$$y = 2(1) - 5$$
$$y = -3$$

The solution is $(1, -3)$.

47.

$$
\begin{cases}
y = 5.1x + 14.56 \\
y = -2x - 3.9
\end{cases}
$$

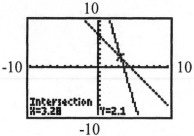

The solution of the system is $(-2.6, 1.3)$.

49.

$$
\begin{cases}
3x + 2y = 14.04 \\
5x + y = 18.5
\end{cases}
$$

$$y_1 = -\frac{3}{2}x + 7.02 \quad \text{and} \quad y_2 = -5x + 18.5$$

The solution of the system is $(3.28, 2.1)$.

51.a.

$$
\begin{cases}
y = -0.52x + 24.89 \\
y = 0.76x + 8.97
\end{cases}
$$

Substitute $0.76x + 8.97$ for y in the first equation.

$$0.76x + 8.97 = -0.52x + 24.89$$
$$1.28x = 15.92$$
$$x = 12.4375$$

Let $x = 12.4375$ in $y = 0.76x + 8.97$

$$y = 0.76(12.4375) + 8.97$$
$$y = 18.4225$$

The solution is $(12, 18)$.

b. In $1970 + 12 = 1982$, 18% of the households used electricity and 18% of the households used fuel oil to heat their homes.

c.

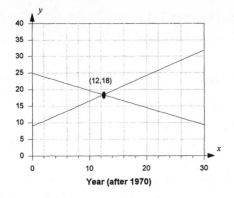

Year (after 1970)

Between 1970 and 1999 the percentage
use of fuel oil for heating decreased
and the percentage use of electricity
for heating increased.

Practice Problems 7.3

1. $\begin{cases} x+y=13 \\ x-y=5 \end{cases}$

$x+y=13$

$\underline{x-y=5}$

$2x=18$

$x=9$

Let $x = 9$ in the first equation.

$9+y=13$

$y=4$

The solution of the system is $(9,4)$

2. $\begin{cases} 2x-y=-6 \\ -x+4y=17 \end{cases}$

Multiply the second equation by 2.

$2x-y=-6$

$\underline{-2x+8y=34}$

$7y=28$

$y=4$

Let $y = 4$ in the second equation.

$-x+4(4)=17$

$-x+16=17$

$-x=1$

$x=-1$

The solution of the system is $(-1,4)$.

3. $\begin{cases} x-3y=-2 \\ -3x+9y=5 \end{cases}$

Multiply the first equation by 3.

$3x-9y=-6$

$\underline{-3x+9y=5}$

$0=-1$

The system has no solution.

4. $\begin{cases} 2x+5y=1 \\ -4x-10y=-2 \end{cases}$

Multiply the first equation by 2.

$4x+10y=2$

$\underline{-4x-10y=-2}$

$0=0$

The equations in the original system
are equivalent and there are an infinite
number of solutions..

5. $\begin{cases} 4x+5y=14 \\ 3x-2y=-1 \end{cases}$

Multiply the first equation by 2 and
the second equation by 5.

$8x+10y=28$

$\underline{15x-10y=-5}$

$23x=23$

$x=1$

Let $x = 1$ in the first equation.

$$4(1) + 5y = 14$$
$$4 + 5y = 14$$
$$5y = 10$$
$$y = 2$$

The solution of the system is $(1, 2)$.

6. $\begin{cases} -\dfrac{x}{3} + y = \dfrac{4}{3} \\ \dfrac{x}{2} - \dfrac{5}{2}y = -\dfrac{1}{2} \end{cases}$

Multiply the first equation by 3 and the second equation by 2.

$$-x + 3y = 4$$
$$\underline{x - 5y = -1}$$
$$-2y = 3$$
$$y = -\dfrac{3}{2}$$

Let $y = -\dfrac{3}{2}$ in the first equation.

$$-\dfrac{x}{3} + \left(-\dfrac{3}{2}\right) = \dfrac{4}{3}$$
$$6\left(-\dfrac{x}{3}\right) + 6\left(-\dfrac{3}{2}\right) = 6\left(\dfrac{4}{3}\right)$$
$$-2x - 9 = 8$$
$$-2x = 17$$
$$x = -\dfrac{17}{2}$$

The solution of the system is $\left(-\dfrac{17}{2}, -\dfrac{3}{2}\right)$.

Exercise Set 7.3

1. $\begin{cases} 3x + y = 5 \\ 6x - y = 4 \end{cases}$

$$3x + y = 5$$
$$\underline{6x - y = 4}$$
$$9x \quad = 9$$
$$x \quad = 1$$

Let $x = 1$ in the first equation.

$$3(1) + y = 5$$
$$3 + y = 5$$
$$y = 2$$

The solution of the system is $(1, 2)$

3. $\begin{cases} x - 2y = 8 \\ -x + 5y = -17 \end{cases}$

$$x - 2y = \quad 8$$
$$\underline{-x + 5y = -17}$$
$$3y = -9$$
$$y = -3$$

Let $y = -3$ in the first equation.

$$x - 2(-3) = 8$$
$$x + 6 = 8$$
$$x = 2$$

The solution of the system is $(2, -3)$.

5. $\begin{cases} 3x + 2y = 11 \\ 5x - 2y = 29 \end{cases}$

$$3x + \quad y = 11$$
$$\underline{5x - 2y = 29}$$
$$8x \quad = 40$$
$$x \quad = 5$$

Let $x = 5$ in the first equation.

$3(5) + 2y = 11$

$15 + 2y = 11$

$2y = -4$

$y = -2$

The solution of the system is $(5, -2)$

7. $\begin{cases} x + y = 6 \\ x - y = 6 \end{cases}$

$x + y = 6$

$\underline{x - y = 6}$

$2x \quad = 12$

$x \quad = 6$

Let $x = 6$ in the first equation.

$6 + y = 6$

$y = 0$

The solution of the system is $(6, 0)$

9. $\begin{cases} 3x + y = -11 \\ 6x - 2y = -2 \end{cases}$

Multiply the first equation by 2.

$6x + 2y = -22$

$\underline{6x - 2y = -2}$

$12x \quad = -24$

$x \quad = -2$

Let $x = -2$ in the first equation.

$3(-2) + y = -11$

$-6 + y = -11$

$y = -5$

The solution of the system is $(-2, -5)$.

11. $\begin{cases} x + 5y = 18 \\ 3x + 2y = -11 \end{cases}$

Multiply the first equation by -3.

$-3x - 15y = -54$

$\underline{3x + 2y = -11}$

$-13y = -65$

$y = 5$

Let $y = 5$ in the first equation.

$x + 5(5) = 18$

$x + 25 = 18$

$x = -7$

The solution of the system is $(-7, 5)$.

13. $\begin{cases} 2x - 5y = 4 \\ 3x - 2y = 4 \end{cases}$

Multiply the first equation by -3 and the second equation by 2.

$-6x + 15y = -12$

$\underline{6x - 4y = \quad 8}$

$11y = -4$

$y = -\dfrac{4}{11}$

Let $y = -\dfrac{4}{11}$ in the first equation.

$2x - 5\left(-\dfrac{4}{11}\right) = 4$

$2x + \dfrac{20}{11} = 4$

$$11(2x)+11\left(\frac{20}{11}\right)=11(4)$$

$$22x+20=44$$

$$22x=24$$

$$x=\frac{12}{11}$$

The solution of the system is $\left(\frac{12}{11},-\frac{4}{11}\right)$.

Let $x=2$ in the first equation.

$$3(2)-2y=7$$

$$6-2y=7$$

$$-2y=1$$

$$y=-\frac{1}{2}$$

The solution of the system is $\left(2,-\frac{1}{2}\right)$.

15. $\begin{cases} 2x+3y=0 \\ 4x+6y=3 \end{cases}$

Multiply the first equation by -2.

$$-4x-6y=0$$

$$\underline{4x+6y=3}$$

$$0=3$$

The system has no solution.

17. $\begin{cases} 3x+y=4 \\ 9x+3y=6 \end{cases}$

Multiply the first equation by -3.

$$-9x-3y=-12$$

$$\underline{9x+3y=\quad 6}$$

$$0=-6$$

The system has no solution.

19. $\begin{cases} 3x-2y=7 \\ 5x+4y=8 \end{cases}$

Multiply the first equation by 2.

$$6x-4y=14$$

$$\underline{5x+4y=8}$$

$$11x\quad\ \ =22$$

$$x\quad\ \ =2$$

21. $\begin{cases} \dfrac{2}{3}x+4y=-4 \\ 5x+6y=18 \end{cases}$

Multiply the first equation by 3 and the second equation by -2.

$$2x+12y=-12$$

$$\underline{-10x-12y=\ \ 36}$$

$$-8x\qquad\quad =-48$$

$$x\qquad\quad =6$$

Let $x=6$ in the first equation.

$$\frac{2}{3}(6)+4y=-4$$

$$4+4y=-4$$

$$4y=-8$$

$$y=-2$$

The solution of the system is $(6,-2)$.

23. $\begin{cases} 4x-6y=8 \\ 6x-9y=12 \end{cases}$

Multiply the first equation by 3 and the second equation by -2.

$$12x-18y=24$$

$$\underline{-12x+18y=\ \ 24}$$

$$0=0$$

The equations in the original system are equivalent and there are an infinite number of solutions..

25. $\begin{cases} 8x = -11y - 16 \\ 8x + 11y = -16 \\ \\ 2x + 3y = -4 \end{cases}$

Multiply the second equation by -4.

$8x + 11y = -16$
$\underline{-8x - 12y = 16}$
$-y = 0$
$y = 0$

Let $y = 0$ in the second equation.

$2x + 3(0) = -4$
$2x = -4$
$x = -2$

The solution of the system is $(-2, 0)$.

27. Answers may vary.

29. $\begin{cases} \dfrac{x}{3} + \dfrac{y}{6} = 1 \\ \dfrac{x}{2} - \dfrac{y}{5} = 0 \end{cases}$

Multiply the first equation by 6 and the second equation by 4.

$\begin{cases} 2x + y = 6 \\ 2x - y = 0 \end{cases}$ Simplified system

$4x = 6$
$x = \dfrac{3}{2}$

Multiply the second equation of the simplified system by -1.

$\begin{cases} 2x + y = 6 \\ \underline{-2x + y = 0} \end{cases}$

$2y = 6$
$y = 3$

The solution of the system is $\left(\dfrac{3}{2}, 3 \right)$.

31. $\begin{cases} x - \dfrac{y}{3} = -1 \\ -\dfrac{x}{2} + \dfrac{y}{8} = \dfrac{1}{4} \end{cases}$

Multiply the first equation by 3 and the second equation by 8.

$\begin{cases} 3x - y = -3 \\ \underline{-4x + y = 2} \end{cases}$ Simplified system

$-x = -1$
$x = 1$

Multiply the first equation of the simplified system by 4 and the second equation by 3.

$\begin{cases} 12x - 4y = -12 \\ \underline{-12x + 3y = 6} \end{cases}$

$-y = -6$
$y = 6$

The solution of the system is $(1, 6)$.

33. $\begin{cases} \dfrac{x}{3} - y = 2 \\ -\dfrac{x}{2} + \dfrac{3y}{2} = -3 \end{cases}$

Multiply the first equation by 3 and the second equation by 2.

$\begin{cases} x - 3y = 6 \\ \underline{-x + 3y = -6} \end{cases}$ Simplified system

$$0 = 0$$

The equations in the original system are equivalent and there are an infinite number of solutions..

35. $\begin{cases} \dfrac{3}{5}x - y = -\dfrac{4}{5} \\ 3x + \dfrac{y}{2} = -\dfrac{9}{5} \end{cases}$

Multiply the first equation by 5 and the second equation by 10.

$\begin{cases} 3x - 5y = -4 \\ \underline{30x + 5y = -18} \end{cases}$ Simplified system

$$33x = -22$$

$$x = -\dfrac{2}{3}$$

Multiply the first equation of the simplified system by -10.

$\begin{cases} -30x + 50y = 40 \\ \underline{30x + 5y = -18} \end{cases}$

$$55y = 22$$

$$y = \dfrac{2}{5}$$

The solution of the system is $\left(-\dfrac{2}{3}, \dfrac{2}{5}\right)$.

37. $\begin{cases} 3.5x + 2.5y = 17 \\ -1.5x - 7.5y = -33 \end{cases}$

Multiply the first equation by 3.

$\begin{cases} 10.5x + 7.5y = 51 \\ \underline{-1.5x - 7.5y = -33} \end{cases}$ Simplified system

$$9x = 18$$

$$x = 2$$

Multiply the second equation of the simplified system by 7.

$\begin{cases} 10.5x + 7.5y = 51 \\ \underline{-10.5x - 52.5y = -231} \end{cases}$

$$-45y = -180$$

$$y = 4$$

The solution of the system is $(2, 4)$.

39. $\begin{cases} 0.02x + 0.04y = 0.09 \\ -0.1x + 0.3y = 0.8 \end{cases}$

Multiply the first equation by 100 and the second equation by 20.

$\begin{cases} 2x + 4y = 9 \\ \underline{-2x + 6y = 16} \end{cases}$ Simplified system

$$10y = 25$$

$$y = 2.5$$

Multiply the first equation of the simplified system by 3 and the second equation by -2.

$\begin{cases} 6x + 12y = 27 \\ \underline{4x - 12y = -32} \end{cases}$

$$10x = -5$$

$$x = -0.5$$

The solution of the system is $(-0.5, 2.5)$.

41. Let x = a number.

$2x + 6 = x - 3$

43. Let x = a number.

$20 - 3x = 2$

45. Let x = a number.

$4(x + 6) = 2x$

47. $\begin{cases} x + y = 5 \\ 3x + 3y = b \end{cases}$

Multiply the first equation by -3.

$\begin{aligned} -3x - 3y &= -15 \\ \underline{3x + 3y = \quad b} \\ 0 &= b - 15 \end{aligned}$

a. The system has an infinite number of solutions if this statement is true. $b = 15$

b. The system has no solution if this statement is false. b = any real number except 15.

49. $\begin{cases} 2x + 3y = 14 \\ 3x - 4y = -69.1 \end{cases}$

Multiply the first equation by 3 and the second equation by -2.

$\begin{aligned} 6x + 9y &= \quad 42 \\ \underline{-6x + 8y = 138.2} \\ 17y &= 180.2 \\ y &= 10.6 \end{aligned}$

Let $y = 10.6$ in the first equation.

$\begin{aligned} 2x + 3(10.6) &= 14 \\ 2x + 31.8 &= 14 \\ 2x &= -17.8 \\ x &= -8.9 \end{aligned}$

The solution of the system is $(-8.9, 10.6)$.

51. b. $4x - 8y = 6$

Answers may vary.

53.a. $\begin{cases} -19x + 10y = 5428 \\ 70x - 5y = -2520 \end{cases}$

Multiply the second equation by 2.

$\begin{aligned} -19x + 10y &= \quad 5428 \\ \underline{140x - 10y = -5040} \\ 121x \qquad &= 388 \\ x \qquad &\approx 3.2 \end{aligned}$

Let $x = 3.2$ in the first equation.

$\begin{aligned} -19(3.2) + 10y &= 5428 \\ -60.8 + 10y &= 5428 \\ 10y &= 5488.8 \\ y &\approx 548.88 \end{aligned}$

The solution of the system is $(3, 549)$.

b. Answers may vary

c. Since there were more VHF stations in 1988 (543 compared to 504 UHF), and they were equal 3 years later, then from $1988 + 4 = 1992$ to 2000 there were more UHF stations.

Integrated Review 7.3

1. $\begin{cases} 2x - 3y = -11 \\ y = 4x - 3 \end{cases}$

Substitute $4x - 3$ for y in the first equation.

$2x - 3(4x - 3) = -11$

$2x - 12x + 9 = -11$

$-10x = -20$

$x = 2$

Let $x = 2$ in the second equation.

$y = 4(2) - 3$

$y = 5$

The solution is $(2, 5)$.

2. $\begin{cases} 4x - 5y = 6 \\ y = 3x - 10 \end{cases}$

Substitute $3x - 10$ for y in the first equation.

$4x - 5(3x - 10) = 6$

$4x - 15x + 50 = 6$

$-11x = -44$

$x = 4$

Let $x = 4$ in the second equation.

$y = 3(4) - 10$

$y = 2$

The solution is $(4, 2)$.

3. $\begin{cases} x + y = 3 \\ x - y = 7 \end{cases}$

$\begin{array}{rl} 2x & = 10 \\ x & = 5 \end{array}$

Let $x = 5$ in the first equation.

$5 + y = 3$

$y = -2$

The solution of the system is $(5, -2)$

4. $\begin{cases} x - y = 20 \\ x + y = -8 \end{cases}$

$\begin{array}{rl} 2x & = 12 \\ x & = 6 \end{array}$

Let $x = 6$ in the second equation.

$6 + y = -8$

$y = -14$

The solution of the system is $(6, -14)$

5. $\begin{cases} x + 2y = 1 \\ 3x + 4y = -1 \end{cases}$

Solve the first equation for x.

$x = 1 - 2y$

Substitute $1 - 2y$ for x in the second equation.

$3(1 - 2y) + 4y = -1$

$3 - 6y + 4y = -1$

$-2y = -4$

$y = 2$

Let $y = 2$ in $x = 1 - 2y$.

$x = 1 - 2(2)$

$x = -3$

The solution is $(-3, 2)$.

6. $\begin{cases} x+3y=5 \\ 5x+6y=-2 \end{cases}$

Solve the first equation for x.

$x = 5-3y$

Substitute $5-3y$ for x in the second equation.

$5(5-3y)+6y=-2$

$25-15y+6y=-2$

$-9y=-27$

$y=3$

Let $y=3$ in $x=5-3y$.

$x=5-3(3)$

$x=-4$

The solution is $(-4,3)$.

7. $\begin{cases} y=x+3 \\ 3x-2y=-6 \end{cases}$

Substitute $x+3$ for y in the second equation.

$3x-2(x+3)=-6$

$3x-2x-6=-6$

$x=0$

Let $x=0$ in the first equation.

$y=0+3$

$y=3$

The solution is $(0,3)$.

8. $\begin{cases} y=-2x \\ 2x-3y=-16 \end{cases}$

Substitute $-2x$ for y in the second equation.

$2x-3(-2x)=-16.$

$2x+6x=-16$

$8x=-16$

$x=-2$

Let $x=-2$ in the first equation.

$y=-2(-2)$

$y=4$

The solution is $(-2,4)$.

9. $\begin{cases} y=2x-3 \\ y=5x-18 \end{cases}$

Substitute $5x-18$ for y in the first equation.

$5x-18=2x-3$

$3x=15$

$x=5$

Let $x=5$ in the second equation.

$y=5(5)-18$

$y=7$

The solution is $(5,7)$.

10. $\begin{cases} y=6x-5 \\ y=4x-11 \end{cases}$

Substitute $6x-5$ for y in the second equation.

$6x-5=4x-11$

$2x=-6$

$x=-3$

Let $x=-3$ in the first equation.

$y=6(-3)-5$

$y=-23$

The solution is $(-3,-23)$.

11. $\begin{cases} x + \dfrac{1}{6}y = \dfrac{1}{2} \\ 3x + 2y = 3 \end{cases}$

Multiply the first equation by 6.

$\begin{cases} 6x + y = 3 \\ 3x + 2y = 3 \end{cases}$ Simplified system

Multiply the first equation of the simplified system by -2.

$\begin{cases} -12x - 2y = -6 \\ \underline{3x + 2y = 3} \end{cases}$

$\begin{array}{ll} -9x & = -3 \\ x & = \dfrac{1}{3} \end{array}$

Multiply the second equation of the simplified system by -2.

$\begin{cases} 6x + y = 3 \\ \underline{-6x - 4y = -6} \end{cases}$

$\begin{array}{l} -3y = -3 \\ y = 1 \end{array}$

The solution of the system is $\left(\dfrac{1}{3}, 1 \right)$.

12. $\begin{cases} x + \dfrac{1}{3}y = \dfrac{5}{12} \\ 8x + 3y = 4 \end{cases}$

Multiply the first equation by 12.

$\begin{cases} 12x + 4y = 5 \\ 8x + 3y = 4 \end{cases}$ Simplified system

Multiply the first equation of the simplified system by 2 and the second equation by -3.

$\begin{cases} 24x + 8y = 10 \\ \underline{-24x - 9y = -12} \end{cases}$

$\begin{array}{l} -y = -2 \\ y = 2 \end{array}$

Multiply the first equation of the simplified system by 3 and the second equation by 4.

$\begin{cases} 36x + 12y = 15 \\ \underline{-32x - 12y = -16} \end{cases}$

$\begin{array}{ll} 4x & = -1 \\ x & = -\dfrac{1}{4} \end{array}$

The solution of the system is $\left(-\dfrac{1}{4}, 2 \right)$.

13. $\begin{cases} x - 5y = 1 \\ -2x + 10y = 3 \end{cases}$

Multiply the first equation by 2.

$\begin{array}{l} 2x - 10y = 2 \\ \underline{-2x + 10y = 3} \\ 0 = 5 \end{array}$

The system has no solution.

14. $\begin{cases} -x + 2y = 3 \\ 3x - 6y = -9 \end{cases}$

Multiply the first equation by 3.

$\begin{array}{l} -3x + 6y = 9 \\ \underline{3x - 6y = -9} \\ 0 = 0 \end{array}$

The equations in the original system are equivalent and there are an infinite number of solutions..

15. $\begin{cases} 0.2x - 0.3y = -0.95 \\ 0.4x + 0.1y = 0.55 \end{cases}$

Multiply both equations by 10.

$\begin{cases} 2x - 3y = -9.5 \\ 4x + y = 5.5 \end{cases}$ Simplified system

Multiply the first equation of the simplified system by -2.

$\begin{cases} -4x + 6y = 19 \\ \underline{4x + \ y = 5.5} \end{cases}$

$\qquad 7y = 24.5$

$\qquad\quad y = 3.5$

Multiply the second equation of the simplified system by 3.

$\begin{cases} \ 2x - 3y = -9.5 \\ 12x + 3y = 16.5 \end{cases}$

$\quad 14x \quad\ = 7$

$\qquad x \quad\ = 0.5$

The solution of the system is $(0.5, 3.5)$.

16. $\begin{cases} 0.08x - 0.04y = -0.11 \\ 0.02x - 0.06y = -0.09 \end{cases}$

Multiply both equations by 100.

$\begin{cases} 8x - 4y = -11 \\ 2x - 6y = -9 \end{cases}$ Simplified system

Multiply the second equation of the simplified system by -4.

$\begin{cases} \ 8x - \ 4y = -11 \\ -8x + 24y = \ 36 \end{cases}$

$\qquad 20y = 25$

$\qquad\quad y = 1.25$

Multiply the first equation of the simplified system by -3 and the second equation by 2.

$\begin{cases} -24x + 12y = \ 33 \\ \underline{\ \ 4x - 12y = -18} \end{cases}$

$-20x \qquad = 15$

$\quad x \qquad\ = -0.75$

The solution of the system is $(-0.75, 1.25)$.

17. $\begin{cases} x = 3y - 7 \\ 2x - 6y = -14 \end{cases}$

Substitute $3y - 7$ for x in the second equation.

$$2(3y - 7) - 6y = -14$$
$$6y - 14 - 6y = -14$$
$$0 = 0$$

The equations in the original system are equivalent and there are an infinite number of solutions..

18. $\begin{cases} y = \dfrac{x}{2} - 3 \\ 2x - 4y = 0 \end{cases}$

Substitute $\dfrac{x}{2} - 3$ for y in the second equation.

$$2x - 4\left(\frac{x}{2} - 3\right) = 0$$
$$2x - 2x + 12 = 0$$
$$12 = 0$$

There is no solution.

19. Answers may vary.

20. Answers may vary.

Practice Problems 7.4

1. Let x = the first number and
y = the second number.
$$\begin{cases} x+y=50 \\ x-y=22 \end{cases}$$
$$2x \quad = 72$$
$$x \quad = 36$$
Let $x=36$ in the first equation.
$$36+y=50$$
$$y=14$$
The numbers are 36 and 14.

2. Let C = the number of children and
A = the number of adults.
$$\begin{cases} 5C+7A=3379 \\ C+A=587 \end{cases}$$
Solve the second equation for A.
$$A=587-C$$
Substitute $587-C$ for A in the
first equation.
$$5C+7(587-C)=3379$$
$$5C+4109-7C=3379$$
$$-2C=-730$$
$$C=365$$
Let $C=365$ in $A=587-C$.
$$A=587-365$$
$$A=222$$
There were 365 children and 222 adults.

3. Let x = the speed of the faster car and
y = the speed of the slower car.

	r	$\cdot$	t	$=$	d
Faster car	x		3		$3x$
Slower car	y		3		$3y$

$$\begin{cases} x=y+10 \\ 3x+3y=440 \end{cases}$$
Substitute $y+10$ for x in the
second equation.
$$3(y+10)+3y=440$$
$$3y+30+3y=440$$
$$6y=410$$
$$y=\frac{410}{6}=68\frac{1}{3}$$
Let $y=68\frac{1}{3}$ in the first equation.
$$x=68\frac{1}{3}+10=78\frac{1}{3}$$
The speed of the faster car is $68\frac{1}{3}$ mph.

The speed of the slower car is $78\frac{1}{3}$ mph.

4. Let x = liters of 20% solution and
y = liters of 70% solution.

	Concentration Rate	Liters of Solution	Liters of Pure Alcohol
First solution	20%	x	$0.2x$
Second solution	70%	y	$0.7y$
Mixture	60%	50	$0.6(50)$

$$\begin{cases} x + y = 50 \\ 0.2x + 0.7y = 0.6(50) \end{cases}$$

Multiply the first equation by -2 and the second equation by 10.

$$-2x - 2y = -100$$
$$\underline{2x + 7y = 300}$$
$$5y = 200$$
$$y = 40$$

Let $y = 40$ in the first equation.

$$x + 40 = 50$$
$$x = 10$$

10 liters of 20% solution and 40 liters of 70% solution.

Mental Math 7.4

1. c

2. b

3. b

4. c

5. a

6. c

Exercise Set 7.4

1. Let $x =$ the first number and $y =$ the second number.
$$\begin{cases} x + y = 15 \\ x - y = 7 \end{cases}$$

3. Let $x =$ the amount invested in the larger account and $y =$ the amount invested in the smaller account.
$$\begin{cases} x + y = 6500 \\ x = y + 800 \end{cases}$$

5. Let $x =$ the first number and $y =$ the second number.
$$\begin{cases} x + y = 83 \\ x - y = 17 \end{cases}$$
$$2x = 100$$
$$x = 50$$

Let $x = 50$ in the first equation.
$$50 + y = 83$$
$$y = 33$$

The numbers are 50 and 33.

7. Let $x =$ the first number and $y =$ the second number.
$$\begin{cases} x + 2y = 8 \\ 2x + y = 25 \end{cases}$$

Multiply the first equation by -2.
$$-2x - 4y = -16$$
$$\underline{2x + y = 25}$$
$$-3y = 9$$
$$y = -3$$

Let $y = -3$ in the first equation.
$$x + 2(-3) = 8$$
$$x - 6 = 8$$
$$x = 14$$

The numbers are 14 and -3.

9. Let x = points scored by Swoopes and y = points scored by Smith.

$$\begin{cases} x + y = 1289 \\ y = x + 3 \end{cases}$$

Substitute $x + 3$ for y in the first equation.

$$x + (x + 3) = 1289$$
$$x + x + 3 = 1289$$
$$2x = 1286$$
$$x = 643$$

Let $x = 643$ in the second equation.

$$y = 643 + 3$$
$$y = 646$$

Swoopes scored 643 points and Smith scored 646 points.

11. Let x = the price of an adult's ticket and y = the price of a child's ticket.

$$\begin{cases} 3x + 4y = 159 \\ 2x + 3y = 112 \end{cases}$$

Multiply the first equation by -2 and the second equation by 3.

$$\begin{array}{r} -6x - 8y = -318 \\ 6x + 9y = 336 \\ \hline y = 18 \end{array}$$

Let $y = 18$ in the first equation.

$$3x + 4(18) = 159$$
$$3x + 72 = 159$$
$$3x = 87$$
$$x = 29$$

An adult's ticket is \$29 and a child's ticket is \$18.

13. Let x = the number of quarters and y = the number of nickles.

$$\begin{cases} x + y = 80 \\ 0.25x + 0.05y = 14.6 \end{cases}$$

Solve the first equation for y.

$$y = 80 - x$$

Substitute $80 - x$ for y in the second equation.

$$0.25x + 0.05(80 - x) = 14.6$$
$$0.25x + 4 - 0.05x = 14.6$$
$$0.20x = 10.6$$
$$x = 53$$

Let $x = 53$ in $y = 80 - x$.

$$y = 80 - 53$$
$$y = 27$$

There are 53 quarters and 27 nickles.

15. Let x = price of Ohio Art stock and y = price of General Electric stock.

$$\begin{cases} 55x + 30y = 2348.10 \\ y = x + 35.77 \end{cases}$$

Substitute $x + 35.77$ for y in the first equation.

$$55x + 30(x + 35.77) = 2348.10$$
$$55x + 30x + 1073.10 = 2348.10$$
$$85x = 1275$$
$$x = 15$$

Let $x = 15$ in the second equation.

$$y = 15 + 35.77$$
$$y = 50.77$$

Ohio Art was \$15 and General Electric was \$50.77

17. Let x = the cost per hour of labor and y = the cost per ton of material.

$$\begin{cases} 65x + 3y = 1702.50 \\ 49x + \dfrac{5}{2}y = 1349 \end{cases}$$

Multiply the second equation by 2.

$$\begin{cases} 65x + 3y = 1702.50 \\ 98x + 5y = 2698 \end{cases} \quad \text{Simplified system}$$

Multiply the first equation of the simplified system by 5 and the second equation by -3.

$$325x + 15y = 8512.5$$
$$-294x - 15y = -8094$$
$$\overline{31x = 418.5}$$
$$x = 13.5$$

Let $x = 13.5$ in the first equation.

$$65(13.5) + 3y = 1702.5$$
$$877.5 + 3y = 1702.5$$
$$3y = 825$$
$$y = 275$$

Labor costs $13.50 per hour and material costs $275 per ton.

19.

	d	$=$	r	$\cdot$	t
Downstream	18		$x+y$		2
Upstream	18		$x-y$		$4\frac{1}{2}$

$$\begin{cases} 2(x+y) = 18 \\ \dfrac{9}{2}(x-y) = 18 \end{cases}$$

Multiply the first equation by $\dfrac{1}{2}$ and the second equation by $\dfrac{2}{9}$.

$$\begin{cases} x + y = 9 \\ x - y = 4 \end{cases} \quad \text{Simplified system}$$

$$2x = 13$$
$$x = 6.5$$

Multiply the second equation of the simplified system by -1.

$$\begin{cases} x + y = 9 \\ -x + y = -4 \end{cases}$$
$$\overline{2y = 5}$$
$$y = 2.5$$

Pratap can row 6.5 mph in still water. The rate of the current is 2.5 mph.

21.

	d	$=$	r	$\cdot$	t
With the wind	780		$x+y$		$1\frac{1}{2}$
Into the wind	780		$x-y$		2

$$\begin{cases} \dfrac{3}{2}(x+y) = 780 \\ 2(x-y) = 780 \end{cases}$$

Multiply the first equation by $\dfrac{2}{3}$ and the second equation by $\dfrac{1}{2}$.

$$\begin{cases} x + y = 520 \\ x - y = 390 \end{cases} \quad \text{Simplified system}$$

$$2x = 910$$
$$x = 455$$

Multiply the second equation of the simplified system by -1.

$$\begin{cases} x + y = 520 \\ -x + y = -390 \end{cases}$$

$$2y = 130$$
$$y = 65$$

The plane can fly 455 mph in still air. The speed of the wind is 65 mph.

23. Let $x =$ the time spent walking and $y =$ the time spent on the bicycle.

	r	$\cdot$ t	$=$ d
Walking	4	x	$4x$
Biking	40	y	$40y$

$$\begin{cases} x + y = 6 \\ 4x + 40y = 186 \end{cases}$$

Multiply the first equation by -4.

$$-4x - 4y = -24$$
$$4x + 40y = 186$$

$$36y = 162$$
$$y = 4.5$$

He spent $4\frac{1}{2}$ hours on the bicycle.

25. Let $x =$ liters of 4% solution and $y =$ liters of 12% solution.

	Concentration Rate	Ounces of Solution	Ounces of Pure Acid
First solution	0.04	x	$0.04x$
Second solution	0.12	y	$0.12y$
Mixture	0.09	12	$0.09(12)$

$$\begin{cases} x + y = 12 \\ 0.04x + 0.12y = 0.09(12) \end{cases}$$

Multiply the first equation by -4 and the second equation by 100.

$$-4x - 4y = -48$$
$$4x + 12y = 108$$

$$8y = 60$$
$$y = 7.5$$

Let $y = 7.5$ in the first equation.

$$x + 7.5 = 12$$
$$x = 4.5$$

$4\frac{1}{2}$ ounces of 4% solution and

$7\frac{1}{2}$ ounces of 12% solution.

27. Let $x =$ pounds of $4.95 per pound beans and $y =$ pounds of $2.65 per pound beans.

	Cost Rate	Pounds of Beans	Dollars Cost
High Quality	4.95	x	$4.95x$
Low Quality	2.65	y	$2.65y$
Mixture	3.95	200	$3.95(200)$

$$\begin{cases} x + y = 200 \\ 4.95x + 2.65y = 3.95(200) \end{cases}$$

Solve the first equation for y.

$$y = 200 - x$$

Substitute $200 - x$ for y in the second equation.

$$4.95x + 2.65(200 - x) = 3.95(200)$$
$$4.95x + 530 - 2.65x = 790$$
$$2.30x = 260$$
$$x = 113.04$$

Let $x = 113.04$ in the first equation.

$113.04 + y = 200$

$y = 86.96$

He needs 113 pounds of $4.95 per pound beans and 87 pounds of $2.65 per pound beans.

29. Let $x =$ the first angle and $y =$ the second angle.

$$\begin{cases} x + y = 90 \\ x = 2y \end{cases}$$

Substitute $2y$ for x in the first equation.

$2y + y = 90$

$3y = 90$

$y = 30$

Let $y = 30$ in the second equation.

$x = 2(30)$

$x = 60$

The angles are 60° and 30°.

31. Let $x =$ the first angle and $y =$ the second angle.

$$\begin{cases} x + y = 90 \\ x = 3y + 10 \end{cases}$$

Substitute $3y + 10$ for x in the first equation.

$3y + 10 + y = 90$

$4y = 80$

$y = 20$

Let $y = 20$ in the second equation.

$x = 3(20) + 10$

$x = 70$

The angles are 70° and 20°.

33. Let $x =$ the number sold at $9.50 and $y =$ the number sold at $7.50.

$$\begin{cases} x + y = 90 \\ 9.5x + 7.5y = 721 \end{cases}$$

Solve the first equation for y.

$y = 90 - x$

Substitute $90 - x$ for y in the second equation.

$9.5x + 7.5(90 - x) = 721$

$9.5x + 675 - 7.5x = 721$

$2x = 46$

$x = 23$

Let $x = 23$ in $y = 90 - x$.

$y = 90 - 23$

$y = 67$

They sold 23 at $9.50 and 67 at $7.50.

35. Let $x =$ the rate of the faster group and $y =$ the rate of the slower group.

	r	$\cdot$ t	$=$ d
Slower group	x	240	$240x$
Faster group	y	240	$240y$

$$\begin{cases} x = y - \dfrac{1}{2} \\ 240x + 240y = 1200 \end{cases}$$

Substitute $y - \dfrac{1}{2}$ for x in the second equation.

$$240\left(y - \frac{1}{2}\right) + 240y = 1200$$

$$240y - 120 + 240y = 1200$$

$$480y = 1320$$

$$y = \frac{1320}{480} = 2\frac{3}{4}$$

Let $y = 2\frac{3}{4}$ in the first equation.

$$x = 2\frac{3}{4} - \frac{1}{2} = 2\frac{1}{4}$$

The rate of the faster group is $2\frac{3}{4}$ mph.

The rate of the slower group is $2\frac{1}{4}$ mph.

37. Let x = gallons of 30% solution and y = gallons of 60% solution.

	Concentration Rate	Gallons of Solution	Gallons of Pure Fertilizer
First solution	0.30	x	$0.30x$
Second solution	0.60	y	$0.60y$
Mixture	0.50	150	$0.50(150)$

$$\begin{cases} x + y = 150 \\ 0.30x + 0.60y = 0.50(150) \end{cases}$$

Multiply the first equation by -3 and the second equation by 10.

$$-3x - 3y = -450$$
$$\underline{3x + 6y = 750}$$
$$3y = 300$$
$$y = 100$$

Let $y = 100$ in the first equation.

$$x + 100 = 150$$
$$x = 50$$

50 gallons of 30% solution and 100 gallons of 60% solution.

39. Let x = the width and y = the length.

$$\begin{cases} 2x + 2y = 144 \\ y = x + 12 \end{cases}$$

Substitute $x + 12$ for y in the first equation.

$$2x + 2(x + 12) = 144$$
$$2x + 2x + 24 = 144$$
$$4x = 120$$
$$x = 30$$

Let $x = 30$ in the second equation.

$$y = 30 + 12$$
$$y = 42$$

Width = 30 inches, length = 42 inches.

41. $4^2 = 16$

43. $(6x)^2 = 36x^2$

45. $\left(10y^3\right)^2 = 100y^6$

47. Let x = the width and y = the length.

$$\begin{cases} 2x + y = 33 \\ y = 2x - 3 \end{cases}$$

Substitute $2x - 3$ for y in the first equation.

$$2x + 2x - 3 = 33$$
$$4x = 36$$
$$x = 9$$

Let $x = 9$ in the second equation.

$$y = 2(9) - 3$$
$$y = 15$$

Width = 9 feet, length = 15 feet.

Chapter 7 Review

1. a. Let $x = 12$ and $y = 4$.

$$2x - 3y = 12 \qquad 3x + 4y = 1$$
$$2(12) - 3(4) \overset{?}{=} 12 \qquad 3(12) + 4(4) \overset{?}{=} 1$$
$$24 - 12 \overset{?}{=} 12 \qquad 36 + 16 \overset{?}{=} 1$$
$$12 = 12 \qquad 52 = 1$$
$$\text{True} \qquad\qquad \text{False}$$

$(12, 4)$ is not a solution of the system.

b. Let $x = 3$ and $y = -2$.

$$2x - 3y = 12 \qquad 3x + 4y = 1$$
$$2(3) - 3(-2) \overset{?}{=} 12 \qquad 3(3) + 4(-2) \overset{?}{=} 1$$
$$6 + 6 \overset{?}{=} 12 \qquad 9 - 8 \overset{?}{=} 1$$
$$2 = 12 \qquad 1 = 1$$
$$\text{True} \qquad\qquad \text{True}$$

$(3, -2)$ is a solution of the system

2. a. Let $x = \dfrac{3}{4}$ and $y = -3$.

$$4x + y = 0 \qquad -8x - 5y = 9$$
$$4\left(\dfrac{3}{4}\right) - 3 \overset{?}{=} 0 \qquad -8\left(\dfrac{3}{4}\right) - 5(-3) \overset{?}{=} 9$$
$$3 - 3 \overset{?}{=} 0 \qquad -6 + 15 \overset{?}{=} 9$$
$$0 = 0 \qquad 9 = 9$$
$$\text{True} \qquad\qquad \text{True}$$

$\left(\dfrac{3}{4}, -3\right)$ is a solution of the system.

b. Let $x = -2$ and $y = 8$.

$$4x + y = 0 \qquad -8x - 5y = 9$$
$$4(-2) + 8 \overset{?}{=} 0 \qquad -8(-2) - 5(8) \overset{?}{=} 9$$
$$-8 + 8 \overset{?}{=} 0 \qquad 16 - 40 \overset{?}{=} 9$$
$$0 = 0 \qquad -24 = 9$$
$$\text{True} \qquad\qquad \text{False}$$

$(-2, 8)$ is not a solution of the system

3. a. Let $x = -6$ and $y = -8$.

$$5x - 6y = 18 \qquad 2y - x = -4$$
$$5(-6) - 6(-8) \overset{?}{=} 18 \qquad 2(-8) - (-6) \overset{?}{=} -4$$
$$-30 + 48 \overset{?}{=} 18 \qquad -16 + 6 \overset{?}{=} -4$$
$$18 = 18 \qquad -10 = -4$$
$$\text{True} \qquad\qquad \text{False}$$

$(-6, -8)$ is not a solution of the system.

b. Let $x = 3$ and $y = \dfrac{5}{2}$.

$$5x - 6y = 18 \qquad 2y - x = -4$$
$$5(3) - 6\left(\dfrac{5}{2}\right) \overset{?}{=} 18 \qquad 2\left(\dfrac{5}{2}\right) - 3 \overset{?}{=} -4$$
$$15 - 15 \overset{?}{=} 18 \qquad 5 - 3 \overset{?}{=} -4$$
$$0 = 18 \qquad 2 = -4$$
$$\text{False} \qquad\qquad \text{False}$$

$\left(3, \dfrac{5}{2}\right)$ is not a solution of the system

4. a. Let $x = 2$ and $y = 2$.

$$2x + 3y = 1 \qquad\qquad 3y - x = 4$$

$$2(2) + 3(2) \overset{?}{=} 1 \qquad 3(2) - (2) \overset{?}{=} 4$$

$$4 + 6 \overset{?}{=} 1 \qquad\qquad 6 - 2 \overset{?}{=} 4$$

$$10 = 1 \qquad\qquad\qquad 4 = 4$$

$$\text{False} \qquad\qquad\qquad \text{True}$$

$(2, 2)$ is not a solution of the system.

b. Let $x = -1$ and $y = 1$.

$$2x + 3y = 1 \qquad\qquad 3y - x = 4$$

$$2(-1) + 3(1) \overset{?}{=} 1 \qquad 3(1) - (-1) \overset{?}{=} 4$$

$$-2 + 3 \overset{?}{=} 1 \qquad\qquad 3 + 1 \overset{?}{=} 4$$

$$1 = 1 \qquad\qquad\qquad 4 = 4$$

$$\text{True} \qquad\qquad\qquad \text{True}$$

$(-1, 1)$ is a solution of the system

5. $\begin{cases} x + y = 5 \\ x - y = 1 \end{cases}$

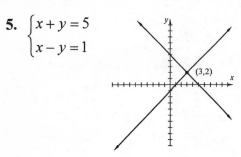

The solution of the system is $(3, 2)$.

6. $\begin{cases} x + y = 3 \\ x - y = -1 \end{cases}$

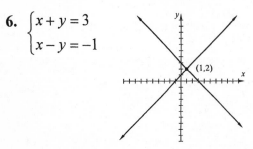

The solution of the system is $(1, 2)$.

7. $\begin{cases} x = 5 \\ y = -1 \end{cases}$

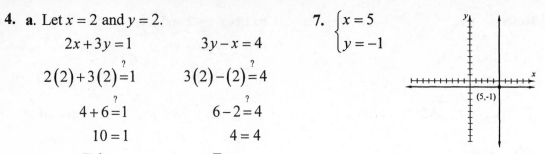

The solution of the system is $(5, -1)$.

8. $\begin{cases} x = -3 \\ y = 2 \end{cases}$

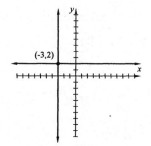

The solution of the system is $(-3, 2)$.

9. $\begin{cases} 2x + y = 5 \\ x = -3y \end{cases}$

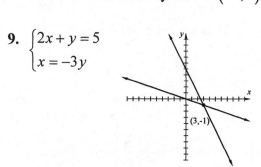

The solution of the system is $(3, -1)$.

10. $\begin{cases} 3x + y = -2 \\ y = -5x \end{cases}$

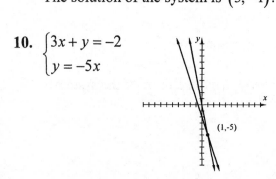

The solution of the system is $(1, -5)$.

11. $\begin{cases} y = 2x + 4 \\ y = -x - 5 \end{cases}$

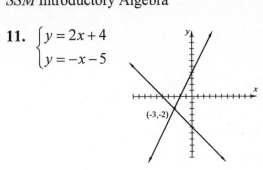

(-3,-2)

The solution of the system is $(-3, -2)$.

12. $\begin{cases} y = x - 5 \\ y = -2x + 2 \end{cases}$

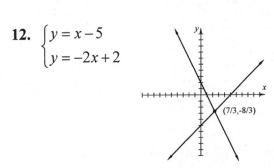

(7/3,-8/3)

The solution of the system is $\left(\dfrac{7}{3}, -\dfrac{8}{3} \right)$.

13. $\begin{cases} y = 3x \\ -6x + 2y = 6 \end{cases}$

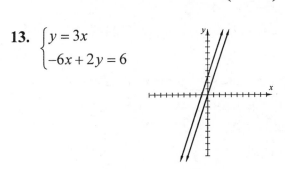

There is no solution.

14. $\begin{cases} x - 2y = 2 \\ -2x + 4y = -4 \end{cases}$

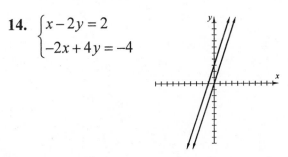

There are an infinite number of solutions.

15. $\begin{cases} x = 2y \\ 2x - 3y = 2 \end{cases}$

Substitute $2y$ for x in the second equation.

$$2(2y) - 3y = 2$$
$$4y - 3y = 2$$
$$y = 2$$

Let $y = 2$ in the first equation.

$$x = 2(2)$$
$$x = 4$$

The solution is $(4, 2)$.

16. $\begin{cases} x = 5y \\ x - 4y = 1 \end{cases}$

Substitute $5y$ for x in the second equation.

$$5y - 4y = 1$$
$$y = 1$$

Let $y = 1$ in the first equation.

$$x = 5(1)$$
$$x = 5$$

The solution is $(5, 1)$.

17. $\begin{cases} y = 2x + 6 \\ 3x - 2y = -11 \end{cases}$

Substitute $2x + 6$ for y in the second equation.

$$3x - 2(2x + 6) = -11$$
$$3x - 4x - 12 = -11$$
$$-x = 1$$
$$x = -1$$

Let $x = -1$ in the first equation.

$y = 2(-1) + 6$

$y = 4$

The solution is $(-1, 4)$.

18. $\begin{cases} y = 3x - 7 \\ 2x - 3y = 7 \end{cases}$

Substitute $3x - 7$ for y in the second equation.

$2x - 3(3x - 7) = 7$

$2x - 9x + 21 = 7$

$-7x = -14$

$x = 2$

Let $x = 2$ in the first equation.

$y = 3(2) - 7$

$y = -1$

The solution is $(2, -1)$.

19. $\begin{cases} x + 3y = -3 \\ 2x + y = 4 \end{cases}$

Solve the first equation for x.

$x = -3 - 3y$

Substitute $-3 - 3y$ for x in the second equation.

$2(-3 - 3y) + y = 4$

$-6 - 6y + y = 4$

$-5y = 10$

$y = -2$

Let $y = -2$ in $x = -3 - 3y$.

$x = -3 - 3(-2)$

$x = 3$

The solution is $(3, -2)$.

20. $\begin{cases} 3x + y = 11 \\ x + 2y = 12 \end{cases}$

Solve the first equation for y.

$y = 11 - 3x$

Substitute $11 - 3x$ for y in the second equation.

$x + 2(11 - 3x) = 12$

$x + 22 - 6x = 12$

$-5x = -10$

$x = 2$

Let $x = 2$ in $y = 11 - 3x$.

$y = 11 - 3(2)$

$y = 5$

The solution is $(2, 5)$.

21. $\begin{cases} 4y = 2x - 3 \\ x - 2y = 4 \end{cases}$

Solve the second equation for x.

$x = 4 + 2y$

Substitute $4 + 2y$ for x in the first equation.

$4y = 2(4 + 2y) - 3$

$4y = 8 + 4y - 3$

$0 = 5$

The system has no solution.

22. $\begin{cases} 2x = 3y - 18 \\ x + 4y = 2 \end{cases}$

Solve the second equation for x.

$x = 2 - 4y$

Substitute $2 - 4y$ for x in the first equation.

$2(2 - 4y) = 3y - 18$

$\quad 4 - 8y = 3y - 18$

$\quad\quad -11y = -22$

$\quad\quad\quad\; y = 2$

Let $y = 2$ in $x = 2 - 4y$.

$x = 2 - 4(2)$

$x = -6$

The solution is $(-6, 2)$.

23. $\begin{cases} x + y = 6 \\ y = -x - 4 \end{cases}$

Substitute $-x - 4$ for y in the first equation.

$x + (-x - 4) = 6$

$\quad x - x - 4 = 6$

$\quad\quad\quad -4 = 6$

There is no solution.

24. $\begin{cases} -3x + y = 6 \\ y = 3x + 2 \end{cases}$

Substitute $3x + 2$ for y in the first equation.

$-3x + (3x + 2) = 6$

$\quad -3x + 3x + 2 = 6$

$\quad\quad\quad\quad\quad 2 = 6$

There is no solution.

25. $\begin{cases} x + y = 14 \\ \underline{x - y = 18} \end{cases}$

$2x \quad\;\; = 32$

$\;x \quad\;\; = 16$

Let $x = 16$ in the first equation.

$16 + y = 14$

$\quad\;\; y = -2$

The solution of the system is $(16, -2)$.

26. $\begin{cases} x + y = 9 \\ \underline{x - y = 13} \end{cases}$

$2x \quad\;\; = 22$

$\;x \quad\;\; = 11$

Let $x = 11$ in the first equation.

$11 + y = 9$

$\quad\;\; y = -2$

The solution of the system is $(11, -2)$.

27. $\begin{cases} 2x + 3y = -6 \\ \underline{\;\; x - 3y = -12} \end{cases}$

$3x \quad\;\; = -18$

$\;x \quad\;\; = -6$

Let $x = -6$ in the first equation.

$2(-6) + 3y = -6$

$\quad -12 + 3y = -6$

$\quad\quad\quad 3y = 6$

$\quad\quad\quad\; y = 2$

The solution of the system is $(-6, 2)$.

28. $\begin{cases} 4x + y = 15 \\ -4x + 3y = -19 \end{cases}$

$$\overline{ 4y = -4}$$

$$y = -1$$

Let $y = -1$ in the first equation.

$$4x + (-1) = 15$$

$$4x - 1 = 15$$

$$4x = 16$$

$$x = 4$$

The solution of the system is $(4, -1)$.

29. $\begin{cases} 2x - 3y = -15 \\ x + 4y = 31 \end{cases}$

Multiply the second equation by -2.

$$2x - 3y = -15$$

$$\underline{-2x - 8y = -62}$$

$$-11y = -77$$

$$y = 7$$

Let $y = 7$ in the second equation.

$$x + 4(7) = 31$$

$$x + 28 = 31$$

$$x = 3$$

The solution of the system is $(3, 7)$.

30. $\begin{cases} x - 5y = -22 \\ 4x + 3y = 4 \end{cases}$

Multiply the first equation by -4.

$$-4x + 20y = 88$$

$$\underline{4x + 3y = 4}$$

$$23y = 92$$

$$y = 4$$

Let $y = 4$ in the first equation.

$$x - 5(4) = -22$$

$$x - 20 = -22$$

$$x = -2$$

The solution of the system is $(-2, 4)$.

31. $\begin{cases} 2x - 6y = -1 \\ -x + 3y = \dfrac{1}{2} \end{cases}$

Multiply the second equation by 2.

$$2x - 6y = -1$$

$$\underline{-2x + 6y = 1}$$

$$0 = 0$$

There are an infinite number of solutions.

32. $\begin{cases} -4x - 6y = 8 \\ 2x + 3y = -3 \end{cases}$

Multiply the second equation by 2.

$$-4x - 6y = 8$$

$$\underline{4x + 6y = -6}$$

$$0 = 2$$

The system has no solution.

33. $\begin{cases} \dfrac{3}{4}x + \dfrac{2}{3}y = 2 \\ x + \dfrac{y}{3} = 6 \end{cases}$

Multiply the first equation by 12 and the second equation by -9.

$$9x + 8y = 24$$

$$\underline{-9x - 3y = -54}$$

$$5y = -30$$

$$y = -6$$

Let $y = -6$ in the second equation.

$$x + \left(\frac{-6}{3}\right) = 6$$
$$x - 2 = 6$$
$$x = 8$$

The solution of the system is $(8, -6)$.

34. $\begin{cases} \dfrac{2}{5}x + \dfrac{3}{4}y = 1 \\ x + 3y = -2 \end{cases}$

Multiply the first equation by 20 and the second equation by -8.

$$8x + 15y = 20$$
$$\underline{-8x - 24y = 16}$$
$$-9y = 36$$
$$y = -4$$

Let $y = -4$ in the second equation.

$$x + 3(-4) = -2$$
$$x - 12 = -2$$
$$x = 10$$

The solution of the system is $(10, -4)$.

35. $\begin{cases} 10x + 2y = 0 \\ 3x + 5y = 33 \end{cases}$

Multiply the first equation by 5 and the second equation by -2.

$$50x + 10y = 0$$
$$\underline{-6x - 10y = -66}$$
$$44x = -66$$
$$x = -\frac{3}{2}$$

Let $x = -\dfrac{3}{2}$ in the first equation.

$$10\left(-\frac{3}{2}\right) + 2y = 0$$
$$-15 + 2y = 0$$
$$2y = 15$$
$$y = \frac{15}{2}$$

The solution of the system is $\left(-\dfrac{3}{2}, \dfrac{15}{2}\right)$.

36. $\begin{cases} 0.6x - 0.3y = -1.5 \\ 0.04x - 0.02y = -0.1 \end{cases}$

Multiply the first equation by 10 and the second equation by 100.

$\begin{cases} 6x - 3y = -15 \\ 4x - 2y = -10 \end{cases}$ Simplified system

Multiply the first equation by 2 and the second equation by -3.

$$12x - 6y = -30$$
$$\underline{-12x + 6y = 30}$$
$$0 = 0$$

There are an infinite number of solutions..

37. Let x = the larger number and y = the smaller number.

$\begin{cases} x + y = 16 \\ 3x - y = 72 \end{cases}$

$$4x = 88$$
$$x = 22$$

Let $x = 22$ in the first equation.

$$22 + y = 16$$
$$y = -6$$

The numbers are -6 and 22.

38. Let x = the number of orchestra seats and y = the number of balcony seats.

$$\begin{cases} x + y = 360 \\ 45x + 35y = 15{,}150 \end{cases}$$

Solve the first equation for x.

$x = 360 - y$

Substitute $360 - y$ for x in the second equation.

$45(360 - y) + 35y = 15{,}150$

$16{,}200 - 45y + 35y = 15{,}150$

$-10y = -1050$

$y = 105$

Let $y = 105$ in $x = 360 - y$.

$x = 360 - 105$

$x = 255$

There were 255 orchestra seats and 105 balcony seats.

39. Let x = the riverboat's speed in still water and y = the rate of the current.

	d	$=$	r	$\cdot$	t
Downriver	340		$x + y$		14
Upriver	340		$x - y$		19

$$\begin{cases} 14(x + y) = 340 \\ 19(x - y) = 340 \end{cases}$$

Multiply the first equation by $\dfrac{1}{14}$ and the second equation by $\dfrac{1}{19}$.

$$\begin{cases} x + y = \dfrac{340}{14} \approx 24.29 \\ x - y = \dfrac{340}{19} \approx 17.89 \end{cases} \quad \text{Simplified system}$$

$$\begin{array}{ll} 2x & \approx 42.18 \\ x & \approx 21.09 \end{array}$$

Multiply the second equation of the simplified system by -1.

$$\begin{cases} x + y \approx 24.29 \\ -x + y \approx -17.89 \end{cases}$$

$2y \approx 6.4$

$y \approx 3.2$

The riverboat's speed in still water is 21.1 mph. The rate of the current is 3.2 mph.

40. Let x = amount invested at 6% and y = amount invested at 10%.

$$\begin{cases} x + y = 9000 \\ 0.06x + 0.10y = 652.80 \end{cases}$$

Multiply the first equation by -6 and the second equation by 100.

$$\begin{array}{l} -6x - 6y = -54{,}000 \\ 6x + 10y = 65{,}280 \\ \hline 4y = 11{,}280 \\ y = 2820 \end{array}$$

Let $y = 2820$ in the first equation.

$x + 2820 = 9000$

$x = 6180$

$6180 invested at 6% and $2820 invested at 10%.

41. Let x = the width and y = the length.

$$\begin{cases} 2x + 2y = 6 \\ y = 1.6x \end{cases}$$

Substitute $1.6x$ for y in the first equation.

$$2x + 2(1.6x) = 6$$
$$2x + 3.2x = 6$$
$$5.2x = 6$$
$$x \approx 1.154$$

Let $x = 1.154$ in the second equation.

$$y = 1.6(1.154)$$
$$y \approx 1.846$$

Width $= 1.15$ feet, length $= 1.85$ feet.

42. Let x = liters of 6% solution and y = liters of 14% solution.

	Concentration Rate	Ounces of Solution	Ounces of Pure Acid
First solution	0.06	x	$0.06x$
Second solution	0.14	y	$0.14y$
Mixture	0.12	50	$0.12(50)$

$$\begin{cases} x + y = 50 \\ 0.06x + 0.14y = 0.12(50) \end{cases}$$

Multiply the first equation by -6 and the second equation by 100.

$$\begin{array}{r} -6x - 6y = -300 \\ 6x + 14y = 600 \\ \hline 8y = 300 \\ y = 37.5 \end{array}$$

Let $y = 37.5$ in the first equation.

$$x + 37.5 = 50$$
$$x = 12.5$$

$12\dfrac{1}{2}$ cc of 6% solution and

$37\dfrac{1}{2}$ cc of 14% solution.

43. Let x = the cost of an egg and y = the cost of a strip of bacon.

$$\begin{cases} 3x + 4y = 3.80 \\ 2x + 3y = 2.75 \end{cases}$$

Multiply the first equation by -2 and the second equation by 3.

$$\begin{array}{r} -6x - 8y = -7.60 \\ 6x + 9y = 8.25 \\ \hline y = 0.65 \end{array}$$

Let $y = 0.65$ in the first equation.

$$3x + 4(0.65) = 3.80$$
$$3x + 2.60 = 3.80$$
$$3x = 1.20$$
$$x = 0.40$$

An egg costs 40¢ and a strip of bacon costs 65¢.

44. Let x = the time spent walking and y = the time spent jogging.

	r	$\cdot$	t	$=$	d
Walking	4		x		$4x$
Jogging	7.5		y		$7.5y$

$$\begin{cases} x + y = 3 \\ 4x + 7.5y = 15 \end{cases}$$

Multiply the first equation by -4.

$$-4x - 4y = -12$$
$$\underline{4x + 7.5y = 15}$$
$$3.5y = 3$$
$$y \approx 0.857$$

Let $y = 0.857$ in the first equation.

$$x + 0.857 = 3$$
$$x = 2.143$$

He spent 2.14 hours walking and 0.86 hours jogging.

Chapter 7 Test

1. $\begin{cases} x - y = 2 \\ 3x - y = -2 \end{cases}$

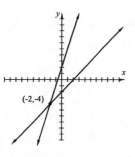

(-2,-4)

The solution of the system is $(-2, -4)$.

2. $\begin{cases} y = -3x \\ 3x + y = 6 \end{cases}$

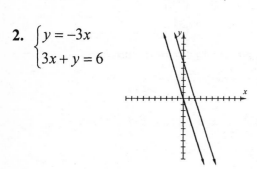

There is no solution.

3. $\begin{cases} 3x - 2y = -14 \\ y = x + 5 \end{cases}$

Substitute $x + 5$ for y in the first equation.

$$3x - 2(x + 5) = -14$$
$$3x - 2x - 10 = -14$$
$$x = -4$$

Let $x = -4$ in the second equation.

$$y = -4 + 5$$
$$y = 1$$

The solution is $(-4, 1)$.

4. $\begin{cases} 3x + y = 7 \\ 4x + 3y = 1 \end{cases}$

Solve the first equation for y.

$$y = 7 - 3x$$

Substitute $7 - 3x$ for y in the second equation.

$$4x + 3(7 - 3x) = 1$$
$$4x + 21 - 9x = 1$$
$$-5x = -20$$
$$x = 4$$

Let $x = 4$ in $y = 7 - 3x$.

$$y = 7 - 3(4)$$
$$y = -5$$

The solution is $(4, -5)$.

5. $\begin{cases} x - y = 4 \\ x - 2y = 11 \end{cases}$

Solve the first equation for x.

$x = y + 4$

Substitute $y + 4$ for x in the second equation.

$y + 4 - 2y = 11$

$-y = 7$

$y = -7$

Let $y = -7$ in $x = y + 4$.

$x = -7 + 4$

$x = -3$

The solution is $(-3, -7)$.

6. $\begin{cases} 8x - 4y = 12 \\ y = 2x - 3 \end{cases}$

Substitute $2x - 3$ for y in the first equation.

$8x - 4(2x - 3) = 12$

$8x - 8x + 12 = 12$

$12 = 12$

There are an infinite number of solutions.

7. $\begin{cases} x + y = 28 \\ x - y = 12 \end{cases}$

$2x \quad\;\; = 40$

$x \quad\;\; = 20$

Let $x = 20$ in the first equation.

$20 + y = 28$

$y = 8$

The solution is $(20, 8)$

8. $\begin{cases} y - x = 6 \\ y + 2x = -6 \end{cases}$

Multiply the first equation by -1.

$-y + x = -6$

$\underline{y + 2x = -6}$

$3x = -12$

$x = -4$

Let $x = -4$ in the first equation.

$y - (-4) = 6$

$y + 4 = 6$

$y = 2$

The solution is $(-4, 2)$

9. $\begin{cases} 5x - 6y = 7 \\ 7x - 4y = 12 \end{cases}$

Multiply the first equation by -2 and the second equation by 3.

$-10x + 12y = -14$

$\underline{21x - 12y = \;\; 36}$

$11x \qquad\quad = 22$

$x \qquad\quad = 2$

Let $x = 2$ in the first equation.

$5(2) - 6y = 7$

$10 - 6y = 7$

$-6y = -3$

$y = \dfrac{1}{2}$

The solution is $\left(2, \dfrac{1}{2} \right)$.

10. $\begin{cases} x - \dfrac{2}{3}y = 3 \\ -2x + 3y = 10 \end{cases}$

Multiply the first equation by 3.

$\begin{cases} 3x - 2y = 9 \\ -2x + 3y = 10 \end{cases}$ Simplified system

Multiply the first equation of the simplified system by 2 and the second equation by 3.

$\begin{cases} 6x - 4y = 18 \\ -6x + 9y = 30 \end{cases}$
$\underline{}$
$5y = 48$

$y = \dfrac{48}{5} = 9\dfrac{3}{5}$

Multiply the first equation of the simplified system by 3 and the second equation by 2.

$\begin{cases} 9x - 6y = 27 \\ -4x + 6y = 20 \end{cases}$
$\underline{}$
$5x = 47$

$x = \dfrac{47}{5} = 9\dfrac{2}{5}$

The solution of the system is $\left(9\dfrac{2}{5}, 9\dfrac{3}{5}\right)$.

11. $\begin{cases} 0.01x - 0.06y = -0.23 \\ 0.2x + 0.4y = 0.2 \end{cases}$

Multiply the first equation by 100 and the second equation by 10.

$\begin{cases} x - 6y = -23 \\ 2x + 4y = 2 \end{cases}$ Simplified system

Multiply the first equation of the simplified system by -2.

$\begin{cases} -2x + 12y = 46 \\ 2x + 4y = 2 \end{cases}$
$\underline{}$
$16y = 48$
$y = 3$

Multiply the first equation of the simplified system by 2 and the second equation by 3.

$\begin{cases} 2x - 12y = -46 \\ 6x + 12y = 6 \end{cases}$
$\underline{}$
$8x = -40$
$x = -5$

The solution is $(-5, 3)$.

12. $\begin{cases} 6x - y = 0 \\ \dfrac{3}{2}x - \dfrac{y}{4} = -3 \end{cases}$

Multiply the second equation by -4.

$\begin{cases} 6x - y = 0 \\ -6x + y = 12 \end{cases}$ Simplified system
$\underline{}$
$0 = 12$

There is no solution..

13. Let $x =$ the first number and $y =$ the second number.

$\begin{cases} x + y = 124 \\ x - y = 32 \end{cases}$
$\underline{}$
$2x = 156$
$x = 78$

Let $x = 78$ in the first equation.

$78 + y = 124$
$y = 46$

The numbers are 78 and 46.

14. Let $x =$ the number of \$1 bills and $y =$ the number of \$5 bills.

$$\begin{cases} x + y = 62 \\ 1x + 5y = 230 \end{cases}$$

Solve the first equation for y.

$$y = 62 - x$$

Substitute $62 - x$ for y in the second equation.

$$x + 5(62 - x) = 230$$
$$x + 310 - 5x = 230$$
$$-4x = -80$$
$$x = 20$$

Let $x = 20$ in $y = 62 - x$.

$$y = 62 - 20$$
$$y = 42$$

She had 20 \$1 bills and 42 \$5 bills.

15. Let $x =$ liters of 30% solution and $y =$ liters of 70% solution.

	Concentration Rate	Liters of Solution	Liters of Pure Alcohol
First solution	30%	x	$0.3x$
Second solution	70%	y	$0.7y$
Mixture	40%	10	$0.4(10)$

$$\begin{cases} x + y = 10 \\ 0.3x + 0.7y = 0.4(10) \end{cases}$$

Multiply the first equation by -3 and the second equation by 10.

$$\begin{array}{r} -3x - 3y = -30 \\ 3x + 7y = 40 \\ \hline 4y = 10 \\ y = 2.5 \end{array}$$

Let $y = 2.5$ in the first equation.

$$x + 2.5 = 10$$
$$x = 7.5$$

2.5 liters of 30% solution and 7.5 liters of 70% solution.

16. Let $x =$ the rate of the faster hiker and $y =$ the rate of the slower hiker.

	r	$\cdot$	t	$=$	d
Slower hiker	x		4		$4x$
Faster hiker	y		4		$4y$

$$\begin{cases} y = 2x \\ 4x + 4y = 36 \end{cases}$$

Substitute $2x$ for y in the second equation.

$$4x + 4(2x) = 36$$
$$4x + 8x = 36$$
$$12x = 36$$
$$x = 3$$

Let $x = 3$ in the first equation.

$$y = 2(3)$$
$$y = 6$$

The rate of the faster hiker is 6 mph.
The rate of the slower hiker is 3 mph.

17. 1999

18. 1991-1999

Cumulative Review Chapter 7

1. **a.** $-14-8+10-(-6)$

    $= -14+(-8)+10+6$

    $= -6$

    b. $1.6-(-10.3)+(-5.6)$

    $= 1.6+10.3+(-5.6)$

    $= 6.3$

2. The reciprocal of 22 is $\dfrac{1}{22}$

    since $22 \cdot \dfrac{1}{22} = 1$.

3. The reciprocal of $\dfrac{3}{16}$ is $\dfrac{16}{3}$

    since $\dfrac{3}{16} \cdot \dfrac{16}{3} = 1$.

4. The reciprocal of -10 is $-\dfrac{1}{10}$

    since $-10 \cdot -\dfrac{1}{10} = 1$.

5. The reciprocal of $-\dfrac{9}{13}$ is $-\dfrac{13}{9}$

    since $-\dfrac{9}{13} \cdot -\dfrac{13}{9} = 1$.

6. The reciprocal of 1.7 is $\dfrac{1}{1.7}$

    since $1.7 \cdot \dfrac{1}{1.7} = 1$.

7. **a.** $8-3$

    b. $8-x$

8. $-2(x-5)+10 = -3(x+2)+x$

    $-2x+10+10 = -3x-6+x$

    $-2x+20 = -2x-6$

    $20 = -6$

    There is no solution

9. **a.** $\dfrac{2}{5}$

    b. $2 \text{ feet} = 2 \text{ feet} \cdot \left(\dfrac{12 \text{ inches}}{1 \text{ foot}} \right) = 24 \text{ inches}$

    $\dfrac{18 \text{ inches}}{2 \text{ feet}} = \dfrac{18}{24} = \dfrac{3}{4}$

10. $-5x+7 < 2(x-3)$

    $-5x+7 < 2x-6$

    $-7x < -13$

    $\dfrac{-7x}{-7} > \dfrac{-13}{-7}$

    $x > \dfrac{13}{7}$

11. $\left(\dfrac{m}{n} \right)^7 = \dfrac{m^7}{n^7}, \ n \neq 0$

12. $\left(\dfrac{2x^4}{3y^5} \right)^4 = \dfrac{2^4 (x^4)^4}{3^4 (y^5)^4} = \dfrac{16x^{16}}{81y^{20}}, \ y \neq 0$

13. $(2x^3 + 8x^2 - 6x) - (2x^3 - x^2 + 1)$

    $= 2x^3 + 8x^2 - 6x - 2x^3 + x^2 - 1$

    $= 2x^3 - 2x^3 + 8x^2 + x^2 - 6x - 1$

    $= 9x^2 - 6x - 1$

14.

$$\begin{array}{r} 2x+4 \\ 3x-1\overline{)6x^2+10x-5} \end{array}$$

$$\begin{array}{r} 6x^2-\ 2x \\ \hline 12x-5 \\ 12x-4 \\ \hline -1 \end{array}$$

$$\frac{6x^2+10x-5}{3x-1}=2x+4-\frac{1}{3x-1}$$

15.
$$x(2x-7)=4$$
$$2x^2-7x=4$$
$$2x^2-7x-4=0$$
$$(2x+1)(x-4)=0$$
$$2x+1=0 \quad \text{or} \quad x-4=0$$
$$x=-\frac{1}{2} \qquad x=4$$

The solutions are $-\dfrac{1}{2}$ and 4.

16. Let x = the length of the shorter leg,
$x+2$ = the length of the longer leg, and
$x+4$ = the length of the hypotenuse.

$$(x)^2+(x+2)^2=(x+4)^2$$
$$x^2+x^2+4x+4=x^2+8x+16$$
$$2x^2+4x+4=x^2+8x+16$$
$$x^2-4x-12=0$$
$$(x+2)(x-6)=0$$
$$x+2=0 \quad \text{or} \quad x-6=0$$
$$x=-2 \qquad x=6$$

The solutions are -2 and 6.

17. $\dfrac{2y}{2y-7}-\dfrac{7}{2y-7}=\dfrac{2y-7}{2y-7}=1$

18.
$$\frac{\dfrac{x}{y}+\dfrac{3}{2x}}{\dfrac{x}{2}+y}=\frac{\dfrac{x}{y}+\dfrac{3}{2x}}{\dfrac{x}{2}+y}\cdot\frac{\dfrac{2xy}{1}}{\dfrac{2xy}{1}}$$

$$=\frac{\dfrac{x}{y}\left(\dfrac{2xy}{1}\right)+\dfrac{3}{2x}\left(\dfrac{2xy}{1}\right)}{\dfrac{x}{2}\left(\dfrac{2xy}{1}\right)+y\left(\dfrac{2xy}{1}\right)}$$

$$=\frac{2x^2+3y}{x^2y+2xy^2}$$

19. Since $y=-1$ for all x, use $(0,-1)$
and $(2,-1)$.

$(\ )$ and $(\ )$

$$m=\frac{y_2-y_1}{x_2-x_1}=\frac{-1-(-1)}{2-0}=\frac{0}{2}=0$$

20. $(2,5)$ and $(-3,4)$

$$m=\frac{y_2-y_1}{x_2-x_1}=\frac{4-5}{-3-2}=\frac{-1}{-5}=\frac{1}{5}$$

$$m=\frac{1}{5}; (2,5)$$

$$y-y_1=m(x-x_1)$$

$$y-5=\frac{1}{5}(x-2)$$

$$5(y-5)=1(x-2)$$

$$5y-25=x-2$$

$$-x+5y=23$$

$$x-5y=-23$$

21. Domain is $\{-1,0,3\}$
Range is $\{-2,0,2,3\}$

22. Let $x = 12$ and $y = 6$

$$2x - 3y = 6 \qquad\qquad x = 2y$$

$$2(12) - 3(6) \overset{?}{=} 6 \qquad 12 \overset{?}{=} 2(6)$$

$$24 - 18 \overset{?}{=} 6 \qquad\quad 12 = 12$$

$$6 = 6 \qquad\qquad\quad \text{True}$$

$$\text{True}$$

$(12, 6)$ is a solution of the system.

23. $\begin{cases} x + 2y = 7 \\ 2x + 2y = 13 \end{cases}$

Solve the first equation for x.

$$x = 7 - 2y$$

Substitute $7 - 2y$ for x in the second equation.

$$2(7 - 2y) + 2y = 13$$

$$14 - 4y + 2y = 13$$

$$-2y = -1$$

$$y = \frac{1}{2}$$

Let $y = \frac{1}{2}$ in $x = 7 - 2y$.

$$x = 7 - 2\left(\frac{1}{2}\right)$$

$$x = 6$$

The solution is $\left(6, \frac{1}{2}\right)$.

24. $\begin{cases} -x - \dfrac{y}{2} = \dfrac{5}{2} \\ \dfrac{x}{6} - \dfrac{y}{2} = 0 \end{cases}$

Multiply the first equation by -6 and the second equation by 6.

25. (continued, right column)

$\begin{cases} 6x + 3y = -15 \\ x - 3y = 0 \end{cases}$ Simplified system

$$7x \qquad\quad = -15$$

$$x \qquad\quad = -\frac{15}{7}$$

Multiply the second equation of the simplified system by -6.

$$\begin{cases} 6x + 3y = -15 \\ -6x + 18y = 0 \end{cases}$$

$$21y = -15$$

$$y = -\frac{5}{7}$$

The solution of the system is $\left(-\dfrac{15}{7}, -\dfrac{5}{7}\right)$.

25. Let $x =$ the first number and $y =$ the second number.

$$\begin{cases} x + y = 37 \\ x - y = 21 \end{cases}$$

$$2x \qquad\quad = 58$$

$$x \qquad\quad = 29$$

Let $x = 29$ in the first equation.

$$29 + y = 37$$

$$y = 8$$

The numbers are 29 and 8.

Chapter 8

Chapter 8 Pretest

1. $-\sqrt{49} = -7$

2. $\sqrt{\dfrac{4}{25}} = \dfrac{2}{5}$

3. $\sqrt[3]{-64} = -4$

4. $\sqrt{120} = \sqrt{4 \cdot 30} = \sqrt{4} \cdot \sqrt{30} = 2\sqrt{30}$

5. $\sqrt{\dfrac{24}{y^6}} = \dfrac{\sqrt{24}}{\sqrt{y^6}} = \dfrac{\sqrt{4} \cdot \sqrt{6}}{\sqrt{\left(y^3\right)^2}} = \dfrac{2\sqrt{6}}{y^3}$

6. $\sqrt[3]{112} = \sqrt[3]{8} \cdot \sqrt[3]{14} = 2\sqrt[3]{14}$

7. $\sqrt{15} + 2\sqrt{15} - 6\sqrt{15} = (1 + 2 - 6)\sqrt{15} = -3\sqrt{15}$

8. $3\sqrt{12} - 2\sqrt{27} = 3\sqrt{4} \cdot \sqrt{3} - 2\sqrt{9} \cdot \sqrt{3}$
$$= 6\sqrt{3} - 6\sqrt{3}$$
$$= 0$$

9. $\sqrt{\dfrac{7}{4}} + \sqrt{\dfrac{7}{25}} = \dfrac{\sqrt{7}}{\sqrt{4}} + \dfrac{\sqrt{7}}{\sqrt{25}} = \dfrac{\sqrt{7}}{2} + \dfrac{\sqrt{7}}{5}$
$$= \dfrac{5\sqrt{7}}{10} + \dfrac{2\sqrt{7}}{10} = \dfrac{(5+2)\sqrt{7}}{10} = \dfrac{7\sqrt{7}}{10}$$

10. $\sqrt{6} \cdot \sqrt{18} = \sqrt{6 \cdot 18} = \sqrt{108} = \sqrt{36 \cdot 3} = 6\sqrt{3}$

11. $\sqrt{2}\left(\sqrt{14} - \sqrt{5}\right) = \sqrt{2} \cdot \sqrt{14} - \sqrt{2} \cdot \sqrt{5}$
$$= \sqrt{28} - \sqrt{10} = \sqrt{4 \cdot 7} - \sqrt{10}$$
$$= 2\sqrt{7} - \sqrt{10}$$

12. $\left(\sqrt{y} - 3\right)^2 = \left(\sqrt{y}\right)^2 - 2(3)\sqrt{y} + (3)^2$
$$= y - 6\sqrt{y} + 9$$

13. $\dfrac{\sqrt{56x^5}}{\sqrt{2x^3}} = \sqrt{\dfrac{56x^5}{2x^3}} = \sqrt{28x^2} = \sqrt{4 \cdot 7x^2}$
$$= 2x\sqrt{7}$$

14. $\sqrt{\dfrac{5}{11}} = \dfrac{\sqrt{5}}{\sqrt{11}} = \dfrac{\sqrt{5}}{\sqrt{11}} \cdot \dfrac{\sqrt{11}}{\sqrt{11}} = \dfrac{\sqrt{55}}{11}$

15. $\dfrac{16}{\sqrt{2a}} = \dfrac{16}{\sqrt{2a}} \cdot \dfrac{\sqrt{2a}}{\sqrt{2a}} = \dfrac{16\sqrt{2a}}{2a} = \dfrac{8\sqrt{2a}}{a}$

16. $\dfrac{3}{2 - \sqrt{x}} = \dfrac{3}{2 - \sqrt{x}} \cdot \dfrac{2 + \sqrt{x}}{2 + \sqrt{x}} = \dfrac{3\left(2 + \sqrt{x}\right)}{4 - x}$
$$= \dfrac{6 + 3\sqrt{x}}{4 - x}$$

17. $\sqrt{x} + 9 = 16$
$$\sqrt{x} = 7$$
$$\left(\sqrt{x}\right)^2 = 7^2$$
$$x = 49$$

18. $\sqrt{x+4} = \sqrt{x} + 1$
$$\left(\sqrt{x+4}\right)^2 = \left(\sqrt{x}+1\right)^2$$
$$x + 4 = x + 2\sqrt{x} + 1$$
$$3 = 2\sqrt{x}$$
$$\dfrac{3}{2} = \sqrt{x}$$

$$\left(\frac{3}{2}\right)^2 = \left(\sqrt{x}\right)^2$$

$$\frac{9}{4} = x$$

19. Let b = the length of the unknown leg.

$$a^2 + b^2 = c^2$$
$$6^2 + b^2 = 14^2$$
$$36 + b^2 = 196$$
$$b^2 = 160$$
$$b = \sqrt{160}$$
$$b = 4\sqrt{10}$$

The length of the leg is $4\sqrt{10}$ cm.

20. Let $S = 80$.

$$r = \sqrt{\frac{S}{4\pi}}$$

$$r = \sqrt{\frac{80}{4\pi}} = \sqrt{\frac{20}{\pi}} = \frac{2\sqrt{5}}{\sqrt{\pi}} \approx 2.52$$

The radius is about 2.52 inches.

Practice Problems 8.1

1. $\sqrt{100} = 10$, because $10^2 = 100$ and 10 is positive.

2. $\sqrt{9} = 3$, because $3^2 = 9$ and 3 is positive.

3. $-\sqrt{36} = -6$, because $6^2 = 36$ and the negative sign indicates the negative square root.

4. $\sqrt{\frac{25}{81}} = \frac{5}{9}$, because $\left(\frac{5}{9}\right)^2 = \frac{25}{81}$ and $\frac{5}{9}$ is positive.

5. $\sqrt{1} = 1$, because $1^2 = 1$ and 1 is positive.

6. $\sqrt[3]{27} = 3$, because $3^3 = 27$.

7. $\sqrt[3]{-8} = -2$, because $(-2)^3 = -8$.

8. $\sqrt[3]{\frac{1}{64}} = \frac{1}{4}$, because $\left(\frac{1}{4}\right)^3 = \frac{1}{64}$.

9. $\sqrt[4]{-16}$ is not a real number.

10. $\sqrt[5]{-1} = -1$, because $(-1)^3 = -1$.

11. $\sqrt[4]{81} = 3$, because $3^4 = 81$.

12. $\sqrt[6]{-64}$ is not a real number.

13. $\sqrt{10} \approx 3.162$

14. $\sqrt{x^2} = x$, because $(x)^2 = x^2$.

15. $\sqrt{x^{20}} = x^{10}$, because $\left(x^{10}\right)^2 = x^{20}$.

16. $\sqrt{4x^6} = 2x^3$, because $\left(2x^3\right)^2 = 4x^6$.

17. $\sqrt[3]{8y^{12}} = 2y^4$, because $\left(2y^4\right)^3 = 8y^{12}$.

Calculator Explorations 8.1

1. $\sqrt{7} \approx 2.646$

2. $\sqrt{14} \approx 3.742$

3. $\sqrt{11} \approx 3.317$

4. $\sqrt{200} \approx 14.142$

5. $\sqrt{82} \approx 9.055$

6. $\sqrt{46} \approx 6.782$

7. $\sqrt[3]{40} \approx 3.420$

8. $\sqrt[3]{71} \approx 4.141$

9. $\sqrt[4]{20} \approx 2.115$

10. $\sqrt[4]{15} \approx 1.968$

11. $\sqrt[5]{18} \approx 1.783$

12. $\sqrt[6]{2} \approx 1.122$

Exercise Set 8.1

1. $\sqrt{16} = 4$, because $4^2 = 16$ and 4 is positive.

3. $\sqrt{81} = 9$, because $9^2 = 81$ and 9 is positive.

5. $\sqrt{\dfrac{1}{25}} = \dfrac{1}{5}$, because $\left(\dfrac{1}{5}\right)^2 = \dfrac{1}{25}$ and $\dfrac{1}{5}$ is positive.

7. $-\sqrt{100} = -10$, because $10^2 = 100$ and the negative sign indicates the negative square root.

9. $\sqrt{-4}$ is not a real number.

11. $-\sqrt{121} = -11$, because $11^2 = 121$ and the negative sign indicates the negative square root.

13. $\sqrt{\dfrac{9}{25}} = \dfrac{3}{5}$, because $\left(\dfrac{3}{5}\right)^2 = \dfrac{9}{25}$ and $\dfrac{3}{5}$ is positive.

15. $\sqrt{900} = 30$, because $30^2 = 900$ and 30 is positive.

17. $\sqrt{144} = 12$, because $12^2 = 144$ and 12 is positive.

19. $\sqrt{\dfrac{1}{100}} = \dfrac{1}{10}$, because $\left(\dfrac{1}{10}\right)^2 = \dfrac{1}{100}$ and $\dfrac{1}{10}$ is positive.

21. $\sqrt[3]{125} = 5$, because $(5)^3 = 125$.

23. $\sqrt[3]{-64} = -4$, because $(-4)^3 = -64$.

25. $-\sqrt[3]{8} = -2$, because $\sqrt[3]{8} = 2$.

27. $\sqrt[3]{\dfrac{1}{8}} = \dfrac{1}{2}$, because $\left(\dfrac{1}{2}\right)^3 = \dfrac{1}{8}$.

29. $\sqrt[3]{-125} = -5$, because $(-5)^3 = -125$.

31. Answers may vary.

33. $\sqrt[5]{32} = 2$, because $(2)^5 = 32$.

35. $\sqrt[4]{-16}$ is not a real number.

37. $-\sqrt[4]{625} = -5$, because $\sqrt[4]{625} = 5$.

39. $\sqrt[6]{1} = 1$, because $(1)^6 = 1$.

41. $\sqrt{7} \approx 2.646$

43. $\sqrt{12} \approx 3.464$

45. $\sqrt{37} \approx 6.083$

47. $\sqrt{136} \approx 11.662$

49. $\sqrt{2} \approx 1.41$
$90\sqrt{2} \approx 90 \cdot 1.41 = 126.90$ feet

51. $\sqrt{z^2} = z$, because $(z)^2 = z^2$.

53. $\sqrt{x^4} = x^2$, because $(x^2)^2 = x^4$.

55. $\sqrt{9x^8} = 3x^4$, because $(3x^4)^2 = 9x^8$.

57. $\sqrt{81x^2} = 9x$, because $(9x)^2 = 81x^2$.

59. $\sqrt{a^2 b^4} = ab^2$, because $(ab^2)^2 = a^2 b^4$.

61. $\sqrt{16a^6 b^4} = 4a^3 b^2$,
because $(4a^3 b^2)^2 = 16a^6 b^4$.

63. $50 = 25 \cdot 2$

65. $32 = 16 \cdot 2$ or $32 = 4 \cdot 8$

67. $28 = 4 \cdot 7$

69. $27 = 9 \cdot 3$

71. Let $A = 49$
The length of a side $= \sqrt{A}$
$\sqrt{A} = \sqrt{49} = 7$
The length of a side $= 7$ miles

73. Let $A = 9.61$
The length of a side $= \sqrt{A}$
$\sqrt{A} = \sqrt{9.61} = 3.1$
The length of a side $= 3.1$ inches.

75. $\sqrt{\sqrt{81}} = \sqrt{9} = 3$

77. $y = \sqrt{x}$

x	y
0	0
1	1
3	1.7
4	2
9	3

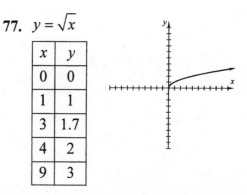

79. $y = \sqrt{x-2}$

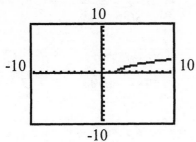

The graph starts at $(2, 0)$ because

$x - 2 \geq 0$ for $x \geq 2$

81. $y = \sqrt{x+4}$

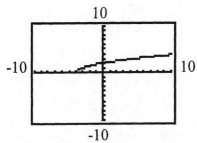

The graph starts at $(-4, 0)$ because

$x + 4 \geq 0$ for $x \geq -4$

83. $\sqrt[3]{195,112} = 58$

The length of a side = 58 feet.

Practice Problems 8.2

1. $\sqrt{40} = \sqrt{4 \cdot 10} = \sqrt{4} \cdot \sqrt{10} = 2\sqrt{10}$

2. $\sqrt{18} = \sqrt{9 \cdot 2} = \sqrt{9} \cdot \sqrt{2} = 3\sqrt{2}$

3. $\sqrt{700} = \sqrt{100 \cdot 7} = \sqrt{100} \cdot \sqrt{7} = 10\sqrt{7}$

4. $\sqrt{15}$ can't be simplified.

5. $\sqrt{\dfrac{16}{81}} = \dfrac{\sqrt{16}}{\sqrt{81}} = \dfrac{4}{9}$

6. $\sqrt{\dfrac{2}{25}} = \dfrac{\sqrt{2}}{\sqrt{25}} = \dfrac{\sqrt{2}}{5}$

7. $\sqrt{\dfrac{45}{49}} = \dfrac{\sqrt{45}}{\sqrt{49}} = \dfrac{\sqrt{9} \cdot \sqrt{5}}{7} = \dfrac{3\sqrt{5}}{7}$

8. $\sqrt{x^{11}} = \sqrt{x^{10} \cdot x} = \sqrt{x^{10}} \cdot \sqrt{x} = x^5 \sqrt{x}$

9. $\sqrt{18x^4} = \sqrt{9 \cdot 2x^4} = \sqrt{9x^4} \cdot \sqrt{2} = 3x^2 \sqrt{2}$

10. $\sqrt{\dfrac{27}{x^8}} = \dfrac{\sqrt{27}}{\sqrt{x^8}} = \dfrac{\sqrt{9} \cdot \sqrt{3}}{x^4} = \dfrac{3\sqrt{3}}{x^4}$

11. $\sqrt[3]{40} = \sqrt[3]{8 \cdot 5} = \sqrt[3]{8} \cdot \sqrt[3]{5} = 2\sqrt[3]{5}$

12. $\sqrt[3]{50}$ can't be simplified.

13. $\sqrt[3]{\dfrac{10}{27}} = \dfrac{\sqrt[3]{10}}{\sqrt[3]{27}} = \dfrac{\sqrt[3]{10}}{3}$

14. $\sqrt[3]{\dfrac{81}{8}} = \dfrac{\sqrt[3]{81}}{\sqrt[3]{8}} = \dfrac{\sqrt[3]{27 \cdot 3}}{2} = \dfrac{\sqrt[3]{27} \cdot \sqrt[3]{3}}{2} = \dfrac{3\sqrt[3]{3}}{2}$

Mental Math 8.2

1. $\sqrt{4 \cdot 9} = 6$

2. $\sqrt{9 \cdot 36} = 18$

3. $\sqrt{x^2} = x$

4. $\sqrt{y^4} = y^2$

5. $\sqrt{0} = 0$

6. $\sqrt{1} = 1$

7. $\sqrt{25x^4} = 5x^2$

8. $\sqrt{49x^2} = 7x$

Exercise Set 8.2

1. $\sqrt{20} = \sqrt{4 \cdot 5} = \sqrt{4} \cdot \sqrt{5} = 2\sqrt{5}$

3. $\sqrt{18} = \sqrt{9 \cdot 2} = \sqrt{9} \cdot \sqrt{2} = 3\sqrt{2}$

5. $\sqrt{50} = \sqrt{25 \cdot 2} = \sqrt{25} \cdot \sqrt{2} = 5\sqrt{2}$

7. $\sqrt{33}$ can't be simplified.

9. $\sqrt{60} = \sqrt{4 \cdot 15} = \sqrt{4} \cdot \sqrt{15} = 2\sqrt{15}$

11. $\sqrt{180} = \sqrt{36 \cdot 5} = \sqrt{36} \cdot \sqrt{5} = 6\sqrt{5}$

13. $\sqrt{52} = \sqrt{4 \cdot 13} = \sqrt{4} \cdot \sqrt{13} = 2\sqrt{13}$

15. $\sqrt{\dfrac{8}{25}} = \dfrac{\sqrt{8}}{\sqrt{25}} = \dfrac{\sqrt{4} \cdot \sqrt{2}}{5} = \dfrac{2\sqrt{2}}{5}$

17. $\sqrt{\dfrac{27}{121}} = \dfrac{\sqrt{27}}{\sqrt{121}} = \dfrac{\sqrt{9} \cdot \sqrt{3}}{11} = \dfrac{3\sqrt{3}}{11}$

19. $\sqrt{\dfrac{9}{4}} = \dfrac{\sqrt{9}}{\sqrt{4}} = \dfrac{3}{2}$

21. $\sqrt{\dfrac{125}{9}} = \dfrac{\sqrt{125}}{\sqrt{9}} = \dfrac{\sqrt{25} \cdot \sqrt{5}}{3} = \dfrac{5\sqrt{5}}{3}$

23. $\sqrt{\dfrac{11}{36}} = \dfrac{\sqrt{11}}{\sqrt{36}} = \dfrac{\sqrt{11}}{6}$

25. $-\sqrt{\dfrac{27}{144}} = -\dfrac{\sqrt{27}}{\sqrt{144}} = -\dfrac{\sqrt{9} \cdot \sqrt{3}}{12} = -\dfrac{3\sqrt{3}}{12}$

27. $\sqrt{x^7} = \sqrt{x^6 \cdot x} = \sqrt{x^6} \cdot \sqrt{x} = x^3 \sqrt{x}$

29. $\sqrt{x^{13}} = \sqrt{x^{12} \cdot x} = \sqrt{x^{12}} \cdot \sqrt{x} = x^6 \sqrt{x}$

31. $\sqrt{75x^2} = \sqrt{25x^2 \cdot 3} = \sqrt{25x^2} \cdot \sqrt{3} = 5x\sqrt{3}$

33. $\sqrt{96x^4} = \sqrt{16x^4 \cdot 6} = \sqrt{16x^4} \cdot \sqrt{6} = 4x^2 \sqrt{6}$

35. $\sqrt{\dfrac{12}{y^2}} = \dfrac{\sqrt{12}}{\sqrt{y^2}} = \dfrac{\sqrt{4} \cdot \sqrt{3}}{y} = \dfrac{2\sqrt{3}}{y}$

37. $\sqrt{\dfrac{9x}{y^2}} = \dfrac{\sqrt{9x}}{\sqrt{y^2}} = \dfrac{\sqrt{9} \cdot \sqrt{x}}{y} = \dfrac{3\sqrt{x}}{y}$

39. $\sqrt{\dfrac{88}{x^4}} = \dfrac{\sqrt{88}}{\sqrt{x^4}} = \dfrac{\sqrt{4} \cdot \sqrt{22}}{x^2} = \dfrac{2\sqrt{22}}{x^2}$

41. $\sqrt[3]{24} = \sqrt[3]{8 \cdot 3} = \sqrt[3]{8} \cdot \sqrt[3]{3} = 2\sqrt[3]{3}$

43. $\sqrt[3]{250} = \sqrt[3]{125 \cdot 2} = \sqrt[3]{125} \cdot \sqrt[3]{2} = 5\sqrt[3]{2}$

45. $\sqrt[3]{\dfrac{5}{64}} = \dfrac{\sqrt[3]{5}}{\sqrt[3]{64}} = \dfrac{\sqrt[3]{5}}{4}$

47. $\sqrt[3]{\dfrac{7}{8}} = \dfrac{\sqrt[3]{7}}{\sqrt[3]{8}} = \dfrac{\sqrt[3]{7}}{2}$

49. $\sqrt[3]{\dfrac{15}{64}} = \dfrac{\sqrt[3]{15}}{\sqrt[3]{64}} = \dfrac{\sqrt[3]{15}}{4}$

51. $\sqrt[3]{80} = \sqrt[3]{8 \cdot 10} = \sqrt[3]{8} \cdot \sqrt[3]{10} = 2\sqrt[3]{10}$

53. $6x + 8x = (6+8)x = 14x$

55. $(2x+3)(x-5) = 2x^2 - 10x + 3x - 15$
$$= 2x^2 - 7x - 15$$

57. $9y^2 - 9y^2 = 0$

59. $\sqrt{x^6 y^3} = \sqrt{x^6 y^2 y} = \sqrt{x^6 y^2} \cdot \sqrt{y} = x^3 y\sqrt{y}$

61. $\sqrt{x^2 + 4x + 4} = \sqrt{(x+2)^2} = x+2$

63. $\sqrt[3]{80} = \sqrt[3]{8 \cdot 10} = \sqrt[3]{8} \cdot \sqrt[3]{10} = 2\sqrt[3]{10}$

The length of each side is $2\sqrt[3]{10}$ inches.

65. Let $A = 594$

The length of a side $= \sqrt{\dfrac{A}{6}}$

$\sqrt{\dfrac{A}{6}} = \sqrt{\dfrac{594}{6}} = \sqrt{99} = \sqrt{9} \cdot \sqrt{11} = 3\sqrt{11}$

The length of a side $= 3\sqrt{11}$ feet

67. Let $A = 150$

The length of a side $= \sqrt{\dfrac{A}{6}}$

$\sqrt{\dfrac{A}{6}} = \sqrt{\dfrac{150}{6}} = \sqrt{25} = 5$

The length of a side $= 5$ inches.

69. Let $n = 1000$
$$C = 100\sqrt[3]{n} + 700$$
$$C = 100\sqrt[3]{1000} + 700$$
$$= 100(10) + 700$$
$$= 1700$$
The cost is $1700

71. Answers may vary.

73. Let $h = 169$ and $w = 64$.

$B = \sqrt{\dfrac{hw}{3600}}$

$B = \sqrt{\dfrac{(169)(64)}{3600}} = \sqrt{\dfrac{10,816}{3600}} = \sqrt{\dfrac{676}{225}}$

$= \dfrac{26}{15} \approx 1.7$

The surface area is about 1.7 sq. m.

Practice Problems 8.3

1. $6\sqrt{11} + 9\sqrt{11} = (6+9)\sqrt{11} = 15\sqrt{11}$

2. $\sqrt{7} - 3\sqrt{7} = (1-3)\sqrt{7} = -2\sqrt{7}$

3. $\sqrt{2} + \sqrt{2} = (1+1)\sqrt{2} = 2\sqrt{2}$

4. $3\sqrt{3} - 3\sqrt{2}$ cannot be simplified.

5. $\sqrt{27} + \sqrt{75} = \sqrt{9} \cdot \sqrt{3} + \sqrt{25} \cdot \sqrt{3}$
$$= 3\sqrt{3} + 5\sqrt{3}$$
$$= 8\sqrt{3}$$

6. $3\sqrt{20} - 7\sqrt{45} = 3\sqrt{4} \cdot \sqrt{5} - 7\sqrt{9} \cdot \sqrt{5}$
$$= 3(2)\sqrt{5} - 7(3)\sqrt{5}$$
$$= 6\sqrt{5} - 21\sqrt{5}$$
$$= -15\sqrt{5}$$

7. $\sqrt{36} - \sqrt{48} - 4\sqrt{3} - \sqrt{9}$
$$= 6 - \sqrt{16} \cdot \sqrt{3} - 4\sqrt{3} - 3$$
$$= 6 - 4\sqrt{3} - 4\sqrt{3} - 3$$
$$= 3 - 8\sqrt{3}$$

8. $\sqrt{9x^4} - \sqrt{36x^3} + \sqrt{x^3}$
$$= 3x^2 - \sqrt{36x^2} \cdot \sqrt{x} + \sqrt{x^2} \cdot \sqrt{x}$$
$$= 3x^2 - 6x\sqrt{x} + x\sqrt{x}$$
$$= 3x^2 - 5x\sqrt{x}$$

Mental Math 8.3

1. $3\sqrt{2} + 5\sqrt{2} = 8\sqrt{2}$

2. $3\sqrt{5} + 7\sqrt{5} = 10\sqrt{5}$

3. $5\sqrt{x} + 2\sqrt{x} = 7\sqrt{x}$

4. $8\sqrt{x} + 3\sqrt{x} = 11\sqrt{x}$

5. $5\sqrt{7} - 2\sqrt{7} = 3\sqrt{7}$

6. $8\sqrt{6} - 5\sqrt{6} = 3\sqrt{6}$

Exercise Set 8.3

1. $4\sqrt{3} - 8\sqrt{3} = (4 - 8)\sqrt{3} = -4\sqrt{3}$

3. $3\sqrt{6} + 8\sqrt{6} - 2\sqrt{6} - 5 = (3 + 8 - 2)\sqrt{6} - 5$
$$= 9\sqrt{6} - 5$$

5. $6\sqrt{5} - 5\sqrt{5} + \sqrt{2} = (6 - 5)\sqrt{5} + \sqrt{2}$
$$= \sqrt{5} + \sqrt{2}$$

7. $2\sqrt{3} + 5\sqrt{3} - \sqrt{3} = (2 + 5 - 1)\sqrt{3} = 6\sqrt{3}$

9. $2\sqrt{2} - 7\sqrt{2} - 6 = (2 - 7)\sqrt{2} - 6$
$$= -5\sqrt{2} - 6$$

11. $12\sqrt{5} - \sqrt{5} - 4\sqrt{5} = (12 - 1 - 4)\sqrt{5} = 7\sqrt{5}$

13. $\sqrt{5} + \sqrt{5} = (1 + 1)\sqrt{5} = 2\sqrt{5}$

15. $6 - 2\sqrt{3} - \sqrt{3} = 6 + (-2 - 1)\sqrt{3} = 6 - 3\sqrt{3}$

17. Answers may vary.

19. $\sqrt{12} + \sqrt{27} = \sqrt{4 \cdot 3} + \sqrt{9 \cdot 3}$
$$= \sqrt{4} \cdot \sqrt{3} + \sqrt{9} \cdot \sqrt{3}$$
$$= 2\sqrt{3} + 3\sqrt{3} = 5\sqrt{3}$$

21. $\sqrt{45} + 3\sqrt{20} = \sqrt{9 \cdot 5} + 3\sqrt{4 \cdot 5}$
$$= \sqrt{9} \cdot \sqrt{5} + 3\sqrt{4} \cdot \sqrt{5}$$
$$= 3\sqrt{5} + 3(2)\sqrt{5}$$
$$= 3\sqrt{5} + 6\sqrt{5}$$
$$= 9\sqrt{5}$$

23. $2\sqrt{54} - \sqrt{20} + \sqrt{45} - \sqrt{24}$

$= 2\sqrt{9 \cdot 6} - \sqrt{4 \cdot 5} + \sqrt{9 \cdot 5} - \sqrt{4 \cdot 6}$

$= 2\sqrt{9} \cdot \sqrt{6} - \sqrt{4} \cdot \sqrt{5} + \sqrt{9} \cdot \sqrt{5} - \sqrt{4} \cdot \sqrt{6}$

$= 2(3)\sqrt{6} - 2\sqrt{5} + 3\sqrt{5} - 2\sqrt{6}$

$= 6\sqrt{6} - 2\sqrt{5} + 3\sqrt{5} - 2\sqrt{6}$

$= 4\sqrt{6} + \sqrt{5}$

25. $4x - 3\sqrt{x^2} + \sqrt{x} = 4x - 3x + \sqrt{x} = x + \sqrt{x}$

27. $\sqrt{25x} + \sqrt{36x} - 11\sqrt{x}$

$= \sqrt{25} \cdot \sqrt{x} + \sqrt{36} \cdot \sqrt{x} - 11\sqrt{x}$

$= 5\sqrt{x} + 6\sqrt{x} - 11\sqrt{x}$

$= 0$

29. $3\sqrt{x^3} - x\sqrt{4x} = 3\sqrt{x^2 \cdot x} - x\sqrt{4x}$

$= 3\sqrt{x^2} \cdot \sqrt{x} - x\sqrt{4} \cdot \sqrt{x}$

$= 3x\sqrt{x} - x(2)\sqrt{x}$

$= x\sqrt{x}$

31. $\sqrt{75} + \sqrt{48} = \sqrt{25} \cdot \sqrt{3} + \sqrt{16} \cdot \sqrt{3}$

$= 5\sqrt{3} + 4\sqrt{3}$

$= 9\sqrt{3}$

33. $\sqrt{8} + \sqrt{9} + \sqrt{18} + \sqrt{81}$

$= \sqrt{4} \cdot \sqrt{2} + 3 + \sqrt{9} \cdot \sqrt{2} + 9$

$= 2\sqrt{2} + 3 + 3\sqrt{2} + 9$

$= 5\sqrt{2} + 12$

35. $\sqrt{\dfrac{5}{9}} + \sqrt{\dfrac{5}{81}} = \dfrac{\sqrt{5}}{\sqrt{9}} + \dfrac{\sqrt{5}}{\sqrt{81}} = \dfrac{\sqrt{5}}{3} + \dfrac{\sqrt{5}}{9}$

$= \dfrac{3\sqrt{5}}{9} + \dfrac{\sqrt{5}}{9} = \dfrac{3\sqrt{5} + \sqrt{5}}{9} = \dfrac{4\sqrt{5}}{9}$

37. $\sqrt{\dfrac{3}{4}} - \sqrt{\dfrac{3}{64}} = \dfrac{\sqrt{3}}{\sqrt{4}} - \dfrac{\sqrt{3}}{\sqrt{64}} = \dfrac{\sqrt{3}}{2} - \dfrac{\sqrt{3}}{8}$

$= \dfrac{4\sqrt{3}}{8} - \dfrac{\sqrt{3}}{8} = \dfrac{4\sqrt{3} - \sqrt{3}}{8} = \dfrac{3\sqrt{3}}{8}$

39. $2\sqrt{45} - 2\sqrt{20} = 2\sqrt{9} \cdot \sqrt{5} - 2\sqrt{4} \cdot \sqrt{5}$

$= 2(3)\sqrt{5} - 2(2)\sqrt{5}$

$= 6\sqrt{5} - 4\sqrt{5}$

$= 2\sqrt{5}$

41. $\sqrt{35} - \sqrt{140} = \sqrt{35} - \sqrt{4} \cdot \sqrt{35}$

$= \sqrt{35} - 2\sqrt{35}$

$= -\sqrt{35}$

43. $3\sqrt{9x} + 2\sqrt{x} = 3\sqrt{9} \cdot \sqrt{x} + 2\sqrt{x}$

$= 3(3)\sqrt{x} + 2\sqrt{x}$

$= 9\sqrt{x} + 2\sqrt{x}$

$= 11\sqrt{x}$

45. $\sqrt{9x^2} + \sqrt{81x^2} - 11\sqrt{x}$

$= \sqrt{9} \cdot \sqrt{x^2} + \sqrt{81} \cdot \sqrt{x^2} - 11\sqrt{x}$

$= 3x + 9x - 11\sqrt{x}$

$= 12x - 11\sqrt{x}$

47. $\sqrt{3x^3} + 3x\sqrt{x} = \sqrt{x^2 \cdot 3x} + 3x\sqrt{x}$

$= \sqrt{x^2} \cdot \sqrt{3x} + 3x\sqrt{x}$

$= x\sqrt{3x} + 3x\sqrt{x}$

49. $\sqrt{32x^2} + \sqrt{32x^2} + \sqrt{4x^2}$

$= \sqrt{16} \cdot \sqrt{x^2} \cdot \sqrt{2} + \sqrt{16} \cdot \sqrt{x^2} \cdot \sqrt{2} + \sqrt{4} \cdot \sqrt{x^2}$

$= 4x\sqrt{2} + 4x\sqrt{2} + 2x$

$= 8x\sqrt{2} + 2x$

51. $\sqrt{40x} + \sqrt{40x^4} - 2\sqrt{10x} - \sqrt{5x^4}$

$= \sqrt{4} \cdot \sqrt{10x} + \sqrt{4x^4} \cdot \sqrt{10} - 2\sqrt{10x} - \sqrt{x^4} \cdot \sqrt{5}$

$= 2\sqrt{10x} + 2x^2\sqrt{10} - 2\sqrt{10x} - x^2\sqrt{5}$

$= 2x^2\sqrt{10} - x^2\sqrt{5}$

53. $(x+6)^2 = x^2 + 2(6)x + 6^2$

$\qquad\qquad = x^2 + 12x + 36$

55. $(2x-1)^2 = (2x)^2 + 2(-1)(2x) + (-1)^2$

$\qquad\qquad = 4x^2 - 4x + 1$

57. $\begin{cases} x = 2y \\ x + 5y = 14 \end{cases}$

Substitute $2y$ for x in the second equation.

$2y + 5y = 14$

$\qquad 7y = 14$

$\qquad\ y = 2$

Let $y = 2$ in the first equation.

$x = 2(2) = 4$

The solution is $(4, 2)$

59. Let $l = 3\sqrt{5}$ and $w = \sqrt{5}$

Perimeter $= 2l + 2w$

$\qquad\qquad = 2(3\sqrt{5}) + 2(\sqrt{5})$

$\qquad\qquad = 6\sqrt{5} + 2\sqrt{5}$

$\qquad\qquad = 8\sqrt{5}$ inches

61. Let $l = 8$ and $w = 3$

Area = area of 2 triangles

$\qquad\qquad$ + area of 2 rectangles

$= 2\left(\dfrac{3\sqrt{27}}{4}\right) + 2lw$

$= \dfrac{3\sqrt{9} \cdot \sqrt{3}}{2} + 2(8)(3)$

$= \dfrac{9\sqrt{3}}{2} + 48$ square feet

Practice Problems 8.4

1. $\sqrt{5} \cdot \sqrt{2} = \sqrt{5 \cdot 2} = \sqrt{10}$

2. $\sqrt{6} \cdot \sqrt{3} = \sqrt{6 \cdot 3} = \sqrt{18} = \sqrt{9} \cdot \sqrt{2} = 3\sqrt{2}$

3. $\sqrt{10x} \cdot \sqrt{2x} = \sqrt{10x \cdot 2x} = \sqrt{20x^2}$

$\qquad\quad = \sqrt{4x^2} \cdot \sqrt{5} = 2x\sqrt{5}$

4. a. $\sqrt{7}\left(\sqrt{7} - \sqrt{3}\right) = \sqrt{7} \cdot \sqrt{7} - \sqrt{7} \cdot \sqrt{3}$

$\qquad\qquad = \sqrt{49} - \sqrt{21} = 7 - \sqrt{21}$

b. $\left(\sqrt{x} + \sqrt{5}\right)\left(\sqrt{x} - \sqrt{3}\right)$

$\qquad = \sqrt{x} \cdot \sqrt{x} - \sqrt{x} \cdot \sqrt{3} + \sqrt{5} \cdot \sqrt{x} - \sqrt{5} \cdot \sqrt{3}$

$\qquad = \sqrt{x^2} - \sqrt{3x} + \sqrt{5x} - \sqrt{15}$

$\qquad = x - \sqrt{3x} + \sqrt{5x} - \sqrt{15}$

5. a. $\left(\sqrt{3} + 6\right)\left(\sqrt{3} - 6\right) = \left(\sqrt{3}\right)^2 - 6^2$

$\qquad\qquad = 3 - 36$

$\qquad\qquad = -33$

b. $\left(\sqrt{5x} + 4\right)^2 = \left(\sqrt{5x}\right)^2 + 2(4)\sqrt{5x} + 4^2$

$\qquad\qquad = 5x + 8\sqrt{5x} + 16$

6. $\dfrac{\sqrt{15}}{\sqrt{3}} = \sqrt{\dfrac{15}{3}} = \sqrt{5}$

7. $\dfrac{\sqrt{90}}{\sqrt{2}} = \sqrt{\dfrac{90}{2}} = \sqrt{45} = \sqrt{9} \cdot \sqrt{5} = 3\sqrt{5}$

8. $\dfrac{\sqrt{75x^3}}{\sqrt{5x}} = \sqrt{\dfrac{75x^3}{5x}} = \sqrt{15x^2}$
$= \sqrt{x^2} \cdot \sqrt{15} = x\sqrt{15}$

9. $\dfrac{5}{\sqrt{3}} = \dfrac{5}{\sqrt{3}} \cdot \dfrac{\sqrt{3}}{\sqrt{3}} = \dfrac{5\sqrt{3}}{\sqrt{9}} = \dfrac{5\sqrt{3}}{3}$

10. $\dfrac{\sqrt{7}}{\sqrt{20}} = \dfrac{\sqrt{7}}{\sqrt{4 \cdot 5}} = \dfrac{\sqrt{7}}{2\sqrt{5}} = \dfrac{\sqrt{7}}{2\sqrt{5}} \cdot \dfrac{\sqrt{5}}{\sqrt{5}}$
$= \dfrac{\sqrt{35}}{2\sqrt{25}} = \dfrac{\sqrt{35}}{10}$

11. $\dfrac{\sqrt{2}}{\sqrt{45x}} = \dfrac{\sqrt{2}}{\sqrt{9} \cdot \sqrt{5x}} = \dfrac{\sqrt{2}}{3\sqrt{5x}} = \dfrac{\sqrt{2}}{3\sqrt{5x}} \cdot \dfrac{\sqrt{5x}}{\sqrt{5x}}$
$= \dfrac{\sqrt{10x}}{3\sqrt{25x^2}} = \dfrac{\sqrt{10x}}{15x}$

12. $\dfrac{3}{1+\sqrt{7}} = \dfrac{3}{1+\sqrt{7}} \cdot \dfrac{1-\sqrt{7}}{1-\sqrt{7}} = \dfrac{3\left(1-\sqrt{7}\right)}{1^2 - \left(\sqrt{7}\right)^2}$
$= \dfrac{3\left(1-\sqrt{7}\right)}{1-7} = \dfrac{3\left(1-\sqrt{7}\right)}{-6} = \dfrac{1-\sqrt{7}}{-2}$
$= \dfrac{-1+\sqrt{7}}{2}$

13. $\dfrac{\sqrt{2}+5}{\sqrt{2}-1} = \dfrac{\sqrt{2}+5}{\sqrt{2}-1} \cdot \dfrac{\sqrt{2}+1}{\sqrt{2}+1}$
$= \dfrac{2+\sqrt{2}+5\sqrt{2}+5}{2-1}$
$= 7+6\sqrt{2}$

14. $\dfrac{7}{2-\sqrt{x}} = \dfrac{7}{2-\sqrt{x}} \cdot \dfrac{2+\sqrt{x}}{2+\sqrt{x}} = \dfrac{7\left(2+\sqrt{x}\right)}{2^2 - \left(\sqrt{x}\right)^2}$
$= \dfrac{7\left(2+\sqrt{x}\right)}{4-x}$

Mental Math 8.4

1. $\sqrt{2} \cdot \sqrt{3} = \sqrt{6}$

2. $\sqrt{5} \cdot \sqrt{7} = \sqrt{35}$

3. $\sqrt{1} \cdot \sqrt{6} = \sqrt{6}$

4. $\sqrt{7} \cdot \sqrt{x} = \sqrt{7x}$

5. $\sqrt{10} \cdot \sqrt{y} = \sqrt{10y}$

6. $\sqrt{x} \cdot \sqrt{y} = \sqrt{xy}$

Exercise Set 8.4

1. $\sqrt{8} \cdot \sqrt{2} = \sqrt{8 \cdot 2} = \sqrt{16} = 4$

3. $\sqrt{10} \cdot \sqrt{5} = \sqrt{10 \cdot 5} = \sqrt{50} = \sqrt{25} \cdot \sqrt{2} = 5\sqrt{2}$

5. $\sqrt{6} \cdot \sqrt{6} = \sqrt{6 \cdot 6} = \sqrt{36} = 6$

7. $\sqrt{2x} \cdot \sqrt{2x} = \sqrt{2x \cdot 2x} = \sqrt{4x^2} = 2x$

9. $\left(2\sqrt{5}\right)^2 = 2^2\left(\sqrt{5}\right)^2 = 4(5) = 20$

11. $\left(6\sqrt{x}\right)^2 = 6^2\left(\sqrt{x}\right)^2 = 36x$

13. $\sqrt{3y}\cdot\sqrt{6x} = \sqrt{3y\cdot 6x} = \sqrt{18xy}$

$\qquad = \sqrt{9}\cdot\sqrt{2xy} = 3\sqrt{2xy}$

15. $\sqrt{2xy^2}\cdot\sqrt{8xy} = \sqrt{2xy\cdot 8xy^2} = \sqrt{16x^2y^3}$

$\qquad = \sqrt{16x^2y^2}\cdot\sqrt{y} = 4xy\sqrt{y}$

17. $\sqrt{2}\left(\sqrt{5}+1\right) = \sqrt{2}\cdot\sqrt{5} + \sqrt{2}\cdot 1$

$\qquad = \sqrt{2\cdot 5} + \sqrt{2\cdot 1} = \sqrt{10} + \sqrt{2}$

19. $\sqrt{10}\left(\sqrt{2}+\sqrt{5}\right) = \sqrt{10}\cdot\sqrt{2} + \sqrt{10}\cdot\sqrt{5}$

$\qquad = \sqrt{20} + \sqrt{50} = \sqrt{4}\cdot\sqrt{5} + \sqrt{25}\cdot\sqrt{2}$

$\qquad = 2\sqrt{5} + 5\sqrt{2}$

21. $\sqrt{6}\left(\sqrt{5}+\sqrt{7}\right) = \sqrt{6}\cdot\sqrt{5} + \sqrt{6}\cdot\sqrt{7}$

$\qquad\qquad = \sqrt{30} + \sqrt{42}$

23. $\left(\sqrt{3}+6\right)\left(\sqrt{3}-6\right) = \left(\sqrt{3}\right)^2 - (6)^2$

$\qquad = 3 - 36 = -33$

25. $\left(\sqrt{3}+\sqrt{5}\right)\left(\sqrt{2}-\sqrt{5}\right)$

$\qquad = \sqrt{3}\cdot\sqrt{2} - \sqrt{3}\cdot\sqrt{5} + \sqrt{5}\cdot\sqrt{2} - \left(\sqrt{5}\right)^2$

$\qquad = \sqrt{6} - \sqrt{15} + \sqrt{10} - 5$

27. $\left(2\sqrt{11}+1\right)\left(\sqrt{11}-6\right)$

$\qquad = 2\left(\sqrt{11}\right)^2 - 12\sqrt{11} + 1\sqrt{11} - 6$

$\qquad = 2(11) - 11\sqrt{11} - 6$

$\qquad = 16 - 11\sqrt{11}$

29. $\left(\sqrt{x}+6\right)\left(\sqrt{x}-6\right) = \left(\sqrt{x}\right)^2 - (6)^2 = x - 36$

31. $\left(\sqrt{x}-7\right)^2 = \left(\sqrt{x}\right)^2 - 2(7)\sqrt{x} + (7)^2$

$\qquad\qquad = x - 14\sqrt{x} + 49$

33. $\left(\sqrt{6y}+1\right)^2 = \left(\sqrt{6y}\right)^2 + 2(1)\sqrt{6y} + (1)^2$

$\qquad\qquad = 6y + 2\sqrt{6y} + 1$

35. $\dfrac{\sqrt{32}}{\sqrt{2}} = \sqrt{\dfrac{32}{2}} = \sqrt{16} = 4$

37. $\dfrac{\sqrt{21}}{\sqrt{3}} = \sqrt{\dfrac{21}{3}} = \sqrt{7}$

39. $\dfrac{\sqrt{90}}{\sqrt{5}} = \sqrt{\dfrac{90}{5}} = \sqrt{18} = \sqrt{9}\cdot\sqrt{2} = 3\sqrt{2}$

41. $\dfrac{\sqrt{75y^5}}{\sqrt{3y}} = \sqrt{\dfrac{75y^5}{3y}} = \sqrt{25y^4} = 5y^2$

43. $\dfrac{\sqrt{150}}{\sqrt{2}} = \sqrt{\dfrac{150}{2}} = \sqrt{75} = \sqrt{25}\cdot\sqrt{3} = 5\sqrt{3}$

45. $\dfrac{\sqrt{72y^5}}{\sqrt{3y^3}} = \sqrt{\dfrac{72y^5}{3y^3}} = \sqrt{24y^2}$

$\qquad\qquad = \sqrt{4y^2}\cdot\sqrt{6} = 2y\sqrt{6}$

47. $\dfrac{\sqrt{24x^3y^4}}{\sqrt{2xy}} = \sqrt{\dfrac{24x^3y^4}{2xy}} = \sqrt{12x^2y^3}$

$$= \sqrt{4x^2y^2} \cdot \sqrt{3y} = 2xy\sqrt{3y}$$

49. $\dfrac{\sqrt{3}}{\sqrt{5}} = \dfrac{\sqrt{3}}{\sqrt{5}} \cdot \dfrac{\sqrt{5}}{\sqrt{5}} = \dfrac{\sqrt{15}}{\sqrt{25}} = \dfrac{\sqrt{15}}{5}$

51. $\dfrac{7}{\sqrt{2}} = \dfrac{7}{\sqrt{2}} \cdot \dfrac{\sqrt{2}}{\sqrt{2}} = \dfrac{7\sqrt{2}}{\sqrt{4}} = \dfrac{7\sqrt{2}}{2}$

53. $\dfrac{1}{\sqrt{6y}} = \dfrac{1}{\sqrt{6y}} \cdot \dfrac{\sqrt{6y}}{\sqrt{6y}} = \dfrac{\sqrt{6y}}{6y}$

55. $\sqrt{\dfrac{5}{18}} = \dfrac{\sqrt{5}}{\sqrt{18}} = \dfrac{\sqrt{5}}{\sqrt{9} \cdot \sqrt{2}} = \dfrac{\sqrt{5}}{3\sqrt{2}}$

$$= \dfrac{\sqrt{5}}{3\sqrt{2}} \cdot \dfrac{\sqrt{2}}{\sqrt{2}} = \dfrac{\sqrt{10}}{3(2)} = \dfrac{\sqrt{10}}{6}$$

57. $\sqrt{\dfrac{3}{x}} = \dfrac{\sqrt{3}}{\sqrt{x}} = \dfrac{\sqrt{3}}{\sqrt{x}} \cdot \dfrac{\sqrt{x}}{\sqrt{x}} = \dfrac{\sqrt{3x}}{x}$

59. $\sqrt{\dfrac{1}{8}} = \dfrac{\sqrt{1}}{\sqrt{8}} = \dfrac{1}{\sqrt{4} \cdot \sqrt{2}} = \dfrac{1}{2\sqrt{2}}$

$$= \dfrac{1}{2\sqrt{2}} \cdot \dfrac{\sqrt{2}}{\sqrt{2}} = \dfrac{\sqrt{2}}{2(2)} = \dfrac{\sqrt{2}}{4}$$

61. $\sqrt{\dfrac{2}{15}} = \dfrac{\sqrt{2}}{\sqrt{15}} = \dfrac{\sqrt{2}}{\sqrt{15}} \cdot \dfrac{\sqrt{15}}{\sqrt{15}} = \dfrac{\sqrt{30}}{15}$

63. $\sqrt{\dfrac{3}{20}} = \dfrac{\sqrt{3}}{\sqrt{20}} = \dfrac{\sqrt{3}}{\sqrt{4} \cdot \sqrt{5}} = \dfrac{\sqrt{3}}{2\sqrt{5}}$

$$= \dfrac{\sqrt{3}}{2\sqrt{5}} \cdot \dfrac{\sqrt{5}}{\sqrt{5}} = \dfrac{\sqrt{15}}{2(5)} = \dfrac{\sqrt{15}}{10}$$

65. $\dfrac{3x}{\sqrt{2x}} = \dfrac{3x}{\sqrt{2x}} \cdot \dfrac{\sqrt{2x}}{\sqrt{2x}} = \dfrac{3x\sqrt{2x}}{2x} = \dfrac{3\sqrt{2x}}{2}$

67. $\dfrac{8y}{\sqrt{5}} = \dfrac{8y}{\sqrt{5}} \cdot \dfrac{\sqrt{5}}{\sqrt{5}} = \dfrac{8y\sqrt{5}}{5}$

69. $\sqrt{\dfrac{y}{12x}} = \dfrac{\sqrt{y}}{\sqrt{12x}} = \dfrac{\sqrt{y}}{\sqrt{4} \cdot \sqrt{3x}} = \dfrac{\sqrt{y}}{2\sqrt{3x}}$

$$= \dfrac{\sqrt{y}}{2\sqrt{3x}} \cdot \dfrac{\sqrt{3x}}{\sqrt{3x}} = \dfrac{\sqrt{3xy}}{2(3x)} = \dfrac{\sqrt{3xy}}{6x}$$

71. $\dfrac{3}{\sqrt{2}+1} = \dfrac{3}{\sqrt{2}+1} \cdot \dfrac{\sqrt{2}-1}{\sqrt{2}-1} = \dfrac{3(\sqrt{2}-1)}{(\sqrt{2})^2 - 1^2}$

$$= \dfrac{3(\sqrt{2}-1)}{2-1} = \dfrac{3(\sqrt{2}-1)}{1} = 3\sqrt{2}-3$$

73. $\dfrac{4}{2-\sqrt{5}} = \dfrac{4}{2-\sqrt{5}} \cdot \dfrac{2+\sqrt{5}}{2+\sqrt{5}} = \dfrac{4(2+\sqrt{5})}{2^2 - (\sqrt{5})^2}$

$$= \dfrac{4(2+\sqrt{5})}{4-5} = \dfrac{4(2+\sqrt{5})}{-1} = -8-4\sqrt{5}$$

75. $\dfrac{\sqrt{5}+1}{\sqrt{6}-\sqrt{5}} = \dfrac{\sqrt{5}+1}{\sqrt{6}-\sqrt{5}} \cdot \dfrac{\sqrt{6}+\sqrt{5}}{\sqrt{6}+\sqrt{5}}$

$$= \dfrac{\sqrt{30}+5+\sqrt{6}+\sqrt{5}}{(\sqrt{6})^2 - (\sqrt{5})^2}$$

$$= \dfrac{\sqrt{30}+5+\sqrt{6}+\sqrt{5}}{6-5}$$

$$= \sqrt{30}+5+\sqrt{6}+\sqrt{5}$$

77. $\dfrac{\sqrt{3}+1}{\sqrt{2}-1} = \dfrac{\sqrt{3}+1}{\sqrt{2}-1} \cdot \dfrac{\sqrt{2}+1}{\sqrt{2}+1}$

$\qquad = \dfrac{\sqrt{6}+\sqrt{3}+\sqrt{2}+1}{2-1}$

$\qquad = \sqrt{6}+\sqrt{3}+\sqrt{2}+1$

79. $\dfrac{5}{2+\sqrt{x}} = \dfrac{5}{2+\sqrt{x}} \cdot \dfrac{2-\sqrt{x}}{2-\sqrt{x}} = \dfrac{5\left(2-\sqrt{x}\right)}{2^2-\left(\sqrt{x}\right)^2}$

$\qquad = \dfrac{10-5\sqrt{x}}{4-x}$

81. $\dfrac{3}{\sqrt{x}-4} = \dfrac{3}{\sqrt{x}-4} \cdot \dfrac{\sqrt{x}+4}{\sqrt{x}+4} = \dfrac{3\left(\sqrt{x}+4\right)}{\left(\sqrt{x}\right)^2-4^2}$

$\qquad = \dfrac{3\sqrt{x}+12}{x-16}$

83. $x+5 = 7^2$

$\qquad x+5 = 49$

$\qquad x = 44$

85. $4z^2+6z-12 = \left(2z\right)^2$

$\qquad 4z^2+6z-12 = 4z^2$

$\qquad 6z-12 = 0$

$\qquad 6z = 12$

$\qquad z = 2$

87. $9x^2+5x+4 = \left(3x+1\right)^2$

$\qquad 9x^2+5x+4 = 9x^2+6x+1$

$\qquad -x = -3$

$\qquad x = 3$

89. Let $l = 13\sqrt{2}$ and $w = 5\sqrt{6}$.

$\quad A = lw$

$\qquad = 13\sqrt{2} \cdot 5\sqrt{6} = 65\sqrt{12} = 65\sqrt{4} \cdot \sqrt{3}$

$\qquad = 65\left(2\right)\sqrt{3} = 130\sqrt{3}$ square meters

91. Answers may vary.

93. $\dfrac{\sqrt{3}+1}{\sqrt{2}-1} = \dfrac{\sqrt{3}+1}{\sqrt{2}-1} \cdot \dfrac{\sqrt{3}-1}{\sqrt{3}-1}$

$\qquad = \dfrac{3-1}{\sqrt{6}-\sqrt{2}-\sqrt{3}+1}$

$\qquad = \dfrac{2}{\sqrt{6}-\sqrt{2}-\sqrt{3}+1}$

Integrated Review 8.4

1. $\sqrt{36} = 6$, because $6^2 = 36$ and 6 is positive.

2. $\sqrt{48} = \sqrt{16} \cdot \sqrt{3} = 4\sqrt{3}$

3. $\sqrt{x^4} = x^2$, because $\left(x^2\right)^2 = x^4$.

4. $\sqrt{y^7} = \sqrt{y^6}\sqrt{y} = y^3\sqrt{y}$

5. $\sqrt{16x^2} = 4x$, because $\left(4x\right)^2 = 16x^2$.

6. $\sqrt{18x^{11}} = \sqrt{9x^{10}}\sqrt{2x} = 3x^5\sqrt{2x}$

7. $\sqrt[3]{8} = 2$, because $\left(2\right)^3 = 8$.

8. $\sqrt[4]{81} = 3$, because $\left(3\right)^4 = 81$.

9. $\sqrt[3]{-27} = -3$, because $\left(-3\right)^3 = -27$.

10. $\sqrt{-4}$ is not a real number.

11. $\sqrt{\dfrac{11}{9}} = \dfrac{\sqrt{11}}{\sqrt{9}} = \dfrac{\sqrt{11}}{3}$

12. $\sqrt[3]{\dfrac{7}{64}} = \dfrac{\sqrt[3]{7}}{\sqrt[3]{64}} = \dfrac{\sqrt[3]{7}}{4}$

13. $-\sqrt{16} = -4$

14. $-\sqrt{25} = -5$

15. $\sqrt{\dfrac{9}{49}} = \dfrac{3}{7}$

16. $\sqrt{\dfrac{1}{64}} = \dfrac{1}{8}$

17. $\sqrt{a^8 b^2} = a^4 b$

18. $\sqrt{x^{10} y^{20}} = x^5 y^{10}$

19. $\sqrt{25 m^6} = 5 m^3$

20. $\sqrt{9 n^{16}} = 3 n^8$

21. $5\sqrt{7} + \sqrt{7} = (5+1)\sqrt{7} = 6\sqrt{7}$

22. $\sqrt{50} - \sqrt{8} = \sqrt{25} \cdot \sqrt{2} - \sqrt{4} \cdot \sqrt{2}$
$= 5\sqrt{2} - 2\sqrt{2} = (5-2)\sqrt{2} = 3\sqrt{2}$

23. $5\sqrt{2} - 5\sqrt{3}$ cannot be simplified.

24. $2\sqrt{x} + \sqrt{25x} - \sqrt{36x} + 3x$
$= 2\sqrt{x} + \sqrt{25} \cdot \sqrt{x} - \sqrt{36} \cdot \sqrt{x} + 3x$
$= 2\sqrt{x} + 5\sqrt{x} - 6\sqrt{x} + 3x$
$= (2+5-6)\sqrt{x} + 3x$
$= \sqrt{x} + 3x$

25. $\sqrt{2} \cdot \sqrt{15} = \sqrt{2 \cdot 15} = \sqrt{30}$

26. $\sqrt{3} \cdot \sqrt{3} = \sqrt{3 \cdot 3} = \sqrt{9} = 3$

27. $\left(2\sqrt{7}\right)^2 = 2^2 \left(\sqrt{7}\right)^2 = 4(7) = 28$

28. $\left(3\sqrt{5}\right)^2 = 3^2 \left(\sqrt{5}\right)^2 = 9(5) = 45$

29. $\sqrt{3}\left(\sqrt{11} + 1\right) = \sqrt{3} \cdot \sqrt{11} + \sqrt{3} \cdot 1$
$= \sqrt{33} + \sqrt{3}$

30. $\sqrt{6}\left(\sqrt{3} - 2\right) = \sqrt{6} \cdot \sqrt{3} - \sqrt{6} \cdot 2$
$= \sqrt{18} - 2\sqrt{6} = \sqrt{9} \cdot \sqrt{2} - 2\sqrt{6}$
$= 3\sqrt{2} - 2\sqrt{6}$

31. $\sqrt{8y} \cdot \sqrt{2y} = \sqrt{8y \cdot 2y} = \sqrt{16 y^2} = 4y$

32. $\sqrt{15 x^2} \cdot \sqrt{3 x^2} = \sqrt{15 x^2 \cdot 3 x^2} = \sqrt{45 x^4}$
$= \sqrt{9 x^4} \cdot \sqrt{5} = 3 x^2 \sqrt{5}$

33. $\left(\sqrt{x} - 5\right)\left(\sqrt{x} + 2\right) = \sqrt{x^2} + 2\sqrt{x} - 5\sqrt{x} - 10$
$= x - 3\sqrt{x} - 10$

34. $\left(3+\sqrt{2}\right)^2 = 3^2 + 2(3)\sqrt{2} + \left(\sqrt{2}\right)^2$

$$= 9 + 6\sqrt{2} + 2$$

$$= 11 + 6\sqrt{2}$$

35. $\dfrac{\sqrt{8}}{\sqrt{2}} = \sqrt{\dfrac{8}{2}} = \sqrt{4} = 2$

36. $\dfrac{\sqrt{45}}{\sqrt{15}} = \sqrt{\dfrac{45}{15}} = \sqrt{3}$

37. $\dfrac{\sqrt{24x^5}}{\sqrt{2x}} = \sqrt{\dfrac{24x^5}{2x}} = \sqrt{12x^4} = \sqrt{4x^4} \cdot \sqrt{3}$

$$= 2x^2\sqrt{3}$$

38. $\dfrac{\sqrt{75a^4b^5}}{\sqrt{5ab}} = \sqrt{\dfrac{75a^4b^5}{5ab}} = \sqrt{15a^3b^4}$

$$= \sqrt{a^2b^4} \cdot \sqrt{15a} = ab^2\sqrt{15a}$$

39. $\sqrt{\dfrac{1}{6}} = \dfrac{\sqrt{1}}{\sqrt{6}} = \dfrac{1}{\sqrt{6}} \cdot \dfrac{\sqrt{6}}{\sqrt{6}} = \dfrac{\sqrt{6}}{6}$

40. $\dfrac{x}{\sqrt{20}} = \dfrac{x}{\sqrt{4}\cdot\sqrt{5}} = \dfrac{x}{2\sqrt{5}} = \dfrac{x}{2\sqrt{5}} \cdot \dfrac{\sqrt{5}}{\sqrt{5}}$

$$= \dfrac{x\sqrt{5}}{2(5)} = \dfrac{x\sqrt{5}}{10}$$

41. $\dfrac{4}{\sqrt{6}+1} = \dfrac{4}{\sqrt{6}+1} \cdot \dfrac{\sqrt{6}-1}{\sqrt{6}-1} = \dfrac{4\left(\sqrt{6}-1\right)}{6-1}$

$$= \dfrac{4\sqrt{6}-4}{5}$$

42. $\dfrac{\sqrt{2}+1}{\sqrt{x}-5} = \dfrac{\sqrt{2}+1}{\sqrt{x}-5} \cdot \dfrac{\sqrt{x}+5}{\sqrt{x}+5}$

$$= \dfrac{\sqrt{2x}+5\sqrt{2}+\sqrt{x}+5}{x-25}$$

Practice Problems 8.5

1. $\quad \sqrt{x-2} = 7$

$$\left(\sqrt{x-2}\right)^2 = 7^2$$

$$x - 2 = 49$$

$$x = 51$$

2. $\quad \sqrt{x} + 9 = 2$

$$\sqrt{x} = -7$$

The square root cannot be negative, therefore there is no solution.

3. $\quad \sqrt{6x-1} = \sqrt{x}$

$$\left(\sqrt{6x-1}\right)^2 = \left(\sqrt{x}\right)^2$$

$$6x - 1 = x$$

$$5x = 1$$

$$x = \dfrac{1}{5}$$

4. $\quad \sqrt{9y^2 + 2y - 10} = 3y$

$$\left(\sqrt{9y^2 + 2y - 10}\right)^2 = \left(3y\right)^2$$

$$9y^2 + 2y - 10 = 9y^2$$

$$2y - 10 = 0$$

$$2y = 10$$

$$y = 5$$

5. $\sqrt{x+1} - x = -5$

$\sqrt{x+1} = x - 5$

$\left(\sqrt{x+1}\right)^2 = (x-5)^2$

$x + 1 = x^2 - 10x + 25$

$0 = x^2 - 11x + 24$

$0 = (x-3)(x-8)$

$x - 3 = 0$ or $x - 8 = 0$

$x = 3$ $x = 8$

Check:

$\sqrt{3+1} - 3 \overset{?}{=} -5$ $\sqrt{8+1} - 8 \overset{?}{=} -5$

$\sqrt{4} - 3 \overset{?}{=} -5$ $\sqrt{9} - 8 \overset{?}{=} -5$

$2 - 3 \overset{?}{=} -5$ $3 - 8 \overset{?}{=} -5$

$-1 \neq -5$ $-5 = -5$

False   True

The solution is 8.

6. $\sqrt{x} + 3 = \sqrt{x+15}$

$\left(\sqrt{x}+3\right)^2 = \left(\sqrt{x+15}\right)^2$

$x + 6\sqrt{x} + 9 = x + 15$

$6\sqrt{x} = 6$

$\sqrt{x} = 1$

$\left(\sqrt{x}\right)^2 = (1)^2$

$x = 1$

Exercise Set 8.5

1. $\sqrt{x} = 9$

$\left(\sqrt{x}\right)^2 = 9^2$

$x = 81$

3. $\sqrt{x+5} = 2$

$\left(\sqrt{x+5}\right)^2 = 2^2$

$x + 5 = 4$

$x = -1$

5. $\sqrt{2x+6} = 4$

$\left(\sqrt{2x+6}\right)^2 = 4^2$

$2x + 6 = 16$

$2x = 10$

$x = 5$

7. $\sqrt{x} - 2 = 5$

$\sqrt{x} = 7$

$\left(\sqrt{x}\right)^2 = 7^2$

$x = 49$

9. $3\sqrt{x} + 5 = 2$

$3\sqrt{x} = -3$

The square root cannot be negative, therefore there is no solution.

11. $\sqrt{x+6} + 1 = 3$

$\sqrt{x+6} = 2$

$\left(\sqrt{x+6}\right)^2 = 2^2$

$x + 6 = 4$

$x = -2$

13. $\sqrt{2x+1}+3=5$

$\sqrt{2x+1}=2$

$\left(\sqrt{2x+1}\right)^2=2^2$

$2x+1=4$

$2x=3$

$x=\dfrac{3}{2}$

15. $\sqrt{x}+3=7$

$\sqrt{x}=4$

$\left(\sqrt{x}\right)^2=4^2$

$x=16$

17. $\sqrt{x+6}+5=3$

$\sqrt{x+6}=-2$

The square root cannot be negative, therefore there is no solution.

19. $\sqrt{4x-3}=\sqrt{x+3}$

$\left(\sqrt{4x-3}\right)^2=\left(\sqrt{x+3}\right)^2$

$4x-3=x+3$

$3x=6$

$x=2$

21. $\sqrt{x}=\sqrt{3x-8}$

$\left(\sqrt{x}\right)^2=\left(\sqrt{3x-8}\right)^2$

$x=3x-8$

$-2x=-8$

$x=4$

23. $\sqrt{4x}=\sqrt{2x+6}$

$\left(\sqrt{4x}\right)^2=\left(\sqrt{2x+6}\right)^2$

$4x=2x+6$

$2x=6$

$x=3$

25. $\sqrt{9x^2+2x-4}=3x$

$\left(\sqrt{9x^2+2x-4}\right)^2=\left(3x\right)^2$

$9x^2+2x-4=9x^2$

$2x-4=0$

$2x=4$

$x=2$

27. $\sqrt{16x^2-3x+6}=4x$

$\left(\sqrt{16x^2-3x+6}\right)^2=\left(4x\right)^2$

$16x^2-3x+6=16x^2$

$-3x+6=0$

$-3x=-6$

$x=2$

29. $\sqrt{16x^2+2x+2}=4x$

$\left(\sqrt{16x^2+2x+2}\right)^2=\left(4x\right)^2$

$16x^2+2x+2=16x^2$

$2x+2=0$

$2x=-2$

$x=-1$

A check shows that $x=-1$ is an extraneous solution. Therefore, there is no solution.

31. $\sqrt{2x^2 + 6x + 9} = 3$

$\left(\sqrt{2x^2 + 6x + 9}\right)^2 = (3)^2$

$2x^2 + 6x + 9 = 9$

$2x^2 + 6x = 0$

$2x(x + 3) = 0$

$2x = 0$ or $x + 3 = 0$

$x = 0$ $x = -3$

33. $\sqrt{x + 7} = x + 5$

$\left(\sqrt{x + 7}\right)^2 = (x + 5)^2$

$x + 7 = x^2 + 10x + 25$

$0 = x^2 + 9x + 18$

$0 = (x + 3)(x + 6)$

$x + 3 = 0$ or $x + 6 = 0$

$x = -3$ $x = -6 \,(\text{extraneous})$

35. $\sqrt{x} = x - 6$

$\left(\sqrt{x}\right)^2 = (x - 6)^2$

$x = x^2 - 12x + 36$

$0 = x^2 - 13x + 36$

$0 = (x - 9)(x - 4)$

$x - 9 = 0$ or $x - 4 = 0$

$x = 9$ $x = 4 \,(\text{extraneous})$

37. $\sqrt{2x + 1} = x - 7$

$\left(\sqrt{2x + 1}\right)^2 = (x - 7)^2$

$2x + 1 = x^2 - 14x + 49$

$0 = x^2 - 16x + 48$

$0 = (x - 12)(x - 4)$

$x - 12 = 0$ or $x - 4 = 0$

$x = 12$ $x = 4 \,(\text{extraneous})$

39. $x = \sqrt{2x - 2} + 1$

$x - 1 = \sqrt{2x - 2}$

$(x - 1)^2 = \left(\sqrt{2x - 2}\right)^2$

$x^2 - 2x + 1 = 2x - 2$

$x^2 - 4x + 3 = 0$

$(x - 1)(x - 3) = 0$

$x - 1 = 0$ or $x - 3 = 0$

$x = 1$ $x = 3$

41. $\sqrt{1 - 8x} - x = 4$

$\sqrt{1 - 8x} = x + 4$

$\left(\sqrt{1 - 8x}\right)^2 = (x + 4)^2$

$1 - 8x = x^2 + 8x + 16$

$0 = x^2 + 16x + 15$

$0 = (x + 1)(x + 15)$

$x + 1 = 0$ or $x + 15 = 0$

$x = -1$ $x = -15$

                (extraneous)

43. $\sqrt{2x + 5} - 1 = x$

$\sqrt{2x + 5} = x + 1$

$\left(\sqrt{2x + 5}\right)^2 = (x + 1)^2$

$2x + 5 = x^2 + 2x + 1$

$0 = x^2 - 4$

$0 = (x - 2)(x + 2)$

$x - 2 = 0$ or $x + 2 = 0$

$x = 2$ $x = -2$

            (extraneous)

45.
$$\sqrt{x-7} = \sqrt{x} - 1$$
$$\left(\sqrt{x-7}\right)^2 = \left(\sqrt{x}-1\right)^2$$
$$x - 7 = x - 2\sqrt{x} + 1$$
$$2\sqrt{x} = 8$$
$$\sqrt{x} = 4$$
$$\left(\sqrt{x}\right)^2 = (4)^2$$
$$x = 16$$

47.
$$\sqrt{x} + 3 = \sqrt{x+15}$$
$$\left(\sqrt{x}+3\right)^2 = \left(\sqrt{x+15}\right)^2$$
$$x + 6\sqrt{x} + 9 = x + 15$$
$$6\sqrt{x} = 6$$
$$\sqrt{x} = 1$$
$$\left(\sqrt{x}\right)^2 = (1)^2$$
$$x = 1$$

49.
$$\sqrt{x+8} = \sqrt{x} + 2$$
$$\left(\sqrt{x+8}\right)^2 = \left(\sqrt{x}+2\right)^2$$
$$x + 8 = x + 4\sqrt{x} + 4$$
$$4 = 4\sqrt{x}$$
$$1 = \sqrt{x}$$
$$1^2 = \left(\sqrt{x}\right)^2$$
$$1 = x$$

51.
$$3x - 8 = 19$$
$$3x = 27$$
$$x = 9$$

53. Let x = width and $2x$ = length.
$$2(2x + x) = 24$$
$$2(3x) = 24$$
$$6x = 24$$
$$x = 4$$
$$2x = 2(4) = 8$$
The length is 8 inches.

55. $b = \sqrt{\dfrac{V}{2}}$

a. $b = \sqrt{\dfrac{20}{2}} \approx 3.2$

$b = \sqrt{\dfrac{200}{2}} = 10$

$b = \sqrt{\dfrac{2000}{2}} \approx 31.6$

V	20	200	2000
b	3.2	10	31.6

b. No; it increases by a factor of $\sqrt{10}$.

57. Answers may vary.

59. $\sqrt{x+1} = 2x - 3$, $y_1 = \sqrt{x+1}$, $y_2 = 2x - 3$

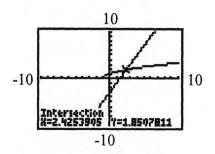

The solution is 2.43.

61. $-\sqrt{x+5} = -7x+1$

$y_1 = -\sqrt{x+5}, \; y_2 = -7x+1$

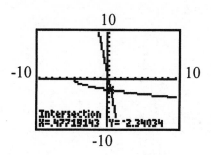

The solution is 0.48.

Practice Problems 8.6

1. $a^2 + b^2 = c^2$

$3^2 + 4^2 = c^2$

$9 + 16 = c^2$

$25 = c^2$

$5 = c$

The length is 5 centimeters

2. $a^2 + b^2 = c^2$

$3^2 + b^2 = 6^2$

$9 + b^2 = 36$

$b^2 = 27$

$b = \sqrt{27}$

$b = 3\sqrt{3}$

The length is $3\sqrt{3}$ miles ≈ 5.20 miles.

3. $a^2 + b^2 = c^2$

$40^2 + b^2 = 65^2$

$1600 + b^2 = 4225$

$b^2 = 2625$

$b = \sqrt{2625}$

$b = 5\sqrt{105}$

The distance is $5\sqrt{105}$ feet ≈ 51.2 feet.

4. $v = \sqrt{2gh}$

$= \sqrt{2(32)(20)}$

$= \sqrt{1280}$

$= 16\sqrt{5}$

The velocity is $16\sqrt{5}$ feet per second

≈ 35.8 feet per second.

Exercise Set 8.6

1. $a^2 + b^2 = c^2$

$2^2 + 3^2 = c^2$

$4 + 9 = c^2$

$13 = c^2$

$\sqrt{13} = c$

The length is $\sqrt{13} \approx 3.61$.

3. $a^2 + b^2 = c^2$

$3^2 + b^2 = 6^2$

$9 + b^2 = 36$

$b^2 = 27$

$b = \sqrt{27}$

$b = 3\sqrt{3}$

The length is $3\sqrt{3} \approx 5.20$.

5. $a^2 + b^2 = c^2$

$7^2 + 24^2 = c^2$

$49 + 576 = c^2$

$625 = c^2$

$\sqrt{625} = c$

$25 = c$

The length is 25.

7. $a^2 + b^2 = c^2$

$a^2 + \left(\sqrt{3}\right)^2 = 5^2$

$a^2 + 3 = 25$

$a^2 = 22$

$a = \sqrt{22}$

The length is $\sqrt{22} \approx 4.69$.

9. $a^2 + b^2 = c^2$

$4^2 + b^2 = 13^2$

$16 + b^2 = 169$

$b^2 = 153$

$b = \sqrt{153}$

$b = 3\sqrt{17}$

The length is $3\sqrt{17} \approx 12.37$.

11. $a^2 + b^2 = c^2$

$4^2 + 5^2 = c^2$

$16 + 25 = c^2$

$41 = c^2$

$\sqrt{41} = c$

The length is $\sqrt{41} \approx 6.40$.

13. $a^2 + b^2 = c^2$

$a^2 + 2^2 = 6^2$

$a^2 + 4 = 36$

$a^2 = 32$

$a = \sqrt{32}$

$a = 4\sqrt{2}$

The length is $4\sqrt{2} \approx 5.66$.

15. $a^2 + b^2 = c^2$

$\left(\sqrt{10}\right)^2 + b^2 = 10^2$

$10 + b^2 = 100$

$b^2 = 90$

$b = \sqrt{90}$

$b = 3\sqrt{10}$

The length is $3\sqrt{10} \approx 9.49$.

17. $a^2 + b^2 = c^2$

$5^2 + 20^2 = c^2$

$25 + 400 = c^2$

$425 = c^2$

$\sqrt{425} = c$

The length is $\sqrt{425} \approx 20.6$ feet.

19. $a^2 + b^2 = c^2$

$6^2 + 10^2 = c^2$

$36 + 100 = c^2$

$136 = c^2$

$\sqrt{136} = c$

The length is $\sqrt{136} \approx 11.7$ feet.

21. $b = \sqrt{\dfrac{3V}{h}}$

$6 = \sqrt{\dfrac{3V}{2}}$

$6^2 = \left(\sqrt{\dfrac{3V}{2}}\right)^2$

$36 = \dfrac{3V}{2}$

$24 = V$

The volume is 24 cubic feet.

23. $s = \sqrt{30\,fd}$

$s = \sqrt{30(0.35)(280)}$

$\quad = \sqrt{2940}$

$\quad \approx 54$

It was moving at 54 mph.

25. $v = \sqrt{2.5r}$

$v = \sqrt{2.5(300)}$

$\quad = \sqrt{750}$

$\quad \approx 27$

It can travel at 27 mph.

27. $d = 3.5\sqrt{h}$

$d = 3.5\sqrt{285.4}$

$\quad \approx 59.1$

You can see 59.1 km.

29. $3^2 = 9,\ (-3)^2 = 9$

The numbers are 3 and -3.

31. $10^2 = 100,\ (-10)^2 = 100$

The numbers are 10 and -10.

33. $8^2 = 64,\ (-8)^2 = 64$

The numbers are 8 and -8.

35. Let y = length of whole base and

z = length of unlabeled section of base.

Find y:

$y^2 + 3^2 = 7^2$

$y^2 + 9 = 49$

$y^2 = 40$

$y = \sqrt{40} = 2\sqrt{10}$

Find z

$z^2 + 3^2 = 5^2$

$z^2 + 9 = 25$

$z^2 = 16$

$z = \sqrt{16} = 4$

Find x:

$x = y - z$

$\quad = 2\sqrt{10} - 4$

37. $\qquad\qquad a^2 + b^2 = c^2$

$\left[60(3)\right]^2 + \left[30(3)\right]^2 = c^2$

$\qquad\quad 180^2 + 90^2 = c^2$

$\qquad 32,400 + 8100 = c^2$

$\qquad\qquad\quad 40,500 = c^2$

$\qquad\qquad \sqrt{40,500} = c$

$\qquad\qquad\qquad 201 \approx c$

They are about 201 miles apart.

39. Answers may vary.

Chapter 8 Review

1. $\sqrt{81} = 9,$ because $9^2 = 81$ and

9 is positive.

2. $-\sqrt{49} = -7$, because $\sqrt{49} = 7$.

3. $\sqrt[3]{27} = 3$, because $(3)^3 = 27$.

4. $\sqrt[4]{16} = 2$, because $2^4 = 16$.

5. $-\sqrt{\dfrac{9}{64}} = -\dfrac{3}{8}$, because $\sqrt{\dfrac{9}{64}} = \dfrac{3}{8}$.

6. $\sqrt{\dfrac{36}{81}} = \dfrac{6}{9} = \dfrac{2}{3}$, because $\left(\dfrac{6}{9}\right)^2 = \dfrac{36}{81}$.

7. $\sqrt[4]{16} = 2$, because $2^4 = 16$.

8. $\sqrt[3]{-8} = -2$, because $(-2)^3 = -8$.

9. c

10. a, c

11. $\sqrt{x^{12}} = x^6$, because $\left(x^6\right)^2 = x^{12}$.

12. $\sqrt{x^8} = x^4$, because $\left(x^4\right)^2 = x^8$.

13. $\sqrt{9y^2} = 3y$, because $(3y)^2 = 9y^2$.

14. $\sqrt{25x^4} = 5x^2$, because $\left(5x^2\right)^2 = 25x^4$.

15. $\sqrt{40} = \sqrt{4\cdot10} = \sqrt{4}\cdot\sqrt{10} = 2\sqrt{10}$

16. $\sqrt{24} = \sqrt{4\cdot6} = \sqrt{4}\cdot\sqrt{6} = 2\sqrt{6}$

17. $\sqrt{54} = \sqrt{9\cdot6} = \sqrt{9}\cdot\sqrt{6} = 3\sqrt{6}$

18. $\sqrt{88} = \sqrt{4\cdot22} = \sqrt{4}\cdot\sqrt{22} = 2\sqrt{22}$

19. $\sqrt{x^5} = \sqrt{x^4\cdot x} = \sqrt{x^4}\cdot\sqrt{x} = x^2\sqrt{x}$

20. $\sqrt{y^7} = \sqrt{y^6\cdot y} = \sqrt{y^6}\cdot\sqrt{y} = y^3\sqrt{y}$

21. $\sqrt{20x^2} = \sqrt{4x^2\cdot5} = \sqrt{4x^2}\cdot\sqrt{5} = 2x\sqrt{5}$

22. $\sqrt{50y^4} = \sqrt{25y^4\cdot2} = \sqrt{25y^4}\cdot\sqrt{2} = 5y^2\sqrt{2}$

23. $\sqrt[3]{54} = \sqrt[3]{27\cdot2} = \sqrt[3]{27}\cdot\sqrt[3]{2} = 3\sqrt[3]{2}$

24. $\sqrt[3]{88} = \sqrt[3]{8\cdot11} = \sqrt[3]{8}\cdot\sqrt[3]{11} = 2\sqrt[3]{11}$

25. $\sqrt{\dfrac{18}{25}} = \dfrac{\sqrt{18}}{\sqrt{25}} = \dfrac{\sqrt{9}\cdot\sqrt{2}}{5} = \dfrac{3\sqrt{2}}{5}$

26. $\sqrt{\dfrac{75}{64}} = \dfrac{\sqrt{75}}{\sqrt{64}} = \dfrac{\sqrt{25}\cdot\sqrt{3}}{8} = \dfrac{5\sqrt{3}}{8}$

27. $-\sqrt{\dfrac{50}{9}} = -\dfrac{\sqrt{50}}{\sqrt{9}} = -\dfrac{\sqrt{25}\cdot\sqrt{2}}{3} = -\dfrac{5\sqrt{2}}{9}$

28. $-\sqrt{\dfrac{12}{49}} = -\dfrac{\sqrt{12}}{\sqrt{49}} = -\dfrac{\sqrt{4}\cdot\sqrt{3}}{7} = -\dfrac{2\sqrt{3}}{7}$

29. $\sqrt{\dfrac{11}{x^2}} = \dfrac{\sqrt{11}}{\sqrt{x^2}} = \dfrac{\sqrt{11}}{x}$

30. $\sqrt{\dfrac{7}{y^4}} = \dfrac{\sqrt{7}}{\sqrt{y^4}} = \dfrac{\sqrt{7}}{y^2}$

31. $\sqrt{\dfrac{y^5}{100}} = \dfrac{\sqrt{y^5}}{\sqrt{100}} = \dfrac{\sqrt{y^4}\cdot\sqrt{y}}{10} = \dfrac{y^2\sqrt{y}}{10}$

32. $\sqrt{\dfrac{x^3}{81}} = \dfrac{\sqrt{x^3}}{\sqrt{81}} = \dfrac{\sqrt{x^2}\cdot\sqrt{x}}{9} = \dfrac{x\sqrt{x}}{9}$

33. $5\sqrt{2} - 8\sqrt{2} = (5-8)\sqrt{2} = -3\sqrt{2}$

34. $\sqrt{3} - 6\sqrt{3} = (1-6)\sqrt{3} = -5\sqrt{3}$

35. $6\sqrt{5} + 3\sqrt{6} - 2\sqrt{5} + \sqrt{6}$
$= (6-2)\sqrt{5} + (3+1)\sqrt{6}$
$= 4\sqrt{5} + 4\sqrt{6}$

36. $-\sqrt{7} + 8\sqrt{2} - \sqrt{7} - 6\sqrt{2}$
$= (-1-1)\sqrt{7} + (8-6)\sqrt{2}$
$= -2\sqrt{7} + 2\sqrt{2}$

37. $\sqrt{28} + \sqrt{63} + \sqrt{56}$
$= \sqrt{4}\cdot\sqrt{7} + \sqrt{9}\cdot\sqrt{7} + \sqrt{4}\cdot\sqrt{14}$
$= 2\sqrt{7} + 3\sqrt{7} + 2\sqrt{14}$
$= 5\sqrt{7} + 2\sqrt{14}$

38. $\sqrt{75} + \sqrt{48} - \sqrt{16}$
$= \sqrt{25}\cdot\sqrt{3} + \sqrt{16}\cdot\sqrt{3} - 4$
$= 5\sqrt{3} + 4\sqrt{3} - 4$
$= 9\sqrt{3} - 4$

39. $\sqrt{\dfrac{5}{9}} - \sqrt{\dfrac{5}{36}} = \dfrac{\sqrt{5}}{\sqrt{9}} - \dfrac{\sqrt{5}}{\sqrt{36}} = \dfrac{\sqrt{5}}{3} - \dfrac{\sqrt{5}}{6}$
$= \dfrac{2\sqrt{5}}{6} - \dfrac{\sqrt{5}}{6} = \dfrac{2\sqrt{5}-\sqrt{5}}{6} = \dfrac{\sqrt{5}}{6}$

40. $\sqrt{\dfrac{11}{25}} + \sqrt{\dfrac{11}{16}} = \dfrac{\sqrt{11}}{\sqrt{25}} + \dfrac{\sqrt{11}}{\sqrt{16}} = \dfrac{\sqrt{11}}{5} + \dfrac{\sqrt{11}}{4}$
$= \dfrac{4\sqrt{11}}{20} + \dfrac{5\sqrt{11}}{20} = \dfrac{4\sqrt{11}+5\sqrt{11}}{20} = \dfrac{9\sqrt{11}}{20}$

41. $\sqrt{45x^2} + 3\sqrt{5x^2} - 7x\sqrt{5} + 10$
$= \sqrt{9x^2}\cdot\sqrt{5} + 3\sqrt{x^2}\cdot\sqrt{5} - 7x\sqrt{5} + 10$
$= 3x\sqrt{5} + 3x\sqrt{5} - 7x\sqrt{5} + 10$
$= -x\sqrt{5} + 10$
$= 10 - x\sqrt{5}$

42. $\sqrt{50x} - 9\sqrt{2x} + \sqrt{72x} - \sqrt{3x}$
$= \sqrt{25}\cdot\sqrt{2x} - 9\sqrt{2x} + \sqrt{36}\cdot\sqrt{2x} - \sqrt{3x}$
$= 5\sqrt{2x} - 9\sqrt{2x} + 6\sqrt{2x} - \sqrt{3x}$
$= 2\sqrt{2x} - \sqrt{3x}$

43. $\sqrt{3}\cdot\sqrt{6} = \sqrt{18} = \sqrt{9}\cdot\sqrt{2} = 3\sqrt{2}$

44. $\sqrt{5}\cdot\sqrt{15} = \sqrt{75} = \sqrt{25}\cdot\sqrt{3} = 5\sqrt{3}$

45. $\sqrt{2}\left(\sqrt{5} - \sqrt{7}\right) = \sqrt{10} - \sqrt{14}$

46. $\sqrt{5}\left(\sqrt{11} + \sqrt{3}\right) = \sqrt{55} + \sqrt{15}$

47. $\left(\sqrt{3} + 2\right)\left(\sqrt{6} - 5\right)$
$= \sqrt{18} - 5\sqrt{3} + 2\sqrt{6} - 10$
$= \sqrt{9}\cdot\sqrt{2} - 5\sqrt{3} + 2\sqrt{6} - 10$
$= 3\sqrt{2} - 5\sqrt{3} + 2\sqrt{6} - 10$

48. $\left(\sqrt{5}+1\right)\left(\sqrt{5}-3\right) = \sqrt{25}-3\sqrt{5}+\sqrt{5}-3$
$$= 5-2\sqrt{5}-3$$
$$= 2-2\sqrt{5}$$

49. $\left(\sqrt{x}-2\right)^2 = \left(\sqrt{x}\right)^2 -2(2)\sqrt{x}+(2)^2$
$$= x-4\sqrt{x}+4$$

50. $\left(\sqrt{y}+4\right)^2 = \left(\sqrt{y}\right)^2 +2(4)\sqrt{y}+(4)^2$
$$= y+8\sqrt{y}+16$$

51. $\dfrac{\sqrt{27}}{\sqrt{3}} = \sqrt{\dfrac{27}{3}} = \sqrt{9} = 3$

52. $\dfrac{\sqrt{20}}{\sqrt{5}} = \sqrt{\dfrac{20}{5}} = \sqrt{4} = 2$

53. $\dfrac{\sqrt{160}}{\sqrt{8}} = \sqrt{\dfrac{160}{8}} = \sqrt{20} = \sqrt{4}\cdot\sqrt{5} = 2\sqrt{5}$

54. $\dfrac{\sqrt{96}}{\sqrt{3}} = \sqrt{\dfrac{96}{3}} = \sqrt{32} = \sqrt{16}\cdot\sqrt{2} = 4\sqrt{2}$

55. $\dfrac{\sqrt{30x^6}}{\sqrt{2x^3}} = \sqrt{\dfrac{30x^6}{2x^3}} = \sqrt{15x^3} = \sqrt{x^2}\cdot\sqrt{15x}$
$$= x\sqrt{15x}$$

56. $\dfrac{\sqrt{54x^5y^2}}{\sqrt{3xy^2}} = \sqrt{\dfrac{54x^5y^2}{3xy^2}} = \sqrt{18x^4}$
$$= \sqrt{9x^4}\cdot\sqrt{2} = 3x^2\sqrt{2}$$

57. $\dfrac{\sqrt{2}}{\sqrt{11}} = \dfrac{\sqrt{2}}{\sqrt{11}}\cdot\dfrac{\sqrt{11}}{\sqrt{11}} = \dfrac{\sqrt{22}}{\sqrt{121}} = \dfrac{\sqrt{22}}{11}$

58. $\dfrac{\sqrt{3}}{\sqrt{13}} = \dfrac{\sqrt{3}}{\sqrt{13}}\cdot\dfrac{\sqrt{13}}{\sqrt{13}} = \dfrac{\sqrt{39}}{\sqrt{169}} = \dfrac{\sqrt{39}}{13}$

59. $\sqrt{\dfrac{5}{6}} = \dfrac{\sqrt{5}}{\sqrt{6}} = \dfrac{\sqrt{5}}{\sqrt{6}}\cdot\dfrac{\sqrt{6}}{\sqrt{6}} = \dfrac{\sqrt{30}}{\sqrt{36}} = \dfrac{\sqrt{30}}{6}$

60. $\sqrt{\dfrac{7}{10}} = \dfrac{\sqrt{7}}{\sqrt{10}} = \dfrac{\sqrt{7}}{\sqrt{10}}\cdot\dfrac{\sqrt{10}}{\sqrt{10}} = \dfrac{\sqrt{70}}{\sqrt{100}} = \dfrac{\sqrt{70}}{10}$

61. $\dfrac{1}{\sqrt{5x}} = \dfrac{1}{\sqrt{5x}}\cdot\dfrac{\sqrt{5x}}{\sqrt{5x}} = \dfrac{\sqrt{5x}}{5x}$

62. $\dfrac{5}{\sqrt{3y}} = \dfrac{5}{\sqrt{3y}}\cdot\dfrac{\sqrt{3y}}{\sqrt{3y}} = \dfrac{5\sqrt{3y}}{3y}$

63. $\sqrt{\dfrac{3}{x}} = \dfrac{\sqrt{3}}{\sqrt{x}} = \dfrac{\sqrt{3}}{\sqrt{x}}\cdot\dfrac{\sqrt{x}}{\sqrt{x}} = \dfrac{\sqrt{3x}}{x}$

64. $\sqrt{\dfrac{6}{y}} = \dfrac{\sqrt{6}}{\sqrt{y}} = \dfrac{\sqrt{6}}{\sqrt{y}}\cdot\dfrac{\sqrt{y}}{\sqrt{y}} = \dfrac{\sqrt{6y}}{y}$

65. $\dfrac{3}{\sqrt{5}-2} = \dfrac{3}{\sqrt{5}-2}\cdot\dfrac{\sqrt{5}+2}{\sqrt{5}+2} = \dfrac{3\left(\sqrt{5}+2\right)}{\left(\sqrt{5}\right)^2-2^2}$
$$= \dfrac{3\left(\sqrt{5}+2\right)}{5-4} = \dfrac{3\left(\sqrt{5}+2\right)}{1} = 3\sqrt{5}+6$$

66. $\dfrac{8}{\sqrt{10}-3} = \dfrac{8}{\sqrt{10}-3}\cdot\dfrac{\sqrt{10}+3}{\sqrt{10}+3} = \dfrac{8\left(\sqrt{10}+3\right)}{\left(\sqrt{10}\right)^2-3^2}$
$$= \dfrac{8\left(\sqrt{10}+3\right)}{10-9} = \dfrac{8\left(\sqrt{10}+3\right)}{1} = 8\sqrt{10}+24$$

67. $\dfrac{\sqrt{2}+1}{\sqrt{3}-1} = \dfrac{\sqrt{2}+1}{\sqrt{3}-1} \cdot \dfrac{\sqrt{3}+1}{\sqrt{3}+1}$

$\qquad = \dfrac{\sqrt{6}+\sqrt{2}+\sqrt{3}+1}{3-1}$

$\qquad = \dfrac{\sqrt{6}+\sqrt{2}+\sqrt{3}+1}{2}$

68. $\dfrac{\sqrt{3}-2}{\sqrt{5}+2} = \dfrac{\sqrt{3}-2}{\sqrt{5}+2} \cdot \dfrac{\sqrt{5}-2}{\sqrt{5}-2}$

$\qquad = \dfrac{\sqrt{15}-2\sqrt{3}-2\sqrt{5}+4}{5-4}$

$\qquad = \sqrt{15}-2\sqrt{3}-2\sqrt{5}+4$

69. $\dfrac{10}{\sqrt{x}+5} = \dfrac{10}{\sqrt{x}+5} \cdot \dfrac{\sqrt{x}-5}{\sqrt{x}-5} = \dfrac{10\left(\sqrt{x}-5\right)}{x-25}$

$\qquad = \dfrac{10\sqrt{x}-50}{x-25}$

70. $\dfrac{8}{\sqrt{x}-1} = \dfrac{8}{\sqrt{x}-1} \cdot \dfrac{\sqrt{x}+1}{\sqrt{x}+1} = \dfrac{8\left(\sqrt{x}+1\right)}{x-1}$

$\qquad = \dfrac{8\sqrt{x}+8}{x-1}$

71. $\sqrt{2x} = 6$

$\qquad \left(\sqrt{2x}\right)^2 = 6^2$

$\qquad 2x = 36$

$\qquad x = 18$

72. $\sqrt{x+3} = 4$

$\qquad \left(\sqrt{x+3}\right)^2 = 4^2$

$\qquad x+3 = 16$

$\qquad x = 13$

73. $\sqrt{x}+3 = 8$

$\qquad \sqrt{x} = 5$

$\qquad \left(\sqrt{x}\right)^2 = 5^2$

$\qquad x = 25$

74. $\sqrt{x}+8 = 3$

$\qquad \sqrt{x} = -5$

The square root cannot be negative, therefore there is no solution.

75. $\sqrt{2x+1} = x-7$

$\qquad \left(\sqrt{2x+1}\right)^2 = (x-7)^2$

$\qquad 2x+1 = x^2 -14x+49$

$\qquad 0 = x^2 -16x+48$

$\qquad 0 = (x-12)(x-4)$

$\qquad x-12 = 0 \quad \text{or} \quad x-4 = 0$

$\qquad x = 12 \qquad\qquad x = 4$

$\qquad\qquad\qquad\qquad \text{(extraneous)}$

76. $\sqrt{3x+1} = x-1$

$\qquad \left(\sqrt{3x+1}\right)^2 = (x-1)^2$

$\qquad 3x+1 = x^2 -2x+1$

$\qquad 0 = x^2 -5x$

$\qquad 0 = x(x-5)$

$\qquad x = 0 \quad \text{or} \quad x-5 = 0$

$\qquad x = 0 \qquad\qquad x = 5$

$\qquad \text{(extraneous)}$

77.
$$\sqrt{x} + 3 = \sqrt{x+15}$$
$$\left(\sqrt{x}+3\right)^2 = \left(\sqrt{x+15}\right)^2$$
$$x + 6\sqrt{x} + 9 = x + 15$$
$$6\sqrt{x} = 6$$
$$\sqrt{x} = 1$$
$$\left(\sqrt{x}\right)^2 = (1)^2$$
$$x = 1$$

78.
$$\sqrt{x-5} = \sqrt{x} - 1$$
$$\left(\sqrt{x-5}\right)^2 = \left(\sqrt{x}-1\right)^2$$
$$x - 5 = x - 2\sqrt{x} + 1$$
$$-6 = -2\sqrt{x}$$
$$3 = \sqrt{x}$$
$$3^2 = \left(\sqrt{x}\right)^2$$
$$9 = x$$

79.
$$a^2 + b^2 = c^2$$
$$5^2 + b^2 = 9^2$$
$$25 + b^2 = 81$$
$$b^2 = 56$$
$$b = \sqrt{56}$$
$$b = 2\sqrt{14}$$
The length is $2\sqrt{14} \approx 7.48$.

80.
$$a^2 + b^2 = c^2$$
$$6^2 + 9^2 = c^2$$
$$36 + 81 = c^2$$
$$117 = c^2$$
$$\sqrt{117} = c$$
The length is $\sqrt{117} \approx 10.82$.

81.
$$a^2 + b^2 = c^2$$
$$20^2 + 12^2 = c^2$$
$$400 + 144 = c^2$$
$$544 = c^2$$
$$\sqrt{544} = c$$
$$4\sqrt{34} = c$$
They are $4\sqrt{34}$ feet apart.

82.
$$a^2 + b^2 = c^2$$
$$a^2 + 5^2 = 10^2$$
$$a^2 + 25 = 100$$
$$a^2 = 75$$
$$a = \sqrt{75}$$
$$a = 5\sqrt{3}$$
The length is $5\sqrt{3}$ inches.

83.
$$r = \sqrt{\frac{S}{4\pi}}$$
$$r = \sqrt{\frac{72}{4\pi}} \approx 2.4$$
The radius is about 2.4 inches.

84.
$$r = \sqrt{\frac{S}{4\pi}}$$
$$6 = \sqrt{\frac{S}{4\pi}}$$
$$6^2 = \left(\sqrt{\frac{S}{4\pi}}\right)^2$$
$$36 = \frac{S}{4\pi}$$
$$144\pi = S$$
The surface area is 144π square inches.

Chapter 8 Test

1. $\sqrt{16} = 4$, because $4^2 = 16$ and 4 is positive.

2. $\sqrt[3]{125} = 5$, because $(5)^3 = 125$.

3. $\sqrt[4]{81} = 3$, because $3^4 = 81$.

4. $\sqrt{\dfrac{9}{16}} = \dfrac{3}{4}$, because $\left(\dfrac{3}{4}\right)^2 = \dfrac{9}{16}$ and $\dfrac{3}{4}$ is positive.

5. $\sqrt[4]{-81}$ is not a real number.

6. $\sqrt{x^{10}} = x^5$, because $\left(x^5\right)^2 = x^{10}$.

7. $\sqrt{54} = \sqrt{9} \cdot \sqrt{6} = 3\sqrt{6}$

8. $\sqrt{92} = \sqrt{4} \cdot \sqrt{23} = 2\sqrt{23}$

9. $\sqrt{y^7} = \sqrt{y^6} \cdot \sqrt{y} = y^3 \sqrt{y}$

10. $\sqrt{24x^8} = \sqrt{4x^8} \cdot \sqrt{6} = 2x^4 \sqrt{6}$

11. $\sqrt[3]{27} = 3$

12. $\sqrt[3]{16} = \sqrt[3]{8} \cdot \sqrt[3]{2} = 2\sqrt[3]{2}$

13. $\sqrt{\dfrac{5}{16}} = \dfrac{\sqrt{5}}{\sqrt{16}} = \dfrac{\sqrt{5}}{4}$

14. $\sqrt{\dfrac{y^3}{25}} = \dfrac{\sqrt{y^3}}{\sqrt{25}} = \dfrac{\sqrt{y^2} \cdot \sqrt{y}}{5} = \dfrac{y\sqrt{y}}{5}$

15. $\sqrt{13} + \sqrt{13} - 4\sqrt{13} = -2\sqrt{13}$

16. $\sqrt{18} - \sqrt{75} + 7\sqrt{3} - \sqrt{8}$
$= \sqrt{9} \cdot \sqrt{2} - \sqrt{25} \cdot \sqrt{3} + 7\sqrt{3} - \sqrt{4} \cdot \sqrt{2}$
$= 3\sqrt{2} - 5\sqrt{3} + 7\sqrt{3} - 2\sqrt{2}$
$= \sqrt{2} + 2\sqrt{3}$

17. $\sqrt{\dfrac{3}{4}} + \sqrt{\dfrac{3}{25}} = \dfrac{\sqrt{3}}{\sqrt{4}} + \dfrac{\sqrt{3}}{\sqrt{25}} = \dfrac{\sqrt{3}}{2} + \dfrac{\sqrt{3}}{5}$
$= \dfrac{5\sqrt{3}}{10} + \dfrac{2\sqrt{3}}{10} = \dfrac{5\sqrt{3} + 2\sqrt{3}}{10} = \dfrac{7\sqrt{3}}{10}$

18. $\sqrt{7} \cdot \sqrt{14} = \sqrt{98} = \sqrt{49} \cdot \sqrt{2} = 7\sqrt{2}$

19. $\sqrt{2}\left(\sqrt{6} - \sqrt{5}\right) = \sqrt{12} - \sqrt{10}$
$= \sqrt{4} \cdot \sqrt{3} - \sqrt{10}$
$= 2\sqrt{3} - \sqrt{10}$

20. $\left(\sqrt{x} + 2\right)\left(\sqrt{x} - 3\right) = \sqrt{x^2} - 3\sqrt{x} + 2\sqrt{x} - 6$
$= x - \sqrt{x} - 6$

21. $\dfrac{\sqrt{50}}{\sqrt{10}} = \sqrt{\dfrac{50}{10}} = \sqrt{5}$

22. $\dfrac{\sqrt{40x^4}}{\sqrt{2x}} = \sqrt{\dfrac{40x^4}{2x}} = \sqrt{20x^3} = \sqrt{4x^2} \cdot \sqrt{5x}$
$= 2x\sqrt{5x}$

23. $\sqrt{\dfrac{2}{3}} = \dfrac{\sqrt{2}}{\sqrt{3}} = \dfrac{\sqrt{2}}{\sqrt{3}} \cdot \dfrac{\sqrt{3}}{\sqrt{3}} = \dfrac{\sqrt{6}}{\sqrt{9}} = \dfrac{\sqrt{6}}{3}$

24. $\dfrac{8}{\sqrt{5y}} = \dfrac{8}{\sqrt{5y}} \cdot \dfrac{\sqrt{5y}}{\sqrt{5y}} = \dfrac{8\sqrt{5y}}{5y}$

25. $\dfrac{8}{\sqrt{6}+2} = \dfrac{8}{\sqrt{6}+2} \cdot \dfrac{\sqrt{6}-2}{\sqrt{6}-2} = \dfrac{8\left(\sqrt{6}-2\right)}{\left(\sqrt{6}\right)^2 - 2^2}$

$= \dfrac{8\left(\sqrt{6}-2\right)}{6-4} = \dfrac{8\left(\sqrt{6}-2\right)}{2} = 4\sqrt{6}-8$

26. $\dfrac{1}{3-\sqrt{x}} = \dfrac{1}{3-\sqrt{x}} \cdot \dfrac{3+\sqrt{x}}{3+\sqrt{x}} = \dfrac{3+\sqrt{x}}{9-x}$

27. $\sqrt{x}+8 = 11$

$\sqrt{x} = 3$

$\left(\sqrt{x}\right)^2 = 3^2$

$x = 9$

28. $\sqrt{3x-6} = \sqrt{x+4}$

$\left(\sqrt{3x-6}\right)^2 = \left(\sqrt{x+4}\right)^2$

$3x-6 = x+4$

$2x = 10$

$x = 5$

29. $\sqrt{2x-2} = x-5$

$\left(\sqrt{2x-2}\right)^2 = \left(x-5\right)^2$

$2x-2 = x^2 -10x+25$

$0 = x^2 -12x+27$

$0 = \left(x-9\right)\left(x-3\right)$

$x-9 = 0 \quad \text{or} \quad x-3 = 0$

$x = 9 \qquad\qquad x = 3$

$\qquad\qquad\qquad\quad$ (extraneous)

30. $a^2 + b^2 = c^2$

$8^2 + b^2 = 12^2$

$64 + b^2 = 144$

$b^2 = 80$

$b = \sqrt{80}$

$b = 4\sqrt{5}$

The length is $4\sqrt{5}$ inches.

31. $r = \sqrt{\dfrac{A}{\pi}}$

$r = \sqrt{\dfrac{15}{\pi}} \approx 2.19$

The radius is about 2.19 meters

Cumulative Review Chapter 8

1. $-5\left(-10\right) = 50$

2. $-\dfrac{2}{3} \cdot \dfrac{4}{7} = -\dfrac{8}{21}$

3. $4\left(2x-3\right)+7 = 3x+5$

$8x-12+7 = 3x+5$

$8x-5 = 3x+5$

$5x = 10$

$x = 2$

4. a. 17%

b. $17\% + 4\% = 21\%$

c. Let x = the unknown number

$x = 0.17\left(253\right) = 43$

43 are traveling soley for business.

5. a. $1.02 \times 10^5 = 102,000$

   b. $7.358 \times 10^{-3} = 0.007358$

   c. $8.4 \times 10^7 = 84,000,000$

   d. $3.007 \times 10^{-5} = 0.00003007$

6. $(3x+2)(2x-5) = 6x^2 - 15x + 4x - 10$

$$= 6x^2 - 11x - 10$$

7. $xy + 2x + 3y + 6 = x(y+2) + 3(y+2)$

$$= (y+2)(x+3)$$

8. $3x^2 + 11x + 6 = (3x+2)(x+3)$

9. a. When $x - 3 = 0, x = 0.$

   b. When $x^2 - 3x + 2 = 0,$

$$(x-1)(x-2) = 0$$

$$x = 1 \quad \text{or} \quad x = 2.$$

   c. None, since 3 cannot be zero.

10. $\dfrac{x^2 + 4x + 4}{x^2 + 2x} = \dfrac{(x+2)(x+2)}{x(x+2)} = \dfrac{x+2}{x}$

11. a. $\dfrac{a}{4} - \dfrac{2a}{8} = \dfrac{a}{4} - \dfrac{a}{4} = \dfrac{a-a}{4} = \dfrac{0}{4} = 0$

   b. $\dfrac{3}{10x^2} + \dfrac{7}{25x} = \dfrac{3 \cdot 5}{10x^2 \cdot 5} + \dfrac{7 \cdot 2x}{25x \cdot 2x}$

$$= \dfrac{15}{50x^2} + \dfrac{14x}{50x^2} = \dfrac{14x + 15}{50x^2}$$

12. $\dfrac{4x}{x^2 + x - 30} + \dfrac{2}{x-5} = \dfrac{1}{x+6}$

$$(x-5)(x+6)\left(\dfrac{4x}{x^2+x-30} + \dfrac{2}{x-5}\right)$$

$$= (x-5)(x+6)\left(\dfrac{1}{x+6}\right)$$

$$4x + 2(x+6) = 1(x-5)$$

$$4x + 2x + 12 = x - 5$$

$$5x = -17$$

$$x = -\dfrac{17}{5}$$

13. $y = -3$

14. $m = \dfrac{1}{4}, \; b = -3$

$$y = mx + b$$

$$y = \dfrac{1}{4}x - 3$$

15. $\begin{cases} 3x + 4y = 13 \\ 5x - 9y = 6 \end{cases}$

Multiply the first equation by 5 and the second equation by -3.

$$15x + 20y = 65$$

$$\underline{-15x + 27y = -18}$$

$$47y = 47$$

$$y = 1$$

Let $y = 1$ in the first equation.

$3x + 4(1) = 13$

$3x + 4 = 13$

$3x = 9$

$x = 3$

The solution of the system is $(3, 1)$.

16. Let x = Alfredo's rate and

y = Betsy's rate.

	r	$\cdot$	t	$=$	d
Alfredo	x		2		$2x$
Betsy	y		2		$2y$

$$\begin{cases} y = x + 1 \\ 2x + 2y = 15 \end{cases}$$

Substitute $x + 1$ for y in the second equation.

$2x + 2(x + 1) = 15$

$2x + 2x + 2 = 15$

$4x = 13$

$x = \dfrac{13}{4} = 3.25$

Let $x = 3.25$ in the first equation.

$y = 3.25 + 1 = 4.25$

Alfredo walks at 3.25 mph and Betsy walks at 4.25 mph.

17. $\sqrt[3]{1} = 1$

18. $\sqrt[3]{-27} = -3$

19. $\sqrt[3]{\dfrac{1}{125}} = \dfrac{1}{5}$

20. $\sqrt{54} = \sqrt{9} \cdot \sqrt{6} = 3\sqrt{6}$

21. $\sqrt{200} = \sqrt{100} \cdot \sqrt{2} = 10\sqrt{2}$

22. $7\sqrt{12} - \sqrt{75} = 7\sqrt{4} \cdot \sqrt{3} - \sqrt{25} \cdot \sqrt{3}$

$= 7(2)\sqrt{3} - 5\sqrt{3} = 14\sqrt{3} - 5\sqrt{3} = 9\sqrt{3}$

23. $2\sqrt{x^2} - \sqrt{25x} + \sqrt{x} = 2x - 5\sqrt{x} + \sqrt{x}$

$= 2x - 4\sqrt{x}$

24. $\dfrac{2}{\sqrt{7}} = \dfrac{2}{\sqrt{7}} \cdot \dfrac{\sqrt{7}}{\sqrt{7}} = \dfrac{2\sqrt{7}}{7}$

25. $\sqrt{x} = \sqrt{5x - 2}$

$\left(\sqrt{x}\right)^2 = \left(\sqrt{5x - 2}\right)^2$

$x = 5x - 2$

$-4x = -2$

$x = \dfrac{1}{2}$

Chapter 9

Chapter 9 Pretest

1. $a^2 - 6a = 0$

$a(a-6) = 0$

$a - 6 = 0 \quad \text{or} \quad a = 0$

$a = 6$

The solutions are 0 and 6.

2. $2x^2 - 11x = 6$

$2x^2 - 11x - 6 = 0$

$(2x-1)(x-6) = 0$

$2x - 1 = 0 \quad \text{or} \quad x - 6 = 0$

$2x = -1 \qquad\qquad x = 6$

$x = -\dfrac{1}{2}$

The solutions are $-\dfrac{1}{2}$ and 6.

3. $b^2 = 144$

$b = \sqrt{144} \quad \text{or} \quad b = -\sqrt{144}$

$b = 12 \qquad\qquad b = -12$

4. $(2x-7)^2 = 24$

$2x - 7 = \sqrt{24} \quad \text{or} \quad 2x - 7 = -\sqrt{24}$

$2x - 7 = 2\sqrt{6} \qquad 2x - 7 = -2\sqrt{6}$

$2x = 7 + 2\sqrt{6} \qquad 2x = 7 - 2\sqrt{6}$

$x = \dfrac{7 + 2\sqrt{6}}{2} \qquad x = \dfrac{7 - 2\sqrt{6}}{2}$

The solutions are $\dfrac{7 + 2\sqrt{6}}{2}$ and $\dfrac{7 - 2\sqrt{6}}{2}$.

5. $x^2 - 14x + 48 = 0$

$x^2 - 14x = -48$

$x^2 - 14x + 49 = -48 + 49$

$(x-7)^2 = 1$

$x - 7 = \sqrt{1} \quad \text{or} \quad x - 7 = -\sqrt{1}$

$x = 7 + 1 \qquad\qquad x = 7 - 1$

$x = 8 \qquad\qquad\quad x = 6$

The solutions are 6 and 8.

6. $3x^2 - 5x = 2$

$x^2 - \dfrac{5}{3}x = \dfrac{2}{3}$

$x^2 - \dfrac{5}{3}x + \dfrac{25}{36} = \dfrac{2}{3} + \dfrac{25}{36}$

$\left(x - \dfrac{5}{6}\right)^2 = \dfrac{49}{36}$

$x - \dfrac{5}{6} = \sqrt{\dfrac{49}{36}} \quad \text{or} \quad x - \dfrac{5}{6} = -\sqrt{\dfrac{49}{36}}$

$x - \dfrac{5}{6} = \dfrac{7}{6} \qquad\qquad x - \dfrac{5}{6} = -\dfrac{7}{6}$

$x = \dfrac{12}{6} \qquad\qquad\quad x = -\dfrac{2}{6}$

$x = 2 \qquad\qquad\qquad x = -\dfrac{1}{3}$

The solutions are $-\dfrac{1}{3}$ and 2.

7. $x^2 - 6x - 27 = 0$

$a = 1, b = -6,$ and $c = -27$

$$x = \frac{-b \pm \sqrt{b^2 - 4ac}}{2a}$$

$$x = \frac{-(-6) \pm \sqrt{(-6)^2 - 4(1)(-27)}}{2(1)}$$

$$x = \frac{6 \pm \sqrt{36 + 108}}{2}$$

$$x = \frac{6 \pm \sqrt{144}}{2}$$

$$x = \frac{6 \pm 12}{2}$$

$$x = \frac{6 + 12}{2} = 9 \quad \text{or} \quad x = \frac{6 - 12}{2} = -3$$

The solutions are -3 and 9.

8. $m^2 - \dfrac{7}{4}m - \dfrac{3}{2} = 0$

$a = 1, b = -\dfrac{7}{4},$ and $c = -\dfrac{3}{2}$

$$m = \frac{-b \pm \sqrt{b^2 - 4ac}}{2a}$$

$$m = \frac{-\left(-\dfrac{7}{4}\right) \pm \sqrt{\left(-\dfrac{7}{4}\right)^2 - 4(1)\left(-\dfrac{3}{2}\right)}}{2(1)}$$

$$= \frac{\dfrac{7}{4} \pm \sqrt{\dfrac{49}{16} + \dfrac{12}{2}}}{2} = \frac{\dfrac{7}{4} \pm \sqrt{\dfrac{145}{16}}}{2}$$

$$= \frac{\dfrac{7}{4} \pm \dfrac{\sqrt{145}}{4}}{2} = \frac{7 \pm \sqrt{145}}{8}$$

The solutions are $\dfrac{7 + \sqrt{145}}{8}$ and $\dfrac{7 - \sqrt{145}}{8}$.

9. $(2x + 3)(x - 1) = 6$

$2x^2 + x - 3 = 6$

$2x^2 + x - 9 = 0$

$a = 2, b = 1,$ and $c = -9$

$$x = \frac{-b \pm \sqrt{b^2 - 4ac}}{2a}$$

$$x = \frac{-(1) \pm \sqrt{(1)^2 - 4(2)(-9)}}{2(2)}$$

$$= \frac{-1 \pm \sqrt{1 + 72}}{4} = \frac{-1 \pm \sqrt{73}}{4}$$

The solutions are $\dfrac{-1 + \sqrt{73}}{4}$ and $\dfrac{-1 - \sqrt{73}}{4}$.

10. $(5x + 3)^2 = 18$

$5x + 3 = \sqrt{18} \quad \text{or} \quad 5x + 3 = -\sqrt{18}$

$5x + 3 = 3\sqrt{2} \qquad 5x + 3 = -3\sqrt{2}$

$5x = -3 + 3\sqrt{2} \qquad 5x = -3 - 3\sqrt{2}$

$$x = \frac{-3 + 3\sqrt{2}}{5} \qquad x = \frac{-3 - 3\sqrt{2}}{5}$$

The solutions are $\dfrac{-3 + 3\sqrt{2}}{5}$ and $\dfrac{-3 - 3\sqrt{2}}{5}$.

11. $8x^2 + 18x + 9 = 0$

$a = 8, b = 18,$ and $c = 9$

$$x = \frac{-b \pm \sqrt{b^2 - 4ac}}{2a}$$

$$x = \frac{-(18) \pm \sqrt{(18)^2 - 4(8)(9)}}{2(8)}$$

$$= \frac{-18 \pm \sqrt{324 - 288}}{16} = \frac{-18 \pm \sqrt{36}}{16}$$

$$= \frac{-18 \pm 6}{16}$$

$$x = \frac{-18 + 6}{16} = -\frac{3}{4} \quad \text{or} \quad x = \frac{-18 - 6}{16} = -\frac{3}{2}$$

The solutions are -3 and 9.

12.
$$m^2 - 6m = -3$$
$$m^2 - 6m + 9 = -3 + 9$$
$$(m - 3)^2 = 6$$
$$m - 3 = \sqrt{6} \quad \text{or} \quad m - 3 = -\sqrt{6}$$
$$m = 3 + \sqrt{6} \qquad m = 3 - \sqrt{6}$$

The solutions are $3 + \sqrt{6}$ and $3 - \sqrt{6}$.

13.
$$\frac{1}{4}x^2 + x - \frac{1}{8} = 0$$
$$x^2 + 4x - \frac{1}{2} = 0$$
$$x^2 + 4x = \frac{1}{2}$$
$$x^2 + 4x + 4 = \frac{1}{2} + 4$$
$$(x + 2)^2 = \frac{9}{2} = \frac{18}{4}$$
$$x + 2 = \sqrt{\frac{18}{4}} \quad \text{or} \quad x + 2 = -\sqrt{\frac{18}{4}}$$
$$x = -2 + \frac{3\sqrt{2}}{2} \qquad x = -2 - \frac{3\sqrt{2}}{2}$$

The solutions are $\dfrac{-4 + 3\sqrt{2}}{4}$ and $\dfrac{-4 - 3\sqrt{2}}{4}$.

14.
$$(y + 7)^2 - 5 = 0$$
$$(y + 7)^2 = 5$$
$$y + 7 = \sqrt{5} \quad \text{or} \quad y + 7 = -\sqrt{5}$$
$$y = -7 + \sqrt{5} \qquad y = -7 - \sqrt{5}$$

The solutions are $-7 + \sqrt{5}$ and $-7 + \sqrt{5}$

15. $y = -3x^2$

x	y
0	0
1	-3
2	-12
-1	-3
-2	-12

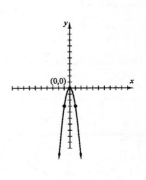

16. $y = x^2 + 3$

x	y
-2	7
-1	4
0	3
1	4
2	7

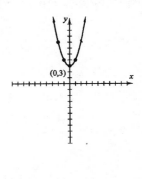

17. $y = x^2 + 4x$

x	y
-4	0
-3	-3
-2	-4
-1	-3
0	0

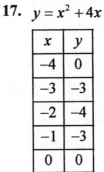
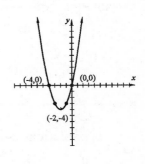

18. $y = x^2 + 2x - 3$

x	y
-3	0
-2	-3
-1	-4
0	-3
1	0

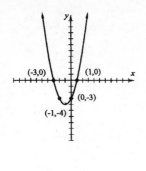

Practice Problems 9.1

1. $x^2 - 25 = 0$

$(x+5)(x-5) = 0$

$x + 5 = 0$ or $x - 5 = 0$

$x = -5$ $x = 5$

The solutions are -5 and 5

2. $2x^2 - 3x = 9$

$2x^2 - 3x - 9 = 0$

$(2x+3)(x-3) = 0$

$2x + 3 = 0$ or $x - 3 = 0$

$x = -\dfrac{3}{2}$ $x = 3$

The solutions are $-\dfrac{3}{2}$ and 3.

3. $x^2 - 16 = 0$

$x^2 = 16$

$x = \sqrt{16} = 4$ or $x = -\sqrt{16} = -4$

The solutions are -4 and 4.

4. $3x^2 = 11$

$x^2 = \dfrac{11}{3}$

$x = \sqrt{\dfrac{11}{3}}$ or $x = -\sqrt{\dfrac{11}{3}}$

$x = \sqrt{\dfrac{11}{3}} \cdot \dfrac{\sqrt{3}}{\sqrt{3}}$ $x = -\sqrt{\dfrac{11}{3}} \cdot \dfrac{\sqrt{3}}{\sqrt{3}}$

$x = \dfrac{\sqrt{33}}{3}$ $x = -\dfrac{\sqrt{33}}{3}$

The solutions are $-\dfrac{\sqrt{33}}{3}$ and $-\dfrac{\sqrt{33}}{3}$.

5. $(x-4)^2 = 49$

$x - 4 = \sqrt{49}$ or $x - 4 = -\sqrt{49}$

$x - 4 = 7$ $x - 4 = -7$

$x = 4 + 7 = 11$ $x = 4 - 7 = -3$

The solutions are -3 and 11.

6. $(x-5)^2 = 18$

$x - 5 = \sqrt{18}$ or $x - 5 = -\sqrt{18}$

$x - 5 = 3\sqrt{2}$ $x - 5 = -3\sqrt{2}$

$x = 5 + 3\sqrt{2}$ $x = -5 + 3\sqrt{2}$

The solutions are $-5 \pm 3\sqrt{2}$.

7. $(x+3)^2 = -5$

This equation has no real solution because $\sqrt{-5}$ is not a real number.

8. $(4x+1)^2 = 15$

$$4x+1 = \sqrt{15} \quad \text{or} \quad 4x+1 = -\sqrt{15}$$

$$4x = -1+\sqrt{15} \qquad 4x = -1-\sqrt{15}$$

$$x = \frac{-1+\sqrt{15}}{4} \qquad x = \frac{-1-\sqrt{15}}{4}$$

The solutions are $\dfrac{-1\pm\sqrt{15}}{4}$.

Exercise Set 9.1

1. $k^2 - 9 = 0$

$$(k+3)(k-3) = 0$$

$$k+3 = 0 \quad \text{or} \quad k-3 = 0$$

$$k = -3 \qquad k = 3$$

The solutions are -3 and 3.

3. $m^2 + 2m = 15$

$$m^2 + 2m - 15 = 0$$

$$(m+5)(m-3) = 0$$

$$m+5 = 0 \quad \text{or} \quad m-3 = 0$$

$$m = -5 \qquad m = 3$$

The solutions are -5 and 3.

5. $2x^2 - 32 = 0$

$$2(x^2 - 16) = 0$$

$$2(x+4)(x-4) = 0$$

$$x+4 = 0 \quad \text{or} \quad x-4 = 0$$

$$x = -4 \qquad x = 4$$

The solutions are -4 and 4.

7. $4a^2 - 36 = 0$

$$4(a^2 - 9) = 0$$

$$4(a+3)(a-3) = 0$$

$$a+3 = 0 \quad \text{or} \quad a-3 = 0$$

$$a = -3 \qquad a = 3$$

The solutions are -3 and 3.

9. $x^2 + 7x = -10$

$$x^2 + 7x + 10 = 0$$

$$(x+5)(x+2) = 0$$

$$x+5 = 0 \quad \text{or} \quad x+2 = 0$$

$$x = -5 \qquad x = -2$$

The solutions are -5 and -2.

11. $x^2 = 64$

$$x = \sqrt{64} = 8 \quad \text{or} \quad x = -\sqrt{64} = -8$$

The solutions are ± 8.

13. $x^2 = 21$

$$x = \sqrt{21} \quad \text{or} \quad x = -\sqrt{21}$$

The solutions are $\pm\sqrt{21}$.

15. $x^2 = \dfrac{1}{25}$

$$x = \sqrt{\frac{1}{25}} = \frac{1}{5} \quad \text{or} \quad x = -\sqrt{\frac{1}{25}} = -\frac{1}{5}$$

The solutions are $\pm\dfrac{1}{5}$.

17. $x^2 = -4$

This equation has no real solution because $\sqrt{-4}$ is not a real number.

19. $3x^2 = 13$

$$x^2 = \frac{13}{3}$$

$$x = \sqrt{\frac{13}{3}} \quad \text{or} \quad x = -\sqrt{\frac{13}{3}}$$

$$x = \sqrt{\frac{13}{3}} \cdot \frac{\sqrt{3}}{\sqrt{3}} \qquad x = -\sqrt{\frac{13}{3}} \cdot \frac{\sqrt{3}}{\sqrt{3}}$$

$$x = \frac{\sqrt{39}}{3} \qquad\qquad x = -\frac{\sqrt{39}}{3}$$

The solutions are $\pm \dfrac{\sqrt{39}}{3}$.

21. $7x^2 = 4$

$$x^2 = \frac{4}{7}$$

$$x = \sqrt{\frac{4}{7}} \quad \text{or} \quad x = -\sqrt{\frac{4}{7}}$$

$$x = \frac{2}{\sqrt{7}} \cdot \frac{\sqrt{7}}{\sqrt{7}} \qquad x = -\frac{2}{\sqrt{7}} \cdot \frac{\sqrt{7}}{\sqrt{7}}$$

$$x = \frac{2\sqrt{7}}{7} \qquad\qquad x = -\frac{2\sqrt{7}}{7}$$

The solutions are $\pm \dfrac{2\sqrt{7}}{7}$.

23. $x^2 - 2 = 0$

$$x^2 = 2$$

$$x = \sqrt{2} \quad \text{or} \quad x = -\sqrt{2}$$

The solutions are $\pm\sqrt{2}$.

25. Answers may vary.

27. $(x-5)^2 = 49$

$$x - 5 = \sqrt{49} \quad \text{or} \quad x - 5 = -\sqrt{49}$$

$$x - 5 = 7 \qquad\qquad x - 5 = -7$$

$$x = 5 + 7 = 12 \qquad x = 5 - 7 = -2$$

The solutions are -2 and 12.

29. $(x+2)^2 = 7$

$$x + 2 = \sqrt{7} \quad \text{or} \quad x + 2 = -\sqrt{7}$$

$$x = -2 + \sqrt{7} \qquad x = -2 - \sqrt{7}$$

The solutions are $-2 \pm \sqrt{7}$.

31. $\left(m - \dfrac{1}{2}\right)^2 = \dfrac{1}{4}$

$$m - \frac{1}{2} = \sqrt{\frac{1}{4}} \quad \text{or} \quad m - \frac{1}{2} = -\sqrt{\frac{1}{4}}$$

$$m - \frac{1}{2} = \frac{1}{2} \qquad\qquad m - \frac{1}{2} = -\frac{1}{2}$$

$$m = \frac{1}{2} + \frac{1}{2} = 1 \qquad m = \frac{1}{2} - \frac{1}{2} = 0$$

The solutions are 0 and 1.

33. $(p+2)^2 = 10$

$$p + 2 = \sqrt{10} \quad \text{or} \quad p + 2 = -\sqrt{10}$$

$$p = -2 + \sqrt{10} \qquad p = -2 - \sqrt{10}$$

The solutions are $-2 \pm \sqrt{10}$.

35. $(3y+2)^2 = 100$

$$3y+2 = \sqrt{100} \quad \text{or} \quad 3y+2 = -\sqrt{100}$$
$$3y+2 = 10 \qquad\qquad 3y+2 = -10$$
$$3y = -2+10 \qquad 3y = -2-10$$
$$y = \frac{-2+10}{3} \qquad y = \frac{-2-10}{3}$$
$$y = \frac{8}{3} \qquad\qquad y = -4$$

The solutions are -4 and $\dfrac{8}{3}$

37. $(z-4)^2 = -9$

This equation has no real solution because $\sqrt{-9}$ is not a real number.

39. $(2x-11)^2 = 50$

$$2x-11 = \sqrt{50} \quad \text{or} \quad 2x-11 = -\sqrt{50}$$
$$2x-11 = 5\sqrt{2} \qquad 2x-11 = -5\sqrt{2}$$
$$2x = 11+5\sqrt{2} \qquad 2x = 11-5\sqrt{2}$$
$$x = \frac{11+5\sqrt{2}}{2} \qquad x = \frac{11-5\sqrt{2}}{2}$$

The solutions are $\dfrac{11\pm5\sqrt{2}}{2}$.

41. $(3x-7)^2 = 32$

$$3x-7 = \sqrt{32} \quad \text{or} \quad 3x-7 = -\sqrt{32}$$
$$3x-7 = 4\sqrt{2} \qquad 3x-7 = -4\sqrt{2}$$
$$3x = 7+4\sqrt{2} \qquad 3x = 7-4\sqrt{2}$$
$$x = \frac{7+4\sqrt{2}}{3} \qquad x = \frac{7-4\sqrt{2}}{3}$$

The solutions are $\dfrac{7\pm4\sqrt{2}}{3}$.

43. Let $h = 87.6$

$$h = 16t^2$$
$$87.6 = 16t^2$$
$$\frac{87.6}{16} = t^2$$
$$5.475 = t^2$$
$$\sqrt{5.475} = t \quad \text{or} \quad -\sqrt{5.475} = t$$
$$2.3 \approx t \qquad\qquad -2.3 \approx t$$

The length of the dive is not a negative number so the dive lasted approximately 2.3 seconds.

45. $16 \text{ mi} = 16 \text{ mi} \cdot \dfrac{5280 \text{ ft}}{1 \text{ mi}} = 84,480 \text{ ft}$

Let $h = 84,480$

$$h = 16t^2$$
$$84,480 = 16t^2$$
$$\frac{84,480}{16} = t^2$$
$$5280 = t^2$$
$$\sqrt{5280} = t \quad \text{or} \quad -\sqrt{5280} = t$$
$$72.7 \approx t \qquad\qquad -72.7 \approx t$$

The length of the fall is not a negative number so the fall lasted approximately 72.7 seconds.

47. Let $A = 20$

$$A = s^2$$
$$20 = s^2$$
$$\sqrt{20} = s \quad \text{or} \quad -\sqrt{20} = s$$
$$4.47 \approx s \qquad -4.47 \approx s$$

The length of a side is not a negative number so the length is approximately 4.47 inches.

49. Let $A = 20$

$$A = s^2$$

$$3039 = s^2$$

$$\sqrt{3039} = s \quad \text{or} \quad -\sqrt{3039} = s$$

$$55.13 \approx s \qquad\qquad -55.13 \approx s$$

The length of a side is not a negative number so the length is approximately 55.13 feet.

51. $x^2 + 6x + 9 = (x)^2 + 2(3)x + (3)^2$

$$= (x+3)^2$$

53. $x^2 - 4x + 4 = (x)^2 - 2(2)x + (2)^2$

$$= (x-2)^2$$

55. $x^2 + 4x + 4 = 16$

$$(x+2)^2 = 16$$

$$x + 2 = \sqrt{16} \quad \text{or} \quad x + 2 = -\sqrt{16}$$

$$x + 2 = 4 \qquad\qquad x + 2 = -4$$

$$x = 2 \qquad\qquad x = -6$$

The solutions are -6 and 2

57. Let $A = 36\pi$

$$A = \pi r^2$$

$$36\pi = \pi r^2$$

$$36 = r^2$$

$$\sqrt{36} = r \quad \text{or} \quad -\sqrt{36} = r$$

$$6 = r \qquad\qquad -6 = r$$

The radius of a circle is not a negative number so the radius is 6 inches.

59. Let $d = 400$

$$d = 16t^2$$

$$400 = 16t^2$$

$$\frac{400}{16} = t^2$$

$$25 = t^2$$

$$\sqrt{25} = t \quad \text{or} \quad -\sqrt{25} = t$$

$$5 = t \qquad\qquad -5 = t$$

The length of time is not a negative number so the fall lasted 5 seconds.

61. $(x - 1.37)^2 = 5.71$

$$x - 1.37 = \sqrt{5.71} \quad \text{or} \quad x - 1.37 = -\sqrt{5.71}$$

$$x - 1.37 = 2.39 \qquad\qquad x - 1.37 = -2.39$$

$$x = 3.76 \qquad\qquad\qquad x = -1.02$$

63.   Let $y = 17,000$

$$y = -200(x - 1.75)^2 + 19,112.5$$

$$17,000 = -200(x - 1.75)^2 + 19,112.5$$

$$-2112.5 = -200(x - 1.75)^2$$

$$10.5625 = (x - 1.75)^2$$

$$x - 1.75 = \pm\sqrt{10.5625}$$

$$x = 1.75 \pm 3.25$$

$$x = 5 \text{ or } x = -1.5$$

Since years cannot be negative, $x = 5$

The year will be $1998 + 5 = 2003$.

Practice Problems 9.2

1.
$$x^2 + 8x + 1 = 0$$
$$x^2 + 8x = -1$$
$$x^2 + 8x + 16 = -1 + 16$$
$$(x+4)^2 = 15$$
$$x + 4 = \pm\sqrt{15}$$
$$x = -4 \pm \sqrt{15}$$
The solutions are $-4 \pm \sqrt{15}$.

2.
$$x^2 - 14x = -32$$
$$x^2 - 14x + 49 = -32 + 49$$
$$(x-7)^2 = 17$$
$$x - 7 = \pm\sqrt{17}$$
$$x = 7 \pm \sqrt{17}$$
The solutions are $7 \pm \sqrt{17}$.

3. $4x^2 - 16x - 9 = 0$
$$4x^2 - 16x = 9$$
$$x^2 - 4x = \frac{9}{4}$$
$$x^2 - 4x + 4 = \frac{9}{4} + 4$$
$$(x-2)^2 = \frac{25}{4}$$
$$x - 2 = \pm\sqrt{\frac{25}{4}}$$
$$x = 2 + \frac{5}{2} \quad \text{or} \quad x = 2 - \frac{5}{2}$$
$$x = \frac{9}{2} \qquad\qquad x = -\frac{1}{2}$$
The solutions are $-\dfrac{1}{2}$ and $\dfrac{9}{2}$.

4.
$$2x^2 + 10x = -13$$
$$x^2 + 5x = -\frac{13}{2}$$
$$x^2 + 5x + \frac{25}{4} = -\frac{13}{2} + \frac{25}{4}$$
$$(x+5)^2 = -\frac{1}{4}$$
This equation has no real solution because $\sqrt{-\dfrac{1}{4}}$ is not a real number.

5.
$$2x^2 = -3x + 2$$
$$x^2 = -\frac{3}{2}x + 1$$
$$x^2 + \frac{3}{2}x = 1$$
$$x^2 + \frac{3}{2}x + \frac{9}{16} = 1 + \frac{9}{16}$$
$$\left(x + \frac{3}{4}\right)^2 = \frac{25}{16}$$
$$x + \frac{3}{4} = \pm\sqrt{\frac{25}{16}}$$
$$x = -\frac{3}{4} \pm \frac{5}{4}$$
$$x = -\frac{3}{4} + \frac{5}{4} \quad \text{or} \quad x = -\frac{3}{4} - \frac{5}{4}$$
$$x = \frac{1}{2} \qquad\qquad x = -2$$
The solutions are -2 and $\dfrac{1}{2}$.

Mental Math 9.2

1. $p^2 + 8p$
$$\left(\frac{8}{2}\right)^2 = 4^2 = 16$$

2. $p^2 + 6p$

$$\left(\frac{6}{2}\right)^2 = 3^2 = 9$$

3. $x^2 + 20x$

$$\left(\frac{20}{2}\right)^2 = 10^2 = 100$$

4. $x^2 + 18x$

$$\left(\frac{18}{2}\right)^2 = 9^2 = 81$$

5. $y^2 + 14y$

$$\left(\frac{14}{2}\right)^2 = 7^2 = 49$$

6. $y^2 + 2y$

$$\left(\frac{2}{2}\right)^2 = 1^2 = 1$$

Exercise Set 9.2

1.
$$x^2 + 8x = -12$$
$$x^2 + 8x + 16 = -12 + 16$$
$$(x+4)^2 = 4$$
$$x + 4 = \pm\sqrt{4}$$
$$x = -4 \pm 2$$
$$x = -4 + 2 \quad \text{or} \quad x = -4 - 2$$
$$x = -2 \qquad\qquad x = -6$$

The solutions are -6 and -2.

3.
$$x^2 + 2x - 5 = 0$$
$$x^2 + 2x = 5$$
$$x^2 + 2x + 1 = 5 + 1$$
$$(x+1)^2 = 6$$
$$x + 1 = \pm\sqrt{6}$$
$$x = -1 \pm \sqrt{6}$$

The solutions are $-1 \pm \sqrt{6}$.

5.
$$x^2 - 6x = 0$$
$$x^2 - 6x + 9 = 0 + 9$$
$$(x-3)^2 = 9$$
$$x - 3 = \pm\sqrt{9}$$
$$x = 3 \pm 3$$
$$x = 3 + 3 \quad \text{or} \quad x = 3 - 3$$
$$x = 6 \qquad\qquad x = 0$$

The solutions are 0 and 6.

7.
$$z^2 + 5z = 7$$
$$z^2 + 5z + \frac{25}{4} = 7 + \frac{25}{4}$$
$$\left(z + \frac{5}{2}\right)^2 = \frac{53}{4}$$
$$z + \frac{5}{2} = \pm\sqrt{\frac{53}{4}}$$
$$z = -\frac{5}{2} \pm \frac{\sqrt{53}}{2}$$
$$z = \frac{-5 \pm \sqrt{53}}{2}$$

The solutions are $\dfrac{-5 \pm \sqrt{53}}{2}$.

9.
$$x^2 - 2x - 1 = 0$$
$$x^2 - 2x = 1$$
$$x^2 - 2x + 1 = 1 + 1$$
$$(x-1)^2 = 2$$
$$x - 1 = \pm\sqrt{2}$$
$$x = 1 \pm \sqrt{2}$$
The solutions are $1 \pm \sqrt{2}$.

11.
$$y^2 + 5y + 4 = 0$$
$$y^2 + 5y = -4$$
$$y^2 + 5y + \frac{25}{4} = -4 + \frac{25}{4}$$
$$\left(y + \frac{5}{2}\right)^2 = \frac{9}{4}$$
$$y + \frac{5}{2} = \pm\sqrt{\frac{9}{4}}$$
$$y = -\frac{5}{2} \pm \frac{3}{2}$$
$$y = -\frac{5}{2} + \frac{3}{2} \quad \text{or} \quad y = -\frac{5}{2} - \frac{3}{2}$$
$$y = -1 \qquad\qquad y = -4$$
The solutions are -4 and -1.

13.
$$x^2 + 6x - 25 = 0$$
$$x^2 + 6x = 25$$
$$x^2 + 6x + 9 = 25 + 9$$
$$(x+3)^2 = 34$$
$$x + 3 = \pm\sqrt{34}$$
$$x = -3 \pm \sqrt{34}$$
The solutions are $-3 \pm \sqrt{34}$.

15.
$$x^2 - 3z - 3 = 0$$
$$x^2 - 3x = 3$$
$$x^2 - 3x + \frac{9}{4} = 3 + \frac{9}{4}$$
$$\left(x - \frac{3}{2}\right)^2 = \frac{21}{4}$$
$$x - \frac{3}{2} = \pm\sqrt{\frac{21}{4}}$$
$$x = \frac{3}{2} \pm \frac{\sqrt{21}}{2}$$
$$x = \frac{3 \pm \sqrt{21}}{2}$$
The solutions are $\dfrac{3 \pm \sqrt{21}}{2}$.

17.
$$x(x+3) = 18$$
$$x^2 + 3x = 18$$
$$x^2 + 3x + \frac{9}{4} = 18 + \frac{9}{4}$$
$$\left(x + \frac{3}{2}\right)^2 = \frac{81}{4}$$
$$x + \frac{3}{2} = \pm\sqrt{\frac{81}{4}}$$
$$x = -\frac{3}{2} \pm \frac{9}{2}$$
$$x = -\frac{3}{2} + \frac{9}{2} \quad \text{or} \quad x = -\frac{3}{2} - \frac{9}{2}$$
$$x = 3 \qquad\qquad x = -6$$
The solutions are -6 and 3.

19. $3x^2 - 6x = 24$

$x^2 - 2x = 8$

$x^2 - 2x + 1 = 8 + 1$

$(x-1)^2 = 9$

$x - 1 = \pm\sqrt{9}$

$x = 1 \pm 3$

$x = 1 + 3 \quad \text{or} \quad x = 1 - 3$

$x = 4 \qquad\qquad x = -2$

The solutions are -2 and 4.

21. $5x^2 + 10x + 6 = 0$

$5x^2 + 10x = -6$

$x^2 + 2x = -\dfrac{6}{5}$

$x^2 + 2x + 1 = -\dfrac{6}{5} + 1$

$(x+1)^2 = -\dfrac{1}{5}$

This equation has no real solution

because $\sqrt{-\dfrac{1}{5}}$ is not a real number.

23. $2x^2 = 6x + 5$

$2x^2 - 6x = 5$

$x^2 - 3x = \dfrac{5}{2}$

$x^2 - 3x + \dfrac{9}{4} = \dfrac{5}{2} + \dfrac{9}{4}$

$\left(x - \dfrac{3}{2}\right)^2 = \dfrac{19}{4}$

$x - \dfrac{3}{2} = \pm\sqrt{\dfrac{19}{4}}$

$x = \dfrac{3}{2} \pm \dfrac{\sqrt{19}}{2}$

The solutions are $\dfrac{3 \pm \sqrt{19}}{2}$

25. $2y^2 + 8y + 5 = 0$

$2y^2 + 8y = -5$

$y^2 + 4y = -\dfrac{5}{2}$

$y^2 + 4y + 4 = -\dfrac{5}{2} + 4$

$(y+2)^2 = \dfrac{3}{2}$

$y + 2 = \pm\sqrt{\dfrac{3}{2}}$

$y = -2 \pm \sqrt{\dfrac{3}{2}}$

$y = -2 \pm \sqrt{\dfrac{3}{2}} \cdot \sqrt{\dfrac{2}{2}}$

$y = -2 \pm \dfrac{\sqrt{6}}{2}$

The solutions are $-2 \pm \dfrac{\sqrt{6}}{2}$.

27. $2y^2 - 3y + 1 = 0$

$2y^2 - 3y = -1$

$y^2 - \dfrac{3}{2}y = -\dfrac{1}{2}$

$y^2 - \dfrac{3}{2}y + \dfrac{9}{16} = -\dfrac{1}{2} + \dfrac{9}{16}$

$\left(y - \dfrac{3}{4}\right)^2 = \dfrac{1}{16}$

$$y - \frac{3}{4} = \pm\sqrt{\frac{1}{16}}$$

$$y = \frac{3}{4} \pm \frac{1}{4}$$

$$y = \frac{3}{4} + \frac{1}{4} \quad \text{or} \quad y = \frac{3}{4} - \frac{1}{4}$$

$$y = 1 \qquad\qquad y = \frac{1}{2}$$

The solutions are $\frac{1}{2}$ and 1.

29. Answers may vary.

31. $\dfrac{3}{4} - \sqrt{\dfrac{25}{16}} = \dfrac{3}{4} - \dfrac{5}{4} = -\dfrac{2}{4} = -\dfrac{1}{2}$

33. $\dfrac{1}{2} - \sqrt{\dfrac{9}{4}} = \dfrac{1}{2} - \dfrac{3}{2} = -\dfrac{2}{2} = -1$

35. $\dfrac{6 + 4\sqrt{5}}{2} = \dfrac{2\left(3 + 2\sqrt{5}\right)}{2} = 3 + 2\sqrt{5}$

37. $\dfrac{3 - 9\sqrt{2}}{6} = \dfrac{3\left(1 - 3\sqrt{2}\right)}{3 \cdot 2} = \dfrac{1 - 3\sqrt{2}}{2}$

39. $x^2 + kx + 16$

$$\left(\frac{k}{2}\right)^2 = 16$$

$$\frac{k^2}{4} = 16$$

$$k^2 = 64$$

$$k = \pm\sqrt{64}$$

$$k = \pm 8$$

41. Let $y = 47,390$

$$y = 268x^2 + 720x + 13,390$$

$$47,390 = 268x^2 + 720x + 13,390$$

$$0 = 268x^2 + 720x - 34,000$$

$$0 = 67x^2 + 180x - 8500$$

$$0 = \left(67x + 850\right)\left(x - 10\right)$$

$$67x + 850 = 0 \quad \text{or} \quad x - 10 = 0$$

$$x = -\frac{850}{67} \qquad x = 10$$

The number of years cannot be negative so the year will be $1998 + 10 = 2008$.

43. $x^2 + 8x = -12$

$y_1 = x^2 + 8x$

$y_2 = -12$

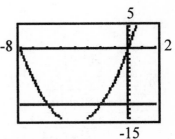

The x-coordinates of the intersections, -6 and -2, are the solutions.

45. $2x^2 = 6x + 5$

$y_1 = 2x^2$

$y_2 = 6x + 5$

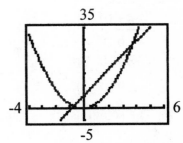

The x-coordinates of the intersections, -0.68 and 3.68, are the solutions.

Practice Problems 9.3

1. $2x^2 - x - 5 = 0$

    $a = 2, b = -1,$ and $c = -5$

    $$x = \frac{-b \pm \sqrt{b^2 - 4ac}}{2a}$$

    $$x = \frac{-(-1) \pm \sqrt{(-1)^2 - 4(2)(-5)}}{2(2)}$$

    $$= \frac{1 \pm \sqrt{1 + 40}}{4} = \frac{1 \pm \sqrt{41}}{4}$$

    The solutions are $\dfrac{1 \pm \sqrt{41}}{4}$.

2. $3x^2 + 8x = 3$

    $3x^2 + 8x - 3 = 0$

    $a = 3, b = 8,$ and $c = -3$

    $$x = \frac{-b \pm \sqrt{b^2 - 4ac}}{2a}$$

    $$x = \frac{-(8) \pm \sqrt{(8)^2 - 4(3)(-3)}}{2(3)}$$

    $$x = \frac{-8 \pm \sqrt{64 + 36}}{6}$$

    $$x = \frac{-8 \pm \sqrt{100}}{6}$$

    $$x = \frac{-8 \pm 10}{6}$$

    $$x = \frac{-8 + 10}{6} = \frac{1}{3} \quad \text{or} \quad x = \frac{-8 - 10}{6} = -3$$

    The solutions are -3 and $\dfrac{1}{3}$.

3. $5x^2 = 2$

    $5x^2 - 2 = 0$

    $a = 5, b = 0,$ and $c = -2$

    $$x = \frac{-b \pm \sqrt{b^2 - 4ac}}{2a}$$

    $$x = \frac{-(0) \pm \sqrt{(0)^2 - 4(5)(-2)}}{2(5)}$$

    $$= \frac{\pm\sqrt{40}}{10} = \frac{\pm 2\sqrt{10}}{10} = \pm\frac{\sqrt{10}}{5}$$

    The solutions are $\pm \dfrac{\sqrt{10}}{5}$.

4. $x^2 = -2x - 3$

    $x^2 + 2x + 3 = 0$

    $a = 1, b = 2,$ and $c = 3$

    $$x = \frac{-b \pm \sqrt{b^2 - 4ac}}{2a}$$

    $$x = \frac{-(2) \pm \sqrt{(2)^2 - 4(1)(3)}}{2(1)}$$

    $$x = \frac{-2 \pm \sqrt{-8}}{2}$$

    This equation has no real solution because $\sqrt{-8}$ is not a real number.

5. $\dfrac{1}{3}x^2 - x = 1$

    $\dfrac{1}{3}x^2 - x - 1 = 0$

    $x^2 - 3x - 3 = 0$

    $a = 1, b = -3,$ and $c = -3$

    $$x = \frac{-b \pm \sqrt{b^2 - 4ac}}{2a}$$

$$x = \frac{-(-3) \pm \sqrt{(-3)^2 - 4(1)(-3)}}{2(1)}$$

$$= \frac{3 \pm \sqrt{9+12}}{2} = \frac{3 \pm \sqrt{21}}{2}$$

The solutions are $\dfrac{3 \pm \sqrt{21}}{2}$

Mental Math 9.3

1. $2x^2 + 5x + 3 = 0$

$a = 2, b = 5, c = 3$

2. $5x^2 - 7x + 1 = 0$

$a = 5, b = -7, c = 1$

3. $10x^2 - 13x - 2 = 0$

$a = 10, b = -13, c = -2$

4. $x^2 + 3x - 7 = 0$

$a = 1, b = 3, c = -7$

5. $x^2 - 6 = 0$

$a = 1, b = 0, c = -6$

6. $9x^2 - 4 = 0$

$a = 9, b = 0, c = -4$

Exercise Set 9.3

1. $x^2 - 3x + 2 = 0$

$a = 1, b = -3,$ and $c = 2$

$$x = \frac{-b \pm \sqrt{b^2 - 4ac}}{2a}$$

$$x = \frac{-(-3) \pm \sqrt{(-3)^2 - 4(1)(2)}}{2(1)}$$

$$= \frac{3 \pm \sqrt{9-8}}{2} = \frac{3 \pm \sqrt{1}}{2} = \frac{3 \pm 1}{2}$$

$$x = \frac{3+1}{2} = 2 \quad \text{or} \quad x = \frac{3-1}{2} = 1$$

The solutions are 1 and 2.

3. $3k^2 + 7x + 1 = 0$

$a = 3, b = 7,$ and $c = 1$

$$k = \frac{-b \pm \sqrt{b^2 - 4ac}}{2a}$$

$$k = \frac{-(7) \pm \sqrt{(7)^2 - 4(3)(1)}}{2(3)}$$

$$= \frac{-7 \pm \sqrt{49-12}}{6} = \frac{-7 \pm \sqrt{37}}{6}$$

The solutions are $\dfrac{-7 \pm \sqrt{37}}{6}$.

5. $49x^2 - 4 = 0$

$a = 49, b = 0,$ and $c = -4$

$$x = \frac{-b \pm \sqrt{b^2 - 4ac}}{2a}$$

$$x = \frac{-(0) \pm \sqrt{(0)^2 - 4(49)(-4)}}{2(49)}$$

$$= \frac{\pm\sqrt{784}}{98} = \frac{\pm 28}{98} = \pm\frac{2}{7}$$

The solutions are $\pm\dfrac{2}{7}$.

7. $5z^2 - 4z + 3 = 0$

$a = 5, b = -4,$ and $c = 3$

$$z = \frac{-(-4) \pm \sqrt{(-4)^2 - 4(5)(3)}}{2(5)}$$

$$= \frac{4 \pm \sqrt{16 - 60}}{10} = \frac{4 \pm \sqrt{-44}}{10}$$

There is no real solution because $\sqrt{-44}$ is not a real number.

9. $y^2 = 7y + 30$

$y^2 - 7y - 30 = 0$

$a = 1, b = -7,$ and $c = -30$

$$y = \frac{-(-7) \pm \sqrt{(-7)^2 - 4(1)(-30)}}{2(1)}$$

$$= \frac{7 \pm \sqrt{49 + 120}}{2} = \frac{7 \pm \sqrt{169}}{2}$$

$$= \frac{7 \pm 13}{2}$$

$$y = \frac{7 + 13}{2} = 10 \quad \text{or} \quad y = \frac{7 - 13}{2} = -3$$

The solutions are -3 and 10.

11. $2x^2 = 10$

$2x^2 - 10 = 0$

$a = 2, b = 0,$ and $c = -10$

$$x = \frac{-(0) \pm \sqrt{(0)^2 - 4(2)(-10)}}{2(2)}$$

$$= \frac{\pm\sqrt{80}}{4} = \frac{\pm 4\sqrt{5}}{4} = \pm\sqrt{5}$$

The solutions are $\pm\sqrt{5}$.

13. $m^2 - 12 = m$

$m^2 - m - 12 = 0$

$a = 1, b = -1,$ and $c = -12$

$$m = \frac{-(-1) \pm \sqrt{(-1)^2 - 4(1)(-12)}}{2(1)}$$

$$= \frac{1 \pm \sqrt{1 + 48}}{2} = \frac{1 \pm \sqrt{49}}{2} = \frac{1 \pm 7}{2}$$

$$m = \frac{1 + 7}{2} = 4 \quad \text{or} \quad m = \frac{1 - 7}{2} = -3$$

The solutions are -3 and 4.

15. $3 - x^2 = 4x$

$-x^2 - 4x + 3 = 0$

$a = -1, b = -4,$ and $c = 3$

$$x = \frac{-(-4) \pm \sqrt{(-4)^2 - 4(-1)(3)}}{2(-1)}$$

$$= \frac{4 \pm \sqrt{16 + 12}}{-2} = \frac{4 \pm \sqrt{28}}{-2}$$

$$= \frac{4 \pm 2\sqrt{7}}{-2} = -2 \pm \sqrt{7}$$

The solutions are $-2 \pm \sqrt{7}$.

17. $6x^2 + 9x = 2$

$6x^2 + 9x - 2 = 0$

$a = 6, b = 9,$ and $c = -2$

$$x = \frac{-(9) \pm \sqrt{(9)^2 - 4(6)(-2)}}{2(6)}$$

$$= \frac{-9 \pm \sqrt{81 + 48}}{12} = \frac{-9 \pm \sqrt{129}}{12}$$

The solutions are $\dfrac{-9 \pm \sqrt{129}}{12}$.

19.
$$7p^2 + 2 = 8p$$
$$7p^2 - 8p + 2 = 0$$
$$a = 7, b = -8, \text{ and } c = 2$$
$$p = \frac{-(-8) \pm \sqrt{(-8)^2 - 4(7)(2)}}{2(7)}$$
$$= \frac{8 \pm \sqrt{64 - 56}}{14} = \frac{8 \pm \sqrt{8}}{14}$$
$$= \frac{8 \pm 2\sqrt{2}}{14} = \frac{4 \pm \sqrt{2}}{7}$$

The solutions are $\dfrac{4 \pm \sqrt{2}}{7}$.

21. $a^2 - 6a + 2 = 0$
$$a = 1, b = -6, \text{ and } c = 2$$
$$a = \frac{-(-6) \pm \sqrt{(-6)^2 - 4(1)(2)}}{2(1)}$$
$$= \frac{6 \pm \sqrt{36 - 8}}{2} = \frac{6 \pm \sqrt{28}}{2}$$
$$= \frac{6 \pm 2\sqrt{7}}{2} = 3 \pm \sqrt{7}$$

The solutions are $3 \pm \sqrt{7}$.

23. $2x^2 - 6x + 3 = 0$
$$a = 2, b = -6, \text{ and } c = 3$$
$$x = \frac{-(-6) \pm \sqrt{(-6)^2 - 4(2)(3)}}{2(2)}$$
$$= \frac{6 \pm \sqrt{36 - 24}}{4} = \frac{6 \pm \sqrt{12}}{4}$$
$$= \frac{6 \pm 2\sqrt{3}}{4} = \frac{3 \pm \sqrt{3}}{2}$$

The solutions are $\dfrac{3 \pm \sqrt{3}}{2}$.

25.
$$3x^2 = 1 - 2x$$
$$3x^2 + 2x - 1 = 0$$
$$a = 3, b = 2, \text{ and } c = -1$$
$$x = \frac{-(2) \pm \sqrt{(2)^2 - 4(3)(-1)}}{2(3)}$$
$$= \frac{-2 \pm \sqrt{4 + 12}}{6} = \frac{-2 \pm \sqrt{16}}{6} = \frac{-2 \pm 4}{6}$$
$$x = \frac{-2 + 4}{6} = \frac{1}{3} \quad \text{or} \quad x = \frac{-2 - 4}{6} = -1$$

The solutions are -1 and $\dfrac{1}{3}$.

27.
$$4y^2 = 6y + 1$$
$$4y^2 - 6y - 1 = 0$$
$$a = 4, b = -6, \text{ and } c = -1$$
$$y = \frac{-(-6) \pm \sqrt{(-6)^2 - 4(4)(-1)}}{2(4)}$$
$$= \frac{6 \pm \sqrt{36 + 16}}{8} = \frac{6 \pm \sqrt{52}}{8}$$
$$= \frac{6 \pm 2\sqrt{13}}{8} = \frac{3 \pm \sqrt{13}}{4}$$

The solutions are $\dfrac{3 \pm \sqrt{13}}{4}$.

29.
$$20y^2 = 3 - 11y$$
$$20y^2 + 11y - 3 = 0$$
$$a = 20, b = 11, \text{ and } c = -3$$
$$y = \frac{-(11) \pm \sqrt{(11)^2 - 4(20)(-3)}}{2(20)}$$
$$= \frac{-11 \pm \sqrt{121 + 240}}{40} = \frac{-11 \pm \sqrt{361}}{40}$$
$$= \frac{-11 \pm 19}{40}$$

$$y = \frac{-11+19}{40} = \frac{1}{5} \quad \text{or} \quad y = \frac{-11-19}{40} = -\frac{3}{4}$$

The solutions are $-\dfrac{3}{4}$ and $\dfrac{1}{5}$.

31. $x^2 + x + 2 = 0$

$a = 1, b = 1,$ and $c = 2$

$$x = \frac{-(1) \pm \sqrt{(1)^2 - 4(1)(2)}}{2(1)}$$

$$= \frac{-1 \pm \sqrt{1-8}}{2} = \frac{-1 \pm \sqrt{-7}}{2}$$

There is no real solution because $\sqrt{-7}$ is not a real number.

33. $3p^2 - \dfrac{2}{3}p + 1 = 0$

$9p^2 - 2p + 3 = 0$

$a = 9, b = -2,$ and $c = 3$

$$p = \frac{-(-2) \pm \sqrt{(-2)^2 - 4(9)(3)}}{2(9)}$$

$$= \frac{2 \pm \sqrt{4-108}}{18} = \frac{2 \pm \sqrt{-104}}{18}$$

There is no real solution because $\sqrt{-104}$ is not a real number.

35. $\dfrac{m^2}{2} = m + \dfrac{1}{2}$

$m^2 = 2m + 1$

$m^2 - 2m - 1 = 0$

$a = 1, b = -2,$ and $c = -1$

$$m = \frac{-(-2) \pm \sqrt{(-2)^2 - 4(1)(-1)}}{2(1)}$$

$$= \frac{2 \pm \sqrt{4+4}}{2} = \frac{2 \pm \sqrt{8}}{2}$$

$$= \frac{2 \pm 2\sqrt{2}}{2} = 1 \pm \sqrt{2}$$

The solutions are $1 \pm \sqrt{2}$.

37. $4p^2 + \dfrac{3}{2} = -5p$

$8p^2 + 3 = -10p$

$8p^2 + 10p + 3 = 0$

$a = 8, b = 10,$ and $c = 3$

$$p = \frac{-(10) \pm \sqrt{(10)^2 - 4(8)(3)}}{2(8)}$$

$$= \frac{-10 \pm \sqrt{100-96}}{16} = \frac{-10 \pm \sqrt{4}}{16}$$

$$= \frac{-10 \pm 2}{16}$$

$$p = \frac{-10+2}{16} = -\frac{1}{2} \quad \text{or} \quad p = \frac{-10-2}{16} = -\frac{3}{4}$$

The solutions are $-\dfrac{3}{4}$ and $-\dfrac{1}{2}$.

39. $5x^2 = \dfrac{7}{2}x + 1$

$10x^2 = 7x + 2$

$10x^2 - 7x - 2 = 0$

$a = 10, b = -7,$ and $c = -2$

$$x = \frac{-(-7) \pm \sqrt{(-7)^2 - 4(10)(-2)}}{2(10)}$$

$$= \frac{7 \pm \sqrt{49+80}}{20} = \frac{7 \pm \sqrt{129}}{20}$$

The solutions are $\dfrac{7 \pm \sqrt{129}}{20}$.

41. $28x^2 + 5x + \dfrac{11}{4} = 0$

$112x^2 + 20x + 11 = 0$

$a = 112, b = 20,$ and $c = 11$

$p = \dfrac{-(20) \pm \sqrt{(20)^2 - 4(112)(11)}}{2(112)}$

$= \dfrac{-20 \pm \sqrt{400 - 4928}}{224} = \dfrac{-20 \pm \sqrt{-4528}}{224}$

There is no real solution because

$\sqrt{-4528}$ is not a real number.

43. $5z^2 - 2z = \dfrac{1}{5}$

$25z^2 - 10z = 1$

$25z^2 - 10z - 1 = 0$

$a = 25, b = -10,$ and $c = -1$

$x = \dfrac{-(-10) \pm \sqrt{(-10)^2 - 4(25)(-1)}}{2(25)}$

$= \dfrac{10 \pm \sqrt{100 + 100}}{50} = \dfrac{10 \pm \sqrt{200}}{50}$

$= \dfrac{10 \pm 10\sqrt{2}}{50} = \dfrac{1 \pm \sqrt{2}}{5}$

The solutions are $\dfrac{1 \pm \sqrt{2}}{5}$.

45. $y = -3$

for all values of x.

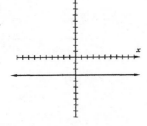

47. $y = 3x - 2$

x	y
3	7
0	−2

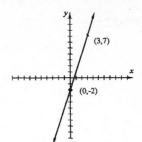

49. $a^2 + b^2 = c^2$

$x^2 + 7^2 = 10^2$

$x^2 + 49 = 100$

$x^2 = 51$

$x = \sqrt{51}$

The length is $\sqrt{51}$ meters

51.   Let x = the width then, $x + 5$ = the length.

$A = lw$

$35 = x(x + 5)$

$35 = x^2 + 5x$

$0 = x^2 + 5x - 35$

$a = 1,\ b = 5,\ c = -35$

$x = \dfrac{-(5) \pm \sqrt{(5)^2 - 4(1)(-35)}}{2(1)}$

$= \dfrac{-5 \pm \sqrt{25 + 140}}{2} = \dfrac{-5 \pm \sqrt{165}}{2}$

Because the width cannot be negative,

$x = \dfrac{-5 + \sqrt{165}}{2} \approx 3.9$

$x + 5 \approx 3.9 + 5 = 8.9$

Length = 8.9 ft., width = 3.9 ft.

53. $x^2 + 3\sqrt{2}\,x - 5 = 0$

$a = 1, b = 3\sqrt{2}$, and $c = -5$

$$x = \frac{-\left(3\sqrt{2}\right) \pm \sqrt{\left(3\sqrt{2}\right)^2 - 4(1)(-5)}}{2(1)}$$

$$= \frac{-3\sqrt{2} \pm \sqrt{18+20}}{2} = \frac{-3\sqrt{2} \pm \sqrt{38}}{2}$$

The solutions are $\dfrac{-3\sqrt{2} \pm \sqrt{38}}{2}$.

55. Answers may vary.

57. $y^2 - y = 11$

$y^2 - y - 11 = 0$

$a = 1, b = -1$, and $c = -11$

$$y = \frac{-(-1) \pm \sqrt{(-1)^2 - 4(1)(-11)}}{2(1)}$$

$$= \frac{1 \pm \sqrt{1+44}}{2} = \frac{1 \pm \sqrt{45}}{2}$$

$$y = \frac{1 + \sqrt{45}}{2} \approx 3.9 \quad \text{or} \quad y = \frac{1 - \sqrt{45}}{2} \approx -2.9$$

The solutions are -2.9 and 3.9.

59. $7.3z^2 + 5.4z - 1.1 = 0$

$a = 7.3, b = 5.4$, and $c = -1.1$

$$z = \frac{-(5.4) \pm \sqrt{(5.4)^2 - 4(7.3)(-1.1)}}{2(7.3)}$$

$$= \frac{-5.4 \pm \sqrt{29.16 + 32.12}}{14.6}$$

$$= \frac{-5.4 \pm \sqrt{61.28}}{14.6}$$

$$z = \frac{-5.4 + \sqrt{61.28}}{14.6} \approx 0.2 \quad \text{or}$$

$$z = \frac{-5.4 - \sqrt{61.28}}{14.6} \approx -0.9$$

The solutions are -0.9 and 0.2.

61. Let $h = 0$

$h = -16t^2 + 120t + 80$

$0 = -16t^2 + 120t + 80$

$a = -16, b = 120$, and $c = 80$

$$t = \frac{-(120) \pm \sqrt{(120)^2 - 4(-16)(80)}}{2(-16)}$$

$$= \frac{-120 \pm \sqrt{14,400 + 5120}}{-32}$$

$$= \frac{-120 \pm \sqrt{19,520}}{-32}$$

Since the time cannot be negative,

$$t = \frac{-120 - \sqrt{19,520}}{-32} \approx 8.1$$

It strikes the ground after 8.1 seconds.

63. Let $y = 3,695,000$

$y = 57,000x^2 - 14,000x + 1,000,000$

$3,695,000 = 57,000x^2 - 14,000x + 1,000,000$

$0 = 57,000x^2 - 14,000x - 2,695,000$

$a = 57,000, b = -14,000,$

and $c = -2,695,000$

$\sqrt{b^2 - 4ac}$

$= \sqrt{(-14,000)^2 - 4(57,000)(-2,695,000)}$

$= 784,000$

$$x = \frac{-(-14,000) \pm 784,000}{2(57,000)}$$

$$= \frac{14,000 \pm 784,000}{114,000}$$

Since time cannot be negative,

$$t = \frac{14,000 + 784,000}{114,000} = 7$$

It will be the year $1998 + 7 = 2005$.

Integrated Review 9.3

1. $5x^2 - 11x + 2 = 0$

$(5x - 1)(x - 2) = 0$

$5x - 1 = 0$ or $x - 2 = 0$

$5x = 1$ $x = 2$

$x = \frac{1}{5}$

The solutions are $\frac{1}{5}$ and 2.

2. $5x^2 + 13x - 6 = 0$

$(5x - 2)(x + 3) = 0$

$5x - 2 = 0$ or $x + 3 = 0$

$5x = 2$ $x = -3$

$x = \frac{2}{5}$

The solutions are $\frac{2}{5}$ and -3.

3. $x^2 - 1 = 2x$

$x^2 - 2x = 1$

$x^2 - 2x + 1 = 1 + 1$

$(x - 1)^2 = 2$

$x - 1 = \pm\sqrt{2}$

$x = 1 \pm \sqrt{2}$

The solutions are $1 \pm \sqrt{2}$.

4. $x^2 + 7 = 6x$

$x^2 - 6x = -7$

$x^2 - 6x + 9 = -7 + 9$

$(x - 3)^2 = 2$

$x - 3 = \pm\sqrt{2}$

$x = 3 \pm \sqrt{2}$

The solutions are $3 \pm \sqrt{2}$.

5. $a^2 = 20$

$a = \pm\sqrt{20}$

$= \pm 2\sqrt{5}$

The solutions are $\pm 2\sqrt{5}$.

6. $a^2 = 72$

$a = \pm\sqrt{72}$

$= \pm 6\sqrt{2}$

The solutions are $\pm 6\sqrt{2}$.

7. $x^2 - x + 4 = 0$

$x^2 - x = -4$

$x^2 - x + \frac{1}{4} = -4 + \frac{1}{4}$

$\left(x - \frac{1}{2}\right)^2 = -\frac{15}{4}$

There is no real solution.

8. $x^2 - 2x + 7 = 0$

$x^2 - 2x = -7$

$x^2 - 2x + 1 = -7 + 1$

$(x-1)^2 = -6$

There is no real solution.

9. $3x^2 - 12x + 12 = 0$

$x^2 - 4x + 4 = 0$

$(x-2)^2 = 0$

$x - 2 = 0$

$x = 2$

The solution is 2.

10. $5x^2 - 30x + 45 = 0$

$x^2 - 6x + 9 = 0$

$(x-3)^2 = 0$

$x - 3 = 0$

$x = 3$

The solution is 3.

11. $9 - 6p + p^2 = 0$

$(p-3)^2 = 0$

$p - 3 = 0$

$p = 3$

The solution is 3.

12. $49 - 28p + 4p^2 = 0$

$(2p-7)^2 = 0$

$2p - 7 = 0$

$2p = 7$

$p = \dfrac{7}{2}$

The solution is $\dfrac{7}{2}$.

13. $\qquad 4y^2 - 16 = 0$

$\qquad 4y^2 = 16$

$\qquad y^2 = 4$

$\qquad y = \pm\sqrt{4}$

$\qquad y = \pm 2$

The solutions are ± 2.

14. $\qquad 3y^2 - 27 = 0$

$\qquad 3y^2 = 27$

$\qquad y^2 = 9$

$\qquad y = \pm\sqrt{9}$

$\qquad y = \pm 3$

The solutions are ± 3.

15. $\quad x^4 - 3x^3 + 2x^2 = 0$

$\quad x^2\left(x^2 - 3x + 2\right) = 0$

$\quad x^2(x-1)(x-2) = 0$

$\quad x^2 = 0 \quad\text{or}\quad x-1 = 0 \quad\text{or}\quad x-2 = 0$

$\qquad x = 0 \qquad\quad x = 1 \qquad\quad x = 2$

The solutions are 0, 1, and 2.

16. $\quad x^3 + 7x^2 + 12x = 0$

$\quad x\left(x^2 + 7x + 12\right) = 0$

$\quad x(x+4)(x+3) = 0$

$\quad x = 0 \quad\text{or}\quad x+4 = 0 \quad\text{or}\quad x+3 = 0$

$\qquad x = 0 \qquad\quad x = -4 \qquad\quad x = -3$

The solutions are -4, -3, and 0.

17. $(2x+5)^2 = 25$

$$2x+5 = \pm\sqrt{25}$$

$$2x = -5 \pm 5$$

$$x = \frac{-5 \pm 5}{2}$$

$$x = \frac{-5-5}{2} = -5 \quad \text{or} \quad x = \frac{-5+5}{2} = 0$$

The solutions are 0 and -5.

18. $(3z-4)^2 = 16$

$$3z-4 = \pm\sqrt{16}$$

$$3z = 4 \pm 4$$

$$z = \frac{4 \pm 4}{3}$$

$$z = \frac{4-4}{3} = 0 \quad \text{or} \quad z = \frac{4+4}{3} = \frac{8}{3}$$

The solutions are 0 and $\frac{8}{3}$.

19. $\qquad 30x = 25x^2 + 2$

$$0 = 25x^2 - 30x + 2 = 0$$

$$a = 25, b = -30, \text{ and } c = 2$$

$$x = \frac{-(-30) \pm \sqrt{(-30)^2 - 4(25)(2)}}{2(25)}$$

$$= \frac{30 \pm \sqrt{900-200}}{50} = \frac{30 \pm \sqrt{700}}{50}$$

$$= \frac{30 \pm 10\sqrt{7}}{50} = \frac{3 \pm \sqrt{7}}{5}$$

The solutions are $\dfrac{3 \pm \sqrt{7}}{5}$.

20. $\qquad 12x = 4x^2 + 4$

$$0 = 4x^2 - 12x + 4$$

$$0 = x^2 - 3x + 1$$

$$a = 1, b = -3, \text{ and } c = 1$$

$$x = \frac{-(-3) \pm \sqrt{(-3)^2 - 4(1)(1)}}{2(1)}$$

$$= \frac{3 \pm \sqrt{9-4}}{2} = \frac{3 \pm \sqrt{5}}{2}$$

The solutions are $\dfrac{3 \pm \sqrt{5}}{2}$.

21. $\dfrac{2}{3}m^2 - \dfrac{1}{3}m - 1 = 0$

$$2m^2 - m - 3 = 0$$

$$(2m-3)(m+1) = 0$$

$$2m-3 = 0 \quad \text{or} \quad m+1 = 0$$

$$2m = 3 \qquad\qquad m = -1$$

$$m = \frac{3}{2}$$

The solutions are -1 and $\dfrac{3}{2}$.

22. $\dfrac{5}{8}m^2 + m - \dfrac{1}{2} = 0$

$$5m^2 + 8m - 4 = 0$$

$$(5m-2)(m+2) = 0$$

$$5m-2 = 0 \quad \text{or} \quad m+2 = 0$$

$$5m = 2 \qquad\qquad m = -2$$

$$m = \frac{2}{5}$$

The solutions are -2 and $\dfrac{2}{5}$.

23. $x^2 - \dfrac{1}{2}x - \dfrac{1}{5} = 0$

$10x^2 - 5x - 2 = 0$

$a = 10, b = -5,$ and $c = -2$

$x = \dfrac{-(-5) \pm \sqrt{(-5)^2 - 4(10)(-2)}}{2(10)}$

$= \dfrac{5 \pm \sqrt{25 + 80}}{20} = \dfrac{5 \pm \sqrt{105}}{20}$

The solutions are $\dfrac{5 \pm \sqrt{105}}{20}$.

24. $x^2 + \dfrac{1}{2}x - \dfrac{1}{8} = 0$

$8x^2 + 4x - 1 = 0$

$a = 8, b = 4,$ and $c = -1$

$x = \dfrac{-(4) \pm \sqrt{(4)^2 - 4(8)(-1)}}{2(8)}$

$= \dfrac{-4 \pm \sqrt{16 + 32}}{16} = \dfrac{-4 \pm \sqrt{48}}{16}$

$= \dfrac{-4 \pm 4\sqrt{3}}{16} = \dfrac{-1 \pm \sqrt{3}}{4}$

The solutions are $\dfrac{-1 \pm \sqrt{3}}{4}$.

25. $4x^2 - 27x + 35 = 0$

$(4x - 7)(x - 5) = 0$

$4x - 7 = 0$ or $x - 5 = 0$

$4x = 7$ $x = 5$

$x = \dfrac{7}{4}$

The solutions are $\dfrac{7}{4}$ and 5.

26. $4x^2 - 27x + 35 = 0$

$(4x - 7)(x - 5) = 0$

$4x - 7 = 0$ or $x - 5 = 0$

$4x = 7$ $x = 5$

$x = \dfrac{7}{4}$

The solutions are $\dfrac{7}{4}$ and 5.

27. $(7 - 5x)^2 = 18$

$7 - 5x = \pm\sqrt{18}$

$7 - 5x = \pm 3\sqrt{2}$

$-5x = -7 \pm 3\sqrt{2}$

$\dfrac{-5x}{-5} = \dfrac{-7 \pm 3\sqrt{2}}{-5}$

$x = \dfrac{7 \pm 3\sqrt{2}}{5}$

The solutions are $\dfrac{7 \pm 3\sqrt{2}}{5}$.

28. $(5 - 4x)^2 = 75$

$5 - 4x = \pm\sqrt{75}$

$5 - 4x = \pm 5\sqrt{3}$

$-4x = -5 \pm 5\sqrt{3}$

$\dfrac{-4x}{-4} = \dfrac{-5 \pm 5\sqrt{3}}{-5}$

$x = \dfrac{5 \pm 5\sqrt{3}}{4}$

The solutions are $\dfrac{5 \pm 5\sqrt{3}}{4}$.

29. $3z^2 - 7z = 12$

$3z^2 - 7z - 12 = 0$

$a = 3, b = -7$, and $c = -12$

$$z = \frac{-(-7) \pm \sqrt{(-7)^2 - 4(3)(-12)}}{2(3)}$$

$$= \frac{7 \pm \sqrt{49 + 144}}{6} = \frac{7 \pm \sqrt{193}}{6}$$

The solutions are $\dfrac{7 \pm \sqrt{193}}{6}$.

30. $6z^2 + 7z = 6$

$6z^2 + 7z - 6 = 0$

$a = 6, b = 7$, and $c = -6$

$$z = \frac{-(7) \pm \sqrt{(7)^2 - 4(6)(-6)}}{2(6)}$$

$$= \frac{-7 \pm \sqrt{49 + 144}}{12} = \frac{-7 \pm \sqrt{193}}{12}$$

The solutions are $\dfrac{-7 \pm \sqrt{193}}{12}$.

31. $x = x^2 - 110$

$0 = x^2 - x - 110$

$0 = (x + 10)(x - 11)$

$x + 10 = 0$ or $x - 11 = 0$

$x = -10$ $x = 11$

The solutions are -10 and 11.

32. $x = 56 - x^2$

$x^2 + x - 56 = 0$

$(x + 8)(x - 7) = 0$

$x + 8 = 0$ or $x - 7 = 0$

$x = -8$ $x = 7$

The solutions are -8 and 7.

33. $\dfrac{3}{4}x^2 - \dfrac{5}{2}x - 2 = 0$

$3x^2 - 10x - 8 = 0$

$(3x + 2)(x - 4) = 0$

$3x + 2 = 0$ or $x - 4 = 0$

$3x = -2$ $x = 4$

$x = -\dfrac{2}{3}$

The solutions are $-\dfrac{2}{3}$ and 4.

34. $x^2 - \dfrac{6}{5}x - \dfrac{8}{5} = 0$

$5x^2 - 6x - 8 = 0$

$(5x + 4)(x - 2) = 0$

$5x + 4 = 0$ or $x - 2 = 0$

$5x = -4$ $x = 2$

$x = -\dfrac{4}{5}$

The solutions are $-\dfrac{4}{5}$ and 2.

35. $x^2 - 0.6x + 0.05 = 0$

$100x^2 - 60x + 5 = 0$

$20x^2 - 12x + 1 = 0$

$(10x - 1)(2x - 1) = 0$

$10x - 1 = 0$ or $2x - 1 = 0$

$10x = 1$ $2x = 1$

$x = \dfrac{1}{10} = 0.1$ $x = \dfrac{1}{2} = 0.5$

The solutions are 0.1 and 0.5.

36. $x^2 - 0.1x + 0.06 = 0$

$100x^2 - 10x + 6 = 0$

$50x^2 - 5x + 3 = 0$

$(5x+1)(10x-3) = 0$

$5x+1 = 0$ 　or　 $10x-3 = 0$

$5x = -1$ 　　　　　$10x = 3$

$x = -\dfrac{1}{5} = -0.2$ 　 $x = \dfrac{3}{10} = 0.3$

The solutions are -0.2 and 0.3.

37. $10x^2 - 11x + 2 = 0$

$a = 10, b = -11,$ and $c = 2$

$x = \dfrac{-(-11) \pm \sqrt{(-11)^2 - 4(10)(2)}}{2(10)}$

$= \dfrac{11 \pm \sqrt{121 - 80}}{20} = \dfrac{11 \pm \sqrt{41}}{20}$

The solutions are $\dfrac{11 \pm \sqrt{41}}{20}$.

38. $20x^2 - 11x + 1 = 0$

$a = 20, b = -11,$ and $c = 1$

$x = \dfrac{-(-11) \pm \sqrt{(-11)^2 - 4(20)(1)}}{2(20)}$

$= \dfrac{11 \pm \sqrt{121 - 80}}{40} = \dfrac{11 \pm \sqrt{41}}{40}$

The solutions are $\dfrac{11 \pm \sqrt{41}}{40}$.

39. $\dfrac{1}{2}z^2 - 2z + \dfrac{3}{4} = 0$

$z^2 - 4z = -\dfrac{3}{2}$

$z^2 - 4z + 4 = -\dfrac{3}{2} + 4$

$(z-2)^2 = \dfrac{5}{2}$

$z - 2 = \pm\sqrt{\dfrac{5}{2}}$

$z = 2 \pm \sqrt{\dfrac{5}{2}} = 2 \pm \dfrac{\sqrt{10}}{2}$

$= \dfrac{4 \pm \sqrt{10}}{2}$

The solutions are $\dfrac{4 \pm \sqrt{10}}{2}$.

40. $\dfrac{1}{5}z^2 - \dfrac{1}{2}z - 2 = 0$

$2z^2 - 5z - 20 = 0$

$a = 2, b = -5,$ and $c = -20$

$z = \dfrac{-(-5) \pm \sqrt{(-5)^2 - 4(2)(-20)}}{2(2)}$

$= \dfrac{5 \pm \sqrt{25 + 160}}{4} = \dfrac{5 \pm \sqrt{185}}{4}$

The solutions are $\dfrac{5 \pm \sqrt{185}}{4}$.

41. Answers may vary.

Practice Problems 9.4

1. $y = -3x^2$

x	y
-2	-12
-1	-3
0	0
1	-3
2	-12

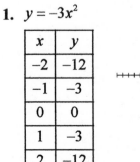

2. $y = x^2 - 9$

    y-intercept: $x = 0,\ y = 0^2 - 9 = -9,\ (0,-9)$

    x-intercepts: $y = 0,$

    $0 = x^2 - 9$

    $0 = (x+3)(x-3)$

    $x + 3 = 0$ or $x - 3 = 0$

      $x = -3$ $x = 3$

    $(-3,0)$ and $(3,0)$

x	y
-1	0
0	-3
1	-4
2	-3
3	0

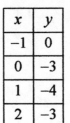
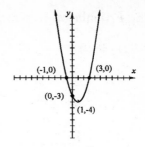

x	y
-4	7
-3	0
0	-9
3	0
4	7

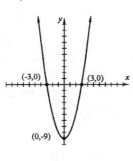

3. $y = x^2 - 2x - 3$

    vertex: $x = -\dfrac{b}{2a} = -\dfrac{-2}{2(1)} = 1 \left.\begin{array}{c}\\[2ex]\end{array}\right\}(1,4)$

      $y = (1)^2 - 2(1) - 3 = -4$

    y-intercept: $x = 0,\ y = 0^2 - 2(0) - 3 = -3,$

         $(0,-9)$

    x-intercepts: $y = 0,$

    $0 = x^2 - 2x - 3$

    $0 = (x+1)(x-3)$

    $x = -1$ or $x = 3$

    $(-1,0)$ and $(3,0)$

4. $y = x^2 - 3x + 1$

    vertex: $x = -\dfrac{b}{2a} = -\dfrac{-3}{2(1)} = \dfrac{3}{2} \left.\begin{array}{c}\\[3ex]\end{array}\right\} \left(\dfrac{3}{2}, -\dfrac{5}{4}\right)$

      $y = \left(\dfrac{3}{2}\right)^2 - 3\left(\dfrac{3}{2}\right) + 1 = -\dfrac{5}{4}$

    y-intercept: $x = 0,\ y = 0^2 - 3(0) + 1 = 1,$

         $(0,1)$

    x-intercepts: $y = 0,$

    $0 = x^2 - 3x + 1$

    $x = \dfrac{-(-3) \pm \sqrt{(-3)^2 - 4(1)(1)}}{2(1)} = \dfrac{3 \pm \sqrt{5}}{2}$

    $x = \dfrac{3 - \sqrt{5}}{2} \approx 0.4$ or $x = \dfrac{3 + \sqrt{5}}{2} \approx 2.6$

    $\left(\dfrac{3 - \sqrt{5}}{2}, 0\right)$ and $\left(\dfrac{3 + \sqrt{5}}{2}, 0\right)$

x	y
0	1
0.4	0
$3/2$	$-5/4$
2.6	0
3	1

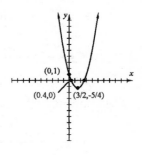

Graphing Calculator Explorations 9.4

1. $x^2 - 7x - 3 = 0$

   $y_1 = x^2 - 7x - 3$

   $y_2 = 0$

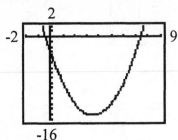

The x-coordinates of the intersections, -0.41 and 7.41, are the solutions.

2. $2x^2 - 11x - 1 = 0$

   $y_1 = 2x^2 - 11x - 1$

   $y_2 = 0$

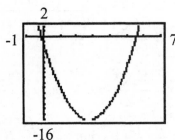

The x-coordinates of the intersections, -0.09 and 5.59, are the solutions.

3. $-1.7x^2 + 5.6x - 3.7 = 0$

   $y_1 = -1.7x^2 + 5.6x - 3.7$

   $y_2 = 0$

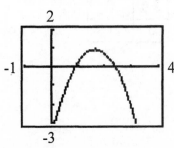

The x-coordinates of the intersections, 0.91 and 2.38, are the solutions.

4. $-5.8x^2 + 2.3x - 3.9 = 0$

   $y_1 = -5.8x^2 + 2.3x - 3.9$

   $y_2 = 0$

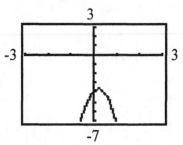

There are no x-intercepts so there are no real solutions.

5. $5.8x^2 - 2.6x - 1.9 = 0$

   $y_1 = 5.8x^2 - 2.6x - 1.9$

   $y_2 = 0$

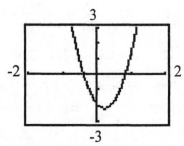

The x-coordinates of the intersections, -0.39 and 0.84, are the solutions.

6. $7.5x^2 - 3.7x - 1.1 = 0$

   $y_1 = 7.5x^2 - 3.7x - 1.1$

   $y_2 = -12$

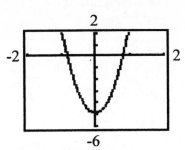

The x-coordinates of the intersections, -0.21 and 0.70, are the solutions.

Exercise Set 9.4

1. $y = 2x^2$

x	y
-2	8
-1	2
0	0
1	2
2	8

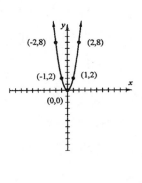

3. $y = -x^2$

x	y
-2	-4
-1	-1
0	0
1	-1
2	-4

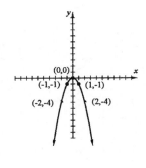

5. $y = \dfrac{1}{3}x^2$

x	y
-6	12
-3	3
0	0
3	3
6	12

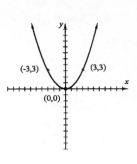

7. $y = x^2 - 1$

y-intercept: $x = 0$, $y = 0^2 - 1 = -1$, $(0, -1)$

vertex: $(0, -1)$

x-intercepts: $y = 0$,

$0 = x^2 - 1$

$0 = (x+1)(x-1)$

$x + 1 = 0 \quad$ or $\quad x - 1 = 0$

$\quad x = -1 \qquad\qquad x = 1$

$(-1, 0)$ and $(1, 0)$

x	y
-2	3
-1	0
0	-1
1	0
2	3

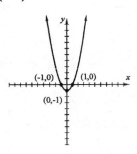

9. $y = x^2 + 4$

y-intercept: $x = 0$, $y = 0^2 + 4 = 4$, $(0, 4)$

vertex: $(0, 4)$

x-intercepts: $y = 0$,

$0 = x^2 + 4$

$-4 = x^2$

There are no x-intercepts because there is no real solution to this equation.

x	y
-2	8
-1	5
0	4
1	5
2	8

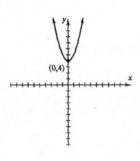

11. $y = x^2 + 6x$

vertex: $x = -\dfrac{b}{2a} = -\dfrac{6}{2(1)} = -3$ $\left.\right\}$ $(-3, -9)$

$\quad y = (-3)^2 + 6(-3) = -9$

y-intercept: $x = 0$, $y = 0^2 + 6(0) = 0$,

$(0, 0)$

x-intercepts: $y = 0$,

$0 = x^2 + 6x$

$0 = x(x + 6)$

$x = -6$ or $x = 0$

$(-6, 0)$ and $(0, 0)$

x	y
-7	7
-6	0
-3	-9
0	0
1	7

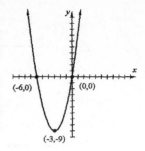

13. $y = x^2 + 2x - 8$

vertex: $x = -\dfrac{b}{2a} = -\dfrac{2}{2(1)} = -1$ $\left.\right\}$ $(-1, -9)$

$\quad y = (-1)^2 + 2(-1) - 8 = -9$

y-intercept: $x = 0$, $y = 0^2 + 2(0) - 8 = -8$,

$(0, -8)$

x-intercepts: $y = 0$,

$0 = x^2 + 2x - 8$

$0 = (x + 4)(x - 2)$

$x = -4$ or $x = 2$

$(-4, 0)$ and $(2, 0)$

x	y
-4	0
-2	-8
-1	-9
0	-8
2	0

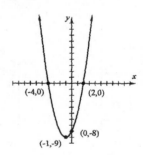

15. $y = -x^2 + x + 2$

vertex: $x = -\dfrac{b}{2a} = -\dfrac{1}{2(-1)} = \dfrac{1}{2}$ $\left.\right\}$ $\left(\dfrac{1}{2}, \dfrac{9}{4}\right)$

$\quad y = -\left(\dfrac{1}{2}\right)^2 + \left(\dfrac{1}{2}\right) + 2 = \dfrac{9}{4}$

y-intercept: $x = 0,\ y = -0^2 + (0) + 2 = 2,$

$$(0,2)$$

x-intercepts: $y = 0,$

$$0 = -x^2 + x + 2$$

$$0 = x^2 - x - 2$$

$$0 = (x+1)(x-2)$$

$$x = -1 \quad \text{or} \quad x = 2$$

$$(-1,0) \text{ and } (2,0)$$

x	y
−1	0
0	2
1/2	9/4
1	2
2	0

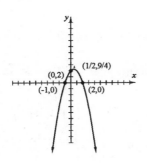

17. $y = x^2 + 5x + 4$

vertex: $x = -\dfrac{b}{2a} = -\dfrac{5}{2(1)} = -\dfrac{5}{2}$

$$y = \left(-\frac{5}{2}\right)^2 + 5\left(-\frac{5}{2}\right) + 4 = -\frac{9}{4}$$

$$\left(-\frac{5}{2}, -\frac{9}{4}\right)$$

y-intercept: $x = 0,\ y = 0^2 + 5(0) + 4 = 4,$

$$(0,4)$$

x-intercepts: $y = 0,$

$$0 = x^2 + 5x + 4$$

$$0 = (x+4)(x+1)$$

$$x = -4 \quad \text{or} \quad x = -1$$

$$(-4,0) \text{ and } (-1,0)$$

x	y
−5	4
−4	0
−5/2	−9/4
−1	0
0	4

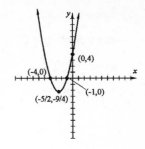

19. $y = x^2 - 4x + 5$

vertex: $x = -\dfrac{b}{2a} = -\dfrac{-4}{2(1)} = 2$, $(2,1)$
$y = (2)^2 - 4(2) + 5 = 1$

y-intercept: $x = 0,\ y = 0^2 - 4(0) + 5 = 5,$

$$(0,5)$$

x-intercepts: $y = 0,$

$$0 = x^2 - 4x + 5$$

$$x = \frac{-(-4) \pm \sqrt{(-4)^2 - 4(1)(5)}}{2(1)}$$

$$= \frac{4 \pm \sqrt{-4}}{2}$$

There are no *x*-intercepts because there is no real solution to the equation.

x	y
0	5
1	2
2	1
3	2
4	5

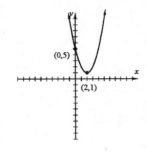

21. $y = 2 - x^2$

y-intercept: $x = 0$, $y = 2 - 0^2 = 2$, $(0, 2)$

vertex: $(0, 2)$

x-intercepts: $y = 0$,

$0 = 2 - x^2$

$x^2 = 2$

$x = \pm\sqrt{2} \approx \pm 1.4$

$\left(-\sqrt{2}, 0\right)$ and $\left(\sqrt{2}, 0\right)$

x	y
-3	-7
-1.4	0
0	2
1.4	0
3	-7

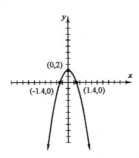

23. $y = 2x^2 - 11x + 5$

vertex: $x = -\dfrac{b}{2a} = -\dfrac{-11}{2(2)} = \dfrac{11}{4}$

$y = 2\left(\dfrac{11}{4}\right)^2 - 11\left(\dfrac{11}{4}\right) + 5 = -\dfrac{81}{8}$

$\left(\dfrac{11}{4}, -\dfrac{81}{8}\right)$

y-intercept: $x = 0$,

$y = 2(0)^2 - 11(0) + 5 = 5$,

$(0, 5)$

x-intercepts: $y = 0$,

$0 = 2x^2 - 11x + 5$

$0 = (2x - 1)(x - 5)$

$x = \dfrac{1}{2}$ or $x = 5$

$\left(\dfrac{1}{2}, 0\right)$ and $(5, 0)$

x	y
0	5
$1/2$	0
$11/4$	$-81/8$
5	0
$11/2$	5

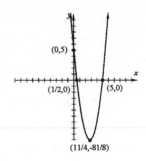

25. $y = -x^2 + 4x - 3$

vertex: $x = -\dfrac{b}{2a} = -\dfrac{4}{2(-1)} = 2$ $\left. \right\}$ $(2, 1)$

$y = -(2)^2 + 4(2) - 3 = 1$

y-intercept: $x = 0$, $y = -0^2 + 4(0) - 3 = -3$,

$(0, -3)$

x-intercepts: $y = 0$,

$0 = -x^2 + 4x - 3$

$0 = x^2 - 4x + 3$

$0 = (x - 1)(x - 3)$

$x = 1$ or $x = 3$

$(1, 0)$ and $(3, 0)$

x	y
0	-3
1	0
2	1
3	0
4	-3

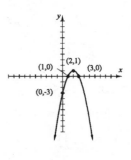

27. $\dfrac{\frac{1}{7}}{\frac{2}{5}} = \dfrac{1}{7} \cdot \dfrac{5}{2} = \dfrac{5}{14}$

29. $\dfrac{\frac{1}{x}}{\frac{2}{x^2}} = \dfrac{1}{x} \cdot \dfrac{x^2}{2} = \dfrac{x}{2}$

31. $\dfrac{2x}{1-\frac{1}{x}} = \dfrac{2x}{\frac{x-1}{x}} = \dfrac{2x}{1} \cdot \dfrac{x}{x-1} = \dfrac{2x^2}{x-1}$

33. $\dfrac{\frac{a-b}{2b}}{\frac{b-a}{8b^2}} = \dfrac{a-b}{2b} \cdot \dfrac{8b^2}{b-a} = \dfrac{a-b}{2b} \cdot \dfrac{8b^2}{-1(a-b)} = -4b$

35.   **a.** 256 feet

     b. 4 seconds

     c. 8 seconds

37. $a < 0$, one x-intercept

     E

39. $a > 0$, no x-intercept

     C

41. $a < 0$, two x-intercepts

     B

Chapter 9 Review

1. $(x-4)(5x+3) = 0$

$$5x+3 = 0 \quad \text{or} \quad x-4 = 0$$
$$x = -\dfrac{3}{5} \qquad x = 4$$

     The solutions are $-\dfrac{3}{5}$ and 4.

2. $(x+7)(3x+4) = 0$

$$3x+4 = 0 \quad \text{or} \quad x+7 = 0$$
$$x = -\dfrac{4}{3} \qquad x = -7$$

     The solutions are $-\dfrac{4}{3}$ and -7.

3. $\qquad 3m^2 - 5m = 2$

$$3m^2 - 5m - 2 = 0$$
$$(m-2)(3m+1) = 0$$
$$m-2 = 0 \quad \text{or} \quad 3m+1 = 0$$
$$m = 2 \qquad\qquad m = -\dfrac{1}{3}$$

     The solutions are $-\dfrac{1}{3}$ and 2.

4. $\qquad 7m^2 + 2m = 5$

$$7m^2 + 2m - 5 = 0$$
$$(m+1)(7m-5) = 0$$
$$m+1 = 0 \quad \text{or} \quad 7m-5 = 0$$
$$m = -1 \qquad m = \dfrac{5}{7}$$

     The solutions are $\dfrac{5}{7}$ and -1.

5. $\qquad 6x^3 - 54x = 0$

$$6x(x^2 - 9) = 0$$
$$6x(x+3)(x-3) = 0$$
$$6x = 0 \quad \text{or} \quad x+3 = 0 \quad \text{or} \quad x-3 = 0$$
$$x = 0 \qquad x = -3 \qquad x = 3$$

     The solutions are 0, -3, and 3.

6. $\qquad 2x^2 - 8 = 0$

$$2(x^2 - 4) = 0$$
$$2(x+2)(x-2) = 0$$
$$x+2 = 0 \quad \text{or} \quad x-2 = 0$$
$$x = -2 \qquad x = 2$$

     The solutions are -2 and 2.

7. $x^2 = 36$

$x = \pm\sqrt{36}$

$= \pm 6$

The solutions are ± 6.

8. $x^2 = 81$

$x = \pm\sqrt{81}$

$= \pm 9$

The solutions are ± 9.

9. $k^2 = 50$

$k = \pm\sqrt{50}$

$= \pm 5\sqrt{2}$

The solutions are $\pm 5\sqrt{2}$.

10. $k^2 = 45$

$k = \pm\sqrt{45}$

$= \pm 3\sqrt{5}$

The solutions are $\pm 3\sqrt{5}$.

11. $(x-11)^2 = 49$

$x - 11 = \pm\sqrt{49}$

$x - 11 = \pm 7$

$x = 11 \pm 7$

$x = 11 - 7 = 4$ or $x = 11 + 7 = 18$

The solutions are 4 and 18.

12. $(x+3)^2 = 100$

$x + 3 = \pm\sqrt{100}$

$x + 3 = \pm 10$

$x = -3 \pm 10$

$x = -3 - 10 = -13$ or $x = -3 + 10 = 7$

The solutions are -13 and 7.

13. $(4p+2)^2 = 100$

$4p + 2 = \pm\sqrt{100}$

$4p + 2 = \pm 10$

$4p = -2 \pm 10$

$p = \dfrac{-2 \pm 10}{4}$

$p = \dfrac{-2-10}{4} = -3$ or $p = \dfrac{-2+10}{4} = 2$

The solutions are -3 and 2.

14. $(3p+6)^2 = 81$

$3p + 6 = \pm\sqrt{81}$

$3p + 6 = \pm 9$

$3p = -6 \pm 9$

$p = \dfrac{-6 \pm 9}{3}$

$p = \dfrac{-6-9}{3} = -5$ or $p = \dfrac{-6+9}{3} = 1$

The solutions are -5 and 1.

15. Let $h = 100$

$h = 16t^2$

$16t^2 = h$

$16t^2 = 100$

$t^2 = \dfrac{100}{16}$

$t = \pm\sqrt{\dfrac{100}{16}} = \pm\dfrac{10}{4} = \pm 2.5$

The length of time is not a negative number so the dive lasted 2.5 seconds.

16. Let $h = 5 \cdot 5280 = 26,400$

$$h = 16t^2$$
$$16t^2 = h$$
$$16t^2 = 26,400$$
$$t^2 = \frac{26,400}{16} = 1650$$
$$t = \pm\sqrt{1650} = \pm 40.6$$

The length of time is not a negative number so the fall lasted 2.5 seconds.

17.
$$x^2 + 4x = 1$$
$$x^2 + 4x + 4 = 1 + 4$$
$$(x+2)^2 = 5$$
$$x + 2 = \pm\sqrt{5}$$
$$x = -2 \pm \sqrt{5}$$

The solutions are $-2 \pm \sqrt{5}$.

18.
$$x^2 - 8x = 3$$
$$x^2 - 8x + 16 = 3 + 16$$
$$(x-4)^2 = 19$$
$$x - 4 = \pm\sqrt{19}$$
$$x = 4 \pm \sqrt{19}$$

The solutions are $4 \pm \sqrt{19}$.

19.
$$x^2 - 6x + 7 = 0$$
$$x^2 - 6x = -7$$
$$x^2 - 6x + 9 = -7 + 9$$
$$(x-3)^2 = 2$$
$$x - 3 = \pm\sqrt{2}$$
$$x = 3 \pm \sqrt{2}$$

The solutions are $3 \pm \sqrt{2}$.

20.
$$x^2 + 6x + 7 = 0$$
$$x^2 + 6x = -7$$
$$x^2 + 6x + 9 = -7 + 9$$
$$(x+3)^2 = 2$$
$$x + 3 = \pm\sqrt{2}$$
$$x = -3 \pm \sqrt{2}$$

The solutions are $-3 \pm \sqrt{2}$.

21.
$$2y^2 + y - 1 = 0$$
$$y^2 + \frac{1}{2}y - \frac{1}{2} = 0$$
$$y^2 + \frac{1}{2}y = \frac{1}{2}$$
$$y^2 + \frac{1}{2}y + \frac{1}{16} = \frac{1}{2} + \frac{1}{16}$$
$$\left(y + \frac{1}{4}\right)^2 = \frac{9}{16}$$
$$y + \frac{1}{4} = \pm\sqrt{\frac{9}{16}}$$
$$y = -\frac{1}{4} \pm \frac{3}{4}$$
$$y = -\frac{1}{4} + \frac{3}{4} \quad \text{or} \quad y = -\frac{1}{4} - \frac{3}{4}$$
$$y = \frac{1}{2} \qquad\qquad\qquad y = -1$$

The solutions are $\frac{1}{2}$ and -1.

22.
$$y^2 + 3y - 1 = 0$$
$$y^2 + 3y = 1$$
$$y^2 + 3y + \frac{9}{4} = 1 + \frac{9}{4}$$

$$\left(y+\frac{3}{2}\right)^2=\frac{13}{4}$$

$$y+\frac{3}{2}=\pm\sqrt{\frac{13}{4}}$$

$$y=-\frac{3}{2}\pm\frac{\sqrt{13}}{2}$$

$$y=\frac{-3\pm\sqrt{13}}{2}$$

The solutions are $\dfrac{-3\pm\sqrt{13}}{2}$.

23. $x^2-10x+7=0$

$a=1, b=-10,$ and $c=7$

$$x=\frac{-(-10)\pm\sqrt{(-10)^2-4(1)(7)}}{2(1)}$$

$$=\frac{10\pm\sqrt{100-28}}{2}=\frac{10\pm\sqrt{72}}{2}$$

$$=\frac{10\pm6\sqrt{2}}{2}=5\pm3\sqrt{2}$$

The solutions are $5\pm3\sqrt{2}$.

24. $x^2+4x-7=0$

$a=1, b=4,$ and $c=-7$

$$x=\frac{-(4)\pm\sqrt{(4)^2-4(1)(-7)}}{2(1)}$$

$$=\frac{-4\pm\sqrt{16+28}}{2}=\frac{-4\pm\sqrt{44}}{2}$$

$$=\frac{-4\pm2\sqrt{11}}{2}=-2\pm\sqrt{11}$$

The solutions are $-2\pm\sqrt{11}$.

25. $2x^2+x-1=0$

$a=2, b=1,$ and $c=-1$

$$x=\frac{-(1)\pm\sqrt{(1)^2-4(2)(-1)}}{2(2)}$$

$$=\frac{-1\pm\sqrt{1+8}}{4}=\frac{-1\pm\sqrt{9}}{4}=\frac{-1\pm3}{4}$$

$$x=\frac{-1+3}{4}=\frac{1}{2} \text{ or } x=\frac{-1-3}{4}=-1$$

The solutions are -1 and $\dfrac{1}{2}$.

26. $x^2+3x-1=0$

$a=1, b=3,$ and $c=-1$

$$x=\frac{-(3)\pm\sqrt{(3)^2-4(1)(-1)}}{2(1)}$$

$$=\frac{-3\pm\sqrt{9+4}}{2}=\frac{-3\pm\sqrt{13}}{2}$$

The solutions are $\dfrac{-3\pm\sqrt{13}}{2}$.

27. $9x^2+30x+25=0$

$a=9, b=30,$ and $c=25$

$$x=\frac{-(30)\pm\sqrt{(30)^2-4(9)(25)}}{2(9)}$$

$$=\frac{-30\pm\sqrt{900-900}}{18}=\frac{-30\pm\sqrt{0}}{18}=-\frac{5}{3}$$

The solution is $-\dfrac{5}{3}$.

28. $16x^2 - 72x + 81 = 0$

$a = 16, b = -72,$ and $c = 81$

$$x = \frac{-(-72) \pm \sqrt{(-72)^2 - 4(16)(81)}}{2(16)}$$

$$= \frac{72 \pm \sqrt{5184 - 5184}}{32} = \frac{72 \pm \sqrt{0}}{32} = \frac{9}{4}$$

The solution is $\dfrac{9}{4}$.

29. $15x^2 + 2 = 11x$

$15x^2 - 11x + 2 = 0$

$a = 15, b = -11,$ and $c = 2$

$$x = \frac{-(-11) \pm \sqrt{(-11)^2 - 4(15)(2)}}{2(15)}$$

$$= \frac{11 \pm \sqrt{121 - 120}}{30} = \frac{11 \pm \sqrt{1}}{30} = \frac{11 \pm 1}{30}$$

$$x = \frac{11 + 1}{30} = \frac{2}{5} \quad \text{or} \quad x = \frac{11 - 1}{30} = \frac{1}{3}$$

The solutions are $\dfrac{2}{5}$ and $\dfrac{1}{3}$.

30. $15x^2 + 2 = 13x$

$15x^2 - 13x + 2 = 0$

$a = 15, b = -13,$ and $c = 2$

$$x = \frac{-(-13) \pm \sqrt{(-13)^2 - 4(15)(2)}}{2(15)}$$

$$= \frac{13 \pm \sqrt{169 - 120}}{30} = \frac{13 \pm \sqrt{49}}{30} = \frac{13 \pm 7}{30}$$

$$x = \frac{13 + 7}{30} = \frac{2}{3} \quad \text{or} \quad x = \frac{13 - 7}{30} = \frac{1}{5}$$

The solutions are $\dfrac{2}{3}$ and $\dfrac{1}{5}$.

31. $2x^2 + x + 5 = 0$

$a = 2, b = 1,$ and $c = 5$

$$x = \frac{-(1) \pm \sqrt{(1)^2 - 4(2)(5)}}{2(2)}$$

$$= \frac{-1 \pm \sqrt{1 - 40}}{4} = \frac{-1 \pm \sqrt{-39}}{4}$$

There is no real solution because $\sqrt{-39}$ is not a real number.

32. $7x^2 - 3x + 1 = 0$

$a = 7, b = -3,$ and $c = 1$

$$x = \frac{-(-3) \pm \sqrt{(-3)^2 - 4(7)(1)}}{2(7)}$$

$$= \frac{3 \pm \sqrt{9 - 28}}{14} = \frac{3 \pm \sqrt{-19}}{14}$$

There is no real solution because $\sqrt{-19}$ is not a real number.

33. Let $y = 1687$

$y = 25x^2 - 54x + 519$

$1687 = 25x^2 - 54x + 519$

$0 = 25x^2 - 54x - 1168$

$a = 25, b = -54,$ and $c = -1168$

$$x = \frac{-(-54) \pm \sqrt{(-54)^2 - 4(25)(-1168)}}{2(25)}$$

$$= \frac{54 \pm \sqrt{2916 + 116{,}800}}{50}$$

$$= \frac{54 \pm \sqrt{119{,}716}}{50} = \frac{54 \pm 346}{50}$$

$x = \dfrac{54+346}{50} = 8$ or $x = \dfrac{54-346}{50} \approx -5.8$

The number of years cannot be negative so the year will be $1996 + 8 = 2004$.

34. Let $y = 670$

$y = 5x^2 - 6x + 398$

$670 = 5x^2 - 6x + 398$

$0 = 5x^2 - 6x - 272$

$a = 5, b = -6,$ and $c = -272$

$x = \dfrac{-(-6) \pm \sqrt{(-6)^2 - 4(5)(-272)}}{2(5)}$

$= \dfrac{6 \pm \sqrt{36 + 5440}}{10}$

$= \dfrac{6 \pm \sqrt{5476}}{10} = \dfrac{6 \pm 74}{50}$

$x = \dfrac{6+74}{10} = 8$ or $x = \dfrac{6-74}{10} \approx -6.8$

The number of years cannot be negative so the year will be $1996 + 8 = 2004$.

35. $y = 3x^2$

vertex: $x = -\dfrac{0}{2(3)} = 0 \left.\vphantom{\dfrac{0}{2(3)}}\right\}$ $(0,0)$

$\quad\quad\quad y = 3(0)^2 = 0$

x	y
-2	12
-1	3
0	0
1	3
2	12

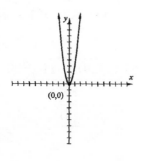

36. $y = -\dfrac{1}{2}x^2$

vertex: $x = -\dfrac{0}{2(-1/2)} = 0 \left.\vphantom{\dfrac{0}{2(-1/2)}}\right\}$ $(0,0)$

$\quad\quad\quad y = -\dfrac{1}{2}(0)^2 = 0$

x	y
-4	-8
-2	-2
0	0
2	-2
4	-8

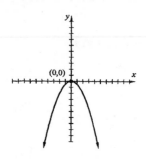

37. $y = x^2 - 25$

vertex: $x = -\dfrac{b}{2a} = -\dfrac{0}{2(1)} = 0 \left.\vphantom{\dfrac{b}{2a}}\right\}$ $(0,-25)$

$\quad\quad\quad y = (0)^2 - 25 = -25$

y-intercept: $x = 0,\ y = -25,\ (0,-25)$

x-intercepts: $y = 0,$

$0 = x^2 - 25$

$0 = (x+5)(x-5)$

$x = -5$ or $x = 5$

$(-5,0)$ and $(5,0)$

x	y
-7	24
-5	0
0	-25
5	0
7	24

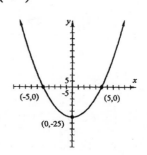

38. $y = x^2 - 36$

vertex: $x = -\dfrac{b}{2a} = -\dfrac{0}{2(1)} = 0 \left.\begin{array}{c}\\\\\end{array}\right\} (0, -36)$

$\qquad y = (0)^2 - 36 = -36$

y-intercept: $x = 0$, $y = -36$, $(0, -36)$

x-intercepts: $y = 0$,

$0 = x^2 - 36$

$0 = (x + 6)(x - 6)$

$x = -6 \quad \text{or} \quad x = 6$

$(-6, 0)$ and $(6, 0)$

x	y
-8	28
-6	0
0	-36
6	0
8	28

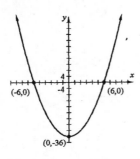

39. $y = x^2 + 3$

vertex: $x = -\dfrac{b}{2a} = -\dfrac{0}{2(1)} = 0 \left.\begin{array}{c}\\\\\end{array}\right\} (0, 3)$

$\qquad y = (0)^2 + 3 = 3$

y-intercept: $x = 0$, $y = 0^2 + 3 = 3$, $(0, 3)$

x-intercepts: $y = 0$,

$0 = x^2 + 3$

$-3 = x^2$

There are no x-intercepts because there is no real solution to this equation.

x	y
-2	7
-1	4
0	3
1	4
2	7

40. $y = x^2 + 8$

vertex: $x = -\dfrac{b}{2a} = -\dfrac{0}{2(1)} = 0 \left.\begin{array}{c}\\\\\end{array}\right\} (0, 8)$

$\qquad y = (0)^2 + 8 = 8$

y-intercept: $x = 0$, $y = 0^2 + 8 = 8$, $(0, 8)$

x-intercepts: $y = 0$,

$0 = x^2 + 8$

$-8 = x^2$

There are no x-intercepts because there is no real solution to this equation.

x	y
-2	12
-1	9
0	8
1	9
2	12

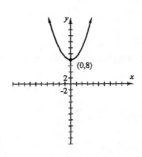

41. $y = -4x^2 + 8$

    y-intercept: $x = 0$, $y = -4(0)^2 + 8 = 8$,

$$(0, 8)$$

    vertex: $(0, 8)$

    x-intercepts: $y = 0$,

$$0 = -4x^2 + 8$$

$$4x^2 = 8$$

$$x^2 = 2$$

$$x = \pm\sqrt{2} \approx \pm 1.4$$

$$\left(-\sqrt{2}, 0\right) \text{ and } \left(\sqrt{2}, 0\right)$$

x	y
-2	-8
-1.4	0
0	8
1.4	0
2	-8

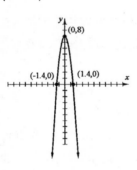

x	y
-2	-3
-1.7	0
0	9
1.7	0
2	-3

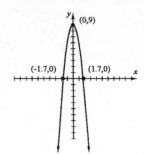

42. $y = -3x^2 + 9$

    y-intercept: $x = 0$, $y = -3(0)^2 + 9 = 9$,

$$(0, 9)$$

    vertex: $(0, 9)$

    x-intercepts: $y = 0$,

$$0 = -3x^2 + 9$$

$$3x^2 = 9$$

$$x^2 = 3$$

$$x = \pm\sqrt{3} \approx \pm 1.7$$

$$\left(-\sqrt{3}, 0\right) \text{ and } \left(\sqrt{3}, 0\right)$$

43. $y = x^2 + 3x - 10$

    vertex: $x = -\dfrac{b}{2a} = -\dfrac{3}{2(1)} = -\dfrac{3}{2}$

$$y = \left(-\frac{3}{2}\right)^2 + 3\left(-\frac{3}{2}\right) - 10 = -\frac{49}{4}$$

$$\left(-\frac{3}{2}, -\frac{49}{4}\right)$$

    y-intercept: $x = 0$, $y = 0^2 + 3(0) - 10$

$$= -10, \ (0, -10)$$

    x-intercepts: $y = 0$, $0 = x^2 + 3x - 10$

$$0 = (x + 5)(x - 2)$$

$$x = -5 \quad \text{or} \quad x = 2$$

$$(-5, 0) \text{ and } (2, 0)$$

x	y
-5	0
-3	-10
$-3/2$	$-49/4$
0	-10
2	0

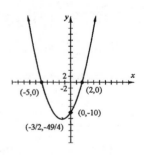

410

44. $y = x^2 + 3x - 4$

vertex: $x = -\dfrac{b}{2a} = -\dfrac{3}{2(1)} = -\dfrac{3}{2}$

$y = \left(-\dfrac{3}{2}\right)^2 + 3\left(-\dfrac{3}{2}\right) - 4 = -\dfrac{25}{4}$

$\left(-\dfrac{3}{2}, -\dfrac{25}{4}\right)$

y-intercept: $x = 0$, $y = 0^2 + 3(0) - 4$

$\qquad = -4,\ (0, -4)$

x-intercepts: $y = 0$,

$0 = x^2 + 3x - 4$

$0 = (x + 4)(x - 1)$

$x = -4$ or $x = 1$

$(-4, 0)$ and $(1, 0)$

x	y
-4	0
-3	-4
$-3/2$	$-25/4$
0	-4
1	0

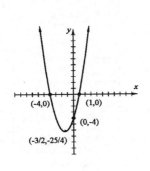

45. $y = -x^2 - 5x - 6$

vertex: $x = -\dfrac{b}{2a} = -\dfrac{-5}{2(-1)} = -\dfrac{5}{2}$

$y = -\left(-\dfrac{5}{2}\right)^2 - 5\left(-\dfrac{5}{2}\right) - 6 = \dfrac{1}{4}$

$\left(-\dfrac{5}{2}, \dfrac{1}{4}\right)$

y-intercept: $x = 0$, $y = -0^2 - 5(0) - 6$

$\qquad = -6,\ (0, -6)$

x-intercepts: $y = 0$,

$0 = -x^2 - 5x - 6$

$0 = x^2 + 5x + 6$

$0 = (x + 3)(x + 2)$

$x = -3$ or $x = -2$

$(-3, 0)$ and $(-2, 0)$

x	y
-5	-6
-3	0
$-5/2$	$1/4$
-2	0
0	-6

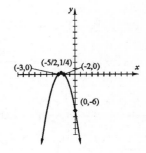

46. $y = -x^2 + 4x + 8$

vertex: $x = -\dfrac{b}{2a} = -\dfrac{4}{2(-1)} = 2$ $\left.\right\}\ (2, 12)$

$y = -(2)^2 + 4(2) + 8 = 12$

y-intercept: $x = 0$, $y = 8$, $(0, 8)$

x-intercepts: $y = 0$,

$0 = -x^2 + 4x + 8$

$x = \dfrac{-(4) \pm \sqrt{(4)^2 - 4(-1)(8)}}{2(-1)}$

$= \dfrac{-4 \pm \sqrt{48}}{-2} = \dfrac{-4 \pm 4\sqrt{3}}{-2} = 2 \pm 2\sqrt{3}$

$x = 2 + 2\sqrt{3} \approx 5.5$ or $x = 2 - 2\sqrt{3} \approx -1.5$

$\left(2 - 2\sqrt{3}, 0\right)$ and $\left(2 + 2\sqrt{3}, 0\right)$

x	y
-1.5	0
0	8
2	12
4	8
5.5	0

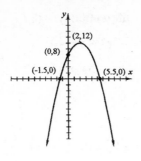

48. $y = 3x^2 - x - 2$

vertex: $x = -\dfrac{b}{2a} = -\dfrac{-1}{2(3)} = \dfrac{1}{6}$

$$y = 3\left(\frac{1}{6}\right)^2 - \left(\frac{1}{6}\right) - 2 = -\frac{25}{12}$$

$$\left(\frac{1}{6}, -\frac{25}{12}\right)$$

y-intercept: $x = 0$, $y = -2$, $(0, -2)$

x-intercepts: $y = 0$,

$0 = 3x^2 - x - 2$

$0 = (3x + 2)(x - 1)$

$x = -\dfrac{2}{3}$ or $x = 1$

$\left(-\dfrac{2}{3}, 0\right)$ and $(1, 0)$

x	y
$-2/3$	0
0	-2
$1/6$	$-25/12$
1	0

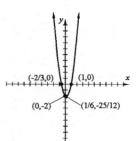

47. $y = 2x^2 - 11x - 6$

vertex: $x = -\dfrac{b}{2a} = -\dfrac{-11}{2(2)} = \dfrac{11}{4}$

$$y = 2\left(\frac{11}{4}\right)^2 - 11\left(\frac{11}{4}\right) - 6 = -\frac{169}{8}$$

$$\left(\frac{11}{4}, -\frac{169}{8}\right)$$

y-intercept: $x = 0$, $y = -6$, $(0, -6)$

x-intercepts: $y = 0$,

$0 = 2x^2 - 11x - 6$

$0 = (2x + 1)(x - 6)$

$x = -\dfrac{1}{2}$ or $x = 6$

$\left(-\dfrac{1}{2}, 0\right)$ and $(6, 0)$

x	y
$-1/2$	0
0	-6
$11/4$	$-169/8$
$11/2$	-6
6	0

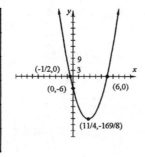

49. The equation has one solution because the graph intersects the x-axis at one point $(-2, 0)$.

50. The equation has two solutions because the graph intersects the x-axis at two points: $\left(-\dfrac{3}{2}, 0\right)$ and $(3, 0)$.

51. The equation has no real solution because the graph does not intersect the x-axis.

52. The equation has two solutions because the graph intersects the x-axis at two points: $(-2, 0)$ and $(2, 0)$.

53. $y = 2x^2$

A

54. $y = -x^2$

D

55. $y = x^2 + 4x + 4$

B

56. $y = x^2 + 5x + 4$

C

Chapter 9 Test

1.
$$2x^2 - 11x = 21$$
$$2x^2 - 11x - 21 = 0$$
$$(2x + 3)(x - 7) = 0$$
$$2x + 3 = 0 \quad \text{or} \quad x - 7 = 0$$
$$x = -\frac{3}{2} \qquad x = 7$$

The solutions are $-\dfrac{3}{2}$ and 7.

2.
$$x^4 + x^3 - 2x^2 = 0$$
$$x^2 \left(x^2 + x - 2\right) = 0$$
$$x^2 \left(x + 2\right)\left(x - 1\right) = 0$$
$$x^2 = 0 \quad \text{or} \quad x + 2 = 0 \quad \text{or} \quad x - 1 = 0$$
$$x = 0 \qquad x = -2 \qquad x = 1$$

The solutions are 0, 1, and -2.

3.
$$5k^2 = 80$$
$$k^2 = 16$$
$$k = \pm\sqrt{16}$$
$$k = \pm 4$$

The solutions are ± 4.

4. $\left(3m - 5\right)^2 = 8$
$$3m - 5 = \pm\sqrt{8}$$
$$3m - 5 = \pm 2\sqrt{2}$$
$$3m = 5 \pm 2\sqrt{2}$$
$$m = \frac{5 \pm 2\sqrt{2}}{3}$$

The solutions are $\dfrac{5 \pm 2\sqrt{2}}{3}$.

5. $x^2 - 26x + 160 = 0$
$$x^2 - 26x = -160$$
$$x^2 - 26x + 169 = -160 + 169$$
$$\left(x - 13\right)^2 = 9$$
$$x - 13 = \pm\sqrt{9}$$
$$x = 13 \pm 3$$
$$x = 13 - 3 \quad \text{or} \quad x = 13 + 3$$
$$x = 10 \qquad x = 16$$

The solutions are -6 and -2.

6. $5x^2 + 9x = 2$

$$x^2 + \frac{9}{5}x = \frac{2}{5}$$

$$x^2 + \frac{9}{5}x + \frac{81}{100} = \frac{2}{5} + \frac{81}{100}$$

$$\left(x + \frac{9}{10}\right)^2 = \frac{121}{100}$$

$$x + \frac{9}{10} = \pm\sqrt{\frac{121}{100}}$$

$$x = -\frac{9}{10} \pm \frac{11}{10}$$

$$x = -\frac{9}{10} - \frac{11}{10} = -2$$

$$\text{or }\; x = -\frac{9}{10} + \frac{11}{10} = \frac{1}{5}$$

The solutions are -2 and $\frac{1}{5}$.

7. $x^2 - 3x - 10 = 0$

$a = 1, b = -3,$ and $c = -10$

$$x = \frac{-(-3) \pm \sqrt{(-3)^2 - 4(1)(-10)}}{2(1)}$$

$$= \frac{3 \pm \sqrt{9 + 40}}{2} = \frac{3 \pm \sqrt{49}}{2} = \frac{3 \pm 7}{2}$$

$$x = \frac{3 - 7}{2} = -2 \;\text{ or }\; x = \frac{3 + 7}{2} = 5$$

The solutions are -2 and 5.

8. $p^2 - \frac{5}{3}p - \frac{1}{3} = 0$

$3p^2 - 5p - 1 = 0$

$a = 3, b = -5,$ and $c = -1$

$$p = \frac{-(-5) \pm \sqrt{(-5)^2 - 4(3)(-1)}}{2(3)}$$

$$= \frac{5 \pm \sqrt{25 + 12}}{6} = \frac{5 \pm \sqrt{37}}{6}$$

The solutions are $\dfrac{5 \pm \sqrt{37}}{6}$.

9. $(3x - 5)(x + 2) = -6$

$$3x^2 + x - 10 = -6$$

$$3x^2 + x - 4 = 0$$

$$(3x + 4)(x - 1) = 0$$

$$3x + 4 = 0 \;\text{ or }\; x - 1 = 0$$

$$x = -\frac{4}{3} \qquad\qquad x = 1$$

The solutions are $-\dfrac{4}{3}$ and 1.

10. $(3x - 1)^2 = 16$

$$3x - 1 = \pm\sqrt{16}$$

$$3x = 1 \pm 4$$

$$x = \frac{1 \pm 4}{3}$$

$$x = \frac{1 - 4}{3} = -1 \;\text{ or }\; x = \frac{1 + 4}{3} = \frac{5}{3}$$

The solutions are -1 and $\dfrac{5}{3}$.

11. $3x^2 - 7x - 2 = 0$

$a = 3, b = -7,$ and $c = -2$

$$z = \frac{-(-7) \pm \sqrt{(-7)^2 - 4(3)(-2)}}{2(3)}$$

$$= \frac{7 \pm \sqrt{49 + 24}}{6} = \frac{7 \pm \sqrt{73}}{6}$$

The solutions are $\dfrac{7 \pm \sqrt{73}}{6}$.

12. $x^2 - 4x - 5 = 0$

$(x+1)(x-5) = 0$

$x + 1 = 0$　or　$x - 5 = 0$

$x = -1$　　　　$x = 5$

The solutions are -1 and 5.

13. $3x^2 - 7x + 2 = 0$

$(3x-1)(x-2) = 0$

$3x - 1 = 0$　or　$x - 2 = 0$

$x = \dfrac{1}{3}$　　　$x = 2$

The solutions are $\dfrac{1}{3}$ and 2.

14. $2x^2 - 6x + 1 = 0$

$a = 2, b = -6,$ and $c = 1$

$x = \dfrac{-(-6) \pm \sqrt{(-6)^2 - 4(2)(1)}}{2(2)}$

$= \dfrac{6 \pm \sqrt{36 - 8}}{4} = \dfrac{6 \pm \sqrt{28}}{4}$

$= \dfrac{6 \pm 2\sqrt{7}}{4} = \dfrac{3 \pm \sqrt{7}}{2}$

The solutions are $\dfrac{3 \pm \sqrt{7}}{2}$.

15. Let $x =$ the base, then $4x =$ the height.

$A = \dfrac{1}{2}bh$

$18 = \dfrac{1}{2}x(4x)$

$18 = 2x^2$

$9 = x^2$

$x = \pm\sqrt{9} = \pm 3$

Because the base cannot be negative,

$x = 3$

$4x = 4(3) = 12$

Base $= 3$ ft., height $= 12$ ft.

16. $y = -5x^2$

vertex: $x = -\dfrac{0}{2(-5)} = 0$　$\left.\begin{array}{}\\ \\ \\ \end{array}\right\}$ $(0,0)$

$y = -5(0)^2 = 0$

x	y
-1	-5
$-1/5$	$-1/5$
0	0
$1/5$	$-1/5$
1	-5

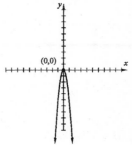

17. $y = x^2 - 4$

vertex: $x = -\dfrac{b}{2a} = -\dfrac{0}{2(1)} = 0$　$\left.\begin{array}{}\\ \\ \\ \end{array}\right\}$ $(0, -4)$

$y = (0)^2 - 4 = -4$

y-intercept: $x = 0, \; y = -4, \; (0, -4)$

x-intercepts: $y = 0$,

$0 = x^2 - 4$

$0 = (x+2)(x-2)$

$x = -2$　or　$x = 2$

$(-2, 0)$ and $(2, 0)$

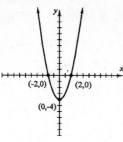

x	y
-3	5
-2	0
0	-4
2	0
3	5

18. $y = x^2 - 7x + 10$

vertex: $x = -\dfrac{b}{2a} = -\dfrac{-7}{2(1)} = \dfrac{7}{2}$

$$y = \left(\frac{7}{2}\right)^2 - 7\left(\frac{7}{2}\right) + 10 = -\frac{9}{4}$$

$$\left(\frac{7}{2}, -\frac{9}{4}\right)$$

y-intercept: $x = 0$, $y = 10$, $(0, 10)$

x-intercepts: $y = 0$,

$0 = x^2 - 7x + 10$

$0 = (x-2)(x-5)$

$x = 2$ or $x = 5$

$(2, 0)$ and $(5, 0)$

x	y
0	10
2	0
$7/2$	$-9/45$
5	0
7	10

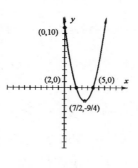

19. $y = 2x^2 + 4x - 1$

$\left.\begin{array}{l} \text{vertex: } x = -\dfrac{b}{2a} = -\dfrac{4}{2(2)} = -1 \\[3mm] \quad y = 2(-1)^2 + 4(-1) - 1 = -3 \end{array}\right\}(-1, -3)$

y-intercept: $x = 0$, $y = -1$, $(0, -1)$

x-intercepts: $y = 0$,

$0 = 2x^2 + 4x - 1$

$$x = \frac{-(4) \pm \sqrt{(4)^2 - 4(2)(-1)}}{2(2)}$$

$$= \frac{-4 \pm \sqrt{24}}{4} = \frac{-4 \pm 2\sqrt{6}}{4} = \frac{-2 \pm \sqrt{6}}{2}$$

$$x = \frac{-2 + \sqrt{6}}{2} \approx 0.2 \text{ or } x = \frac{-2 - \sqrt{6}}{2} \approx -2.2$$

$$\left(\frac{-2 - \sqrt{6}}{2}, 0\right) \text{ and } \left(\frac{-2 + \sqrt{6}}{2}, 0\right)$$

x	y
-2.2	0
-2	-1
-1	-3
0	-1
0.2	0

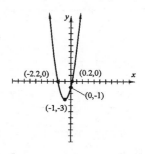

20. Let $d = 9$

$$d = \frac{n^2 - 3n}{2}$$

$$9 = \frac{n^2 - 3n}{2}$$

$$18 = n^2 - 3n$$

$$0 = n^2 - 3n - 18$$

$$0 = (n+3)(n-6)$$

$n = -3$ or $n = 6$

Since the number of diagonals cannot be negative, there are 6 diagonals.

21. Let $h = 120.75$

$$h = 16t^2$$

$$16t^2 = h$$

$$16t^2 = 120.75$$

$$t^2 = \frac{120.75}{16}$$

$$t = \pm\sqrt{\frac{120.75}{16}} \approx \pm 2.7$$

The length of time is not a negative number so the dive lasted 2.7 seconds.

22. Let $y = 1003$

$$y = 28x^2 + 555$$

$$1003 = 28x^2 + 555$$

$$448 = 28x^2$$

$$16 = x^2$$

$$\pm\sqrt{16} = x$$

$$\pm 4 = x$$

The number of years cannot be negative so the year will be $1996 + 4 = 2000$.

Cumulative Review Chapter 9

1. $y + 0.6 = -1.0$

$\qquad y = -1.6$

2. $8(2 - t) = -5t$

$\qquad 16 - 8t = -5t$

$\qquad 16 = 3t$

$\qquad \dfrac{16}{3} = t$

3. Let $x =$ the number of minutes used, then
$0.36x =$ the charge for the minutes used.

$$50 + 0..36x = 99.68$$

$$0.36x = 49.68$$

$$x = 138$$

She used the phone for 138 minutes.

4. $3^0 = 1$

5. $\left(5x^3y^2\right)^0 = 1$

6. $-4^0 = -1$

7. $(3y + 2)^2 = (3y)^2 + 2(3y)(2) + (2)^2$
$\qquad\qquad\quad = 9y^2 + 12y + 4$

8.

$$
\begin{array}{r}
x + 4 \\
x + 3 \overline{)\, x^2 + 7x + 12} \\
\underline{x^2 + 3x} \\
4x + 12 \\
\underline{4x + 12} \\
0
\end{array}
$$

$$\frac{x^2 + 7x + 12}{x + 3} = x + 4$$

9. $r^2 - r - 42 = (r - 7)(r + 6)$

10. $10x^2 - 13xy - 3y^2 = (2x - 3y)(5x + y)$

11. $8x^2 - 14x + 5 = 8x^2 - 10x - 4x + 5$
$\qquad\qquad\qquad\quad = 2x(4x - 5) - (4x - 5)$
$\qquad\qquad\qquad\quad = (2x - 1)(4x - 5)$

12. a. $4x^3 - 49x = x\left(4x^2 - 49\right)$

$$= x\left[\left(2x\right)^2 - \left(7\right)^2\right]$$

$$= x\left(2x + 7\right)\left(2x - 7\right)$$

b. $162x^4 - 2 = 2\left(81x^4 - 1\right)$

$$= 2\left[\left(9x^2\right)^2 - \left(1\right)^2\right]$$

$$= 2\left(9x^2 + 1\right)\left(9x^2 - 1\right)$$

$$= 2\left(9x^2 + 1\right)\left[\left(3x\right)^2 - \left(1\right)^2\right]$$

$$= 2\left(9x^2 + 1\right)\left(3x + 1\right)\left(3x - 1\right)$$

13. $\left(5x - 1\right)\left(2x^2 + 15x + 18\right) = 0$

$$\left(5x - 1\right)\left(2x + 3\right)\left(x + 6\right) = 0$$

$$5x - 1 = 0 \quad \text{or} \quad 2x + 3 = 0 \quad \text{or} \quad x + 6 = 0$$

$$x = \frac{1}{5} \qquad\qquad x = -\frac{3}{2} \qquad x = -6$$

The solutions are $-6, -\dfrac{3}{2},$ and $\dfrac{1}{5}$.

14. $\dfrac{x^2 + 8x + 7}{x^2 - 4x - 5} = \dfrac{\left(x + 7\right)\left(x + 1\right)}{\left(x - 5\right)\left(x + 1\right)} = \dfrac{x + 7}{x - 5}$

15. Let $x = $ the unknown number.

$$\frac{x}{6} - \frac{5}{3} = \frac{x}{2}$$

$$6\left(\frac{x}{6} - \frac{5}{3}\right) = 6\left(\frac{x}{2}\right)$$

$$x - 10 = 3x$$

$$-10 = 2x$$

$$-5 = x$$

The number is -5.

16.

	x	y
a.	-1	-3
b.	0	0
c.	-3	-9

17.a $y = -\dfrac{1}{5}x + 1,\ m_1 = -\dfrac{1}{5}$

$$2x + 10y = 3,\ 10y = -2x + 3,$$

$$y = -\frac{2}{10}x + \frac{3}{10},\ m_2 = -\frac{2}{10} = \frac{1}{5}$$

$m_1 = m_2$, parallel

b. $x + y = 3,\ y = -x + 3,\ m_1 = -1$

$$-x + y = 4,\ y = x + 4,\ m_2 = 1$$

$$m_1 m_2 = \left(-1\right)\left(1\right) = -1,\ \text{perpendicular}$$

c. $3x + y = 5,\ y = -3x + 5,\ m_1 = -3$

$$2x + 3y = 6,\ 3y = -2x + 6,$$

$$y = -\frac{2}{3}x + 2,\ m_2 = -\frac{2}{3}$$

$m_1 \neq m_2$ and $m_1 m_2 \neq -1$, neither

18.a. Every point has a unique x-value: it is a function.

b. Two points have the same x-value: it is not a function.

19. $\begin{cases} 2x + y = 10 \\ x = y + 2 \end{cases}$

Substitute $y + 2$ for x in the first equation.

$2(y + 2) + y = 10$

$2y + 4 + y = 10$

$3y = 6$

$y = 2$

Let $y = 2$ in the second equation.

$x = 2 + 2$

$x = 4$

The solution is $(4, 2)$.

20. $\begin{cases} 2x - y = 7 \\ 8x - 4y = 1 \end{cases}$

Multiply the first equation by -4.

$8x + 4y = -28$

$\underline{8x - 4y = 1}$

$ 0 = -27$

Since $0 = -27$ is a false statement,

the system has no solution.

21. $\sqrt{36} = 6$

22. $\sqrt{\dfrac{9}{100}} = \dfrac{3}{10}$

23. $\dfrac{2}{1+\sqrt{3}} = \dfrac{2(1-\sqrt{3})}{(1+\sqrt{3})(1-\sqrt{3})} = \dfrac{2(1-\sqrt{3})}{1^2 - (\sqrt{3})^2}$

$ = \dfrac{2(1-\sqrt{3})}{1-3} = \dfrac{2(1-\sqrt{3})}{-2}$

$ = -1 + \sqrt{3}$

24. $(x - 3)^2 = 16$

$x - 3 = \pm\sqrt{16}$

$x = 3 \pm 4$

$x = 3 - 4 = -1$ or $x = 3 + 4 = 7$

The solutions are -1 and 7.

25. $\dfrac{1}{2}x^2 - x = 2$

$x^2 - 2x = 4$

$x^2 - 2x - 4 = 0$

$a = 1, b = -2,$ and $c = -4$

$x = \dfrac{-(-2) \pm \sqrt{(-2)^2 - 4(1)(-4)}}{2(1)}$

$ = \dfrac{2 \pm \sqrt{4+16}}{2} = \dfrac{2 \pm \sqrt{20}}{2}$

$ = \dfrac{2 \pm 2\sqrt{5}}{2} = 1 \pm \sqrt{5}$

The solutions are $1 \pm \sqrt{5}$.